Data Flow Analysis

Theory and Practice

Data Flow Analysis

Theory and Practice

Uday P. Khedker
Amitabha Sanyal
Bageshri Karkare

CRC Press
Taylor & Francis Group
Boca Raton London New York

CRC Press is an imprint of the
Taylor & Francis Group, an **informa** business

CRC Press
Taylor & Francis Group
6000 Broken Sound Parkway NW, Suite 300
Boca Raton, FL 33487-2742

International Standard Book Number-13: 978-0-8493-2880-0 (Hardcover)

Library of Congress Cataloging-in-Publication Data

Khedker, Uday.
Data flow analysis : theory and practice / Uday Khedker, Amitabha Sanyal, Bageshri Karkare.
p. cm.
Includes bibliographical references and index.
ISBN 978-0-8493-2880-0 (hardcover : alk. paper)
1. Compilers (Computer programs) 2. Data flow computing. 3. Software engineering. 4. Computer software--Verification. I. Sanyal, Amitabha. II. Karkare, Bageshri. III. Title.

QA76.76.C65K54 2009
004'.35--dc22 2009002056

Visit the Taylor & Francis Web site at
http://www.taylorandfrancis.com

and the CRC Press Web site at
http://www.crcpress.com

Preface

Data flow analysis is a classical static analysis technique that has been used to discover useful properties of programs being analyzed. It has found many useful applications ranging from compiler optimizations to software engineering to software verification. Modern compilers use this technique to produce code that maximize performance. In software engineering, it is used to re-engineer or reverse engineer programs. Finally, data flow analysis based techniques are used in software verification to prove the soundness of programs with respect to properties of interest.

This book provides a detailed treatment of data flow analysis. Although we explain it in the context of compiler optimizations, the concepts are general enough to be used for other applications. This is possible because we use a general model of data flow equations to represent the specification of data flow analysis. These data flow equations are defined in terms of constant and dependent *Gen* and *Kill* components. For classical bit vector frameworks, the constant *Gen* and *Kill* suffice; dependent parts are required for frameworks like constant propagation, points-to analysis etc. Such a modeling explicates the inter-dependence of data flow values and leads to an orthogonal generality that models flow functions in terms of a rather small set of constituent functions called *entity functions*. On the one hand, modeling flow functions in terms of entity functions allows us to define *information flow paths* that explain empirical observations for a large class of data flow frameworks and facilitate tight complexity bounds on solution procedures for data flow equations. On the other hand, this modeling also allows reasoning about the feasibility of constructing summary flow functions.

The book is organized in three parts: The first part deals with the specification of data flow frameworks and the solution process at the intraprocedural level. This part presents the lattice theoretic modeling of data flow frameworks apart from the generalizations of constant and dependent parts in flow functions and entity functions as constituents of flow functions. It shows how these generalizations lead to tight complexity bounds. This part also presents a large number of data flow frameworks. The diversity of these analyses is an evidence of the wide applicability of the generalizations presented. The final chapter of the first part presents SSA representation of programs. This is interesting because it builds an additional layer of abstraction over the control flow graph representation of programs and directly relates the definition points and the use points of data. This increases the efficiency with which a class of optimizations can be performed.

The second part of the book presents interprocedural data flow analysis. As a matter of choice, we avoid methods that are specific to a particular application or a particular data flow framework and instead, focus on generic approaches. The first approach is a *functional* approach that constructs context independent summary flow functions of procedures. These flow functions are used at the call points to incorporate the effects of procedure calls. The second approach is a *value-based* approach that computes distinct values for distinct calling contexts; this is achieved by augmenting the data flow values with context information.

The third part of the book describes the implementation of a generic data flow analyzer for bit vector frameworks in GCC and shows how it can be instantiated to a given framework.

This book is an outcome of our notes for the course *CS618: Program Analysis* which is a graduate course at the Department of Computer Science and Engineering, IIT Bombay. The slides used in the course and the source of the generic data flow analyzer *gdfa* are available at the web page of the book:

`http://www.cse.iitb.ac.in/~uday/dfaBook-web`

As errors are discovered, we will upload an errata on the above web page. Any additional material that we find relevant to a course based on this book will also be made available on the same web page.

Many people have gone through the earlier versions of this manuscript. The registrants of CS618 were our captive audience for testing our examples—some examples tested their patience in the examinations of CS618. The following students of CS618 pointed out errors to us: Abhishek Shrivastav, Amitraj Singh Chouhan, Dhritiman Das, Harshada Gune, Md. Naseerunddin, Nilesh Padariya, Prashima Sharma, and Pushpraj Agrawal. Among others, Jaishri Waghmare, Prashant Singh Rawat, Sameera Deshpande, Santosh Sonawane, and Seema Ravandale read some chapters and gave valuable comments. Seema extended *gdfa* to include support for reaching definitions analysis. Sameera's help in preparing the first draft of the index is gratefully acknowledged.

Finally, this book would not have been possible without the patience and constant encouragement of our families. They have gracefully tolerated our mental, if not physical, absence, relieving us from a sense of guilt. We express a deep sense of gratitude for their support.

Uday P. Khedker, Amitabha Sanyal, and Bageshri Karkare

To my mother Rajani and the memory of my father Prabhakar Khedker

Uday Khedker

To my parents Arunojjwal and Prakriti Sanyal

Amitabha Sanyal

Contents

1

An Introduction to Data Flow Analysis

Data flow analysis is a process of deriving information about the run time behaviour of a program.

This chapter introduces the basic concepts of data flow analysis through a contemporary optimization. Then we describe common properties of program analyses at an abstract level and instantiate them for data flow analysis.

1.1 A Motivating Example

We present a data flow analysis for optimizing heap memory usage in programs to free heap cells as soon as possible. Formal details of the analysis are postponed to Section 4.4. In this section we perform the required analysis and explain the issues involved intuitively. The result of intraprocedural data flow analysis of this program using the formal theory is presented in Section 4.4.5 whereas Section 9.5 presents the result of interprocedural data flow analysis.

1.1.1 Optimizing for Heap Memory

Figure 1.1(b) provides a program to traverse a tree in depth first order. The data structure used for representing the input tree is illustrated in Figure 1.1(a). Function `dfTraverse` recursively descends down a tree node and prints node numbers while unwinding from recursion. Figure 1.1(c) provides its *control flow graph*. The nodes in this graph represent statements and the edges represent control transfers between the statements. Observe that the `while` loop, which is a compound statement, has been translated in terms of a conditional branch (out edges of block n_2) and an unconditional branch (out edge of block n_5).

For simplicity of descriptions, we assume that reading a pointer is equivalent to reading the data pointed to by the pointer. Further, when we say that a given data object is read, we mean that *some* pointer which points to the data object is read; when a data object is not read, *no* pointer which points to the data object is read.

Figure 1.2 provides the execution trace of `dfTraverse` on the input tree in Figure 1.1(a). It is clear from the trace that the data object pointed to by pointer `succ` is last read in block n_4. Thus it is desirable that the heap memory allocated for this

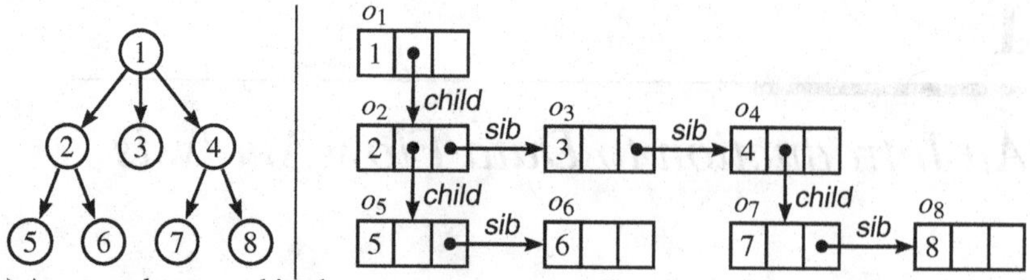

(a) An example tree and its data structure representation. Each object contains a pointer to its first child. Other children are siblings of the first child.

```
void main()
{ Tree *tree;
   tree = createTree();
   dfTraverse(tree);
}
void dfTraverse(Tree *n)
{ Tree *succ, *next;
   succ = n->child;
   while (succ != NULL);
   { dfTraverse(succ);
      next = succ->sib;
      free(succ);
      succ = next;
   }
   printf("%d\n",n->num);
}
```

(b) A tree traversal program

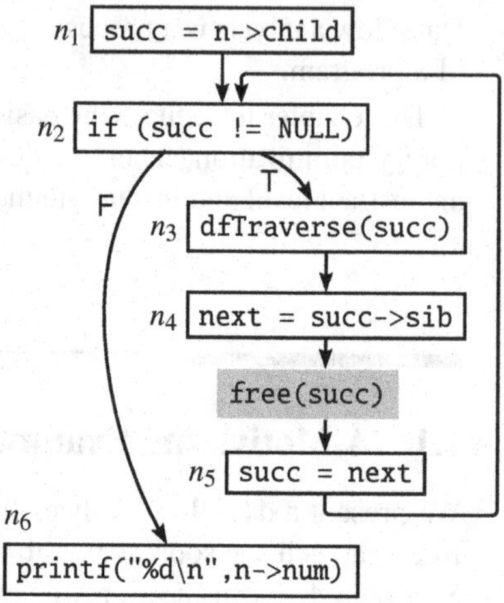

(c) CFG of dfTraverse

FIGURE 1.1

An example of heap memory optimization. Various nodes of `tree` are freed as shown in the gray boxes as soon as their traversal is over.

data object be reclaimed as soon as possible and added to the free pool for a possible subsequent allocation. The statement which performs the suggested deallocation has been shown in gray box and is not part of the original program. Observe that this deallocation cannot be performed through garbage collection because all these data objects are reachable from the root variable `tree` in the program.

This particular instance of optimization can be summarized as follows:

> Pointer variable `succ` is not live at the entry of n_5 and is not aliased to any live pointer. Hence the data can be deallocated at the entry of n_5.

The properties of *liveness* and *aliasing* of pointers are defined as:

Liveness of a pointer. A pointer is live at a program point u if the address that it holds at u is read along some path starting at u.

Aliasing of pointers. Two pointers are aliased to each other at a program point u if they hold the same address in some execution instance of u.

n_1:o_1,o_2:n->child	n_5:NULL:next	n_1:o_7,NULL:n->child
n_2:o_2:succ	n_2:NULL:succ	n_2:NULL:succ
n_3:o_2:succ	n_6:o_2:n	n_6:o_7:n
n_1:o_2,o_5:n->child	n_4:o_2,o_3:succ->sib	n_4:o_7:succ->sib
n_2:o_5:succ	n_5:o_3:next	n_5:o_8:next
n_3:o_5:succ	n_2:o_3:succ	n_2:o_8:succ
n_1:o_5,NULL:n->child	n_3:o_3:succ	n_3:o_8:succ
n_2:NULL:succ	n_1:o_3,NULL:n->child	n_1:o_8,NULL:n->child
n_6:o_5:n	n_2:NULL:succ	n_2:NULL:succ
n_4:o_5,o_6:succ->sib	n_6:o_3:n	n_6:o_8:n
n_5:o_6:next	n_4:o_3,o_4:succ->sib	n_4:o_8:succ->sib
n_2:o_6:succ	n_5:o_4:next	n_5:NULL:next
n_3:o_6:succ	n_2:o_4:succ	n_2:NULL:succ
n_1:o_6,NULL:n->child	n_3:o_4:succ	n_6:o_4:n
n_2:NULL:succ	n_1:o_4,o_7:n->child	n_4:o_4:succ->sib
n_6:o_6:n	n_2:o_7:succ	n_5:NULL:next
n_4:o_6,NULL:succ->sib	n_3:o_7:succ	n_2:NULL:succ

FIGURE 1.2
Execution trace of function `dfTraverse` on the input tree in Figure 1.1(a). Each entry is of the form $x : y : z$ where y is the list of objects read using the pointer sequence z in block x. Entries with gray background correspond to the last use of the first object in the list. Nested activations have been shown by nested indentations.

The final data flow information which enables this optimization has been provided in Figure 1.4 (Section 1.1.4).

The liveness and alias analyses required for performing optimization such as above use the concept of an *access path* which is a sequence of pointers representing a path in the memory. The first pointer in the sequence is a local or global variable whereas all subsequent pointers are field members of structures. In our example, when succ points to object o_2, objects o_3, o_4, o_5, o_6 can be accessed using access paths *succ→sib*, *succ→sib→sib*, *succ→child*, and *succ→child→sib*; we say that objects o_3, o_4, o_5, and o_6 are *targets* of access paths *succ→sib*, *succ→sib→sib*, *succ→child*, and *succ→child→sib* respectively.

For the purpose of this chapter, we do not distinguish between access paths beyond two levels of pointer indirections. Access paths with three or more pointers are summarized by suffixing a $\star$ after the first two pointers. Thus *succ→sib→sib* and *succ→sib→child* are both represented by *succ→sib→*$\star$. A more precise and formal method of summarization of access paths using graphs is presented in Section 4.4.3.

Our analyses extend the concept of liveness and aliasing of pointer variables to liveness and aliasing of access paths.

1.1.2 Computing Liveness

The liveness information at a program point is represented by a set of live access paths where liveness of an access path is defined as follows:

Liveness of access paths. An access path ρ is live at a program point u if the targets of all prefixes of ρ are read along some control flow path starting at u.

Clearly, liveness sets are prefix-closed. For notational convenience, we retain only those access paths which are not prefixes of other access paths.

Since liveness information at u represents possible uses beyond u, it is computed from the liveness information at the successors of u. For an access path to be live at u, it is sufficient that it is live at any successor of u. Hence the set of live access paths at u is a union of the corresponding sets at successors of u. In our example, the liveness set at the exit of n_2 is computed by taking a union of the sets of live access paths at the entries of n_6 and n_3.

The sets of live access paths are computed by successive refinements starting from a conservative initial value of $\emptyset$. The initial value chosen is $\emptyset$ because it is the identity of union operation. We choose an iterative traversal over the CFG for each step of refinement. Since liveness at a program point depends on the successor points, we traverse the CFG against the direction of control flow. For our example, this implies the following order of computing liveness sets: n_6, n_5, n_4, n_3, n_2, and n_1. This method is called the *round-robin iterative* method of performing data flow analysis. We will use this method in the rest of the book to present our examples. Sections 3.4, 3.5, and 5.2 define this method formally and analyze its complexity.

Modelling Interprocedural Effects

The data flow information within a function is influenced by interprocedural effects arising out of function calls. In particular, the data flow information in function f is influenced by the caller functions of f as well as by the functions called by f. If the interprocedural effects are ignored during intraprocedural analysis, it could lead to incorrect results. This can be avoided by either performing interprocedural analysis or by approximating the interprocedural effects.

Figure 1.3 models the above situations for our example program. Figure 1.3(a) illustrates the situation when the interprocedural effects are ignored: The call statement in block n_3 is modeled as reading merely the actual parameter `succ`. Further it is assumed that no access path rooted at the formal parameter `n` is live at the exit of `dfTraverse`. Figure 1.3(b) shows a safe approximation of liveness for handling interprocedural effects: In block n_3, it is assumed that any access path rooted at the actual parameter `succ` becomes live due to the call made in n_3. Similarly, it is assumed that any path rooted at the formal parameter `n` is live at end of `dfTraverse` because it may be accessed in a caller's body using the actual parameter.

Figure 1.3(c) shows how the function `dfTraverse` can be represented to facilitate interprocedural analysis. It models function calls by splitting them into a call node and a return node and by adding an edge from the call node to the start of the

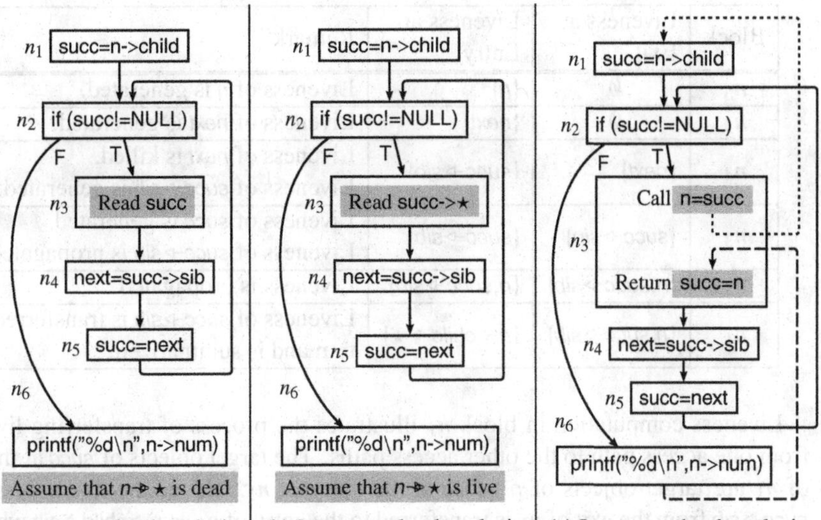

(a) Intraprocedural analysis ignoring interprocedural effects.

(b) Intraprocedural analysis with interprocedural approximation.

(c) Interprocedural analysis. Function main has not been shown.

FIGURE 1.3

Modelling interprocedural effects in liveness analysis for the program in Figure 1.1.

called procedure and an edge from the end of the called procedure to the return node. A call node maps the actual parameters to the formal parameters. During liveness analysis, the call node in block n_3 transfers the liveness of the formal parameter `n` in the callee's body (`dfTraverse`) to the liveness of the actual parameter `succ` in the caller's body (also `dfTraverse`). In our example, the callee does not return any value. However, since the parameter of `dfTraverse` is a pointer variable, the return node in block n_3 transfers the liveness of the actual parameter `succ` in the caller's body to the liveness of the formal parameter `n` in the callee's body.

For simplicity of exposition, we first show the liveness analysis for simple intraprocedural analysis (modeled in Figure 1.3(a)). Then we show the effect of incorporating the interprocedural approximation (modeled in Figure 1.3(b)). Finally we show a simple interprocedural liveness analysis (modeled in Figure 1.3(c)).

In the later part of the book, a solution of the simple intraprocedural liveness analysis of our example program as well as intraprocedural liveness analysis with interprocedural summarization has been presented in Section 4.4.5. Common variants of interprocedural data flow analysis are later introduced in Section 7.6 and Section 9.5 presents interprocedural liveness analysis of our example.

Simple Intraprocedural Liveness Analysis

As described before, simple intraprocedural analysis disregards the interprocedural effects completely. Thus it is assumed that no access path is live at the end of the procedure. Liveness information at the end of the first iteration is:

Block	Liveness at Exit	Liveness at Entry	Remark
n_6	∅	{n}	Liveness of n is generated.
n_5	∅	{next}	Liveness of next is generated.
n_4	{next}	{succ→sib}	Liveness of next is killed. Liveness of succ→sib is generated.
n_3	{succ→sib}	{succ→sib}	Liveness of succ is generated. Liveness of succ→sib is propagated.
n_2	{n,succ→sib}	{n,succ→sib}	Liveness is propagated.
n_1	{n,succ→sib}	{n→child→★}	Liveness of succ→sib is transferred to n and is summarized.

Liveness computation in block n_1 illustrates the process of transferring liveness from one access path to the other access paths. The target objects of *succ* at the exit of n_1 are target objects of *n→child* at the entry of n_1. Hence the live access path *succ→sib* from the exit of n_1 is transferred to the entry of n_1 as *n→child→sib* which is then summarized to *n→child→★*; this also subsumes the unchanging live access path *n*. The process of transfer is described as follows:

> If access path $a \rightarrow \sigma$ is live after an assignment a = b, then σ is transferred to b and the access path $b \rightarrow \sigma$ becomes live before the assignment.

Data flow information converges in the third iteration as shown below. In the second iteration, liveness information {*n,succ→sib*} at the entry of n_2 is propagated to the exit of n_5 along the back edge. The assignment in n_5 does not affect *n*, but the access paths *succ→sib* cease to be live before n_5 due to the assignment to `succ` and the liveness of *succ→sib* is transferred as the liveness of *next→sib* before the assignment. Computing liveness in n_4 involves transfer followed by summarization.

Block	Liveness in iteration 2		Liveness in iteration 3	
	At Exit	At Entry	At Exit	At Entry
n_6	∅	{n}	∅	{n}
n_5	{n,succ→sib}	{n,next→sib}	{n,succ→sib→★}	{n,next→sib★}
n_4	{n,next→sib}	{n,succ→sib→★}	{n,next→sib★}	{n,succ→sib→★}
n_3	{n,succ→sib→★}	{n,succ→sib→★}	{n,succ→sib→★}	{n,succ→sib→★}
n_2	{n,succ→sib→★}	{n,succ→sib→★}	{n,succ→sib→★}	{n,succ→sib→★}
n_1	{n,succ→sib→★}	{n→child→★}	{n,succ→sib→★}	{n→child→★}

Intraprocedural Analysis with Interprocedural Approximation

Interprocedural approximation assumes that *n→★* is live at the end of `dfTraverse` and *succ→★* is live just before the recursive call. Due to this approximation, the analysis terminates in two iterations.

Block	Liveness in iteration 2		Liveness in iteration 3	
	At Exit	At Entry	At Exit	At Entry
n_6	{n→★}	{n→★}	{n→★}	{n→★}
n_5	∅	{next}	{n→★,succ→★}	{n→★,next→★}
n_4	{next}	{succ→sib}	{n→★,next→★}	{n→★,succ→★}
n_3	{succ→sib}	{succ→★}	{n→★,succ→★}	{n→★,succ→★}
n_2	{n→★,succ→★}	{n→★,succ→★}	{n→★,succ→★}	{n→★,succ→★}
n_1	{n→★,succ→★}	{n→★}	{n→★,succ→★}	{n→★}

Interprocedural Analysis

For interprocedural analysis, we split block n_3 into a call block n_3.call and a return block n_3.ret and compute liveness at the entries and exits of these blocks. The initial value is ∅. No access path is live after the call to `dfTraverse` in function `main`. The liveness information after first two iterations is:

Block	Liveness in iteration 2		Liveness in iteration 3	
	At Exit	At Entry	At Exit	At Entry
n_6	∅	{n}	{n→sib}	{n→sib}
n_5	∅	{next}	{n,succ}	{n,next}
n_4	{next}	{succ→sib}	{n,next}	{n,succ→sib}
n_3.ret	{succ→sib}	{n→sib}	{n,succ→sib}	{n→sib}
n_3.call	∅	∅	{n→child}	{succ→child}
n_2	{n}	{n,succ}	{n→sib,succ→child}	{n→sib,succ→child}
n_1	{n,succ}	{n→child}	{n→sib,succ→child}	{n→sib,n→child→★}

In the second iteration, {n→sib} is propagated from the entry of n_3.ret to the exit of n_6 and {n→child} is propagated from the entry of n_1 to the exit of n_3.call. Further, the transfer in block n_1 causes summarization in the second iteration.

	Block	At Exit	At Entry
Iteration 3	n_6	{n→sib}	{n→sib}
	n_5	{n→sib,succ→child}	{n→sib,next→child}
	n_4	{n→sib,next→child}	{n→sib,succ→sib→★}
	n_3.ret	{n→sib,succ→sib→★}	{n→sib→★}
	n_3.call	{n→sib,n→child→★}	{succ→sib,succ→child→★}
	n_2	{n→sib,succ→sib,succ→child→★}	{n→sib,succ→sib,succ→child→★}
	n_1	{n→sib,succ→sib,succ→child→★}	{n→sib,n→child→★}
Iteration 4	n_6	{n→sib→★}	{n→sib→★}
	n_5	{n→sib,succ→sib,succ→child→★}	{n→sib,next→sib,next→child→★}
	n_4	{n→sib,next→sib,next→child→★}	{n→sib,succ→sib→★}
	n_3.ret	{n→sib,succ→sib→★}	{n→sib→★}
	n_3.call	{n→sib,n→child→★}	{succ→sib,succ→child→★}
	n_2	{n→sib→★,succ→sib, succ→child→★}	{n→sib→★,succ→sib, succ→child→★}
	n_1	{n→sib→★,succ→sib, succ→child→★}	{n→★}

	Block	At Exit	At Entry
Iteration 5	n_6	{n->sib->★}	{n->sib->★}
	n_5	{n->sib->★,succ->sib, succ->child->★}	{n->sib->★,next->sib, next->child->★}
	n_4	{n->sib->★,next->sib,next->child->★}	{n->sib->★,succ->sib->★}
	n_3.ret	{n->sib->★,succ->sib->★}	{n->sib->★}
	n_3.call	{n->★}	{succ->★}
	n_2	{n->sib->★,succ->★}	{n->sib->★,succ->★}
	n_1	{n->sib->★,succ->★}	{n->★}
Iteration 6	n_6	{n->sib->★}	{n->sib->★}
	n_5	{ n->sib->★,succ->★}	{ n->sib->★,next->★}
	n_4	{ n->sib->★,next->★}	{ n->sib->★,succ->sib->★}
	n_3.ret	{ n->sib->★,succ->sib->★}	{n->sib->★}
	n_3.call	{n->★}	{succ->★}
	n_2	{ n->sib->★,succ->★}	{ n->sib->★,succ->★}
	n_1	{ n->sib->★,succ->★}	{n->★}

It can be verified that the seventh iteration results in the same liveness at each program point indicating convergence.

A Comparison of Liveness Computed by Three Methods

We reproduce below the liveness information computed by the three methods.

Program Point		Intraprocedural Analysis		Interprocedural Analysis
		Simple	Interprocedural Approximation	
n_6	Exit	∅	∅	{n->sib->★}
	Entry	{n}	{n->★}	{n->sib->★}
n_5	Exit	{n, succ->sib->★}	{n->★, succ->★}	{ n->sib->★, succ->★}
	Entry	{n, next->sib★}	{n->★, next->★}	{ n->sib->★, next->★}
n_4	Exit	{n, next->sib★}	{n->★, next->★}	{ n->sib->★, next->★}
	Entry	{n, succ->sib->★}	{n->★, succ->★}	{ n->sib->★,succ->sib->★}
n_3	Exit	{n, succ->sib->★}	{n->★, succ->★}	{ n->sib->★,succ->sib->★}
	Entry	{n, succ->sib->★}	{n->★, succ->★}	{succ->★}
n_2	Exit	{n, succ->sib->★}	{n->★, succ->★}	{ n->sib->★, succ->★}
	Entry	{n, succ->sib->★}	{n->★, succ->★}	{ n->sib->★, succ->★}
n_1	Exit	{n, succ->sib->★}	{n->★, succ->★}	{ n->sib->★, succ->★}
	Entry	{n->child->★}	{n->★}	{n->★}

It is easy to see that the simple intraprocedural analysis fails to record some access paths as live. For example, access path *n->sib* is live at the end of `dfTraverse`. This is because the procedure traverses the next sibling of `n` after traversing `n`. However, the simple intraprocedural analysis concludes that it is not live. When interprocedural summarization is included, it records *n->sib* as live at the end of the procedure but it also marks *n->child* as live. The interprocedural analysis correctly recognizes that only *n->sib* is live at the end of the procedure.

1.1.3 Computing Aliases

Computing alias information is simpler compared to liveness for this example because there are no interprocedural effects. This is because unlike liveness which is a property of an access path, aliasing at a program point is a relation between two access paths that are visible at that program point. Since there are no global variables, and no assignments to formal parameter in our example, aliases created in `dfTraverse` are restricted to a single activation.

Aliasing of access paths. Access path ρ_1 and ρ_2 are aliased to each other at a program point u, denoted $\rho_1 \doteq \rho_2$, if their targets are same at u along some control flow path reaching u.

Aliasing information at a program point is represented using a set of alias pairs $\rho_1 \doteq \rho_2$. Since an alias holds at a program point u if it holds along some predecessor of u, we use union to combine sets of alias pairs and use its identity ($\emptyset$) as the initial value. Unlike liveness analysis, aliasing information at a program point u depends on the aliases at predecessors of u. Hence we traverse control flow graph along the control flow for faster convergence of successive refinements. This implies the following order: n_1, n_2, n_3, n_4, n_5, and n_6.

The aliases at the end of first iteration are as shown below:

Block	Aliases at Entry	Aliases at Exit	Remark
n_1	$\emptyset$	{*succ* ≐ *n->child*}	Generation
n_2	{*succ* ≐ *n->child*}	{*succ* ≐ *n->child*}	Propagation
n_3	{*succ* ≐ *n->child*}	{*succ* ≐ *n->child*}	Propagation
n_4	{*succ* ≐ *n->child*}	{*succ* ≐ *n->child*, *next* ≐ *succ->sib* *next* ≐ *n->child->* ★}	Propagation, transfer and summarization
n_5	{*succ* ≐ *n->child*, *next* ≐ *succ->sib* *next* ≐ *n->child->* ★}	{*succ* ≐ *next*, *succ* ≐ *n->child->* ★, *next* ≐ *n->child->* ★}	Generation, killing and transfer
n_6	{*succ* ≐ *n->child*}	{*succ* ≐ *n->child*}	Propagation

Observe the effect of assignment `next = succ->sib` in block n_4 on the aliases at the entry of n_4. Since *succ* is aliased to *n->child*, *next* gets aliased to *n->child->* ★. This is analogous to the transfer in liveness. In n_5, since assignment `succ = next` modifies `succ`, alias *succ* ≐ *n->child* ceases to hold at the exit of n_6. Two new aliases *succ* ≐ *next* and *succ* ≐ *n->child->* ★ are created.

The second iteration causes aliases from the exit of n_5 to be propagated to the entry of n_2 and some more aliases to be generated as a consequence of transfer. Since *succ* is aliased to *n->child->* ★ in block n_4, *next* gets aliased to *n->child->* ★.

Block	Aliases at Entry	Aliases at Exit
n_1	∅	{succ ≐ n-▷child}
n_2	{succ ≐ next, succ ≐ n-▷child-▷⋆ next ≐ n-▷child-▷⋆}	{succ ≐ next, succ ≐ n-▷child-▷⋆, next ≐ n-▷child-▷⋆}
n_3	{succ ≐ next, succ ≐ n-▷child-▷⋆, next ≐ n-▷child-▷⋆}	{succ ≐ next, succ ≐ n-▷child-▷⋆, next ≐ n-▷child-▷⋆}
n_4	{succ ≐ next, succ ≐ n-▷child-▷⋆, next ≐ n-▷child-▷⋆}	{succ ≐ n-▷child-▷⋆, next ≐ succ-▷sib, next ≐ n-▷child-▷⋆}
n_5	{succ ≐ n-▷child-▷⋆, next ≐ succ-▷sib, next ≐ n-▷child-▷⋆}	{succ ≐ next, succ ≐ n-▷child-▷⋆, next ≐ n-▷child-▷⋆}
n_6	{succ ≐ next, succ ≐ n-▷child-▷⋆, next ≐ n-▷child-▷⋆}	{succ ≐ next, succ ≐ n-▷child-▷⋆, next ≐ n-▷child-▷⋆}

It can be verified that the third iteration does not compute any new aliases.

1.1.4 Performing Optimization

Figure 1.4 summarizes the final data flow information which enables the desired optimization. Access path *succ* is not live at the exit of n_4 and the entry of n_5. Further at these points none of the access paths that it is aliased to are live. Thus the object pointed to by it can be freed. Although *next* is not live in blocks n_2, n_3, and n_4, it is aliased to a live access path and hence its target cannot be freed. An alternative place for deallocating `succ` is block n_6. The difference between the two deallocations is that the former will be performed after a call to `dfTraverse` is over while the latter will be performed just before the end of a call.

1.1.5 General Observations

At the entry of n_5, access path *succ* is not live. It is aliased to *n-▷child* which is not live either. If function `main` is modified to access `tree->child` after the call to `dfTraverse` as shown below, then *n-▷child* will be live at the exit of n_6.

```
void main()
{  Tree *tree;
    tree = createTree();
    printEdges(tree);
    printf("%d\n",tree->child->num);
}
```

Since liveness of *n-▷child* is not affected by the assignment in n_5, it will be live at the entry of n_5 too. Thus, with this change, *succ* cannot be freed. Interestingly, this change accesses only object o_2 outside of function `dfTraverse` but prohibits freeing any object in `dfTraverse`. This is because the same statements in `dfTraverse` are used to access all objects and unless the code is rewritten to access o_2 and other objects differently, selective freeing is not feasible.

Program Point		Interprocedural Liveness	Aliases
n_1	Entry	{n->sib->★}	∅
	Exit	{n->sib->★,succ->★}	{succ ≐ n->child}
n_2	Entry	{n->sib->★,succ->★}	{succ ≐ next, succ ≐ n->child->★, next ≐ n->child->★}
	Exit	{n->sib->★,succ->★}	{succ ≐ next, succ ≐ n->child->★, next ≐ n->child->★}
n_3	Entry	{succ->★}	{succ ≐ next, succ ≐ n->child->★, next ≐ n->child->★}
	Exit	{n->sib->★,succ->sib->★}	{succ ≐ next, succ ≐ n->child->★, next ≐ n->child->★}
n_4	Entry	{n->sib->★,succ->sib->★}	{succ ≐ next, succ ≐ n->child->★, next ≐ n->child->★}
	Exit	{n->sib->★,next->★}	{succ ≐ n->child->★, next ≐ succ->sib, next ≐ n->child->★}
n_5	Entry	{n->sib->★,next->★}	{succ ≐ n->child->★, next ≐ succ->sib, next ≐ n->child->★}
	Exit	{n->sib->★,succ->★}	{succ ≐ next, succ ≐ n->child->★, next ≐ n->child->★}
n_6	Entry	{n->sib->★}	{succ ≐ next, succ ≐ n->child->★, next ≐ n->child->★}
	Exit	{n->sib->★}	{succ ≐ next, succ ≐ n->child->★, next ≐ n->child->★}

FIGURE 1.4

Liveness and alias information in function `dfTraverse`.

This brings out the concept of safety of data flow analysis and the conservative approximations which are used to achieve safety. Since liveness is used to prohibit freeing of objects, it is safer to include spurious access paths as live. Missing a live access path could lead to incorrect optimization. Data flow information is required to represent all possible executions on all possible inputs. Hence the concept of approximation depends on the intended use of the data flow information. Approximations performed by data flow analysis can be characterized by the following two properties: *exhaustiveness* and *safety*. Data flow information is exhaustive if it does not miss any optimization opportunity; it is safe if it does not enable optimizations that do not preserve program semantics. In the context of liveness analysis, exclusion of an access path that is actually live is an approximation towards exhaustiveness because it facilitates freeing a larger number of objects; however, this may be unsafe. In contrast, inclusion of an access path that is not live is an approximation towards safety because it prohibits freeing objects thereby preserving program semantics. The goal of data flow analysis is to compute the most exhaustive safe information.

The interprocedural analysis performed by us is *context insensitive* because it does not distinguish between different calling contexts. In our original example, *n* becomes live at the exit of `dfTraverse` in those activations of `dfTraverse` that are invoked through the recursive call. It is not live at the end of the outermost activation of `dfTraverse` made through `main`. A *context sensitive* interprocedural analysis can make this distinction. However, exploiting this distinction requires rewriting the code in a non-trivial manner. Otherwise, the data flow information reaching at a program point along different contexts will have to be merged. This highlights the limitation of transformations performed statically. In any case, merging the information discovered by context sensitive analysis generally results in more precise information than the information computed by context insensitive analysis.

The alias analysis performed by us is *flow sensitive* because it propagates aliases along the control flow. A flow insensitive alias analysis disregards the control flow and assumes that the aliases discovered hold at all program points. Such an analysis visits each block only once and accumulates the aliases discovered, no aliases can be killed. For our example, the flow insensitive aliases are: $succ \doteq n\text{-}{\triangleright}child\text{-}{\triangleright}\star$, $succ \doteq next$, $next \doteq succ\text{-}{\triangleright}sib$, and $next \doteq n\text{-}{\triangleright}child\text{-}{\triangleright}\star$. This alias information prohibits freeing the target of *succ* at the entry of n_5 because it is aliased to *next* which is live at that point.

We have summarized the access paths *n*, *n-▷child*, *n-▷child-▷sib*, *n-▷child-▷child*, *n-▷child-▷sib-▷sib*, ... by $n\text{-}{\triangleright}child\text{-}{\triangleright}\star$. It is clear that some kind of summarization is essential because statically it is not possible to know how many such access paths need to be created by analysis. However for precision, the process of summarization should keep as many access paths distinct in the summary information as is possible. Further, these summaries have to be constructed automatically by data flow analysis. Ensuring convergence on safe summaries requires creating suitable representation for data flow information and devising appropriate operations on the chosen representation. In the case of stack and static data, building summaries is simpler because the mapping between names and addresses does not change during the lifetime of a name and hence names can be directly used to represent data. Section 4.4.3 shows how access paths for heap data can be summarized using graphs.

1.2 Program Analysis: The Larger Perspective

Program analyses cover a large spectrum of motivations, basic principles, and methods. Different approaches to program analysis differ in details but at a conceptual level, almost all program analyses are characterized by some common properties. Although these properties are abstract, they provide useful insights about a particular analysis. A deeper understanding of the analysis would require exploring many more analysis-specific details.

Applications of Analysis

The uses of information derived by program analyses can be broadly classified as:

- *Determining the validity of a program.* An analysis may be used to validate programs with regard to some desired properties (viz. type correctness).
- *Understanding the behaviour of a program.* An analysis may discover useful properties of programs required for debugging, maintenance, verification, or testing etc. Abstract interpretation, slicing, ripple analysis, test data generation etc. are the common examples of such analyses.
- *Transforming a program.* Most analyses enable useful transformations to be performed on programs. Traditionally, the term program analysis has been used for the analyses that facilitate transforming a program within the same given representation. These transformations may be aimed at optimizing the program for space, time, or power consumption. Note that analyses such as lexical and syntax analyses transform a program representation into another representation and are not included in the class of program analyses.
- *Enabling program execution.* Program analysis can also be used for determining the operations implied by a program so that the program can be executed (viz. dynamic type inferencing).

Approaches to Program Analysis

Some of the common paradigms of program analysis are:

- *Inference Systems* consisting of a set of axioms and inductive and compositional definitions constituting rules of inference.

  In such systems, the properties are *inferred* by repeatedly discovering the premises that are satisfied by the program components of interest and by invoking appropriate rules of inference. Note that there is no algorithm that suggests appropriate choice of rules; it is left to the creativity of the user of such a system. As a consequence, such systems may not be decidable.

  Typically, the inference systems are converted to constraint based system (described below) and constraint resolution algorithms are used for inference.

- *Constraint Resolution Systems* consisting of a constraint store and a logic for solving constraints.

  In such systems, a program component *constrains* the semantic properties. These constraints are expressed in form of inequalities and the semantics properties are derived by finding a solution which satisfies all the constraints.

  Often these constraints take advantage of the temporal or spatial structures of data and operations by grouping the related constraints together. Traditionally they have been unconditional, and are called *flow*-based constraints because they have been solved by traversals over trees or general graphs. Grouping of structured constraints often leads to replacing groups of related inequalities by equations. Structured constraints often lead to more efficient analyses, both in terms of time as well as space.

- *Model Checking* requires creating suitable abstractions of programs as *models* and the desired properties are expressed in terms of boolean formulae. A model checking algorithm then discovers the states in the mode that satisfy the given formulae.

- *Abstract Interpretations* use abstraction functions to map the concrete semantics values to abstract semantics, perform the computations on the abstract semantics, and use concretization functions to map the abstract semantics back to the concrete semantics. The theory of abstract interpretation provides mechanisms to show the soundness of the abstraction functions. The most interesting aspect of this approach is that the algorithms for performing analysis emerge from the construction of abstraction functions.

  This is unlike inference systems, constraints resolution systems, and model checking, where the specifications of analysis are generally based on intuitions of semantics instead of being derived formally from concrete semantics. Hence these three approaches require separate algorithms that perform the specified analyses.

Other approaches like those involving denotational semantics or logic are relatively less common.

In general an analysis can be expressed in any of the above approaches.

Time of Performing Analysis

An analysis performed before the execution of a program is termed *static analysis*, whereas an analysis performed during the execution of a program (in an interleaved fashion) is termed *dynamic analysis*. Thus an interpreter can perform static analysis (by analyzing a program just before execution) as well as dynamic analysis (by analyzing the program during execution). A compiler, however, can perform static analysis only; for dynamic analysis, a compiler must embed extra code in the compiled program as a part of run time support.

In principle, the choice between static and dynamics analysis is governed by the availability of information on which the analysis depends, the amount of precision required and the permissible run time overheads.

An analysis which depends on run time information is inherently dynamic. For example, if type annotations can be omitted in a language and type associations could change at run time, types can be discovered only at run time. This requires dynamic type inferencing. If some amount of imprecision can be tolerated (viz. if precise types are not expected but it is only expected to constrain the set of possible types by ruling out some types before execution), it may be possible to perform an *approximate* static analysis for an otherwise inherently dynamic analysis. This obviates dynamic analysis *only* if a compromise on the precision of information is acceptable; otherwise it requires a subsequent dynamic analysis. In any case, it reduces the amount of dynamic analysis and hence, run time overheads.

If run time overheads are a matter of concern, dynamic analyses should be either avoided or preceded by corresponding (approximate) static analyses. This often is the case and it should not come as a surprise that, in practice a majority of analyses performed by language processors are indeed static. Besides, many dynamic analyses have a static counterpart. For instance, many languages require array bounds to be checked at run time; optimizing compilers can minimize these checks by a static array bound checking optimization.

Scope of Analysis

Programs can be viewed as hierarchical constructions consisting of structures and sub-structures. Program analyses try to discover information about a program structure by correlating the information discovered for constituent sub-structures. As such, an analysis may be confined to a small sub-structure like an expression, a statement, or to larger sub-structure like a group of statements or function/procedure blocks, or to still larger structures like modules or entire programs. The nature of analysis for the structures and the sub-structures may be different. The sub-structures that belong to the same structure are analyzed independently. Analysis of a structure and its sub-structure may be interleaved or may be non-overlapping (and cascaded); in either case, the larger structure can be analyzed only after their constituent sub-structures. For example, the liveness analysis performed in Section 1.1 requires analysis of basic blocks to discover their effects.

Flow Sensitivity of Analysis

If the information discovered by an analysis at a program point depends on the control flow paths involving the program point and could vary from one program point to another, then the analysis is *flow sensitivity*. Otherwise, it is flow insensitive. Type inferencing in C is flow insensitive whereas that in Ruby is flow sensitive. In general, flow insensitivity is a compromise on precision for achieving efficiency.

Context Sensitivity of Analysis

If the information discovered by an interprocedural analysis for a function could vary from one calling context of the function to another, then the analysis is *context sensitive*. A *context insensitive* analysis does not distinguish between different calling contexts and computes the same information for all calling contexts of a function. Context insensitivity is also a compromise on precision for achieving efficiency.

Granularity of Performing Analysis

An *exhaustive* analysis derives information starting from scratch whereas an *incremental* analysis updates the previously derived information to incorporate the effect of some changes in the programs. These changes may be caused by transformations (typically for optimization) or by user edits (typically in programming environments). In general, an incremental analysis must be preceded by at least one instance of the corresponding exhaustive analysis.

Program Representations Used for Analysis

An analysis is typically performed on an intermediate representation of the program. Though the theoretical discussions of many analyses are in terms of the source code (viz. in the case of parallelization), in practice these analyses are performed on a suitable internal representation.

These internal representations differ in their "shapes": They may be either linear data structures (viz. a sequence of quadruples), hierarchical data structures (viz. abstract syntax trees), or general non-linear structures (viz. graphs). The graphs may capture linear abstractions of control flow (as in CFGs) or hierarchical abstractions of control flow (as in call graphs).

Single Static Assignment (SSA) form is an interesting representation that does not belong to the above category. SSA form is used for optimization rather than analysis. As a matter of fact, it can be viewed as the result of a different kind of data flow analysis that explicates the data flow information in a CFG.

Representations of Information

Most common representations of information are sets. The elements of these sets may be of states of a model that satisfy given formulae, or program entities that satisfy the given constraints, or facts that hold at a given program point, or trees or graphs representing types. In many cases these elements may be pairs of program entities and the representations of their properties.

Most analyses require these sets to be finite. Some form of summarization may be required if these sets are not finite. Further the representations of individual properties must also be bounded.

1.3 Characteristics of Data Flow Analysis

Data flow analysis statically computes information about the flow of data (i.e., uses and definitions of data) for each program point in the program being analyzed. This information is required to be a safe approximation of the desired properties of the run time behaviour of the program during each possible execution of that program point on all possible inputs.

Data flow analysis is a special case of program analysis and is characterized by the following:

- *Applications*. Data flow analysis can be used for

- Determining the semantic validity of a program (viz. type correctness based on inferencing, prohibiting the use of uninitialized variables etc.)
- Understanding the behaviour of a program for debugging, maintenance, verification, or testing.
- Transforming a program. This is the classical application of data flow analysis and data flow analysis was originally conceived in this context.

- *Approach of Program Analysis.* Data flow analysis uses constraint resolution systems based on equalities. These constraints are often unconditional. The constraints are called Data Flow Equations.

- *Time.* Data flow analysis is mostly static analysis. The Just-In-Time (JIT) compilation and dynamic slicing etc. involve dynamic data flow analysis.

- *Scope.* Data flow analysis may be performed at almost all levels of scope in a program. Traditionally the following terms have been associated with data flow analysis for different scopes in the domain of imperative languages:

  - Across statements but confined to a maximal sequence of statements with no control transfer other than fall through (i.e., within a *basic block*): Local Data Flow Analysis.
  - Across basic blocks but confined to a function/procedure: Global (intraprocedural) Data Flow Analysis.
  - Across functions/procedures: Interprocedural Data Flow Analysis.

  It is also common to use the term local data flow analysis for analysis of a single statement and global data flow analysis for analysis across statements in a function/procedure. Effectively, the basic blocks for such analyses consist of a single statement.

- *Flow Sensitivity.* Data flow analysis is almost always flow sensitive in that it computes point-specific information. In some cases like alias analysis, flow insensitive analyses are also common.

- *Context Sensitivity.* Interprocedural data flow analysis can be context sensitive as well as context insensitive. In general, fully context sensitive analysis is very inefficient and most practical algorithms employ a limited amount of context sensitivity. Context insensitive data flow analysis is also very common.

- *Granularity.* Data flow analysis can have exhaustive as well as incremental versions. Incremental versions of data flow analysis are conceptually more difficult compared to exhaustive data flow analysis.

- *Program Representations.* The possible internal representations for data flow analysis are abstract syntax trees (ASTs), directed acyclic graphs (DAGs), control flow graphs (CFGs), program flow graphs (PFGs), call multigraphs (CGs), program dependence graphs (PDGs), static single assignment (SSA) forms etc. The most common representations for global data flow analysis are CFGs, PFGs, SSA, and PDGs whereas interprocedural data flow analyses use a combination of CGs (and CFGs or PFGs). Though ASTs can and have been used for data flow analysis, they are not common since they do not exhibit control flow explicitly.

In this book, we restrict ourselves to CFGs and supergraphs created by connecting CFGs of different procedures.

- *Representation of Data Flow Information.* The most common representations are sets of program entities such as variables or expressions satisfying the given property. These sets are implemented using bit vectors. Some analyses use sets of pairs of entities and their properties. For example, constant propagation stores a constantness value for each expression. Some other form of representations such as access paths require summarization.

1.4 Summary and Concluding Remarks

Data flow analysis is a technique of discovering useful information from programs without executing them. This information can be put to a variety of uses. Data flow analysis was conceived in the context of optimization performed by compilers and to date this remains its most dominant application.

Data flow analysis constructs a static summary of the information that represents run time behaviour of a program. Precision of this information depends on the formulation of analysis in terms of the representation of information, rules of summarization, and the algorithms used to compute the information. This chapter has presented a contemporary optimization that demonstrates the importance of these aspects of data flow analysis. We use access paths as a unit of data flow information and summarization is based on treating all access paths beyond two field names as identical.

Our formulation of liveness analysis uses sets of access paths as data flow information; at a given program point, the data flow information depends on the computations that occur after the program point in some execution path. The effect of a statement on the incoming data flow information is incorporated by applying a flow function. In the case of alias analysis, the data flow information is a set of pairs of access paths; at a given program point this information depends on the computations that precede the program point in some execution path. In either case, the data flow information along different paths is combined by taking a union of the sets.

We have also seen that data flow analysis can be restricted to a single procedure by ignoring function calls or can be performed across procedure boundaries. In the latter situation, the calling context of a procedure influences data flow information and for precision, such an analysis should be context sensitive.

This book builds on the above theme in the following manner:

- Part I presents analysis formulations at the intraprocedural level. This part describes a large number of data flow problems ranging from the classical problems to contemporary problems. It also presents generalizations underlying these problems. In particular, it presents the lattice theoretic modeling of data flow frameworks apart from the generalizations of constant and dependent parts in flow functions and entity functions as constituents of flow functions. It shows how these generalizations lead to tight complexity bounds.

  The final chapter of the first part presents SSA representation of programs which builds an additional layer of abstraction over the control flow graph representation of programs and directly relates the definition points and the use points of data.

- Part II shows how an intraprocedural formulation can be used for interprocedural analysis. The main theme of this part is that the two are orthogonal and hence we avoid methods that are specific to a particular application or a particular data flow framework. This part presents two generic approaches. The first approach is a *functional* approach that constructs context independent summary flow functions of procedures. These flow functions are used at the call points to incorporate the effects of procedure calls. The second approach is a *value-based* approach that computes distinct values for distinct calling contexts; this is achieved by augmenting the data flow values with context information.

- Part III describes the implementation of a GCC based generic data flow analyzer for bot vectors and shows how particular data flow analyses can be implemented by writing simple specifications.

1.5 Bibliographic Notes

Most texts on compilers discuss data flow analysis in varying lengths [3, 10, 40, 75, 76, 105]. Some of them discuss details [3, 10, 76]. An advanced treatment of data flow analysis can be found in the books by Hecht [44], Muchnick and Jones [77], and F. Nielson, H. R. Nielson and Hankin [80].

Historically, the practice of data flow analysis precedes the theory. Hecht [44] reports that the round-robin method of performing data flow analysis can be traced back to Vyssotsky and Wegner [101]. It was an attempt to discover uses of variables that were potentially uninitialized in a Bell Laboratories 7090 Fortran II compiler. This was the first variant of an analysis that later came to be known as *reaching definitions analysis*. We describe this analysis in Chapter 2. A more powerful variant of this analysis considers transitive effects of assignments and is described in Chapter 4.

The problem of early deallocation of heap memory is an important optimization and has been attempted in many different ways. The fact that there is ample scope for performing such an optimization has been well established [1, 90, 91, 89, 52]. Some approaches to this optimization attempt to allocate objects on stack when possible [73, 81, 15, 16, 23]. This ensures that the memory is automatically deallocated when activation records are popped off the control stack.

Among earliest data flow analyses, Kennedy [55] presented liveness analysis for scalar variables and since then it has been discussed thoroughly in the literature. Liveness of heap data was first approximated by Agesen, Detlefs and Moss [1] by performing liveness of root variables on the stack that point to heap data. A more precise liveness analysis for heap cells was formulated recently by Khedker, Sanyal and Karkare [62].

The concept of aliasing was first studied in the context of interprocedural analysis for discovering the side effects of function calls. Cooper [25] introduced aliasing in the context formal parameters. Later aliasing of pointers was studied in details. We list references in the bibliographic notes of Chapter 4.

Cocke [24], Ullman [100], Allen [4, 5], and Kennedy [55, 56] were the earliest researchers in intraprocedural data flow analysis. The most influential work in intraprocedural analysis is the classical work by Kildall [63] and Kam and Ullman [49].

Spillman [94], Allen [6], Barth [13] and Banning [12] were the earliest researchers to study interprocedural data flow analysis. This was motivated by the side effect analysis. The most influential work on interprocedural data flow analysis is the classical work by Sharir and Pnueli [93].

Part I

Intraprocedural Data Flow Analysis

2

Classical Bit Vector Data Flow Analysis

Data flow analysis originated with what was later termed as "bit vector" data flow frameworks. The term "bit vector" arises from the fact that not only can the data flow information be represented using bit vectors, it can also be computed using bit vector operations alone. There are data flow former for which although the data flow information can be represented using bit vectors, computing it requires additional operations. We make this notion more precise in the chapter summary with the help of the examples presented in the chapter.

2.1 Basic Concepts and Notations

Data flow analysis views computation of data through expressions and transition of data through assignments to variables. Properties of programs are defined in terms of properties of program entities such as expressions, variables, and definitions appearing in a program. In this chapter, we restrict expressions to primitive expressions involving a single operator. Variables are restricted to scalar variables and definitions are restricted to assignments made to scalar variables. Data flow analyses of other program entities such as composite expressions, array variables, pointer variables, statement numbers etc. have also been devised; we present some of them in later chapters.

For a given program entity such as an expression, data flow analysis of a program involves the following two steps (a) discovering the effect of individual statements on the expression, and (b) relating these effects across statements in the program. For reasons of efficiency, both these steps are often carried over a *basic block* instead of a single statement. A basic block is a maximal group of consecutive statements that are always executed together with a strictly sequential control flow between them. Step (a) is called *local* data flow analysis and is performed for a basic block only once. Step (b) constitutes *global* data flow analysis* and may require repeated traversals over basic blocks in a CFG. Since global analysis correlates local properties, combining local analysis of several statements together and performing global

*Observe that the term global data flow analysis is restricted to data flow analysis of a single procedure.

analysis over the resulting basic blocks rather than individual statements implies lesser work for global analysis.

Relating the effects across basic blocks involves propagating data flow information from a basic block to another along the direction of control flow or against it. Propagation along the direction of control flow constitutes a *forward flow* whereas propagation against the direction of control flow constitutes a *backward flow*. As observed in Sections 1.1.2 and 1.1.3, liveness analysis involves backward flows and alias analysis involves forward flows.

Global data flow information is associated with the entry and exit points of a basic block. For block n these points are denoted by $\mathsf{Entry}(n)$ and $\mathsf{Exit}(n)$; they represent the possible states of the program just before the execution of the first statement and the just after the execution of the last statement in block n. Data flow information associated with them is usually denoted by In_n and Out_n. For bit vector frameworks, the local data flow information is usually expressed in terms of Gen_n and Kill_n. Gen_n denotes the data flow information which is generated within block n whereas Kill_n denotes the data flow information which becomes invalid in block n.

The relationship between local and global data flow information for a block (i.e., Gen_n, Kill_n, In_n, and Out_n) and between global data flow information across different blocks is captured by a system of linear simultaneous equations called *data flow equations*. In general, these equations have multiple solutions. This makes it important to choose the initial values of In_n and Out_n carefully.

Edges in CFGs denote the *predecessor* and *successor* relationships: If there is an edge $n_1 \rightarrow n_2$, then n_1 is a predecessor of n_2 and n_2 is a successor of n_1. Observe that this is different from the notions of *ancestors* and *descendants* which are the transitive closures of predecessors and successors respectively. Predecessors and successors of a block n are denoted by $\mathsf{pred}(n)$ and $\mathsf{succ}(n)$ respectively.

We assume that the CFG has two distinguished unique nodes: *Start* which has no predecessor and *End* which has no successor. If such nodes do not exist, dummy nodes can be added without affecting the program semantics. It is further assumed that every basic block n is reachable from the *Start* block and that the *End* block is reachable from n. We use the terms nodes and blocks interchangeably.

2.2 Discovering Local Data Flow Information

The manner in which the effect of a statement is modeled varies from one analysis to another. In any case, there is a common pattern of generation of data flow information or invalidation of data flow information. In this chapter we are interested in the following entities and operations related to data flow analysis:

Entity	Operations	
Variable $x \in \mathbb{V}\text{ar}$	Reading the value of x	Modifying the value of x
Expression $e \in \mathbb{E}\text{xpr}$	Computing e	Modifying an operand of e
Definition $d_i : x = e$, $d_i \in \mathbb{D}\text{efs}$, $x \in \mathbb{V}\text{ar}$, $e \in \mathbb{E}\text{xpr}$	Occurrence of d_i	Any definition of x

Reading the value of a variable is also termed as the *use* of the variable. A variable may be used or an expression may be computed (a) in the right hand side of an assignment statement, (b) in a condition for altering flow of control, (c) as an actual parameter in a function call, or (d) as a return value from a function. All other operations in the above table involve an assignment statement to a relevant variable. Note that reading a value of a variable from input can be safely considered as an assignment statement assigning an unknown value to the variable.

The set Gen_n and Kill_n are computed from the operations described above. It is easy to see that the operation in one column nullifies the effect of the operation in the other column. From that viewpoint, the operation in one column is an inverse of the operation in the other column. Computing Gen_n and Kill_n requires identifying operations that are exposed in the direction of analysis i.e., are not followed by the inverse operation in the direction of analysis. For forward problems, we are interested in the operations that are *downwards exposed* and for the backward problems we are interested in the operations that are *upwards exposed.* This is illustrated by the following example.

Example 2.1

Consider an assignment statement $x = x + 1$. In this statement, the use of variable x and the computation of expression $x + 1$ are upwards exposed because they are not preceded by a modification of the value of x. They are not downwards exposed because they are followed by a modification of the value of x. As a contrasting example, the use of x and computation of $x + 1$ are both upwards and downwards exposed in an assignment $y = x + 1$ if x and y do not have the same address (i.e., they are not aliased). □

Traditionally, the definitions of Gen_n and Kill_n have not been symmetric with respect to the chosen operation. In particular, the operations which contribute to Gen_n are required to be downwards exposed for forward flows and upwards exposed for backward flows. The operations which contribute to Kill_n may be preceded or followed by their inverses. We explain this asymmetry later in the specific contexts of the data flow problems presented in this chapter.

Local property computation isolates global analysis from the intermediate representation (IR) in that it is the former which needs to examine the IR statements. In practice, IRs in real compilers are very complicated since they need to store a lot of information about each statement across different phases of a compiler. Hence local property computations are tedious and error-prone. Global data flow analyzers are relatively much simpler and cleaner.

2.3 Discovering Global Properties of Variables

In this section, we describe two analyses involving variables: *Live Variables Analysis* and *Reaching Definitions Analysis*. Although we have listed a definition as a separate entity, here we club its analysis with those of variables.

2.3.1 Live Variables Analysis

Section 1.1.2 has introduced liveness analysis for heap data. Liveness analysis for scalar variables essentially involves determining whether a variable is used in future and is relatively much simpler because it does not have to consider pointer dereferencing.

DEFINITION 2.1 *A variable $x \in \mathsf{Var}$ is live at a program point u if some path from u to End contains a use of x which is not preceded by its definition.*

The data flow equations which define live variables analysis are:

$$\mathit{In}_n = (\mathit{Out}_n - \mathit{Kill}_n) \cup \mathit{Gen}_n \tag{2.1}$$

$$\mathit{Out}_n = \begin{cases} \mathit{BI} & n \text{ is } \mathsf{End} \text{ block} \\ \bigcup_{s \in succ(n)} \mathit{In}_s & \text{otherwise} \end{cases} \tag{2.2}$$

where In_n, Out_n, Gen_n, Kill_n, and BI are sets of variables.

Liveness at $\mathit{Exit}(\mathsf{End})$ is represented by BI. This is required because different categories of variables have to be treated differently. Local variables are not live at $\mathit{Exit}(\mathsf{End})$ whereas liveness of the return value, global variables, and parameters passed by reference depends on the calling contexts. If there is no interprocedural analysis, all variables other than local variables are assumed to be live. We assume that all our analyses in Part I are restricted to local entities only. Thus we will define BI for local entities only. Under the assumption of parameter passing by value as in C, this also allows us to ignore function calls completely.

Observe the use of $\cup$ in Equation (2.2). It essentially means that the liveness information at $\mathit{Exit}(n)$ is a superset of the liveness information at $\mathit{Entry}(s)$ where s is a successor of n. This is consistent with the "any path" nature of the definition of liveness: Subsequent use along a single path is sufficient to make a variable live. Further, since data flow information at a node depends on the successor nodes, this is a backward data flow problem.

Gen_n contains the variables whose liveness is generated within n. Clearly, these variables have upwards exposed uses in n. Kill_n contains the variables whose liveness is killed in n. These are the variables which appear on the left hand side of an assignment anywhere in n. Observe that Gen_n and Kill_n need not be mutually exclusive.

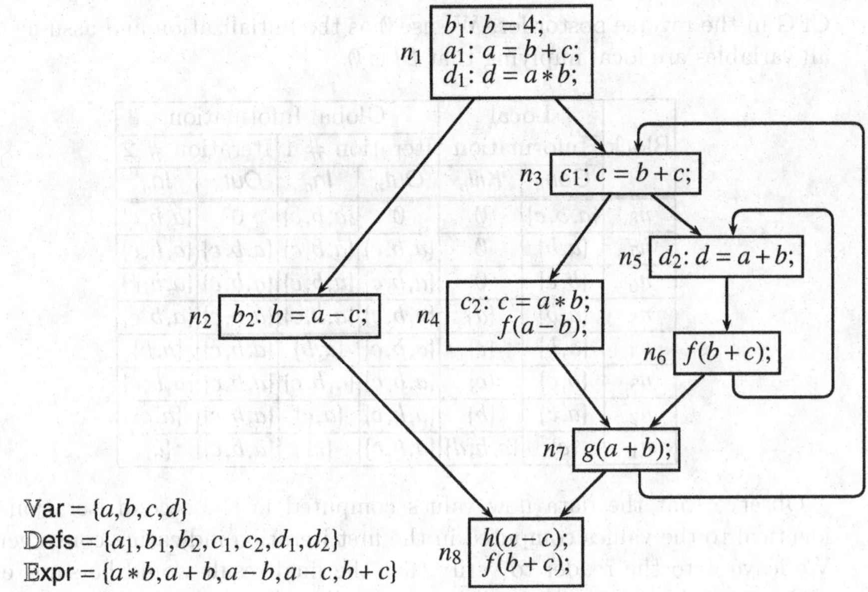

FIGURE 2.1
Program for illustrating bit vector data flow frameworks.

Example 2.2
In Figure 2.1, variable c is contained in both Gen_{n_3} and $Kill_{n_3}$. □

In general, assuming that variable x is live at $Exit(n)$, there are four possibilities with four distinct semantics:

Case	Local Information		Effect on Liveness
1	$x \notin Gen_n$	$x \notin Kill_n$	Liveness of x is unaffected in block n
2	$x \in Gen_n$	$x \notin Kill_n$	Liveness of x is generated in block n
3	$x \notin Gen_n$	$x \in Kill_n$	Liveness of x is killed in block n
4	$x \in Gen_n$	$x \in Kill_n$	Liveness of x is unaffected in block n in spite of x being modified in n.

Variable x is live at $Entry(n)$ in cases 1, 2, and 4 but the reason for its liveness is different in each case. In particular, case 4 captures the fact that the liveness of x is killed in n but is re-generated within n. The reason why this needs to be distinguished from case 1 and case 2 is that in some instances, it is important to know whether the value of a variable is modified in a block or not.

Example 2.3
We provide a trace of liveness analysis for the program flow graph in Figure 2.1. Since this analysis involves backward flows, we prefer to traverse the

CFG in the reverse postorder. We use $\emptyset$ as the initialization and assume that all variables are local implying that *BI* is $\emptyset$.

Block	Local Information		Global Information			
			Iteration # 1		Iteration # 2	
	Gen_n	$Kill_n$	Out_n	In_n	Out_n	In_n
n_8	$\{a,b,c\}$	$\emptyset$	$\emptyset$	$\{a,b,c\}$	$\emptyset$	$\{a,b,c\}$
n_7	$\{a,b\}$	$\emptyset$	$\{a,b,c\}$	$\{a,b,c\}$	$\{a,b,c\}$	$\{a,b,c\}$
n_6	$\{b,c\}$	$\emptyset$	$\{a,b,c\}$	$\{a,b,c\}$	$\{a,b,c\}$	$\{a,b,c\}$
n_5	$\{a,b\}$	$\{d\}$	$\{a,b,c\}$	$\{a,b,c\}$	$\{a,b,c\}$	$\{a,b,c\}$
n_4	$\{a,b\}$	$\{c\}$	$\{a,b,c\}$	$\{a,b\}$	$\{a,b,c\}$	$\{a,b\}$
n_3	$\{b,c\}$	$\{c\}$	$\{a,b,c\}$	$\{a,b,c\}$	$\{a,b,c\}$	$\{a,b,c\}$
n_2	$\{a,c\}$	$\{b\}$	$\{a,b,c\}$	$\{a,c\}$	$\{a,b,c\}$	$\{a,c\}$
n_1	$\{c\}$	$\{a,b,d\}$	$\{a,b,c\}$	$\{c\}$	$\{a,b,c\}$	$\{c\}$

Observe that the data flow values computed in the second iteration are identical to the values computed in the first iteration indicating convergence. We leave it to the reader to verify that the final result would be same even if the graph is traversed in postorder; the only difference is that it will take many more iterations.

Observe that the result would be different if we had used the universal set (in this case $\{a,b,c,d\}$) as the initialization. Then, d would have been live at $Exit(n_7)$ whereas d is not used anywhere in the program. □

For brevity, we will show only new values computed in an iteration in subsequent examples—if a value is same as in the previous iteration, we will not show it explicitly. Hence we will not show the data flow values in the last iteration.

Two major applications of liveness analysis are in *register allocation* and *dead code elimination*. If a variable x is live at a program point, the current value of x is likely to be used along some execution path and hence x is a potential candidate for being allocated a register. On the other hand, if x is not live, the register allocated to x can be allocated to some other variable without the need of storing the value of x in memory. If x is not live at a exit of an assignment of x, then this assignment can be safely deleted.[†] For example, in Figure 2.1, variable d is not live anywhere. Thus all assignments of d can be safely eliminated.

In some cases deleting such assignments can have a transitive effect because the variables used in the right hand side of such an assignment may cease to be live. Instead of repeating the sequence of liveness analysis and dead code elimination, it is possible to discover such transitive effects through a single data flow analysis before dead code elimination is performed. This analysis is called *faint variables analysis* and will be presented in Chapter 4. Note that such an analysis cannot be restricted to a single variable at a time because the liveness of variables occurring on

[†]Deletion of code which is unreachable is also called dead code elimination but we will restrict dead code elimination to deletion of assignments to values which have no further use.

the right hand side of an assignment now also depends on the liveness of the variable on the left hand side. Such analyses are not bit vector analyses in spite of the fact that some of them use bit vector representation for data flow information. This is because the effect of basic blocks in these analyses are not expressible in terms of constant functions defined using *Gen* and *Kill* due to inter-dependence of various entities. Such frameworks are called non-separable. We describe them in Chapter 4.

For a given variable x, liveness analysis discovers a set of *liveness paths.* Each liveness path is a sequence of blocks $(b_1, b_2, \ldots, b_k)$ which is a prefix of some potential execution path starting at b_1 such that:

- b_k contains an upwards exposed use of x, and
- b_1 is either *Start* or contains an assignment to x, and
- no other block on the path contains an assignment to x.

Example 2.4
Some liveness paths for variable c in our example program are: (n_4, n_7, n_8), $(n_3, n_5, n_6, n_7, n_8)$, $(n_3, n_5, n_6, n_5, n_6, n_7, n_8)$, and (n_1, n_2, n_8). ☐

2.3.2 Dead Variables Analysis

A variable is dead (i.e., not live) if it is dead along all paths. If we wish to perform dead variables analysis instead of live variables analysis, the interpretation of In_n and Out_n changes: If a variable is contained in In_n or Out_n, it is dead instead of being live. This requires the following changes:

- The definitions of Gen_n and Kill_n will change. Gen_n will now contain all variables whose values are modified in the block such that the modifications are upwards exposed (i.e., are not preceded by a use of the variable). Kill_n will contain variables which are used anywhere regardless of what precedes or follows the uses. Observe that this is different from merely swapping Gen_n and Kill_n of liveness analysis.
- We will have to use $\cap$ rather than $\cup$ for merging information.
- We will have to use the universal set as initialization rather than empty set. Similarly, *BI* will now have a different set of variables.

2.3.3 Reaching Definitions Analysis

A definition of a variable x is a statement which assigns a value to x. For the purpose of analysis, a unique label is associated with each assignment and these labels are used to represent the definitions. As a consequence, different occurrences of the same assignment become different definitions. This is different from uses of variables or computation of expressions—labels are not associated with them and hence lexically same computations are not treated as different entities for analysis.

DEFINITION 2.2 *A definition $d_i \in \mathbb{D}\mathsf{efs}$ of a variable $x \in \mathbb{V}\mathsf{ar}$ reaches a program point u if d_i occurs on some path from* **Start** *to u and is not followed by any other definition of x on this path.*

The data flow equations which define the required analysis are:

$$\mathit{In}_n = \begin{cases} \mathit{BI} & n \text{ is } \mathit{Start} \text{ block} \\ \bigcup\limits_{p \in pred(n)} \mathit{Out}_p & \text{otherwise} \end{cases} \tag{2.3}$$

$$\mathit{Out}_n = (\mathit{In}_n - \mathit{Kill}_n) \cup \mathit{Gen}_n \tag{2.4}$$

where In_n, Out_n, Gen_n, Kill_n, and BI are sets of definitions. Observe the use of $\cup$ to capture the "any path" nature of data flow. This is similar to liveness analysis except that now the data flow is forward rather than backward.

For every local variables x, it is assumed that a fictitious definition $x = \mathit{undef}$ reaches *Entry*(*Start*). This is required for the optimization of copy propagation (described in Section 2.3.4). If definition $x = \mathit{undef}$ reaches a use of x, it suggests a potential use before definition. Whether this happens at run time depends on the actual results of conditions along the path taken to reach the program point.

Gen_n contains downwards exposed definitions in n whereas Kill_n contains all definitions of all variables modified in n. Thus $\mathit{Gen}_n \subseteq \mathit{Kill}_n$ for reaching definitions analysis.

Example 2.5

The labels of assignments in the program in Figure 2.1 consist of variable names and an instance number. We use them to represent the definitions in the programs. Definitions a_0, b_0, c_0, and d_0 represent the special definitions $a = \mathit{undef}$, $b = \mathit{undef}$, $c = \mathit{undef}$, and $d = \mathit{undef}$ respectively. Since the confluence operation is $\cup$, the initial value at each program point is $\emptyset$.

The result of performing reaching definitions analysis has been shown in Figure 2.2. The definitions which reach $\mathit{Exit}(n_6)$ and $\mathit{Exit}(n_7)$ in first iteration have to be propagated to $\mathit{Entry}(n_5)$ and $\mathit{Entry}(n_3)$ respectively requiring an additional iteration. □

Reaching definitions analysis is used for constructing *use-def* and *def-use* chains which connect definitions to their uses as illustrated in the following example. These chains facilitate several optimizing transformations.

Example 2.6

Figure 2.3 shows the use-def and def-use chains of variables a and c in our example program. For simplicity, we have not shown the chains for other

Block	Local Information		Global Information			
			Iteration # 1		Changed values in iteration # 2	
	Gen_n	$Kill_n$	In_n	Out_n	In_n	Out_n
n_1	$\{a_1, b_1, d_1\}$	$\{a_0, a_1, b_0, b_1, b_2, d_0, d_1, d_2\}$	$\{a_0, b_0, c_0, d_0\}$	$\{a_1, b_1, c_0, d_1\}$		
n_2	$\{b_2\}$	$\{b_0, b_1, b_2\}$	$\{a_1, b_1, c_0, d_1\}$	$\{a_1, b_2, c_0, d_1\}$		
n_3	$\{c_1\}$	$\{c_0, c_1, c_2\}$	$\{a_1, b_1, c_0, d_1\}$	$\{a_1, b_1, c_1, d_1\}$	$\{a_1, b_1, c_0, c_1, c_2, d_1, d_2\}$	$\{a_1, b_1, c_1, d_1, d_2\}$
n_4	$\{c_2\}$	$\{c_0, c_1, c_2\}$	$\{a_1, b_1, c_1, d_1\}$	$\{a_1, b_1, c_2, d_2\}$	$\{a_1, b_1, c_1, d_1, d_2\}$	$\{a_1, b_1, c_2, d_1, d_2\}$
n_5	$\{d_2\}$	$\{d_0, d_1, d_2\}$	$\{a_1, b_1, c_1, d_1\}$	$\{a_1, b_1, c_1, d_2\}$	$\{a_1, b_1, c_1, d_1, d_2\}$	
n_6	$\emptyset$	$\emptyset$	$\{a_1, b_1, c_1, d_2\}$	$\{a_1, b_1, c_1, d_2\}$		
n_7	$\emptyset$	$\emptyset$	$\{a_1, b_1, c_1, c_2, d_1, d_2\}$	$\{a_1, b_1, c_1, c_2, d_1, d_2\}$		
n_8	$\emptyset$	$\emptyset$	$\{a_1, b_1, b_2, c_0, c_1, c_2, d_1, d_2\}$	$\{a_1, b_1, b_2, c_0, c_1, c_2, d_1, d_2\}$		

FIGURE 2.2
Reaching definitions analysis for Example 2.5.

variables. Observe that the definition c_0 reaches some uses of c. This suggests a potential use before any assigning meaningful value. This, in turn, makes variable b potentially undefined. □

Transitive effects of undefined variables are captured by *possibly uninitialized variables analysis*. Similar to faint variables analysis which captures transitive effect of dead variables, possibly uninitialized variables analysis is also non-separable—whether a variable is possibly undefined may depend on whether other variables are possibly undefined.

For definition x_i of variable x, reaching definitions analysis discovers a set of *definition reaching paths*. This path is a sequence of blocks $(b_1, b_2, \ldots, b_k)$ which is a prefix of some potential execution path starting at b_1 such that:

- b_1 contains the definition x_i
- b_k is either *End* or contains a definition of x
- no other block in the path contains a definition of x.

Example 2.7
Some definition reaching paths for variable c in our example program are: (n_4, n_7, n_3), $(n_3, n_5, n_6, n_5, n_6, n_7, n_8)$, and $(n_3, n_5, n_6, n_7, n_3)$. □

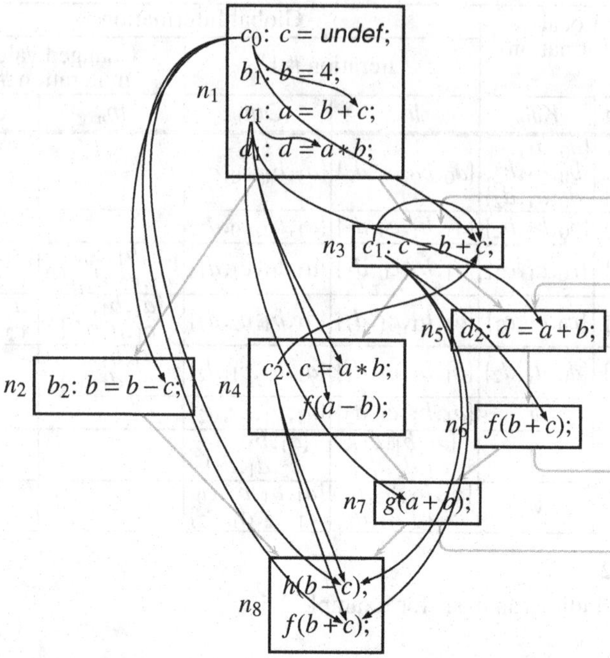

FIGURE 2.3
Def-use chains of variables a and c in our example program.

2.3.4 Reaching Definitions for Copy Propagation

Another application of reaching definitions analysis is in performing *copy propagation*. A definition of the form $x = y$ is called a *copy* because it merely copies the value of y to x. When such a definition reaches a use of x, and no other definition of x reaches that use then the use of x can be replaced by y.

Example 2.8
Copy $b = 4$ in block n_1 in our example program is the only definition which reached the uses of b in blocks n_3, n_4, n_5, n_6 and n_7. Thus all these uses can be replaced by constant 4. ▯

In the above example, the right hand side value is constant. When they are variables, as in $x = y$, replacing the uses of x by y requires an additional check that the value of y has not been modified along the path from the copy to the use. We can define a variant of reaching definitions analysis to accomplish this. The main difference between this variant and the analysis presented in Section 2.3.3 is that we restrict the definitions to copies and a definition $x = y$ is contained in

- Gen_n if it is downwards exposed in n in the sense of not being followed by a definition of x or y, and in

- $Kill_b$ if n contains a definition of x or y.

With these changes, we can now perform reaching definitions analysis. If one definition reaches a use, we can perform copy propagation.

Note that this optimization does not improve the program on its own but it has the potential of creating dead code: When copy propagation is performed using $x = y$, it is possible that all uses of x are replaced by y thus making x dead after the assignment. Thus this assignment can be safely deleted.

We leave it for the reader to define a variant of copy propagation analysis using intersection rather than union.

2.4 Discovering Global Properties of Expressions

In this section we present analyses for eliminating redundant computations of expressions. Our first analysis involves replacing an expression by its precomputed value. The remaining analyses facilitate *code movement* which involve advancing computation an expression to earlier points in control flow paths.

2.4.1 Available Expressions Analysis

Given a program point u, this analysis discovers the expressions whose results at u are same as the their previously computed values regardless of the execution path taken to reach u.

DEFINITION 2.3 *An expression $e \in$ Expr is available at a program point u if all paths from Start to u contain a computation of e which is not followed by an assignment to any of its operands.*

The data flow equations which define available expressions analysis are:

$$In_n = \begin{cases} BI & n \text{ is } Start \text{ block} \\ \bigcap_{p \in pred(n)} Out_p & \text{otherwise} \end{cases} \tag{2.5}$$

$$Out_n = (In_n - Kill_n) \cup Gen_n \tag{2.6}$$

where In_n, Out_n, Gen_n, $Kill_n$, and BI are sets of expressions. Observe the use of $\cap$ to capture the "all paths" nature of data flow. This is different from liveness and reaching definitions analyses. However, similar to reaching definitions analysis, the direction of data flow is forward.

BI assumes that expressions involving local variables are not available at entry of *Start* since the local variables come into existence with function invocations.[‡] Gen_n contains downwards exposed expressions in n whereas $Kill_n$ contains all expressions whose operands are modified in n.

The availability information is useful in an optimization called *common subexpression elimination* in which computation of an expression is marked as redundant if the expression is available at that point. Let the set of expressions whose upwards exposed computations exist in block n be denoted by $AntGen_n$[§]. Let $Redundant_n$ denote expressions which can be eliminated in block n. Then,

$$Redundant_n = AntGen_n \cap In_n \tag{2.7}$$

Values of the previous computations are stored in a temporary variable and the redundant computations are replaced by that temporary variable. Most production compilers such as gcc perform common subexpression elimination.

Example 2.9

The program in Figure 2.1 contains expressions $(a*b)$, $(a+b)$, $(a-b)$, $(a-c)$, and $(b+c)$. We represent the set of expression by a bit vector; the position a bit indicates the expression which it represents as shown below.

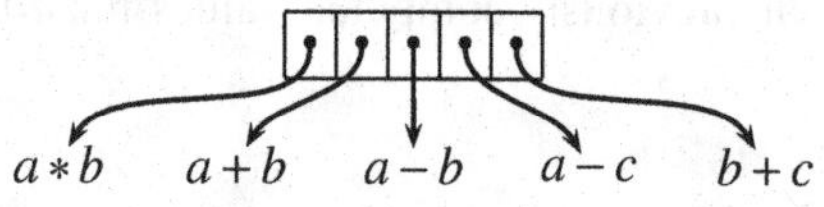

Bit string 11111 represents the set $\{a*b, a+b, a-b, a-c, b+c\}$ whereas bit string 00000 represents $\emptyset$. The result of available expressions analysis has been shown below. Since this is an all paths analysis, the initial value at each

‡There could be exceptions to this in languages which allocate activation records in static area instead of stack e.g., FORTRAN IV.

§*AntGen* is the *Gen* set for Anticipability analysis described in Section 2.4.3. Here we use a different name to avoid confusion with *Gen* of the current analysis.

program point is the universal set (i.e., 11111).

Block	Local Information			Global Information				
				Iteration # 1		Changed values in iteration # 2		
	Gen$_n$	*Kill*$_n$	*AntGen*$_n$	*In*$_n$	*Out*$_n$	*In*$_n$	*Out*$_n$	*Redundant*$_n$
n_1	10001	11111	00000	00000	10001			00000
n_2	00010	11101	00010	10001	00010			00000
n_3	00000	00011	00001	10001	10000	10000		00000
n_4	10100	00011	10100	10000	10100			10000
n_5	01000	00000	01000	10000	11000			00000
n_6	00001	00000	00001	11000	11001			00000
n_7	01000	00000	01000	10000	11000			00000
n_8	00011	00000	00011	00000	00011			00000

Expression $(a * b)$ in n_4 is redundant. Its value can be stored in a temporary variable say t_0. Then the assignment $d = a * b$ in n_1 can be replaced by $d = t_0$ and the assignment $c = a * b$ in n_4 can be replaced by $c = t_0$.

If we had used 00000 as the initial value, expression $(a * b)$ would not have been available anywhere in the loops except at *Exit*(n_4). Thus we would have missed the opportunity of eliminating the computation of $(a * b)$ in n_4. □

For a given expression e, available expressions analysis discovers a set of *availability paths*. Each availability path is a sequence of blocks $(b_1, b_2, \ldots, b_k)$ which is a prefix of some potential execution path starting at b_1 such that:

- b_1 contains a downwards exposed computation of e,
- b_k is either *End* or contains a computation of e, or an assignment to some operand of e,
- no block in the path contains a computation of e, or an assignment to any operand of e, and
- every path ending on b_k is an availability path for e.

Note that because of the last condition, we cannot talk about an availability path in isolation from other paths ending on a node—we must talk about a group of availability paths.

In terms of availability paths, common subexpression elimination in block n involves storing the value of redundant expression in a temporary at the start of every availability path terminating at n and replacing the computation of the expression in n by the temporary.

Example 2.10
Some availability paths for expression $(a * b)$ in our example program are: (n_1, n_3, n_4), $(n_1, n_3, n_5, n_6, n_7, n_3, n_4)$, and (n_4, n_7, n_3, n_4). □

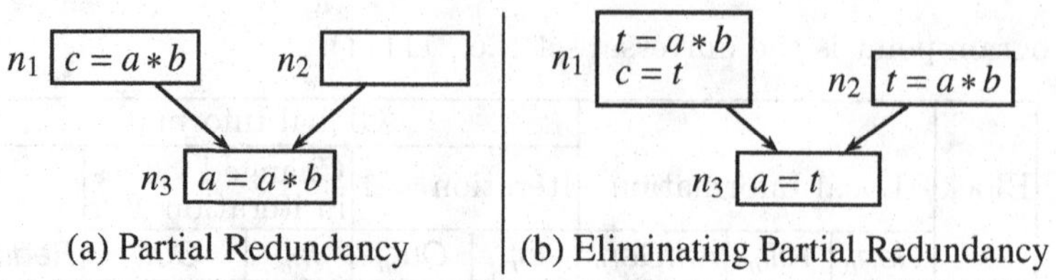

n_1 $c = a * b$
n_2
n_3 $a = a * b$
(a) Partial Redundancy
n_1 $t = a * b$ $c = t$
n_2 $t = a * b$
n_3 $a = t$
(b) Eliminating Partial Redundancy

FIGURE 2.4
Partial availability and partial redundancy.

2.4.2 Partially Available Expressions Analysis

An important variant of available expressions analysis relaxes the condition that an expression should be available along all paths—it is sufficient if the expression is available along some path.

If a block contains an upwards exposed computation of an expression and the expression is available at the entry of the block, then the upwards exposed computation is totally redundant. If the expression is partially available at the entry of the block, then the upwards exposed computation is partially redundant as illustrated in Figure 2.4. This information is used in partial redundancy elimination described in Section 2.4.4.

We need to make a simple change in available expressions analysis to discover partially available expressions: Data flow information should be merged using $\cup$ instead of $\cap$. This also means that the initial value is $\emptyset$ instead of the universal set.

Partially redundant computations in block n are defined by

$$\mathit{ParRedund}_n = \mathit{AntGen}_n \cap \mathit{In}_n \tag{2.8}$$

where AntGen_n denotes the set of expressions whose upwards exposed computations exist in block n.

Example 2.11

The result of partially available expressions analysis on our example program has been shown below. Since the confluence operation is $\cup$, the initial value of In_i and Out_i for all i is 00000.

Block	Local Information			Global Information				
				Iteration # 1		Changed values in iteration # 2		
	Gen_n	$Kill_n$	$AntGen_n$	In_n	Out_n	In_n	Out_n	$ParRedund_n$
n_1	10001	11111	00000	00000	10001			00000
n_2	00010	11101	00010	10001	00010			00000
n_3	00000	00011	00001	10001	10000	11101	11100	00001
n_4	10100	00011	10100	10000	10100	11100	11100	10100
n_5	01000	00000	01000	10000	11000	11101	11101	01000
n_6	00001	00000	00001	11000	11001	11101	11101	00001
n_7	01000	00000	01000	11101	11101			01000
n_8	00011	00000	00011	11111	11111			00011

Observe that for every n, $ParRedund_n \supseteq Redundant_n$ suggesting partial redundancies subsume total redundancies. Also note that in our program, there are many partial redundancies which are not total. □

The paths discovered by partial available expressions analysis are a special case of the availability paths discovered by available expressions analysis: The last condition in the definition of availability paths does not apply to partial availability paths. Thus unlike availability paths, we can talk about individual partial availability paths.

2.4.3 Anticipable Expressions Analysis

Common subexpression elimination explained in Section 2.4.1 involves "in-place" transformation. As observed in the beginning of Section 2.4, some transformations involve inserting expressions at program points where they were not computed in the original program. Preserving the semantics of programs requires ensuring that a computation should not be inserted in a path along which the computation was not performed in the original program.

Example 2.12
Consider our running example of Figure 2.1. It is easy to see that expression $(a+b)$ is invariant in both the loops and it is desirable to move it out of the loops and place it at $Exit(n_1)$. However, the control flow path $n_1 \rightarrow n_2 \rightarrow n_8$ does not have any computation of the expression. Hence inserting the expression at $Exit(n_1)$ is not safe. □

The decision such as above can be arrived at by performing *anticipable expressions analysis* (also called *very busy expressions* analysis).

DEFINITION 2.4 *An expression* $e \in \mathbb{E}\text{xpr}$ *is anticipable at a program*

Block	Local Information		Global Information			
			Iteration # 1		Changed values in iteration # 2	
	Gen_n	$Kill_n$	Out_n	In_n	Out_n	In_n
n_8	00011	00000	00000	00011		
n_7	01000	00000	00011	01011	00001	01001
n_6	00001	00000	01011	01011	01001	01001
n_5	01000	00000	01011	01011	01001	01001
n_4	10100	00011	01011	11100	01001	11100
n_3	00001	00011	01000	01001	01000	01001
n_2	00010	11101	00011	00010		
n_1	00000	11111	00000	00000		

FIGURE 2.5
Anticipable expressions analysis for Example 2.13.

point u if every path from u to End contains a computation of e which is not preceded by an assignment to any operand of e.

The data flow equations which define anticipable expressions analysis are:

$$In_n = (Out_n - Kill_n) \cup Gen_n \tag{2.9}$$

$$Out_n = \begin{cases} BI & n \text{ is } End \text{ block} \\ \bigcap_{s \in succ(n)} In_s & \text{otherwise} \end{cases} \tag{2.10}$$

where In_n, Out_n, Gen_n, $Kill_n$, and BI are sets of expressions. Similar to available expressions analysis, these equations use $\cap$ to capture the "all paths" nature of data flow. However, the data flow is backward similar to live variables analysis.

BI assumes that the expressions involving local variables are not anticipated at $Exit(End)$. Gen_n contains upwards exposed expressions in n whereas $Kill_n$ contains all expressions whose operands are modified in n.

Example 2.13
The result of anticipable expressions analysis on our example program has been shown in Figure 2.5. Since the confluence operation is $\cap$, the initial value of In_i and Out_i for all i is 11111. □

For a given expression e, anticipable expressions analysis discovers a set of *anticipability paths*. Each anticipability path is a sequence of blocks $(b_1, b_2, \ldots, b_k)$ which is a prefix of some potential execution path starting at b_1 such that:

- b_k contains an upwards exposed computation of e,

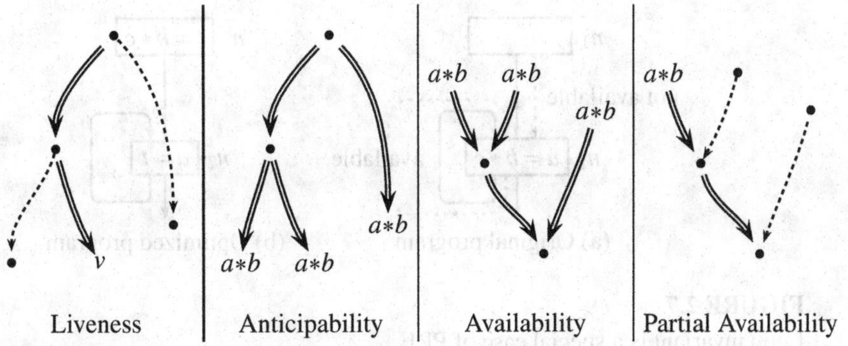

FIGURE 2.6
Data flow paths discovered by data flow analysis (shown by double lines).

- b_1 is either *Start* or contains a computation of e, or an assignment to some operand of e,
- no block in the path contains a computation of e, or an assignment to any operand of e, and
- every path starting at b_1 is an anticipability path.

Similar to availability paths, we talk about a group of anticipability paths rather than a single anticipability path.

Example 2.14
Some anticipability paths for expression $(a+b)$ in our example program are: (n_5,n_6,n_5), (n_5,n_6,n_7), (n_3,n_4,n_7), and (n_3,n_5). Note that $(a+b)$ is not anticipable at *Exit*(n_1). □

2.4.4 Classical Partial Redundancy Elimination

This section presents the classical approach to *partial redundancy elimination* (PRE) which involves a *bidirectional* formulation of data flows. This section also describes its limitations and shows how they are overcome by some of its variants.

The basic principle of PRE has been illustrated in Figure 2.4. It can be viewed as an instance of *code hoisting* along a *hosting path*. This hoisting subsumes loop invariant movement and common subexpression elimination.

Example 2.15
In Figure 2.4 the hoisting path is (n_2,n_3); path (n_1,n_3) is an availability path. In Figure 2.7, expression $b*c$ is loop invariant and is partially available due the availability path along the back edge. This is a special case of partial redundancy and can be eliminated along the hoisting path (n_1,n_2). □

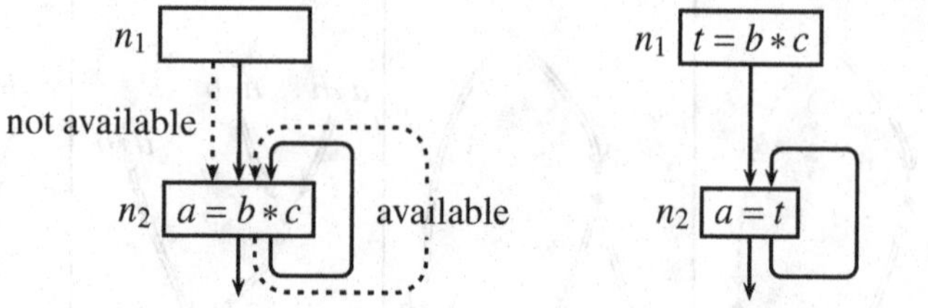

(a) Original program (b) Optimized program

FIGURE 2.7
Loop invariant is a special case of PRE.

Hoisting Path of an Expression

Informally, the safety and desirability of hoisting an expression are defined as follows: An expression can be safely hoisted to a program point u if it is anticipable at u. It should be hoisted to ancestors of u if it is partially available at u.

For an expression e, a hoisting path is a maximal sequence of blocks $(b_1, b_2, \ldots, b_k)$ which is a prefix of a potential execution path starting at b_1 such that:

- b_k contains an upwards exposed computation of e,
- e is anticipable and partially available at $\mathit{Entry}(b_i)$ and $\mathit{Exit}(b_i)$ of each block b_i (other than b_1 and b_k), and at $\mathit{Entry}(b_k)$,
- e is not available at $\mathit{Exit}(b_1)$, or can be hoisted to $\mathit{Entry}(b_1)$, and
- no block in the path contains a computation of e, or an assignment to any operand of e.

A key design idea in defining a hoisting path is that an expression is hoisted to $\mathit{Entry}(n)$ only if it can be hoisted out of n into its predecessors. This means that if an expression has to be inserted at the start of a hoisting path, it is inserted at the exit of the first block rather than at its entry. The conditions for hoisting an expression into and out of a block are defined as follows:

- *Safety of hoisting to* $\mathit{Exit}(n)$.

  An expression e should be hoisted to $\mathit{Exit}(n)$ only if

  (S.1) it can be hoisted to $\mathit{Entry}(s)$ for every successor s of n.

  This is captured by the equation:

$$\mathit{Out}_n = \begin{cases} \mathit{BI} & n \text{ is } \mathit{End} \text{ block} \\ \bigcap_{s \in succ(n)} \mathit{In}_s & \text{otherwise} \end{cases} \tag{2.11}$$

- *Safety of hoisting to Entry(n).*

  An expression e should be hoisted to $Entry(n)$ only if

  (S.2) n contains an upwards exposed computation of e, or

  (S.3) e can be hoisted to $Exit(n)$ and n does not contain an assignment to any operand of e.

  Condition S.2 is satisfied by Gen_n of Anticipability analysis which is denoted by $AntGen_n$ to distinguish it from Gen_n of other analyses. Condition S.3 is satisfied by the term $(Out_n - Kill_n)$.¶ Thus the safety of placement at $Entry(n)$ is captured by the term

$$In_n \subseteq (AntGen_n \cup (Out_n - Kill_n)) \tag{2.12}$$

- *Desirability of hoisting.*

  By design, an expression e should be hoisted to $Entry(n)$ only if it can be hoisted out of it into a predecessor of n. If it can be hoisted into some predecessor but not all predecessors then safety requires that one evaluation of the expression should be made in n and then it is not profitable to hoist it into any predecessor.

  Further, if it is not partially available, hoisting it does not eliminate any partial redundancy. Hence an expression e should be hoisted to $Entry(n)$ only if

  (D.1) e is partially available at $Entry(n)$, and

  (D.2) for each predecessor p of n,

  (D.2.a) e can be hoisted to $Exit(p)$, or

  (D.2.b) e is available at $Exit(p)$ (and hence need not be inserted at $Exit(n)$).

  Condition D.1 is captured by the term

$$In_n \subseteq PavIn_n \tag{2.13}$$

  Condition D.2 is captured by the term

$$In_n \subseteq \bigcap_{p \in pred(n)} \left(Out_p \cup AvOut_p\right) \tag{2.14}$$

Combining Conditions (2.12), (2.13), and (2.14) results in Equation (2.15) below which defines In_n. Out_n is defined by Equation (2.11).

¶Note that $Kill_n$ is same for all analyses involving expressions: Available expressions analysis, partially available expressions analysis, anticipable expressions analysis, and PRE.

Block	Local information		Constant information		Global Information					
					Iteration # 1		Changes in iteration # 2		Changes in iteration # 3	
	Gen_n	$Kill_n$	$PavIn_n$	$AvOut_n$	Out_n	In_n	Out_n	In_n	Out_n	In_n
n_8	00011	00000	11111	00011	00000	00011				00001
n_7	01000	00000	11101	11000	00011	01001	00001			
n_6	00001	00000	11101	11001	01001	01001			01000	
n_5	01000	00000	11101	11000	01001	01001		01000		
n_4	10100	00011	11100	10100	01001	11100		11000		
n_3	00001	00011	11101	10000	01000	01001		00001		
n_2	00010	11101	10001	00010	00011	00000			00001	
n_1	00000	11111	00000	10001	00000	00000				

FIGURE 2.8
Partial redundancy elimination.

$$In_n = PavIn_n \cap (AntGen_n \cup (Out_n - Kill_n)) \cap \bigcap_{p \in pred(n)} \left(Out_p \cup AvOut_p\right) \quad (2.15)$$

Observe that if we drop the desirability terms from Equations (2.11) and (2.15), they reduce to the anticipability equations (Equations 2.9 and 2.10).

Example 2.16
We illustrate the conditions defining hosting criteria with the help of expression $(a+b)$ in our running example of Figure 2.1. Since this expression is not computed along path (n_1, n_2, n_8), it is not anticipable at the exit of n_1. Hence inserting it at the exit of n_1 violates safety. However, it is anticipable at the exit of n_3 and inserting it there is safe. Feasibility condition S.2 for $(a+b)$ is satisfied by block n_7 and n_5 whereas condition S.3 is satisfied by block n_4. Condition D.1 is satisfied by blocks n_4, n_5, n_6, and n_7. Condition D.2.a is satisfied by n_3 whereas Condition D.2.b is satisfied by n_7. ▯

Example 2.17
The computation of PRE data flow properties of our running example is shown in Figure 2.8. Since the confluence operation is $\cap$, the initial value of In_i and Out_i for all i is 11111.

Figure 2.9 shows the hoisting paths in our example. Observe that there is no hoisting path for expression $(a*b)$ since it is totally redundant and

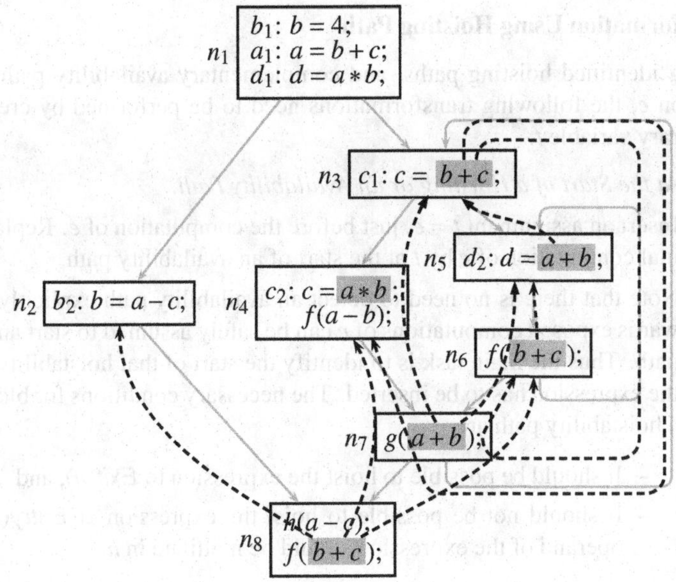

FIGURE 2.9
Hoisting paths in PRE of the running example.

need not be inserted anywhere. For expression $(a+b)$ there are three hoisting paths: (n_3, n_4, n_7), (n_3, n_5) and (n_5, n_6, n_7). Since the last path also happens to be an availability path, there is no need to insert the expression in n_5. Expression $(b+c)$ has the following hoisting paths: (n_2, n_8), (n_6, n_7, n_8), (n_6, n_7, n_3), (n_4, n_7, n_8), (n_4, n_7, n_3), and (n_5, n_6). Observe that there is no hoisting path for expressions $(a-b)$ and $(a-c)$.

Also observe the need of the third iteration for suppressing the hoisting of expressions $(a-c)$, and $(b+c)$. The initial values of the bits corresponding to these expressions is 1 in *In*/*Out* values. Expression $(a-c)$ cannot be hoisted out of the outer loop because it is neither partially available anywhere in the loop nor is it invariant in the loop due to assignment to c. Thus the bit corresponding to this expression becomes 0 in In_{n_3} in the first iteration. The fact that it cannot be placed at *Exit*(n_7) because of this reason, can be discovered only in the second iteration when its bit in Out_{n_7} becomes 0. Its hoisting out of n_8 is suppressed in the third iteration when its bit in In_{n_8} becomes 0 in the third iteration.

Expression $(b+c)$ is not anticipated at *Exit*(n_3) and hence its bit in Out_{n_3} becomes 0 in the first iteration. Setting the corresponding bit in In_{n_5} to 0 requires the second iteration. Its placement at *Exit*(n_6) is suppressed in the third iteration. □

Transformation Using Hoisting Path

Having identified hoisting paths, and complementary availability paths for an expression e, the following transformations need to be performed by creating a new temporary variable t:

- *At the Start of a Hoisting or an Availability Path.*

  Insert an assignment $t = e$, just before the computation of e. Replace the original computation of e by t at the start of an availability path.

  Note that there is no need to detect an availability path explicitly. All downwards exposed computations of e can be safely assumed to start an availability path. Thus the main task is to identify the start of that hoistability path where the expression has to be inserted. The necessary conditions for block n to start a hoistability path are:

  - It should be possible to hoist the expression to $\mathit{Exit}(n)$, and
  - It should not be possible to hoist the expression at $\mathit{Entry}(n)$, or some operand of the expression should be modified in n.

  These conditions are captured by the following:

$$\mathit{Insert}_n = \mathit{Out}_n \cap (\neg \mathit{In}_n \cup \mathit{Kill}_n) \tag{2.16}$$

- *At the End of a Hoisting Path.*

  Replace the original computation of e by t.

  Identifying this is easy: It should be possible to hoist e to $\mathit{Entry}(n)$ and there should be an upwards exposed computation of e in n. These conditions are captured by the following:

$$\mathit{Replace}_n = \mathit{In}_n \cap \mathit{AntGen}_n \tag{2.17}$$

Example 2.18

In our running example, the data flow information which enables the transformation is:

Block	Local Information		Global Information			
			Iteration # 3			
	AntGen_n	Kill_n	In_n	Out_n	$\mathit{Replace}_n$	Insert_n
n_1	00000	11111	00000	00000	00000	00000
n_2	00010	11101	00000	00001	00000	00001
n_3	00001	00011	00001	01000	00001	01000
n_4	10100	00011	11000	01001	10000	00001
n_5	01000	00000	01000	01001	01000	00001
n_6	00001	00000	01001	01000	00001	00000
n_7	01000	00000	01001	00001	01000	00000
n_8	00011	00000	00001	00000	00001	00000

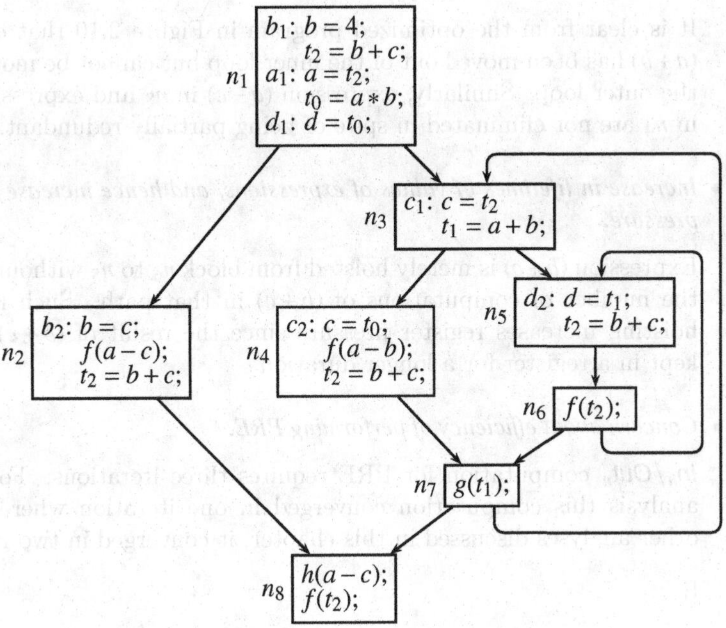

FIGURE 2.10
Optimized program after PRE.

Figure 2.10 shows the optimized program after performing PRE. □

An important property of this transformation is that on any path in the program, the number of computations in the optimized program is guaranteed to not exceed the number of computations in the original program.

Limitations of Partial Redundancy Elimination

PRE combines many flows: Partial availability is a forward flow with union as the confluence, total availability is a forward flow with intersection as the confluence, and anticipability is backward flow with intersection as the confluence. Combining these flows results in conservative approximations. Thus in some cases, partial redundancies cannot be eliminated; in some cases, elimination causes some undesirable side effects; and in most cases, efficiency of performing analysis is a matter of concern.

Example 2.19
We illustrate the above limitations with our running example.

- *Inability to eliminate all partial redundancies.*

It is clear from the optimized program in Figure 2.10 that expression $(a+b)$ has been moved out of the inner loop but cannot be moved out of the outer loop. Similarly, expression $(a-c)$ in n_8 and expression $(a-b)$ in n_4 are not eliminated in spite of being partially redundant.

- *Increase in lifetimes of values of expressions, and hence increase in register pressure.*

  Expression $(b+c)$ is merely hoisted from block n_6 to n_5 without reducing the number of computations of $(b+c)$ in that path. Such redundant hoisting increases register pressure since the result of $(b+c)$ must be kept in a register for a longer duration.

- *Concern about efficiency of performing PRE.*

  $\mathsf{In}_n/\mathsf{Out}_n$ computation for PRE requires three iterations. For liveness analysis this computation converged in one iteration whereas for all other analyses discussed in this chapter, it converged in two iterations.

□

PRE is blocked by a combination of data flows in the presence of the following two structures in CFGs: *Critical edges*, and *critical nodes*. A critical edge is an edge that runs from a *fork node* (i.e., a node with more than one successor) to a *join node* (i.e., a node with more than one predecessor). A critical node is a fork node which has multiple paths reaching it.

Figure 2.11 illustrates the effect of critical edges and nodes on hoisting. Edge $n_1 \rightarrow n_2$ in Figure 2.11(a) is a critical edge whereas node n_2 in Figure 2.11(b) is a critical node. In each case, expression e is a possible candidate for hoisting from $\mathsf{Entry}(n_2)$ to $\mathsf{Exit}(n_1)$ but is not anticipated at $\mathsf{Exit}(n_1)$. In the case of a critical edge, e is partially available at $\mathsf{Entry}(n_2)$ due to another predecessor of n_2 whereas in the case of a critical node, e is partially available at $\mathsf{Entry}(n_2)$ due to n_1.

Observe that if e were available at $\mathsf{Exit}(n_1)$, the critical edge or critical node would not have any adverse effect because there would be no need of hoisting e out of n_2; it would be totally redundant in n_2. Alternatively, if e were anticipated at $\mathsf{Exit}(n_1)$, then e would be hoisted out of n_2—in the case of critical edge, it would be placed in n_1 and in the case of critical node, it would be hoisted further out of n_1.

Example 2.20

Edges $n_1 \rightarrow n_3$, $n_3 \rightarrow n_5$, $n_6 \rightarrow n_5$, $n_6 \rightarrow n_7$, and $n_7 \rightarrow n_8$ in our running example are critical edges. Nodes n_3, n_6, and n_7 are critical nodes. Edge $n_1 \rightarrow n_3$ blocks hoisting expression $(a+b)$ from n_3 to n_1, $n_3 \rightarrow n_5$, blocks hoisting expression $(b+c)$ from n_5 to n_3, and $n_7 \rightarrow n_8$, blocks hoisting expression $(a-c)$ from n_8 to n_7. Critical node n_3 blocks hoisting expression $(a-b)$ from n_4 to n_3. □

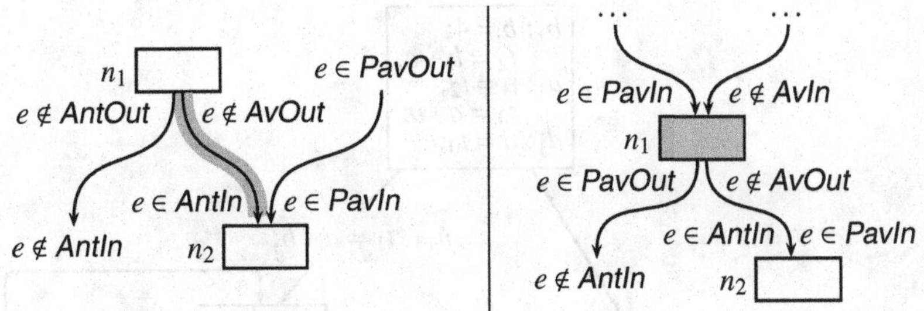

(a) Edge $n_1 \rightarrow n_2$ is a critical edge (b) Block n_1 is a critical node

FIGURE 2.11
Critical edges and critical nodes block PRE. Expression e cannot be hoisted out of n_2 into the exit of n_1.

Handling Critical Edges

A careful examination of the effect of critical edges reveals that this limitation arises due to the fact that the data flow value represented by In_n plays a dual role: It captures the property of safety of placement (Constraint 2.12) as well as the desirability of placement (Constraints 2.13 and 2.14).

In Figure 2.11(a), the bit corresponding to e becomes 0 in Out_{n_1} due to safety constraint ($e \notin AntIn$ of the successor on the left). This makes the corresponding bit 0 in In_{n_2} due to desirability constraint which in turn make the corresponding bit 0 in Out of the right predecessor of n_2. If a new node n_{12} is inserted along edge $n_1 \rightarrow n_2$ in Figure 2.11, the repercussions of the desirability constraint are restricted to $In_{n_{12}}$ since it does not have any predecessor other than n_1. Further, since $e \in AntOut_{n_{12}}$ even if $e \notin AntOut_{n_1}$, it becomes possible to hoist e out of n_2 into the newly created node n_{12}. Note that this hoisting is not redundant because e is not partially available in n_{12}.

Example 2.21
Figure 2.12 shows PRE after splitting critical edges in our running example. This allows hoisting $(b+c)$ out of the inner loop and $(a+b)$ out of the outer loop. Besides, $(a-c)$ is hoisted out of n_8. Note that this has no effect on the placement of loop invariant expression $(a-b)$. □

Edge splitting has a pleasant side effect of increasing the efficiency of analysis. Intuitively, an all-path analysis can be seen as optimistically assuming bits to be 1 in the CFG and then resetting them to 0 due to the influence of corresponding bits at neighbouring program point. Thus analysis involves propagating 0 in the graph along arbitrarily long paths. The corresponding view for any-path analyses assumes the bits to be 0 initially and then propagates 1 in the graph. Edge splitting prunes this propagation for PRE because it prohibits the repercussions of the desirability

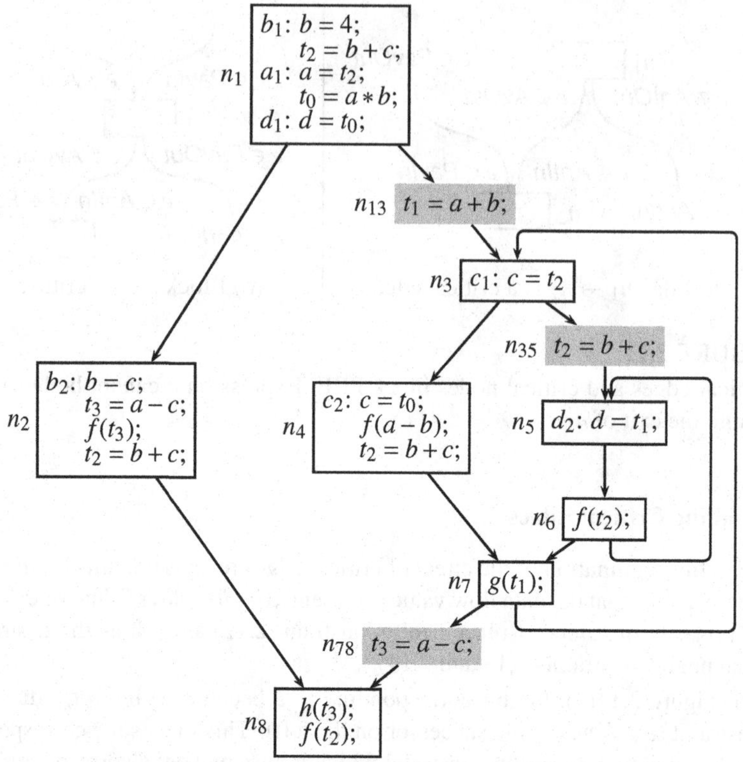

FIGURE 2.12
PRE after splitting critical edges. Among the new blocks, we have retained only non-empty blocks.

constraints: Propagation of 0 from Out_{n_1} to In_{n_2} is truncated at $In_{n_{12}}$: $Out_{n_{12}}$ cannot become 0 even if $In_{n_{12}}$ becomes 0 and hence In_{n_2} remains 1.

A variant of edge-splitting is *edge-placement* which essentially achieves the same effect except that instead of splitting critical edges a-priori, the approach is to change data flow analysis to discover the edges along which expressions should be placed. Then the required edges are split and expressions placed in the new node. Thus this can be seen as edge-splitting on demand.

Handling Critical Nodes

Edge splitting does not help in the case of critical nodes even if we decide to split the out edges of critical nodes regardless of whether these edges are critical or not. If we split edge $n_1 \rightarrow n_2$ in Figure 2.11(b), it would be possible to hoist e from n_2 into the new node but it will continue to be partially redundant. What is required is a transformation which will enable hoisting e out of n_1 to those ancestors m of n_1 such that $e \notin \mathit{PavOut}_m$.

A transformation which achieves this involves duplicating the critical node, and along with it some other nodes such that in one copy of these nodes, the expression is available whereas in the other copy, the expression is not available. The region in which the expression is available does not need hoisting since the expression becomes totally redundant. The region in which the expression is not available can be optimized by edge-splitting.

Example 2.22

Figure 2.13 shows code duplication involving a critical node which blocks hoisting. The basic idea is to identify *code motion preventing* (*CMP*) region which is a set of nodes characterized by the following:

$$n \in \mathit{CMP}(e) \Leftrightarrow e \in (\mathit{PantOut}_n \cap \mathit{PavOut}_n \cap \mathit{PantIn}_n \cap \mathit{PavIn}_n)$$

For our running example,

$$\mathit{CMP}(a-b) = \{n_3, n_{35}, n_5, n_6, n_7\}$$

A critical node is that node in *CMP* where the expression is not anticipated along one set of out edges and is anticipated along the other set of edges. It is this node which blocks the hoisting of expressions into the region. In our case n_3 is the critical node.

The transformation involves duplicating each *CMP* region such that for one copy the expression is available and for the other copy it is not available. This involves retaining the availability edge in one copy and not in the other. In our example, the expression is available in the nodes with dashed labels through edge $n_4 \rightarrow n_7'$. Note that the other copy does not have the corresponding edge.

There are two copies of the critical node and since their out edges are retained, the out edges along which the expression is anticipated become critical edges because these edges go to a unique node out of *CMP* region. Splitting these edges facilitates hoisting into a new successor of the critical node. □

2.4.5 Lazy Code Motion

This section presents an alternative approach to PRE which minimizes lifetimes by separating safety and desirability constraints. It allows placement of expressions at the entry of a block and incorporates the desirability through separate analyses. These analyses employ a stronger notion of desirability to minimize the lifetimes of temporary variables. Unlike the classical formulation of PRE, all analyses involved in this approach are unidirectional.

This approach is called *lazy* code motion because it performs as little code motion as possible suppressing it where it does not result in profitable placement. The main steps of this approach are:

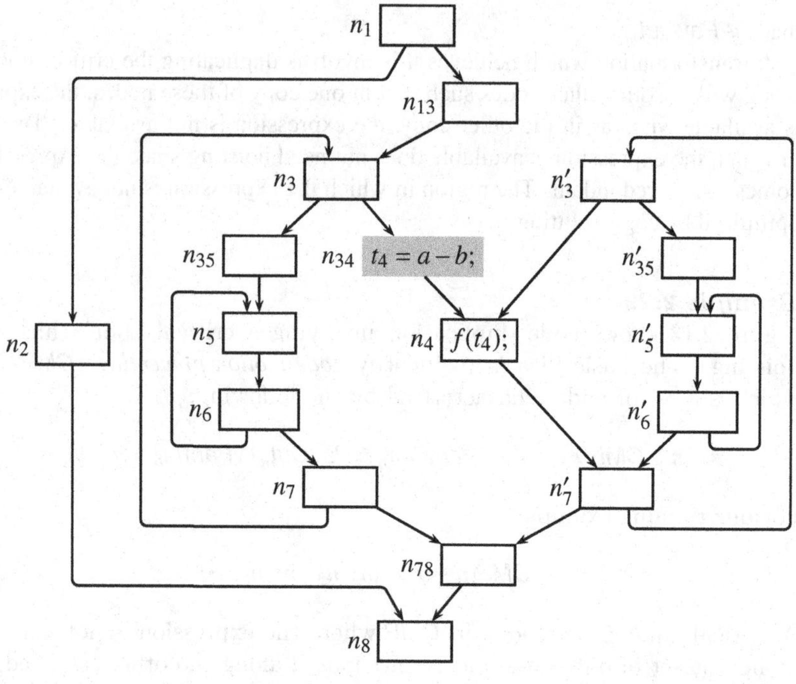

FIGURE 2.13
PRE after duplicating a code motion preventing region rooted at a critical node (n_3). Duplicate copies have dashed labels. Additional edge-splitting is required for the technique to work.

1. Splitting critical edges. Observe that in classical PRE, edge-splitting only enhances the effectiveness of redundancy elimination but is not required for its correctness. However, it is crucial for the correctness of this approach.

2. Discovering a region of safe placement of expressions.

   This involves anticipability analysis (Section 2.4.3) for discovering hoisting paths where the expressions could be placed anywhere to make the original computations redundant. A safe region of placement for an expression e is the set of program points where the expression is anticipable. Equations (2.10) and (2.9) are used to discover the region of safe placement.

3. Discovering entry points of region of safe placements.

   Entry points of a region of safe placement are the points in the region where the expression can be inserted in order to make the original computations in the region totally redundant.

   Entry points are the earliest points and form the smallest such set where expressions can be placed. These points are discovered by combining the results of availability analysis (Section 2.4.1) with the result of anticipability analysis. Placing expressions at earliest points amounts to hoisting them from their original points of computation.

We use the prefix *Ant* and *Av* to denote data flow values in anticipability and availability. Let $\mathit{EarliestIn}_n$ and $\mathit{EarliestOut}_n$ denote the entry points. Then,

$$\mathit{EarliestIn}_n = \mathit{AntIn}_n \cap \left(\bigcap_{p \in pred(n)} \neg\left(\mathit{AvOut}_p \cup \mathit{AntOut}_p\right)\right) \tag{2.18}$$

$$\mathit{EarliestOut}_n = (\mathit{AntOut}_n \cup \mathit{AvGen}_n) \cap \mathit{Kill}_n \tag{2.19}$$

Availability is computed using Equations (2.5) and (2.6).

Edge splitting ensures that *AntOut* of all predecessors of a node is identical. Thus the earliest points are

- *Entry*(n) of block n where it is safe to insert the expression, cannot be hoisted into any predecessor, and is not available along any predecessor.
- *Exit*(n) of block n that contains a downwards exposed computation of the expression such that it cannot be hoisted to *Entry*(n) due the presence of an assignment to some operand of the expression.

Note that it is possible that both *Exit*(n) and *Entry*(n) are earliest points for some expression e. This happens when e is anticipable at *Exit*(n) and n contains both downwards and upwards exposed computations of e and an assignment to an operand of e.

4. Discovering the latest points of region of safe placements.
   In order to minimize the lifetimes of temporary variables, the expressions placed at earliest points can be *sunk* to later points along the control flow in the region of safe placements. This analysis is an all-paths forward analysis:

$$\mathit{SinkIn}_n = \mathit{EarliestIn}_n \cup \begin{cases} \emptyset & n \text{ is } \mathit{Start} \text{ block} \\ \bigcap_{p \in pred(n)} (\mathit{SinkOut}_p - \mathit{AvGen}_p) & \text{otherwise} \end{cases} \tag{2.20}$$

$$\mathit{SinkOut}_n = \mathit{EarliestOut}_n \cup (\mathit{SinkIn}_n - \mathit{AntGen}_n) \tag{2.21}$$

Sinking begins at the earliest points of placements and discovered path along which the expressions can be sunk. The latest placement points of expressions are the end points of these paths and are defined by:

$$\mathit{LatestIn}_n = \mathit{SinkIn}_n \cap \mathit{AntGen}_n \quad (2.22)$$

$$\mathit{LatestOut}_n = \mathit{SinkOut}_n \cap \left(\mathit{AvGen}_n \cup \left(\bigcup_{s \in succ(n)} \neg \mathit{SinkIn}_s \right) \right) \quad (2.23)$$

The above equations use AntGen_n and AvGen_n to ensure that sinking is applicable only to new placements—an original computation in a block cannot be sunk.

5. Discovering those expressions whose values need not be preserved in temporary variables.

   When the expressions are sunk to their latest points, some computations might have only a local use within a block. Such computations need not be preserved in a temporary variable. Discovering the variables whose values need not be preserved is a simple variation of deadness analysis.

$$\mathit{NoUseIn}_n = \mathit{EarliestIn}_n \cup \mathit{NoUseOut}_n \quad (2.24)$$

$$\mathit{NoUseOut}_n = \bigcap_{s \in succ(n)} (\mathit{EarliestIn}_s \cup (\mathit{NoUseIn}_s - \mathit{AntGen}_s)) \quad (2.25)$$

6. Inserting assignments to temporary variables at insertion points and replacing original expressions by temporary variables.

   The values of expressions should be stored in temporary variables at the latest computation points provided the values have some use in future. This is identified by

$$\mathit{InsertIn}_n = \mathit{LatestIn}_n - \mathit{NoUseIn}_n \quad (2.26)$$

$$\mathit{InsertOut}_n = \mathit{LatestOut}_n - \mathit{NoUseOut}_n \quad (2.27)$$

   The original computations which should be replaced by temporary variables are defined by the following:

$$\mathit{ReplaceIn}_n = \mathit{AntGen}_n - (\mathit{LatestIn}_n \cap \mathit{NoUseIn}_n) \quad (2.28)$$

$$\mathit{ReplaceOut}_n = \mathit{AvGen}_n - (\mathit{LatestOut}_n \cap \mathit{NoUseOut}_n) \quad (2.29)$$

Example 2.23
Consider our running example after edge splitting: Edge $n_1 \rightarrow n_3$ in Figure 2.1 is split to create node n_{13}, edge $n_3 \rightarrow n_5$ is split to create node n_{35}, and edge

Block		Availability			Anticipability			Earliest Placement	
	Kill	*AvGen*	*AvIn*	*AvOut*	*AntGen*	*AntIn*	*AntOut*	*EarliestIn*	*EarliestOut*
n_1	11111	10001	00000	10001	00000	00000	00000	00000	10001
n_2	11101	00010	10001	00010	00010	00010	00011	00010	00001
n_{13}	00000	00000	10001	10001	00000	01001	01001	01000	00000
n_3	00011	00000	10000	10000	00001	01001	01000	00000	00000
n_{35}	00000	00000	10000	10000	00000	01001	01001	00001	00000
n_4	00011	10100	10000	10100	10100	11100	01001	00100	00001
n_5	00000	01000	10000	11000	01000	01001	01001	00000	00000
n_6	00000	00001	11000	11001	00001	01001	01001	00000	00000
n_7	00000	01000	10000	11000	01000	01001	00001	00000	00000
n_{78}	00000	00000	11000	11000	00000	00011	00011	00010	00000
n_8	00000	00011	00000	00011	00011	00011	00000	00000	00000

FIGURE 2.14

Early placement points for lazy code motion.

$n_7 \rightarrow n_8$ is split to create node n_{78}. The early placement points are shown in Figure 2.14. As shown in Figure 2.15, the earliest placement points also happen to be the latest points for this particular example. This is because of the early placement opportunities created by edge splitting. The optimized program after lazy code motion is identical to that shown in Figure 2.12. □

Example 2.24

If we do not split critical edges in our running example, lazy code motion replaces all occurrence of expressions $(a-c)$ and $(a+b)$ by temporaries. However, the value of $(a-c)$ is stored in its temporary only in n_2 and hence it is not available along the paths reaching n_8 from n_7. The value of $(a+b)$ is not stored in its temporary anywhere. □

2.5 Combined *May-Must* Analyses

Classical PRE requires both total availability and partial availability analysis. Such a need is not uncommon and often both any-path and all-paths variants of information are required. The all-path variant of data flow information is also called *must* information. Analogously, the any-path variant of data flow information is called *may*

Block	*SinkIn*	*SinkOut*	*LatestIn*	*LatestOut*	*NoUseIn*	*NoUseOut*
n_1	00000	10001	00000	10001	11101	01100
n_2	00010	00001	00010	00001	11101	11100
n_{13}	01000	01000	00000	01000	00100	00100
n_3	00000	00000	00000	00000	00100	00100
n_{35}	00001	00001	00000	00001	00100	00100
n_4	00100	00001	00100	00001	00101	00100
n_5	00000	00000	00000	00000	00100	00100
n_6	00000	00000	00000	00000	00100	00100
n_7	00000	00000	00000	00000	00100	00100
n_{78}	00010	00010	00000	00010	11100	11100
n_8	00000	00000	00000	00000	11111	11111

FIGURE 2.15
Latest placement points for lazy code motion.

information. It is possible to define a single analysis which discovers both *may* and *must* information. We explain this with the help of availability analysis.

Defining *may-must* availability analysis requires us to define four possible values which can be associated an expression at any program point. For an expression e, the value *unknown* at a program point u indicates that sufficient information is not available at u; the value *must* indicates that e is available along all paths reaching u; the value *may* indicates that e is available along some but not along all paths reaching u; and the value *no* indicates that e is not available along any path reaching u. We view them as *degrees of certainty*. We define a new confluence operation which combines the degree of certainties of a given expression e as shown in Figure 2.16.

These values can be represented using 2 bits. If we represent *unknown* by 11, *must* by 10, *no* by 01, and *may* by 00, then $\sqcap$ can be implemented using simple bitwise AND. An alternative representation is to swap the bit strings for *unknown* and *may* and use bitwise OR for $\sqcap$.

The data flow information is defined in terms of sets of pairs $\langle e, d_e \rangle$ where d_e is the degree of certainty of expression e. The local data flow information is defined as follows:

$$\begin{aligned} \mathit{Kill}_n &= \{\langle e,d\rangle \mid e \in (\mathit{AvGen}_n \cup \mathit{AvKill}_n), d \in \{\mathit{may},\mathit{must},\mathit{no},\mathit{unknown}\}\} \\ \mathit{Gen}_n &= \{\langle e,\mathit{must}\rangle \mid e \in \mathit{AvGen}_n\} \cup \{\langle e,\mathit{no}\rangle \mid e \in \mathit{AvKill}_n\} \end{aligned}$$

where AvGen_n and AvKill_n represent Gen_n and Kill_n for availability (or partial availability) analysis.

Observe that when an expression e is in AvGen_n or AvKill_n, it belongs to both Gen_n as well as Kill_n. This is because the local effect of block n may change the degree of certainty of e. Effectively, the pairs are neither removed nor added to in In_n and Out_n—only the degrees of certainties change. In other words, these sets have the

$\sqcap$	$\langle e, unknown\rangle$	$\langle e, must\rangle$	$\langle e, no\rangle$	$\langle e, may\rangle$
$\langle e, unknown\rangle$	$\langle e, unknown\rangle$	$\langle e, must\rangle$	$\langle e, no\rangle$	$\langle e, may\rangle$
$\langle e, must\rangle$	$\langle e, must\rangle$	$\langle e, must\rangle$	$\langle e, may\rangle$	$\langle e, may\rangle$
$\langle e, no\rangle$	$\langle e, no\rangle$	$\langle e, may\rangle$	$\langle e, no\rangle$	$\langle e, may\rangle$
$\langle e, may\rangle$	$\langle e, may\rangle$	$\langle e, may\rangle$	$\langle e, may\rangle$	$\langle e, may\rangle$

FIGURE 2.16
Confluence operation for combined *may* and *must* analysis.

same size at each program point. This is different from other bit vector frameworks which we have seen in this chapter,

Since the un-availability of an expression e is reflected by recording its degree of certainty as *no* instead of removing it from the set, $Kill_n$ does not imply that e ceases to be available; it captures the fact that the data flow information of e is killed.

The data flow equations are defined in the usual manner. The confluence $\sqcap$ defined over pairs $\langle e, d_e\rangle$ is lifted to the sets by applying it to pairs of the same expression.

$$In_n = \begin{cases} \{\langle e, no\rangle \mid e \in \mathbb{E}\mathsf{xpr}\} & n \text{ is } Start \\ \displaystyle\bigsqcap_{p \in pred(n)} Out_p & \text{otherwise} \end{cases} \tag{2.30}$$

$$Out_n = (In_n - Kill_n) \cup Gen_n \tag{2.31}$$

Example 2.25
For brevity, we represent the sets of pairs $\langle e, d_e\rangle$ in terms of vectors of d_e such that there is a positional correspondence between e and d_e. We retain the order of expressions as described in Example 2.9 except that now there are two bits for every expression instead of a single bit. The boundary information *BI* is $\langle no, no, no, no, no\rangle$ and the initial value of In_n and Out_n for all n is the tuple $\langle unknown, unknown, unknown, unknown, unknown\rangle$. With our first choice of representation, these values are represented by $\langle 01, 01, 01, 01, 01\rangle$ and $\langle 11, 11, 11, 11, 11\rangle$ respectively.

The data flow values are presented in Figure 2.17. Note that this information is same as availability and partial availability information computed in Example 2.9 and 2.11 except that partial availability includes total availability whereas *may* and *must* availabilities are mutually exclusive. □

An efficient implementation of the computation of Out_n is as follows:

$$Out_n = \{\langle e, \widehat{f}_n(e, X)\rangle \mid e \in \mathbb{E}\mathsf{xpr}\} \tag{2.32}$$

where $\widehat{f}_n(e, X)$ represents the local effect of a block on the availability of expression e. The actual implementation of $\widehat{f}_n$ in terms of bit vector operations depends on

Block	Iteration #1		Iteration #2	
	In_n	Out_n	In_n	Out_n
n_1	⟨01,01,01,01,01⟩	⟨10,01,01,01,10⟩		
n_2	⟨10,01,01,01,10⟩	⟨01,01,01,10,01⟩		
n_3	⟨10,01,01,01,10⟩	⟨10,01,01,01,01⟩	⟨10,00,00,01,00⟩	⟨10,00,00,01,01⟩
n_4	⟨10,01,01,01,01⟩	⟨10,01,10,01,01⟩	⟨10,00,01,01,01⟩	⟨10,00,10,01,01⟩
n_5	⟨10,01,01,01,01⟩	⟨10,10,01,01,01⟩	⟨10,00,00,01,01⟩	⟨10,10,00,01,01⟩
n_6	⟨10,10,01,01,01⟩	⟨10,10,01,01,10⟩	⟨10,10,00,01,01⟩	⟨10,10,00,01,10⟩
n_7	⟨10,00,00,01,00⟩	⟨10,10,00,01,00⟩		
n_8	⟨00,10,00,00,00⟩	⟨00,10,00,10,10⟩		

FIGURE 2.17
Combined *may* and *must* availability analysis.

the choice of representation for the degrees of certainty. Assuming that we use the representation *unknown* ≡ 11, *must* ≡ 10, *no* ≡ 01, and *may* ≡ 00, and use bitwise AND as $\sqcap$, $\widehat{f}_n$ can be implemented as follows:

$$\widehat{f}_n(e,X) = A_e + B_e \cdot d_e \tag{2.33}$$

where $\langle e, d_e\rangle \in X$, "+" denotes bitwise OR and "·" denotes bitwise AND. The values of A_e and B_e are governed by local information:

Local Information of e		A_e	B_e
$e \in AvGen_n$	$e \in Kill_n$	10	00
$e \in AvGen_n$	$e \notin Kill_n$	10	00
$e \notin AvGen_n$	$e \in Kill_n$	01	00
$e \notin AvGen_n$	$e \notin Kill_n$	00	11

2.6 Summary and Concluding Remarks

It is clear from the data flow frameworks presented in this chapter that data flow equations have a common form which can be customized for each analysis. The customization of this common form involves specifying the direction of flow, the confluence operation, and the flow functions which are defined in terms of Gen_n and $Kill_n$ components.

All flow functions in this chapter can be implemented using the bitwise operations AND and OR (or set operations ∩ and ∪). There are two important points associated with this observation:

- Kill_n used in the operation $X - \mathit{Kill}_n$ is a constant value. Thus set complement (or bitwise NOT) is applied only to constant value. This computation can be performed once and the desired operation can be applied during the data flow analysis by $X \cap \neg \mathit{Kill}_n$.

- Gen_n and Kill_n do not depend on In_n and Out_n and are purely local effects. Since Gen_n and Kill_n are constant values, In_n and Out_n can be computed unconditionally without examining the operands.

In summary, in bit vector frameworks, the data flow information can be represented and computed using aggregate operations on bits; there is no need to examine the bits individually. Although the data flow value of an entity in common bit vector frameworks is a boolean value and hence can be represented by a single bit, this is neither necessary nor sufficient for a framework to qualify as a bit vector framework. For example, the combined *may-must* availability analysis described in Section 2.5 requires two bits but is a bit vector framework. Chapter 4 presents faint variables analysis in which data flow value is boolean and hence can be represented using a single bit. However, it is not a bit vector framework.

Subsequent chapters relax both these constraints and describe frameworks which capture more powerful semantics.

2.7 Bibliographic Notes

Bit vector frameworks are some of the oldest data flow problems. Among the initial works that introduced most common bit vector problems, Cocke [24] and Ullman [100] described available expressions analysis and its use in common subexpression elimination, Allen [4, 5] presented reaching definitions analysis, and live variables analysis was described by Kennedy [55, 56]. Partial redundancy elimination was introduced by Morel and Renvoise [74]. Bodik, Gupta and Soffa [17] discuss a combination of *must* and *may* availability and its use in complete removal of redundancies. Knoop, Rüthing and Steffen [65] introduced lazy code motion. Almost every book on compiler construction discusses bit vector data flow frameworks. A detailed treatment can be found in the advanced texts on compilers such as Aho, Lam, Sethi, and Ullman [3], Appel [10], or Muchnick [76] or in the books devoted to static analysis such as by Hecht [44], Muchnick and Jones [77], and F. Nielson, H. R. Nielson and Hankin [80]. The first formal definition of bit vector frameworks was provided by Khedker and Dhamdhere [60].

3

Theoretical Abstractions in Data Flow Analysis

The study of several examples of data flow problems suggests that they share similar features in terms of their specifications, their formulations as data flow equations, and their solution methods. In this chapter, we describe a general framework so that most of the data flow problems that we have seen earlier can be viewed as instances of this framework. Doing so yields two important benefits.

The first benefit is that which results from any generalization. When a data flow problem is shown to be an instance of the framework, it also suggests a solution method whose properties are apparent. We do not have to separately prove the correctness or estimate the complexity of the solution method.

The second benefit is that the generalization leads to the design of data flow analyzer generators, much in the way that lexer generators and parser generators have emerged from the study of formal languages. Instead of implementing each data flow analyzer separately, a general solution method that is parametrized with respect to the specific details of any analysis is implemented. When the specifics of a data flow analysis are supplied to this solution method, it yields a data flow analyzer for the particular analysis. This results in a rapid method of implementing data flow analyzers. Further, the reliability of the generated analyzers is related to the reliability of the generator. As the generator becomes more reliable through usage, the generated analyzers are likely to become more reliable than hand-coded analyzers.

This chapter deals with unidirectional data flow problems; generalizations for handling bidirectional data flow problems have been presented in Chapter 5. Further, although our descriptions are in terms of forward unidirectional problems, they are uniformly applicable to backward data flow problems. For such problems, the propagation of data flow information begins from the *End* node of the CFG instead of the *Start* node and computation of the data flow value at a node is in terms of its successors instead of its predecessors.

3.1 Graph Properties Relevant to Data Flow Analysis

Programs and their properties are often represented by directed or undirected graphs. A *path* in a directed graph is a sequence of nodes $(n_0, n_1, \ldots, n_k)$ such that there is an

Input: A CFG G with N nodes.
Output: A DFST T for G and an array *rpo*[1..N] representing a reverse postorder listing of nodes in the graph.
Algorithm:

```
function dfstMain()
{ i = N
    make root(G) the root of T
    dfst(root(G))
}
function dfst(currnode)
{ mark currnode
    while there are unmarked successors of currnode do
    { let child be an unmarked successor of currnode in
        { add the edge (currnode → child) to T
            dfst(child)
        }
    }
    rpo[currnode] = i
    i = i − 1
}
```

FIGURE 3.1
An algorithm to compute a depth first spanning tree.

edge between any two consecutive nodes in the sequence. An edge between nodes n and m is denoted as $n \rightarrow m$. A non-null path whose starting and ending nodes are n and m is denoted as $n \xrightarrow{+} m$, and the corresponding unrestricted path as $n \xrightarrow{*} m$, i.e., we denote the path from n to n with no edges between them as $n \xrightarrow{*} n$. An edge connecting n to m in an undirected graph is denoted as $n — m$. The corresponding unrestricted path and non-null paths are denoted as $n \overset{*}{—} m$ and $n \overset{+}{—} m$. The *length* of the path $n_0, n_1, \ldots, n_k$ is k.

Recall that data flow analysis models programs in terms of CFGs which have been described in Section 2.1. As described in Chapter 2, data flow equations are defined by associating variables In_n and Out_n with every node n in the CFG. The variables are related through data flow equations. In the examples presented in Chapter 2, the equations were solved using a round-robin iterative algorithm which traversed the CFG in a fixed order.

In this section, we present some properties of CFGs that are relevant to round-robin iterative data flow analysis. Since we restrict ourselves to CFGs, these properties are defined for connected directed graphs with a unique *Start* node.

A *spanning tree* of a directed graph G is a connected subgraph of G that includes all nodes of G and is a tree. The root of a spanning tree is the same as the *Start* node of the graph. A *depth first spanning tree (DFST)* of G is a spanning tree rooted at *Start* that is constructed by the algorithm in Figure 3.1.

DEFINITION 3.1 *Given a graph G and its DFST T, the edges of G can be categorized as follows:*

- *Tree edges are the edges that are in T.*
- *Backward edges are the edges from a node to one of its tree ancestors in T. A loop from a node to itself is also classified as a backward edge.*
- *Forward edges are the edges not in T that connect a node to one of its tree descendants.*
- *Cross edges are the edges connecting nodes that are not related by the ancestor-descendant relation in the tree.*

The classification of edges allows us to define the following order of traversal over CFGs.

DEFINITION 3.2 *Given a graph G and its DFST, consider the subgraph G′ obtained by eliminating the back edges of G. A reverse postorder is a topological sort of the nodes of G′.*

The algorithm shown in Figure 3.1 computes a reverse postorder listing of the input graph in the array *rpo*. The position of the node n in this listing is $\mathsf{rpo}[n]$. The nodes of the example graph of Figure 3.2 have been numbered in reverse postorder, i.e., $\mathsf{rpo}[i]$ is i for all nodes.

As we shall see later, the process of equation solving converges faster for forward data flow problems when the round-robin iterative algorithm traverses the CFGs graphs in reverse postorder. For backward data flow problems, the preferred order of traversal is a postorder traversal.

OBSERVATION 3.1 *Let G be a graph and T be a DFST of G. Then,*

1. *An edge $x \rightarrow y$ of G is a back edge iff $\mathsf{rpo}[x] \geq \mathsf{rpo}[y]$.*
2. *Every cycle of G contains at least one back edge.*

Back edges are important for unidirectional data flow problems since they propagate data flow information in a direction which is opposite to the chosen direction of graph traversal. Therefore, they may add to the number of iterations required for convergence of the analyses.

DEFINITION 3.3 *Let G be a graph and T be a DFST of G. The loop connectedness (more often called depth) of G with respect to T, denoted as d(G,T), is the largest number of back edges in any acyclic path in G.*

The depth of a graph could be different for different DFSTs. There is a special class of graphs called *reducible* graphs for which the choice of DFST does not matter because every DFST identifies exactly the same set of back edges.

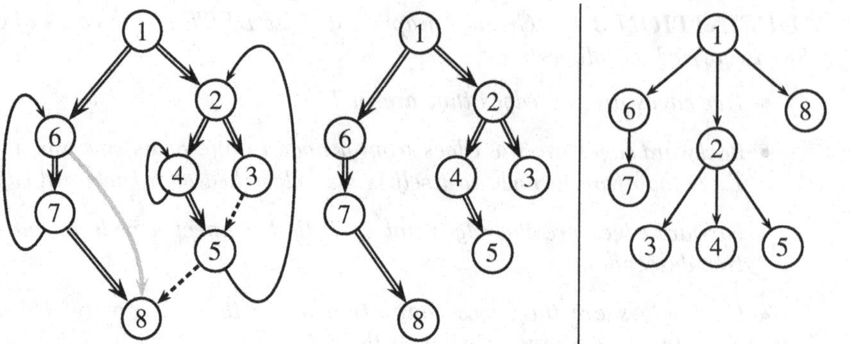

(a) G and one of its DFSTs. Tree edges in G are shown by double lines, back edges by single black lines, the forward edge by a gray line, and cross edges by dashed lines.

(b) Dominator tree of G. Given an edge $x \rightarrow y$, $x = idom(y)$.

FIGURE 3.2
A graph, its depth first spanning tree and its dominator tree.

DEFINITION 3.4 *A graph G is reducible if and only if it does not contain the forbidden subgraph shown in Figure 3.3 on the next page.*

The forbidden subgraph is characterized by presence of a cycle that has two distinct entry points for paths from a node that does not appear in the cycle. The common control constructs in programs result in reducible control flow graphs. However, a compiler inserts *gotos* liberally in a program being compiled. The CFG of such a program could become irreducible after optimizations.

DEFINITION 3.5 *Let n and m be nodes in the CFG. The node n is said to dominate m, denoted $n \geq m$, if every path from* **Start** *to m passes through n.*

Dominance is, by definition, reflexive. It is also transitive. Figure 3.2(b) shows the dominator tree for our example graph.

We now prove an important result that relates dominance and reducibility.

LEMMA 3.1
A graph G is reducible iff the head of every back edge in G dominates its tail.

PROOF *If part*: We show that if G is not reducible then there is a back edge in G whose head does not dominate its tail. Indeed if G is irreducible then it must contain the forbidden subgraph shown in Figure 3.3. Without any loss of generality, let us consider $b \rightarrow c$ to be a back edge. Then there is a path from ***Start*** to b through a which does not pass through c.

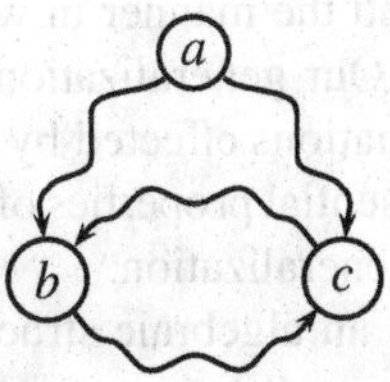

FIGURE 3.3
The forbidden subgraph for reducibility.

Only if part: We now show that if there is a back edge in G whose head does not dominate its tail, G is irreducible. Assume that $b \to c$ is such a back edge. Since c does not dominate b, there is a path from *Start* to b which bypasses c. Further, there is also a path from *Start* to c which bypasses b, or else b would have been visited before c in any depth first traversal and $b \to c$ would not have been a back edge. Thus G contains a forbidden subgraph with *Start*, b and c as the constituent nodes. ∎

The graph in Figure 3.2(a) is reducible. Some examples of edges whose addition could make it irreducible are: $1 \to 7$, $1 \to 3$, and $1 \to 5$.

3.2 Data Flow Framework

As we have said earlier, given a data flow problem, we associate data flow variables with entry and exit points of each basic block. The data flow variables are related through equations which are then solved to get data flow values at the program points. To obtain a solution of these equations, each data flow variable is initialized with a value, and the equations are iterated over till the value of each data flow variable converges.

Recall that in the case of available expressions analysis, the value of a data flow variable during an iteration is a subset of the value in the preceding iteration. In general there is an order between the values that a data flow variable takes in successive iterations during the solution process. In fact, one can impose an order on the entire space of data flow values. The order is related to the notion of approximation of data flow values that we discussed in Section 1.1.5 and is also important in reasoning about the termination of the solution procedure. Therefore the first step in the generalization of data flow problems and their solutions is to formalize this notion of order in the space of data flow values. A general way to express an order between objects is to embed them in a mathematical structure called a lattice.

The analyses studied in the previous chapter also illustrated the effect of a basic block on data flow values and the manner in which data flow values arriving along different paths are merged. Our generalization includes both these aspects of data flow analysis. The transformations effected by basic blocks on data flow values are called *flow functions*. The essential properties of flow functions and merge operations are identified as part of the generalization.

A data flow framework is an algebraic structure consisting of a set of data flow values, a set of flow functions and a merge operator.

3.2.1 Modeling Data Flow Values Using Lattices

Systematic computation of data flow values requires that the concept of approximations of data flow values and the operation of merging data flow values should satisfy certain properties. In this section we provide a lattice theoretic basis of these properties.

Partially Ordered Sets

The relation of partial order, defined below, captures the notion of approximations amongst data flow values.

DEFINITION 3.6 *A partial order* $\sqsubseteq$ *on a set* S *is a relation over* $S \times S$ *that is*

1. *Reflexive. For all elements* $x \in S : x \sqsubseteq x$.

2. *Transitive. For all elements* $x, y, z \in S : x \sqsubseteq y$ *and* $y \sqsubseteq z$ *implies* $x \sqsubseteq z$.

3. *Anti-symmetric. For all elements* $x, y \in S : x \sqsubseteq y$ *and* $y \sqsubseteq x$ *implies* $x = y$.

A partially ordered set (abbreviated as poset), denoted by $(S, \sqsubseteq)$, *is a set* S *with a partial order* $\sqsubseteq$.

We shall read $x \sqsubseteq y$ as "x is weaker than y". If $x \sqsubseteq y$ and $x \neq y$, we shall say that "x is strictly weaker than y", and denote this as $x \sqsubset y$. If $x \sqsubseteq y$ ($x \sqsubset y$), we shall also equivalently write $y \sqsupseteq x$ ($y \sqsupset x$) and read it as "y is stronger than (strictly stronger than) x". The posets that we shall deal with will often have an element which is weaker than any other element in the poset. Such an element, if it exists, is called the *least element* and denoted as $\bot$. The *greatest element*, defined similarly, will be denoted as $\top$.

Example 3.1

The poset of data flow values in live variables analysis is shown in Figure 3.4 on the facing page. Here, the set of all data flow values, denoted by L_{lv}, is $2^{\mathbb{V}\mathsf{ar}}$, where $\mathbb{V}\mathsf{ar}$ denotes the set of variables in a program. The partial order is: For x_i and x_j in L_{lv}, $x_i \sqsubseteq_{lv} x_j$ iff $x_i \supseteq x_j$. The greatest element of this poset is $\emptyset$ and the least element is $\mathbb{V}\mathsf{ar}$. □

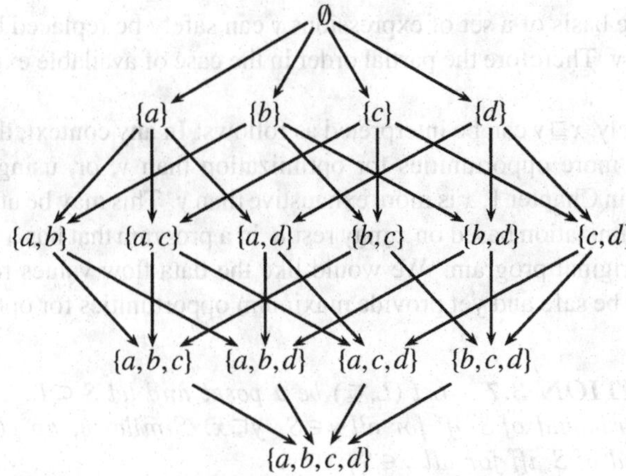

FIGURE 3.4
L_{lv} as a partially ordered set.

In the representation of the poset as a directed graph, $x_i \sqsubseteq x_j$, if there is a directed path from x_j to x_i. Since paths of length 0 are also possible, for every element x_i, $x_i \sqsubseteq x_i$. Such representations of posets are called Hasse diagrams*.

Example 3.2
As a dual example, consider the poset of data flow values for available expressions analysis. If we denote the set of all expressions occurring in the program as $\mathbb{E}\mathsf{xpr}$, then the set of data flow values, L_{av}, is $2^{\mathbb{E}\mathsf{xpr}}$, the set of all subsets of $\mathbb{E}\mathsf{xpr}$. Consider the partial order $\sqsubseteq_{av}$ defined as: for all x_i and x_j in L_{av}, $x_i \sqsubseteq_{av} x_j$ iff $x_i \subseteq x_j$. The least element of this poset is the empty set $\emptyset$ and the top element is $\mathbb{E}\mathsf{xpr}$. □

In the context of data flow analysis, the relation $\sqsubseteq$ can be interpreted as "a conservative (safe) approximation of". If $x \sqsubseteq y$, then, in any context, the data flow value x can be used in place of y for optimization without affecting the correctness of the optimized program. As an example, consider the use of liveness analysis for either dead code elimination (Section 2.3.1) or freeing memory objects (Section 1.1.5). If y is the set of variables that are actually live, then performing an optimization on the basis of a set x that is larger than y will not make the optimization unsafe. It is for this reason that the $\sqsubseteq$ relation in the case of live variables analysis is $\supseteq$. Similarly, for optimizations which are based on available expressions analysis like common subexpression or partial redundancy elimination, an optimization performed at a program

*Traditionally, Hasse diagrams are undirected graphs with the implicit assumption that $x_i \sqsubseteq x_j$ if x_j is drawn at a higher level in the diagram than x_i. We have, instead, chosen to make the graph directed with the hope that this lends to clarity.

point on the basis of a set of expressions y can safely be replaced by one based on a subset x of y. Therefore the partial order in the case of available expressions analysis is $\subseteq$.

Conversely, $x \sqsupseteq y$ can be interpreted as follows: In any context, the data flow value x provides more opportunities for optimization than y, or, using the terminology introduced in Chapter 1, x is more exhaustive than y. This may be at the cost of safety, i.e., the optimization based on x may result in a program that has a behavior different from the original program. We would like the data flow values resulting from our analyses to be safe and yet provide maximum opportunities for optimization.

DEFINITION 3.7 *Let $(L, \sqsubseteq)$ be a poset and let $S \subseteq L$. An element $x \in L$ is an upper bound of S iff for all $y \in S$, $y \sqsubseteq x$. Similarly, an element $x \in L$ is a lower bound of S iff for all $y \in S$, $x \sqsubseteq y$.*

In the graphical representation of a poset, x is an upper bound of S iff there are paths from x to each element of S. Similarly, x is an lower bound of S iff there are paths from each element of S to x. Also note that the definition above does not require the upper bound of a set to be in the set itself. As an example, let $S = \{\{a,b\},\{b,c\}\}$ in Figure 3.4. Then none of the upper or lower bounds of S are in S.

DEFINITION 3.8 *The least upper bound (lub) of a set S is an element x such that (i) x is an upper bound of S, and (ii) for all other upper bounds y of S, $x \sqsubseteq y$. The greatest lower bound (glb) of a set is an element x such that (i) x is a lower bound of S, and (ii) for all other lower bounds y of S, $y \sqsubseteq x$.*

Referring once again to Figure 3.4 on the previous page, $\{a,b\}$, $\{a\}$, $\{b\}$ are all upper bounds of the set $\{\{a,b,c\},\{a,b,d\}\}$. However the *lub* of this set is $\{a,b\}$.

The *lub* of a set S is also called the *join* of S and is denoted as $\bigsqcup S$. The *glb* of a set S is also called the *meet* of S and is denoted as $\bigsqcap S$. $\bigsqcup$ can also be used as an infix operator; $x \sqcup y$ denotes the *lub* of the two elements x and y. The *lub* (*glb*) of a set, if it exists, is unique. It can be verified that the join (and meet) operator has the following properties:

1. *Idempotence.* $\forall x \in S : x \sqcap x = x$.

2. *Commutativity.* $\forall x, y \in S : x \sqcap y = y \sqcap x$.

3. *Associativity.* $\forall x, y, z \in S : (x \sqcap y) \sqcap z = x \sqcap (y \sqcap z)$.

In the context of data flow analysis, the meet operator is used to merge data flow values along different paths and reaching a join node of the underlying CFG. The result of the meet operation is the most exhaustive safe approximation of data flow values along each of the paths.

***OBSERVATION 3.2** Let L be a poset and S be a subset of L whose glb exists. Let $x \in L$. If $x \sqsubseteq y$ for each $y \in S$, then $x \sqsubseteq \sqcap S$. This is just a restatement of the fact that any lower bound of a poset is weaker than the glb of the poset.*

It is important to mention that the posets that represent data flow values may be infinite. However, since each data flow value is a finite quantity, the posets are countable. Since we want to present algorithms that search for solutions of equations in posets which may be countably infinite, we have to impose additional constraints on these posets to ensure termination of the algorithms.

***DEFINITION 3.9** A chain S is a subset of a poset which is totally ordered, i.e., $\forall x, y \in S : x \sqsubseteq y$ or $y \sqsubseteq x$. A descending chain is a sequence of elements $\{x_1, x_2, \ldots\}$ from a poset such that $i \leq j$ implies $x_i \sqsupseteq x_j$.*

***DEFINITION 3.10** A descending chain $\{x_1, x_2, \ldots\}$ stabilizes eventually iff $\exists n, \forall m > n : x_m = x_n$.*

***DEFINITION 3.11** A poset satisfies the descending chain condition iff every descending chain in the poset stabilizes eventually.*

The importance of the descending chain condition is that it allows us to extend the guarantee of existence of meets to countably infinite sets. Let $S = \{x_1, x_2, x_3, \ldots\}$ be such a set. Then the values $\bigsqcap_{i=1}^{k} x_i$, $k = 1, 2, \ldots$, form a chain. Because of the descending chain condition, there is an m such that for any $n > m$, $\bigsqcap_{i=1}^{m} x_i = \bigsqcap_{i=1}^{n} x_i$. Then $\bigsqcap_{i=1}^{m} x_i$ is the *glb* of S.

Analogous to the descending chain condition, we can also define the ascending chain condition. However, since data flow analysis uses the meet operator for confluence, the result of merging is a lower bound of the data flow values being merged. Hence we are interested in the descending chain condition rather than the ascending chain condition. In the rest of the chapter we restrict the discussions to posets that satisfy the descending chain condition.

Lattices and Complete Lattices

During data flow analysis, we have to merge sets of data flow values. Therefore it is important to ensure that the meet of such sets exists.

***DEFINITION 3.12** A poset $(L, \sqsubseteq)$ is a lattice, iff, for each non-empty finite subset S of L, both $\sqcup S$ and $\sqcap S$ are in L. L is a complete lattice, iff, for each subset S of L, both $\sqcup S$ and $\sqcap S$ are in L.*

The condition that every non-empty finite subset must have a *glb* and a *lub* in L is equivalent to the condition that for any pair of elements x and y, both $x \sqcup y$ and $x \sqcap y$ should be in L. For the lattice L to be complete, even $\emptyset$ and infinite subsets of L must have a *glb* and *lub* in L.

Example 3.3

The posets $(L_{lv}, \sqsubseteq_{lv})$ and $(L_{av}, \sqsubseteq_{av})$ are complete lattices. An example of a lattice which is not complete is the set of natural numbers $\mathbb{N} = \{0, 1, 2, 3, \ldots\}$, ordered by $\leq$. In fact, any infinite set in this lattice does not have a *lub*. This set can be converted to a complete lattice by adding the element ∞ with the property that for any $x \in \mathbb{N}, x \leq \infty$. □

For a poset L, the conditions (i) $\bigsqcup S \in L$ for every subset S of L and (ii) $\bigsqcap S \in L$ for every subset S of L are equivalent. Thus for a poset to be a complete lattice, it is enough to require one of the two conditions to hold, the other is automatically satisfied. To see this, assume that the *glb* of every subset of L exists in L. We have to show that for an arbitrary $S \subseteq L$, the *lub* of S exists. Consider the set B of all upper bounds of S. Since every element of S is a lower bound of B, from Observation 3.2 $\bigsqcap B$ is an upper bound of S. In particular, it is the least upper bound of S.

If L is a complete lattice, then we denote the top element of the lattice, $\bigsqcup L$, by $\top$. Similarly, the bottom element of the lattice, $\bigsqcap L$ is denoted by $\bot$. Since every subset of L must have a *glb* and a *lub*, $\emptyset$ must also have a *glb* and a *lub*. It turns out that $\bigsqcap \emptyset$ is $\top$ and $\bigsqcup \emptyset$ is $\bot$. To see this, consider the definition of a lower bound of S: x is a lower bound of S iff $\forall y \in S : x \sqsubseteq y$. When S is $\emptyset$, every element of L is vacuously a lower bound of S. The greatest among them, $\top$, is the *glb* of $\emptyset$. For similar reasons $\bot$ is the same as $\bigsqcup \emptyset$. Observe that $\emptyset$ cannot be a complete lattice; the smallest poset which is complete must contain at least one element which can serve as both $\top$ and $\bot$.

Very often we shall consider tuples of values, each component of the tuple coming from a complete lattice. In such a case, the tuples themselves also form a complete lattice.

DEFINITION 3.13 *Let L_i, $1 \leq i \leq m$ be complete lattices with the partial order $\sqsubseteq_i$ and meet $\sqcap_i$. Then the cross-product $L = L_1 \times L_2 \times \ldots \times L_m$ is also a complete lattice with the partial order:*

$$\langle x_1, x_2, \ldots, x_m \rangle \sqsubseteq \langle y_1, y_2, \ldots, y_m \rangle \text{ iff } x_i \sqsubseteq_i y_i \text{ for all } i,\ 1 \leq i \leq m$$

and the induced meet

$$\langle x_1, x_2, \ldots, x_m \rangle \sqcap \langle y_1, y_2, \ldots, y_m \rangle = \langle x_1 \sqcap_1 y_1,\ x_2 \sqcap_2 y_2,\ \ldots,\ x_n \sqcap_n y_n \rangle$$

The L_is are called the components of the product lattice L.

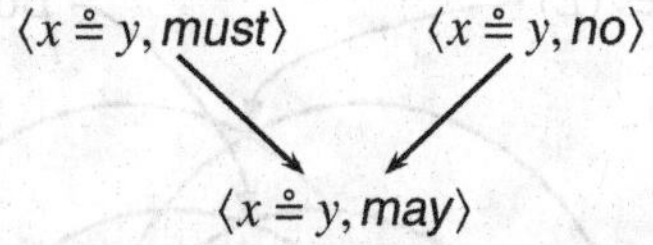

FIGURE 3.5
A meet semilattice for *may-must* alias analysis.

Meet Semilattices

Although the data flow values of most of the analyses can be modeled as a complete lattice, there are analyses whose data flow values cannot be modeled even as a lattice. Hence we need a structure which is less restrictive than a lattice.

Example 3.4
As an example of a data flow analysis problem which cannot be modeled naturally as a lattice, consider the combined *may-must* alias analysis problem. This is a similar to the combined *may-must* analysis described in Section 2.5. Assume that a program has just two pointer variables x and y. The data flow values for this problem can be modeled as a pair $(x \doteq y, d)$, where d is one of the three values *must*, *may* and *no*. The data flow value $(x \doteq y, \textsf{must})$ at a program point p indicates that x and y are aliased along all paths reaching p, $(x \doteq y, \textsf{may})$ indicates that x and y are aliased along some paths and not along all paths reaching p, and $(x \doteq y, \textsf{no})$ indicates that x and y are not aliased along any path reaching p. The poset of these data flow values is shown in Figure 3.5. □

In particular, we shall consider posets in which subsets have a *glb* but drop the requirement that they have a *lub* as well. Thus these lattices may not have a $\top$ element. The poset in Figure 3.5 is an example of a meet semilattice.

DEFINITION 3.14 *A poset $(L, \sqsubseteq)$ is a meet semilattice, iff, for each non-empty finite subset S of L, $\sqcap S$ is in L.*

We are interested in meet semilattices that satisfy the descending chain condition. Further, some of the algorithms that we discuss (algorithm in Figure 3.9, for example) assume the existence of the greatest element $\top$. In general, it is possible to modify these algorithms to avoid using $\top$ (algorithm in Figure 3.15). However, it is often convenient to use an element outside of the meet semilattice and give it the status of the $\top$ element. As an example, the algorithm used for *may-must* availability analysis in Section 2.5 required a $\top$ and hence a fictitious value *unknown* was added to the meet semilattice. Adding a new value requires us to define all flow functions for the value. We shall assume that for all functions f, $f(\top) = \top$. This extension preserves monotonicity of functions. Adding a $\top$ element to a meet semilattice results

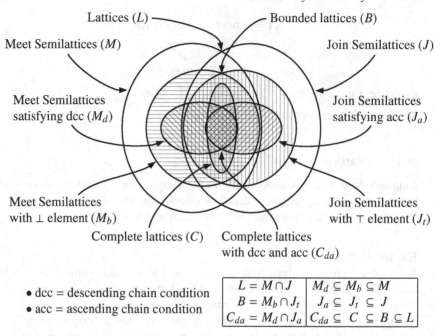

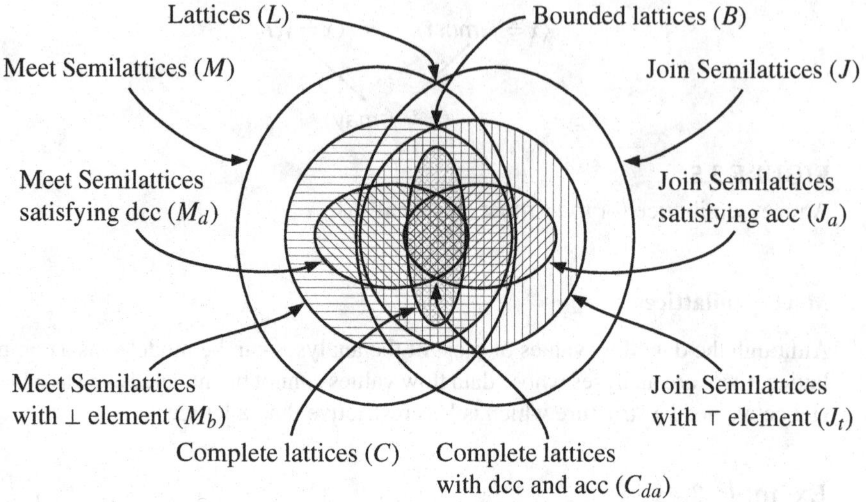

- dcc = descending chain condition
- acc = ascending chain condition

$L = M \cap J$	$M_d \subseteq M_b \subseteq M$
$B = M_b \cap J_t$	$J_a \subseteq J_t \subseteq J$
$C_{da} = M_d \cap J_a$	$C_{da} \subseteq C \subseteq B \subseteq L$

FIGURE 3.6
Relationships between different types of posets. The posets are assumed to be countable.

in a bounded lattice, i.e., a lattice with $\top$ and $\bot$ elements. Note that a bounded lattice need not be complete because arbitrary subsets may not have a *lub* or *glb*.

Example 3.5

Consider the poset $(A, \subseteq)$ of all finite subsets of the set of integers $\mathbb{I}$. Since every element of A is a subset of $\mathbb{I}$, the poset $(A \cup \{\mathbb{I}\}, \subseteq)$ is a bounded lattice with $\mathbb{I}$ and $\emptyset$ as $\top$ and $\bot$. However, it is not a complete lattice because the join ($\cup$) of arbitrary subsets of $A \cup \{\mathbb{I}\}$ may not exist in $A \cup \{\mathbb{I}\}$. For example, the union of all sets that do not contain a given number (say 1) does not exist in $A \cup \{\mathbb{I}\}$. □

It is possible to define a join semilattice much in the same way as a meet semilattice. Figure 3.6 illustrates the relationships between different kinds of posets.

3.2.2 Modeling Flow Functions

Recall that the data flow equations for reaching definitions analysis are:

$$In_n = \begin{cases} BI & n \text{ is } Start \text{ block} \\ \bigcup_{p \in pred(n)} Out_p & \text{otherwise} \end{cases} \tag{3.1}$$

$$Out_n = (In_n - Kill_n) \cup Gen_n \tag{3.2}$$

where In_n and Out_n are data flow variables, whose values are being defined by the data flow equations and Gen_n and $Kill_n$ are constants whose values depend on the contents of node n. BI is the information that is available at the *Start* block of the CFG.

For unidirectional problems, having two sets of variables In_n and Out_n is not essential—it just increases the readability of the equations. To avoid proliferation of variables in the ensuing discussion, we substitute for Out in the equations for In, and get

$$In_n = \begin{cases} BI & n \text{ is } Start \text{ block} \\ \bigcup_{p \in pred(n)} (In_p - Kill_p) \cup Gen_p & \text{otherwise} \end{cases} \tag{3.3}$$

Expressing $(In_p - Kill_p) \cup Gen_p$ as the application of a flow function f_p on In_p, we have:

$$In_n = \begin{cases} BI & n \text{ is } Start \text{ block} \\ \bigcup_{p \in pred(n)} f_p(In_p) & \text{otherwise} \end{cases} \tag{3.4}$$

We generalize Equations (3.4) so that the set of equations for any data flow analysis can be seen as an instance of the general set of equations shown below:

$$In_n = \begin{cases} BI & n \text{ is } Start \text{ block} \\ \bigsqcap_{p \in pred(n)} f_p(In_p) & \text{otherwise} \end{cases} \tag{3.5}$$

In Equation (3.5), $\sqcap$ is the meet operator used to merge data flow information along different paths. If the set of data flow values is L, then $f_n : L \mapsto L$ represents the transformation of the data flow values that reach the basic block n by the statements in n. These functions are called *flow functions.* Two important and related properties of flow functions are monotonicity and distributivity.

DEFINITION 3.15 *A function $f : L \mapsto L$ is called monotonic iff*

$$\forall x, y \in L : \; x \sqsubseteq y \Rightarrow f(x) \sqsubseteq f(y)$$

Monotonicity implies that the flow functions are well-behaved in the sense that they preserve the order of approximations.

DEFINITION 3.16 *A function $f : L \mapsto L$ is called distributive iff*

$$\forall x, y \in L: \; f(x \sqcap y) = f(x) \sqcap f(y)$$

OBSERVATION 3.3 *If f is monotonic then $f(x \sqcap y) \sqsubseteq f(x) \sqcap f(y)$.*

OBSERVATION 3.4 *Every distributive function is also monotonic. If $x \sqsubseteq y$, then $x = x \sqcap y$ and distributivity gives $f(x) = f(x) \sqcap f(y)$. This implies $f(x) \sqsubseteq f(y)$.*

Distributivity is a stronger condition than monotonicity. A distributive function not only preserves the order of approximations but also guarantees that merging information before function application does not result in any loss of precision.

In our generalization we shall assume that the set of flow functions F has the following properties:

1. The identity function $id \in F$. This is the flow function for the empty block of statements.

2. If $f \in F$ and $g \in F$, then $f \circ g \in F$. Composing the flow functions transformations of two basic blocks results in a flow function.

3. The functions in F are monotonic.

4. For every $x \in L$, there is a finite set of flow functions $\{f_1, f_2, \ldots f_m\}$ such that $x = \bigsqcap_{1 \le i \le m} f_i(\mathit{BI})$. This condition arises from the fact that solution procedures can only compute data flow values which are expressible as a finite meet of flow functions applied to BI. This condition can be seen either as a minimality condition on the set of data flow values or as a sufficiency condition on the set of flow functions.

The above four conditions characterize the set of admissible functions for data flow analysis.

3.2.3 Data Flow Frameworks

Having discussed lattice theoretic modeling of data flow values and the admissible flow functions, we now combine the two to present a generalization called data flow frameworks.

DEFINITION 3.17 *A data flow framework is a tuple $(L_{\mathcal{G}}, \sqcap_{\mathcal{G}}, F_{\mathcal{G}})$, where $\mathcal{G}$ is a symbol standing for a unspecified CFG, and :*

- $L_\mathcal{G}$ *is a description of a meet semilattice that represents the data flow values relevant to the problem.* $L_\mathcal{G}$ *must satisfy the descending chain condition.*

- $\sqcap_\mathcal{G}$ *is a description of the meet operator of the semilattice.* $\sqcap_\mathcal{G}$ *is, of course, derivable from* $L_\mathcal{G}$.

- $F_\mathcal{G}$ *is a description of the set of admissible flow functions from* $L_\mathcal{G}$ *to* $L_\mathcal{G}$. *Each flow function has an associated direction which could be along the control flow in the unspecified CFG* $\mathcal{G}$ *or against it.*

Forward flow functions indicate flow of information along the flow of control: The data flow information associated with a node is influenced by its predecessors. *Backward* flow functions indicate flow of information against the flow of control: The data flow information at a node is influenced by its successors. In *unidirectional* data flow frameworks, all functions have the same direction; *bidirectional* frameworks have a combination of flow functions in both directions.

Since we assume that the set of admissible functions are monotonic, we call the framework a *monotone data flow framework*. If the admissible functions are distributive, we call the framework a *distributive data flow framework*.

Example 3.6

As an example of a monotone data flow framework, consider available expressions analysis. In this framework $L_\mathcal{G}$ is $2^{\mathbb{E}\mathsf{xpr}}$, where $\mathbb{E}\mathsf{xpr}$ is the set of all expressions occurring in $\mathcal{G}$, $\sqcap_\mathcal{G}$ is $\cap$, and $F_\mathcal{G}$ consists of functions f such that $f(X) = (X - \mathit{Kill}) \cup \mathit{Gen}$ for arbitrary subsets Kill and Gen of $\mathbb{E}\mathsf{xpr}$. When $\mathit{Kill} = \mathit{Gen} = \emptyset$, f is the identity function. □

OBSERVATION 3.5 *Bit vector frameworks are distributive, i.e., if the flow functions* $f : L \mapsto L$ *of a framework can be expressed as* $f(x) = (x - \mathit{Kill}) \cup \mathit{Gen}$ *where* $\mathit{Kill}, \mathit{Gen} \in L$, *then*

$$\forall x, y \in L : \; f(x \sqcap y) = f(x) \sqcap f(y)$$

It follows that bit vector frameworks are also monotonic.

DEFINITION 3.18 *An instance of a data flow framework is an instantiation of the framework to a particular CFG. It is a pair* $\langle \mathbb{G}, M_\mathbb{G} \rangle$ *where*

- $\mathbb{G} = \langle \mathsf{Nodes}, \mathsf{Edges} \rangle$ *is an instance of* $\mathcal{G}$. *This yields concrete values* $L_\mathbb{G}$, $\sqcap_\mathbb{G}$ *and* $F_\mathbb{G}$ *for* $L_\mathcal{G}$, $\sqcap_\mathcal{G}$ *and* $F_\mathcal{G}$.

- $M_\mathbb{G}$ *is a mapping from blocks in* $\mathbb{G}$ *to* $F_\mathbb{G}$.

Example 3.7
An instance of the available expression analysis is a pair consisting of a concrete CFG $\mathbb{G}$ and a mapping function $M_{\mathbb{G}}$. A basic block consisting of a single statement $a = b * c$ would be mapped to the following function by $M_{\mathbb{G}}$.

$$f(X) = X - \mathbb{E}\mathsf{xpr}_a \cup \{b * c\}$$

where $\mathbb{E}\mathsf{xpr}_a$ is the set of all expressions in $\mathbb{G}$ that have a as an operand. □

Example 3.8
As a more interesting example, consider the *may* alias problem for a CFG $\mathbb{G}$. The goal here is to find at each program point the set of pointer variables whose values are the same, i.e., they point to the same location. The result of this analysis is used to sharpen the effect of optimizations in the presence of pointers. As an example, the fact that a and b are *not may* aliased ensures that the assignment $*b = 5$ does not kill the expression $*a + c$. Thus the expression $*a + c$ can be discovered as a common sub-expression.

- The meet semilattice $L_{\mathbb{G}}$ consists of sets of pairs $e_1 \doteq e_2$, where e_1 and e_2 are pointer expressions. The data flow value at a program point p containing this pair indicates a possible aliasing of the expressions e_1 and e_2 at p.

- Since a larger set of *may* aliases represent safer approximation by disabling more optimization opportunities, the partial order is: $X \sqsubseteq_{\mathbb{G}} Y$ iff $X \supseteq Y$. Thus $\sqcap_{\mathbb{G}}$ is $\cup$.

- Apart from the identity function, $F_{\mathbb{G}}$ consists of functions f such that $f(X) = X - \mathit{Kill}(X) \cup \mathit{Gen}(X)$. Notice that unlike available expressions analysis the *Kill* and *Gen* sets are dependent on X.

Consider a basic block consisting of a single assignment statement $*x = y$. $\mathit{Kill}(X)$ consists of the set of pairs in X, one of whose components has $*x$ as a prefix.[†] $\mathit{Gen}(X)$ consists of all pairs $(*e_1 \doteq e_2)$ such that $e_1 \doteq x$ and $e_2 \doteq y$ in X. □

3.3 Data Flow Assignments

Given an instance of a data flow framework, the desired data flow information is represented by the values of data flow variables In_n for every node n. We define

[†] A more precise definition of $\mathit{Kill}(X)$ would include all those pairs in X, one of whose components has a prefix that is *must* aliased to $*x$.

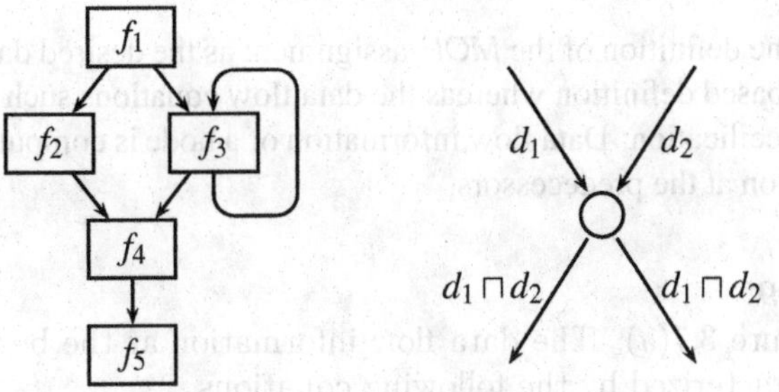

(a) Example CFG (b) Merging information at a join node

FIGURE 3.7
Example to illustrate *MOP* assignment value and fixed point assignment.

a *data flow assignment* (or simply *assignment*) as a mapping from each data flow variable In_n to a data flow value.

3.3.1 Meet Over Paths Assignment

Let $\mathit{paths}(p)$ denote the set of paths from *Start* to p. Given a path $\rho \in \mathit{paths}(p)$ consisting of basic blocks $(n_1, n_2 \ldots n_i)$, let f_ρ denote the composition of functions corresponding to the blocks in ρ, i.e., $f_\rho = f_{n_{i-1}} \circ \ldots \circ f_2 \circ f_1$. If ρ is a path (n) consisting of a single block, f_ρ is the identity function.

DEFINITION 3.19 *An assignment represented by the values of data flow variables In_n is safe iff*

$$\forall n \in \mathsf{Nodes}: \ \mathsf{In}_n \sqsubseteq \bigsqcap_{\rho \in \mathit{paths}(n)} f_\rho(\mathit{BI}) \tag{3.6}$$

Observe that the informal definitions of analyses (2.1), (2.2) and (2.3) in Chapter 2 have been given in terms of paths from *Start* to p.

DEFINITION 3.20 *A Meet Over Paths assignment, denoted* MOP*, is the maximum safe assignment.*

$$\forall n \in \mathsf{Nodes}: \ \mathit{MOP}_n = \bigsqcap_{\rho \in \mathit{paths}(n)} f_\rho(\mathit{BI}) \tag{3.7}$$

The existence of a *MOP* assignment follows from the closure and monotonicity properties of flow functions and the descending chain condition of the lattice of data flow values. A safe assignment is an approximation of the MOP assignment.

3.3.2 Fixed Point Assignment

Observe that the definition of the *MOP* assignment as the desired data flow information is a path-based definition whereas the data flow equations such as (3.5) form an edge-based specification: Data flow information of a node is computed from the data flow information at the predecessors.

Example 3.9
Consider Figure 3.7(a). The data flow information at the beginning of node 5 can be characterized by the following equations.

$$\begin{aligned} In_1 &= BI \\ In_2 &= f_1(In_1) \\ In_3 &= f_1(In_1) \sqcap f_3(In_3) \\ In_4 &= f_2(In_2) \sqcap f_3(In_3) \\ In_5 &= f_4(In_4) \end{aligned}$$

Unfolding the right hand side of In_5 partially, we get:

$$f_4(f_2(f_1(BI)) \sqcap (f_3(f_1(BI) \sqcap f_3(In_3)))) \tag{3.8}$$

The expression, represented as a tree in Figure 3.8(a), gives an idea of the nature of the solution of the equations. The solution computed by data flow equations at p consider all paths to p starting from the *Start* block and computes the data flow information along all these paths. However it merges the information at join nodes as shown in part (b) of Figure 3.7 on the previous page. The data flow information d_1 and d_2 is merged at the join node and the merged information $d_1 \sqcap d_2$ is propagated along all edges beyond the join node.

In contrast, the computation of *MOP* assignment does not involve merging values at intermediate points as shown in part (b) of Figure 3.8 on the facing page. ☐

As we shall see, merging is important for the existence of an algorithm for obtaining a solution. However it can also imply a potential loss of information.

To investigate whether the system of equations described by (3.5) have a solution, we first convert it into a single equation. The equations are of the form:

$$\begin{aligned} In_1 &= \mathbf{f}_1(In_1, \ldots, In_N) \\ In_2 &= \mathbf{f}_2(In_1, \ldots, In_N) \\ &\ldots \\ In_N &= \mathbf{f}_N(In_1, \ldots, In_N) \end{aligned}$$

where $In_i \in L_i$. Let the product lattice $L_1 \times L_2 \times \ldots L_N$ be denoted by $\overrightarrow{\mathbf{L}}$. Observe the difference between f_i and $\mathbf{f}_i$. $f_i \in F : L_i \mapsto L_i$ is a flow function, whereas $\mathbf{f}_i : \overrightarrow{\mathbf{L}} \mapsto L_i$

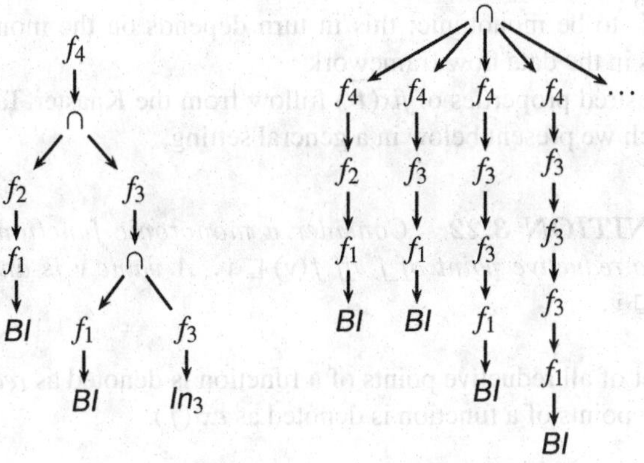

(a) Expression tree for *MFP* (b) Expression tree for *MOP*

FIGURE 3.8
Unfoldings of In_5.

is formed by composing flow functions and the meet operator. The system of simultaneous equations can be rewritten as the single equation

$$\overrightarrow{\mathbf{In}} = \overrightarrow{\mathbf{f}}\,(\overrightarrow{\mathbf{In}}) \tag{3.9}$$

where $\overrightarrow{\mathbf{In}} \in \overrightarrow{\mathbf{L}}$ and $\overrightarrow{\mathbf{f}} : \overrightarrow{\mathbf{L}} \mapsto \overrightarrow{\mathbf{L}}$ is defined as

$$\overrightarrow{\mathbf{f}}\,(\overrightarrow{\mathbf{In}}) = \left\langle \mathbf{f}_1(\overrightarrow{\mathbf{In}}), \mathbf{f}_2(\overrightarrow{\mathbf{In}}), \ldots \mathbf{f}_N(\overrightarrow{\mathbf{In}}) \right\rangle$$

A solution of Equation (3.9) represents the data flow information computed by solving data flow equations.

DEFINITION 3.21 *A fixed point of a function $f : L \mapsto L$ is a value $v \in L$ that satisfies $f(v) = v$.*

A *fixed point* assignment is a solution of the data flow equations represented by (3.9). For a fixed point assignment *FP*, we denote the value of variable In_n by FP_n. The *maximum fixed point* assignment is a fixed point assignment *MFP* such that for any fixed point assignment *FP*,

$$\forall n \in \text{Nodes} : FP_n \sqsubseteq MFP_n$$

3.3.3 Existence of Fixed Point Assignment

The set of all fixed points of f is denoted by *fix*(f). We are interested in the existence and structure of *fix*($\overrightarrow{\mathbf{f}}$) where $\overrightarrow{\mathbf{f}}$ is the function used for defining Equation (3.9). We require $\overrightarrow{f}$ to be monotonic; this in turn depends on the monotonicity of the flow functions in the data flow framework.

The desired properties of $fix(\overrightarrow{f})$ follow from the Knaster-Tarski fixed point theorem which we present below in a general setting.

DEFINITION 3.22 *Consider a monotonic function $f : L \mapsto L$. A value $v \in L$ is a reductive point of f iff $f(v) \sqsubseteq v$. A value v is an extensive point of f iff $f(v) \sqsupseteq v$.*

The set of all reductive points of a function is denoted as $red(f)$ and the set of all extensive points of a function is denoted as $ext(f)$.

THEOREM 3.1 (Knaster-Tarski fixed point theorem)
Let $f : L \mapsto L$ be a monotonic function on a complete lattice L. Then

1. $\bigsqcap red(f) \in fix(f)$ *and* $\bigsqcap fix(f) = \bigsqcap red(f)$.
2. $\bigsqcup ext(f) \in fix(f)$ *and* $\bigsqcup fix(f) = \bigsqcup ext(f)$.
3. $fix(f)$ *is a complete lattice.*

PROOF

1. Let $\bigsqcap red(f)$ be l. We first prove that l is a fixed point, i.e., $f(l) = l$. To show $f(l) \sqsubseteq l$, consider any element $x \in red(f)$. Since $l \sqsubseteq x$, $f(l) \sqsubseteq f(x)$ because of monotonicity of f. Further, since $x \in red(f)$, $f(x) \sqsubseteq x$. Therefore $f(l) \sqsubseteq x$. Since x was an arbitrary element in $red(f)$, $f(l) \sqsubseteq l$ by Observation 3.2.
   We now show $l \sqsubseteq f(l)$. Interestingly, this can be derived from $f(l) \sqsubseteq l$. Because of monotonicity, $f(f(l)) \sqsubseteq f(l)$. Thus $f(l)$ is a reductive point of $red(f)$. Since l is $\bigsqcap red(f)$, we have $l \sqsubseteq f(l)$.
   Since $fix(f) \subseteq red(f)$, $\bigsqcap red(f)$ is a lower bound of $fix(f)$. Further, since $\bigsqcap red(f) \in fix(f)$, $\bigsqcap red(f) = \bigsqcap fix(f)$.
2. Similar to 1.
3. Consider any arbitrary subset Y of $fix(f)$. It is enough to show that $\bigsqcap Y$ exists in $fix(f)$. Let $X = \{x \mid x \sqsubseteq \bigsqcap Y, x \in L\}$. Since L is a complete lattice, it is easy to see that X is a complete lattice with $\bigsqcap Y$ as the top element and the bottom of L as the bottom element of X. Now consider a restriction of f to X called f'. f' is a monotonic function on the complete lattice X. Clearly $fix(f') \subseteq fix(f)$. Further, $fix(f') \subseteq X$. Thus every fixed point of f' is weaker than $\bigsqcap Y$. Since $fix(f') \subseteq fix(f)$, $\bigsqcap Y$ is contained in $fix(f)$.

∎

Input: An instance $(\mathbb{G}, M_{\mathbb{G}})$ of a monotone data flow framework $(L_G, \sqcap_G, F_G)$. The function to which $M_{\mathbb{G}}$ maps a node n is denoted as f_n. The *Start* node is numbered 0. The rest of the nodes are arbitrarily ordered from 1 to $N-1$.

Output: $In_k, 0 \leq k \leq N-1$ giving the output of the data flow analysis for each node.

Algorithm:

```
 0  function dfaMain()
 1  {  In_0 = BI
 2     for all j, j ≠ 0 do In_j = ⊤
 3     change = true
 4     while change do
 5     {  change = false
 6        for j = 1 to N−1 do
 7        {  temp =    ⊓       f_p(In_p)
                    p∈pred(j)
 8           if temp ≠ In_j then
 9           {  In_j = temp
10              change = true
11           }
12        }
13     }
14  }
```

FIGURE 3.9
Round-robin iterative algorithm for computing *MFP* assignment for frameworks with a complete lattice.

3.4 Computing Data Flow Assignments

Given a complete lattice and a monotonic function defining data flow equations (which, in our case, is $\overrightarrow{f}$), the Knaster-Tarski fixed point theorem guarantees existence of fixed points. In this section we present an algorithm for computing the *MFP* assignment and show the computability of *MFP* assignment and undecidability of *MOP* assignment.

3.4.1 Computing *MFP* Assignment

Figure 3.9 provides an algorithm to solve the data flow equations. The iterations of lines 7-12 can be indexed using a pair (i, j), where i, starting with 1, is the iteration number of the **while** loop, and j is the iteration number (the index) of the **for** loop. Given an iteration (i, j), we shall denote the next iteration in lexicographical ordering as $N(i, j)$ and the value of In_m before the (i, j)th iteration as $In_m^{(i,j)}$.

LEMMA 3.2
The algorithm shown in Figure 3.9 terminates.

PROOF We shall first show that the value of a data flow variable decreases across successive iterations. In other words, for all m

$$\mathit{In}_m^{(i,j)} \sqsupseteq \mathit{In}_m^{\mathcal{N}(i,j)} \tag{3.10}$$

This must be true for $m = 0$ for all (i, j) as its value remains constant at BI. For other values of m, we show (3.10) by induction on the iteration count (i, j).

Basis: True, because the value of $\mathit{In}_m^{\mathcal{N}(1,1)}$ is $\top$.

Inductive Step: Assume as the inductive hypothesis that $\mathit{In}_m^{(i,j)} \sqsupseteq \mathit{In}_m^{\mathcal{N}(i,j)}$ for all m. From monotonicity, it follows that

$$\forall m \in \mathsf{Nodes} : f_m\left(\mathit{In}_m^{(i,j)}\right) \sqsupseteq f_m\left(\mathit{In}_m^{\mathcal{N}(i,j)}\right) \tag{3.11}$$

We have to show that

$$\forall m \in \mathsf{Nodes} : \; \mathit{In}_m^{\mathcal{N}(i,j)} \sqsupseteq \mathit{In}_m^{\mathcal{N}(\mathcal{N}(i,j))} \tag{3.12}$$

The second component of $\mathcal{N}(i, j)$ gives the block number whose data flow variable is examined on line 8 in $\mathcal{N}(i, j)$th iteration. We shall denote this block number as l. If this is not the same as m, or, if the value of In_m is the same since it was last examined, there is nothing to be proven. Otherwise, by lines 7 and 9 of the algorithm, the proof obligation (3.12) reduces to

$$\prod_{p \in pred(l)} f_p\left(\mathit{In}_p^{(i,j)}\right) \sqsupseteq \prod_{p \in pred(l)} f_p\left(\mathit{In}_p^{(\mathcal{N}(i,j))}\right) \tag{3.13}$$

The inductive step then follows from (3.11) and Observation 3.2.

The termination of the algorithm follows directly from (3.10) and the descending chain condition. ∎

We next show that algorithm (3.9) computes the *MFP* assignment of the associated data flow equations.

LEMMA 3.3
The algorithm in Figure 3.9 computes the MFP *assignment of the data flow equations represented by (3.5).*

PROOF The convergence of the algorithm implies that the values of In found by the algorithm form a fixed point assignment of the equations represented by (3.5). We have to prove that it is the maximum fixed point by showing that for any other fixed point assignment FP, $\mathit{FP}_m \sqsubseteq \mathit{In}_m$ for every node m. We do this by showing that the value of In_m computed at each step

(i, j) of the algorithm is stronger than FP_m. This is true of FP_0 and In_0 since the value of FP_0 is BI and so is the value of In_0 in each step of the algorithm. We therefore prove the lemma for values of m other than 0. The proof is by induction on (i, j).

Basis: Follows from the fact that $In_m(1,1) = \top$

Inductive step: We have to show that $FP_m \sqsubseteq In_m{}^{N(i,j)}$. Since FP is a fixed point assignment of Equation (3.5), $FP_m = \bigsqcap_{p \in pred(m)} f_p(FP_p)$. Further, from line 7 of the algorithm, $In_m{}^{N(i,j)} = \bigsqcap_{p \in pred(m)} f_p\left(In_p{}^{(i,j)}\right)$. Therefore we have to show that

$$\bigsqcap_{p \in pred(m)} f_p(FP_p) \sqsubseteq \bigsqcap_{p \in pred(m)} f_p\left(In_p{}^{(i,j)}\right) \tag{3.14}$$

This once again follows from the induction hypothesis, monotonicity of the flow functions and Observation 3.2. ∎

3.4.2 Comparing *MFP* and *MOP* Assignments

In this section we show that the *MFP* assignment computed by the algorithm in Figure 3.9 is weaker than the *MOP* assignment. We also show examples of frameworks in which the *MFP* is strictly weaker than the *MOP* assignment.

LEMMA 3.4

When the algorithm in Figure 3.9 terminates, $\forall m \in \text{Nodes}$, $In_m \sqsubseteq MOP_m$.

PROOF Let $paths_l(m)$ denote the set of all paths of length l from *Start* to m. We want to show by induction on l that $In_m \sqsubseteq \bigsqcap_{\rho \in paths_l(m)} f_\rho(BI)$.

Basis: $l = 1$. In this case the path being considered has the single node *Start*. The lemma holds because In_0, which represents the data flow value at the beginning of *Start* is held constant at BI.

Inductive step: We have to show that

$$In_m \sqsubseteq \bigsqcap_{\rho \in paths_l(m)} f_\rho(BI) \tag{3.15}$$

From Equation (3.5), we also have

$$In_m = \bigsqcap_{p \in pred(m)} f_p(In_p)$$

and as the induction hypothesis, we can assume that for all $p \in pred(m)$,

$$In_p \sqsubseteq \bigsqcap_{\rho \in paths_{l-1}(p)} f_\rho(BI)$$

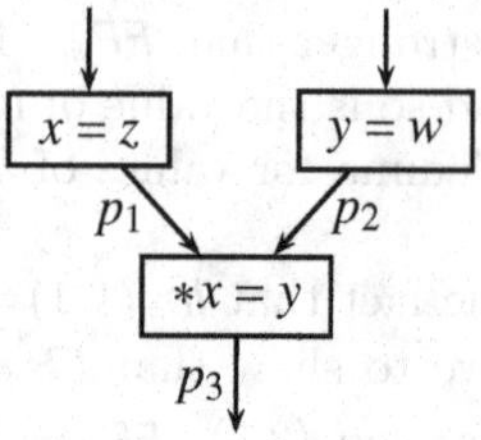

FIGURE 3.10
CFG illustrating the non-distributivity of *may* alias framework.

Monotonicity of flow functions gives

$$f_p(In_p) \sqsubseteq f_p\left(\bigsqcap_{\rho \in paths_{l-1}(p)} f_\rho(BI)\right)$$

And from Observation 3.3,

$$f_p(In_p) \sqsubseteq \bigsqcap_{\rho \in paths_{l-1}(p)} f_p\left(f_\rho(BI)\right)$$

Since ρ is a path of length $l-1$ and p is a predecessor of m, the composition $f_p \circ f_\rho$ corresponds to a path of length l reaching m and

$$f_p(In_p) \sqsubseteq \bigsqcap_{\rho \in paths_l(m)} f_\rho(BI)$$

Therefore

$$In_m = \bigsqcap_{p \in pred(m)} f_p(In_p) \sqsubseteq \bigsqcap_{\rho \in paths_l(m)} f_\rho(BI) \sqsubseteq MOP_m$$

∎

We now show that for some data flow frameworks, the *MFP* assignment is strictly weaker than the *MOP* assignment.

Example 3.10
Consider a CFG fragment shown in Figure 3.10 as an instance of the *may* alias analysis framework. The data flow values at p_1 and p_2 are $\{x \doteq z\}$ and $\{y \doteq w\}$. While computing the *MFP* assignment, these data flow values will be merged to obtain the value $\{x \doteq z, y \doteq w\}$ at the input of the block containing the assignment $*x = y$. The flow function of this assignment will add to this value the cross product of all aliases of $*x$ and all aliases of y. The data flow value at p_3 is thus $\{x \doteq z, y \doteq w, *x \doteq y, *x \doteq w, *z \doteq y, *z \doteq w\}$.

The *MOP* assignment on the other hand finds the effect of the assignment $*x = y$ on the incoming data flow values $\{x \doteq z\}$ and $\{y \doteq w\}$ separately. This yields the sets $\{x \doteq z, *x \doteq y, *z \doteq y\}$ and $\{*x \doteq y, *x \doteq w, y \doteq w\}$. The value at p_3 is a union of the two sets, and this is clearly stronger than the corresponding *MFP* value. The *MFP* value includes an alias $*z \doteq w$ which is not possible along any execution path. □

In Chapter 4 we will see other examples of data flow frameworks for which the *MFP* assignment is strictly weaker than *MOP* assignment. We now show that the *MFP* and the *MOP* assignments coincide for distributive frameworks.

LEMMA 3.5
For distributive frameworks, $\forall m \in \mathsf{Nodes}$, $\mathit{In}_m = \mathit{MOP}_m$.

PROOF We replay the proof of Lemma 3.4 with $\sqsubseteq$ substituted by $=$ in (3.15). As the induction hypothesis, we can assume that for all $p \in \mathit{pred}(m)$,

$$\mathit{In}_p = \bigsqcap_{\rho \in \mathit{paths}_{l-1}(p)} f_\rho(\mathit{BI})$$

Applying f_p to both sides of the equation, we have:

$$f_p(\mathit{In}_p) = f_p\left(\bigsqcap_{\rho \in \mathit{paths}_{l-1}(p)} f_\rho(\mathit{BI})\right)$$

Because f_p is distributive, we have

$$f_p(\mathit{In}_p) = \bigsqcap_{\rho \in \mathit{paths}_{l-1}(p)} f_p\left(f_\rho(\mathit{BI})\right)$$

which simplifies to

$$f_p(\mathit{In}_p) = \bigsqcap_{\rho \in \mathit{paths}_l(m)} f_\rho(\mathit{BI})$$

Therefore

$$\mathit{In}_m = \bigsqcap_{p \in \mathit{pred}(m)} f_p(\mathit{In}_p) = \bigsqcap_{\rho \in \mathit{paths}_l(m)} f_\rho(\mathit{BI})$$

■

3.4.3 Undecidability of *MOP* Assignment Computation

We have seen that if a framework is not distributive, then the algorithm shown in Figure 3.9 on page 79 may produce a solution which is strictly weaker than the *MOP* value. Thus it is interesting to investigate whether there exists an algorithm which can compute the *MOP* of an arbitrary monotone data flow framework. We now show that the problem of finding the *MOP* value of a monotone data flow framework is undecidable. To do this we reduce an instance of an undecidable problem called the *Modified Post's Correspondence Problem (MPCP)* to an instance of a monotone data flow framework. MPCP is a decision problem defined as follows:

DEFINITION 3.23 *Given lists* $A = [a_1, a_2, \ldots, a_k]$ *and* $B = [b_1, b_2, \ldots, b_k]$, *where* a_i *and* b_i *are strings of 0's and 1's, is there an index list* $[1, i_1, i_2, \ldots, i_r]$ *such that* $a_1 a_{i_1} a_{i_2} \ldots a_{i_r} = b_1 b_{i_1} b_{i_2} \ldots b_{i_r}$?

In the above definition, juxtaposition of strings denotes their concatenation. Given an instance I of MPCP, we convert it into an instance of a monotone data flow framework as follows:

- The meet semilattice L of data flow values consists of lists of integers between 1 and k. These play the role of index lists. The semilattice also includes $\perp$ and the special element \$ indicating that the instance of MPCP has no solution.

- The relation $\sqsubseteq_I$ is defined as $x \sqsubseteq_I y$ *iff* $x = y$ *or* $x = \perp$.

- The set of flow functions F is formed by composing the following functions:

  1. The identity function *id*.
  2. A class of functions $f_i, 1 \leq i \leq k$, such that:

  $$f_i(\alpha) = \begin{cases} \perp, & \alpha \text{ is } \perp \\ \$, & \alpha \text{ is } \$ \\ \alpha\#i & \text{otherwise} \end{cases}$$

  $\alpha\#i$ extends the index list α by adding the integer i at the end.

  3. A function g such that

  $$g(\alpha) = \begin{cases} \perp, & \text{the index list } \alpha \text{ is a solution of the} \\ & \text{MPCP instance } I \\ \$ & \text{otherwise} \end{cases}$$

- *BI* is the singleton list containing 1.

- The CFG is shown in Figure 3.11.

LEMMA 3.6
The data flow framework defined above is monotone.

PROOF Obvious. ∎

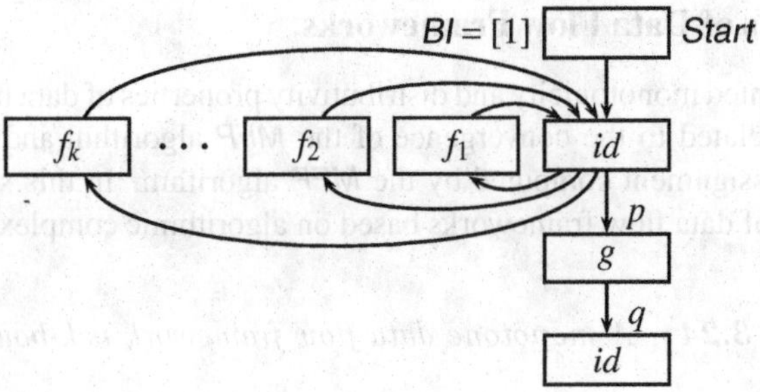

FIGURE 3.11
CFG for showing undecidability of *MOP* computation.

THEOREM 3.1
The problem of finding the MOP assignment for any monotone data flow framework is undecidable.

PROOF Given an MPCP instance I, we define an instance of a monotone data flow framework using the above construction. Each path to the program point p generates a distinct index list as the data flow value. Conversely, for each possible index list there is a path to p that generates the list. The function g checks whether each of these lists is a possible solution of the MPCP instance. Therefore, the *MOP* value at the program point q is \$ iff there is a solution to the MPCP instance, and $\perp$ otherwise. If an algorithm to compute the *MOP* assignment existed, we could use it to find a solution of the MPCP instance I. However, since MPCP is known to be undecidable, the problem of finding *MOP* for any monotone data flow framework is also undecidable. ∎

3.5 Complexity of Data Flow Analysis for Rapid Frameworks

Recall that the *MFP* algorithm presented in Figure 3.9 on page 79 does not assume an a-priori order in which nodes of the input CFG are visited during an iteration. In order to estimate the complexity of data flow analysis, we now consider a specialization of the *MFP* algorithm in which the nodes of the CFG are visited in reverse postorder. We also consider special properties of data flow frameworks that make the algorithm amenable to complexity analysis.

3.5.1 Properties of Data Flow Frameworks

Section 3.2.3 presented monotonicity and distributivity properties of data flow frameworks. They are related to the convergence of the *MFP* algorithm and characterize the data flow assignment computed by the *MFP* algorithm. In this section, we present properties of data flow frameworks based on algorithmic complexity.

DEFINITION 3.24 *A monotone data flow framework is k-bounded iff*

$$\exists k \geq 1 \ s.t. \ \forall f \in F, \forall x \in L: \ f^0(x) \sqcap f^1(x) \sqcap f^2(x) \sqcap \cdots = \prod_{i=0}^{k-1} f^i(x) \qquad (3.16)$$

where f^0 is the identity function and $f^{j+1} = f \circ f^j$.

The unbounded expression $f^0(x) \sqcap f^1(x) \sqcap f^2(x) \sqcap \cdots$ represents the *glb* of the data flow value computed in all possible traversals over a loop and is called the *loop closure* of f. Since we require L to satisfy the descending chain condition, all loop closures are bounded. For a framework to be k-bounded, the loop closures must be bounded by a constant k.

A 2-bounded framework is called a *fast* framework. It can be shown that a framework is fast iff

$$\forall f \in F, \forall x \in L : f^2(x) \sqsupseteq x \sqcap f(x) \qquad (3.17)$$

Intuitively, a single traversal over a loop is sufficient for computing loop closure.

LEMMA 3.7
Bit vector frameworks are fast.

PROOF Recall that the flow functions in bit vector frameworks can be expressed as $f(x) = (x - \mathit{Kill}) \cup \mathit{Gen}$ where $\mathit{Kill}, \mathit{Gen} \in L$. For such functions,

$$\begin{aligned} f^2(x) &= f((x - \mathit{Kill}) \cup \mathit{Gen}) \\ &= (((x - \mathit{Kill}) \cup \mathit{Gen}) - \mathit{Kill}) \cup \mathit{Gen} \\ &= (x - \mathit{Kill}) \cup (\mathit{Gen} - \mathit{Kill}) \cup \mathit{Gen} \\ &= (x - \mathit{Kill}) \cup \mathit{Gen} \\ &= f(x) \end{aligned}$$

This implies $f^2(x) \sqsupseteq x \sqcap f(x)$. ∎

There is an important subclass of fast frameworks called *rapid* frameworks in which traversing the loop independently of the value at the entry of the loop is sufficient for computing the final value at the entry of the loop.

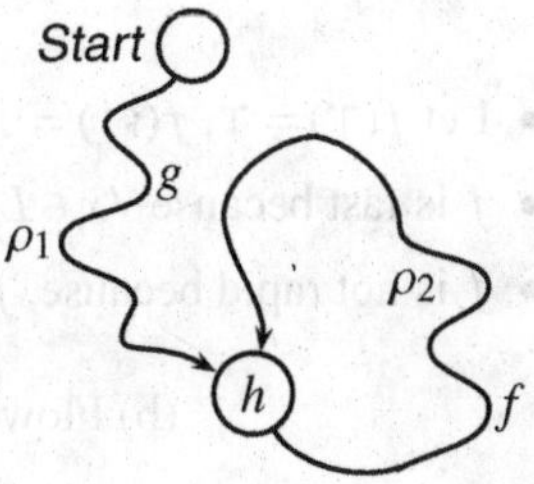

FIGURE 3.12
The significance of the rapidity condition.

DEFINITION 3.25 *A data flow framework is rapid, iff*

$$(\forall f, g \in F)\,(\forall x, \mathit{BI} \in L) : f(g(\mathit{BI})) \sqsupseteq g(\mathit{BI}) \sqcap f(x) \sqcap x \tag{3.18}$$

The condition is significant for paths which include loops. Figure 3.12 shows an example of such a path whose initial segment ρ_1 is from the *Start* node to the header h of a loop. The second segment ρ_2 is from h back to h along the looping path. The flow functions corresponding to the two segments are g and f. The result of $f(g(\mathit{BI}))$ represents the data flow value at h along the path $\rho_1\rho_2$. The rapidity condition says that this is safely approximated by combining the data flow value generated along ρ_1 and the value obtained by traversing the loop with *any* data flow x available at h. The important point is that the data value $g(\mathit{BI})$ may take several iterations to reach h from *Start* because of the presence of back edges in ρ_1. However, the rapidity condition ensures that it is enough to traverse the loop with a data flow value that has reached h earlier, say, through a back edge free path from *Start* to h.

We now state and prove a condition that is equivalent to Condition (3.18).

LEMMA 3.8
The rapid condition (3.18) is equivalent to:

$$(\forall f \in F)\,(\forall x, y \in L) : f(y) \sqsupseteq y \sqcap f(x) \sqcap x \tag{3.19}$$

PROOF It is easy to derive (3.18) from (3.19). If (3.19) holds for any y, in particular it holds for values expressible as $g(\mathit{BI})$ for any choice of g and BI. To derive (3.19) from (3.18), we show that for arbitrary f, y and x,

$$f(y) \sqsupseteq y \sqcap f(x) \sqcap x$$

Since any value y can be expressed as $\bigsqcap_{i=0}^{k} g_i(\mathit{BI})$, our proof obligation becomes:

$$f\Big(\bigsqcap_{i=0}^{k} g_i(\mathit{BI})\Big) \sqsupseteq \bigsqcap_{i=0}^{k} g_i(\mathit{BI}) \sqcap f(x) \sqcap x$$

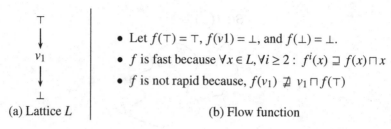

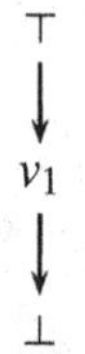

(a) Lattice L

- Let $f(\top) = \top$, $f(v1) = \bot$, and $f(\bot) = \bot$.
- f is fast because $\forall x \in L, \forall i \geq 2 : \ f^i(x) \sqsupseteq f(x) \sqcap x$
- f is not rapid because, $f(v_1) \not\sqsupseteq v_1 \sqcap f(\top)$

(b) Flow function

FIGURE 3.13
A fast function need not be rapid.

Because of monotonicity, this is the same as

$$\prod_{i=0}^{k} f(g_i(BI)) \sqsupseteq \prod_{i=0}^{k} g_i(BI) \sqcap f(x) \sqcap x \tag{3.20}$$

Because of (3.18), $f(g_i(BI)) \sqsupseteq g_i(BI) \sqcap f(x) \sqcap x$ holds for each i. Therefore (3.20) holds because of Observation 3.2. ∎

A consequence of this condition is that it is not necessary for an algorithm to traverse a loop twice. If x is taken as the value at h before iterating over the loop, then setting y to $f(x)$ we have

$$\begin{aligned} f(f(x)) &\sqsupseteq f(x) \sqcap f(x) \sqcap x \\ &\sqsupseteq f(x) \sqcap x \end{aligned}$$

We have just shown that every rapid framework is fast. To show that fastness does not necessarily imply rapidity, it is sufficient to construct a framework with a flow function that is fast but is not rapid. Figure 3.13 defines such a function.

For complete lattices, the rapid condition can also be stated as

$$\forall z \in L, \forall f \in F : \ f(z) \sqsupseteq z \sqcap f(\top) \tag{3.21}$$

This is just an instance of (3.19). Observe this condition also has the same meaning: A loop can be analyzed independently of the incoming information.

We have already shown that bit vector frameworks are fast (Lemma 3.7). Now we show that they are also rapid.

LEMMA 3.9
Bit vector frameworks are rapid.

PROOF We first consider frameworks in which the $\sqsubseteq$ relation is $\subseteq$. For such frameworks, Condition (3.18) reduces to

$$(\forall f, g \in F)\,(\forall x, y \in L) : \ f(g(y)) \supseteq g(y) \cap f(x) \cap x$$

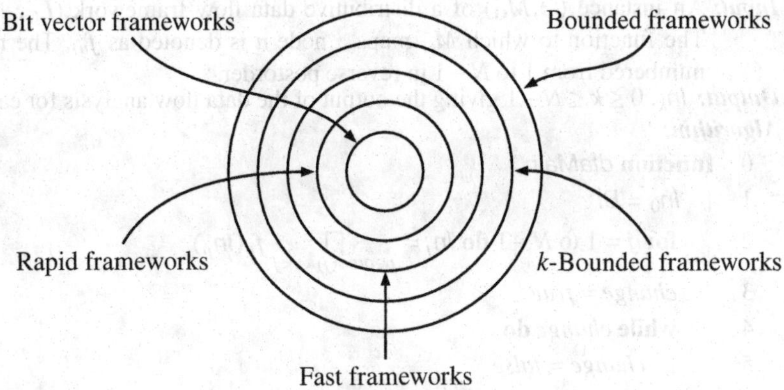

FIGURE 3.14
Monotone data flow frameworks with lattices containing $\top$ and satisfying the descending chain condition.

Let $g(y) = z$. Then our proof obligation becomes

$$(\forall f \in F)\,(\forall x, z \in L):\ f(z) \supseteq z \cap f(x) \cap x$$

The right hand side can be reduced to

$$\begin{aligned} z \cap f(x) \cap x &= z \cap ((x - \mathit{Kill}) \cup \mathit{Gen}) \cap x \\ &= z \cap (x \cap (\neg \mathit{Kill}) \cup \mathit{Gen}) \cap x \\ &= (z \cap (\neg \mathit{Kill}) \cap x) \cup (\mathit{Gen} \cap z \cap x) \\ &\subseteq (z \cap (\neg \mathit{Kill})) \cup (\mathit{Gen}) \\ &\subseteq (z - \mathit{Kill}) \cup \mathit{Gen} \\ &\subseteq f(z) \end{aligned}$$

Rapidity of frameworks in which $\sqsubseteq$ relation is $\supseteq$, can be shown similarly. ∎

Given arbitrary $x \in L$ and arbitrary $f \in F$, we have seen that for fast frameworks, $f^2(x) \sqsupseteq f(x) \sqcap x$ whereas for bit vector frameworks, $f^2(x) = f(x)$. We now show that the rapid frameworks satisfy the condition $f^2(x) \sqsupseteq f(x)$. This condition is stronger than the condition for fast frameworks but weaker that the condition for bit vector frameworks.

LEMMA 3.10
If $f \in F$ is a flow function in a rapid framework and the underlying lattice is complete, then $\forall z \in L:\ f^2(z) \sqsupseteq f(z)$.

PROOF Instantiating g to f, BI to z, and x to $\top$ in the rapid condition (3.18), we have

Input: An instance $(\mathbb{G}, M_{\mathbb{G}})$ of a distributive data flow framework $(L_{\mathcal{G}}, \sqcap_{\mathcal{G}}, F_{\mathcal{G}})$. The function to which $M_{\mathbb{G}}$ maps a node n is denoted as f_n. The nodes are numbered from 1 to $N - 1$ in reverse postorder.

Output: $In_k, 0 \le k \le N - 1$ giving the output of the data flow analysis for each node.

Algorithm:

```
0   function dfaMain()
1   {   In₀ = BI
2       for j = 1 to N − 1 do Inⱼ =        ⊓        fₚ(Inₚ)
                                    p∈pred(j)∧p<j
3       change = true
4       while change do
5       {   change = false
6           for j = 1 to N − 1 do
7           {   temp =    ⊓    fₚ(Inₚ)
                        p∈pred(j)
8               if temp ≠ Inⱼ then
9               {   Inⱼ = temp
10                  change = true
11              }
12          }
13      }
14  }
```

FIGURE 3.15

An efficient and more general version of the *MFP* algorithm.

$$f^2(z) \sqsupseteq f(z) \sqcap f(\top)$$
$$\sqsupseteq f(z \sqcap \top) \sqsupseteq f(z)$$

The second step follows from Observation 3.3 proving the lemma.   ∎

Observe that conditions $f^2(x) \sqsupseteq f(x)$ and $f^2(x) = f(x)$ on rapid and bit vector frameworks respectively are only necessary conditions and are not sufficient. For the function f defined in Figure 3.13 on page 88, $\forall x \in L : f^2(x) = f(x)$ and yet the framework is neither rapid nor bit vector. Figure 3.14 shows the relationship between various frameworks.

3.5.2   Complexity for General CFGs

The complexity analysis in this section is restricted to rapid frameworks that are distributive. The modified algorithm is shown in Figure 3.15. Note that the data flow variables are also initialized differently. Such an initialization obviates the need of the $\top$ element and allows handling frameworks with meet semilattices. This initialization has the effect of assigning to each node except *Start* with $\top$ and propagating the initial values by assuming $f(\top) = \top$.

We count the number of iterations of the algorithm as follows. The initialization of all data flow variables in the **for** loop in line 2 is counted as the first iteration. Following this, each iteration of the **while** loop is counted separately.

To prove the main complexity result, we need a couple of auxiliary results. The first result characterizes the data flow value at any program point after a given number of iterations in terms of paths containing a specified number of back edges. When the number of back edges in paths also needs to be denoted, we extend the notation *paths*(j) to $\mathit{paths}^k(j)$ to denote the set of paths containing at most $k-1$ back edges.

LEMMA 3.11
After k iterations of the algorithm, the data flow value at the entry of block j is given by $\mathit{In}_j = \bigsqcap_{\rho \in \mathit{paths}^k(j)} f_\rho(\mathit{BI})$.

PROOF The proof is by induction on the number of iterations k.

- *Basis:* $k = 1$. This step corresponds to line 2 of the algorithm when we traverse only back edge free paths. To prove this case, we do an inner induction on the visiting order of nodes. The variable j is used to denote the position of the nodes in this order.
  - *Basis:* $j = 0$. The node that is numbered 0 in the visiting order is *Start*. The relevant path in this case is (*Start*). Thus we have $\mathit{In}_0 = \mathit{BI} = f_{(\mathit{Start})}(\mathit{BI})$.
  - *Inductive step:* Recall that the nodes are visited in reverse postorder. Assume that the lemma holds for all nodes whose position in reverse postorder is less than j. Observe that back edge free paths from *Start* to j consist of back edge free paths from *Start* to p, where $p < j$, followed by the forward edge (p, j). Thus:

$$\begin{aligned}\mathit{In}_j &= \bigsqcap_{p \in \mathit{pred}(j) \wedge p<j} f_p(\mathit{In}_p) \\ &= \bigsqcap_{p \in \mathit{pred}(j) \wedge p<j} f_p\Big(\bigsqcap_{\rho \in \mathit{paths}^1(p)} f_\rho(\mathit{BI})\Big) \\ &= \bigsqcap_{p \in \mathit{pred}(j) \wedge p<j} \; \bigsqcap_{\rho \in \mathit{paths}^1(p)} f_p(f_\rho(\mathit{BI})) \\ &= \bigsqcap_{\rho \in \mathit{paths}^1(j)} f_\rho(\mathit{BI})\end{aligned}$$

- *Inductive step:* Assume that the lemma holds for $k-1$ iterations. We once again do an inner induction on the visiting order of nodes.
  - *Basis:* Trivial.

– *Inductive step:* Assume that the lemma holds for k iterations for those nodes whose number in reverse postorder is less than j. Then:

$$\begin{aligned}
In_j &= \bigsqcap_{p\in pred(j)} f_p(In_p) \\
&= \left(\bigsqcap_{p\in pred(j)\wedge p<j} f_p(In_p)\right) \sqcap \left(\bigsqcap_{p\in pred(j)\wedge p\geq j} f_p(In_p)\right) \\
&= \left(\bigsqcap_{p\in pred(j)\wedge p<j} f_p\left(\bigsqcap_{\rho\in paths^k(p)} f_\rho(BI)\right)\right) \\
&\quad \sqcap \left(\bigsqcap_{p\in pred(j)\wedge p\geq j} f_p\left(\bigsqcap_{\rho\in paths^{k-1}(p)} f_\rho(BI)\right)\right) \\
&\quad \{\text{using induction hypothesis}\} \\
&= \left(\bigsqcap_{(p\in pred(j)\wedge p<j)} \ \bigsqcap_{(\rho\in paths^k(p))} f_p(f_\rho(BI))\right) \\
&\quad \sqcap \left(\bigsqcap_{(p\in pred(j)\wedge p\geq j)} \ \bigsqcap_{(\rho\in paths^{k-1}(p))} f_p(f_\rho(BI))\right) \\
&\quad \{\text{distributivity}\} \\
&= \bigsqcap_{\rho\in paths^k(j)} f_\rho(BI)
\end{aligned}$$

The last step is justified because a path from *Start* to j with k back edges could either be made up of (i) a path with k back edges from *Start* to p, where $p < j$, followed by a traversal along the forward edge $p \to j$, or (ii) a path from *Start* to p with $k-1$ back edges, where $p \geq j$, followed by a traversal along the back edge $p \to j$.

Hence the lemma. ∎

Since $paths^{k-1}(j) \subset paths^k(j)$, the data flow value at any node decreases with increasing number of iterations. This is similar to the algorithm shown in Figure 3.9, and is crucial for the termination of the algorithm. Note that the algorithms have this property because of the choice of the initial values.

The second result relates the termination of the algorithm to the data flow values at program points.

LEMMA 3.12
The algorithm terminates within k iterations iff for each block j, each path ρ in paths*(j) and any boundary value* BI*, there exists a finite set of paths $\rho_1, \ldots \rho_r$ from* $paths^{k-1}(j)$ *such that*

$$f_\rho(BI) \sqsupseteq \bigsqcap_{1\leq i\leq r} f_{\rho_i}(BI) \qquad (3.22)$$

PROOF *If part:* Let *BI* be an arbitrary boundary value. Assume that

Condition (3.22) is satisfied after k iterations. Since $\textit{paths}^{k-1}(j) \subseteq \textit{paths}^k(j)$,

$$\bigsqcap_{\rho \in \textit{paths}^k(j)} f_\rho(BI) \sqsubseteq \bigsqcap_{\rho \in \textit{paths}^{k-1}(j)} f_\rho(BI) \qquad (3.23)$$

Further, following Condition (3.22), for each path $\rho \in \textit{paths}^k(j)$ we have a finite set of paths $\rho_1, \ldots \rho_r$ from $\textit{paths}^{k-1}(j)$ such that $f_\rho(BI) \sqsupseteq \bigsqcap_{1 \leq i \leq r} f_{\rho_i}(BI)$. Therefore $f_\rho(BI) \sqsupseteq \bigsqcap_{\rho' \in \textit{paths}^{k-1}(j)} f_{\rho'}(BI)$. Considering all paths in $\textit{paths}^k(j)$ we have:

$$\bigsqcap_{\rho \in \textit{paths}^k(j)} f_\rho(BI) \sqsupseteq \bigsqcap_{\rho \in \textit{paths}^{k-1}(j)} f_\rho(BI) \qquad (3.24)$$

Combining (3.23) and (3.24), we have:

$$\bigsqcap_{\rho \in \textit{paths}^k(j)} f_\rho(BI) = \bigsqcap_{\rho \in \textit{paths}^{k-1}(j)} f_\rho(BI)$$

Therefore the data flow values at the end of iterations $k-1$ and k coincide at every program point and the algorithm terminates.

Only if part: Suppose the algorithm halts after m iterations, where $m \leq k$. From Lemma 3.11, the data flow information at any node j after m iterations is $\bigsqcap_{\rho \in \textit{paths}^m(j)} f_\rho(BI)$. Further, since the data flow framework is assumed to be distributive, the algorithm computes the ***MOP*** solution. Thus

$$In_j = \bigsqcap_{\rho \in \textit{paths}(j)} f_\rho(BI) = \bigsqcap_{\rho \in \textit{paths}^m(j)} f_\rho(BI)$$

Therefore, for an arbitrary path $\rho \in \textit{paths}(j)$,

$$f_\rho(BI) \sqsupseteq \bigsqcap_{\rho \in \textit{paths}^m(j)} f_\rho(BI)$$

We now show that there is a finite set S of paths in $\textit{paths}^m(j)$ such that $\bigsqcap_{\rho \in \textit{paths}^m(j)} f_\rho(BI) = \bigsqcap_{\rho \in S} f_\rho(BI)$. Enumerate the paths in $\textit{paths}^m(j)$ as $\rho_1, \rho_2 \ldots$, and let $x_i = \bigsqcap_{1 \leq n \leq i} f_{\rho_n}(BI)$. It is clear that the x_i's form a chain. Therefore, from the descending chain condition, there is a number i' such that for all $i'' > i'$, $x_{i'} = x_{i''}$. Let S be $\{\rho_1, \rho_2, \ldots \rho_{i'}\}$. We then have:

$$f_\rho(BI) \sqsupseteq \bigsqcap_{\rho \in \textit{paths}^m(j)} f_\rho(BI) = \bigsqcap_{\rho \in S} f_\rho(BI)$$

∎

Now we prove the main complexity result captured by Theorem 3.2. Note that the theorem asserts a property of data flow frameworks and not of particular instances of

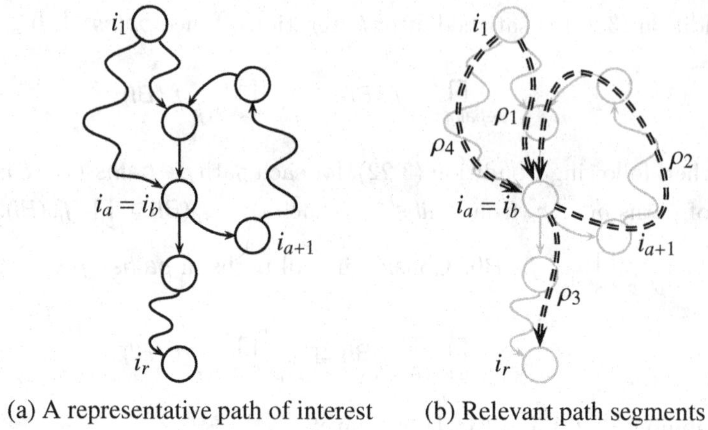

FIGURE 3.16
Paths of interest in the CFG.

the framework. It says that if the framework satisfies the rapid condition, the algorithm will terminate for every instance of the framework within an instance-related bound. Conversely, if the algorithm terminates for every instance of the framework within the specified bound, the framework is rapid. The theorem, however, does not say anything about the precision of the specified bound.

THEOREM 3.2
Let $(\mathbb{G}, M_{\mathbb{G}})$ be an arbitrary instance of a distributive data flow framework $(L, \sqcap, F)$. Assume that the traversal of $\mathbb{G}$ is based on the DFST T. Then the rapid condition is both necessary and sufficient for the algorithm in Figure 3.15 to terminate within $d(\mathbb{G}, T) + 3$ iterations.

PROOF *If part:* Following Lemma 3.12, it is enough to show that for an arbitrary program point j and a path $\rho \in \textsf{paths}(j)$, there exists a set of paths $S = \{\rho_1, \rho_2, \ldots, \rho_m\} \subseteq \textsf{paths}^{d(\mathbb{G},T)+2}(j)$ and

$$f_\rho(BI) \sqsupseteq \bigsqcap_{\rho' \in S} f_{\rho'}(BI)$$

We shall prove the above by induction on the number of back edges l in the path ρ.

Basis: $l \leq d(\mathbb{G}, T) + 1$. In this case ρ itself is in $\textsf{paths}^{d(\mathbb{G},T)+2}(j)$ and $S = \{\rho\}$.

Inductive Step: $l > d(\mathbb{G}, T) + 1$. Since the number of back edges in ρ exceeds the depth $d(\mathbb{G}, T)$, ρ has a cycle. Let us enumerate the program points that constitute ρ as $(i_0, i_1, \ldots, i_a, \ldots, i_b, \ldots, i_r)$, where i_a is the last point in the path that is the same as a later point i_b in the path. This situation is illustrated in Figure 3.16. We now identify the following subpaths of ρ in the graph:

- The path $\rho_1 = (i_1, \dots i_a)$ contains at least one back edge. This is because the path $(i_{a+1}, \dots, i_r)$ is cycle free and contains at most $d(\mathbb{G}, T)$ edges, and even assuming the edge $i_a \to i_{a+1}$ to be a back edge, the number of back edges in $(i_a, \dots, i_r)$ is at most $d(\mathbb{G}, T) + 1$.

- The path $\rho_2 = (i_a, \dots i_b)$ constitutes a cycle and therefore must contain at least one back edge.

- The path $\rho_3 = (i_b, \dots i_r)$ is an acyclic path and therefore contains at most $d(\mathbb{G}, T)$ back edges.

- Let ρ_4 be a back edge free path from i_0 to i_a. Such a path can always be found by following tree edges from i_0 to i_a.

Using the rapid condition, $f_\rho(\mathit{BI})$ can be rewritten as: .

$$\begin{aligned} f_\rho(\mathit{BI}) &= f_{\rho_3}(f_{\rho_2}(f_{\rho_1}(\mathit{BI}))) \\ &\sqsupseteq f_{\rho_3}\left(f_{\rho_1}(\mathit{BI}) \sqcap f_{\rho_2}(x) \sqcap x\right) \end{aligned}$$

for any x. Instantiating x to $f_{\rho_4}(\mathit{BI})$, we have

$$f_\rho(\mathit{BI}) \sqsupseteq f_{\rho_3}\left(f_{\rho_1}(\mathit{BI}) \sqcap f_{\rho_2}(f_{\rho_4}(\mathit{BI})) \sqcap f_{\rho_4}(\mathit{BI})\right)$$

which, because of distributivity, gives

$$f_\rho(\mathit{BI}) \sqsupseteq f_{\rho_3}(f_{\rho_1}(\mathit{BI})) \sqcap f_{\rho_3}(f_{\rho_2}(f_{\rho_4}(\mathit{BI}))) \sqcap f_{\rho_3}(f_{\rho_4}(\mathit{BI}))$$

Recall that the original path $\rho_1\rho_2\rho_3$ had l back edges. We observe that:

- The path $\rho_1\rho_3$ has at most $l-1$ back edges since the path $\rho_2 = (i_a, \dots i_b)$ has at least one back edge.

- The path $\rho_4\rho_2\rho_3$ has at most $l-1$ back edges since ρ_1, which had at least one back edge, has been replaced by ρ_4 which has none.

- The path $\rho_4\rho_3$ has less than $l-1$ back edges.

Thus the induction hypothesis applies and there exists sets S_1, S_2 and S_3, all of them subsets of $\mathit{paths}^{d(\mathbb{G},T)+2}(j)$, such that

$$f_\rho(\mathit{BI}) \sqsupseteq \bigsqcap_{\sigma \in S_1} f_\sigma(\mathit{BI}) \sqcap \bigsqcap_{\sigma \in S_2} f_\sigma(\mathit{BI}) \sqcap \bigsqcap_{\sigma \in S_3} f_\sigma(\mathit{BI})$$

Thus the required set S is $S_1 \cup S_2 \cup S_3$.

Only if part: Assume that condition (3.18) is violated for a data flow framework, i.e.,

$$(\exists f, g \in F)(\exists x, \mathit{BI} \in L) : f(g(\mathit{BI})) \not\sqsupseteq g(\mathit{BI}) \sqcap f(x) \sqcap (x)$$

Using the above f, g, x and BI, we have to create an instance of the framework for which the algorithm takes more than $d(\mathbb{G}, T) + 1$ iterations to terminate.

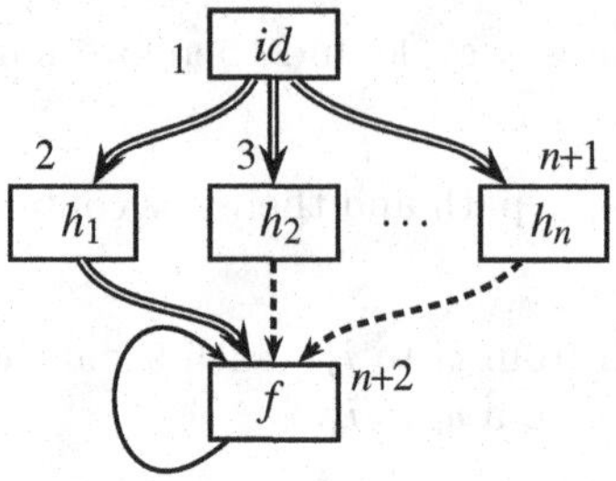

(a) $f(f(x)) \not\sqsupseteq f(x) \sqcap x$

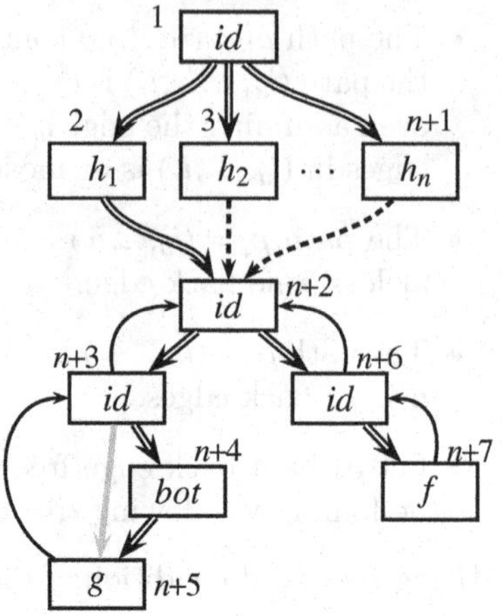

(b) $f(f(x)) \sqsupseteq f(x) \sqcap x$

FIGURE 3.17
Instances that require more than $d(\mathbb{G}, T)$ iterations to converge.

Because of the conditions on the values in the data flow lattice and the admissible flow functions (Section 3.2.2), we can assume that $x = \prod_{1 \le i \le n} h_i(BI)$. There are two cases to consider. If $f(f(x)) \not\sqsupseteq f(x) \sqcap x$ then consider the CFG of part (a) of Figure 3.17. The tree edges are drawn with double lines, back edges are single lines, cross edges are dashed lines, and forward edges are gray lines. The depth of the graph for the indicated DFST is 0.[‡] The data flow values In_{n+2} in the first three iterations are: x, $x \sqcap f(x)$, and $x \sqcap f(x) \sqcap f(f(x))$ respectively. Clearly, the algorithm will not terminate within 3 iterations.

If $f(f(x)) \sqsupseteq f(x) \sqcap x$, then we consider the instance in part (b) of Figure 3.17. The function *bot* in node n+4 is the constant function $\forall x \in L : bot(x) = \bot$. The depth of the graph in this case is 2. Figure 3.18 shows the data flow values at program points of interest in the first four iterations. In the fifth iteration, the data flow value at n+3 is $x \sqcap f(x) \sqcap g(\bot) \sqcap f(g(\bot))$. Under the assumed condition, this value is different from the value at $n+3$ in the fourth iteration. Therefore the algorithm takes at least six iterations to terminate. ∎

Example 3.11

Figure 3.19 provides an instance of a framework that requires $d(G, T) + 3$ iterations. We leave it for the reader to verify that the framework is distributive and rapid. As usual, tree edges have been shown in double lines and back

[‡]Note that this is because we are not distinguishing between *In* and *Out* properties.

Node i	In_i in various iterations			
	#1	#2	#3	#4
n+2	x	x	$x \sqcap f(x) \sqcap g(\bot)$	$x \sqcap f(x) \sqcap g(\bot)$
n+3	x	$x \sqcap g(\bot)$	$x \sqcap f(x) \sqcap g(\bot)$	$x \sqcap f(x) \sqcap g(\bot)$
n+4	x	$x \sqcap g(\bot)$	$x \sqcap f(x) \sqcap g(\bot)$	$x \sqcap f(x) \sqcap g(\bot)$
n+5	$\bot$	$\bot$	$\bot$	$\bot$
n+6	x	$x \sqcap f(x)$	$x \sqcap f(x) \sqcap f(f(x)) \sqcap g(\bot)$ $= x \sqcap f(x) \sqcap g(\bot)$	$x \sqcap f(x) \sqcap g(\bot) \sqcap f(g(\bot))$
n+7	x	$x \sqcap f(x)$	$x \sqcap f(x) \sqcap g(\bot)$	$x \sqcap f(x) \sqcap g(\bot) \sqcap f(g(\bot))$

FIGURE 3.18
First four iterations for the instance in Figure 3.17 on the facing page.

edges are shown in single lines. The value of $d(G,T)$ is 1. The lattice does not have a $\top$ element but the graph is reducible.

As shown in the following table, the data flow values converge in the third iteration—one more iteration is required to detect convergence. This is independent of the BI value because of the presence of function h_1. We leave it for the reader to verify that if L contains $\top$, three iterations are sufficient.

Variables	Values in each iteration			
	Iteration 1	Iteration 2	Iteration 3	Iteration 4
In_1	v_1	v_1	v_1	v_1
In_2	v_1	v_1	$\bot$	$\bot$
In_3	v_0	$\bot$	$\bot$	$\bot$
In_4	v_0	$\bot$	$\bot$	$\bot$

□

An non-rapid fast framework has been illustrated in Figure 5.9 on page 178.

3.5.3 Complexity in Special Cases

First we consider the situation when the CFG is reducible. The modified statement of Theorem (3.2) for reducible CFGs is as follows.

THEOREM 3.3

Let $(\mathbb{G}, M_{\mathbb{G}})$ be an arbitrary instance of a distributive data flow framework $(L, \sqcap, F)$ such that $\mathbb{G}$ is reducible. Assume that the traversal of $\mathbb{G}$ is based on the DFST T. Then the rapid condition is both necessary and sufficient for the algorithm in Figure 3.15 to terminate within $d(\mathbb{G},T)+2$ iterations.

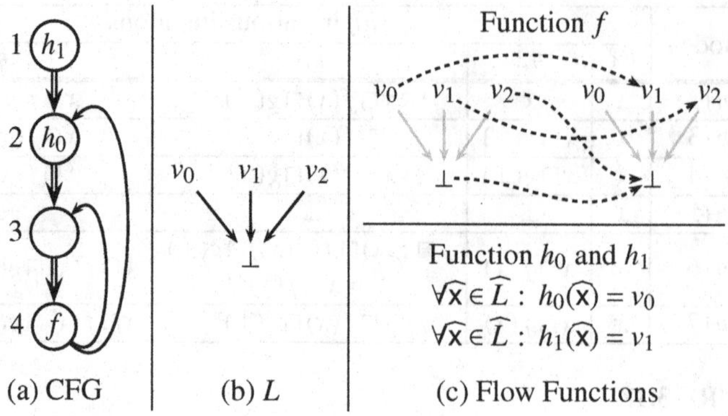

FIGURE 3.19
A instance of a distributive rapid framework that requires $d(G,T)+3$ iterations.

PROOF We replay the earlier proof with the expression $d(\mathbb{G},T)+x$ uniformly replaced by $d(\mathbb{G},T)+(x-1)$. The only change is in the portion of the proof that asserts the sufficiency of the rapid condition (the *if* part).

The basis of the *if* part remains identical. We consider the changes required to prove the inductive case. Reducibility imposes some restrictions on the structure of the path ρ. We consider the following two cases:

- The edge $i_a \rightarrow i_{a+1}$ is not a back edge. Since the path from i_{a+1} to i_r is acyclic, it can have at most $d(\mathbb{G},T)$ back edges. Thus the only way in which the path $\rho_1\rho_2\rho_3$ can have $d(\mathbb{G},T)+1$ back edges is to have at least one back edge in ρ_1. As in the earlier proof, this path can be replaced by a back edge free path and the induction hypothesis applied.

- The edge $i_a \rightarrow i_{a+1}$ is a back edge. Due to reducibility, i_{a+1} must dominate i_a and the path segment ρ_1 must also pass through i_{a+1}. We can then divide the path ρ into path segments as illustrated in Figure 3.20 on the facing page. Due to the back edge $i_a \rightarrow i_{a+1}$, the path ρ is $\rho_1\rho_2\rho_2\rho_3$. Since the path from i_{a+1} to i_r is acyclic, the path $\rho_2\rho_3$ can have at most d back edges. The data flow value along path ρ is:

$$\begin{aligned} f_\rho(BI) &= f_{\rho_3}\left(f_{\rho_2}\left(f_{\rho_2}\left(f_{\rho_1}(BI)\right)\right)\right) \\ &\sqsupseteq f_{\rho_3}\left(f_{\rho_2}\left(f_{\rho_1}(BI)\right)\right) \end{aligned}$$

  since $f^2(x) \sqsupseteq f(x)$ from Lemma 3.10.

  Observe that ρ has been replaced by the path $\rho_1\rho_2\rho_3$ which excludes the back edge $i_a \rightarrow i_{a+1}$ and thus contains one back edge less. Hence, the induction hypothesis applies to the path $\rho_1\rho_2\rho_3$ and the result follows.

■

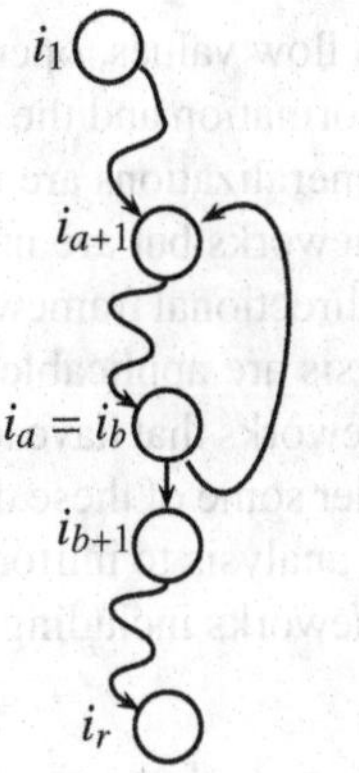

(a) $i_a \to i_{a+1}$ is a back edge and graph is reducible.

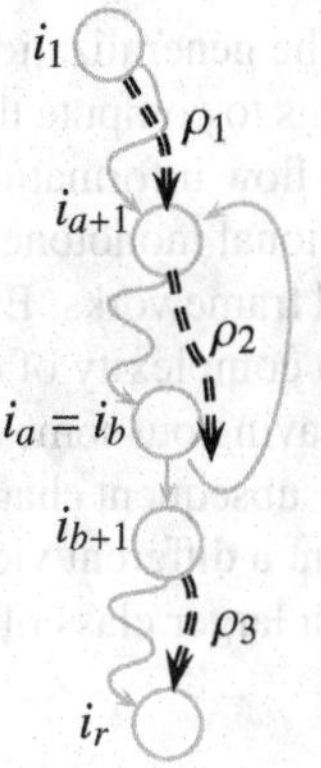

(b) Relevant path segments

FIGURE 3.20
Paths of interest in the CFG.

Now we consider the special case when a $\top$ element exists in the meet semilattice. The bit vector data flow problems fall in this category. In this case, the algorithm in Figure 3.15 can be made more efficient by initializing *In* for each node except *Start* to the value $\top$. This is identical to the initialization on line 2 of Figure 3.9. Thus the two algorithms become similar except for the order of traversal. Only the iterations of the **while** loop are counted—the work done during the initialization step is ignored. This is reasonable because, unlike the algorithm in Figure 3.15, no attempt is being made to propagate the initial values in this step. We merely state the theorem and point to the source of the proof in bibliographic notes.

THEOREM 3.4

Consider an instance $(\mathbb{G}, M_{\mathbb{G}})$ of a distributive data flow framework $(L, \sqcap, F)$, where L has a $\top$ element. The rapid condition is both necessary and sufficient for the algorithm in Figure 3.15 with the modification mentioned above to terminate within $d(\mathbb{G}, T) + 2$ iterations. T is the DFST used for deciding the order of traversal of $\mathbb{G}$.

3.6 Summary and Concluding Remarks

In this chapter, we have presented generalizations of data flow frameworks based on mathematical abstractions and have presented lattice theoretic modelling of data flow frameworks. The generalizations include data flow values, operations to manipulate them, algorithms to compute the data flow information and the characteristics of the computed data flow information. All these generalizations are uniformly applicable to all unidirectional monotone data flow frameworks but are not directly applicable to bidirectional frameworks. Even among unidirectional frameworks, the generalizations related to complexity of data flow analysis are applicable to a limited class of frameworks, leaving out some important frameworks that have arisen in practical situations. In the subsequent chapters, we consider some of these data flow frameworks and then present a different view of data flow analysis to uniformly characterize the complexity of a larger class of data flow frameworks including bidirectional frameworks.

3.7 Bibliographic Notes

Of the graph theoretic concepts introduced early in the chapter, discussion on DFST can be found in the texts by Aho, Hopcroft and Ullman [2] and Cormen, Rivest, Leiserson and Stein [27]. Reducibility was introduced by Allen [4] and is further discussed by Hecht and Ullman in [45, 46]. Dominance was introduced by Lowry and Medlock [70]. Lengauer and Tarjan [68] present an algorithm that can be used to compute dominators efficiently. The text by Davey and Priestley [29] is a good introduction to lattice theory. The presentation of Tarski's fixed point theorem is from Tarski's original paper [99].

The initial attempt to model data flow values in terms of meet semilattices was by Kildall [63]. Kam and Ullman [49] introduced reverse postorder for visiting nodes in the CFG and also introduces the rapidity condition which guarantees convergence within $d(\mathbb{G},T)+3$ iterations. This work has given rise to the folklore that iterative data flow analysis is fast for many data flow frameworks. Much of Section 3.5.2 is based on this paper.

The papers so far dealt with distributive frameworks. Kam and Ullman [50] showed that for montonic frameworks, which are less restrictive then distributive frameworks, a round-robin iterative algorithm computes the MFP solution. However, for a monotonic framework that is not distributive, the MFP solution may be different from the MOP solution. They also showed the undecidability of the problem of finding MOP solution of an arbitrary monotonic data flow problem. Monotonicity of flow functions was also discussed by Graham and Wegman [37] where they introduced the concept of fast frameworks. A detailed treatment of these concepts can also be found in the book by Hecht [44]. Marlowe and Ryder [71] review properties of different data flow frameworks in lattice theoretic settings.

4

General Data Flow Frameworks

In bit vector frameworks the data flow information of different entities is independent of each other. However, there are many situations in which the data flow information of an entity could depend on the data flow information of some other entity. For example, the concept of transfer of liveness was described in Section 1.1.2 as follows:

> If access path $x \rightarrow\!\!\triangleright \sigma$ is live after an assignment x = y, then σ is transferred to x and the access path $y \rightarrow\!\!\triangleright \sigma$ becomes live before the assignment.

Here, the liveness of access path $x \rightarrow\!\!\triangleright \sigma$ depends on the liveness of access path $y \rightarrow\!\!\triangleright \sigma$. Capturing such interdependences requires a more general kind of flow functions and the frameworks involving such flow functions are called non-separable.

4.1 Non-Separable Flow Functions

This section defines the non-separability of flow functions, shows how it can be modeled in terms of *Gen* and *Kill* effects, and describes the limitations it imposes on the nature of basic blocks that can be constructed for performing data flow analysis.

Recall that a data flow framework $(L_{\mathcal{G}}, \sqcap_{\mathcal{G}}, F_{\mathcal{G}})$ is defined in terms of an unspecified CFG $\mathcal{G}$. For convenience, we drop the subscript $\mathcal{G}$ where not required. We assume that the entities occurring in $\mathcal{G}$ that are of interest to us for a given analysis are contained in a set $\Sigma = \{\alpha, \beta, \gamma, \ldots, \omega\}$. A given analysis discovers some properties of interest for a specific kind of entities e.g., expressions, variables, definitions, etc. Thus for any given analysis, all entities are of the same type. The lattice L is a product $\widehat{L}_\alpha \times \widehat{L}_\beta \times \cdots \times \widehat{L}_\omega$ where $\widehat{L}_\alpha$ is the component lattice containing the data flow values of entity α. In general, all $\widehat{L}$s are same. Data flow value $\mathsf{x} \in L$ is a tuple $\langle \widehat{\mathsf{x}}^\alpha, \widehat{\mathsf{x}}^\beta, \ldots, \widehat{\mathsf{x}}^\omega \rangle$.

The motivation behind modeling non-separability explicitly arises from the observation that an element in L is not atomic—it consists of a tuple of separate data flow values for each entity. Thus it is natural to ask if instead of viewing flow functions as atomic, they can also be modeled in terms of functions that compute data flow values of smaller granularities. This view allows us to explicate the dependence of the data flow value of an entity on the data flow values of the other entities. This leads to rich insights that are useful in defining tight complexity bounds as well as the feasibility conditions for systematic reduction of flow function compositions.

DEFINITION 4.1 *A flow function $f : L \mapsto L$ is separable iff it is a tuple $\langle \widehat{f}^{\alpha}, \widehat{f}^{\beta}, \cdots, \widehat{f}^{\omega} \rangle$ of component functions $\widehat{f} : \widehat{L} \mapsto \widehat{L}$. If $\widehat{f}$ is of the form $L \mapsto \widehat{L}$, then f is non-separable.*

A component function $\widehat{f}^{\alpha}$ computes the data flow value of entity α. Similar to the flow function, we use basic block as a subscript of the component function when required.

As the name suggests, separability is based on independence of data flow properties of entities for which data flow analysis is being performed. In order to model non-separable flow functions in terms of *Gen* and *Kill* components, instead of defining constant Gen_n and $Kill_n$, we define them as $Gen_n : L \mapsto L$ and $Kill_n : L \mapsto L$ by allowing dependent parts also:

$$Gen_n(x) = ConstGen_n \cup DepGen_n(x) \tag{4.1}$$

$$Kill_n(x) = ConstKill_n \cup DepKill_n(x) \tag{4.2}$$

The flow function f_n is defined as:

$$f_n(x) = (x - Kill_n(x)) \cup Gen_n(x) \tag{4.3}$$

In bit vector frameworks, the dependent parts are absent resulting in constant *Gen* and *Kill* components. Rapid and fast frameworks require that the flow functions are separable, so that the rapidity condition (3.18) and fastness condition (3.17) are satisfied. In these and other separable frameworks, dependent parts may exist due to a possibility of dependence among data flow values of the same entity at different program points. In non-separable frameworks, the dependence can be of two types: The data flow value of a given entity may depend on the data flow value of the same entity or on data flow value of some other entity. Dependence captured by *DepGen* on the data flow value of the same entity must necessarily be a non-identity dependence because identity dependence is implicitly defined by ensuring that both *Gen* and *Kill* have no effect on the entity. The dependence on other entities may be identity or non-identity dependence. Unlike identity dependence on the same entity, identity dependence on other entities must be explicitly defined. We model these dependences in Section 4.5.

The presence of dependent parts in *Gen* and *Kill* makes it difficult to summarize the effect of multiple statements in a flow function. Hence, basic blocks for non-separable analyses consist of single statements. However, multiple consecutive statements which do not have any data dependence between them can still be combined into a basic block subject to the usual control flow restriction. If two consecutive statements can be executed in any order without affecting program semantics, then they can be grouped into the same basic block for data flow analysis of non-separable flows. Further, a conditional or unconditional jump need not always be a separate block. If it is included in a block, it must be the last statement of the block.

The statements relevant to data flow analysis are divided in the following categories: (a) assignment statements $x = e$ where $x \in \mathbb{V}\text{ar}$, $e \in \mathbb{E}\text{xpr}$, (b) input statements *read*(x) which assign a new value to x, (c) use statements *use*(x) which model uses of x for condition checking, printing and parameter passing etc., and (d) other statements. Since we restrict ourselves to intraprocedural analysis in this part, we assume that there are no function calls. Effectively, $\mathbb{V}\mathsf{ar}$ contains local variables only. Print statements and evaluation of branching condition etc. are modeled in terms of use statements.

4.2 Discovering Properties of Variables

In this section we present analyses to discover whether a given scalar variable is dead, or possibly undefined, or has a constant value.

4.2.1 Faint Variables Analysis

As discussed towards the end of Section 2.3.1, liveness analysis does not take into account interdependence of variables. This section describes a data flow analysis which takes into account such interdependence and discovers the transitive closure of deadness of a variable which is the complement of liveness.

DEFINITION 4.2 *A variable $x \in \mathbb{V}\mathsf{ar}$ is faint at a program point u if along every path from u to* End*, it is either not used before being defined or is used to define a faint variable.*

Clearly, this is a backward data flow problem. However, unlike liveness analysis this is an all-paths analysis. Hence the confluence operation is $\cap$. The lattice is $(2^{\mathbb{V}\mathsf{ar}}, \subseteq)$ and $\top$ is $\mathbb{V}\mathsf{ar}$. The initial value of In_n and Out_n for all n is $\mathbb{V}\mathsf{ar}$.

$$\mathsf{In}_n = f_n(\mathsf{Out}_n) \tag{4.4}$$

$$\mathsf{Out}_n = \begin{cases} \mathsf{BI} & n \text{ is } \mathsf{End} \\ \bigcap_{s \in \mathsf{succ}(n)} \mathsf{In}_s & \text{otherwise} \end{cases} \tag{4.5}$$

All local variables are dead at the end of a procedure and $\mathsf{BI} = \mathbb{V}\mathsf{ar}$.

The constant and dependent parts of $\mathsf{Gen}_n(\mathsf{x})$ component are defined as follows. A variable x becomes faint before every assignment to it. There is no other way in which a variable that is live after a statement, could become faint before the statement.

$$\mathsf{ConstGen}_n = \begin{cases} \{x\} & n \text{ is assignment } x = e,\ x \notin \mathsf{Opd}(e) \\ \{x\} & n \text{ is } read(x) \\ \emptyset & \text{otherwise} \end{cases}$$

$$\mathsf{DepGen}_n(\mathsf{x}) = \emptyset$$

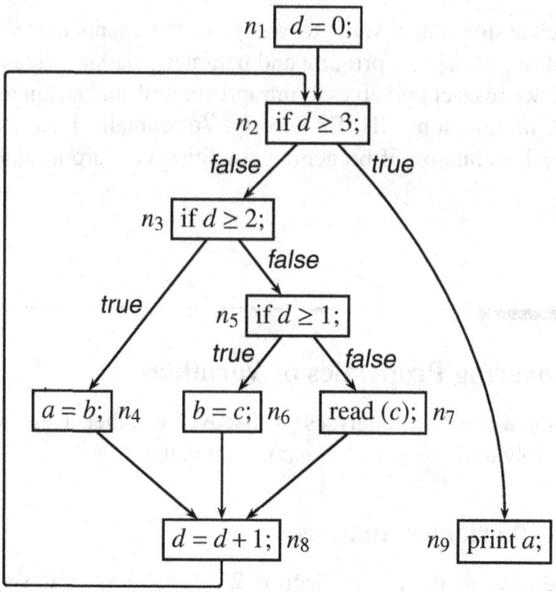

FIGURE 4.1
Program for illustrating faint variables analysis and possibly uninitialized variables analysis.

A variable x could cease to become faint before an assignment statement if it appears on the right hand side and the left hand side variable is faint. Alternatively, it could cease to become faint because of a use statement. The former represents the transitive effect of left hand side variable not being faint and is captured by the dependent part $\mathit{DepKill}_n(\mathsf{x})$ as follows:

$$\mathit{ConstKill}_n = \begin{cases} \{x\} & n \text{ is } \mathit{use}(x) \\ \emptyset & \text{otherwise} \end{cases}$$

$$\mathit{DepKill}_n(\mathsf{x}) = \begin{cases} \mathit{Opd}(e) \cap \mathbb{V}\mathsf{ar} & n \text{ is assignment } x = e,\ x \notin \mathsf{x} \\ \emptyset & \text{otherwise} \end{cases}$$

where $\mathit{Opd}(\mathsf{e})$ denotes the operands of expression e.

Example 4.1
The result of performing faint variables analysis for the program in Figure 4.1 has been shown in Figure 4.2. Since a is used in block n_9, it is not faint. As a consequence, variables b and c cease to be faint. Discovering these facts requires two additional iterations and propagating it against the back edge requires the fourth iteration.

If n_9 did not contain a use of a, the variables a, b, and c would have been

Node	Iteration #1		Changes in Iteration #2		Changes in Iteration #3		Changes in Iteration #4	
	Out_n	In_n	Out_n	In_n	Out_n	In_n	Out_n	In_n
n_9	$\{a,b,c,d\}$	$\{b,c,d\}$						
n_8	$\{a,b,c,d\}$	$\{a,b,c,d\}$	$\{b,c\}$	$\{b,c\}$	$\{c\}$	$\{c\}$	$\emptyset$	$\emptyset$
n_7	$\{a,b,c,d\}$	$\{a,b,c,d\}$	$\{b,c\}$	$\{b,c\}$	$\{c\}$	$\{c\}$	$\emptyset$	
n_6	$\{a,b,c,d\}$	$\{a,b,c,d\}$	$\{b,c\}$	$\{b,c\}$	$\{c\}$	$\emptyset$	$\emptyset$	
n_5	$\{a,b,c,d\}$	$\{a,b,c\}$	$\{b,c\}$	$\{b,c\}$	$\emptyset$	$\emptyset$		
n_4	$\{a,b,c,d\}$	$\{a,b,c,d\}$	$\{b,c\}$	$\{c\}$	$\{c\}$		$\emptyset$	$\emptyset$
n_3	$\{a,b,c\}$	$\{a,b,c\}$	$\{c\}$	$\{c\}$	$\emptyset$	$\emptyset$		
n_2	$\{b,c\}$	$\{b,c\}$	$\{c\}$	$\{c\}$	$\emptyset$	$\emptyset$	$\emptyset$	
n_1	$\{b,c\}$	$\{b,c,d\}$	$\{c\}$	$\{c,d\}$	$\emptyset$	$\{d\}$		

FIGURE 4.2
Performing faint variables analysis of program in Figure 4.1.

discovered to be faint. Liveness analysis would conclude that b and c are live regardless of the use of a in block n_9. □

It is interesting to explore the distributivity, rapidity, and fastness properties of faint variables analysis. Since $\mathit{DepGen}_n(\mathsf{x})$ is $\emptyset$, f_n can be rewritten as:

$$\begin{aligned} f_n(\mathsf{x}) &= (\mathsf{x} - \mathit{Kill}_n(\mathsf{x})) \cup \mathit{Gen}_n(\mathsf{x}) \\ &= (\mathsf{x} - (\mathit{ConstKill}_n \cup \mathit{DepKill}_n(\mathsf{x}))) \cup (\mathit{ConstGen}_n \cup \mathit{DepGen}_n(\mathsf{x})) \\ &= ((\mathsf{x} - \mathit{ConstKill}_n) \cup \mathit{ConstGen}_n) \cup (\mathsf{x} - \mathit{DepKill}_n(\mathsf{x})) \end{aligned}$$

Clearly the constant part of f_n is similar to flow functions in bit vector frameworks and hence is distributive, rapid and fast. Thus, in order to investigate whether these properties hold for f_n, it is sufficient to explore them for $(\mathsf{x} - \mathit{DepKill}_n(\mathsf{x}))$.

LEMMA 4.1
Faint variables analysis is distributive.

PROOF It is sufficient to prove that $\forall \mathsf{x}_1, \mathsf{x}_2 \in L, \forall f_n \in F$:

$$(\mathsf{x}_1 \cap \mathsf{x}_2) - \mathit{DepKill}_n(\mathsf{x}_1 \cap \mathsf{x}_2) = (\mathsf{x}_1 - \mathit{DepKill}_n(\mathsf{x}_1)) \cap (\mathsf{x}_2 - \mathit{DepKill}_n(\mathsf{x}_2))$$

From the definition of $\mathit{DepKill}_n(\mathsf{x})$, there are two cases to consider. First we consider the case when n is an assignment statement $x = e$ and $x \notin \mathsf{x}_1 \cap \mathsf{x}_2$. Assume that x is neither in x_1 nor in x_2.

$$\begin{aligned} (\mathsf{x}_1 \cap \mathsf{x}_2) - \mathit{DepKill}_n(\mathsf{x}_1 \cap \mathsf{x}_2) &= (\mathsf{x}_1 \cap \mathsf{x}_2) - (\mathit{Opd}(e) \cap \mathbb{V}\mathsf{ar}) \\ &= (\mathsf{x}_1 - (\mathit{Opd}(e) \cap \mathbb{V}\mathsf{ar})) \cap (\mathsf{x}_2 - (\mathit{Opd}(e) \cap \mathbb{V}\mathsf{ar})) \\ &= (\mathsf{x}_1 - \mathit{DepKill}_n(\mathsf{x}_1)) \cap (\mathsf{x}_2 - \mathit{DepKill}_n(\mathsf{x}_2)) \end{aligned}$$

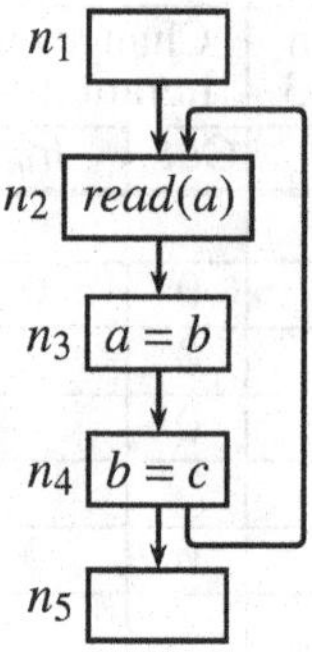

Let $f = f_{n_2} \circ f_{n_3} \circ f_{n_4}$ and let x be $\mathbb{V}$ar. $f^i(\text{x})$ represents the set of faint variables at the entry of n_2 in iteration number i in postorder traversal over the graph.

$$\text{x} = \mathbb{V}\text{ar}$$
$$f(\text{x}) = \mathbb{V}\text{ar} - \{a\}$$
$$f^2(\text{x}) = \mathbb{V}\text{ar} - \{a,b\}$$
$$\forall i \geq 3: \; f^i(\text{x}) = \mathbb{V}\text{ar} - \{a,b,c\}$$
$$\text{x} \sqcap f(\text{x}) \sqcap f^2(\text{x}) \sqcap \ldots \neq \text{x} \sqcap f(\text{x})$$

FIGURE 4.3
Faint variables analysis is not fast.

If $x \notin \text{x}_1$ but $x \in \text{x}_2$, $\mathit{DepKill}_n(\text{x}_2)$ is $\emptyset$ and the proof obligation follows due to $\sqcap$ even if $\mathit{Opd} \cap \mathbb{V}\text{ar}$ is not removed from x_2.

In other situations, $\mathit{DepKill}_n(\text{x})$ is $\emptyset$ and the lemma trivially follows. ∎

Figure 4.3 contains an instance of faint variables analysis to show that it is neither rapid nor fast. It is easy to generalize the example to show that faint variables analysis is not k-bounded. It is bounded by height of the lattice which turns out to be $|\mathbb{V}\text{ar}|$ and depends on the particular instance.

4.2.2 Possibly Uninitialized Variables Analysis

Section 2.3.3 described reaching definitions analysis which is primarily motivated by construction of def-use chains. If we use *BI* to include definitions $x = \mathit{undef}$ for all $x \in \mathit{var}$, reaching definitions analysis also discovers the program points where these definitions reach suggesting the possibility of a use before a variable is initialized. However, the transitive effect of such definitions is not handled by reaching definitions analysis. We present an analysis which handles these effects. Further, unlike reaching definitions analysis, this analysis is aimed at discovering only whether a given variable is possibly uninitialized—It does not collect the definitions of the variable. This simplifies the analysis and makes it very efficient.

DEFINITION 4.3 *A variable $x \in \mathbb{V}\text{ar}$ is possibly uninitialized at a program point u if there exists a path from* Start *to u along which either no definition of the variable has been encountered or the definition uses a possibly uninitialized variable on the right hand side of the assignment.*

Clearly this is a forward data flow problem and uses $\cup$ as the confluence operation.

The lattice is $(2^{\mathbb{V}\mathsf{ar}}, \supseteq)$ and $\top$ is $\emptyset$. The initial value at each node is $\emptyset$.

$$In_n = \begin{cases} BI & n \text{ is } Start \\ \bigcup_{p \in pred(n)} Out_p & \text{otherwise} \end{cases} \tag{4.6}$$

$$Out_n = f_n(In_n) \tag{4.7}$$

Since every local variable is uninitialized at *Entry*(*Start*), $BI = \mathbb{V}\mathsf{ar}$.

An interesting aspect of this analysis is that the possibility of a variable being uninitialized is generated only at *Entry*(*Start*) and no other program point. Hence $ConstGen_n$ is $\emptyset$. The transitive effect of an uninitialized variable appearing on the right hand side of an assignment is captured by $DepGen_n(\mathsf{x})$.

$$ConstGen_n = \emptyset$$

$$DepGen_n(\mathsf{x}) = \begin{cases} \{x\} & n \text{ is assignment } x = e,\ Opd(e) \cap \mathsf{x} \neq \emptyset\} \\ \emptyset & \text{otherwise} \end{cases}$$

A variable ceases to be uninitialized if its value is read from input or a constant value is assigned to it. The transitive effect of such initializations is captured by $DepKill_n(\mathsf{x})$.

$$ConstKill_n = \begin{cases} \{x\} & n \text{ is assignment } x = e,\ Opd(e) \subseteq \mathbb{C}\mathsf{onst} \\ \{x\} & n \text{ is } read(x) \\ \emptyset & \text{otherwise} \end{cases}$$

$$DepKill_n(\mathsf{x}) = \begin{cases} \{x\} & n \text{ is assignment } x = e,\ Opd(e) \cap \mathsf{x} = \emptyset\} \\ \emptyset & \text{otherwise} \end{cases}$$

Example 4.2

For the program in Figure 4.1, the result of possibly uninitialized analysis is: $In_{n_1} = \{a,b,c,d\}$, $Out_{n_4} = \{b,c\}$, $Out_{n_6} = \{a,c\}$, $Out_{n_6} = \{a,b\}$. All other In_n and Out_n are $\{a,b,c\}$. □

LEMMA 4.2

Possibly uninitialized analysis is distributive.

PROOF It is sufficient to show that $\forall \mathsf{x}_1, \mathsf{x}_2 \in L, \forall f_n \in F$:

$$((\mathsf{x}_1 \cup \mathsf{x}_2) - DepKill_n(\mathsf{x}_1 \cup \mathsf{x}_2)) \cup Gen_n(\mathsf{x}_1 \cup \mathsf{x}_2) = (\mathsf{x}_1 - DepKill_n(\mathsf{x}_1)) \cup (\mathsf{x}_2 - DepKill_n(\mathsf{x}_2)) \cup Gen_n(\mathsf{x}_1) \cup Gen_n(\mathsf{x}_2)$$

Further, it is sufficient to consider only the assignment statement $x = e$.

Consider the following three cases:

- $Opd(e) \cap \mathsf{x}_1 = \emptyset$ and $Opd(e) \cap \mathsf{x}_2 = \emptyset$. Thus $Opd(e) \cap (\mathsf{x}_1 \cup \mathsf{x}_2) = \emptyset$.

In this case.

$$\begin{aligned} \mathit{DepKill}_n(x_1 \cup x_1) &= \mathit{DepKill}_n(x_1) &= \mathit{DepKill}_n(x_2) &= \{x\} \\ \mathit{DepGen}_n(x_1 \cup x_1) &= \mathit{DepGen}_n(x_1) &= \mathit{DepGen}_n(x_2) &= \emptyset \end{aligned}$$

Hence the proof obligation is satisfied.

- $\mathit{Opd}(e) \cap x_1 \neq \emptyset$ and $\mathit{Opd}(e) \cap x_2 \neq \emptyset$. Thus $\mathit{Opd}(e) \cap (x_1 \cup x_2) \neq \emptyset$. In this case.

$$\begin{aligned} \mathit{DepKill}_n(x_1 \cup x_1) &= \mathit{DepKill}_n(x_1) &= \mathit{DepKill}_n(x_2) &= \emptyset \\ \mathit{DepGen}_n(x_1 \cup x_1) &= \mathit{DepGen}_n(x_1) &= \mathit{DepGen}_n(x_2) &= \{x\} \end{aligned}$$

Hence the proof obligation is satisfied.

- $\mathit{Opd}(e) \cap x_1 \neq \emptyset$ and $\mathit{Opd}(e) \cap x_2 = \emptyset$. Thus $\mathit{Opd}(e) \cap (x_1 \cup x_2) \neq \emptyset$. In this case.

$$\begin{aligned} \mathit{DepKill}_n(x_1 \cup x_1) &= \mathit{DepKill}_n(x_1) = \emptyset &, \mathit{DepKill}_n(x_2) = \{x\} \\ \mathit{DepGen}_n(x_1 \cup x_1) &= \mathit{DepGen}_n(x_1) = \{x\} &, \mathit{DepKill}_n(x_2) = \emptyset \end{aligned}$$

In this case also, the proof obligation is satisfied.

- $\mathit{Opd}(e) \cap x_1 = \emptyset$ and $\mathit{Opd}(e) \cap x_2 \neq \emptyset$. Thus $\mathit{Opd}(e) \cap (x_1 \cup x_2) \neq \emptyset$.

  This case is similar to the above case.

∎

This framework is not fast, and hence is not rapid. We leave it for the reader to construct suitable examples.

4.2.3 Constant Propagation

If it can be asserted at compile time that a given expression would compute a fixed known value at a given program point in every execution of the program, the expression computation can be replaced by the known constant value. This can then be propagated further as the value of the variable to which the result of the expression is assigned. This can help in identifying if other expressions that involve the variable compute a constant value.

For simplicity, we restrict our discussion to integer constants.

DEFINITION 4.4 *A variable $x \in \mathbb{V}\mathsf{ar}$ has a constant value $c \in \mathbb{C}\mathsf{onst}$ at a program point u if for every path reaching u along which a definition of x reaches u, the value of x is c.*

Note that this definition assumes that the program is correct in the sense that no execution path uses a variable before defining it and if the CFG contains a path

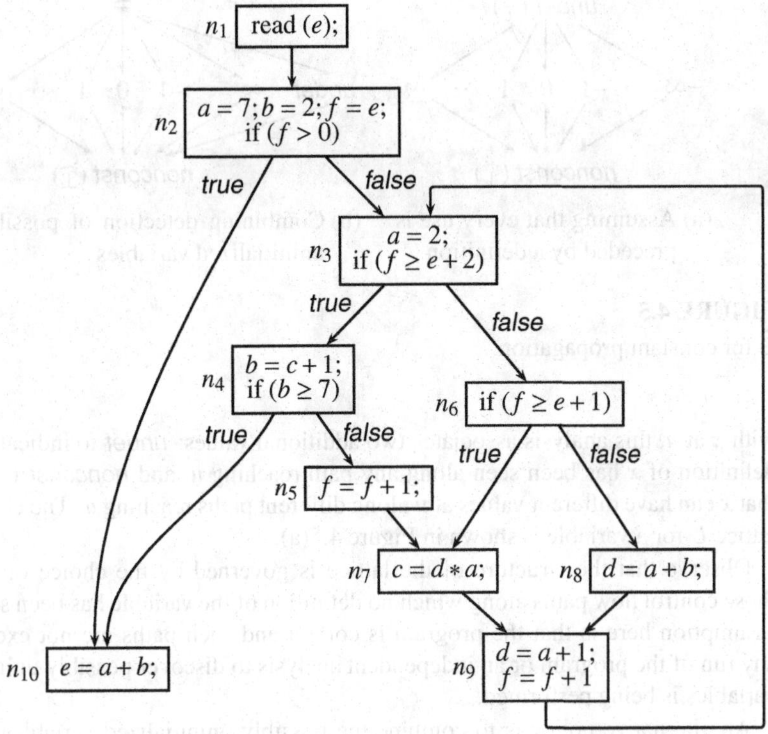

FIGURE 4.4
Program for illustrating constant propagation.

reaching u that does not have any definition of x, such a path can be ignored so long as at least one path containing a definition of x reaches u.

Example 4.3

We use the program in Figure 4.4 as a running example for constant propagation. We have included branching conditions and have labeled out edges of branch nodes with the branch outcomes to emphasize the above assumption about the correctness of program in terms of use and definitions of variables. Observe that, if we ignore the branching conditions, our basic blocks consist of single statements except n_2 and n_9 which contains multiple statements because they are independent of each other. Within the loop, the uses of following variables can be replaced by their statically known values: $a = 2$, $c = 6$, and $d = 3$. Further, $b = 7$ in block n_4. This results in the branching condition in block n_4 being *true* making block n_5 unreachable. □

Given a variable x and a program point u, apart from associating integer constants

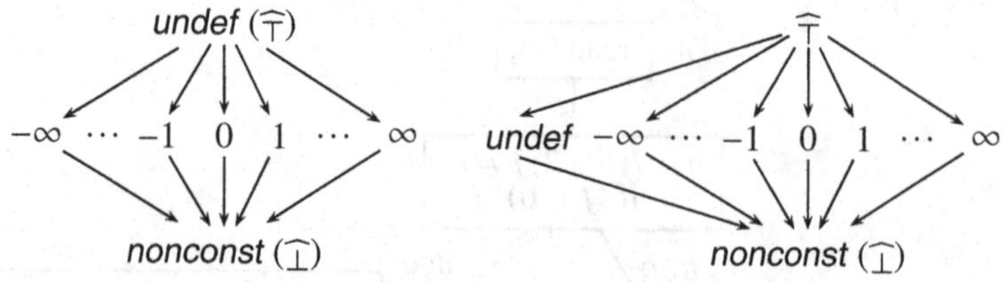

(a) Assuming that every use is preceded by a definition

(b) Combining detection of possibly uninitialized variables

FIGURE 4.5
$\widehat{L}$ for constant propagation.

with x at u, this analysis associates two additional values: *undef* to indicate that no definition of x has been seen along any path reaching u, and *nonconst* to indicate that x can have different values at u along different paths reaching u. The component lattice $\widehat{L}$ for a variable is shown in Figure 4.5(a).

Observe that the structure of the lattice is governed by the choice of ignoring those control flow paths along which no definition of the variable has been seen. The assumption here is that the program is correct and such paths are not executed in any run of the program or an independent analysis to discover possibly uninitialized variables is being performed.

An alternative policy is to combine the possibly uninitialized variables analysis along with constant propagation. This would require declaring a variable to be *nonconst* at a join point if it has a constant value along a path but is undefined along some other path reaching the program point. This is fair under the assumption that all paths are potential execution paths so the value of the variable is known along some paths and is not known along some other paths. This results in a meet semilattice as illustrated in Figure 4.5(b). In this lattice $\top$ is an artificial element and is required for initialization. The flow functions will have to be suitably extended to include this value.

Such an analysis will discover fewer constants in the program and is more conservative compared to the analysis that excludes those paths that do not contain a definition of the variable under consideration. Hence practically, this policy is usually not adopted. In this book, we restrict ourselves to the common policy of assuming that the program is correct in the sense that every use of a variable is preceded by its definition.

Classical Constant Propagation Using Def-Use Chains

Constant propagation can be performed using def-use chains as described below:

1. Create a work list W_l consisting of definitions of the form $x_i : x = c_i$ occurring in the program, where $x \in \mathbb{V}\text{ar}$ and $c_i \in \mathbb{C}\text{onst}$. The *read*($x$) statement should be treated as a definition $x =$ *nonconst* and must be inserted in the work list.

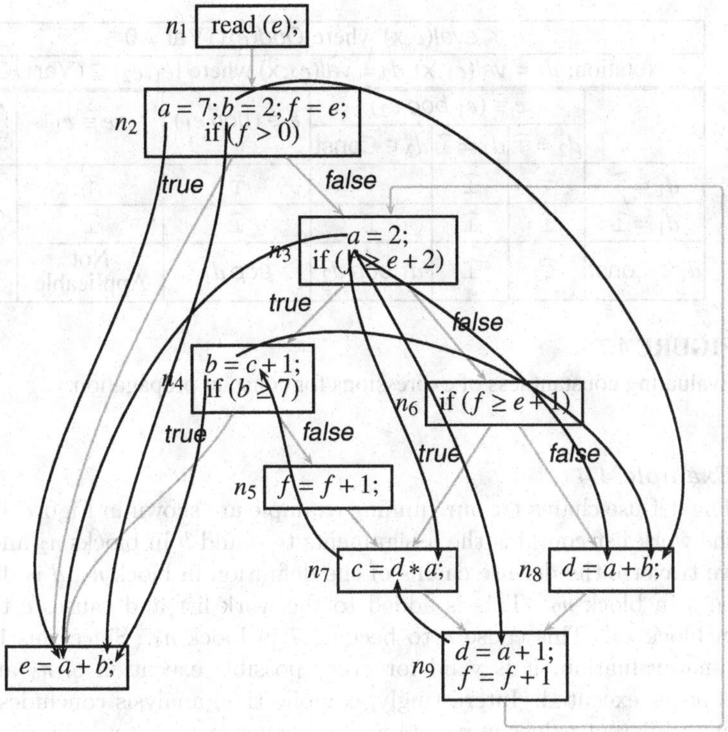

FIGURE 4.6

Def-use chains of variables a, b, c, and d for constant propagation.

Repeat the following step until W_l becomes empty.

2. Remove a definition $x_i : x = c_i$ from W_l. Perform the following steps for each def-use chain of x_i.

   (a) Traverse the def-use chain to locate the use of x reachable by the chain.

   (b) Let the value of the use be denoted by x'. If the use of x has not been replaced by any value, then x' is $\widehat{\top}$.

   (c) Replace the use of x by $x' \widehat{\sqcap} c_i$. This then becomes the value of x.

   (d) Evaluate the expression in which the use of x occurs. If the result is a constant value and the expression appears in the right hand side of an assignment, replace the expression by the constant value and add the definition to W_l. If the result is *nonconst*, then add the definition to W_l without replacing the expression.

$\mathsf{eval}(e,\mathsf{x})$ where $\mathsf{Opd}(e) \cap \mathbb{V}\mathsf{ar} \neq \emptyset$						
Notation: $d_1 = \mathsf{val}(e_1,\mathsf{x}), d_2 = \mathsf{val}(e_2,\mathsf{x})$ where $\{e_1,e_2\} \subseteq (\mathbb{V}\mathsf{ar} \cup \mathbb{C}\mathsf{onst})$						
	$e \equiv (e_1\ \mathsf{bop}\ e_2)$			$e \equiv (\mathsf{uop}\ e_1)$	$e \equiv e_1$	Any other expression
	$d_2 = \widehat{\top}$	$d_2 = \widehat{\bot}$	$d_2 \in \mathbb{C}\mathsf{onst}$			
$d_1 = \widehat{\top}$	$\widehat{\top}$	$\widehat{\bot}$	$\widehat{\top}$	$\widehat{\top}$	$\widehat{\top}$	
$d_1 = \widehat{\bot}$	$\widehat{\bot}$	$\widehat{\bot}$	$\widehat{\bot}$	$\widehat{\bot}$	$\widehat{\bot}$	$\widehat{\bot}$
$d_1 \in \mathbb{C}\mathsf{onst}$	$\widehat{\top}$	$\widehat{\bot}$	$d_1\ \mathsf{bop}\ d_2$	$\mathsf{uop}\ d_1$	Not Applicable	

FIGURE 4.7
Evaluating constantness of expressions for constant propagation.

Example 4.4

The def-use chains for our running example are shown in Figure 4.6. Initially, the work list contains the assignments to a and b in blocks n_2 and n_7. When we traverse the def-use chains of the definition in block n_3, d is discovered to be 3 in block n_9. This is added to the work list and causes c to become 6 in block n_7. This cause b to become 7 in block n_4. Since this is a compile time evaluation, it is valid for every possible execution of n_4 and block n_5 is never executed. Interestingly, compile time analysis concludes that b can have different values in n_8 and n_{10} and hence is $\widehat{\bot}$. For n_8, this is conservative imprecision since the execution never reaches n_8 after b becomes 7 in n_4. ☐

Data Flow Analysis for Constant Propagation

Observe that the specification of constant propagation in terms of def-use chains has a highly operational flavor. Data flow equations provide a declarative mechanism of defining a program analysis and reduce the work to fixed point computation.

Data flow analysis for constant propagation uses an overall lattice L that is a product of $\widehat{L}$. For convenience of defining flow functions, we represent an element in L by sets of pairs $\langle x, d_x \rangle$ where $x \in \mathbb{V}\mathsf{ar}$ and $d_x \in \widehat{L}$.

This is a forward data flow analysis. The data flow equations are:

$$\mathsf{In}_n = \begin{cases} \mathsf{BI} & n \text{ is } \mathsf{Start} \\ \displaystyle\bigsqcap_{p \in \mathsf{pred}(n)} \mathsf{Out}_p & \text{otherwise} \end{cases} \tag{4.8}$$

$$\mathsf{Out}_n = f_n(\mathsf{In}_n) \tag{4.9}$$

BI contains pairs $\langle x, \widehat{\top} \rangle$ for all variables $x \in \mathbb{V}\mathsf{ar}$. The confluence operation $\sqcap$ on elements in L is defined in terms of $\widehat{\sqcap}$ by applying it to pairs of the same variable:

$$\forall \mathsf{x}_1, \mathsf{x}_2 \in L,\ \mathsf{x}_1 \sqcap \mathsf{x}_2 = \{\langle z, d_x \widehat{\sqcap} d_y \rangle \mid \langle z, d_x \rangle \in \mathsf{x}_1, \langle z, d_y \rangle \in \mathsf{x}_2, x \in \mathbb{V}\mathsf{ar}\}$$

$$ConstGen_n = \begin{cases} \{\langle x, eval(e, \top)\rangle\} & n \text{ is assignment } x = e, Opd(e) \subseteq \mathbb{C}\text{onst} \\ \{\langle x, \widehat{\bot}\rangle\} & n \text{ is } read(x) \\ \emptyset & \text{otherwise} \end{cases}$$

$$DepGen_n(\mathsf{x}) = \begin{cases} \{\langle x, eval(e, \mathsf{x})\rangle\} & n \text{ is assignment } x = e, Opd(e) \cap \mathbb{V}\text{ar} \neq \emptyset \\ \emptyset & \text{otherwise} \end{cases}$$

$$ConstKill_n = \emptyset$$

$$DepKill_n(\mathsf{x}) = \begin{cases} \{\langle x, d\rangle\} & n \text{ is assignment } x = e,\ \langle x, d\rangle \in \mathsf{x} \\ \{\langle x, d\rangle\} & n \text{ is } read(x),\ \langle x, d\rangle \in \mathsf{x} \\ \emptyset & \text{otherwise} \end{cases}$$

Function *eval* is defined in Figure 4.7. It uses $val(e, \mathsf{x})$ to denote the value of a simple expression (consisting of a variable or a constant) in the context of the given data flow information x:

$$val(e, \mathsf{x}) = \begin{cases} c & \text{if } e \text{ is } c \in \mathbb{C}\text{onst} \\ d & \text{if } e \text{ is } x \in \mathbb{V}\text{ar},\ \langle x, d\rangle \in \mathsf{x} \end{cases}$$

Example 4.5

The computation of data flow values for our running example of Figure 4.4 has been shown in Figure 4.8. For brevity, we represent the data flow information as a vector $\langle d_a, d_b, d_c, d_d, d_e\rangle$ where d_x represents the constantness value of variable x. BI is $\langle \widehat{\top}, \widehat{\top}, \widehat{\top}, \widehat{\top}, \widehat{\top}\rangle$. The initial value of In_i and Out_i for all i is $\top = \langle \widehat{\top}, \widehat{\top}, \widehat{\top}, \widehat{\top}, \widehat{\top}\rangle$.

Observe that this analysis requires four traversals over the control flow graph in reverse postorder. In the first iteration, d is discovered to be 3 in block n_9. Thus, c is discovered to be 6 block n_7 in the third iteration. This makes b a constant with value 7 at $Exit(n_3)$ in the fourth iteration. At $Entry(n_2)$, b is 2 along the path from n_1 and 7 along the path from n_6. Observe the non-separability of constant propagation: The constantness of b depends on the constantness of a through c and d.

Also note that b is $\widehat{\bot}$ in n_8 due to the effect of n_4 in spite of the fact that control never reaches n_8 after execution n_4. □

Properties of Constant Propagation Data Flow Framework

In this section we show that Constant Propagation framework is monotonic but non-distributive.

THEOREM 4.1

Constant Propagation framework is monotonic.

	Iteration #1	Changes in iteration #2	Changes in iteration #3	Changes in iteration #4
In_{n_1}	$\widehat{\top},\widehat{\top},\widehat{\top},\widehat{\top},\widehat{\top},\widehat{\top}$			
Out_{n_1}	$\widehat{\top},\widehat{\top},\widehat{\top},\widehat{\top},\widehat{\bot},\widehat{\top}$			
In_{n_2}	$\widehat{\top},\widehat{\top},\widehat{\top},\widehat{\top},\widehat{\bot},\widehat{\bot}$			
Out_{n_2}	$7,2,\widehat{\top},\widehat{\top},\widehat{\bot},\widehat{\bot}$			
In_{n_3}	$7,2,\widehat{\top},\widehat{\top},\widehat{\bot},\widehat{\bot}$	$\widehat{\bot},2,\widehat{\top},3,\widehat{\bot},\widehat{\bot}$	$\widehat{\bot},2,6,3,\widehat{\bot},\widehat{\bot}$	$\widehat{\bot},\widehat{\bot},6,3,\widehat{\bot},\widehat{\bot}$
Out_{n_3}	$2,2,\widehat{\top},\widehat{\top},\widehat{\bot},\widehat{\bot}$	$2,2,\widehat{\top},3,\widehat{\bot},\widehat{\bot}$	$2,2,6,3,\widehat{\bot},\widehat{\bot}$	$2,\widehat{\bot},6,3,\widehat{\bot},\widehat{\bot}$
In_{n_4}	$2,2,\widehat{\top},\widehat{\top},\widehat{\bot},\widehat{\bot}$	$2,2,\widehat{\top},3,\widehat{\bot},\widehat{\bot}$	$2,2,6,3,\widehat{\bot},\widehat{\bot}$	$2,\widehat{\bot},6,3,\widehat{\bot},\widehat{\bot}$
Out_{n_4}	$2,\widehat{\top},\widehat{\top},\widehat{\top},\widehat{\bot},\widehat{\bot}$	$2,\widehat{\top},\widehat{\top},3,\widehat{\bot},\widehat{\bot}$	$2,7,6,3,\widehat{\bot},\widehat{\bot}$	
In_{n_5}	$2,\widehat{\top},\widehat{\top},\widehat{\top},\widehat{\bot},\widehat{\bot}$	$2,\widehat{\top},\widehat{\top},3,\widehat{\bot},\widehat{\bot}$	$2,7,6,3,\widehat{\bot},\widehat{\bot}$	
Out_{n_5}	$2,\widehat{\top},\widehat{\top},\widehat{\top},\widehat{\bot},\widehat{\bot}$	$2,\widehat{\top},\widehat{\top},3,\widehat{\bot},\widehat{\bot}$	$2,7,6,3,\widehat{\bot},\widehat{\bot}$	
In_{n_6}	$2,2,\widehat{\top},\widehat{\top},\widehat{\bot},\widehat{\bot}$	$2,2,\widehat{\top},3,\widehat{\bot},\widehat{\bot}$	$2,2,6,3,\widehat{\bot},\widehat{\bot}$	$2,\widehat{\bot},6,3,\widehat{\bot},\widehat{\bot}$
Out_{n_6}	$2,2,\widehat{\top},\widehat{\top},\widehat{\bot},\widehat{\bot}$	$2,2,\widehat{\top},3,\widehat{\bot},\widehat{\bot}$	$2,2,6,3,\widehat{\bot},\widehat{\bot}$	$2,\widehat{\bot},6,3,\widehat{\bot},\widehat{\bot}$
In_{n_7}	$2,2,\widehat{\top},\widehat{\top},\widehat{\bot},\widehat{\bot}$	$2,2,\widehat{\top},3,\widehat{\bot},\widehat{\bot}$	$2,\widehat{\bot},6,3,\widehat{\bot},\widehat{\bot}$	
Out_{n_7}	$2,2,\widehat{\top},\widehat{\top},\widehat{\bot},\widehat{\bot}$	$2,2,6,3,\widehat{\bot},\widehat{\bot}$	$2,\widehat{\bot},6,3,\widehat{\bot},\widehat{\bot}$	
In_{n_8}	$2,2,\widehat{\top},\widehat{\top},\widehat{\bot},\widehat{\bot}$	$2,2,\widehat{\top},3,\widehat{\bot},\widehat{\bot}$	$2,2,6,3,\widehat{\bot},\widehat{\bot}$	$2,\widehat{\bot},6,3,\widehat{\bot},\widehat{\bot}$
Out_{n_8}	$2,2,\widehat{\top},4,\widehat{\bot},\widehat{\bot}$	$2,2,\widehat{\top},4,\widehat{\bot},\widehat{\bot}$	$2,2,6,4,\widehat{\bot},\widehat{\bot}$	$2,\widehat{\bot},6,\widehat{\bot},\widehat{\bot},\widehat{\bot}$
In_{n_9}	$2,2,\widehat{\top},4,\widehat{\bot},\widehat{\bot}$	$2,2,6,\widehat{\bot},\widehat{\bot},\widehat{\bot}$	$2,\widehat{\bot},6,\widehat{\bot},\widehat{\bot},\widehat{\bot}$	
Out_{n_9}	$2,2,\widehat{\top},3,\widehat{\bot},\widehat{\bot}$	$2,2,6,3,\widehat{\bot},\widehat{\bot}$	$2,\widehat{\bot},6,3,\widehat{\bot},\widehat{\bot}$	
$In_{n_{10}}$	$\widehat{\bot},2,\widehat{\top},\widehat{\top},\widehat{\bot},\widehat{\bot}$	$\widehat{\bot},2,\widehat{\top},3,\widehat{\bot},\widehat{\bot}$	$\widehat{\bot},\widehat{\bot},6,3,\widehat{\bot},\widehat{\bot}$	
$Out_{n_{10}}$	$\widehat{\bot},2,\widehat{\top},\widehat{\top},\widehat{\bot},\widehat{\bot}$	$\widehat{\bot},2,\widehat{\top},3,\widehat{\bot},\widehat{\bot}$	$\widehat{\bot},\widehat{\bot},6,3,\widehat{\bot},\widehat{\bot}$	

FIGURE 4.8
Constant propagation data flow analysis for the running example in Figure 4.4.

PROOF Showing monotonicity of $f_n(\mathsf{x})$ requires showing that $(\mathsf{x} - \mathit{DepKill}_n(\mathsf{x}))$ and $\mathit{DepGen}_n(\mathsf{x})$ are monotonic.

$\mathit{DepKill}_n(\mathsf{x})$ is $\{\langle x, d_x \rangle\}$ for assignment $x = e$ or $read(x)$. In all other cases it is $\emptyset$. Since it does not depend on x,

$$\forall \mathsf{x}_1 \sqsubseteq \mathsf{x}_2 \in L : \ (\mathsf{x}_1 - \mathit{DepKill}_n(\mathsf{x}_1)) \ \sqsubseteq \ (\mathsf{x}_2 - \mathit{DepKill}_n(\mathsf{x}_2))$$

Showing monotonicity of $\mathit{DepGen}_n(\mathsf{x})$ reduces to showing

$$\forall e \in \mathbb{E}\mathsf{xpr}, \forall \mathsf{x}_1, \mathsf{x}_2 \in L : \mathsf{x}_1 \sqsubseteq \mathsf{x}_2 \Rightarrow \mathit{eval}(e, \mathsf{x}_1) \ \widehat{\sqsubseteq} \ \mathit{eval}(e, \mathsf{x}_2)$$

Function $\mathit{eval}(e, \mathsf{x})$ examines the data flow values of the operands of e. From its definition in Figure 4.7, it is easy to see that the data flow value computed by $\mathit{eval}(e, \mathsf{x})$ preserves the partial order. ∎

THEOREM 4.2
Constant Propagation framework is non-distributive.

PROOF Using the arguments similar to those in Theorem 4.1, it can be shown in terms of *eval*().

$$\exists e \in \mathbb{E}\text{xpr}, \exists \mathsf{x}_1, \mathsf{x}_2 \in L : eval(e, \mathsf{x}_1 \sqcap \mathsf{x}_2) \neq eval(e, \mathsf{x}_1) \,\widehat{\sqcap}\, eval(e, \mathsf{x}_2)$$

This is demonstrated by expression $(a+b)$ in block n_{10} in the program in Figure 4.4 for $\mathsf{x}_1 = \langle 7, 2, -, -, - \rangle$ and $\mathsf{x}_2 = \langle 2, 7, -, -, - \rangle$ where "−" indicates the values which do not matter. ∎

Presence of non-distributivity shows the limits of static analysis: Unless all paths are traversed independently, which may require exponential amount of work, a static analysis is likely to miss out on useful information even if the information is independent of program execution. This happens because of sharing of information across distinct paths as shown by the following example.

Example 4.6

Only two execution paths reach n_{10}: (n_1, n_2, n_7), and $(n_1, n_2, n_3, n_6, n_8, n_9, n_3, n_6, n_7, n_9, n_3, n_4, n_{10})$. The values of a, b, and e at *Exit*(n_{10}) along the first path are 7, 2, and 9 respectively whereas along the second path they are 2, 7, and 9. Static summary of constantness information should conclude that a and b are $\widehat{\bot}$ and e is 9. However, due to non-distributivity, our analysis concludes that all the three variables are $\widehat{\bot}$. Effectively, the flow function in n_{10} uses all possible combinations of a and b including those across different paths: $a = 7$ and $b = 2$ resulting in $e = 9$; $a = 2$ and $b = 7$ resulting in $e = 9$; $a = 2$ and $b = 2$ resulting in $e = 4$; $a = 7$ and $b = 7$ resulting in $e = 14$. Observe that the last two combinations are infeasible because there is no execution path reaching n_{10} along which a and b can both be 2 or both be 7. Fortunately, the imprecision caused by non-distributivity is safe because a $\widehat{\bot}$ variable does not enable any transformation. □

Constant propagation is not fast, and hence is not rapid. We leave it for the reader to construct suitable examples.

4.2.4 Variants of Constant Propagation

Constant propagation is a very useful analysis in practice. It improves the efficiency of programs by advancing some computations to compile time. It facilitates many other optimizations such as elimination of dead code (i.e., assignments which define variables which are not used later) as well as unreachable code. The latter simplifies control flow and may reduce branch delays on pipelined architectures. It can help in strength reduction and may enable many loop optimizations that require loop iterations bounds to be known at compile time.

It is not surprising that many variants of constant propagation have been proposed. The formulation which we have presented in the preceding sections is called *full* constant propagation to distinguish it from other variants of constant propagation which restrict the analysis in some ways.

Conditional Constant Propagation

As observed in Examples 4.3, 4.4, and 4.5, the value $b = 7$ in n_4 causes the control flow to leave the loop. Block n_5 is never executed and the value 7 does not reach n_8 resulting in both b and d being constant in n_8. Conditional constant propagation can discover this by evaluating the branching conditions appearing on execution paths.

In order to achieve the above, we create a lattice $\{\textsf{reachable}, \textsf{notReachable}\}$ with the partial order $\textsf{notReachable} \sqsubseteq \textsf{reachable}$. Let L be the product lattice of $\widehat{L}$. We create a new product lattice $L_c = \{\textsf{reachable}, \textsf{notReachable}\} \times L$. Values in L_c are pairs $\langle \textsf{status}, \textsf{x} \rangle$ where $\textsf{status}$ is either $\textsf{reachable}$ or $\textsf{notReachable}$ and $\textsf{x}$ is the constantness information as discovered in the unconditional constant propagation. The confluence operation $\sqcap_c$ of values in L_c ignores the values which are not reachable and is as defined below.

$\langle \textsf{status}_1, \textsf{x}_1 \rangle \sqcap_c \langle \textsf{status}_2, \textsf{x}_2 \rangle$		
	$\textsf{status}_2 = \textsf{reachable}$	$\textsf{status}_2 = \textsf{notReachable}$
$\textsf{status}_1 = \textsf{reachable}$	$\langle \textsf{reachable}, \textsf{x}_1 \sqcap \textsf{x}_2 \rangle$	$\langle \textsf{reachable}, \textsf{x}_1 \rangle$
$\textsf{status}_1 = \textsf{notReachable}$	$\langle \textsf{reachable}, \textsf{x}_2 \rangle$	$\langle \textsf{notReachable}, \top \rangle$

Reachability status is determined by evaluating branching conditions using function $\textsf{evalCond}(m, \textsf{x})$ which computes $\textsf{true}$, $\textsf{false}$, or $\textsf{undefined}$ depending upon the following: If basic block m contains a condition at the end and data flow information $\textsf{x}$ contains constant values for all variables required to evaluate the condition, then $\textsf{evalCond}(m, \textsf{x})$ is the result of the condition. Otherwise, $\textsf{evalCond}(m, \textsf{x})$ is $\textsf{undefined}$. Propagation of data flow information along the out edge associated with the outcome is ensured by using an edge flow function.

An alternative to such a data flow analysis is to simply delete the edge that will not be executed instead of qualifying data flow information with $\textsf{reachable}$ and $\textsf{notReachable}$ values. However, this may not be possible if branch outcome is likely to be influenced by calling contexts. In particular, when context sensitive interprocedural data flow analysis is performed a branch outcome may be different in different contexts and deletion of an edge may not be possible. Further, the abstraction of conditional propagation along edges is a powerful mechanism that can compute more precise data flow information for analyses such as *null* pointer analysis: For this analysis, a condition that checks for the nullity of a pointer can propagate different outcomes along the two out edges of a condition.

The propagation function for an edge $m \rightarrow n$, is defined as follows:

$$g_{m\rightarrow n}(\textsf{status}, \textsf{x}) = \begin{cases} \langle \textsf{notReachable}, \top \rangle & \textsf{evalCond}(m, \textsf{x}) \neq \textsf{undefined} \text{ and} \\ & \textsf{evalCond}(m, \textsf{x}) \neq \textsf{label}(m \rightarrow n) \\ \langle \textsf{status}, \textsf{x} \rangle & \text{otherwise} \end{cases}$$

	Iteration #1	Changes in iteration #2	Changes in iteration #3
In_{n_1}	$R,\langle\widehat{\top},\widehat{\top},\widehat{\top},\widehat{\top},\widehat{\top},\widehat{\top}\rangle$		
Out_{n_1}	$R,\langle\widehat{\top},\widehat{\top},\widehat{\top},\widehat{\top},\widehat{\bot},\widehat{\top}\rangle$		
In_{n_2}	$R,\langle\widehat{\top},\widehat{\top},\widehat{\top},\widehat{\top},\widehat{\bot},\widehat{\bot}\rangle$		
Out_{n_2}	$R,\langle 7,2,\widehat{\top},\widehat{\top},\widehat{\bot},\widehat{\bot}\rangle$		
In_{n_3}	$R,\langle 7,2,\widehat{\top},\widehat{\top},\widehat{\bot},\widehat{\bot}\rangle$	$R,\langle\widehat{\bot},2,\widehat{\top},3,\widehat{\bot},\widehat{\bot}\rangle$	$R,\langle\widehat{\bot},2,6,3,\widehat{\bot},\widehat{\bot}\rangle$
Out_{n_3}	$R,\langle 2,2,\widehat{\top},\widehat{\top},\widehat{\bot},\widehat{\bot}\rangle$	$R,\langle 2,2,\widehat{\top},3,\widehat{\bot},\widehat{\bot}\rangle$	$R,\langle 2,2,6,3,\widehat{\bot},\widehat{\bot}\rangle$
In_{n_4}	$R,\langle 2,2,\widehat{\top},\widehat{\top},\widehat{\bot},\widehat{\bot}\rangle$	$R,\langle 2,2,\widehat{\top},3,\widehat{\bot},\widehat{\bot}\rangle$	$R,\langle 2,2,6,3,\widehat{\bot},\widehat{\bot}\rangle$
Out_{n_4}	$R,\langle 2,\widehat{\top},\widehat{\top},\widehat{\top},\widehat{\bot},\widehat{\bot}\rangle$	$R,\langle 2,\widehat{\top},\widehat{\top},3,\widehat{\bot},\widehat{\bot}\rangle$	$R,\langle 2,7,6,3,\widehat{\bot},\widehat{\bot}\rangle$
In_{n_5}	$R,\langle 2,\widehat{\top},\widehat{\top},\widehat{\top},\widehat{\bot},\widehat{\bot}\rangle$	$R,\langle 2,\widehat{\top},\widehat{\top},3,\widehat{\bot},\widehat{\bot}\rangle$	$R,\langle 2,7,6,3,\widehat{\bot},\widehat{\bot}\rangle$
Out_{n_5}	$R,\langle 2,\widehat{\top},\widehat{\top},\widehat{\top},\widehat{\bot},\widehat{\bot}\rangle$	$R,\langle 2,\widehat{\top},\widehat{\top},3,\widehat{\bot},\widehat{\bot}\rangle$	$R,\langle 2,7,6,3,\widehat{\bot},\widehat{\bot}\rangle$
In_{n_6}	$R,\langle 2,2,\widehat{\top},\widehat{\top},\widehat{\bot},\widehat{\bot}\rangle$	$R,\langle 2,2,\widehat{\top},3,\widehat{\bot},\widehat{\bot}\rangle$	$N,\top=\langle\widehat{\top},\widehat{\top},\widehat{\top},\widehat{\top},\widehat{\top},\widehat{\top}\rangle$
Out_{n_6}	$R,\langle 2,2,\widehat{\top},\widehat{\top},\widehat{\bot},\widehat{\bot}\rangle$	$R,\langle 2,2,\widehat{\top},3,\widehat{\bot},\widehat{\bot}\rangle$	$N,\top=\langle\widehat{\top},\widehat{\top},\widehat{\top},\widehat{\top},\widehat{\top},\widehat{\top}\rangle$
In_{n_7}	$R,\langle 2,2,\widehat{\top},\widehat{\top},\widehat{\bot},\widehat{\bot}\rangle$	$R,\langle 2,2,\widehat{\top},3,\widehat{\bot},\widehat{\bot}\rangle$	$R,\langle 2,2,6,3,\widehat{\bot},\widehat{\bot}\rangle$
Out_{n_7}	$R,\langle 2,2,\widehat{\top},\widehat{\top},\widehat{\bot},\widehat{\bot}\rangle$	$R,\langle 2,2,6,3,\widehat{\bot},\widehat{\bot}\rangle$	$R,\langle 2,2,6,3,\widehat{\bot},\widehat{\bot}\rangle$
In_{n_8}	$R,\langle 2,2,\widehat{\top},\widehat{\top},\widehat{\bot},\widehat{\bot}\rangle$	$R,\langle 2,2,\widehat{\top},3,\widehat{\bot},\widehat{\bot}\rangle$	$R,\langle 2,2,6,3,\widehat{\bot},\widehat{\bot}\rangle$
Out_{n_8}	$R,\langle 2,2,\widehat{\top},4,\widehat{\bot},\widehat{\bot}\rangle$	$R,\langle 2,2,\widehat{\top},4,\widehat{\bot},\widehat{\bot}\rangle$	$R,\langle 2,2,6,4,\widehat{\bot},\widehat{\bot}\rangle$
In_{n_9}	$R,\langle 2,2,\widehat{\top},4,\widehat{\bot},\widehat{\bot}\rangle$	$R,\langle 2,2,6,\widehat{\bot},\widehat{\bot},\widehat{\bot}\rangle$	$R,\langle 2,\widehat{\bot},6,\widehat{\bot},\widehat{\bot},\widehat{\bot}\rangle$
Out_{n_9}	$R,\langle 2,2,\widehat{\top},3,\widehat{\bot},\widehat{\bot}\rangle$	$R,\langle 2,2,6,3,\widehat{\bot},\widehat{\bot}\rangle$	$R,\langle 2,\widehat{\bot},6,3,\widehat{\bot},\widehat{\bot}\rangle$
$In_{n_{10}}$	$R,\langle\widehat{\bot},2,\widehat{\top},\widehat{\top},\widehat{\bot},\widehat{\bot}\rangle$	$R,\langle\widehat{\bot},2,\widehat{\top},3,\widehat{\bot},\widehat{\bot}\rangle$	$R,\langle\widehat{\bot},\widehat{\bot},6,3,\widehat{\bot},\widehat{\bot}\rangle$
$Out_{n_{10}}$	$R,\langle\widehat{\bot},2,\widehat{\top},\widehat{\top},\widehat{\bot},\widehat{\bot}\rangle$	$R,\langle\widehat{\bot},2,\widehat{\top},3,\widehat{\bot},\widehat{\bot}\rangle$	$R,\langle\widehat{\bot},\widehat{\bot},6,3,\widehat{\bot},\widehat{\bot}\rangle$

FIGURE 4.9
Conditional constant propagation for the running example in Figure 4.4.

The data flow equations remain much the same except that now they must honor the reachability status as shown below.

$$In_n = \begin{cases} \langle \mathit{reachable}, \mathit{BI} \rangle & n \text{ is } \mathit{Start} \\ \displaystyle\bigsqcap_{C\; p\in pred(n)} g_{p\to n}(Out_p) & \text{otherwise} \end{cases}$$

$$Out_n = \begin{cases} \langle \mathit{reachable}, f_n(\mathsf{x}) \rangle & In_n = \langle \mathit{reachable}, \mathsf{x} \rangle \\ \langle \mathit{notReachable}, \top \rangle & \text{otherwise} \end{cases}$$

In the beginning, only the *Start* block is assumed to be reachable and the initial value associated with all other program points is $\langle \mathit{notReachable}, \top \rangle$. This is required for computing the *MFP* solution. If we use the initial value $\langle \mathit{reachable}, \top \rangle$, the analysis will converge on a fixed point that may not be maximum. The result would be imprecise but safe.

Example 4.7

Figure 4.9 provides the data flow values for conditional constant propagation in our running example. Since the data flow information is not propagated from n_4 to n_5, b remains constant in the loop and analysis converges in three iterations rather than four. □

It is easy to see that conditional constant propagation can discover more precise information than unconditional constant propagation. It is guaranteed to be at least as good, if not better.

Copy Constant Propagation

Copy constant propagation limits the expressions appearing on the right hand side of an assignment to simple variables or constants. Such statements have been called copies in Section 2.3.4 to describe copy propagation using reaching definitions. There are two fundamental differences between the analysis presented here and the copy propagation described in Section 2.3.4: (a) the analysis presented here allows replacement of variables by constants only whereas the earlier analysis allowed replacement of variables by other variables also, and (b) the analysis presented here takes care of transitive effects of replacements whereas the earlier analysis does not do so.

Copy constant propagation does not generate new constants based on the values of variables. Hence it is guaranteed to compute only a finite number of constants. Thus the component lattice $\widehat{L}$ is finite. The flow function does not evaluate any expression involving a variable. Thus the definitions of $\mathsf{ConstKill}_n$ and $\mathsf{DepKill}_n(\mathsf{x})$ do not change. $\mathsf{ConstGen}_n$ and $\mathsf{DepGen}_n(\mathsf{x})$ change in the following manner. $\mathsf{DepGen}_n(\mathsf{x})$ is restricted to copy assignments and $\mathsf{DepGen}_n(\mathsf{x})$ computes $\widehat{\bot}$ value for non-copy assignments. The new definitions are:

$$\mathsf{ConstGen}_n = \begin{cases} \{\langle v, \mathsf{eval}(e, \top)\rangle\} & n \text{ is assignment } v = e, \mathsf{Opd}(e) \subseteq \mathsf{Const} \\ \{\langle v, \widehat{\bot}\rangle\} & n \text{ is } \mathit{read}(v) \text{ or a non-copy assignment to } v \\ \emptyset & \text{otherwise} \end{cases}$$

$$\mathsf{DepGen}_n(\mathsf{x}) = \begin{cases} \{\langle v, d\rangle\} & n \text{ is assignment } v = w,\ \langle w, d\rangle \in \mathsf{x} \\ \emptyset & \text{otherwise} \end{cases}$$

Observe that the expression evaluation in the above definition is restricted to constant operands only.

Full constant propagation is non-distributive due to the use of function $\mathsf{eval}(e, \mathsf{x})$. All other terms involved in defining f_n are distributive. Copy constant propagation is distributive because it does not involve $\mathsf{eval}(e, \mathsf{x})$. However, due to non-separability, the framework remains non-fast.

Since expressions are not evaluated, this analysis finds fewer constants and is limited in scope compared to the full constant propagation.

Linear Constant Propagation

A slightly more general formulation than copy constant propagation allows expressions to appear on the right hand side but these expressions may contain at most a single variable. This requires a restricted version of *eval*. Since this analysis computes new constants, the lattice $\widehat{L}$ is infinite, unlike copy constant propagation. However, similar to copy constant propagation, linear constant propagation is distributive because the number of variables in the right hand side is restricted to one. However, due to non-separability, the framework remains non-fast.

4.3 Discovering Properties of Pointers

Pointers allow indirect modification of data thereby making it difficult to discover useful information from programs. They reduce the effectiveness of program analysis tools. This is because, in the absence of precise analysis of pointer manipulations, program analysis must conservatively assume that any data object could be modified by any pointer. Practically, this can be mitigated somewhat by using type information and by confining the conservative assumptions within variables of the same type. However, if information about the possible manipulations performed through pointers is available, it can enhance the precision of other analyses.

This section presents pointer analyses for stack and static data. These analyses capture relationships between pointers and other variables or pointers. This is different from other analyses which we have seen because the domain of data flow values of an entity did not involve other entities.

Our model of pointer manipulations is based on C except that we do not take into account pointer arithmetic. Since the size of stack and static data is fixed, pointers can point to only a fixed set of locations that are known at compile time. We assume that field references of a structure are flattened out into a new pointer name: A reference like $x.f$ occurring in a statement can be modeled as a new pointer x_f to which the pointer x points to. Further, a *null* assignment to a pointer x is treated as assigning address 0 to x. Thus assignment $x = null$ is treated as $x = \&zero$ where *zero* is a special symbol whose address is 0.

4.3.1 Points-To Analysis of Stack and Static Data

This analysis establishes *points-to* relation between pointer variables and memory locations under the assumption that the program is type correct in terms of pointer manipulations.

DEFINITION 4.5 *A pointer variable x points to variable y at a program point u, denoted $x \rightarrow y$, if it holds the address of variable y at u.* ♦

Points-to relation is neither reflexive (because $x \rightarrow x$ may not hold), nor symmetric (because $x \rightarrow y \not\Rightarrow y \rightarrow x$), nor transitive (because $x \rightarrow y, y \rightarrow z \not\Rightarrow x \rightarrow z$).

We assume that the left hand side of a pointer assignment is either a pointer variable x or a pointer indirection $*x$. The right hand side could be either an address expression $\&x$, a pointer variable x, or a pointer indirection $*x$.

The pointers which are likely to be modified by a pointer assignment are called *left locations* of the assignment. The addresses which may be assigned to the left locations are called the *right locations* of the assignment. Let x be the set representing the points-to relations that hold just before assignment statement n. The left and the right locations of n which depend on x are denoted by $\mathit{DepLeftL}_n(\mathsf{x})$ and $\mathit{DepRightL}_n(\mathsf{x})$. The left and right locations which depend solely on the local effect of n are denoted by $\mathit{ConstLeftL}_n$ and $\mathit{ConstRightL}_n$.

Consider an assignment statement $\mathit{lhs}_n = \mathit{rhs}_n$. The left and the right locations of n are defined as follows:

Left Locations			Right Locations		
lhs_n	$\mathit{ConstLeftL}_n$	$\mathit{DepLeftL}_n(\mathsf{x})$	rhs_n	$\mathit{ConstRightL}_n$	$\mathit{DepRightL}_n(\mathsf{x})$
x	$\{x\}$	$\emptyset$	x	$\emptyset$	$\{y \mid (x \rightarrow y) \in \mathsf{x}\}$
$*x$	$\emptyset$	$\{y \mid (x \rightarrow y) \in \mathsf{x}\}$	$*x$	$\emptyset$	$\{z \mid \{x \rightarrow y, y \rightarrow z\} \subseteq \mathsf{x}\}$
			$\&x$	$\{x\}$	$\emptyset$

Points-to relation between the left and the right locations is established in terms of new points-to pairs which are generated and the points-to pairs which cease to hold due to the effect of a basic block.

$$
\begin{aligned}
\mathit{ConstGen}_n &= \{x \rightarrow y \mid x \in \mathit{ConstLeftL}_n, y \in \mathit{ConstRightL}_n\} \\
\mathit{DepGen}_n(\mathsf{x}) &= \{x \rightarrow y \mid (x \in \mathit{ConstLeftL}_n, y \in \mathit{DepRightL}_n(\mathsf{x})), \text{ or} \\
&\qquad (x \in \mathit{DepLeftL}_n(\mathsf{x}), y \in \mathit{ConstRightL}_n), \text{ or} \\
&\qquad (x \in \mathit{DepLeftL}_n(\mathsf{x}), y \in \mathit{DepRightL}_n(\mathsf{x}))\} \\
\mathit{ConstKill}_n &= \{x \rightarrow y \mid x \in \mathit{ConstLeftL}_n\} \\
\mathit{DepKill}_n(\mathsf{x}) &= \{x \rightarrow y \mid x \in \mathit{DepLeftL}_n(\mathsf{x})\}
\end{aligned}
$$

$\mathit{DepKill}_n(\mathsf{x})$ depends on $\mathit{DepLeftL}_n(\mathsf{x})$ which involves pointer indirection on the left hand side of a pointer assignment. Thus it captures the indirect effect of an assignment due to pointer indirection and hence the choice of x is critical for ensuring conservative approximation on the safer side. We explain this below.

DEFINITION 4.6 *If a pointer z is modified by a pointer assignment regardless of the execution path taken to reach the assignment, then such a modification is called a strong update of z. If z may be modified by the assignment when the execution reaches along some path and may not be modified when it reaches along some other path, such a modification of z is called a weak update of z.*

An assignment $z = w$ causes a strong update of z. Contrast this with the assignment $*x = w$ such that $x \rightarrow z$ holds along some path reaching the assignment. If the execution follows this path, then the assignment modifies z, otherwise it does not modify z. If $x \rightarrow z$ holds along every path, then z is modified by the assignment in every execution. In order to capture the indirect effect of such an assignment, there is a need to make a distinction between the points-to relations which cause weak updates from those which cause strong updates. The former is called *may* points-to relation while the latter is called *must* points-to relation.

DEFINITION 4.7 *If pointer x holds the address of variable y at program point u along some path from* Start *to u, then x→y at u under* may *points-to relation. If x holds the address of y along every path from* Start *to u, then x→y at u under* must *points-to relation.*

It is easy to see that a *may* points-to relation is weaker than a *must* points-to relation: If x must point to y at u then x may point to y at u but not vice-versa.

Since *may* points-to relations must not miss any points-to pair which may hold at a program point, only the pairs affected by a strong update must be removed. Thus, for computing $MayOut_n$, $DepKill_n$ must depend on $MustIn_n$. Since *must* points-to relations should include a points-to pair only if it is guaranteed to hold, all pairs affected by weak update must be removed. Thus, for computing $MustOut_n$, $DepKill_n$ must depend on $MayIn_n$. We explain this in Example 4.9.

The data flow equations for points-to analysis are:

$$MayIn_n = \begin{cases} BI & n \text{ is } Start \\ \bigcup_{p \in pred(n)} MayOut_n & \text{otherwise} \end{cases} \tag{4.10}$$

$$MayOut_n = f_n(MayIn_n, MustIn_n) \tag{4.11}$$

$$MustIn_n = \begin{cases} BI & n \text{ is } Start \\ \bigcap_{p \in pred(n)} MustOut_n & \text{otherwise} \end{cases} \tag{4.12}$$

$$MustOut_n = f_n(MustIn_n, MayIn_n) \tag{4.13}$$

where flow function f_n is defined as follows:

$$f_n(x_1, x_2) = (x_1 - Kill_n(x_2)) \cup Gen_n(x_1) \tag{4.14}$$

Observe the use of different sets as arguments to $Gen_n(x)$ and $Kill_n(x)$. The $Gen_n(x)$ and $Kill_n(x)$ are defined in the usual manner:

$$Gen_n(x) = ConstGen_n \cup DepGen_n(x)$$
$$Kill_n(x) = ConstKill_n \cup DepKill_n(x)$$

In the intraprocedural context, BI is $\emptyset$ for both *may* and *must* point-to because no pointer points to any variable at *Start*.

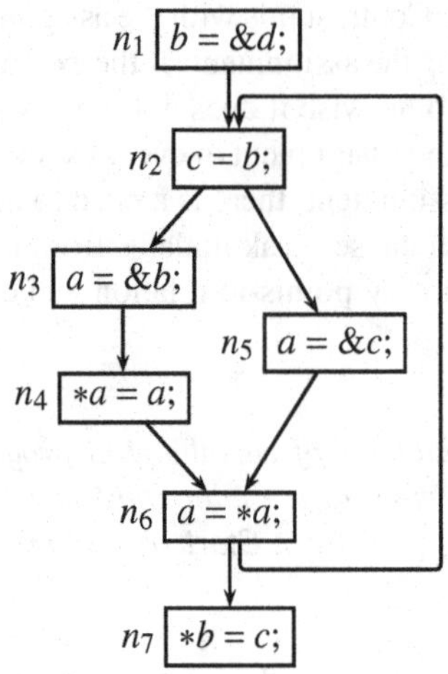

- $\mathbb{V}\text{ar} = \{a, b, c, d\}$
  $\mathbb{U} = \{\ a{\rightarrow}a,\ a{\rightarrow}b,\ a{\rightarrow}c,\ a{\rightarrow}d,\ b{\rightarrow}a,\ b{\rightarrow}b,\ b{\rightarrow}d,\ b{\rightarrow}d,\ c{\rightarrow}a,\ c{\rightarrow}b,\ c{\rightarrow}c,\ c{\rightarrow}d,\ d{\rightarrow}a,\ d{\rightarrow}b,\ d{\rightarrow}c,\ d{\rightarrow}d\ \}$
- $L_{may} = \langle 2^{\mathbb{U}}, \supseteq \rangle,\ \top_{may} = \emptyset, \bot_{may} = \mathbb{U}$
- $L_{must} = \widehat{L}_a \times \widehat{L}_b \times \widehat{L}_c \times \widehat{L}_d$

  We show the component lattice $\widehat{L}_a$:

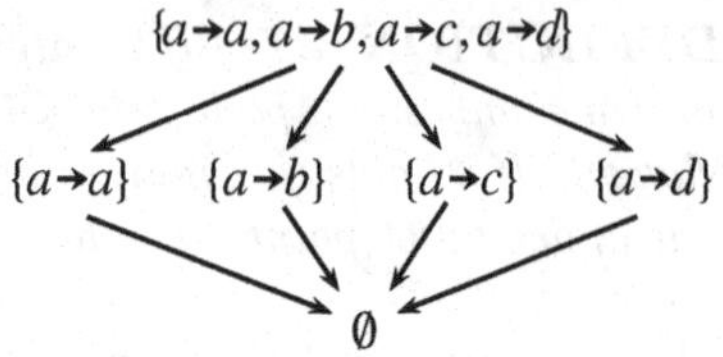

FIGURE 4.10
Example program for points-to analysis.

Figure 4.10 illustrates the lattices for *may* and *must* points-to analysis. Observe that the $\widehat{\top}$ value for *must* points-to in Figure 4.10 is $\{a{\rightarrow}a, a{\rightarrow}b, a{\rightarrow}c, a{\rightarrow}d\}$. It is easy to see to that this is a value that cannot naturally occur in any instance of *must* points-to analysis because a pointer can pointer to at most one location in *must* points-to analysis. This is an example of an artificial value added to a meet semilattice for convenience. Since the descending chain condition is satisfied, the resulting lattice is a complete lattice. By contrast, the lattice for *may* points-to analysis is a naturally complete lattice and its $\widehat{\top}$ element can actually occur during *may* points-to analysis.

Technically, the lattice for *must* points-to analysis is a tuple of values from component lattice. For example, given the lattice in Figure 4.10, if a points to c, b does not point to any location, c points to d, and d points to b, then the *must* points-to information should be represented as $\langle \{a{\rightarrow}b\}, \emptyset, \{c{\rightarrow}d\}, \{d{\rightarrow}b\} \rangle$. However, for compatibility with *may* points-to analysis, we treat it as a flattened set rather than as a vector of sets for each pointer variable. Thus, we represent the same data flow information by $\{a{\rightarrow}b, c{\rightarrow}d, d{\rightarrow}b\}$.

Example 4.8

Consider the example program in Figure 4.10. The computation of *may* and *must* points-to relations has been shown below. The $\top$ for *may* is $\emptyset$ whereas that for *must* is the universal set $\mathbb{U}$ of points-to pairs. The computation of *may* and *must* proceeds in an interleaved fashion.

	Iteration #1	Changes in Iteration #2	Changes in Iteration #3
$MayIn_{n_1}$	$\emptyset$		
$MustIn_{n_1}$	$\emptyset$		
$MayOut_{n_1}$	$\{b \to d\}$		
$MustOut_{n_1}$	$\{b \to d\}$		
$MayIn_{n_2}$	$\{b \to d\}$	$\{a \to b, a \to d, b \to b, b \to d, c \to d\}$	$\{a \to b, a \to d, b \to b, b \to d, c \to b, c \to d\}$
$MustIn_{n_2}$	$\{b \to d\}$	$\emptyset$	
$MayOut_{n_2}$	$\{b \to d, c \to d\}$	$\{a \to b, a \to d, b \to b, b \to d, c \to b, c \to d\}$	
$MustOut_{n_2}$	$\{b \to d, c \to d\}$	$\emptyset$	
$MayIn_{n_3}$	$\{b \to d, c \to d\}$	$\{a \to b, a \to d, b \to b, b \to d, c \to b, c \to d\}$	
$MustIn_{n_3}$	$\{b \to d, c \to d\}$	$\emptyset$	
$MayOut_{n_3}$	$\{a \to b, b \to d, c \to d\}$	$\{a \to b, b \to b, b \to d, c \to b, c \to d\}$	
$MustOut_{n_3}$	$\{a \to b, b \to d, c \to d\}$	$\{a \to b\}$	
$MayIn_{n_4}$	$\{a \to b, b \to d, c \to d\}$	$\{a \to b, b \to b, b \to d, c \to b, c \to d\}$	
$MustIn_{n_4}$	$\{a \to b, b \to d, c \to d\}$	$\{a \to b\}$	
$MayOut_{n_4}$	$\{a \to b, b \to b, c \to d\}$	$\{a \to b, b \to b, c \to b, c \to d\}$	
$MustOut_{n_4}$	$\{a \to b, b \to b, c \to d\}$	$\{a \to b, b \to b\}$	
$MayIn_{n_5}$	$\{b \to d, c \to d\}$	$\{a \to b, a \to d, b \to b, b \to d, c \to b, c \to d\}$	
$MustIn_{n_5}$	$\{b \to d, c \to d\}$	$\emptyset$	
$MayOut_{n_5}$	$\{a \to c, b \to d, c \to d\}$	$\{a \to c, b \to b, b \to d, c \to b, c \to d\}$	
$MustOut_{n_5}$	$\{a \to c, b \to d, c \to d\}$	$\{a \to c\}$	
$MayIn_{n_6}$	$\{a \to b, a \to c, b \to b, b \to d, c \to d\}$	$\{a \to b, a \to c, b \to b, b \to d, c \to b, c \to d\}$	
$MustIn_{n_6}$	$\{c \to d\}$	$\emptyset$	
$MayOut_{n_6}$	$\{a \to b, a \to d, b \to b, b \to d, c \to d\}$	$\{a \to b, a \to d, b \to b, b \to d, c \to b, c \to d\}$	
$MustOut_{n_6}$	$\{c \to d\}$	$\emptyset$	
$MayIn_{n_7}$	$\{a \to b, a \to d, b \to b, b \to d, c \to d\}$	$\{a \to b, a \to d, b \to b, b \to d, c \to b, c \to d\}$	
$MustIn_{n_7}$	$\{c \to d\}$	$\emptyset$	
$MayOut_{n_7}$	$\{a \to b, a \to d, b \to b, b \to d, c \to d, d \to d\}$	$\{a \to b, a \to d, b \to b, b \to d, c \to b, c \to d, d \to b, d \to d\}$	
$MustOut_{n_7}$	$\{c \to d\}$	$\emptyset$	

Since $(a \to b) \in MayIn_{n_4}$, assignment $*a = a$ generates $(b \to b) \in MayOut_{n_4}$. Further, since $(a \to b) \in MustIn_{n_4}$, this assignment causes a strong update of b causing the removal of $b \to d$ from $MayIn_{n_4}$. The third iteration is required $c \to b$ from $MayOut_{n_2}$ to $MayIn_{n_2}$. □

Example 4.9

Consider the program flow graph in Figure 4.11 on the next page which illus-

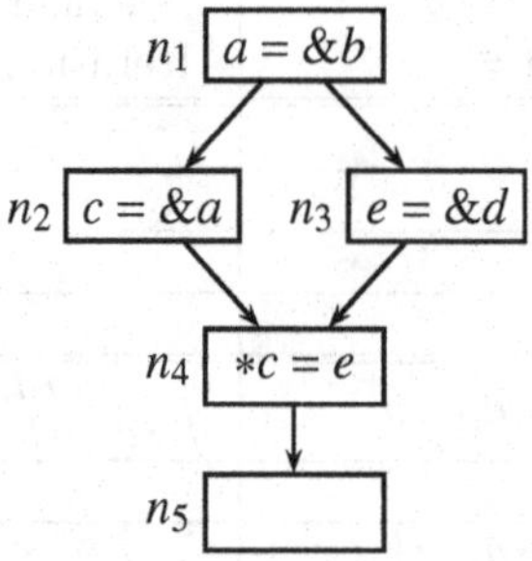

- $a \rightarrow b$ in block 5 along path 1,3,4,5 but not along path 1,2,4,5.
- Required: $a \rightarrow b \in \mathit{MayIn}_{n_5}$ and $a \rightarrow b \notin \mathit{MustIn}_{n_5}$
- If $\mathit{DepKill}_{n_4}$ for MayOut_{n_4} is defined in terms of MayIn_{n_4} then $a \rightarrow b \notin \mathit{MayOut}_{n_4}$ because a is in $\mathit{DepLeftL}_{n_4}(\mathit{MayIn}_{n_4})$
- If $\mathit{DepKill}_{n_4}$ for $\mathit{MustOut}_{n_4}$ is defined in terms of MustIn_{n_4} then $a \rightarrow b \notin \mathit{MustOut}_{n_4}$ because a is in $\mathit{DepLeftL}_{n_4}(\mathit{MustIn}_{n_4})$

FIGURE 4.11
Inverse dependence of *may* and *must* points-to relations for *Kill*.

trates that the dependence between *may* and *must* points-to relations for *Kill* is not only mutual, but is also inverse. In block n_5, the relation $a \rightarrow b$ holds along the path (n_1, n_3, n_4, n_5) but not along the path (n_1, n_2, n_4, n_5). This is because along the latter path, $c \rightarrow a$ and the assignment in n_4 modifies a. Since $c \rightarrow a \in \mathit{MayIn}_{n_4}$ and $c \rightarrow a \notin \mathit{MustIn}_{n_4}$, a is a left location in *may* points-to relation but not in *must* points-to relation. Thus if MayIn_{n_4} is used for defining $\mathit{DepKill}_{n_4}$ for computing MayOut_{n_4}, $a \rightarrow b$ will not exist in MayOut_{n_4} which is incorrect. Similarly, if MustIn_{n_4} is used for defining $\mathit{DepKill}_{n_4}$ for computing $\mathit{MustOut}_{n_4}$, $a \rightarrow b$ will exist in $\mathit{MustOut}_{n_4}$ which is incorrect. □

If *may* and *must* analyses are performed independently, then

$$\begin{aligned} \mathit{MayOut}_n &= f_n(\mathit{MayIn}_n, \emptyset) \\ \mathit{MustOut}_n &= f_n(\mathit{MustIn}_n, \mathbb{U}) \end{aligned}$$

In other words, in the absence of *must* points-to information, no points-to pair can be killed by indirect effect of an assignment since no strong update is known. In the absence of *may* points-to information, every points-to pair must be assumed to be killed by indirect effect of an assignment since no weak update is known.

Observe that unlike any other flow function, the flow function for points-to analysis given by Equation (4.14) is a binary function rather than a unary function. It has been defined so to capture the inverse dependence of *may* and *must* information through the $\mathit{DepKill}_n$ part. The overall lattice for the data flow Equations (4.11) through (4.13) is a product lattice of the lattices for *may* and *must* points-to relations and the flow function is a unary function for the values in this overall lattice. The $\top$ element of the overall lattice is the pair $\langle \emptyset, \mathbb{U} \rangle$ whereas $\bot$ is $\langle \mathbb{U}, \emptyset \rangle$.

Given a constant *must* points-to information, it is easy to see that the flow functions in *may* points-to analysis are monotonic. This is because the $\mathit{DepKill}_n(\mathsf{x})$ component becomes constant and given a larger x, $\mathit{DepGen}_n(\mathsf{x})$ computes a larger set of points-to pairs. Since *must* points-to analysis has also been defined using the same components, given a constant *may* points-to information, the flow functions of *must* points-to analysis are also monotonic.

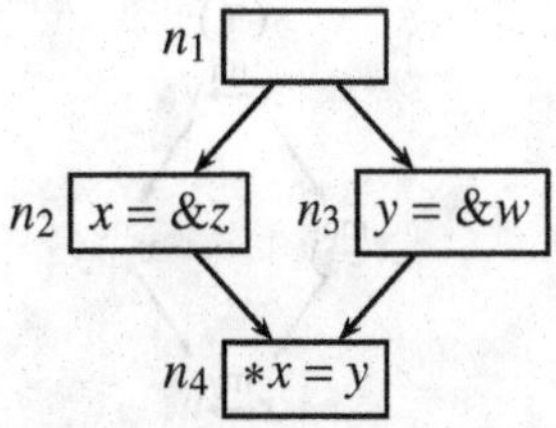

(a) Example for *may* points-to analysis

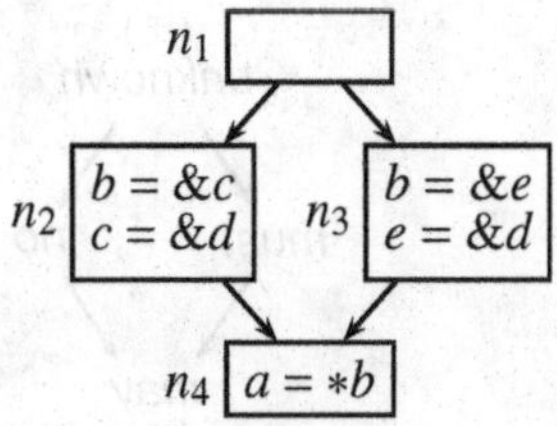

(b) Example for *must* points-to analysis

FIGURE 4.12
Non-distributivity of points-to analysis.

Example 4.10

Figure 4.12 shows the non-distributivity of points-to analysis using the flow function associated with node n_4.

Consider the example for *may* points-to analysis. Assuming that the *must* points-to information is constant, non-distributivity of *may* points-to analysis depends on $DepGen_n(\mathsf{x})$. Let x_1 be the *may* points-to information along the edge $n_2 \rightarrow n_4$ and let x_2 be the *may* points-to information along the edge $n_3 \rightarrow n_4$. Then $\mathsf{x}_1 = \{x \rightarrow y\}$, $\mathsf{x}_2 = \{y \rightarrow w\}$ and:

$$\begin{aligned}
DepGen_n(\mathsf{x}_1 \cup \mathsf{x}_2) &= \{x \rightarrow y, y \rightarrow w, z \rightarrow w\} \\
DepGen_n(\mathsf{x}_1) &= \{x \rightarrow y\} \\
DepGen_n(\mathsf{x}_2) &= \{y \rightarrow w\} \\
DepGen_n(\mathsf{x}_1 \cup \mathsf{x}_2) &\supset DepGen_n(\mathsf{x}_1) \cup DepGen_n(\mathsf{x}_2)
\end{aligned}$$

Consider the example for *must* points-to analysis under similar situations. In this case $\mathsf{x}_1 = \{b \rightarrow c, c \rightarrow d\}$, $\mathsf{x}_2 = \{b \rightarrow e, e \rightarrow d\}$ and:

$$\begin{aligned}
DepGen_n(\mathsf{x}_1 \cap \mathsf{x}_2) &= \emptyset \\
DepGen_n(\mathsf{x}_1) &= \{a \rightarrow d\} \\
DepGen_n(\mathsf{x}_2) &= \{a \rightarrow d\} \\
DepGen_n(\mathsf{x}_1 \cap \mathsf{x}_2) &\subset DepGen_n(\mathsf{x}_1) \cap DepGen_n(\mathsf{x}_2)
\end{aligned}$$

□

We leave it to the reader to construct examples to show that the data flow framework of points-to analysis is not fast.

Points-To Analysis with Degree of Certainty

Instead of computing separate *may* and *must* points-to sets, a points-to pair $x \rightarrow y$ can be qualified with degrees of certainties *may* and *must* and can be denoted $x \xrightarrow{\mathsf{my}} y$ and $x \xrightarrow{\mathsf{mu}} y$. This reduces computation of *may* and *must* points-to sets to a single

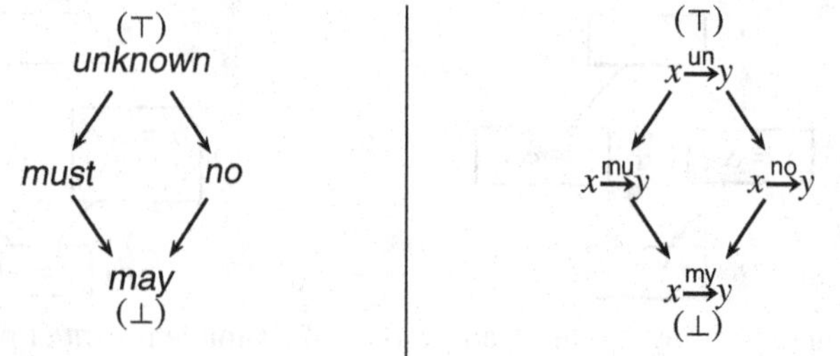

(a) Degree of certainty (b) Points-to relation between x and y

FIGURE 4.13
Lattices for points-to analysis with degree of certainty.

analysis unlike *MayIn*/*MayOut* and *MustIn*/*MustOut*. In order to define data flow analysis, we add two more degrees of certainty: $x \xrightarrow{\text{no}} y$ indicates that x does not point to y and $x \xrightarrow{\text{un}} y$ indicates that nothing is known about the points-to relation between x and y.* This results in the component lattices shown in Figure 4.13. The confluence operations used in defining the data flow analysis are induced by these lattices and are left implicit in the description of the analysis.

The left and right locations are now qualified with degrees of certainty. However, values *unknown* and *no* are irrelevant in the context of a pointer assignment. The left locations are defined as follows:

$\textsf{lhs}_n$	$\textsf{ConstLeftL}_n$	$\textsf{DepLeftL}_n(\textsf{x})$
x	$\{\langle x, \textsf{must}\rangle\}$	$\emptyset$
$*x$	$\emptyset$	$\{\langle y, d\rangle \mid (x \xrightarrow{d} y) \in \textsf{x}, d \in \{\textsf{may}, \textsf{must}\}\}$

The right locations are defined as follows:

$\textsf{rhs}_n$	$\textsf{ConstRightL}_n$	$\textsf{DepRightL}_n(\textsf{x})$
$\&x$	$\{\langle x, \textsf{must}\rangle\}$	$\emptyset$
x	$\emptyset$	$\{\langle y, d\rangle \mid (x \xrightarrow{d} y) \in \textsf{x}, d \in \{\textsf{may}, \textsf{must}\}\}$
$*x$	$\emptyset$	$\{\langle z, d_1 \sqcap d_2\rangle \mid \{x \xrightarrow{d_1} y, y \xrightarrow{d_2} z\} \subseteq \textsf{x}, \{d_1, d_2\} \subseteq \{\textsf{may}, \textsf{must}\}\}$

When the left hand side is variable x, all points-to pairs with x as the source are removed. If the right hand side is an address expression, new *must* and *no* points-

***no* and *unknown* need not be represented explicitly. $x \xrightarrow{\text{no}} y$ can be represented by ensuring that $x \xrightarrow{\text{mu}} y$ or $x \xrightarrow{\text{my}} y$ is not present in the set enumerating the points-to relation. For $x \xrightarrow{\text{un}} y$, it is sufficient to record whether the data flow values associated with a node have been computed or not. While combining the data flow information from predecessors, if the values have not been computed for a predecessor m, it can be ignored in the merge operation; this has the effect of assuming that the data flow information associated with m is $\top$. This has been achieved on line 2 of the algorithm presented in Figure 3.15 on page 90 by excluding the predecessors along a back edge during the initialization.

to pairs are generated purely due to local effect regardless of the existing points-to relations. $\mathsf{ConstGen}_n$ is defined only in the context of assignments such as $x = \&y$ whereas $\mathsf{ConstKill}_n$ is defined only when the left hand side is a variable such as x.

$$\begin{aligned}\mathsf{ConstGen}_n &= \{x \xrightarrow{\mathsf{mu}} y \mid \langle x, \mathsf{must}\rangle \in \mathsf{ConstLeftL}_n, \langle y, \mathsf{must}\rangle \in \mathsf{ConstRightL}_n\} \cup \\ &\quad\ \{x \xrightarrow{\mathsf{no}} z \mid \langle x, \mathsf{must}\rangle \in \mathsf{ConstLeftL}_n, \mathsf{ConstRightL}_n \neq \emptyset, \\ &\quad\ \langle z, d\rangle \notin \mathsf{ConstRightL}_n\} \\ \mathsf{ConstKill}_n &= \{x \xrightarrow{d} y \mid \langle x, \mathsf{must}\rangle \in \mathsf{ConstLeftL}_n\}\end{aligned}$$

In other situations $\mathsf{ConstLeftL}_n \cap \mathsf{ConstRightL}_n = \emptyset$. For these situations let

$$\begin{aligned}\mathsf{Left}_n(\mathsf{x}) &= \mathsf{ConstLeftL}_n \cup \mathsf{DepLeftL}_n(\mathsf{x}) \\ \mathsf{Right}_n(\mathsf{x}) &= \mathsf{ConstRightL}_n \cup \mathsf{DepRightL}_n(\mathsf{x})\end{aligned}$$

The dependent information that is generated and killed by a pointer assignment is defined as follows:

$$\begin{aligned}\mathsf{DepGen}_n(\mathsf{x}) = &\{x \xrightarrow{d} y \mid \langle x, d_l\rangle \in \mathsf{Left}_n(\mathsf{x}), \langle y, d_r\rangle \in \mathsf{Right}_n(\mathsf{x}), d = d_l \sqcap d_r\} \cup \\ &\{x \xrightarrow{\mathsf{my}} y \mid \langle x, \mathsf{may}\rangle \in \mathsf{Left}_n(\mathsf{x}), x \xrightarrow{\mathsf{mu}} y \in \mathsf{x}\} \cup \\ &\{x \xrightarrow{\mathsf{no}} y \mid \langle x, \mathsf{must}\rangle \in \mathsf{Left}_n(\mathsf{x}), \langle y, d\rangle \notin \mathsf{Right}_n(\mathsf{x})\}\end{aligned}$$

The first term in the definition of $\mathsf{DepGen}_n(\mathsf{x})$ is the result of a combination of the left and right hand sides. The second term lowers the degree of certainty of $x \xrightarrow{\mathsf{mu}} y$ in x to $x \xrightarrow{\mathsf{my}} y$ due to a possible modification of x by the assignment. The third term is a replacement of points-to pairs killed by the assignment.

$$\begin{aligned}\mathsf{DepKill}_n(\mathsf{x}) = &\{x \xrightarrow{d} y \mid \langle x, \mathsf{must}\rangle \in \mathsf{DepLeftL}_n(\mathsf{x})\} \cup \\ &\{x \xrightarrow{\mathsf{mu}} y \mid \langle x, \mathsf{may}\rangle \in \mathsf{DepLeftL}_n(\mathsf{x})\}\end{aligned}$$

The first term in $\mathsf{DepKill}_n(\mathsf{x})$ represents the guaranteed modification of x by the pointer assignment n. The second term removes $x \xrightarrow{\mathsf{mu}} y$ so that it can be replaced by the generated pair $x \xrightarrow{\mathsf{my}} y$.

The final data flow equations are:

$$\begin{aligned}\mathsf{In}_n &= \begin{cases} \mathsf{BI} & n \text{ is } \mathsf{Start} \\ \displaystyle\bigsqcap_{p \in \mathsf{pred}(n)} \mathsf{Out}_p & \text{otherwise} \end{cases} \\ \mathsf{Out}_n &= f_n(\mathsf{In}_n) \;=\; (\mathsf{In}_n - \mathsf{Kill}_n(\mathsf{In}_n)) \cup \mathsf{Gen}_n(\mathsf{In}_n)\end{aligned}$$

where $\mathsf{BI} = \{x \xrightarrow{\mathsf{no}} y \mid x \text{ is a pointer variable and } y \text{ is any variable }\}$.

Example 4.11

We show the computation of points-to pairs qualified with the degree of certainty for the example program in Figure 4.10 on page 122. For simplicity, we omit the pairs representing *no* except for In_n where we list the *BI*. Since we perform round-robin analysis and traverse the graph in reverse postorder, the pairs representing *unknown* are required only in the first iteration and only for Out_{n_6}. We leave them also implicit. Observe that now *may* and *must* are mutually exclusive and the resulting information is more precise.

	Iteration #1	Changes in Iteration #2	Changes in Iteration #3
In_{n_1}	$\{x\xrightarrow{no}y \mid x,y \in \{a,b,c,d\}\}$		
Out_{n_1}	$\{b\xrightarrow{mu}d\}$		
In_{n_2}	$\{b\xrightarrow{mu}d\}$	$\{a\xrightarrow{my}b, a\xrightarrow{my}d, b\xrightarrow{my}b, b\xrightarrow{my}d, c\xrightarrow{my}d\}$	$\{a\xrightarrow{my}b, a\xrightarrow{my}d, b\xrightarrow{my}b, b\xrightarrow{my}d, c\xrightarrow{my}b, c\xrightarrow{my}d\}$
Out_{n_2}	$\{b\xrightarrow{mu}d, c\xrightarrow{mu}d\}$	$\{a\xrightarrow{my}b, a\xrightarrow{my}d, b\xrightarrow{my}b, b\xrightarrow{my}d, c\xrightarrow{my}b, c\xrightarrow{my}d\}$	
In_{n_3}	$\{b\xrightarrow{mu}d, c\xrightarrow{mu}d\}$	$\{a\xrightarrow{my}b, a\xrightarrow{my}d, b\xrightarrow{my}b, b\xrightarrow{my}d, c\xrightarrow{my}b, c\xrightarrow{my}d\}$	
Out_{n_3}	$\{a\xrightarrow{mu}b, b\xrightarrow{mu}d, c\xrightarrow{mu}d\}$	$\{a\xrightarrow{mu}b, b\xrightarrow{my}b, b\xrightarrow{my}d, c\xrightarrow{my}b, c\xrightarrow{my}d\}$	
In_{n_4}	$\{a\xrightarrow{mu}b, b\xrightarrow{mu}d, c\xrightarrow{mu}d\}$	$\{a\xrightarrow{mu}b, b\xrightarrow{my}b, b\xrightarrow{my}d, c\xrightarrow{my}b, c\xrightarrow{my}d\}$	
Out_{n_4}	$\{a\xrightarrow{mu}b, b\xrightarrow{mu}b, c\xrightarrow{mu}d\}$	$\{a\xrightarrow{mu}b, b\xrightarrow{mu}b, c\xrightarrow{my}b, c\xrightarrow{my}d\}$	
In_{n_5}	$\{b\xrightarrow{mu}d, c\xrightarrow{mu}d\}$	$\{a\xrightarrow{my}b, a\xrightarrow{my}d, b\xrightarrow{my}b, b\xrightarrow{my}d, c\xrightarrow{my}b, c\xrightarrow{my}d\}$	
Out_{n_5}	$\{a\xrightarrow{mu}c, b\xrightarrow{mu}d, c\xrightarrow{mu}d\}$	$\{a\xrightarrow{mu}c, b\xrightarrow{my}b, b\xrightarrow{my}d, c\xrightarrow{my}b, c\xrightarrow{my}d\}$	
In_{n_6}	$\{a\xrightarrow{my}b, a\xrightarrow{my}c, b\xrightarrow{my}b, b\xrightarrow{my}d, c\xrightarrow{mu}d\}$	$\{a\xrightarrow{my}b, a\xrightarrow{my}c, b\xrightarrow{my}b, b\xrightarrow{my}d, c\xrightarrow{my}b, c\xrightarrow{my}d\}$	
Out_{n_6}	$\{a\xrightarrow{my}b, a\xrightarrow{my}d, b\xrightarrow{my}b, b\xrightarrow{my}d, c\xrightarrow{mu}d\}$	$\{a\xrightarrow{my}b, a\xrightarrow{my}d, b\xrightarrow{my}b, b\xrightarrow{my}d, c\xrightarrow{my}b, c\xrightarrow{my}d\}$	
In_{n_7}	$\{a\xrightarrow{my}b, a\xrightarrow{my}d, b\xrightarrow{my}b, b\xrightarrow{my}d, c\xrightarrow{mu}d\}$	$\{a\xrightarrow{my}b, a\xrightarrow{my}d, b\xrightarrow{my}b, b\xrightarrow{my}d, c\xrightarrow{my}b, c\xrightarrow{my}d\}$	
Out_{n_7}	$\{a\xrightarrow{my}b, a\xrightarrow{my}d, b\xrightarrow{my}b, b\xrightarrow{my}d, c\xrightarrow{mu}d, d\xrightarrow{my}d\}$	$\{a\xrightarrow{my}b, a\xrightarrow{my}d, b\xrightarrow{my}b, b\xrightarrow{my}d, c\xrightarrow{my}b, c\xrightarrow{my}d, d\xrightarrow{my}b, d\xrightarrow{my}d\}$	

The analysis still requires three iterations. □

Example 4.12

We illustrate non-distributivity of points-to analysis with the degree of certainty by enumerating *MOP* and *MFP* assignments for the example in part (a) of Figure 4.12 on page 125.

	MOP Assignment	*MFP* Assignment
Out_{n_2}	$\{x \xrightarrow{mu} z\}$	$\{x \xrightarrow{mu} z\}$
Out_{n_3}	$\{y \xrightarrow{mu} w\}$	$\{y \xrightarrow{mu} w\}$
Out_{n_4}	$\{x \xrightarrow{my} z, y \xrightarrow{my} w\}$	$\{x \xrightarrow{my} z, y \xrightarrow{my} w, z \xrightarrow{my} w\}$

□

4.3.2 Alias Analysis of Stack and Static Data

An alternative way of representing information about pointers is to use the relation of aliasing. Aliasing is defined between pointer expressions which may use dereferencing operations, such as x, $*x$, $**x$ etc.

DEFINITION 4.8 *A pointer expression e_1 is aliased to pointer expression e_2 at program point u, denoted $e_1 \doteq e_2$, if the expressions e_1 and e_2 evaluate to the same address at u.*

A Comparison of Points-to and Alias Relations

Similar to points-to relation, an alias pair $e_1 \doteq e_2$ that holds along all paths reaching u is a *must* alias; if it holds along some paths then it is a *may* alias. The lattices of *may* and *must* aliases are similar to the lattices for *may* and *must* points-to relations illustrated in Figure 4.10.

Aliasing is different from points-to relation in the following sense. Although it is possible to create points-to pairs between pointer expressions such as $(*x) \rightarrow (**y)$, the points-to analysis represents the same information by a pair $z \rightarrow w$, where by construction, z and w are both variable names such that z is the target of x and w is the target of $**y$. This is possible since points-to analysis is defined in terms of locations that are compile time constants whereas aliasing is a relation defined in terms of address expressions that can be evaluated only at run time. This information cannot be represented as an alias by using w because an alias does not relate a pointer expression to the address it holds but relates pointer expressions that hold the same address and the target of the two pointer expressions is left implicit. Hence, alias pair $*x \doteq **y$ needs to be stored.

An alternative way of comparing points-to relations and alias relations is to view them in terms of a memory graph in which edges represent points-to pairs. Alias pairs represent paths that reach the same node in the graph. As a consequence, unlike points-to relation, alias relation is both symmetric and reflexive. *must* aliases are transitive and *may* aliases are not transitive.

$$a = b$$
$$d = \&c$$
$$*a = c$$

(a) Sequence of assignments

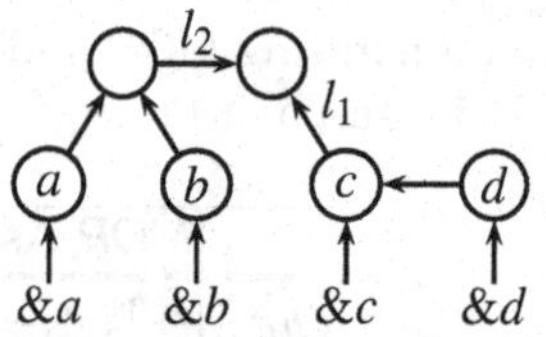

(b) Resulting memory graph

FIGURE 4.14
The need of link aliases in computing node aliases.

The difference that aliasing involves pointer expressions whereas points-to relations involves names of variables implies that in points-to relations, an edge in the memory graph is always represented by a single points-to pair. In the presence of cycles in a data structure, there are an infinite number of paths reaching a node. Thus alias analysis may derive infinite aliases. To see this, consider the assignments sequence $a = \&b$ followed by $b = \&b$ creating a self loop around b. Thus we have an alias $a \doteq *b$. However, since $*b$, $**b$, $***b$ etc. all point to b, we have all possible aliases $a \doteq **b$, $a \doteq ***b$, $b \doteq *b$, $*b \doteq **b$, $**b \doteq *b$, etc. In points-to analysis, the same information is represented by two pairs $a \rightarrow b$ and $b \rightarrow b$.

Due to the presence aliases resulting from pointer indirections, it becomes important to distinguish between *node* and *link* aliases which are defined below.

DEFINITION 4.9 *Pointer expressions e_1 and e_2 are node aliases if their r-values are same but l-values are different; they are link aliases if their l-values are also same. An assignment $a = b$ creates a node alias $a \doteq b$ and link aliases $*a \doteq *b$, $**a \doteq **b$, etc.*

In terms of paths in memory graph, link aliases relate paths that have a non-empty common suffix whereas node aliases relate paths with disjoint non-empty suffixes.

In order to define node aliases for an assignment $a = \&b$, we also introduce a fictitious pointer expression $\&b$ which is assumed to have a unique l-value; its r-value is b. By definition, $*\&b = b$. Assignment $a = \&b$, results in a node alias $a \doteq \&b$. If this is not done, we will have to capture the effect of the assignment by alias pair $*a \doteq b$ which is not a node alias but a link alias.

Link aliases can be computed from node aliases and we restrict our analysis to node aliases only. However, it is necessary to identify link aliases at intermediate stages as explained in the following example. In the rest of this section, we reserve the notation $e_1 \doteq e_2$ to node aliases only; where link aliases are required, they are explicitly defined in terms of node aliases.

Example 4.13
Consider the assignment sequence in Figure 4.14. The assignment $*a = c$ creates the link l_2 in the memory graph thereby creating the node aliases $*a \doteq *d$,

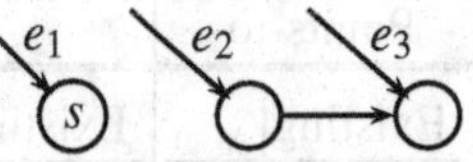

(a) Memory graph before the assignment $s = e_2$

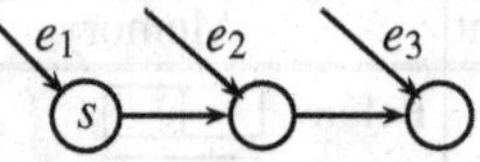

(b) Memory graph after the assignment $s = e_2$

FIGURE 4.15
Direct and indirect node aliases generated as a result of a pointer assignment.

$*b \doteq *d$ and $*b \doteq c$. In order to discover these node aliases, we need to use the fact that $*b$ is a link alias of $*a$ (sharing the link l_2) and $*d$ is a link alias of c (sharing the link l_1). □

In the general situation, given an assignment $\mathit{lhs}_n = \mathit{rhs}_n$ we say that all link aliases of lhs_n get node-aliased to all node and link aliases of rhs_n that are not modified by the assignment. Unlike points-to analysis, alias analysis is significantly influenced by the choice of representation of the alias information. When alias relation is represented in the form of pairs, the node aliases computed by relating appropriate aliases of lhs_n and rhs_n, the resulting aliases are *direct* aliases. However, due to possible indirections of aliases of lhs_n and rhs_n, *indirect* node aliases are also created as explained in the following example.

Example 4.14

Consider the memory graphs in Figure 4.15. As a result of the assignment $s = e_2$, direct aliases $s \doteq e_2$ and $*e_1 \doteq e_2$ are created. However, node aliases $*s \doteq e_3$ and $**e_1 \doteq e_3$ must also be identified. These are examples of indirect node aliases. □

Computing indirect aliases can be avoided by representing alias relations using graphs rather than pairs but the graph representation results in imprecision due to transitivity: When graph representation of two alias pairs $x \doteq y$ and $y \doteq z$ are merged at a join point, their targets are represented by the same node in the graph resulting in a spurious alias $x \doteq z$. This makes the *may* alias information transitive even though the *may* alias relation is not transitive.

Points-to analysis does not have any of the above problems because it is restricted to stack locations and there is a one-to-one mapping between the points-to pairs and the edges in the memory graph. A comparison of points-to relations and alias relations for all possible assignments in our language has been provided in Figure 4.16. It is easy to see that points-to information is much more compact than alias information. On the flip side, using points-to information would require traversing paths in the memory graph; alias information explicates these paths in the pointer expressions used in the alias information.

Statement	Memory	Points-to	Aliases
$x = \&y$	Before After 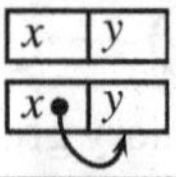	Existing: New: $x \rightarrow y$	Existing: New Direct: $x \doteq \&y$
$x = y$	Before After 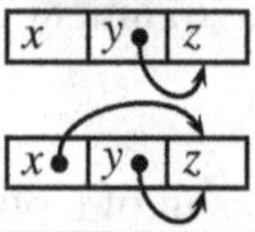	Existing: $y \rightarrow z$ New: $x \rightarrow z$	Existing: $*y \doteq z$ New Direct: $x \doteq y$ New Indirect: $*x \doteq z$
$x = *y$	Before After 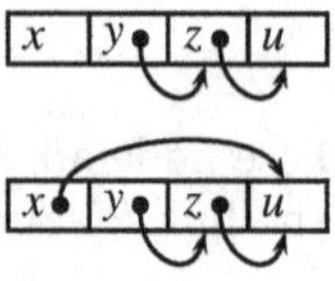	Existing: $y \rightarrow z$, $z \rightarrow u$ New: $x \rightarrow u$	Existing: $*y \doteq z$, $*z \doteq u$, $**y \doteq u$ New Direct: $x \doteq *y$, $x \doteq z$ New Indirect: $*x \doteq u$
$*x = \&y$	Before After 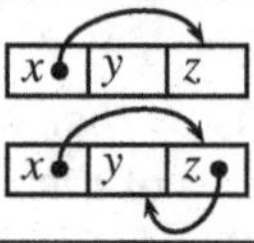	Existing: $x \rightarrow z$ New: $z \rightarrow y$	Existing: $*x \doteq z$ New Direct: $*x \doteq \&y$, $*z \doteq y$
$*x = y$	Before After 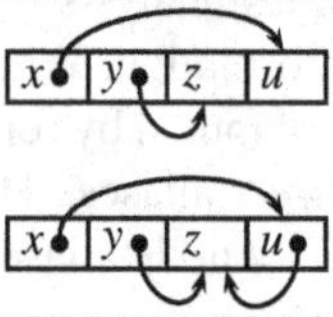	Existing: $x \rightarrow u$, $y \rightarrow z$ New: $u \rightarrow z$	Existing: $*x \doteq u$, $*y \doteq z$ New Direct: $*x \doteq y$, $y \doteq u$ New Indirect: $*u \doteq z$, $**x \doteq z$
$*x = *y$	Before After 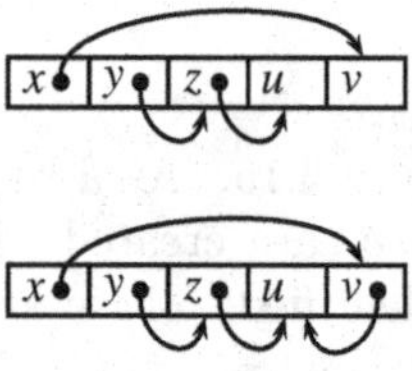	Existing: $x \rightarrow v$, $y \rightarrow z$, $z \rightarrow u$ New: $v \rightarrow u$	Existing: $*x \doteq v$, $*y \doteq z$, $*z \doteq u$, $**y \doteq u$ New Direct: $*x \doteq *y$, $*x \doteq z$, $v \doteq z$, $v \doteq *y$ New Indirect: $**x \doteq u$, $*v \doteq u$

FIGURE 4.16
A comparison of points-to and alias relations.

4.3.3 Formulating Data Flow Equations for Alias Analysis

In order to facilitate creation and detection of link aliases, we define a prefix relation on pointer expressions as follows:

$$e_1 \lessdot^k e_2 \Leftrightarrow e_2 \equiv (*)^k e_1$$

where $(*)^k$ denotes k occurrences of the pointer indirection operator $*$. With this notation $x \lessdot^1 *x$, $x \lessdot^2 **x$, and $*x \lessdot^1 **x$. Observe that $\&b \lessdot^1 b$. We also use the & operator with the following semantics:

$$\&e = \begin{cases} \&x & e \text{ is a pointer variable } x \\ e_1 & \text{otherwise, where } e_1 \lessdot^1 e \end{cases}$$

Given a set of node aliases x, we identify all aliases of a pointer expression e as the maximum fixed point of the equation:

$$\mathit{Aliases}(e,\mathsf{x}) = \begin{cases} \{e_1 \mid e_1 \doteq e \in \mathsf{x}\} & e = \&x, x \in \mathbb{V}\mathrm{ar} \\ \{e_1 \mid e_1 \doteq e \in \mathsf{x}\} \cup \{*e_1 \mid e_1 \in \mathit{Aliases}(\&e,\mathsf{x})\} & \text{otherwise} \end{cases}$$

In the presence of cycles in data structures, $\mathit{Aliases}(e,\mathsf{x})$ could be infinite; this would require employing suitable summarization mechanism. We shall see one such mechanism in the context of heap data analysis.

Now we identify the right and left pointer expressions of a pointer assignment for computing alias relations. Consider a pointer assignment $\mathit{lhs}_n = \mathit{rhs}_n$. The definitions of $\mathit{ConstLeftL}_n$ and $\mathit{ConstRightL}_n$ given below are easy to follow. $\mathit{DepLeftL}_n(\mathsf{x})$ represents the set of all link aliases of lhs_n. They are computed from all link and node aliases of $\&\mathit{lhs}_n$. $\mathit{DepRightL}_n(\mathsf{x})$ represents all node and link aliases of rhs_n.

$$\mathit{ConstLeftL}_n = \{\mathit{lhs}_n\}$$

$$\mathit{ConstRightL}_n = \begin{cases} \emptyset & \mathit{lhs}_n \lessdot \mathit{rhs}_n \\ \{\mathit{rhs}_n\} & \text{otherwise} \end{cases}$$

$$\mathit{DepLeftL}_n(\mathsf{x}) = \begin{cases} \emptyset & \mathit{lhs}_n \text{ is } \&x, x \in \mathbb{V}\mathrm{ar} \\ \{*e \mid e \in \mathit{Aliases}(\&\mathit{lhs}_n,\mathsf{x})\} & \text{otherwise} \end{cases}$$

$$\mathit{DepRightL}_n(\mathsf{x}) = \begin{cases} \emptyset & \mathit{lhs}_n \text{ is } \&x, x \in \mathbb{V}\mathrm{ar} \\ \mathit{Aliases}(\mathit{rhs}_n,\mathsf{x}) & \text{otherwise} \end{cases}$$

Observe that we can use only those right pointer expressions that are not modified by the assignment. The pointer expressions that are modified by the assignment are the pointer expressions that have a prefix that is *must* link aliased to lhs_n.

$$\mathit{Mod}_n(\mathsf{x}_1,\mathsf{x}_2) = \{e \mid e_1 \lessdot^i e,\ i \geq 0,\ e_1 \doteq e_2 \in \mathsf{x}_2,\ e_2 \in (\{\mathit{lhs}_n\} \cup \mathit{DepLeftL}_n(\mathsf{x}_1))\}$$

Similar to the inverse dependence of *may* and *must* points-to relations for *Kill*, if x_1 is the set of *may* aliases, then x_2 is the set of *must* aliases and vice-versa.

In the case of points-to analysis, Mod_n is not required because target of the resulting points-to pair is referred to by a variable name rather than through rhs_n. However, in the case of alias analysis, the pointer expression rhs_n is used in the generated aliases and if the resulting pointer expression is link aliased to lhs_n before the assignment, its target changes due to the assignment. Thus it should not participate in the generation of new alias pairs.

Now we define the flow functions for alias analysis. The generated alias pairs are defined by:

$$\mathit{Gen}_n(\mathsf{x}_1,\mathsf{x}_2) = \mathit{ConstGen}_n \cup \mathit{DepGen}_n^D(\mathsf{x}_1,\mathsf{x}_2) \cup \mathit{DepGen}_n^I(\mathsf{x}_1,\mathsf{x}_2)$$

where $\mathit{DepGen}_n^D(\mathsf{x}_1,\mathsf{x}_2)$ represents the direct aliases and $\mathit{DepGen}_n^I(\mathsf{x}_1,\mathsf{x}_2)$ represents indirect aliases and are defined as follows:

$$\begin{aligned}
\mathit{ConstGen}_n &= \{e_1 \doteq e_2 \mid e_1 \in \mathit{ConstLeftL}_n, e_2 \in \mathit{ConstRightL}_n\} \\
\mathit{DepGen}_n^D(\mathsf{x}_1,\mathsf{x}_2) &= \{e_1 \doteq e_2 \mid e_2 \notin \mathit{Mod}_n(\mathsf{x}_1,\mathsf{x}_2), \text{ and} \\
&\qquad (e_1 \in \mathit{ConstLeftL}_n, e_2 \in \mathit{DepRightL}_n(\mathsf{x}_1)), \text{ or} \\
&\qquad (e_1 \in \mathit{DepLeftL}_n(\mathsf{x}_1), e_2 \in \mathit{ConstRightL}_n), \text{ or} \\
&\qquad (e_1 \in \mathit{DepLeftL}_n(\mathsf{x}_1), e_2 \in \mathit{DepRightL}_n(\mathsf{x}_1))\} \\
\mathit{DepGen}_n^I(\mathsf{x}_1,\mathsf{x}_2) &= \{(*)^k e_1 \doteq e_2 \mid e_2 \notin \mathit{Mod}_n(\mathsf{x}_1,\mathsf{x}_2), (*)^k \mathit{rhs}_n \doteq e_2 \in \mathsf{x}_1,\ k > 0, \\
&\qquad e_1 \in (\mathit{ConstLeftL}_n \cup \mathit{DepLeftL}_n(\mathsf{x}_1))\}
\end{aligned}$$

The aliases killed by the assignment are defined by

$$\mathit{Kill}_n(\mathsf{x}_1,\mathsf{x}_2) = \mathit{ConstKill}_n \cup \mathit{DepKill}_n(\mathsf{x}_1,\mathsf{x}_2)$$

where

$$\begin{aligned}
\mathit{ConstKill}_n &= \{e_1 \doteq e_2 \mid \mathit{lhs}_n <^k e_1,\ k \geq 0\} \\
\mathit{DepKill}_n(\mathsf{x}_1,\mathsf{x}_2) &= \{e_1 \doteq e_2 \mid e_1 \doteq e_2 \in \mathsf{x}_2,\ e_3 <^k e_1,\ k \geq 0,\ e_3 \in \mathit{DepLeftL}_n(\mathsf{x}_1)\}
\end{aligned}$$

The top level data flow equations for alias analysis are identical to that of points-to analysis; the flow function f_n is slightly different.

$$\mathit{MayIn}_n = \begin{cases} \mathit{BI} & n \text{ is } \mathit{Start} \\ \bigcup\limits_{p \in pred(n)} \mathit{MayOut}_p & \text{otherwise} \end{cases} \tag{4.15}$$

$$\mathit{MayOut}_n = f_n(\mathit{MayIn}_n, \mathit{MustIn}_n) \tag{4.16}$$

$$\mathit{MustIn}_n = \begin{cases} \mathit{BI} & n \text{ is } \mathit{Start} \\ \bigcap\limits_{p \in pred(n)} \mathit{MustOut}_p & \text{otherwise} \end{cases} \tag{4.17}$$

$$\mathit{MustOut}_n = f_n(\mathit{MustIn}_n, \mathit{MayIn}_n) \tag{4.18}$$

where flow function f_n is defined as follows:

$$f_n(\mathsf{x}_1,\mathsf{x}_2) = (\mathsf{x}_1 - \mathit{Kill}_n(\mathsf{x}_1,\mathsf{x}_2)) \cup \mathit{Gen}_n(\mathsf{x}_1,\mathsf{x}_2) \tag{4.19}$$

In the intraprocedural context, *BI* is $\emptyset$ because no aliases exist at *Start*.

Example 4.15

Recall that the program in Figure 4.10 on page 122 results in a cycle in the data structure because the assignment $*a = a$ in node 4 creates the points-to pair $b \rightarrow b$ in both *may* and *must* points-to analysis. This results in an infinite number of aliases when *Aliases*(b, x) is computed. Hence we perform *may* alias analysis for a simplified version provided in Figure 4.17 on the facing page. The initialization and *BI* for *may* alias analysis is $\emptyset$. For simplicity, we assume

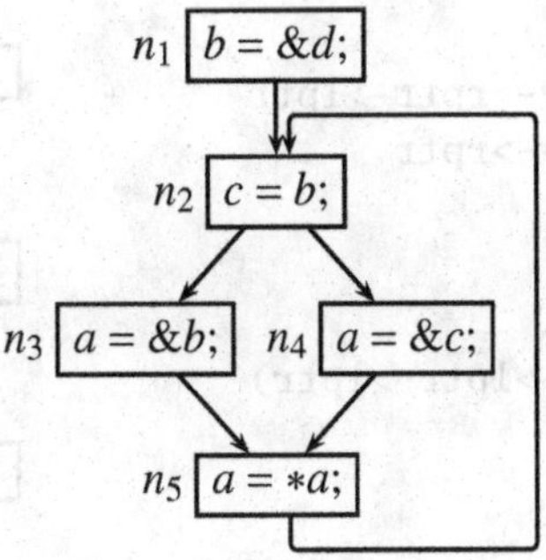

FIGURE 4.17
Example program for alias analysis.

that the *must* alias information is ∅ at each program point; this causes fewer aliases to be killed and hence is a safe approximation for *may* alias analysis.

Node	Iteration #1		Changes in Iteration #2	
	In_n	Out_n	In_n	Out_n
n_2	$\{b \doteq \&d\}$	$\{b \doteq \&d, c \doteq b, c \doteq \&d\}$	$\{b \doteq \&d, c \doteq \&d, c \doteq b, a \doteq c, a \doteq d\}$	
n_3	$\{b \doteq \&d, c \doteq b, c \doteq \&d\}$	$\{b \doteq \&d, c \doteq b, c \doteq \&d, a \doteq \&b, *a \doteq c, *a \doteq \&d\}$		
n_4	$\{b \doteq \&d, c \doteq b, c \doteq \&d\}$	$\{b \doteq \&d, c \doteq b, c \doteq \&d, a \doteq \&c, *a \doteq c, *a \doteq \&d\}$		
n_5	$\{b \doteq \&d, c \doteq b, c \doteq \&d, a \doteq \&c, a \doteq \&b, *a \doteq c, *a \doteq \&d\}$	$\{b \doteq \&d, c \doteq b, c \doteq \&d, a \doteq c, a \doteq d\}$		

Observe that the pairs $*a \doteq c$ and $*a \doteq \&d$ in Out_{n_3} and Out_{n_4} are indirect aliases. All other aliases are direct aliases. □

Similar to points-to analysis, alias analysis is neither fast nor distributive. Example 3.10 in Chapter 3 (Figure 3.10) showed the non-distributivity of *may* alias analysis. We leave it for the reader to construct examples to demonstrate the non-distributivity of *must* alias analysis and non-fastness of *may* and *must* alias analysis.

4.4 Liveness Analysis of Heap Data

The data flow analyses described earlier referred to data objects resident in the stack or the static area. In this section, we describe an analysis for data objects residing

```
     x->succ = y->rptr->lptr
     z->lptr = y->rptr
       ...
p:   ...
       ...
     if (u == z->lptr->lptr)
       ...
```

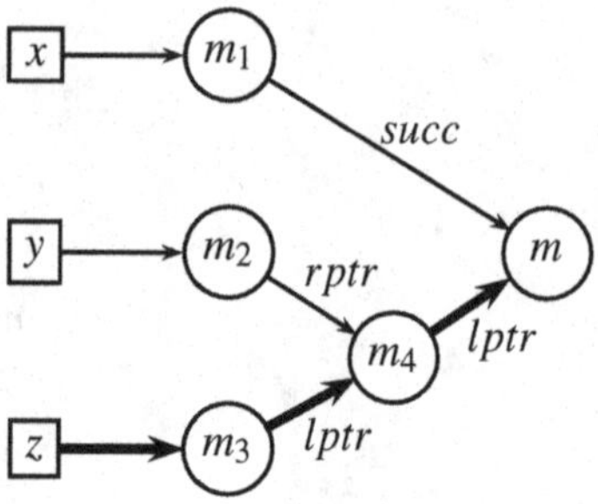

FIGURE 4.18
An example to motivate liveness analysis. The path consisting of thick edges is explicitly live at p.

on the heap. An optimization that requires this analysis was described in Chapter 1. The key idea was to identify heap objects that would not be used in the future, even if they were reachable. Such objects can be freed and the memory space occupied by them can be reused. This optimization brings down the overall memory requirement of the program. If the run time support of the language includes a garbage collector, then the garbage collector can be expected to collect more garbage per collection. Further, if the collector is a copying collector, then the collection itself will be faster since copying collectors process live data only.

To identify the nature of the analysis required for this purpose, consider the example shown in Figure 4.18. The declared variables x, y and z are local or global pointers and accordingly reside in the stack or the static area. We call these *root variables*. The objects pointed to by these variables are on the heap. In this analysis we ignore non-pointer variables. Though our language resembles C, we assume that the programs being analyzed do not make use of the & (address of) operator. Thus root variables cannot point to other root variables. We view the heap at a program point as a directed graph called *memory graph*. The root variables form the entry nodes of the memory graph. Other nodes in the graph correspond to objects on the heap and edges correspond to pointers. The out-edges of entry nodes are labeled by root variable names while out-edges of other nodes are labeled by field names. The edges in the memory graph are called *links*.

Example 4.16

Figure 4.18 shows the memory graph at the program point p. If we can discover that the links $m_4 \rightarrow m$ and $m_1 \rightarrow m$ are never used in any execution path starting from p, then we can free the object m at p by inserting the statements `z->lptr->lptr=NULL` and `x->succ = NULL`. Here, by usage of a link we mean either dereferencing it to access an object or testing it for comparison. In the example shown, the statement `z->lptr->lptr=NULL` cannot be inserted because the link $m_4 \rightarrow m$ is subsequently used by the condition `if (u == z->lptr->rptr)` for comparison. Thus the object m cannot be freed at p. □

In this section, we consider the analysis that discovers whether a link is live i.e., whether it will be used in the sense described above.

4.4.1 Access Expressions and Access Paths

A program accesses data through expressions which have l-values. Such expressions are called *access expressions*. They can be scalar variables such as x, or may involve an array access such as $a[2*i]$, or can be reference expressions such as $*x$ or $y \to rptr \to lptr$. Since we are concerned with analysis of heap-resident data, from now on we shall limit our attention to reference expressions. These are the expressions that are primarily used to access the heap. In Figure 4.18, the access expression $y \to rptr \to lptr$ refers to the heap data denoted as m.

In order to discover liveness and other properties of heap, we need a way of naming links in the memory graph. We do this using access paths. An *access path* ρ_x is a root variable name followed by a sequence of zero or more field names and is denoted by $x \to f_1 \to f_2 \to \cdots \to f_k$. Since an access path represents a path in a memory graph, it can be used for naming links and nodes. An access path consisting of just a root variable name is called a *simple* access path; it represents a path from a root variable to the object pointed to by it. In the context of C, one could think of this as the path followed to access an object using an access expression such as $*x$. $\mathcal{E}$ denotes an empty access path.

The last field name in an access path ρ is called its *frontier* and is denoted by $\textsf{frontier}(\rho)$. The frontier of a simple access path is the root variable name. The access path corresponding to the sequence of names in ρ excluding only its frontier is called its *base* and is denoted by $\textsf{base}(\rho)$. The base of a simple access path is the empty access path $\mathcal{E}$. The object reached by traversing an access path ρ is called the *target* of the access path and is denoted by $\textsf{target}(\rho)$. When we use an access path ρ to refer to a link in a memory graph, it denotes the last link in ρ i.e., the link corresponding to $\textsf{frontier}(\rho)$.

Example 4.17

Consider the access path $\rho_z = z \to lptr \to lptr$ at program point p. $\textsf{target}(\rho_z)$ denotes the node m and $\textsf{frontier}(\rho_z)$ denotes the link $m_4 \to m$. As we have said earlier, access paths are also used to denote links in memory graph. The link denoted by ρ_z is also $m_4 \to m$. $\textsf{base}(\rho_z)$ is the access path $z \to m_3 \to m_4$. □

In the rest of the section, α will denote an access expression, ρ will denote an access path and σ will denote a (possibly empty) sequence of field names separated by $\to$. Let the access expression α_x be $x \to f_1 \to f_2 \ldots \to f_n$. Then, the corresponding access path ρ_x is $x \to f_1 \to f_2 \ldots \to f_n$. When the root variable name is not required, we drop the subscripts from α_x and ρ_x.

We assume that our method does a context insensitive interprocedural analysis. To simplify the description of analysis we assume that the conditions that alter flow of control are made up only of simple variables. If not, the offending reference expression is assigned to a fresh simple variable before the condition and is replaced by the fresh variable in the condition.

The statements that we handle fall in one of the following categories:

- *Function Calls.* These are statements $x = f(\alpha_y, \alpha_z, \ldots)$ where the functions involve access expressions in arguments. The variable x can be a reference or a non-reference variable.

- *Assignment Statements.* These are assignments to references and are denoted by $\alpha_x = \alpha_y$. Only these statements can modify the structure of the heap.

- *Use Statements.* These statements use heap references to access heap data but do not modify heap references. For the purpose of analysis, these statements are abstracted as lists of expressions $\alpha_y.d$ where α_y is an access expression and d is a non-reference.

- *Return Statement* of the type *return* α_x involving reference variable x.

- *Other Statements.* These statements include all statements which do not refer to the heap. We ignore these statements since they do not influence heap reference analysis.

As is customary in static analysis, when we talk about execution paths, we shall refer to a trace of the program that ignores the evaluation of condition checks. For simplicity of exposition, we present the analyses assuming that the program to be analyzed does not create cycles in the heap during execution.

4.4.2 Liveness of Access Paths

A link l is *live* at a program point p if it is used in some control flow path starting from p. As noted earlier, l may be used in two different ways; it may be dereferenced to access an object or tested for comparison. Figure 4.18(b) shows links that are live before program point p by thick arrows. For a link l to be live, there must be at least one access path from some root variable to l such that every link in this path is live. This is the path that is actually traversed while using l.

Since the freeing of nodes is through access paths, we need to express the notion of liveness of links in terms of access paths. An access path is defined to be *live* at p if the link corresponding to its frontier is live along some path starting at p.

We limit ourselves to a subset of live access paths, whose liveness can be determined without taking into account the aliases created before p. These access paths are live solely because of the execution of the program beyond p. We call access paths which are live in this sense as *explicitly live* access paths. An interesting property of explicitly live access paths is that they form the minimal set covering every live link. In this section, we further restrict ourselves to the computation of explicit liveness.

Example 4.18

The access paths z, $z\text{-}\!\!\triangleright lptr$, $z\text{-}\!\!\triangleright lptr\text{-}\!\!\triangleright lptr$ and $y\text{-}\!\!\triangleright rptr\text{-}\!\!\triangleright lptr$ are all live at p. All these paths except $y\text{-}\!\!\triangleright rptr\text{-}\!\!\triangleright lptr$ are also explicitly live. The access path $y\text{-}\!\!\triangleright rptr\text{-}\!\!\triangleright lptr$ is live because of the alias created before p. Also note that if an access path is explicitly live, so are all its prefixes. □

Example 4.19

We illustrate the issues in determining explicit liveness of access paths by considering the assignment $x.r.n = y.n.n$.

- *Killed Access Paths.* Since the assignment modifies $\mathsf{frontier}(x\text{-}\!\!\triangleright r\text{-}\!\!\triangleright n)$, any access path which is live after the assignment and has $x\text{-}\!\!\triangleright r\text{-}\!\!\triangleright n$ as prefix will cease to be live before the assignment. Access paths that are live after the assignment and not killed by it are live before the assignment also.
- *Directly Generated Access Paths.* All prefixes of $x\text{-}\!\!\triangleright r$ and $y\text{-}\!\!\triangleright n$ are explicitly live before the assignment due to the local effect of the assignment.
- *Transferred Access Paths.* If $x\text{-}\!\!\triangleright r\text{-}\!\!\triangleright n\text{-}\!\!\triangleright \sigma$ is live after the assignment, then $y\text{-}\!\!\triangleright n\text{-}\!\!\triangleright n\text{-}\!\!\triangleright \sigma$ will be live before the assignment. For example, if $x\text{-}\!\!\triangleright r\text{-}\!\!\triangleright n\text{-}\!\!\triangleright n$ is live after the assignment, then $y\text{-}\!\!\triangleright n\text{-}\!\!\triangleright n\text{-}\!\!\triangleright n$ will be live before the assignment. The sequence of field names σ is viewed as being *transferred* from $x\text{-}\!\!\triangleright r\text{-}\!\!\triangleright n$ to $y\text{-}\!\!\triangleright n\text{-}\!\!\triangleright n$.

□

We now define liveness by generalizing the above observations. We use the notation $\rho_x\text{-}\!\!\triangleright *$ to enumerate all access paths which have ρ_x as a prefix. The summary liveness information for a set S of access paths is defined as follows:

$$\mathit{summary}(S) = \bigcup_{\rho \in S} \{\rho\text{-}\!\!\triangleright *\}$$

Further, the set of all global variables is denoted by $\mathsf{Globals}$ and the set of formal parameters of the function being analyzed is denoted by Params.

DEFINITION 4.10 *The set of explicitly live access paths at a program point p, denoted by* $\mathsf{liveness}_p$ *is defined as follows.*

$$\mathit{liveness}_p = \bigcup_{\psi \in paths(p)} (\mathit{pathLiveness}_p^{\psi})$$

```
0.    w = x
1.    while (x->data < max)
2.    {
3.       x = x->rptr
4.    }
5.    y = x->lptr
6.    z = malloc(...)
7.    y = y->lptr
8.    z->sum = x->lptr->data
            + y->data
```

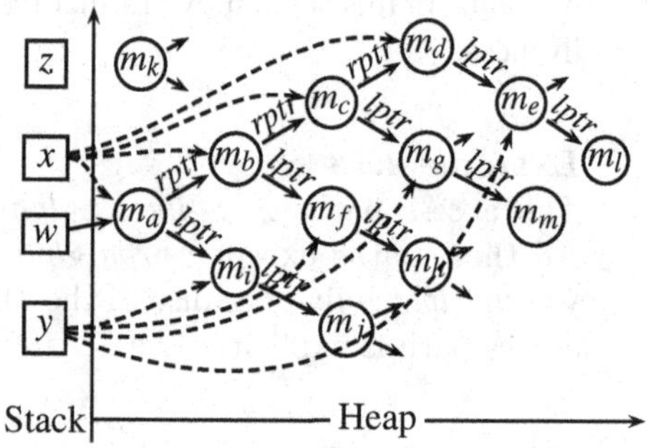

FIGURE 4.19
An example program and possible memory graphs before line 6. Depending on whether the *while* loop is iterated 0, 1, 2, or 3 times, x will point to m_a, m_b, m_c, or m_d. Accordingly y will point to m_i, m_f, m_g, or m_e.

where, $\psi \in paths(p)$ is a control flow path p to Start *and* $\text{pathLiveness}_p^\psi$ *denotes the liveness at p along ψ and is defined as follows. If p is not program exit then let the statement which follows it be denoted by s and the program point immediately following s be denoted by p'. Then,*

$$\text{pathLiveness}_p^\psi = \begin{cases} \emptyset & p = \text{Exit}(main) \\ \text{summary}(\text{Globals}) & p = \text{Exit}(f),\ f \neq main \\ \text{statementLiveness}_s(\text{pathLiveness}_{p'}^\psi) & otherwise \end{cases}$$

where the flow function for s is defined as follows:

$$\text{statementLiveness}_s(X) = (X - \text{LKill}_s) \cup \text{LDirect}_s \cup \text{LTransfer}_s(X)$$

LKill_s *denotes the sets of access paths which cease to be live before statement s,* LDirect_s *denotes the set of access paths which become live due to local effect of s and* $\text{LTransfer}_s(X)$ *denotes the set of access paths which become live before s due to transfer of liveness from live access paths after s. They are defined in Figure 4.20.*

Observe that the definitions of LKill_s, LDirect_s, and LTransfer_s ensure that the liveness_p is prefix-closed.

When we view the above definition in terms of the constant and dependent parts of flow functions as defined in Section 4.1, it is clear that LKill_s represents DepKill_s and ConstKill_s is $\emptyset$. Liveness information is generated by LDirect_s which represents ConstGen_s and LTransfer_s which represents DepGen_s.

Example 4.20
In Figure 4.19, it cannot be statically determined which link is represented by

Statement s	LKill_s	$\mathit{LDirect}_s$	$\mathit{LTransfer}_s(X)$
$\alpha_x = \alpha_y$	$\{\rho_x \rightarrow *\}$	$\mathit{prefixes}(\mathit{base}(\rho_x)) \cup \mathit{prefixes}(\mathit{base}(\rho_y))$	$\{\rho_y \rightarrow \sigma \mid \rho_x \rightarrow \sigma \in X\}$
$\alpha_x = f(\alpha_y)$	$\{\rho_x \rightarrow *\}$	$\mathit{prefixes}(\mathit{base}(\rho_x)) \cup \mathit{prefixes}(\mathit{base}(\rho_y)) \cup \mathit{summary}(\{\rho_y\} \cup \mathit{Globals})$	$\emptyset$
$\alpha_x = \mathit{new}$	$\{\rho_x \rightarrow *\}$	$\mathit{prefixes}(\mathit{base}(\rho_x))$	$\emptyset$
$\alpha_x = \mathit{null}$	$\{\rho_x \rightarrow *\}$	$\mathit{prefixes}(\mathit{base}(\rho_x))$	$\emptyset$
Use $\alpha_y.d$	$\emptyset$	$\mathit{prefixes}(\rho_y)$	$\emptyset$
return α_y	$\emptyset$	$\mathit{prefixes}(\mathit{base}(\rho_y)) \cup \mathit{summary}(\{\rho_y\})$	$\emptyset$
other	$\emptyset$	$\emptyset$	$\emptyset$

FIGURE 4.20
Defining flow functions for liveness. *Globals* denotes the set of global references and *Params* denotes the set of formal parameters. For simplicity, we have shown a single access expression on the RHS.

access expression *x.lptr* at line 5. Depending upon the number of iterations of the while loop, it may be any of the links represented by thick arrows. Thus at line 0, we have to assume that all access paths {*x*→*lptr*→*lptr*, *x*→*rptr*→*lptr*→*lptr*, *x*→*rptr*→*rptr*→*lptr*→*lptr*, ...} are explicitly live. □

4.4.3 Representing Sets of Access Paths by Access Graphs

In the presence of loops, the set of access paths may be infinite and the lengths of access paths may be unbounded. If the algorithm for analysis tries to compute sets of access paths explicitly, termination cannot be guaranteed. We solve this problem by representing a set of access paths by a graph of bounded size. The structure that we use for the representation is called an access graph.

An *access graph*, denoted by G_v, is a directed graph $\langle n_0, N, E\rangle$ representing a set of access paths starting from a root variable v.† N is the set of nodes, $n_0 \in N_F$ is the entry node with no in-edges and E is the set of edges. Every path in the graph represents an access path. The *empty graph* $\mathcal{E}_G$ has no nodes or edges and does not accept any access path.

The entry node of an access graph is labeled with the name of the root variable while the non-entry nodes are labeled with a unique label created as follows: If a field name f is referenced in basic block b, we create an access graph node with a label $\langle f, b, i\rangle$ where i is the instance number used for distinguishing multiple occurrences of the field name f in block b. Note that this implies that the nodes with the same

†Where the root variable name is not required, we drop the subscript v from G_v.

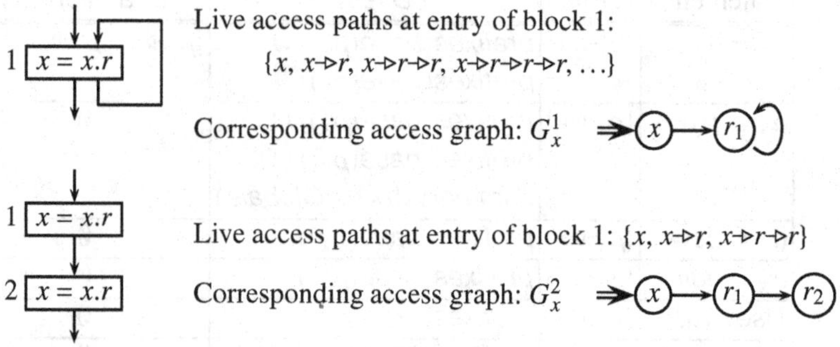

FIGURE 4.21
Approximations in access graphs.

label are treated as being identical. Often, i is 0 and in such a case we denote the label $\langle f, b, 0\rangle$ by f_b for brevity.

A node in the access graph represents one or more links in the memory graph. Additionally, during analysis, it represents a state of access graph construction (explained in Section 4.4.3). An edge $f_n \rightarrow g_m$ in an access graph at program point p indicates that a link corresponding to field f dereferenced in block n may be used to dereference a link corresponding to field g in block m on some path starting at p. This has been used in Section 4.4.4 to argue that the size of access graphs in practical programs is small.

Pictorially, the entry node of an access graph is indicated by an incoming double arrow.

Summarization

Recall that a link is live at a program point p if it is used along some control flow path from p to *Start*. Since different access paths may be live along different control flow paths and there may be infinitely many control flow paths in the case of a loop following p, there may be infinitely many access paths which are live at p. Hence, the lengths of access paths will be unbounded. In such a case summarization is required.

Summarization is achieved by merging appropriate nodes in access graphs, retaining all in and out edges of merged nodes. We explain merging with the help of Figure 4.21:

- Node r_1 in access graph G_x^1 indicates references of n at *different execution instances of the same* program point. Every time this program point is visited during analysis, the same state is reached in that the pattern of references after r_1 is repeated. Thus all occurrences of r_1 are merged into a single state. This creates a cycle which captures the repeating pattern of references.

- In G_x^2, nodes r_1 and r_2 indicate referencing n at *different* program points. Since the references made after these program points may be different, r_1 and r_2 are not merged.

Summarization captures the pattern of heap traversal in the most straightforward way. Traversing a path in the heap requires the presence of reference assignments $\alpha_x = \alpha_y$ such that ρ_x is a proper prefix of ρ_y. Assignments in Figure 4.21 are examples of such assignments. The structure of the flow of control between such assignments in a program determines the pattern of heap traversal. Summarization captures this pattern without the need of control flow analysis and the resulting structure is reflected in the access graphs as can be seen in Figure 4.21. More examples of the resemblance of program structure and access graph structure can be seen in the access graphs in Figure 4.24.

Operations on Access Graphs

Section 4.4.2 defined liveness by applying certain operations on access paths. In this subsection we define the corresponding operations on access graphs. Unless specified otherwise, the binary operations are applied only to access graphs having same root variable. The auxiliary operations and associated notations are:

- *root*(ρ) denotes the root variable of access path ρ, while *root*(G) denotes the root variable of access graph G.

- *field*(n) for a node n denotes the field name component of the label of n.

- *makeGraph*(ρ) constructs access graphs corresponding to ρ. It uses the current basic block number and the field names to create appropriate labels for nodes. The instance number depends on the number of occurrences of a field name in the block. *makeGraph*($\rho$$\rightarrow$$*$) creates an access graph for ρ and connects the final node of the access graph to a special node $n_\star$ called summary node. In addition, there is a self loop over $n_\star$. Both the new edges are assumed to have all field names as labels.

- *lastNode*(G) returns the last node of a *linear graph* G constructed from a given access path ρ.

- *cleanUp*(G) deletes the nodes which are not reachable from the entry node.

- *CN*(G, G', S) computes the set of nodes of G which correspond to the nodes of G' specified in the set S. To compute *CN*(G, G', S), we define *ACN*(G, G'), the set of pairs of *all corresponding nodes*. Let $G \equiv \langle n_0, N, E\rangle$ and $G' \equiv \langle n'_0, N', E'\rangle$. A node n in access graph G corresponds to a node n' in access graph G' if there exists an access path ρ which is represented by a path from n_0 to n in G and a path from n'_0 to n' in G'.

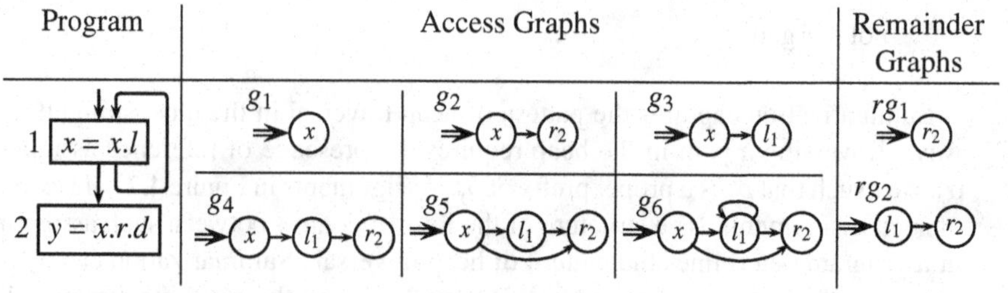

Union	Path Removal	Factorization	Extension
$g_3 \uplus g_4 = g_4$	$g_6 \ominus x \rightarrow l = g_2$	$g_2/(g_1,\{x\}) = \{rg_1\}$	$(g_3,\{l_1\})\#\{rg_1\} = g_4$
$g_2 \uplus g_4 = g_5$	$g_5 \ominus x = \mathcal{E}_G$	$g_5/(g_1,\{x\}) = \{rg_1, rg_2\}$	$(g_3,\{x,l_1\})\#\{rg_1,rg_2\} = g_6$
$g_5 \uplus g_4 = g_5$	$g_4 \ominus x \rightarrow r = g_4$	$g_5/(g_2,\{r_2\}) = \{\epsilon_{RG}\}$	$(g_2,\{r_2\})\#\{\epsilon_{RG}\} = g_2$
$g_5 \uplus g_6 = g_6$	$g_4 \ominus x \rightarrow l = g_1$	$g_4/(g_2,\{r_2\}) = \emptyset$	$(g_2,\{r_2\})\#\emptyset = \mathcal{E}_G$

FIGURE 4.22
Examples of operations on access graphs.

Formally, $\mathsf{ACN}(G,G')$ is the least solution of the following equation:

$$\mathsf{ACN}(G,G') = \begin{cases} \emptyset & \mathsf{root}(G) \neq \mathsf{root}(G') \\ \{\langle n_0, n'_0 \rangle\} \cup \{\langle n_j, n'_j \rangle \mid & \text{otherwise} \\ \quad \mathsf{field}(n_j) = \mathsf{field}(n'_j), & \\ \quad n_i \rightarrow n_j \in E, n'_i \rightarrow n'_j \in E', & \\ \quad \langle n_i, n'_i \rangle \in \mathsf{ACN}(G,G')\} & \end{cases}$$

$$\mathsf{CN}(G,G',S) = \{n \mid \langle n,n' \rangle \in \mathsf{ACN}(G,G'),\ n' \in S\}$$

Note that $\mathsf{field}(n_j) = \mathsf{field}(n'_j)$ would hold even when n_j or n'_j is the summary node $n_\star$.

Let $G \equiv \langle n_0, N, E \rangle$ and $G' \equiv \langle n_0, N', E' \rangle$ be access graphs (having the same entry node). G and G' are equal if $N = N'$ and $E = E'$.

The main operations of interest are defined below and are illustrated in Figure 4.22.

1. *Union* ($\uplus$). $G \uplus G'$ combines access graphs G and G' such that any access path contained in G or G' is contained in the resulting graph.

$$G \uplus G' = \langle n_0, N \cup N', E \cup E' \rangle$$

The operation $N \cup N'$ treats the nodes with the same label as identical. Because of associativity, $\uplus$ can be generalized to arbitrary number of arguments in an obvious manner.

2. *Path Removal* ($\ominus$). The operation $G \ominus \rho$ removes those access paths in G which have ρ as a prefix.

$$G \ominus \rho = \begin{cases} G & \rho = \mathcal{E} \text{ or } \mathsf{root}(\rho) \neq \mathsf{root}(G) \\ \mathcal{E}_G & \rho \text{ is a simple access path} \\ \mathsf{cleanUp}(\langle n_0, N, E - E_{del} \rangle) & \textit{otherwise} \end{cases}$$

where

$$E_{del} = \{n_i \rightarrow n_j \mid n_i \rightarrow n_j \in E, n_i \in \mathsf{CN}(G, G_B, \{\mathsf{lastNode}(G_B)\}), \\ \mathsf{field}(n_j) = \mathsf{frontier}(\rho), G_B = \mathsf{makeGraph}(\mathsf{base}(\rho)), \\ \mathsf{uniqueAccessPath?}(G, n_i)\}$$

$\mathsf{uniqueAccessPath?}(G, n)$ returns true if in G, all paths from the entry node to node n represent the same access path. Note that path removal is conservative in that some paths having ρ as prefix may not be removed. Since an access graph edge may be contained in more than one access path, we have to ensure that access paths which do not have ρ as prefix are not erroneously deleted.

3. *Factorization* (/). Recall that the $\mathsf{LTransfer}$ term in Definition 4.10 requires extracting suffixes of access paths and attaching them to some other access paths. The corresponding operations on access graphs are performed using factorization and extension. Given a node $m \in (N - \{n_0\})$ of an access graph G, the *Remainder Graph* of G at m is the subgraph of G rooted at m and is denoted by $\mathsf{RG}(G, m)$. If m does not have any outgoing edges, then the result is the empty remainder graph ϵ_{RG}. Let M be a subset of the nodes of G' and M' be the set of corresponding nodes in G. Then, $G/(G', M)$ computes the set of remainder graphs of the successors of nodes in M'.

$$G/(G', M) = \{\mathsf{RG}(G, n_j) \mid n_i \rightarrow n_j \in E, n_i \in \mathsf{CN}(G, G', M)\} \qquad (4.20)$$

A remainder graph is similar to an access graph except that (a) its entry node does not correspond to a root variable but to a field name and (b) the entry node can have incoming edges.

4. *Extension*. Extending an empty access graph $\mathcal{E}_G$ results in the empty access graph $\mathcal{E}_G$. For non-empty graphs, this operation is defined as follows.

   (a) *Extension with a remainder graph* ($\cdot$). Let M be a subset of the nodes of G and $R \equiv \langle n', N^R, E^R \rangle$ be a remainder graph. Then, $(G, M) \cdot R$ appends the suffixes in R to the access paths ending on nodes in M.

$$(G, M) \cdot \epsilon_{\mathsf{RG}} = G \\ (G, M) \cdot R = \left\langle n_0, N \cup N^R, E \cup E^R \cup \{n_i \rightarrow n' \mid n_i \in M\} \right\rangle \qquad (4.21)$$

Operation	Access Graphs	Access Paths
Union	$G_3 = G_1 \uplus G_2$	$P(G_3, M_3) \supseteq P(G_1, M_1) \cup P(G_2, M_2)$
Path Removal	$G_2 = G_1 \ominus \rho$	$P(G_2, M_2) \supseteq P(G_1, M_1) - \{\rho \rightarrow \sigma \mid \rho \rightarrow \sigma \in P(G_1, M_1)\}$
Factorization	$S = G_1/(G_2, M)$	$P(S, M_s) = \{\sigma \mid \rho' \rightarrow \sigma \in P(G_1, M_1),\ \rho' \in P(G_2, M)\}$
Extension	$G_2 = (G_1, M)\#S$	$P(G_2, M_2) \supseteq P(G_1, M_1) \cup \{\rho \rightarrow \sigma \mid \rho \in P(G_1, M),\ \sigma \in P(S, M_s)\}$

FIGURE 4.23
Safety of access graph operations. $P(G, M)$ is the set of paths in graph G terminating on nodes in M. For graph G_i, M_i is the set of all nodes in G_i. S is the set of remainder graphs and $P(S, M_s)$ is the set of all paths in all remainder graphs in S.

(b) *Extension with a set of remainder graphs* (#). Let S be a set of remainder graphs. Then, $G\#S$ extends access graph G with every graph in S.

$$
\begin{aligned}
(G, M)\#\emptyset &= \mathcal{E}_G \\
(G, M)\#S &= \biguplus_{R \in S} (G, M) \cdot R
\end{aligned}
\tag{4.22}
$$

Safety of Access Graph Operations

Since access graphs are not exact representations of sets of access paths, the safety of approximations needs to be defined explicitly. The constraints defined in Figure 4.23 capture safety in the context of liveness in the following sense: Every access path which can possibly be live should be retained by each operation. Since the complement of liveness is used to free heap data by nullifying links, this ensures that no live access path is considered for nullification.

4.4.4 Data Flow Analysis for Explicit Liveness

For a given root variable v, $\mathit{ELIn}_v(i)$ and $\mathit{ELOut}_v(i)$ denote the access graphs representing explicitly live access paths at the entry and exit of basic block i. We use $\mathcal{E}_G$ as the initial value for $\mathit{ELIn}_v(i)/\mathit{ELOut}_v(i)$.

$$
\mathit{ELIn}_v(i) = (\mathit{ELOut}_v(i) \ominus \mathit{ELKillPath}_v(i)) \uplus \mathit{ELGen}_v(i) \tag{4.23}
$$

$$
\mathit{ELOut}_v(i) = \begin{cases} \mathit{makeGraph}(v \rightarrow *) & i = \mathit{Start},\ v \in \mathit{Globals} \\ \mathcal{E}_G & i = \mathit{Start},\ v \notin \mathit{Globals} \\ \biguplus_{s \in succ(i)} \mathit{ELIn}_v(s) & \text{otherwise} \end{cases} \tag{4.24}
$$

where

$$\textsf{ELGen}_v(i) = \textsf{LDirect}_v(i) \uplus \textsf{LTransfer}_v(i)$$

The term $\textsf{LDirect}_v(i)$ represents the $\textsf{ConstGen}_i$ component for variable v whereas $\textsf{LTransfer}_v(i)$ represents the $\textsf{DepGen}_i$ component for v. Liveness information is killed using path removal which is implemented by deleting an edge in an access graph. In our case, this edge is $\textsf{frontier}(\rho_x)$ where ρ_x denotes the access path representing the access expression appearing on the left hand side of an assignment. Hence $\textsf{ELKillPath}_v(i)$ represents $\textsf{ConstGen}_i$. This is unlike $\textsf{LKill}_s$ (Definition 4.10 on page 139) which represents $\textsf{DepKill}_s$ rather than $\textsf{ConstKill}_s$. This is because $\textsf{LKill}_s$ is not a fixed set but depends on the liveness information that holds after statement s.

The definitions of $\textsf{ELKillPath}_v(i)$, $\textsf{LDirect}_v(i)$, and $\textsf{LTransfer}_v(i)$ depend on statement i as follows:

1. *Assignment statement* $\alpha_x = \alpha_y$. Apart from defining the desired terms for x and y, we also need to define them for any other variable z. In the following equations, G_x and G_y denote $\textsf{makeGraph}(\rho_x)$ and $\textsf{makeGraph}(\rho_y)$ respectively, whereas M_x denotes $\textsf{lastNode}(\textsf{makeGraph}(\rho_x))$ and M_y denotes $\textsf{lastNode}(\textsf{makeGraph}(\rho_y))$.

$$\begin{aligned}
\textsf{LDirect}_x(i) &= \textsf{makeGraph}(\textsf{base}(\rho_x))\\
\textsf{LDirect}_y(i) &= \begin{cases}\mathcal{E}_G & \alpha_y \text{ is } \textit{New} \ldots \text{ or } \textsf{null}\\ \textsf{makeGraph}(\textsf{base}(\rho_y)) & \text{otherwise}\end{cases}\\
\textsf{LDirect}_z(i) &= \mathcal{E}_G, \text{for any variable } z \text{ other than } x \text{ and } y\\
\textsf{LTransfer}_y(i) &= \begin{cases}\mathcal{E}_G & \alpha_y \text{ is } \textit{New} \text{ or } \textsf{null}\\ (G_y, M_y)\# & \text{otherwise}\\ \quad (\textsf{ELOut}_x(i)/(G_x, M_x)) & \end{cases}\\
\textsf{LTransfer}_z(i) &= \mathcal{E}_G, \text{ for any variable } z \text{ other than } y\\
\textsf{ELKillPath}_x(i) &= \rho_x\\
\textsf{ELKillPath}_z(i) &= \mathcal{E}, \text{ for any variable } z \text{ other than } x
\end{aligned} \tag{4.25}$$

As stated earlier, the path removal operation deletes an edge only if it is contained in a unique path. Thus fewer paths may be killed than desired. This is a safe approximation. Another approximation which is also safe is that only the paths rooted at x are killed. Since assignment to α_x changes the link represented by $\textsf{frontier}(\rho_x)$, for precision, any path which is guaranteed to contain the link represented by $\textsf{frontier}(\rho_x)$ should also be killed. Such paths can be discovered through *must*-alias analysis.

2. *Function call* $\alpha_x = f(\alpha_y)$. We conservatively assume that a function call may make any access path rooted at y or any global reference variable live. Thus

Statement i	ELOut(i)	ELIn(i)
7		$\Rightarrow$(x)$\rightarrow$(l7) $\Rightarrow$(y) $\Rightarrow$(z)
6	$\Rightarrow$(x)$\rightarrow$(l7) $\Rightarrow$(y) $\Rightarrow$(z)	$\Rightarrow$(x)$\rightarrow$(l7) $\Rightarrow$(y)$\rightarrow$(l6) $\Rightarrow$(z)
5	$\Rightarrow$(x)$\rightarrow$(l7) $\Rightarrow$(y)$\rightarrow$(l6) $\Rightarrow$(z)	$\Rightarrow$(x)$\rightarrow$(l7) $\Rightarrow$(y)$\rightarrow$(l6)
4	$\Rightarrow$(x)$\rightarrow$(l7) $\Rightarrow$(y)$\rightarrow$(l6)	$\Rightarrow$(x) $\rightarrow$ (l7); $\rightarrow$ (l4)$\rightarrow$(l6)
3	$\Rightarrow$(x)$\rightarrow$(r3) $\rightarrow$ (l7) loop; (l4)$\rightarrow$(l6)	$\Rightarrow$(x)$\rightarrow$(r3) $\rightarrow$ (l7); (l4)$\rightarrow$(l6)
2	$\Rightarrow$(x)$\rightarrow$(r3) $\rightarrow$ (l7) loop; (l4)$\rightarrow$(l6)	$\Rightarrow$(x)$\rightarrow$(r3) $\rightarrow$ (l7) loop; (l4)$\rightarrow$(l6)
1	$\Rightarrow$(x)$\rightarrow$(r3) $\rightarrow$ (l7) loop; (l4)$\rightarrow$(l6)	$\Rightarrow$(x)$\rightarrow$(r3) $\rightarrow$ (l7) loop; (l4)$\rightarrow$(l6)

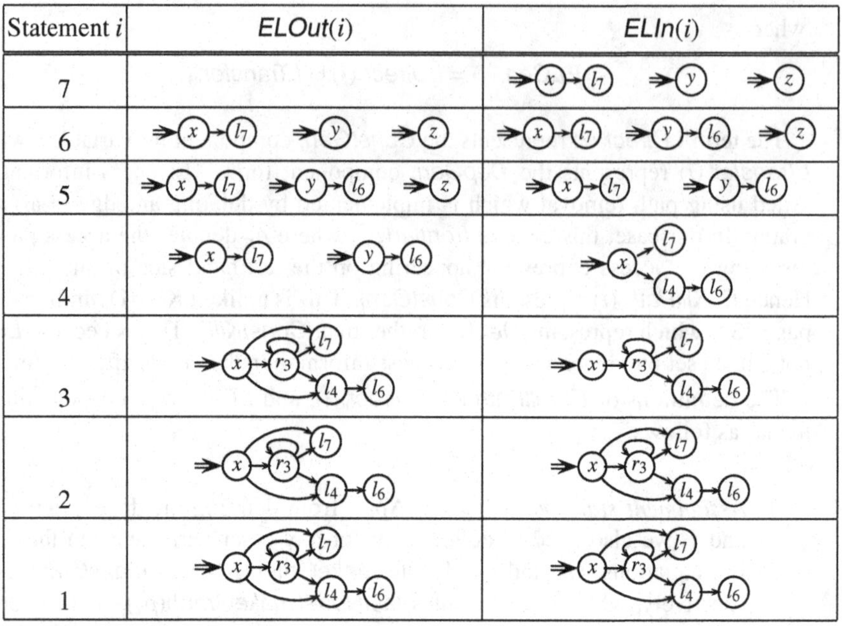

FIGURE 4.24

Explicit liveness for the program in Figure 4.19 on page 140 under the assumption that all variables are local variables.

this version of our analysis is context insensitive.

$$LDirect_x(i) = makeGraph(base(\rho_x))$$

$$LDirect_y(i) = makeGraph(base(\rho_y)) \uplus makeGraph(\rho_y\text{-}\triangleright*)$$

$$LDirect_z(i) = \begin{cases} makeGraph(z\text{-}\triangleright*) & \text{if } z \text{ is a global variable} \\ \mathcal{E}_G & \text{otherwise} \end{cases}$$

$$LTransfer_z(i) = \mathcal{E}_G, \text{ for all variables } z$$

$$ELKillPath_x(i) = \rho_x$$

$$ELKillPath_z(i) = \mathcal{E}, \text{ for any variable } z \text{ other than } x$$

3. *Return Statement* return α_x.

$$LDirect_x(i) = prefixes(base(\rho_x)) \cup makeGraph(\rho_x\text{-}\triangleright*)$$

$$LDirect_z(i) = \begin{cases} makeGraph(z\text{-}\triangleright*) & \text{if } z \text{ is a global variable} \\ \mathcal{E}_G & \text{otherwise} \end{cases}$$

$$LTransfer_z(i) = \mathcal{E}_G, \text{ for any variable } z$$

$$ELKillPath_z(i) = \mathcal{E}, \text{ for any variable } z$$

4. *Use Statements*

$$\begin{aligned}
\textsf{LDirect}_x(i) &= \biguplus \textsf{makeGraph}(\rho_x) \text{ for every } \alpha_x.d \text{ used in } i\\
\textsf{LDirect}_z(i) &= \mathcal{E}_G \text{ for any variable } z \text{ other than } x\\
\textsf{LTransfer}_z(i) &= \mathcal{E}_G, \text{ for every variable } z\\
\textsf{ELKillPath}_z(i) &= \mathcal{E}, \text{ for every variable } z
\end{aligned}$$

Example 4.21

Figure 4.24 lists explicit liveness information at different points of the program in Figure 4.19 on page 140 under the assumption that all variables are local variables. □

Observe that computing liveness using Equations (4.23) and (4.24) results in an *MFP* solution of data flow analysis whereas Definition 4.10 specifies an *MOP* solution of data flow analysis. Since the flow functions are non-distributive, the two solutions may be different.

Convergence of Explicit Liveness Analysis

We now show the termination of explicit liveness analysis using the properties of access graph operations. In particular, we show that the flow functions are monotonic and the data flow values form a finite complete lattice.

For a program there are a finite number of basic blocks, a finite number of fields for any root variable, and a finite number of field names in any access expression. Hence the number of access graphs for a program is finite. Further, the number of nodes and hence the size of each access graph, is bounded by the number of labels which can be created for a program.

Access graphs for a variable x form a complete lattice with a partial order $\sqsubseteq_G$ induced by $\uplus$. Note that $\uplus$ is commutative, idempotent, and associative. Let $G = \langle x, N_F, N_I, E\rangle$ and $G' = \langle x, N'_F, N'_I, E'\rangle$ where subscripts F and I distinguish between the final and intermediate nodes. The partial order $\sqsubseteq_G$ is defined as

$$G \sqsubseteq_G G' \Leftrightarrow \left(N'_F \subseteq N_F\right) \wedge \left(N'_I \subseteq (N_F \cup N_I)\right) \wedge (E' \subseteq E)$$

Clearly, $G \sqsubseteq_G G'$ implies that G contains all access paths of G'. We extend $\sqsubseteq_G$ to a set of access graphs as follows:

$$S_1 \sqsubseteq_S S_2 \Leftrightarrow \forall G_2 \in S_2, \exists G_1 \in S_1 \text{ s.t. } G_1 \sqsubseteq_G G_2$$

It is easy to verify that $\sqsubseteq_G$ is reflexive, transitive, and antisymmetric. For a given variable x, the access graph $\mathcal{E}_G$ forms the $\top$ element of the lattice while the $\bot$ element is a greatest lower bound of all access graphs.

The partial order over access graphs and their sets can be carried over unaltered to remainder graphs ($\sqsubseteq_{RG}$) and their sets ($\sqsubseteq_{RS}$), with the added condition that ϵ_{RG} is incomparable to any other non empty remainder graph.

Operation	Monotonicity
Union	$G_1 \sqsubseteq_G G'_1 \wedge G_2 \sqsubseteq_G G'_2 \Rightarrow G_1 \uplus G_2 \sqsubseteq_G G'_1 \uplus G'_2$
Path Removal	$G_1 \sqsubseteq_G G_2 \Rightarrow G_1 \ominus \rho \sqsubseteq_G G_2 \ominus \rho$
Factorization	$G_1 \sqsubseteq_G G_2 \Rightarrow G_1/(G,M) \sqsubseteq_{RS} G_2/(G,M)$
Extension	$RS_1 \sqsubseteq_{RS} RS_2 \wedge G_1 \sqsubseteq_G G_2 \wedge M_1 \subseteq M_2 \Rightarrow (G_1, M_1)\#RS_1 \sqsubseteq_G (G_2, M_2)\#RS_2$
Link-Alias Closure	$G_1 \sqsubseteq_G G'_1 \wedge G_2 \sqsubseteq_G G'_2 \Rightarrow \mathit{LnG}(G_1, G_2, \langle g_x, g_y\rangle) \sqsubseteq_S \mathit{LnG}(G'_1, G'_2, \langle g_x, g_y\rangle)$

FIGURE 4.25
Monotonicity of access graph operations.

Access graph operations are monotonic as described in Figure 4.25. Path removal is monotonic in the first argument but not in the second argument. Similarly factorization is monotonic in the first argument but not in the second and the third argument. However, we show that in each context where they are used, the resulting functions are monotonic:

1. Path removal is used only for an assignment $\alpha_x = \alpha_y$. It is used in liveness analysis and its second argument is ρ_x which is constant for any assignment statement $\alpha_x = \alpha_y$. Thus the resulting flow functions are monotonic.

2. Factorization is used during liveness analysis. It is used for the flow function corresponding to an assignment $\alpha_x = \alpha_y$. In this context, its second and third arguments are $\mathit{makeGraph}(\rho_x)$ and $\mathit{lastNode}(\mathit{makeGraph}(\rho_x))$. Both these are constants for a given assignment statement $\alpha_x = \alpha_y$. Thus, the resulting flow functions are monotonic.

Thus we conclude that all flow functions are monotonic. Since lattices are finite, termination of explicit liveness analysis follows.

Efficiency of Explicit Liveness Analysis

This section discusses the issues which influence the efficiency of performing explicit liveness analysis.

The data flow frameworks defined in this paper are not *separable* [59] because the data flow information of a variable depends on the data flow information of other variables. Thus the number of iterations over control flow graph is not bounded by the depth of the graph [3, 44, 59] but would also depend on the number of root variables that depend on each other.

The amount of work done in each iteration is not fixed but depends on the size of access graphs. Of all operations performed in an iteration, only $\mathit{CFN}(G, G')$ is costly. In practice, the access graphs are quite small because of the following reason: Recall that edges in access graphs capture dependence of a reference made at one program point on some other reference made at another point (Section 4.4.3). In real programs, traversals involving long dependences are performed using iterative constructs in the program. In such situations, the length of the chain of dependences is limited by the process of summarization because summarization treats nodes with the same label as being identical. Thus, in real programs chains of such dependences, and hence the access graphs, are quite small in size. Hence the complexities of access graph operations is not a matter of concern.

4.4.5 The Motivating Example Revisited

For our motivating example in Section 1.1, we had performed liveness analysis of heap data intuitively. The liveness information was represented using access paths which were summarized by combining all field names beyond the second field by a summary field "⋆". We now present the result of liveness analysis of the program in Figure 1.1 on page 2 in terms of access graphs.

Intraprocedural Analysis by Ignoring the Interprocedural Effects

In this case we treat a function call as a statement that reads its actual parameters and assume that *BI* is $\mathcal{E}_G$.

Node	Out_n	In_n
n_6	$\mathcal{E}_G$	⇒n
n_5	⇒n ⇒next→sib↺	⇒n ⇒next→sib↺
n_4	⇒n ⇒next→sib↺	⇒n ⇒succ→sib↺
n_3	⇒n ⇒succ→sib↺	⇒n ⇒succ→sib↺
n_2	⇒n ⇒succ→sib↺	⇒n ⇒succ→sib↺
n_1	⇒n ⇒succ→sib↺	⇒n→child→sib↺

When we compare these results with the corresponding liveness information computed in Section 1.1.2, we observe that the above access graphs do not include access paths such as *succ→child→sib* or *succ→sib→child* whereas they are included in the liveness information computed in Section 1.1.2. This difference arises because of the difference between the summarization of access paths using access graphs and the summarization by restricting the lengths of access paths.

Intraprocedural Analysis with Conservative Interprocedural Approximation

As described earlier, the effect of the function call in our example can be incorporated conservatively by assuming that every access path rooted at n is live at the exit of `dfTraverse` and that every access path rooted at `succ` is live at the entry of n_3 due to the call. We use the special summary node $n_\star$ defined for access graph to denote any field name. Thus we assume that the function call creates the access graph → succ → $n_\star$ ↺ and *BI* is → n → $n_\star$ ↺. With these assumptions, the data flow information after first iteration is:

Node	Iteration #1	
	Out_n	In_n
n_6	→ n → $n_\star$ ↺	→ n → $n_\star$ ↺
n_5	$\mathcal{E}_G$	$\mathcal{E}_G$
n_4	$\mathcal{E}_G$	$\mathcal{E}_G$
n_3	$\mathcal{E}_G$	→ succ → $n_\star$ ↺
n_2	→ n → $n_\star$ ↺ → succ → $n_\star$ ↺	→ n → $n_\star$ ↺ → succ → $n_\star$ ↺
n_1	→ n → $n_\star$ ↺ → succ → $n_\star$ ↺	→ n → $n_\star$ ↺

If there is an edge $n \rightarrow n_\star$, then n cannot have any other out edge because all its successors are consumed by $n_\star$. The data flow values after second iteration are:

Node	Changes in Iteration #2	
	Out_n	In_n
n_6		
n_5	→ n → $n_\star$ ↺ → succ → $n_\star$ ↺	→ n → $n_\star$ ↺ → next → $n_\star$ ↺
n_4	→ n → $n_\star$ ↺ → next → $n_\star$ ↺	→ n → $n_\star$ ↺ → succ → sib → $n_\star$ ↺
n_3	→ n → $n_\star$ ↺ → succ → sib → $n_\star$ ↺	
n_2		
n_1		

There are no further changes. Observe that the values of In_{n_4} and Out_{n_3} are more precise than those in Section 1.1.2. This is because unlike the earlier summarization, access graphs do not restrict the length of access paths to two.

Interprocedural analysis of this example is presented in Section 9.5.

4.5 Modeling Entity Dependence

Recall that a component function $\widehat{f}^{\,\alpha} : L \mapsto \widehat{L}$ computes the data flow value of entity α. The domain of $\widehat{f}^{\,\alpha}$ is not atomic reflecting the fact that the data flow value of α

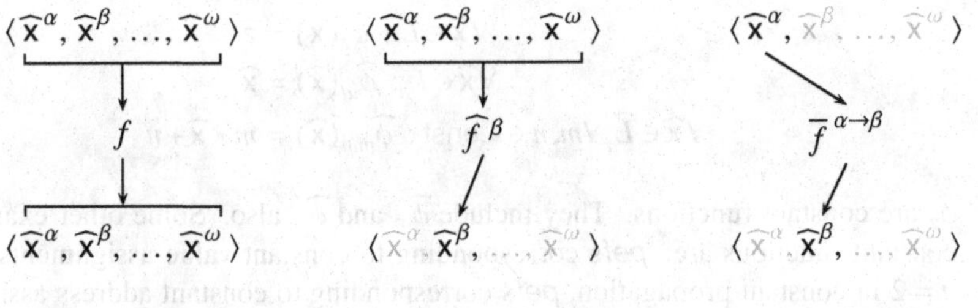

FIGURE 4.26
Defining overall flow function in terms of component and primitive entity functions.

could depend on the data flow values of other entities also. Thus even $\widehat{f}^{\alpha}$ need not be atomic. For some frameworks, it can be defined in terms of simpler functions that use the value of an entity to compute the value of another entity.

4.5.1 Primitive Entity Functions

We define *primitive entity functions* (abbreviated as *pef*) as the functions that compute the data flow value of an entity α from the data flow value of some entity β. We denote such a *pef* by $\overline{f}^{\beta\to\alpha} : \widehat{L}_{\beta} \mapsto \widehat{L}_{\alpha}$. The component function $\widehat{f}^{\alpha}_{u\to v}$ is defined as:

$$\widehat{f}^{\alpha}(\widehat{\mathsf{x}}^{\alpha}) = \prod_{\beta\in\Sigma} \overline{f}^{\beta\to\alpha}(\widehat{\mathsf{x}}^{\beta}) \tag{4.26}$$

Figure 4.26 illustrates how an overall flow function f can be a defined in terms of component functions $\widehat{f}^{\beta}$, and a *pef*s $\overline{f}^{\alpha\to\beta}$. $\mathsf{x} = \langle \widehat{\mathsf{x}}^{\alpha}, \widehat{\mathsf{x}}^{\beta}, \ldots, \widehat{\mathsf{x}}^{\omega} \rangle$ is the input data flow value and $\mathsf{x} = \langle \widehat{\mathsf{x}}^{\alpha}, \widehat{\mathsf{x}}^{\beta}, \ldots, \widehat{\mathsf{x}}^{\omega} \rangle$ is the output data flow value.

Modeling component functions in terms of *pef*s is interesting because it allows the component functions to be defined in terms of a very small set of *pef*s. We explain this by distinguishing between general unspecified functions and specific known functions. Our notation f denotes a general unspecified function. When we wish to denote specific known functions computing specific values, we use the notation ϕ. Unlike the subscript of f which denotes a program point or an edge, the subscript of ϕ distinguishes it from other specific functions. A couple of common special functions are:

$$\forall \mathsf{x} \in L:\ \phi_{id}(\mathsf{x}) = \mathsf{x}$$
$$\forall \mathsf{x} \in L:\ \phi_{\mathsf{z}}(\mathsf{x}) = \mathsf{z}$$

There are two special values of ϕ_{z} that are used very frequently: They are $\phi_{\top}$ and $\phi_{\bot}$. The specific functions that can be used for component functions and *pef*s are denoted by $\widehat{\phi}$ that are defined as follows:

$$\forall \widehat{x} \in \widehat{L} : \widehat{\phi}_z(\widehat{x}) = \widehat{z}$$
$$\forall \widehat{x} \in \widehat{L} : \widehat{\phi}_{id}(\widehat{x}) = \widehat{x}$$
$$\forall \widehat{x} \in \widehat{L}, \forall m, n \in \text{Const} : \widehat{\phi}_{m,n}(\widehat{x}) = m \times \widehat{x} + n$$

$\widehat{\phi}_z$ are constant functions. They include $\widehat{\phi}_\top$ and $\widehat{\phi}_\bot$ also. Some other examples of constant functions are: *pef*s corresponding to constant value assignments such as $a = 2$ in constant propagation, *pef*s corresponding to constant address assignments such as $a = \&b$ in point-to analysis etc. The latter is possible because the address of each named variable is a compile time constant.[‡]

$\widehat{\phi}_{id}$ is an identity *pef*. Note that the domain of $\widehat{\phi}_{id}$ could be $\widehat{L}_\alpha$ and the range could be $\widehat{L}_\beta$. Yet, it is an identity function because the component lattices $\widehat{L}_\alpha$ and $\widehat{L}_\beta$ are identical in terms of values and structure. In separable frameworks, for every identity *pef*, $\alpha = \beta$. Examples of $\widehat{\phi}_{id}$ with $\alpha \neq \beta$ are functions corresponding to copy statements such as $a = b$ in non-separable frameworks like possibly uninitialized variable analysis, constant propagation or points-to analysis.

Together, $\widehat{\phi}_z$ and $\widehat{\phi}_{id}$ cover all bit vector frameworks, all fast frameworks, all non-separable frameworks in which the data flow values can be represented by bit vectors (e.g., faint variables analysis, possibly uninitialized variables analysis), and copy constant propagation. They also cover a restricted points-to analysis if the right hand side does not involve indirection. The last *pef* $\widehat{\phi}_{m,n}$ is included to cover linear constant propagation. It is easy to see that all these *pef*s are distributive and are closed under composition. The frameworks whose component functions can be defined using the above *pef*s are called *primary* frameworks.

If an entity β does not influence α, then $\widehat{f}^{\beta \to \alpha} = \widehat{\phi}_\top$. A separable framework is a special case of non-separable frameworks such that

$$\alpha \neq \beta \Rightarrow \forall \widehat{x}^\beta \in \widehat{L}_\beta, \widehat{f}^{\beta \to \alpha}\left(\widehat{x}^\beta\right) = \widehat{\top}$$

This reduces $\widehat{f}^{\alpha}$ from $L \mapsto \widehat{L}_\alpha$ to $\widehat{L}_\alpha \mapsto \widehat{L}_\alpha$.

Example 4.22

Given an assignment $a = b * c$, some examples of component functions for some data flow frameworks are as follows:

- Available expressions analysis: $\widehat{f}^{b*c} = \widehat{\phi}_\top$; for any expression e that involves a, $\widehat{f}^{e} = \widehat{\phi}_\bot$; and for an expression e that does not involve a, $\widehat{f}^{e} = \widehat{\phi}_{id}$.

‡As is customary, addresses defined in terms of fixed offsets from frame pointers in activations records are considered compile time constants even if the actual address depends on run time.

- Live variables analysis: $\widehat{f}^{\,a} = \widehat{\phi}_{\perp}$; $\widehat{f}^{\,b} = \widehat{f}^{\,c} = \widehat{\phi}_{\top}$; and for any variable x other than a, b, and c, $\widehat{f}^{\,x} = \widehat{\phi}_{id}$.
- Faint variables analysis $\widehat{f}^{\,a} = \widehat{\phi}_{\perp}$; $\widehat{f}^{\,b} = \widehat{\phi}_{id}^{\,b} \sqcap \widehat{\phi}_{id}^{\,a}$; $\widehat{f}^{\,c} = \widehat{\phi}_{id}^{\,c} \sqcap \widehat{\phi}_{id}^{\,a}$; and for any variable x other than a, b, and c, $\widehat{f}^{\,x} = \widehat{\phi}_{id}$.

For an assignment $a = 2$ in constant propagation, $\widehat{f}^{\,a} = \widehat{\phi}_{2}$; for an assignment $a = b$, $\widehat{f}^{\,a} = \widehat{\phi}_{id}^{\,b}$; and for an assignment $a = b + 2$, $\widehat{f}^{\,a} = \widehat{\phi}_{1,2}^{\,b}$. For any variable x other than a, $\widehat{f}^{\,x} = \widehat{\phi}_{id}$. □

Example 4.23

Consider the flow functions in explicit liveness analysis of heap data. An access graph consists of edges between nodes. Since the set of nodes that may occur in any access graph is fixed for an instance of explicit liveness analysis, the set of possible edges is also fixed. Thus we define the following *pef*s for an edge: $\widehat{\phi}_{\perp}$ adds an edge to the given graph, $\widehat{\phi}_{\top}$ removes an edge from the given graph whereas $\widehat{\phi}_{id}$ copies an edge. Thus the flow functions of liveness analysis defined in Section 4.4.4 can be formulated in terms of these three *pef*s. □

4.5.2 Composite Entity Functions

The component functions of full constant propagation and points-to analysis cannot be defined in terms of *pef*s. Such frameworks are not primary frameworks.

Flow functions in full constant propagation evaluate an arithmetic expression and if we wish to define component functions in terms of simpler functions, we will have to use the functions of the form $\widehat{L} \times \widehat{L} \mapsto \widehat{L}$. Such functions are neither distributive nor closed under composition. In points-to analysis a right hand side could involve an indirection like $*x$. In such a situation computing right locations requires collecting points-to information of all z that x could point to. Contrast this with the right hand side x; in this case, the right locations consist of only the points-to information of x. Thus the required function has the form $L \mapsto \widehat{L}$.

The component functions that cannot be defined in terms of primitive entity functions are defined in terms of *composite entity functions* (abbreviated as *cef*) where *cef*s themselves are defined as combinations of *pef*s. For example, addition of two variables in full constant propagation is represented by the composite entity function $\widehat{\phi}_{+}^{\,\alpha,\beta} : \widehat{L} \times \widehat{L} \mapsto \widehat{L}$ defined below:

$$\widehat{\phi}_{+}^{\,\alpha,\beta} = \widehat{\phi}_{id}^{\,\alpha} + \widehat{\phi}_{id}^{\,\beta}$$

Indirection in points-to analysis is defined in terms of composite entity function $\widehat{\phi}_{*}^{\,\alpha} : L \mapsto \widehat{L}$ defined below:

$$\widehat{\phi}_{*}^{\,\alpha} = \bigsqcap_{\alpha \rightarrow \beta} \widehat{\phi}_{id}^{\,\beta}$$

Example 4.24

For an assignment $x = y + z$ in constant propagation, $\widehat{f}^{\,x} = \widehat{\phi}_{+}^{y,z}$ and for every variable w other than x, $\widehat{f}^{\,w} = \widehat{\phi}_{id}$. For an assignment $x = *y$ in points-to analysis, $\widehat{f}^{\,x} = \widehat{\phi}_{*}^{y}$. Observe that modeling assignment $*x = y$ does not require a special function because we define $\widehat{f}^{\,z} = \widehat{\phi}_{id}$ for every z such that $x \rightarrow z$. □

4.6 Summary and Concluding Remarks

In this chapter we have extended the *Gen-Kill* model of bit vector frameworks to general frameworks. The largest class of practical problems that can be described using this extended model are non-separable frameworks. In principle, separable frameworks can also have dependent parts and this model captures such frameworks also. However, the focus of this chapter has been on non-separable frameworks because we are not aware of a practical separable framework that is not a bit vector framework.

The extended *Gen-Kill* model can be seen as a uniform specification model for semantics captured by an analysis. This is useful because it allows flow functions to be decomposed in similar parts so that flow functions of different frameworks can be compared and contrasted. This facilitates modeling flow functions at a finer granularity in terms of primitive and composite entity functions. Surprisingly, a very small set of *pef*s is sufficient to model flow functions in most frameworks despite the diversity of the data flow information. As shown in Section 4.5, four *pef*s are enough to model almost all frameworks except full constant propagation and points-to analysis in which addresses of pointers are taken. This should be contrasted with the conventional modeling where flow functions remain at a much higher level of abstraction $f : L \mapsto L$ and no attempt is made to examine their constituents. Two significant benefits of modeling flow functions in terms of *pef*s are that

- it becomes possible to devise tight complexity bounds for round-robin iterative analysis of a large class of data flow frameworks. We do so in Chapter 5.
- it becomes possible to devise feasibility conditions for systematic reduction of flow function compositions.

4.7 Bibliographic Notes

The term separability was coined by Khedker and Dhamdhere [60]. Separable frameworks were called "decomposable" by Sharir and Pnueli [93] whereas Rosen [84] had called them "factorizable".

Constant propagation was described by Kildall [63] and it has been widely studied in literature. Some important works include conditional constant propagation by Wegman and Zadeck [102] and complexity study of many variants of constant propagation by Müller-Olm and Rüthing [78]. Strongly live variables analysis, which is a dual of faint variables analysis can be found in the text by F. Nielson, H. R. Nielson and Hankin [80].

There is a plethora of literature on pointer analysis. Unlike our presentation which tries to present a clean model of pointer analysis independently of other concerns, most of the works on pointer analysis have almost always given a much higher preference to practical concerns such as efficiency and effectiveness in interprocedural settings. Thus many combinations of flow sensitivity and context sensitivity have been explored. Even among flow insensitive approaches, two separate categories of *equality-based* and *subset-based* methods have been studied. Equality-based method assumes that if a can point to b and c, then b can point to everything that c can point to and vice-versa. Subset-based does not unify the points-to sets of b and c. Equality-based approach was pioneered by Steensgaard [97] whereas subset-based approach was pioneered by Andersen [9]. Fahndrich, Foster, Su and Aiken [35] presented an Andersen style of context insensitive pointer analysis which was followed up by Steensgaard style of context sensitive pointer analysis [36]. Andersen style context sensitive pointer analysis was reported by Whaley and Lam [104]. Among other influential works on pointer analysis, Landi and Ryder [66, 67] have presented flow sensitive pointer analysis which is also context sensitive in non-recursive parts of programs. The work done by Choi, Burke and Carini [21, 48] belongs to the same category. The only pointer analysis that is flow sensitive and also context sensitive for recursive programs is by Emami, Ghiya and Hendren [34]. Our version of points-to analysis is based on its reformulation by Kanade, Khedker and Sanyal [51]. An excellent discussion of the state of art of pointer analysis has been presented by Hind [47].

Liveness analysis of heap data using access graphs is a recent work by Khedker, Sanyal and A. Karkare [62]. We have only presented explicit liveness analysis. Actual nullification requires some other analyses such as alias analysis, availability analysis, anticipability analysis, and nullability analysis [62].

The earlier attempt at discovering the liveness of heap was by Agesen, Detlefs and Moss [1] and was restricted to the liveness of root variables. Our approach of heap data analysis can be seen as some kind of *shape analysis* [88, 106] which is a general method of creating suitable abstractions (called Shape Graphs) of heap memory with respect to the relevant properties. Program execution is then modeled as operations on shape graphs. However, it is not clear how shape analysis can be directly used for discovering future properties like liveness that require analysis against control flow. Shaham, Yahav, Kolodner and Sagiv [92] have devised a restricted version of liveness of heap data using shape analysis.

The concept of modeling flow functions in terms of primitive entity functions has been proposed by B. Karkare [53].

5

Complexity of Iterative Data Flow Analysis

The round-robin iterative method of *MFP* computation presented in Chapter 3, was described in terms of forward data flow problems. It is a general method that can be used with suitable changes for separable and non-separable, forward and backward, unidirectional and bidirectional frameworks. We have already used the method in working out examples of various frameworks in Chapters 1, 2, and 4. However, its complexity was defined only for rapid frameworks (Chapter 3).

In this chapter we present a generic version of round-robin method and define a tight complexity bound for general monotone data flow frameworks. We also introduce work list based iterative algorithm which computes data flow information in a demand driven fashion. This algorithm forms the basis of formalizing the exact amount of work that a data flow analysis algorithm needs to perform.

5.1 Generic Flow Functions and Data Flow Equations

For simplicity of exposition, definitions of flow functions and data flow equations in Chapter 3 were restricted to forward unidirectional frameworks. They are applicable to backward unidirectional frameworks with a simple substitution of In_n by Out_n and $\mathit{pred}(n)$ by $\mathit{succ}(n)$. In either case, the following variations are possible and are equivalent in terms of the data flow information that is computed:

- Data flow equations can be defined in terms of In_n or Out_n. It is not necessary to define both In_n and Out_n. In other words, given a neighbour m of n (i.e., a successor for backward problems and a predecessor for forward problems), In_n can be computed from In_m. Similarly, Out_n can be computed from Out_m.

- The flow functions can be associated with nodes or edges. Thus the following two definitions of In_n are equivalent:

$$\mathit{In}_n = \bigsqcap_{p \in \mathit{pred}(n)} f_p(\mathit{In}_p)$$

$$\mathit{In}_n = \bigsqcap_{p \in \mathit{pred}(n)} f_{p \to n}(\mathit{In}_p)$$

The above variations are possible because the data flow information in unidirectional data flows depends on *either* the predecessors *or* successors but not on both. The

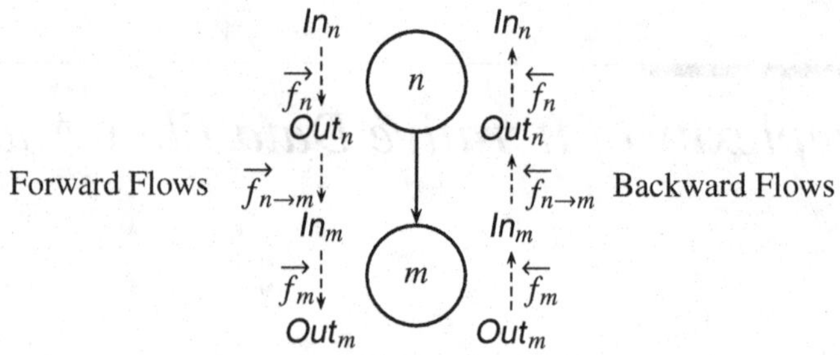

FIGURE 5.1
Associating flow functions with nodes and edges separately.

classical formulation of PRE (Section 2.4.4) does not meet these restrictions because data flow information associated with a node depends on both successors as well as predecessors. In particular, in classical PRE,

- In_n is computed from Out_n and Out_m where $m \in pred(n)$, and
- Out_n is computed from In_s where $s \in succ(n)$.

Such dependencies can be modeled by associating flow functions with nodes and edges separately as illustrated in Figure 5.1. $\overrightarrow{f}$ denotes a forward flow function whereas $\overleftarrow{f}$ denotes a backward flow function. The subscripts used in flow function notation distinguish node flow functions from edge flow functions. Defining separate node and edge flow functions requires explicating In_n and Out_n rather than leaving one of them implicit. This allows modeling the known flows as illustrated in Figure 5.2 by composing the node and edge flow functions appropriately. For forward unidirectional data flows, the forward flow functions associated with edges are identity functions ϕ_{id} and the backward node and edge flow functions are $\phi_\top$. Analogous remarks hold for backward unidirectional data flows. Figure 5.3 shows flow functions in forward, backward and bidirectional bit vector frameworks.

When separate flow functions are associated with nodes and edges, the generic data flow equations can be written as shown below.

$$In_n = \begin{cases} BI_{Start} \sqcap \overleftarrow{f}_n(Out_n) & n = Start \\ \left(\bigsqcap_{m \in pred(n)} \overrightarrow{f}_{m\to n}(Out_m) \right) \sqcap \overleftarrow{f}_n(Out_n) & \text{otherwise} \end{cases} \tag{5.1}$$

$$Out_n = \begin{cases} BI_{End} \sqcap \overrightarrow{f}_n(In_n) & n = End \\ \left(\bigsqcap_{m \in succ(n)} \overleftarrow{f}_{m\to n}(In_m) \right) \sqcap \overrightarrow{f}_n(In_n) & \text{otherwise} \end{cases} \tag{5.2}$$

These equations compute the MFP solution of an instance of a data flow framework. They can be written at an abstract level in terms of program points rather

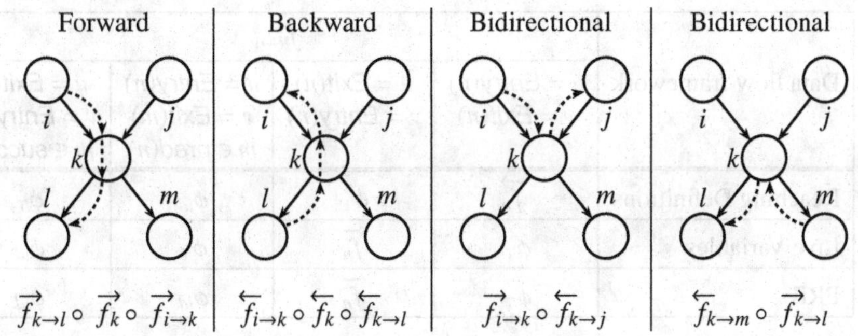

FIGURE 5.2
Representing different kinds of flows by composing node and edge flow functions.

than basic blocks as follows: Let $\mathbb{P}$**oints** denote the set of all program points in a given CFG and $\mathsf{x}_v \in L$ denote the data flow information associated with program point $v \in \mathbb{P}\mathsf{oints}$. Let **neighbours**(v) denote the set of program points adjacent to v. Then,

$$\mathsf{x}_v = \mathit{Initial}_v \sqcap \left(\bigsqcap_{u \in \mathsf{neighbours}(v)} f_{u\to v}(\mathsf{x}_u) \right) \tag{5.3}$$

where $\mathit{Initial}_v$ is defined as

$$\mathit{Initial}_v = \begin{cases} \mathit{BI}_{\mathit{Start}} & v = \mathit{Entry}(\mathit{Start}) \\ \mathit{BI}_{\mathit{End}} & v = \mathit{Exit}(\mathit{End}) \\ \top & \text{otherwise} \end{cases}$$

$f_{u\to v}$ is a forward/backward node/edge flow function depending upon u and v as described below:

u	v	$f_{u\to v}$
$\mathit{Entry}(n)$	$\mathit{Exit}(n)$	$\overrightarrow{f}_n$
$\mathit{Exit}(n)$	$\mathit{Entry}(n)$	$\overleftarrow{f}_n$
$\mathit{Exit}(m)$	$\mathit{Entry}(n), m \in \mathsf{pred}(n)$	$\overrightarrow{f}_{m\to n}$
$\mathit{Entry}(m)$	$\mathit{Exit}(n), m \in \mathsf{succ}(n)$	$\overleftarrow{f}_{n\to m}$

This generalization can be viewed as replacing basic blocks by their entry and exit points with conceptual edges between them. The direction of these edges indicates the direction in which flow functions are applied. A given edge $u \to v$ represents a node flow function if u and v are the two end-points of the same basic block; otherwise it represents an edge flow function.

In Section 3.3.1 we have defined $\mathsf{paths}(n)$ as the paths starting from *Start* reaching basic block n. We generalize this notion to define $\mathsf{paths}(u)$ as the set of paths in the underlying undirected graph. These paths begin either at *Start* or *End* and

Data flow framework	$f_{u \to v}$			
	$u = \mathsf{Entry}(n)$ $v = \mathsf{Exit}(n)$	$u = \mathsf{Exit}(n)$ $v = \mathsf{Entry}(n)$	$u = \mathsf{Entry}(n)$ $v = \mathsf{Exit}(m)$ $m \in \mathsf{pred}(n)$	$u = \mathsf{Exit}(n)$ $v = \mathsf{Entry}(m)$ $m \in \mathsf{succ}(n)$
Reaching Definitions	$\overrightarrow{f_n}$	$\phi_\top$	ϕ_{id}	$\phi_\top$
Live Variables	$\phi_\top$	$\overleftarrow{f_n}$	$\phi_\top$	ϕ_{id}
PRE	$\phi_\top$	$\overleftarrow{f_n}$	ϕ_{id}	ϕ_{id}

FIGURE 5.3
Generic flow functions in forward, backward, and bidirectional bit vector frameworks.

reach program point u. We define the path function f_ρ for every path in $\mathsf{paths}(u)$ as composition of generic flow functions along the conceptual edges in ρ.

In unidirectional forward frameworks, the *MOP* solution at node n is defined in terms of all paths in $\mathsf{paths}(n)$. We define *MOP* solution at a program point u using the generalized definition of $\mathsf{paths}(u)$ and generalized path function as follows:

$$\mathit{MOP}_u = \bigsqcap_{\rho \in \mathsf{paths}(u)} f_\rho(\mathit{BI}_\rho) \tag{5.4}$$

where BI_ρ is $\mathit{BI}_{\mathsf{Start}}$ if ρ begins at *Start*, $\mathit{BI}_{\mathsf{End}}$ otherwise.

5.2 Generic Round-Robin Iterative Algorithm

A round-robin iterative algorithm for computing *MFP* assignment for forward data flow problems was described in Figure 3.9. Its version presented in Figure 3.15 uses reverse postorder traversal over the graph. This makes it efficient for forward data flow problems. Both the versions compute the data flow information at entry points of all blocks. We refer to the former version as *RR* (Round-Robin) and the latter version as *rpoRR* (Reverse PostOrder Round-Robin).

We now introduce further generalizations in terms of program points and the order of their traversal which can be chosen according to the data flow problem. We use the term *stoRR* (Specified Traversal Order Round-Robin) to refer to our algorithm. It is presented in Figure 5.4. For simplicity we assume the presence of the $\top$ element in the lattice, unlike *rpoRR*. If the lattice does not contain a $\top$ element, we replace the initialization on Line 5 by

$$\mathsf{x}_u = \mathit{Initial}_u \sqcap \left(\bigsqcap_{j \in \mathsf{neighbours}(i),\, j<i} f_{j \to i}(\mathsf{x}_j) \right) \tag{5.5}$$

Input: An instance $(\mathbb{G}, M_{\mathbb{G}})$ of a monotone data flow framework $(L_{\mathcal{G}}, \sqcap_{\mathcal{G}}, F_{\mathcal{G}})$. Adjacent program points i, j are mapped to $f_{i \to j}$ by $M_{\mathbb{G}}$. Program points are numbered from $0 \ldots N - 1$ according to the chosen order of graph traversal.

Output: $x_i, \forall\, i$ giving the output of the data flow analysis for each program point.

Algorithm:

```
0    function stoRRMain()
1    {  for all i = 0 to N - 1 do
2       {  if i = Start then Initialᵢ = BIStart
3          else if i = End then Initialᵢ = BIEnd
4          else Initialᵢ = ⊤
5          xᵢ = ⊤
6       }
7       change = true
8       while change do
9       {  change = false
10         for all i = 0 to N - 1 do
11         {  temp = Initialᵢ ⊓     ⊓      fⱼ→ᵢ(xⱼ)
                              j∈neighbours(i)
12            if temp ≠ xᵢ then
13            {  xᵢ = temp
14               change = true
15            }
16         }
17      }
18   }
```

FIGURE 5.4

Round-robin algorithm for computing *MFP* assignment at each program point.

The preferred order of traversal depends on the flow functions in the data flow problem. For example, in forward problems, all node and edge flow functions are forward functions, hence reverse postorder is the most efficient order of traversal. In backward problems postorder traversal is preferable. The original bidirectional formulation of PRE contains three types of flow functions: Forward edge flow functions, backward edge flow functions and backward node flow functions. Thus a sequence of consecutive backward flow functions can be composed but a sequence of consecutive forward flow functions cannot be composed. Hence postorder traversal is the most efficient traversal.

Complexity of round-robin method is defined in context of the chosen order of graph traversal. In Chapter 3, depth of the CFG was used to define the complexity bound of round-robin method: The number of iterations required for *MFP* computation was shown to be $2 + d$ for forward bit vector frameworks and $3 + d$ for forward rapid frameworks, assuming a reverse postorder traversal. For other frameworks,

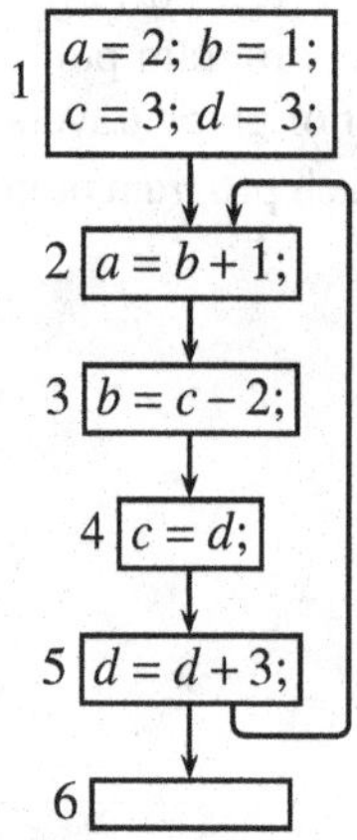

(a) A CFG with $d = 1$

	Iterations				
	1	2	3	4	5
Out_1	$\langle 2,1,3,3\rangle$	$\langle 2,1,3,3\rangle$	$\langle 2,1,3,3\rangle$	$\langle 2,1,3,3\rangle$	$\langle 2,1,3,3\rangle$
In_2	$\langle 2,1,3,3\rangle$	$\langle 2,1,3,\widehat{\bot}\rangle$	$\langle 2,1,\widehat{\bot},\widehat{\bot}\rangle$	$\langle 2,\widehat{\bot},\widehat{\bot},\widehat{\bot}\rangle$	$\langle \widehat{\bot},\widehat{\bot},\widehat{\bot},\widehat{\bot}\rangle$
Out_2	$\langle 2,1,3,3\rangle$	$\langle 2,1,3,\widehat{\bot}\rangle$	$\langle 2,1,\widehat{\bot},\widehat{\bot}\rangle$	$\langle \widehat{\bot},\widehat{\bot},\widehat{\bot},\widehat{\bot}\rangle$	$\langle \widehat{\bot},\widehat{\bot},\widehat{\bot},\widehat{\bot}\rangle$
Out_3	$\langle 2,1,3,3\rangle$	$\langle 2,1,3,\widehat{\bot}\rangle$	$\langle 2,\widehat{\bot},\widehat{\bot},\widehat{\bot}\rangle$	$\langle \widehat{\bot},\widehat{\bot},\widehat{\bot},\widehat{\bot}\rangle$	$\langle \widehat{\bot},\widehat{\bot},\widehat{\bot},\widehat{\bot}\rangle$
Out_4	$\langle 2,1,3,3\rangle$	$\langle 2,1,\widehat{\bot},\widehat{\bot}\rangle$	$\langle 2,\widehat{\bot},\widehat{\bot},\widehat{\bot}\rangle$	$\langle \widehat{\bot},\widehat{\bot},\widehat{\bot},\widehat{\bot}\rangle$	$\langle \widehat{\bot},\widehat{\bot},\widehat{\bot},\widehat{\bot}\rangle$
Out_5	$\langle 2,1,3,6\rangle$	$\langle 2,1,\widehat{\bot},\widehat{\bot}\rangle$	$\langle 2,\widehat{\bot},\widehat{\bot},\widehat{\bot}\rangle$	$\langle \widehat{\bot},\widehat{\bot},\widehat{\bot},\widehat{\bot}\rangle$	$\langle \widehat{\bot},\widehat{\bot},\widehat{\bot},\widehat{\bot}\rangle$

Data flow values of variables a,b,c,d are shown as $\langle \widehat{x}_a,\widehat{x}_b,\widehat{x}_c,\widehat{x}_d\rangle$. Initial values are $\langle \widehat{\top},\widehat{\top},\widehat{\top},\widehat{\top}\rangle$.

(b) Data flow values in round-robin method

FIGURE 5.5
Complexity of round-robin algorithm for constant propagation cannot be defined using depth of CFG.

depth of CFG is not sufficient to define complexity bounds for round-robin method.

Example 5.1

Consider the CFG in Figure 5.5(a). Statements in node 1 do not have any data dependence between them hence for simplicity we have combined them into a single block. Depth of this CFG is 1. Round-robin algorithm for constant propagation on this graph converges in 6 iterations. Part (b) of the figure shows the values at some program points each iteration. The last iteration is not shown since it is required only for detection of fixed point. It is not possible to explain the number of iterations in terms of d. □

5.3 Complexity of Round-Robin Iterative Algorithm

When *stoRR* algorithm is used for performing data flow analysis for a given instance of a framework, x_u values are initialized to $\top$ if $\top$ exists in the lattice of the framework. If the lattice does not contain $\top$, then x_u values are initialized to a suitably high value in the lattice using Equation (5.5). As the algorithm executes, the data flow values gradually change towards $\bot$. The number of iterations required by the algorithm depends on the number of data flow value changes that can be accommodated in a single iteration. In this section we investigate the order of changes in data flow values and their impact on the number of iterations of *stoRR* algorithm.

Two main steps in our treatment of complexity analysis of *stoRR* algorithm are:

- Formalizing the notion of order of dependence of data flow values at different program points in a CFG.
- Devising a measure of how closely the order of traversal specified to the *stoRR* algorithm follows the order of dependences of data flow values.

For the first step, we present an algorithm that directly follows the dependence of data flow values. We show that this algorithm computes the same solution as the *stoRR*. This allows us to define the minimum work that any algorithm of data flow analysis must perform. Based on the observations made in the algorithm, we capture the order of dependence of data flow values at different program points by defining the concept of an *information flow path*. For a given order of traversal, it then becomes possible to quantify how close the order is to the order of the dependence of data flow values.

5.3.1 Identifying the Core Work Using Work List

In this section we describe an iterative algorithm called the *work list* algorithm which follows the order of data flow value changes, and hence is typically more efficient than round-robin method. However, it has an additional overhead of managing the work list. It follows the order of changes by restricting the computation of data flow values to paths along which changes in data flow values take place. This is different from round-robin method where a single change in the data flow information at a program point triggers another iteration which traverses all program points indiscriminately.

Figure 5.6 shows a work list based algorithm for performing data flow analysis using generic flow functions. The organization of the work list influences the efficiency of the algorithm significantly; it can be increased by incorporating heuristics such as insertion of program points in a preferred order of traversal.

Lines 1 to 7 in the algorithm initialize the data flow values at each program point to a value that is computed independently of the other program points. It is assumed that the lattice contains a $\top$ element; if it does not, then the assignment on line 5 must be modified to restrict computation of $f_{u \rightarrow v}$ to only those neighbours of v that have already been visited. Initialization of the work list involves adding the program points with non-$\top$ data flow values to the work list; a $\top$ does not influence any value. From these program points, data flow information is propagated to their neighbouring program point which in turn are added to the work list if their data flow values change.

In *stoRR* algorithm, the data flow value at a program point is *recomputed* in each iteration (line 11, Figure 5.4). This accumulates the effect of all neighbours of a

Input: An instance $(\mathbb{G}, M_{\mathbb{G}})$ of a monotone data flow framework $(L_{\mathcal{G}}, \sqcap_{\mathcal{G}}, F_{\mathcal{G}})$. Adjacent program points u, v are mapped to $f_{u \to v}$ by $M_{\mathbb{G}}$.
Output: $\mathsf{x}_u, \forall\, u$ giving the output of the data flow analysis for each program point.
Algorithm:

```
function worklist_dfaMain()
{  for all u ∈ Points,
   {  if u = Start then Initial_u = BI_Start
      else if u = End then Initial_u = BI_End
      else Initial_u = ⊤
      x_u = Initial_u ⊓ ( ⊓_{v ∈ neighbours(u)} f_{v→u}(⊤) )
      if x_u ⊏ ⊤ then add u to worklist
   }
   while worklist is not empty do
   {  Remove the first program point u from worklist
      for all v ∈ neighbours(u) do
      {  temp = x_v ⊓ f_{u→v}(x_u)
         if temp ⊏ x_v then
         {  x_v = temp
            Add v to worklist
         }
      }
   }
}
```

FIGURE 5.6
Work list algorithm for computing *MFP* assignment at each program point.

program point u on the data flow value x_u. By contrast, in a work list algorithm, a change in a value x_u is propagated to all its neighbours by *refining* their values. Refinement implied merging the old value at that point with the new value obtained from a single neighbour. Because of this difference between the two algorithms, we need to explicitly show that they compute the same assignment of data flow values. We do so by showing three important results:

- A work list algorithm terminates.
- When a work list algorithm terminates, the resulting data flow values constitute a fixed point assignment.
- Finally we show that the resulting fixed point assignment is actually the maximum fixed point assignment.

Since we know that *stoRR* algorithm also computes the *MFP* assignment, and that the *MFP* assignment is unique, it follows that the two algorithms compute identical assignment.

For proving the properties of the work list algorithm, we define the notion of a step of the algorithm as follows. Step 1 refers to the execution of the **for** loop (lines 1 to 7). Each subsequent step corresponds to the refinement of some x_u on lines 11, 12, and 13. Each step i uses the values from step $i-1$; observe that the value used may have been computed in some earlier step. It follows that the values used in step 1 must be values from step 0; since the value used in step 1 is $\top$, we say that $x_u^0 = \top$.

LEMMA 5.1

The work list algorithm terminates.

PROOF Consider some step i in the algorithm. If step i computes x_u, then due to refinement, $x_u^i \sqsubseteq x_u^{i-1}$. If x_u has not been modified in this step, then $x_u^i = x_u^{i-1}$ and u is not put on the work list. However, if x_u is modified and u is put on the work list, then $x_u^i \sqsubset x_u^{i-1}$. Thus the modifications in the value of x_u follow a strictly descending chain. Since all strictly descending chains are finite, each program point can be inserted in the worklist a finite number of times. Eventually the worklist becomes empty and the algorithm terminates. ∎

Now we prove that on termination, the work list algorithm computes a fixed point assignment.

LEMMA 5.2

Let the work list algorithm terminate in n steps. Then,

$$\forall u \in \mathbb{P}\text{oints} : x_u^n \sqsubseteq \mathit{Initial}_u \sqcap \left(\bigsqcap_{v \in \text{neighbours}(u)} f_{v \to u}(x_v^n) \right)$$

PROOF From Lemma 5.1

$$\begin{aligned} & \forall u \in \mathbb{P}\text{oints}, \forall i \geq 1 : x_u^i \sqsubseteq x_i^{i-1} \\ \Rightarrow \quad & \forall u \in \mathbb{P}\text{oints}, \forall i \geq 1 : x_u^i \sqsubseteq \mathit{Initial}_u \qquad (\text{because } \forall u \in \mathbb{P}\text{oints} : x_u^1 \sqsubseteq \mathit{Initial}_u) \end{aligned}$$

Consider an arbitrary program point u and the last step m in which the value of x_u was computed. By the definition of refinement, we have

$$x_u^m = x_u^{m-1} \sqcap f_{v \to u}(x_v^{m-1}) \tag{5.6}$$

$$\Rightarrow \quad x_u^m \sqsubseteq f_{v \to u}(x_v^{m-1})$$

Since this is the last computation of x_u, the effect of changes in other neighbours v' of u has been incorporated by executing (5.6) for some $m' \leq m \leq n$. Hence,

$$x_u^n \sqsubseteq Initial_u \sqcap \left(\bigsqcap_{v \in neighbours(u)} f_{v \to u}(x_v^{n-1}) \right) \qquad (5.7)$$

The algorithm terminates when no program point is added to the work list. Thus,

$$\forall v \in \mathbb{P}oints: \; x_v^n = x_v^{n-1}$$

Substituting the above in (5.7) results in,

$$x_u^n \sqsubseteq Initial_u \sqcap \bigsqcap_{v \in neighbours(u)} f_{v \to u}(x_v^n)$$

∎

LEMMA 5.3
Let the work list algorithm terminate in n steps. Then,

$$\forall u \in \mathbb{P}oints: \; x_u^n \sqsupseteq Initial_u \sqcap \left(\bigsqcap_{v \in neighbours(u)} f_{v \to u}(x_v^n) \right)$$

PROOF We prove this by induction on the number of steps.

1. *Basis:* In step 1, we compute

$$\forall u \in \mathbb{P}oints: \; x_u^1 = Initial_u \sqcap \left(\bigsqcap_{v \in neighbours(u)} f_{v \to u}(x_v^0 = \top) \right)$$

$$\Rightarrow \quad \forall u \in \mathbb{P}oints: \; x_u^1 \sqsupseteq Initial_u \sqcap \left(\bigsqcap_{v \in neighbours(u)} f_{v \to u}(x_v^0 = \top) \right)$$

2. *Inductive step:* Assume that for some step i

$$\forall u \in \mathbb{P}oints: \; x_u^i \sqsupseteq Initial_u \sqcap \left(\bigsqcap_{v \in neighbours(u)} f_{v \to u}(x_v^{i-1}) \right)$$

Consider an arbitrary program point u and step $i+1$. If x_u is not modified in step $i+1$, $x_u^{i+1} = x_u^i$ and by the inductive hypothesis, it trivially follows that,

$$x_u^{i+1} \sqsupseteq Initial_u \sqcap \left(\bigsqcap_{v \in neighbours(u)} f_{v \to u}(x_v^i) \right)$$

Thus the interesting case that needs to be proved is when x_u is modified in step $i+1$. By the definition of refinement,

$$\mathsf{x}_u^{i+1} = \mathsf{x}_u^i \sqcap f_{v\to u}(\mathsf{x}_v^i)$$

Substituting for x_u^i from the inductive hypothesis

$$\mathsf{x}_u^{i+1} \sqsupseteq \mathit{Initial}_u \sqcap \left(\bigsqcap_{v\in\text{neighbours}(u)} f_{v\to u}(\mathsf{x}_v^{i-1}) \right) \sqcap f_{v\to u}(\mathsf{x}_v^i)$$

If the value of every neighbour v was modified in some step $j < i$, then $\mathsf{x}_v^i = \mathsf{x}_v^{i-1}$ and

$$\mathsf{x}_u^{i+1} \sqsupseteq \mathit{Initial}_u \sqcap \left(\bigsqcap_{v\in\text{neighbours}(u)} f_{v\to u}(\mathsf{x}_v^i) \right)$$

and the lemma holds. For the other possibility, let there be a neighbour v' whose value was modified in step i. Then,

$$\mathsf{x}_u^{i+1} \sqsupseteq \mathit{Initial}_u \sqcap \left(\bigsqcap_{v\in\text{neighbours}(u)} f_{v\to u}(\mathsf{x}_v^{i-1}) \right) \sqcap f_{v'\to u}(\mathsf{x}_{v'}^i)$$

We rewrite the meet to separate the term for v'

$$\mathsf{x}_u^{i+1} \sqsupseteq \mathit{Initial}_u \sqcap \left(\bigsqcap_{\substack{v\in\text{neighbours}(u),\\ v\neq v'}} f_{v\to u}(\mathsf{x}_v^{i-1}) \right) \sqcap f_{v'\to u}(\mathsf{x}_{v'}^{i-1}) \sqcap f_{v'\to u}(\mathsf{x}_{v'}^i)$$

However, $\quad f_{v'\to u}(\mathsf{x}_{v'}^i) \sqsubseteq f_{v'\to u}(\mathsf{x}_{v'}^{i-1}) \qquad$ (because $\mathsf{x}_{v'}^i \sqsubseteq \mathsf{x}_{v'}^{i-1}$)

For all other v, the values in $i-1$ and i are same. Hence,

$$\begin{aligned}\mathsf{x}_u^{i+1} &\sqsupseteq \mathit{Initial}_u \sqcap \left(\bigsqcap_{\substack{v\in\text{neighbours}(u),\\ v\neq v'}} f_{v\to u}(\mathsf{x}_v^{i}) \right) \sqcap f_{v'\to u}(\mathsf{x}_{v'}^i) \\ &\sqsupseteq \mathit{Initial}_u \sqcap \left(\bigsqcap_{v\in\text{neighbours}(u)} f_{v\to u}(\mathsf{x}_v^i) \right)\end{aligned}$$

Hence the lemma follows. ∎

LEMMA 5.4
The work list algorithm computes a solution of Equation (5.3).

PROOF Let the work list become empty after n steps. From Lemma (5.2), we know that

$$\forall u \in \mathbb{P}\text{oints} : \mathsf{x}_u^n \sqsubseteq \mathit{Initial}_u \sqcap \left(\bigsqcap_{v\in\text{neighbours}(u)} f_{v\to u}(\mathsf{x}_v^n) \right)$$

and from Lemma (5.3)

$$\forall u \in \mathbb{P}\text{oints}: \ \mathsf{x}_u^n \sqsupseteq \mathit{Initial}_u \sqcap \left(\bigsqcap_{v \in \text{neighbours}(u)} f_{v \to u}(\mathsf{x}_v^n) \right)$$

Hence it follows that,

$$\forall u \in \mathbb{P}\text{oints}: \ \mathsf{x}_u^n = \mathit{Initial}_u \sqcap \left(\bigsqcap_{v \in \text{neighbours}(u)} f_{v \to u}(\mathsf{x}_v^n) \right)$$

▮

LEMMA 5.5
The work list algorithm computes MFP *assignment of Equation (5.3).*

PROOF Consider an arbitrary solution FP of Equation (5.3). Clearly,

$$\forall u \in \mathbb{P}\text{oints}: \ FP_u = \mathit{Initial}_u \sqcap \left(\bigsqcap_{v \in \text{neighbours}(u)} f_{v \to u}(FP_v) \right)$$

Let the work list algorithm terminate after n steps. We need to prove that

$$\forall u \in \mathbb{P}\text{oints}: \ FP_u \sqsubseteq \mathsf{x}_u^n$$

We prove this by induction on step number in the work list algorithm.

1. *Basis:* From the definition of step 1,

$$\forall u \in \mathbb{P}\text{oints}: \ \mathsf{x}_u^1 = \mathit{Initial}_u \sqcap \left(\bigsqcap_{v \in \text{neighbours}(u)} f_{v \to u}(\top) \right)$$

Since $\forall v \in \mathbb{P}\text{oints}: \ FP_v \sqsubseteq \top$, it follows that

$$\forall u, v \in \mathbb{P}\text{oints}: \left(\bigsqcap_{v \in \text{neighbours}(u)} f_{v \to u}(FP_v) \right) \sqsubseteq \left(\bigsqcap_{v \in \text{neighbours}(u)} f_{v \to u}(\top) \right)$$

Since $\mathit{Initial}_v$ is constant,

$$\forall u \in \mathbb{P}\text{oints}: \ FP_u \sqsubseteq \mathsf{x}_u^1$$

2. *Inductive Step:* Assume the inductive hypothesis

$$\forall u \in \mathbb{P}\text{oints}: \ FP_u \sqsubseteq \mathsf{x}_u^i$$

Consider an arbitrary program point u. If x_u is not modified in step $i+1$ then the inductive step trivially follows. Thus we have to show the inductive step when x_u is modified in step $i+1$. From the definition of a fixed point,

$$\forall u \in \mathbb{P}\text{oints}, \ FP_u \sqsubseteq f_{v \to u}(FP_v) \qquad \forall v \in \text{neighbours}(u)$$

By the inductive hypothesis, $FP_v \sqsubseteq x_v^i$ and hence

$$\forall u \in \text{Points}: \; FP_u \sqsubseteq f_{v \to u}(x_v^i) \qquad \forall v \in \text{neighbours}(u)$$

However, from inductive hypothesis we also have

$$\forall u \in \text{Points}: \; FP_u \sqsubseteq x_u^i$$

Combining the two,

$$\forall u \in \text{Points}: \; FP_u \sqsubseteq x_u^i \sqcap f_{v \to u}(x_v^i) \qquad \forall v \in \text{neighbours}(u)$$

From the definition of refinement,

$$x_u^{i+1} = x_u^i \sqcap f_{v \to u}(x_v^i)$$

Hence it follows that

$$\forall u \in \text{Points}: \; FP_u \sqsubseteq x_u^{i+1}$$

Since the assignment computed by the work list algorithm is a fixed point and it contains every possible fixed point FP, it must be the MFP. ■

5.3.2 Information Flow Paths in Bit Vector Frameworks

For simplicity of exposition we begin our discussion with bit vector frameworks in which the data flow values of all entities are independent.

Recall that $\Sigma = \{\alpha, \beta, \ldots, \omega\}$ denotes the set of program entities whose data flow information is computed during data flow analysis. Since bit vector frameworks are separable, flow of information for each entity can be examined independently. Hence the discussion in this section refers to a single entity say α and its lattice $\widehat{L}$. The iterative algorithms defined in Figures 5.4 and 5.6 compute data flow information of all entities simultaneously.

Since $\widehat{L} = \{\widehat{\top}, \widehat{\bot}\}$ in bit vector frameworks, only the following three monotonic flow functions are possible: $\widehat{\phi_\top}$, $\widehat{\phi_\bot}$, and $\widehat{\phi_{id}}$ (Section 4.5). The data flow analysis of bit vector framework involves initializing data flow values to $\widehat{\top}$ and then propagating the $\widehat{\bot}$ value in the graph. The $\widehat{\bot}$ values are generated as a result of local analysis and are propagated to other program points during global analysis. We say that data flow information is *generated* at a program point if the information results from application of a constant function other than $\widehat{\phi_\top}$; in bit vector frameworks a data flow information is generated $\widehat{\phi_\bot}$. The point of generation, called *origin* of information flow is defined as follows.

DEFINITION 5.1 *A program point v is an origin of data flow information for entity α if any of the following conditions is satisfied:*

1. *v is Entry(Start) and* $\widehat{x}_v^\alpha = \widehat{\bot}$ *in* BI_{Start}.

2. *v is Exit(End) and* $\widehat{x}_v^\alpha = \widehat{\bot}$ *in* BI_{End}.

3. *If there exists a pair of adjacent program points u, v such that for some entity α,* $\widehat{f_{u \to v}} = \widehat{\phi_\bot}$.

DEFINITION 5.2 *An information flow path for an entity α in a bit vector framework is defined as a maximal acyclic sequence of adjacent program points $p_0, p_1, \ldots p_m$ such that p_0 is an origin of data flow information for α, and every flow function $\widehat{f_{p_i \to p_{i+1}}}$ is $\widehat{\phi_{id}}$.*

An information flow path represents a single thread of changes in the values of an entity in the program. In general, when there is a change in the data flow at a program point u, the flow of information terminates at u if the change at u does not cause a change in the data flow value of any neighbour v of u. In bit vector frameworks, data flow value of an entity at a program point can change only once. Since an *ifp* propagates a $\widehat{\bot}$ value, no more changes in data flow value are possible at any program point already present in the *ifp*. Hence, *ifp*s in bit vector frameworks are acyclic.

Information flow paths differ from paths in *paths*(u) in many ways: the paths in *paths*(u) always start from *Start* or *End*, *ifp*s may start from any program point. Further, a path in *paths*(u) ends on u, whereas an *ifps* is not defined for a give program point. Paths in *paths*(u) may be cyclic, whereas *ifp*s in bit vector frameworks are always acyclic.

For brevity, we denote *Entry*(n) and *Exit*(n) by I_n and O_n respectively when depicting an information flow path. In Figure 5.2(c), the data flow indicated by the dashed line takes place along the subpath ($O_i \to I_k \to O_j$) of an *ifp*, while the data flow in Figure 5.2(d) takes place along the subpath ($I_l \to O_k \to I_m$) of an *ifp*. Figure 5.7 shows an information flow path in partial redundancy elimination for our example program. In this example, data flow information at *Exit*(n_6) is 0 as a result of assignment to c in n_4. The *ifp* responsible for propagating information from *Entry*(n_4) to *Exit*(n_6) is ($I_{n_4} \to O_{n_3} \to I_{n_5} \to O_{n_6}$) and is shown by a sequence of gray dashed arrows in the figure.

The information flow from p_0 to p_m is realized through the *path flow function* $\widehat{f_\rho}$ of ρ which is a composition of flow functions of all edges in ρ:

$$\widehat{f_\rho} = \widehat{f_{p_{m-1} \to p_m}} \circ \widehat{f_{p_{m-2} \to p_{m-1}}} \circ \cdots \circ \widehat{f_{p_1 \to p_2}} \circ \widehat{f_{p_0 \to p_1}} \tag{5.8}$$

Using the path flow function the data flow information reaching p_m from p_0 can be computed. In bit vector frameworks, the path flow function of an *ifp* is an identity function.

Information Flow Paths and the Work List Algorithm

Observe that the information flow paths in bit vector frameworks correspond to the paths traced by the generic work list based algorithm given in Figure 5.6. Program

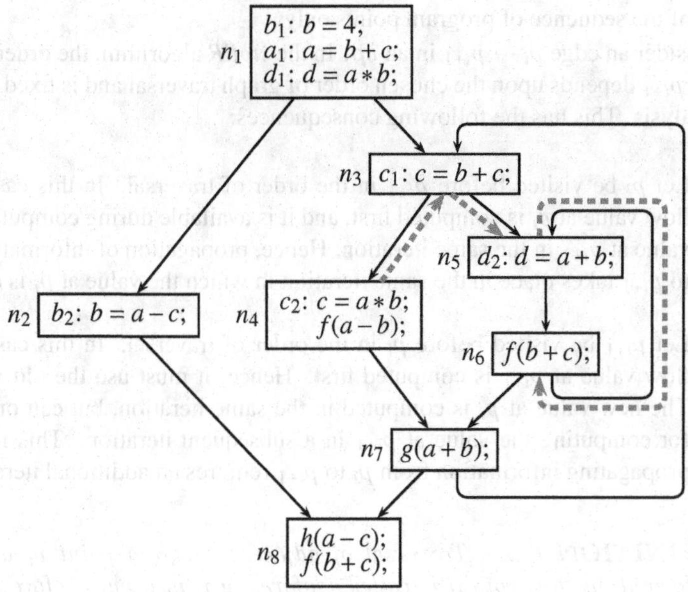

The *ifp* ($I_{n_4} \rightarrow O_{n_3} \rightarrow I_{n_5} \rightarrow O_{n_6}$) (shown in dashed arrows) is responsible for suppressing hoisting of expression $b + c$ at *Exit*(n_6).

FIGURE 5.7
An information flow path in PRE example.

points during initialization are essentially the origins of information flow for some entity. However, since work list algorithm operates on data flow values of all entities simultaneously, the paths traced by work list algorithms may correspond to multiple *ifp*s each referring to a different entity. Further, if a program point is added to the head of the work list, *ifp*s for an entity are traversed independently; if it is added to the rear, *ifp*s of an entity may be traversed in an interleaved fashion.

5.3.3 Defining Complexity Using Information Flow Paths

We now define the complexity of *stoRR* algorithm by relating each iteration of the algorithm to the fragment of an *ifp* that it can cover. Note that we consider the iterations of the **while** loop only; the initialization is not counted in the number of iterations unless the initialization is performed using Equation (5.5).

The discussion in this section is general and is not restricted to bit vector frameworks because it relies on the occurrence of program points in *ifp*s. Later when we define *ifp*s for fast frameworks and non-separable frameworks, the *ifp*s are extended to qualify the program points with additional information. It is done only to identify the relevant sequences of program points and eventually the complexity is defined in terms of the sequence of program points only.

Consider an edge $p_i \rightarrow p_{i+1}$ in an *ifp*. In the *stoRR* algorithm, the order of visiting p_i and p_{i+1} depends upon the chosen order of graph traversal and is fixed throughout the analysis. This has the following consequences:

- Let p_i be visited before p_{i+1} in the order of traversal. In this case, the data flow value at p_i is computed first, and it is available during computation of the value at p_{i+1} in the same iteration. Hence, propagation of information from p_i to p_{i+1} takes place in the same iteration in which the value at p_i is computed.

- Let p_{i+1} be visited before p_i in the order of traversal. In this case, the data flow value at p_{i+1} is computed first. Hence, it must use the old value at p_i. The new value at p_i is computed in the same iteration, but can only be used for computing the value at p_{i+1} in a subsequent iteration. This implies that propagating information from p_i to p_{i+1} requires an additional iteration.

DEFINITION 5.3 *Traversal of adjacent program point p_i and p_{i+1} in an information flow path ρ is called conforming if p_i occurs before p_{i+1} in the chosen order of traversal. Otherwise, it is a non-conforming traversal.*

Conforming traversals do not contribute additional iterations in the *stoRR* algorithm whereas each non-conforming traversal requires one extra iteration.

DEFINITION 5.4 *Width of an information flow path ρ with respect to a given order of traversal is defined as the number of non-conforming traversals in ρ.*

We denote the width of an *ifp* ρ by *width*(ρ). Width is a measure of the number of iterations required by *stoRR* algorithm to propagate information along ρ.

Example 5.2

In Figure 5.7, width of *ifp* ($I_{n_4} \rightarrow O_{n_3} \rightarrow I_{n_5} \rightarrow O_{n_6}$) is 2 since edge traversals $O_{n_3} \rightarrow I_{n_5}$ and $I_{n_5} \rightarrow O_{n_6}$ are non-conforming traversals as the CFG nodes are visited in postorder traversal. ☐

DEFINITION 5.5 *A span is a maximal sequence of conforming edge traversals in an ifp.*

Spans are separated by a non-conforming edge traversal and vice-versa. Thus two successive non-conforming edge traversals have a null span between them. An information flow path may begin and/or end with a null span.

The information along a span can be propagated in a single traversal over the graph. This traversal is same as the traversal of the preceding non-conforming edge.

DEFINITION 5.6 *Width of a CFG for an instance of data flow framework is defined with respect to a given order of traversal as the maximum width of any ifp for the given instance.*

THEOREM 5.1
If the width of a CFG for an instance of a bit vector framework is w then the round-robin iterative method storR *converges in $w+1$ iterations.*

PROOF The information flow can be initiated only after data flow values at all origins are computed. The *stoRR* algorithm achieves this in the first iteration after initialization. The same iteration propagates the information along a non-null span (if any) at the beginning of each *ifp*. Every non-conforming edge traversal and the span following it requires an additional iteration. Thus, $w+1$ iterations are sufficient along the *ifp*s that determine width of the CFG. ∎

Though the *stoRR* algorithm converges in $w+1$ iterations, in practice we do not know the width of a flow graph and the method terminates after discovering that there is no further change. Thus, practically, $w+2$ iterations are required.

The main advantage of using the notion of width is that it is uniformly applicable to general data flow frameworks including bidirectional and non-separable frameworks. Further, it is defined in terms of a specified order and hence explains the difference in the number of iterations when the order of traversal is changed.

Example 5.3
The depth of the program in Figure 5.7 for PRE is 1 whereas its width is 2. Hence the round-robin method requires at most 4 iterations to converge. □

For unidirectional data flow problems, if the direction of graph traversal is same as the direction of the data flows, the width of a graph reduces to its depth. However, depth is applicable to unidirectional data flow problems only.

5.3.4 Information Flow Paths in Fast Frameworks

Fast frameworks are separable 2-bounded frameworks. However, they are more general than bit vector frameworks in that they allow more than two elements in a component lattice, and also allow flow functions that compute incomparable values. The former requires generalizing the definition of origin while the latter requires generalizing the value associated with a program point in an *ifp*.

In fast frameworks, the data flow value at a program point changes due to one of the following reasons: (a) Result of application of a flow function, or (b) Merging incomparable values from neighbours. In bit vector frameworks, the latter situation never arises because the component lattice does not contain incomparable values. In order to handle fast frameworks, the definition of information flow paths must be extended to incorporate merging of information. Also, in bit vector frameworks, an information flow path propagates the same data flow value ($\widehat{\bot}$) from an origin to all possible program points. In fast frameworks, a value at a program point may undergo more than one change due to non-identity non-constant functions and merging.

First we extend the definition of origin to allow the program point to be qualified with the generated data flow value.

DEFINITION 5.7 *A pair $\langle v, \widehat{\mathsf{x}}_v^\alpha \rangle$ is an origin of information flow for entity α if any of the following conditions is satisfied:*

1. *v is* Entry(Start) *and $\widehat{\mathsf{x}}_v^\alpha \neq \widehat{\top}$ in* $\mathsf{BI}_{\mathsf{Start}}$.
2. *v is* Exit(End) *and $\widehat{\mathsf{x}}_v^\alpha \neq \widehat{\top}$ in* $\mathsf{BI}_{\mathsf{End}}$.
3. *If there exists a pair of adjacent program points u, v such that for some entity α, $\widehat{f}_{u \to v}^{\,\alpha}$ is a constant* pef $\widehat{\phi}_{\mathsf{z}}$ *computing the value $\widehat{\mathsf{z}} \neq \widehat{\top}$.*

Apart from recording the data flow value, handling the merging of data flow values intermediate program points requires the following extensions:

- Merging may involve a data flow value generated by some other *ifp* traversed earlier. To remember the values computed by a different *ifp*, we define an *ifp* with respect to a given assignment $A : \mathbb{P}\text{oints} \mapsto \widehat{L} \cup \{\mathit{undef}\}$. A_u^α denotes value of α at program point u in assignment A. Initial assignment is $\forall u \in \mathbb{P}\text{oints}, A_u^\alpha = \widehat{\top}$ if the lattice contains a $\widehat{\top}$ element; it is $\forall u \in \mathbb{P}\text{oints}, A_u^\alpha = \mathit{undef}$ otherwise.
- We need to define a function *latest*() to extract the latest data flow value of α at u when examining an *ifp* ρ.

An *ifp* for a fast framework is defined as follows.

DEFINITION 5.8 *Given an assignment $A : \mathbb{P}\text{oints} \mapsto \widehat{L} \cup \{\mathit{undef}\}$, an information flow path ρ for an entity α in a fast framework is defined as a maximal acyclic sequence of tuples $\langle p_0, \widehat{\mathsf{x}}_0 \rangle, \langle p_1, \widehat{\mathsf{x}}_1 \rangle, \ldots, \langle p_m, \widehat{\mathsf{x}}_m \rangle$ such that $\langle p_0, \widehat{\mathsf{x}}_0 \rangle$ is an origin of information flow for α, and given $\langle p_i, \widehat{\mathsf{x}}_i \rangle$, its successor $\langle p_{i+1}, \widehat{\mathsf{x}}_{i+1} \rangle$ is defined as follows:*

1. *p_i, p_{i+1} are adjacent program points,*
2. *Let ρ' be the prefix of ρ containing i tuples. Then*

$$\widehat{\mathsf{x}}_{i+1} = \widehat{f}_{p_i \to p_{i+1}}(\widehat{\mathsf{x}}_i) \oplus \mathit{latest}(p_{i+1}, \rho')$$

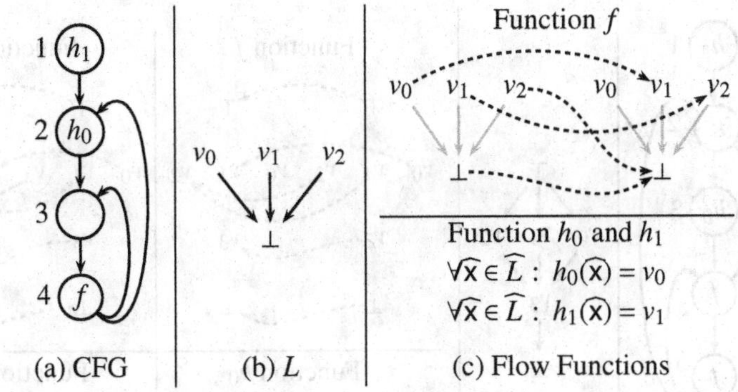

FIGURE 5.8
An instance of a distributive non-bit vector rapid framework reproduced from Figure 3.19. This instance requires $d(G,T)+3$ iterations of a round-robin algorithm with reverse post order traversal.

where

(a) $\widehat{f}^{\alpha}_{p_i \to p_{i+1}}$ *is a non-constant function.*

(b) *latest*(u,ρ') *returns value* $\widehat{x}^{\alpha}_j$ *if* p_j *is the last occurrence of* u *in* ρ'*; if* ρ' *does not contain* u*, then latest*(u,ρ') *returns* A^{α}_u.

(c) $$\widehat{x} \oplus \widehat{x}' = \begin{cases} \widehat{x} & \text{if } \widehat{x}' = \textsf{undef} \\ \widehat{x} \sqcap \widehat{x}' & \text{otherwise} \end{cases}$$

The acyclicity condition prohibits the same pair $\langle p_i, \widehat{x}_i \rangle$ from occurring multiple times in the *ifp*; a program point may appear multiple times in the *ifp*.

Unlike bit vector frameworks, the path flow function $\widehat{f}_{\rho}$ for an *ifp* ρ need not be $\widehat{\phi}_{id}$. An assignment A used to define an *ifp* must be a valid assignment for a correct representation of information flows in a program. If it is arbitrarily chosen, the resulting complexity measures could be incorrect. For the first *ifp* traversed, $A : \forall\, u \in \textsf{Points}, \widehat{x}_u = \top$ is valid if $\top$ exists in the lattice of the framework; otherwise it must be $A : \forall\, u \in \textsf{Points}, \widehat{x}_u = \textsf{undef}$. A must get updated by each subsequent *ifp*.

DEFINITION 5.9 *Given an assignment* $A : \textsf{Points} \mapsto \widehat{L} \cup \{\textsf{undef}\}$*, and an ifp* ρ*, the resulting assignment* A' *is* $\forall u \in \textsf{Points}, A'_u =$ *latest*(u,ρ) *where latest*(u,ρ) *is defined in Definition 5.8.*

Example 5.4
Consider the instance of a data flow framework shown in Figure 5.8 which has been reproduced from Example 3.11 on page 96. For simplicity, we have shown only the non-identity node flow functions and assume that there is

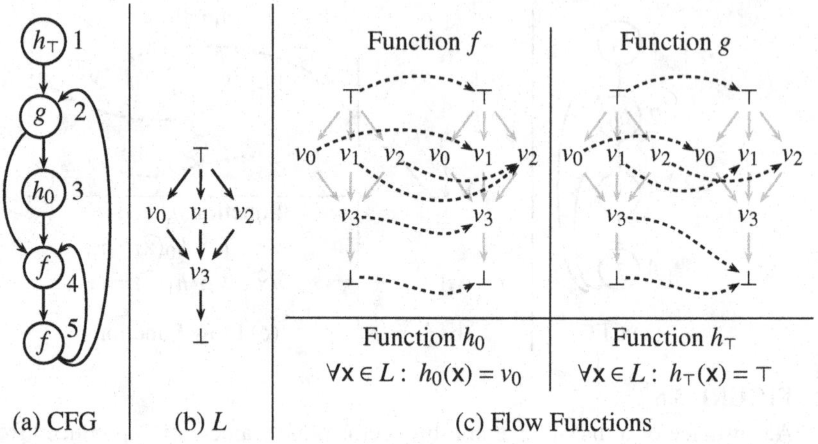

FIGURE 5.9
An instance of a distributive non-rapid fast framework that requires $d(G,T)+4$ iterations of a round-robin algorithm with reverse post order traversal.

a single unspecified entity. All edge flow functions are ϕ_{id}. Let the given assignment be $A : \forall\, u \in \mathbb{P}\text{oints}, x_u = \mathit{undef}$. The constant function h_0 produces data flow value v_0 for entity *en*. Hence $\langle Exit(2), v_0\rangle$ is an origin of information flow. An *ifp* originating at $\langle Exit(2), v_0\rangle$ is

$$(\langle O_2, v_0\rangle \rightarrow \langle I_3, v_0\rangle \rightarrow \langle O_3, v_0\rangle \rightarrow \langle I_4, v_0\rangle \rightarrow \langle O_4, v_1\rangle \rightarrow$$
$$\langle I_3, \bot\rangle \rightarrow \langle O_3, \bot\rangle \rightarrow \langle I_4, \bot\rangle \rightarrow \langle O_4, \bot\rangle \rightarrow \langle I_2, \bot\rangle)$$

The round-robin algorithm requires 4 iterations to converge with a reverse post first order traversal. The data flow value at *Exit*(3) is v_0 in the first iteration. In the second iteration, it changes to $\bot$ as a result of merging the data value of *Exit*(4) and *Exit*(2). The third iteration is required to propagate this value to *Entry*(2) and the final iteration is required to detect convergence.

The depth of the CFG in example in Figure 5.8 is 1. The required number of iterations can be explained in term of width. Width of the above *ifp* is 2 due to the non-conforming edges $O_4 \rightarrow I_3$ and $O_4 \rightarrow I_2$. □

Example 5.5

Consider the instance of a data flow framework shown in Figure 5.9. We leave it for the reader to verify that is a distributive non-rapid fast framework. All edge flow functions are ϕ_{id}. Constant function h_0 produces data flow value v_0. With the initialization $\top$ at all program points, the round-robin algorithm converges in 5 iterations with a reverse post order traversal. The data flow value at *Entry*(4) changes from v_0 to v_3 to $\bot$ in the first three iterations. The fourth iteration is required to propagate this change to $\mathsf{Entry}(2)$ and the fifth iteration is required to detect the fixed point.

The depth of the CFG is 1. The number of iterations can be explained by the following *ifp* whose origin is $\langle \mathsf{Exit}(3), v_0\rangle$.

$$(\langle O_3, v_0\rangle \rightarrow \langle I_4, v_0\rangle \rightarrow \langle O_4, v_0\rangle \rightarrow \langle I_5, v_0\rangle \rightarrow \langle O_5, v_1\rangle \rightarrow \langle I_2, v_1\rangle \rightarrow$$
$$\langle O_2, v_1\rangle \rightarrow \langle I_4, v_3\rangle \rightarrow \langle O_4, v_3\rangle \rightarrow \langle I_5, v_3\rangle \rightarrow \langle O_5, v_3\rangle \rightarrow \langle I_2, v_3\rangle \rightarrow$$
$$\langle O_2, \bot\rangle \rightarrow \langle I_4, \bot\rangle \rightarrow \langle O_4, \bot\rangle \rightarrow \langle I_5, \bot\rangle \rightarrow \langle O_5, \bot\rangle \rightarrow \langle I_2, \bot\rangle)$$

The width of this *ifp* is 3 due to three occurrences of non-conforming edge $O_5 \rightarrow I_2$; observe that the data flow values associated with the multiple occurrence of program points are different. □

5.3.5 Information Flow Paths in Non-separable Frameworks

Recall that in bit vector frameworks, only one change is possible in the data flow value of a given entity α at a given program point u. Further, the value of α at u is influenced only by the value of α at a neighbouring program point v; some other entity β cannot influence the value of α. In fast frameworks, the data flow value of α at u could change multiple times. Hence information flow paths for fast frameworks are defined in terms of a given assignment of values and a program point is qualified with the data flow value. Besides, they are also defined for a given entity due to the independence of entities.

In non-separable frameworks the possible changes in data flow values are still more general. A data flow value of an entity α at a program point u can be influenced by the data flow value of some other entity β at a neighbouring program point v. Similar to fast frameworks, data flow value of an entity could change multiple times. Thus multiple interdependent information flows are simultaneously possible at a given program point.

Example 5.6

Consider the CFG in Figure 5.10 on the next page. In constant propagation framework, the value of variable c in node 4 is influenced by the value of a computed in node 2 (via definition of b in node 5) as well as by the value of b computed in 3. We cover these influences in separate information flow paths. Also, the value of a generated in node 2 is propagated to the entry and exit points of nodes 4, 5, 6. This propagation is covered by a separate *ifp*. □

We continue to define an information flow path for a single thread of information flow. Since an *ifp* is defined in terms of a given assignment, using the data flow value of an entity at a the program point where multiple *ifp*s intersect, allows us to handle interdependence of information flows.

We use the concepts and notations from Section 4.5 that models the component flow functions in non-separable frameworks in terms of primitive and composite

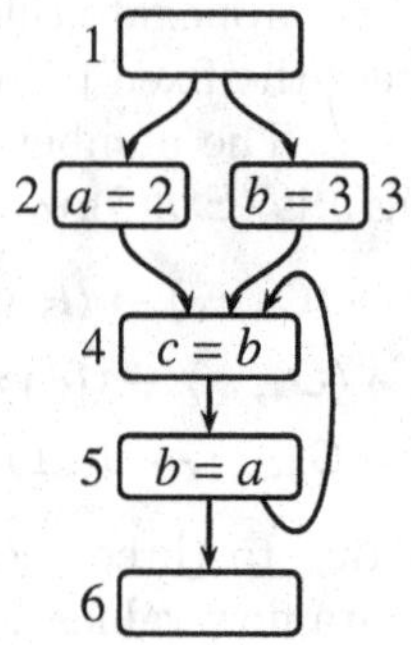

FIGURE 5.10
A CFG to illustrate information flow paths in copy constant propagation.

entity functions. We extend the notation by using program points u and v and edges between them as subscripts of a function. A component function $\widehat{f}^{\alpha}$ that computes the data flow value of an entity α at program point v from the values of other entities at a neighbouring program point u is denoted by $\widehat{f}^{\alpha}_{u\to v}$. If it can be defined in terms of primitive entity functions (*pef*s):

$$\widehat{f}^{\alpha}_{u\to v}(\mathsf{X}_u) = \prod_{\beta\in\Sigma} \overline{f}^{\beta\to\alpha}_{u\to v}\left(\widehat{\mathsf{X}}^{\beta}_{u}\right) \tag{5.9}$$

where Σ is the set of entities, and $\overline{f}^{\beta\to\alpha}_{u\to v}$ is the *pef* that computes the data flow value of α at program point v from the value of β at program point u.

Since we need to handle changes across different entities, we extend the notion of information flow to qualify a program point with the entity also.

DEFINITION 5.10 *A tuple $\left\langle v, \widehat{\mathsf{z}}^{\alpha}_{v}, \alpha\right\rangle$ is an origin of information flow for entity α if any of the following conditions is satisfied:*

1. *v is* Entry(Start) *and $\widehat{\mathsf{X}}^{\alpha}_{v} \neq \widehat{\top}$ in* $\mathsf{BI}_{\mathsf{Start}}$.
2. *v is* Exit(End) *and $\widehat{\mathsf{X}}^{\alpha}_{v} \neq \widehat{\top}$ in* $\mathsf{BI}_{\mathsf{End}}$.
3. *If there exists a pair of adjacent program points u, v such that for some entity $\alpha \in \Sigma$,* pef *$\overline{f}^{\beta\to\alpha}_{u\to v}$ is a constant* pef *$\widehat{\phi}_{\mathsf{z}}$ computing the value $\widehat{\mathsf{z}} \neq \widehat{\top}$ for every $\beta \in \Sigma$.*

Observe that any other *pef* cannot originate the flow of information. Similarly, a composite entity function (*cef*) also cannot originate the flow of information.

At each point in an *ifp*, we record the entity denoted *en* whose data flow value is modified at that point as a result of the application of a non-constant component function, and use it to identify the candidate entity at the subsequent point. Changes in values due to merging of information are computed using the *latest*() function as discussed in the context of fast frameworks.

DEFINITION 5.11 *Given an assignment $A : \mathbb{P}\text{oints} \mapsto L \cup \{\text{undef}\}$, and an origin $\langle p_0, \widehat{x}_0^{\alpha}, \alpha\rangle$ of information flow for some entity α, an information flow path ρ is defined as a maximal acyclic sequence of tuples*

$$(\langle p_0, x_0, \alpha\rangle, \langle p_1, x_1, en_1\rangle, \ldots, \langle p_m, x_m, en_m\rangle)$$

where $\forall \beta \neq \alpha \in \Sigma, \widehat{x}_0^{\beta} = A_0^{\beta}$ and given $\langle p_i, x_i, en_i\rangle$, its successor $\langle p_{i+1}, x_{i+1}, en_{i+1}\rangle$ is defined as follows:

1. *p_i, p_{i+1} are adjacent program points,*
2. *Let ρ' be the prefix of ρ containing i tuples. Select a β such that en_i influences β through a non-constant* pef *or a* cef*. Then,*

$$en_{i+1} = \beta$$

$$\widehat{x}_{i+1}^{\gamma} = \begin{cases} \widehat{f}_{p_i \rightarrow p_{i+1}}^{\beta}(x_i) \oplus latest(p_{i+1}, \rho', \beta) & \gamma = \beta \\ latest(p_{i+1}, \rho', \gamma) & \text{otherwise} \end{cases}$$

where

(a) *latest(u, ρ', β) returns value $\widehat{x}_j^{\beta}$ if p_j is the last occurrence of u in ρ; if ρ does not contain u, then latest(u, ρ', β) returns A_u^{β}.*

(b) $\widehat{x} \oplus \widehat{x}' = \begin{cases} \widehat{x} & \widehat{x}' = \text{undef} \\ \widehat{x} \sqcap \widehat{x}' & \textit{otherwise} \end{cases}$

When the changes in data flow values are not required explicitly, we denote an *ifp* by a sequence of program points $p_0, p_1, \ldots, p_n$. In the presence of cycles, a program point q contained in a cycle may appear multiple times in an *ifp*. The condition of acyclicity in the definition of *ifp* implies that a tuple $\langle u, x_u, en_u\rangle$ cannot appear twice in an *ifp*, although a program point u may appear multiple times.

Example 5.7

Consider the instance of copy constant propagation for the CFG in Figure 5.10 on the facing page. Figure 5.11 on the next page shows some information flow paths for this instance. Changes in data flow values due to application of non-constant component functions are shown by adding edges from $\widehat{x}_u^{\alpha} \rightarrow \widehat{x}_v^{\beta}$ for each edge $\langle u, x_u, \alpha\rangle \rightarrow \langle v, x_v, \beta\rangle$ in the *ifp*. Thick arrows indicate the traversal along the back edge $5 \rightarrow 4$. We leave identification of the *ifp*s beginning at node 3 as an exercise. □

$$A_{I_1} = \langle \top, \top, \top \rangle$$
$$A_{O_1} = \langle \top, \top, \top \rangle$$
$$A_{I_2} = \langle \top, \top, \top \rangle \quad (O_2, \langle 2, \top, \top \rangle, a),$$
$$A_{O_2} = \langle \top, \top, \top \rangle \quad (I_4, \langle 2, \top, \top \rangle, a),$$
$$A_{I_3} = \langle \top, \top, \top \rangle \quad (O_4, \langle 2, \top, \top \rangle, a),$$
$$A_{O_3} = \langle \top, \top, \top \rangle \quad (I_5, \langle 2, \top, \top \rangle, a),$$
$$A_{I_4} = \langle \top, \top, \top \rangle$$
$$A_{O_4} = \langle \top, \top, \top \rangle \quad (O_5, \langle 2, \top, \top \rangle, a),$$
$$A_{I_5} = \langle \top, \top, \top \rangle \quad (I_6, \langle 2, \top, \top \rangle, a),$$
$$A_{O_5} = \langle \top, \top, \top \rangle \quad (O_6, \langle 2, \top, \top \rangle, a)$$
$$A_{I_6} = \langle \top, \top, \top \rangle$$
$$A_{O_6} = \langle \top, \top, \top \rangle$$

Assignment A ifp ρ w.r.t. A

$$A_{I_1} = \langle \top, \top, \top \rangle$$
$$A_{O_1} = \langle \top, \top, \top \rangle \quad (O_2, \langle 2, \top, \top \rangle, a),$$
$$A_{I_2} = \langle \top, \top, \top \rangle \quad (I_4, \langle 2, \top, \top \rangle, a),$$
$$A_{O_2} = \langle 2, \top, \top \rangle \quad (O_4, \langle 2, \top, \top \rangle, a),$$
$$A_{I_3} = \langle \top, \top, \top \rangle \quad (I_5, \langle 2, \top, \top \rangle, a),$$
$$A_{O_3} = \langle \top, \top, \top \rangle$$
$$A_{I_4} = \langle 2, \top, \top \rangle \quad (O_5, \langle 2, 2, \top \rangle, b),$$
$$A_{O_4} = \langle 2, \top, \top \rangle \quad (I_4, \langle 2, 2, \top \rangle, b),$$
$$A_{I_5} = \langle 2, \top, \top \rangle \quad (O_4, \langle 2, 2, \top \rangle, b),$$
$$A_{O_5} = \langle 2, \top, \top \rangle \quad (I_5, \langle 2, 2, \top \rangle, b)$$
$$A_{I_6} = \langle 2, \top, \top \rangle$$
$$A_{O_6} = \langle 2, \top, \top \rangle$$

Assignment A' resulting from A, ρ ifp ρ_1 w.r.t. A'

$$A_{I_1} = \langle \top, \top, \top \rangle \quad (O_2, \langle 2, \top, \top \rangle, a),$$
$$A_{O_1} = \langle \top, \top, \top \rangle \quad (I_4, \langle 2, \top, \top \rangle, a),$$
$$A_{I_2} = \langle \top, \top, \top \rangle \quad (O_4, \langle 2, \top, \top \rangle, a),$$
$$A_{O_2} = \langle 2, \top, \top \rangle$$
$$A_{I_3} = \langle \top, \top, \top \rangle \quad (I_5, \langle 2, \top, \top \rangle, a),$$
$$A_{O_3} = \langle \top, \top, \top \rangle \quad (O_5, \langle 2, 2, \top \rangle, b),$$
$$A_{I_4} = \langle 2, 2, \top \rangle \quad (I_4, \langle 2, 2, \top \rangle, b),$$
$$A_{O_4} = \langle 2, 2, \top \rangle \quad (O_4, \langle 2, 2, 2 \rangle, c),$$
$$A_{I_5} = \langle 2, 2, \top \rangle \quad (I_5, \langle 2, 2, 2 \rangle, c),$$
$$A_{O_5} = \langle 2, 2, \top \rangle \quad (O_5, \langle 2, 2, 2 \rangle, c),$$
$$A_{I_6} = \langle 2, \top, \top \rangle \quad (I_4, \langle 2, 2, 2 \rangle, c)$$
$$A_{O_6} = \langle 2, \top, \top \rangle$$

Assignment A'' resulting from A', ρ_1 ifp ρ_2 w.r.t. A''

$$A_{I_1} = \langle \top, \top, \top \rangle$$
$$A_{O_1} = \langle \top, \top, \top \rangle$$
$$A_{I_2} = \langle \top, \top, \top \rangle \quad (O_3, \langle \top, 2, \top \rangle, b),$$
$$A_{O_2} = \langle 2, \top, \top \rangle \quad (I_4, \langle 2, \bot, \top \rangle, b),$$
$$A_{I_3} = \langle \top, \top, \top \rangle \quad (O_4, \langle 2, 2, \bot \rangle, c),$$
$$A_{O_3} = \langle \top, \top, \top \rangle$$
$$A_{I_4} = \langle 2, 2, 2 \rangle \quad (I_5, \langle 2, 2, \bot \rangle, c),$$
$$A_{O_4} = \langle 2, 2, 2 \rangle \quad (O_5, \langle 2, 2, \bot \rangle, c),$$
$$A_{I_5} = \langle 2, 2, 2 \rangle$$
$$A_{O_5} = \langle 2, 2, 2 \rangle \quad (I_4, \langle 2, \bot, \bot \rangle, c)$$
$$A_{I_6} = \langle 2, \top, \top \rangle$$
$$A_{O_6} = \langle 2, \top, \top \rangle$$

Assignment A''' resulting from A'', ρ_2 ifp ρ_3 w.r.t. A'''

Data flow value x_u is $\langle \widehat{x}_u^a, \widehat{x}_u^b, \widehat{x}_u^c \rangle$ for variables a, b, c.

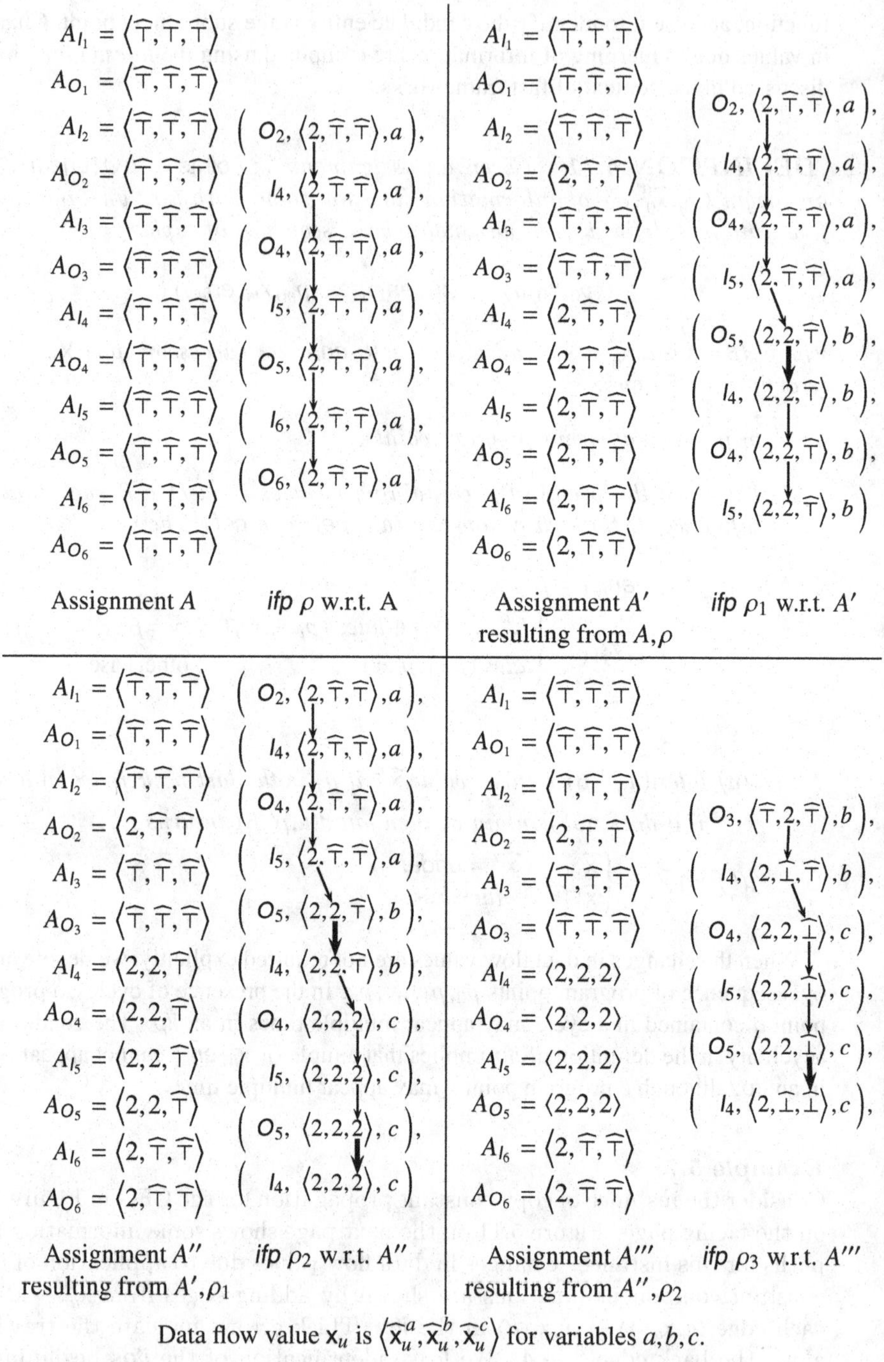

FIGURE 5.11

Some information flow paths in copy constant propagation for CFG in Figure 5.10

$$(O_1, \langle \top,\top,\top,3\rangle, d), \quad (I_2, \langle \top,\top,\bot,\bot\rangle, c),$$
$$(I_2, \langle \top,\top,\top,3\rangle, d), \quad (O_2, \langle \top,\top,\bot,\bot\rangle, c),$$
$$(O_2, \langle \top,\top,\top,3\rangle, d), \quad (I_3, \langle \top,\top,\bot,\bot\rangle, c),$$
$$(I_3, \langle \top,\top,\top,3\rangle, d), \quad (O_3, \langle \top,\bot,\bot,\bot\rangle, b),$$
$$(O_3, \langle \top,\top,\top,3\rangle, d), \quad (I_4, \langle \top,\bot,\bot,\bot\rangle, b),$$
$$(I_4, \langle \top,\top,\top,3\rangle, d), \quad (O_4, \langle \top,\bot,\bot,\bot\rangle, b),$$
$$(O_4, \langle \top,\top,\top,3\rangle, d), \quad (I_5, \langle \top,\bot,\bot,\bot\rangle, b),$$
$$A_{I_1} = \langle \top,\top,\top,\top\rangle \quad (I_5, \langle \top,\top,\top,3\rangle, d), \quad (O_5, \langle \top,\bot,\bot,\bot\rangle, b),$$
$$A_{O_1} = \langle \top,\top,\top,\top\rangle \quad (O_5, \langle \top,\top,\top,6\rangle, d), \quad (I_2, \langle \top,\bot,\bot,\bot\rangle, b),$$
$$A_{I_2} = \langle \top,\top,\top,\top\rangle \quad (I_2, \langle \top,\top,\top,\bot\rangle, d), \quad (O_2, \langle \bot,\bot,\bot,\bot\rangle, a),$$
$$A_{O_2} = \langle \top,\top,\top,\top\rangle \quad (O_2, \langle \top,\top,\top,\bot\rangle, d), \quad (I_3, \langle \bot,\bot,\bot,\bot\rangle, a),$$
$$A_{I_3} = \langle \top,\top,\top,\top\rangle \quad (I_3, \langle \top,\top,\top,\bot\rangle, d), \quad (O_3, \langle \bot,\bot,\bot,\bot\rangle, a),$$
$$A_{O_3} = \langle \top,\top,\top,\top\rangle \quad (O_3, \langle \top,\top,\top,\bot\rangle, d), \quad (I_4, \langle \bot,\bot,\bot,\bot\rangle, a),$$
$$A_{I_4} = \langle \top,\top,\top,\top\rangle \quad (I_4, \langle \top,\top,\top,\bot\rangle, d), \quad (O_4, \langle \bot,\bot,\bot,\bot\rangle, a),$$
$$A_{O_4} = \langle \top,\top,\top,\top\rangle \quad (O_4, \langle \top,\top,\bot,\bot\rangle, c), \quad (I_5, \langle \bot,\bot,\bot,\bot\rangle, a),$$
$$A_{I_5} = \langle \top,\top,\top,\top\rangle \quad (I_5, \langle \top,\top,\bot,\bot\rangle, c), \quad (O_5, \langle \bot,\bot,\bot,\bot\rangle, a),$$
$$A_{O_5} = \langle \top,\top,\top,\top\rangle \quad (O_5, \langle \top,\top,\bot,\bot\rangle, c), \quad (I_2, \langle \bot,\bot,\bot,\bot\rangle, a)$$
$$A_{I_6} = \langle \top,\top,\top,\top\rangle$$
$$A_{O_6} = \langle \top,\top,\top,\top\rangle$$

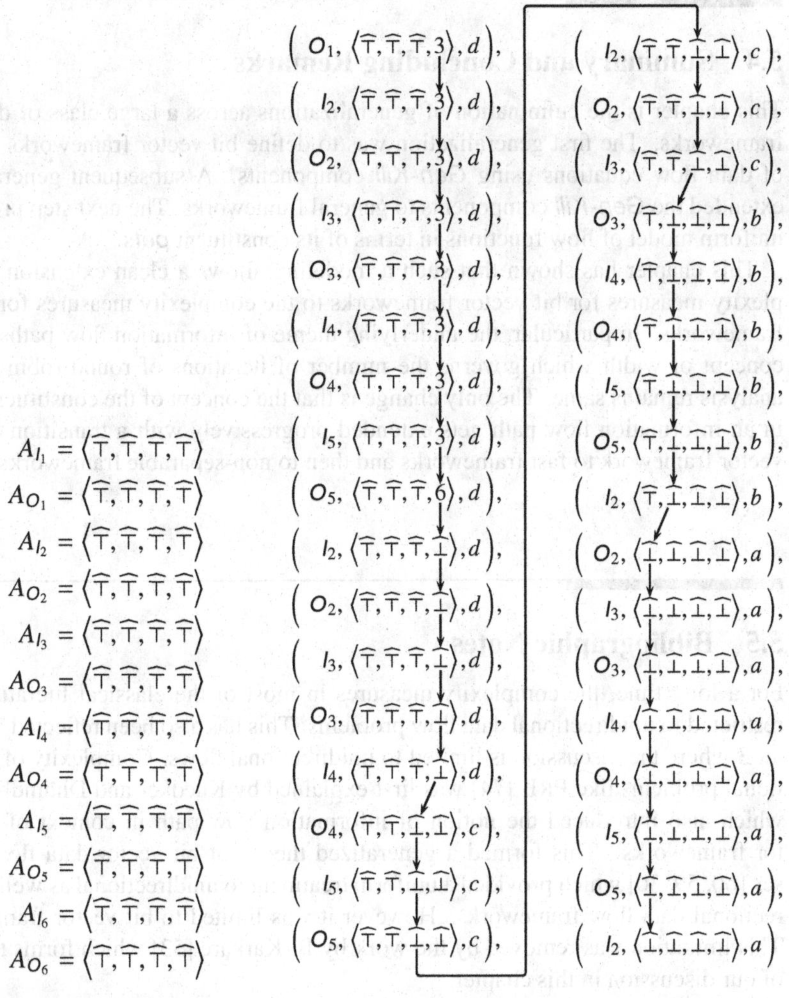

(a) Given assignment A (b) An *ifp* ρ w.r.t. A. *width*$(\rho) = 4$

FIGURE 5.12
A width defining *ifp* in constant propagation problem in Figure 5.5 on page 164.

Example 5.8
Recall that round-robin method requires 6 iterations for Constant Propagation example for CFG with $d = 1$ in Figure 5.5 on page 164. This can be explained using the *ifp* shown in Figure 5.12. In this *ifp*, the non-conforming edge *Exit*(5) → *Entry*(2) appears 4 times, which makes width of this *ifp* 4. ☐

5.4 Summary and Concluding Remarks

This chapter is the culmination of generalizations across a large class of data flow frameworks. The first generalization was to define bit vector frameworks in terms of data flow equations using *Gen-Kill* components. A subsequent generalization extended the *Gen-Kill* components to general frameworks. The next step provided a uniform model of flow functions in terms of its constituent *pef*s.

This chapter has shown that such a modeling allows a clean extension of complexity measures for bit vector frameworks to the complexity measures for general frameworks. In particular, the underlying theme of information flow paths and the concept of width which governs the number of iterations of round-robin iterative analysis remains same. The only change is that the concept of the constituent points in an information flow path gets extended progressively with a transition from bit vector framework to fast frameworks and then to non-separable frameworks.

5.5 Bibliographic Notes

For a long time, the complexity measures in most of the classical literature were restricted to unidirectional data flow problems. This has also been reflected in Chapter 3 where the discussion is limited to unidirectional flows. Complexity of bidirectional problems like PRE [74] was first explained by Khedker and Dhamdhere [60] which also introduced the notion of information flow path in context of bit vector frameworks. This formed a generalized theory of bit vector data flow analyses [60, 59, 30] which provided a uniform treatment to unidirectional as well as bidirectional data flow frameworks. However it was limited to bit vector frameworks. This limitation was removed by the work by B. Karkare [53] which forms the basis of our discussion in this chapter.

We have restricted ourselves to iterative methods of data flow analysis. This is because both round-robin and work list variants of iterative data flow analysis are general methods and can be used for all data flow frameworks. For bit vector frameworks, a much larger class of methods exists. Among them, elimination methods use the structural properties of CFGs and have been widely studied. The pioneering works in elimination methods of data flow analysis are by Allen and Cocke [7], Graham and Wegman [37] and Tarjan [98]. Ryder and Paull [86] describe these methods in details. A much wider range of solution methods have been described by Hecht [44] and Kennedy [57].

6

Single Static Assignment Form as Intermediate Representation

In this chapter we present an intermediate form of programs called single static assignment (SSA) form that is useful for many optimizations. Because of the sparseness of def-use chains in the representation, optimizations based on SSA form can be performed efficiently.

6.1 Introduction

The result of many data flow analyses can be represented by superimposing structures called def-use or use-def chains on the CFG of a program. As mentioned in Section 2.3.3, a def-use chain associates with each definition a list of statements that are reached by the definition and contain uses of the variable being defined. Similarly, a use-def chain associates with each use of a variable, a list of statements containing definitions of the variable that reach the use. Def-use chains can be computed by extending liveness analysis. In this extension, the data flow information is a set of tuples (x,n) where $x \in \mathbb{V}\mathsf{ar}$ and n is a basic block, where it is assumed that each statement forms a basic block by itself. The CFG is traversed backwards as in liveness analysis. The use of a variable x in a statement at n generates the tuple (x,n). If a statement at n' contains a definition of the variable x, then, for each (x,n) in $\mathit{Out}_{n'}$, n' is chained to n. (x,n) is subsequently killed by the statement at n'. Similarly, use-def chains can be found by a minor modification of reaching definitions analysis. Optimizations like dead code elimination make use of def-use chains whereas constant propagation and loop-invariant detection make use of use-def chains. Figure 6.1 shows an example program and its CFG on which the def-use chains have been superimposed. A def-use chain is concretely represented by a set of def-use edges connecting the definition with its uses.

Def-use chains are used to propagate data flow information. A def-use edge may bypass a path through a number of control flow edges and directly connect a definition with its use. Clearly, the time taken for performing an optimization based on def or use-def chains will depend on the number of def-use edges in the graph. Any optimization over the example program shown in Figure 6.1 will have to repeatedly iterate over the 12 chains, propagating a data flow value from a definition to its

```
switch(machineId)
{ case1:
    st = initState1;
    break;
  case2:
    st = initState2;
    break;
  case3:
    st = initState3;
}
while (1)
{ sym = getsym();
  if(isAlpha(sym))
    st = next[st,sym];
  elseif(sym == '\n')
  { printf("%d\n", st);
    nextline();
  }
  else
  { printf("%d\n", st);
    break;
  }
}
```

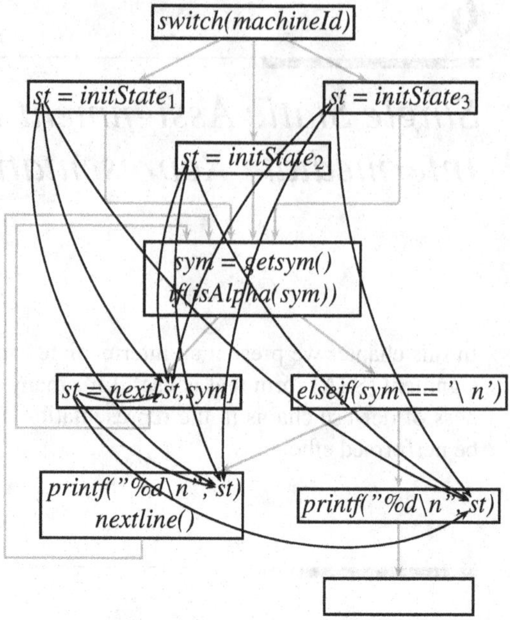

FIGURE 6.1
Example of def-use chains.

corresponding uses in each iteration. The number of def-use edges tend to proliferate when each of several definitions of a variable reach several uses of the same variable through a join node in the CFG. As an example, m definitions reaching each of n uses result in $m \times n$ def-use chains.

6.1.1 An Overview of SSA

A program in SSA form reduces the number of def-use (or use-def) chains by introducing a separate variable version for each definition of the same variable reaching a join node. Thus st_1, st_2, st_3 and st_4 are four different versions of the same variable st. Each version corresponds to a definition of state. The values carried by the four versions are transferred to a new version, st_5, at a join node. This is done using a notational mechanism called a ϕ-instruction. A ϕ-instruction is a special kind of assignment whose right hand side consists of a ϕ-function applied to the incoming variable versions (st_1, st_2, st_3 and st_4 for the example), and the left hand side consists of the new version (st_5). The variable st_5 reaches each of several uses in the original program. These uses are also modified to receive their values from st_5. Thus there are m def-use chains, one for each st_i reaching the ϕ-instruction, and n def-use chains corresponding to the definition involving the ϕ-instruction reaching each of n uses,

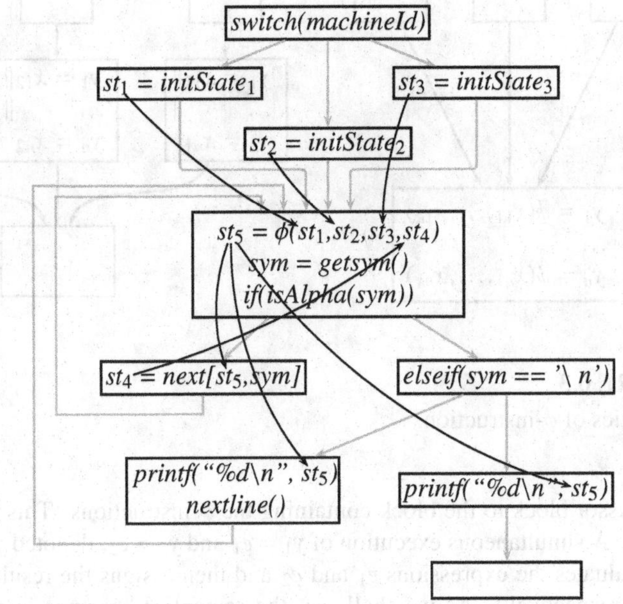

FIGURE 6.2
The earlier example in SSA form.

making up a total of $m+n$ chains. Figure 6.2 shows the earlier program in SSA form. The reduction in the number of def-use chains can be clearly observed.

The variables involved in ϕ-instructions are called ϕ-variables. The variables on the right hand side of a ϕ-instruction are called the *arguments* of the ϕ-instruction and the variable on the left hand side is called the *result*. Since the transformation to SSA form includes insertion of ϕ-instructions, it is important to describe the semantics of the ϕ-instructions. Consider a basic block with k predecessors. Then the block could have several ϕ-instructions, all placed at the beginning of the block. These are denoted as:

$$y_1 = \phi(x_{11}, x_{12}, \ldots, x_{1k})$$
$$y_2 = \phi(x_{21}, x_{12}, \ldots, x_{2k})$$
$$\vdots$$
$$y_n = \phi(x_{n1}, x_{n2}, \ldots, x_{nk})$$

During execution, if the block containing these instructions is reached along predecessor edge j, then the effect of these instructions is that of simultaneously executing the assignment statements $y_1 = x_{1j}$, $y_2 = x_{2j}$, $\ldots$, $y_n = x_{nj}$ along the edge from the jth

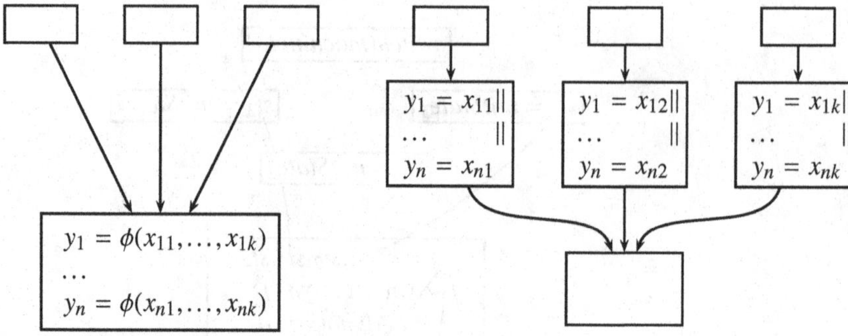

FIGURE 6.3
Semantics of ϕ-instruction.

predecessor block to the block containing the ϕ-instructions. This is shown in Figure 6.3. A simultaneous execution of $y_1 = e_1$ and $y_2 = e_2$, denoted $y_1 = e_1 \parallel y_1 = e_2$, first evaluates the expressions e_1 and e_2 and then assigns the resulting values to y_1 and y_2 respectively. As we shall see, the semantics becomes important when we transform the program into and out of SSA form.

6.1.2 Benefits of SSA Representation

Transformation of a program to SSA form results in a sparser representation of def-use chains. The benefit that results due to this sparsity is an improvement in time to perform the optimization. To see this, consider a generic work list based algorithm that uses def-use edges. Such an algorithm will propagate data flow values from the definition of a variable to its uses. Therefore, we can associate data flow values with the definition end and the use end of each def-use edge. At any point of time, the work list will hold def-use edges for which the data flow value has yet to be propagated from the definition to the use. After this is done, the propagated value is used to compute the value of the definition that depends on this use and, provided this is a new value, all def-use edges which have this definition as the argument are put on the work list.

The algorithm takes time proportional to the product of the total number of def-use edges and the number of times each edge can be inserted in the work list. The number of times each def-use edge can be put on the work list is the same as the maximum number of changes in the data flow value, and this is the same as the height of the data flow lattice. Thus, if we fix the data flow lattice, the time required for the analysis depends on the number of def-use edges in the program representation. As we have argued earlier, the number of def-use edges in a program in SSA form is smaller than the program from which it was constructed, thus reducing the time required for the analysis.

The second benefit is that certain analyses or optimizations become easier due to the nature of the SSA form itself. In a SSA form program, there is exactly one definition reaching each use of a variable. To see a use of this property, consider a method for detection of induction variables in a program. Figure 6.4 shows a program along with its SSA form. The def-use edges from the definitions to the uses of variables are shown explicitly. To discover that i is an induction variable of the original program, we note that statements $i_3 = \phi(i_1, i_2)$ and $i_2 = i_3 + 2$ form a strongly connected region (SCR) involving (versions of) the variable i in the SSA form program. The initial value of the variable is supplied by the statement $i_1 = 0$ and the statements constituting the SCR increase i by a constant in each iteration. In addition, since the SCR passes through the ϕ-instruction, i is identified as an induction variable of the outer loop. This information is not readily available in the original program with def-use chains. By a similar reasoning, j is detected to be an induction variable of the inner loop of the original program. Its increment, i, is detected to be a loop invariant of the inner loop because the definition of i_2 reaching the statement $j_2 = j_3 + i_2$ in the SSA form program is outside the SCR formed by the statements $j_3 = \phi(j_1, j_2)$ and $j_2 = j_3 + i_2$.

A larger example of use of SSA form will be presented later in the chapter when we discuss a method for register allocation that exploits the special properties of SSA form programs.

6.2 Construction of SSA Form Programs

As in reaching definitions analysis (Section 2.3.3), we assume that the node *Start* contains an assignment of the special value *undef* to every variable. Thus along any path in the CFG from *Start* to the use of a variable, there is at least one definition of the variable reaching the use. Programs which satisfy this property are called *strict programs*.

As mentioned earlier, the ϕ-instructions should be inserted where more than one definition coming along different paths converge. We first formalize the notion of converging paths.

DEFINITION 6.1 *Let $\rho_1 = (n_1, n_2, \ldots, o)$ and $\rho_2 = (m_1, m_2, \ldots, o)$ be non-null paths. ρ_1 and ρ_2 are said to converge, if:*

1. *The start nodes of ρ_1 and ρ_2 are different, i.e., $n_1 \neq m_1$.*
2. *The two paths are disjoint except for the node o.*

Note that the common node o could occur in more than one position in the two paths. An interesting example of converging paths for the CFG in Figure 6.5 is (n_1, n_5, n_7) and (n_7, n_9, n_{10}, n_7). If a variable is defined in nodes 1 and 7 of the CFG,

```
i = 0;
while (...)
{  i = i + 2;
   j = i;
   while (...)
       j = j + i;
}
```

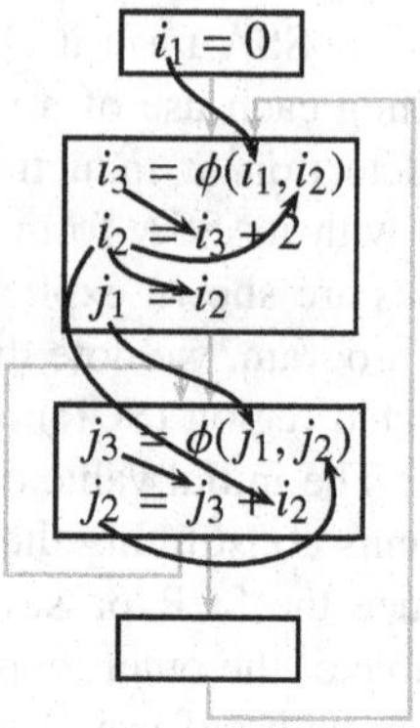

FIGURE 6.4
Detecting induction variables using SSA form.

then there must be a ϕ-instruction for this variable at the entry of 7. The example shows why the end node is allowed to occur in more than one position in the paths—the converging paths may include loops*. The pair of paths (n_5, n_7, n_8, n_{10}) and (n_6, n_7, n_9, n_{10}) is an example of paths that are non-converging.

We now specify the properties of a valid transformation of a program to SSA form. The algorithm that we describe later will be proved to be correct with respect to this specification.

DEFINITION 6.2 *The transformation of a program to another is a valid SSA-transformation, if the following two conditions are satisfied:*

1. *Correctness of form: Each variable mentioned in the transformed program must have exactly one definition.*

2. *Semantic invariance: Consider an execution path leading to a use of a variable x in the original program and a corresponding execution path leading to the variable version x_i in the program in SSA form. Then, under the execution semantics of ϕ-instructions described earlier, the two variables x and x_i must have the same value.*

Unless stated otherwise, by the phrase 'a program in SSA form' we shall mean a program that has been obtained by a valid SSA-transformation of a strict program.

A program in SSA form is *minimal*, if it results from a transformation satisfying the properties listed above and has a minimum number of ϕ-instructions. A program in SSA form is *pruned*, if it has the added restriction that a ϕ-instruction is inserted only if the result variable of the instruction is used later along some path.

*Observe that (n_1, n_5, n_7) and $(n_6, n_7, n_9, n_{10}, n_7)$ are also converging paths by the definition. This is clearly not necessary since their role is subsumed by the pair of paths (n_1, n_5, n_7) and (n_6, n_7).

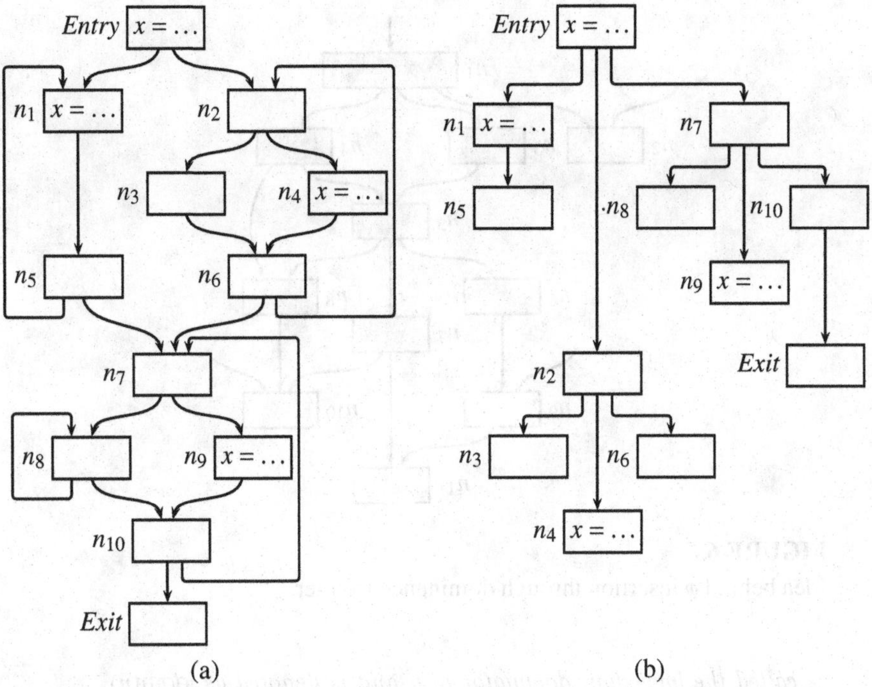

FIGURE 6.5
(a)A CFG and (b) its dominator tree.

To distinguish between the predecessor and successor relation in the CFG and the same relation in the dominator tree, we use the terms *ancestor* and *descendant* in the latter case. An immediate descendant will be called a child.

6.2.1 Dominance Frontier

The key idea behind insertion of ϕ-instructions is that of *dominance frontier*. To develop this idea, we first define the concept of dominance in a graph. Recall the definition of dominance from Section 3.1.

DEFINITION 6.3 *Let n and m be nodes in the CFG. The node n is said to dominate m, denoted $n \geq m$, if every path from* **Start** *to m passes through n.*

We also need a notion of dominance that is not reflexive.

DEFINITION 6.4 *If $n \geq m$ and $n \neq m$, then we say that n strictly dominates m and denote this as $n > m$. Further, the closest strict dominator of a node n*

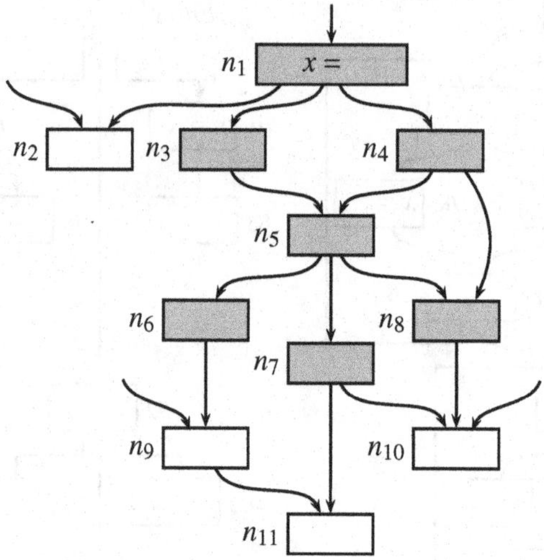

FIGURE 6.6
Idea behind ϕ insertion through dominance frontier.

is called the immediate dominator of n and is denoted as idom(n).

We use the notation $n \not\succ m$ to mean n does not strictly dominate m. Figure 6.5 shows a CFG and its *dominator tree* in which the edges represent immediate dominance. We shall sometimes consider dominance to be a relation between program points instead of nodes.

OBSERVATION 6.1 *If the nodes n and m both dominate a node o then either* $n \succeq m$ *or* $m \succeq n$.

Consider Figure 6.6 in which the node n_1 contains a definition of the variable x. The node n_6 is dominated by n_1 and so are all the shaded nodes in the figure. Each shaded node will have the property of a single definition of x reaching it and will thus not require a ϕ-instruction for x. Now consider the node n_9 which is an immediate successor of n_6 and is not dominated by n_1. This node needs a ϕ-instruction because, apart from the definition in n_1, some other definition, possibly the one that is assumed to initialize the value of x to *undef* at *Start*, will reach n_9. Nodes such as n_9, and n_{10} are said to be in the *dominance frontier* of n_1 and need a ϕ-instruction for the variable x. We shall now formalize this idea.

A straightforward translation of the idea represented by Figure 6.6 gives a first definition of dominance frontier. The dominance frontier of a node n, denoted *df*(n), is given as

$$\mathit{df}(n) = \{m \mid \exists p \in \mathit{pred}(m),\ (n \succeq p \text{ and } n \not\succ m)\}$$

By this definition, a loop header will be included in its own dominance frontier. This is reasonable since a variable in the loop header may have two reaching definitions—one from inside the loop, the other from outside. As an example, if n_1 is a loop header in Figure 6.6, a program point in n_1 before the definition of x will have more than one reaching definition—one reaching from outside the loop and the other from the definition in n_1 itself. In such a situation there will be a ϕ-instruction at the beginning of n_1.

A direct implementation of the above definition will find $\mathit{df}(n)$ by considering each node m dominated by n and checking whether it has an immediate successor in the CFG that is not strictly dominated by n. The problem with this approach is that it finds the dominance frontier of each node independently of the dominance frontier of other nodes. A more efficient algorithm that exploits the relation between dominance frontiers of different nodes is based on the following observations:

1. Consider Figure 6.6 as an example. Nodes that are immediate successors of n_1 and not strictly dominated by n_1 are in $\mathit{df}(n_1)$. An example of such a node is n_2. We call such nodes as $\mathit{df}_{base}(n_1)$ as these nodes are included in what can be considered as the base step of an inductive definition for df.

$$\mathit{df}_{base}(n) = \{m \in \mathit{succ}(n) \mid n \not\succ m\}$$

2. We shall now relate the dominance frontier of n_1 in Figure 6.6 to the dominance frontier of its children. Consider n_5 as an example of a child of n_1. The node n_9, which is in $\mathit{df}(n_5)$, is also in $\mathit{df}(n_1)$. However, n_8, which is also in $\mathit{df}(n_5)$ is not in $\mathit{df}(n_1)$. The reason is that while n_5 does not dominate n_8, its immediate dominator n_1 dominates n_8. We call this component of df as df_{ind}, the inductive step of the definition of df.

$$\mathit{df}_{ind}(n) = \bigcup_{m \in \mathit{children}(n)} \{p \in \mathit{df}(m) \mid \mathit{idom}(m) \not\succ p\}$$

Combining the two:

$$\mathit{df}(n) = \mathit{df}_{base}(n) \cup \mathit{df}_{ind}(n)$$

We can reformulate df_{base} and df_{ind} so that they use the easily checkable $\neq$ relation instead of $\not\succ$. If m is a successor of n then the condition $n \succ m$ is exactly the same as $n = \mathit{idom}(m)$. Thus

$$\mathit{df}_{base}(n) = \{m \in \mathit{succ}(n) \mid n \neq \mathit{idom}(m)\}$$

Similarly, if m is a child of n and p is in $\mathit{df}(m)$, then the condition $n \succ p$ is exactly the same as $n = \mathit{idom}(p)$. To see this, we first observe that any strict dominator of p is also a strict dominator of m. Assume to the contrary that o is a strict dominator of p and either o is the same as m or o is unrelated to m in the dominance relationship. In the first case o cannot dominate p, because p is in $\mathit{df}(o)$. In the second, if o is

Input: A CFG with the dominance frontier for each node.
Output: The dominance frontier of each node n in the CFG computed in a variable DF_n.
Algorithm:

```
for each n in a bottom up traversal of the dominator tree do
{  DF_n = ∅
   for each m ∈ succ(n) do                              /* Calculate df_base */
      if idom(m) ≠ n then DF_n = DF_n ∪ {m};
   for each m ∈ children(n) do                          /* Calculate df_ind */
      for each p ∈ DF_m do
         if idom(p) ≠ n then DF_n = DF_n ∪ {p};
}
```

FIGURE 6.7
The algorithm for dominance frontier.

unrelated to m, o cannot dominate p since there is an alternate path from *Start* to p through m which does not pass through o. Thus we have a contradiction.

Now since n is the closest ancestor of m that strictly dominates p, we must have $n = \mathit{idom}(p)$. Thus we can rewrite df_{ind} as

$$df_{ind}(n) = \bigcup_{m \in children(n)} \{p \in df(m) \mid n \neq idom(p)\}$$

The algorithm in Figure 6.7 computes the dominance frontier using the formulation presented above. The table in Figure 6.8 gives df_{base} and df_{ind} for the nodes in the CFG in Figure 6.5.

Let E and N be the number of edges and nodes in the CFG. To calculate df_{base}, the algorithm clearly visits each edge once, so its complexity is $O(E)$. Let $|df(n)|$ denote the size of dominance frontier of the node n. Then the complexity of the part that calculates df_{ind} is bounded by $O(\Sigma_n|df(n)|)$. This is $O(N^2)$ for arbitrary CFGs, which gives an overall complexity of $O(E+N^2)$. However, it can be shown that for CFGs programs composed of assignments, if-then-else and while-dos, $|df(n)|$ is a constant. For such CFGs, both $O(\Sigma_n|df(n)|)$ and E are $O(N)$. Thus the complexity of the algorithm is also $O(N)$.

6.2.2 Placement of ϕ-instructions

The algorithm for placing ϕ-instructions is shown in Figure 6.9. It considers each variable in turn and maintains a work list for nodes that are yet to be examined. For every variable it starts by inserting the nodes that contain an assignment to the variable in the work list. The dominance frontier of each node in the work list is examined. ϕ-instructions are inserted in the nodes forming the dominance frontier, and these nodes are in turn inserted in the work list.

The algorithm, maintains the following variables.

Node	*Exit*	10	9	8	7	6	5	4	3	2	1	*Entry*
df_{base}	∅	7	8,10	10	∅	7,2	7,1	6	6	∅	∅	∅
df_{ind}	∅	∅	∅	∅	7	∅	∅	∅	∅	7,2	7,1	∅

FIGURE 6.8
df_{base} and df_{ind} for the CFG in Figure 6.5 on page 191.

- *inWorklist*: If $inWorklist_n$ is x, it means that the node n has been inserted in the work list in connection with the variable x.
- *inserted*: If $inserted_n$ is x, it means that a ϕ-instruction has been inserted in node n for the variable x.
- *assign*: $assign_x$ is the set of nodes containing an assignment to the variable x in the original program.

It is possible for the following situation to arise: A node n has been put in the work list in connection with a variable but a ϕ-instruction for the variable has not yet been inserted in n. This could happen, for instance, when the node being examined is a loop header containing an assignment to a variable. Thus $inserted_m$ and $inWorklist_m$ could have different values when entering the body of the **for** loop in line 13 and therefore checking the condition $inWorklist_m \neq x$ in line 16 is not redundant.

For the CFG in Figure 6.5 on page 191, a ϕ-instruction for the variable x is inserted at node 1 since 1 contains a definition of x and is in its own dominance frontier. Similarly a ϕ-instruction is inserted in 6 which is in $df(4)$ and 2 which is in $df(6)$. ϕ-instructions are also inserted in 7 and 10.

From a single node, the notion of dominance frontier can be generalized to a set of nodes in the following way:

$$df(S) = \bigcup_{x \in S} df(x)$$

It is easy to see that df is monotonic, i.e., $S_1 \subseteq S_2$ implies $df(S_1) \subseteq df(S_2)$.

If S_x is the set of nodes containing assignments to the variable x, then the ϕ-instructions placed by the ϕ-placement algorithm is given by the *iterated dominance frontier* of S_x denoted as $idf^+(S_x)$. This is defined as the limit of the increasing sequence $idf^i(S)$:

$$idf^1(S) = df(S) \quad (6.1)$$

$$idf^{i+1}(S) = df(S \cup idf^i(S)) \quad (6.2)$$

Let $A_{orig}(n)$ and $A_{trans}(n)$ represent the number of assignments in node n in the original and the transformed program. Observe that nodes are put in the work list $O(A_{trans})$ number of times, and for each node n that has been put in the work list $O(|df(n)|)$ nodes are examined. Let *avgcost* represent this work averaged over all the assignments in the transformed program. Thus

Input: A CFG with the dominance frontier for each node.
Output: The CFG with the ϕ-instructions inserted but without variable renaming.
Algorithm:

```
0    worklist = ∅
1    for each node n do
2    {  insertedₙ = x₀                    /* x₀ should not occur in the program */
3       inWorklistₙ = x₀
4    }
5    for each variable x do
6        for each n ∈ assign(x) do
7        {  inWorklistₙ = x
8           worklist = worklist ∪ {n}
9        }
10       while worklist ≠ ∅ do
11       {  remove a node n from worklist
12           for each m ∈ dfₙ do
13               if insertedₘ ≠ x then
14               {  place a φ-instruction for x at m
15                   insertedₘ = x
16                   if inWorklistₘ ≠ x then
17                   {  inWorklistₘ = x
18                       worklist = worklist ∪ {m}
19                   }
20               }
21       }
```

FIGURE 6.9

The algorithm for ϕ placement.

$$avgcost = \sum_n (A_{trans}(n) \times |df(n)|)/\Sigma_n(A_{trans}(n))$$

Then the cost for computation of the iterated dominance frontier is $avgcost \times \Sigma_n(A_{trans}(n))$. However, for CFGs consisting of assignments, if-then-else and while-dos, $avgcost$ is a constant and the complexity reduces to $O(\Sigma_n(A_{trans}(n)))$.

6.2.3 Renaming of Variables

The algorithm for renaming is given in Figure 6.11. In order to generate new versions of the variable, the algorithm maintains a counter for each variable. To rename the use of a variable in an assignment, the algorithm needs to keep track of the definition that reaches the use. The algorithm maintains a array of stacks (called *stacks*), one for each variable for this purpose. As the algorithm traverses the program, the version of x that reaches a program point is given by the value of $top(stacks_x)$. In addition, to rename the arguments of a ϕ-function, we need to know the predecessor number

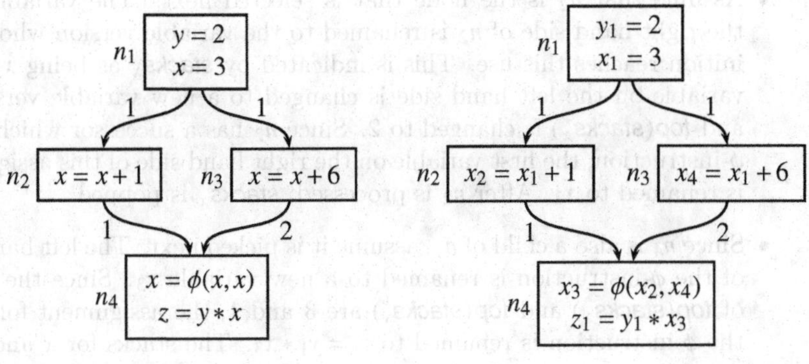

FIGURE 6.10
CFG before and after renaming variables.

of a node with respect to its successor†. This is given by *predNumber*(m,n), where n is a predecessor of m.

Consider a call to *rename*(n). If a variable x is used by an ordinary assignment, it is renamed to the version x_i given by *top*(*stacks*$_x$). The definition of a variable y, whether defined by a ordinary assignment or a ϕ-instruction, is renamed to a new version y_j. The new version number j is inserted in the stack for y. The call to *rename*(n) also renames the arguments of the ϕ-function in each successor m of n. The reason why this is done during a call to *rename*(n) is the following. To rewrite the ith argument of a ϕ-function, we need to know the variable version whose definition reaches the end of the ith predecessor. If x is the current variable being renamed, it is at this point of time that we know that *top*(*stacks*$_x$) is the version of x reaching the end of *predNumber*(m,n). This information is used for renaming. Thus the uses on the right hand side of a ϕ-instruction and an ordinary assignment are renamed during different calls to *rename*.

Example 6.1

We illustrate the algorithm for renaming variables through the example in Figure 6.10. The labels on the edges number the predecessors of a node. Thus n_2 and n_3 are the first and the second predecessors of n_4.

- The algorithm does a reverse postorder traversal of the dominator tree starting with node n_1. The variables on the left hand side of the assignments are renamed to y_1 and x_1. Since none of n_1's successors contain a ϕ-instruction, the children of n_1 are processed next. The values of *top*(*stacks*$_x$) and *top*(*stacks*$_y$) are both 1 at this time.

---

†The predecessors of a node are assumed to be ordered.

- Assume that n_2 is the node that is selected next. The variable x on the right hand side of n_2 is renamed to the variable version whose definition reaches this use. This is indicated by $\textsf{stacks}_x$ as being x_1. The variable on the left hand side is changed to a new variable version x_2 and $\textsf{top}(\textsf{stacks}_x)$ is changed to 2. Since n_2 has a successor which has a ϕ-instruction, the first variable on the right hand side of this assignment is renamed to x_2. After n_2 is processed, $\textsf{stacks}_x$ is popped.

- Since n_4 is also a child of n_1, assume it is picked next. The left hand side of the ϕ-instruction is renamed to a new variable x_3. Since the values of $\textsf{top}(\textsf{stacks}_x)$ and $\textsf{top}(\textsf{stacks}_y)$ are 3 and 1, the assignment following the ϕ-instruction is renamed to $z_1 = y_1 * x_3$. The stacks for x and z are popped.

- Finally, the block n_3 is rewritten as shown in the figure. Since n_4 is a successor of n_3 and this has a ϕ-instruction, the second argument of the ϕ-instruction is renamed to x_4, the version of x reaching this program point.

□

Let $M_{trans}(n)$ denote the number of mentions (uses and definitions) of variables in the block n of the transformed program. Then the algorithm is linear in total number of mentions of variables in the entire transformed program, i.e., the complexity is $O(\Sigma_n(M_{trans}(n)))$.

6.2.4 Correctness of the Algorithm

We now show that the algorithm to calculate the dominance frontier, the ϕ-placement algorithm and the renaming algorithm together satisfy the specification of a valid transformation to SSA form. To do this we first need to prove the following important property regarding placement of ϕ-instructions in the transformed program: If two non-null paths which begin with the definitions of different versions of the same variable converge at a node n, then there is a ϕ-instruction for the variable at n. Note that the definitions at the beginning of the converging paths could themselves involve ϕ-instructions.

DEFINITION 6.5 *Given a set of nodes S, the join of S is defined as:*

$$\textsf{join}(S) = \{n \mid \exists \text{ converging paths } m_1 \xrightarrow{+} n \text{ and } m_2 \xrightarrow{+} n,\ m_1, m_2 \in S\} \tag{6.3}$$

The iterated join of a set of nodes S, denoted $\textsf{ij}^+(S)$, is defined as the limit of the increasing sequence $\textsf{ij}^i(S)$:

$$\textsf{ij}^1(S) = \textsf{join}(S) \tag{6.4}$$

$$\textsf{ij}^{i+1}(S) = \textsf{join}(S \cup \textsf{ij}^i(S)) \tag{6.5}$$

Input: A CFG with ϕ-instruction inserted.
Output: The same CFG with variables renamed.
Algorithm:

```
for each variable x do
{  counter_x = 0; stacks_x = emptyStack
}
rename(Start)

function rename(n)
{  for each assignment a in n do
   {  if a is an ordinary assignment then
         for each variable x in RHS(a) do
            replace x by x_i where i = top(stacks_x)
      let y be LHS(a) in
      {  i = counter_y
         replace y by new variable y_i in y = e
         push i onto stacks_y
         counter_y = i + 1
      }
   }
   for each m ∈ succ(n) do
   {  j = predNumber(m,n)
      for each φ-instruction a in m do
         replace j-th operand x in RHS(a) by x_i, where i = top(stacks_x)
   }
   for each m ∈ children(n) do rename(n)
   for each assignment a in n do
      pop(stacks_z), where z is the original variable of LHS(a)
}
```

FIGURE 6.11
Algorithm for renaming.

The property regarding placement of ϕ-instructions can now be recast as follows: If S_x is the set of definition involving a variable x in the original program, then there must be a ϕ-instruction for x in every node in $ij^+(S_x)$. To prove this, we need a result relating the end node of a non-null path with the iterated dominance frontier of the start node of the path.

LEMMA 6.1
Consider a path $\rho : n \xrightarrow{+} m$. We can find a node n' on ρ such that $n' \in \{n\} \cup idf^+(\{n\})$ and n' dominates m. Further, if n does not dominate each node in ρ, $n' \in idf^+(\{n\})$.

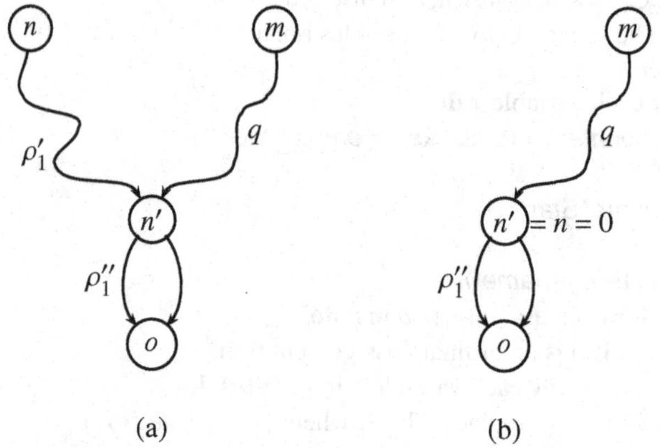

FIGURE 6.12
Figure illustrating Lemma 6.2.

PROOF Clearly, if n dominates each node in ρ, then n' is the same as n. Now assume that there are nodes in ρ that are not dominated by n. Let the path ρ be $(n = n_0, n_1, \ldots, n_k = m)$. Since n does not dominate all nodes in ρ, there will be some nodes in ρ that are in $\mathit{idf}^+(\{n\})$. Let n_j be the node with the largest index j that is in $\mathit{idf}^+(\{n\})$. Claim that n_j is the required n'.

Suppose n_j does not dominate m. Then consider the closest node n_i on ρ that is not dominated by n_j. All nodes in between n_j and n_{i+1} are dominated by n_j. Thus $n_i \in \mathit{df}(\{n_j\})$ and since $n_j \in \mathit{idf}^+(\{n\})$, $n_i \in \mathit{idf}^+(\{n\})$. Thus n_j is not the node with the largest index that is in $\mathit{idf}^+(\{n\})$. ∎

The second lemma shows that a one step join of two nodes is contained in the union of their iterated dominance frontier.

LEMMA 6.2
Let n and m be two distinct nodes in the CFG. Then $\mathit{join}(\{n,m\}) \subseteq \mathit{idf}^+(\{n\}) \cup \mathit{idf}^+(\{m\})$.

PROOF Let $o \in \mathit{join}(\{n,m\})$. Then there are non-null paths $\rho_1 : n \overset{+}{\rightarrow} o$ and $\rho_2 : m \overset{+}{\rightarrow} o$ converging at o. From Lemma 6.1, there is a node n' on ρ_1 and a node m' on ρ_2 such that both n' and m' dominate o. We prove the lemma by case analysis:

1. *n' is also on ρ_2:* The general situation is illustrated by Figure 6.12(a) where ρ_1 is a concatenation of the paths ρ_1' and ρ_1''. Of course, one of the path segments ρ_1' and ρ_1'' could be null. From the definition of convergence, n' is the same as o. If n does not dominate all nodes in ρ_1

then Lemma 6.1 gives us $n' \in \mathit{idf}^+(\{n\})$ and we are through. If n dominates all the nodes in ρ_1 then the situation is illustrated by Figure 6.12(b) obtained by considering ρ_1' to be a null path. Clearly n' and n are the same and $n' \in \mathit{df}(\{n\})$. Therefore $n' \in \mathit{idf}^+(\{n\})$.

2. *m' is also on ρ_1:* The reasoning for this case is similar to the previous case.

3. *n' is not on ρ_2 and m' is not on ρ_1:* We shall show that this is not possible. Since n' and m' both dominate o, from Observation 6.1, either $n' \geq m'$ or $m' \geq n'$. The condition $m' \geq n'$ along with $n' \geq o$ implies that every path from m' to o has n' on it. In particular, n' is on ρ_2. Since this is not the case, the only possibility is $n' \geq m'$. By a symmetrical reasoning, we also have $m' \geq n'$. This gives $n' = m'$ contradicting the initial assumption that n' is not on ρ_2.

∎

It is easy to generalize Lemma 6.2 to any finite set of nodes.

COROLLARY 6.1
For a set of nodes S, $\mathit{join}(S) \subseteq \mathit{idf}^+(S)$.

PROOF Induction on the number of nodes in S and use of Lemma 6.2.
∎

We now show that dominance frontier is contained in joins.

LEMMA 6.3
Let S be a set of CFG nodes that contains the Start *node. Then $\mathit{df}(S) \subseteq \mathit{join}(S)$.*

PROOF Let $n \in S$ and $m \in \mathit{df}(\{n\})$. Then there is a path ρ_1 from n to m in which all the nodes till the predecessor of m are dominated by n. Of course, m could be the same as n. Further, since $m \in \mathit{df}(\{n\})$, there is a path ρ_2 from *Start* to m which does not pass through any node in ρ_1 except m. Since the two paths converge at m, m is in $\mathit{join}(S)$. ∎

We finally show that iterated dominance frontier computes the same set that is specified by iterated joins.

LEMMA 6.4
Let S be a set of nodes in a CFG that contains the **Start** *node. Then*

$$ij^+(S) = idf^+(S)$$

PROOF We first prove

$$ij^+(S) \subseteq idf^+(S)$$

by an induction on the iteration index in the definition of ij^+. Specifically, we show that for all k,

$$ij^k(S) \subseteq idf^+(S)$$

Then, since $ij^+(S) = ij^k(S)$ for some finite k, we shall have shown the containment in the limit.

Basis: Follows from Corollary 6.1.

$$ij(S) = join(S) \subseteq idf^+(S)$$

Inductive step:

$$\begin{aligned}
ij^k(S) &= ij(S \cup ij^k(S)) && \\
&\subseteq ij(S \cup idf^+(S)) && \text{(induction hypothesis, monotonicity of } ij\text{)} \\
&= join(S \cup idf^+(S)) && \text{(definition of } ij\text{)} \\
&\subset idf^+(S \cup idf^+(S)) && \text{(Corollary 6.1)} \\
&= idf^+(S) && \text{(definition of } idf\text{)}
\end{aligned}$$

The proof of $idf^+(S) \subseteq ij^+(S)$ is very similar.
∎

Let S_x represent the set of nodes which contain a definition of x. By our assumption, $Start \in S_x$. Therefore $ij^+(S_x) = idf^+(S_x)$ for any variable x in the program.

We next prove the first condition in the specification of valid SSA-transformation is satisfied by the algorithm.

LEMMA 6.5
Each variable in the SSA form program is assigned exactly once.

PROOF After renaming the definition of a variable x in the original program, $counter_x$ is incremented before renaming the next definition. So there is at most one assignment to a variable x_i. Thus we have to show that for each variable x_i which has a use occurrence in the SSA form program, there is at least one assignment to x_i.

When the renaming algorithm was renaming the use occurrence of x to x_i, the value of $top(stacks_x)$ must have been i. Since $top(stacks_x)$ is set to a value i only after renaming a definition of x to x_i, there is at least one definition of x_i. ∎

For an assignment statement a, let the notations $before(a)$ and $after(a)$ denote program points just before and after a. Similarly, if n is a block then $after(n)$ will denote a program point just after the last statement in n.

Finally we show that the SSA-transformation algorithm maintains semantic invariance. We show that the value of a variable x at a statement in the original program is the same as the renamed variable at the same statement in the SSA form program. This requires us to know what the renamed variable at different program points are. The version of x at the program point p in the transformed program is denoted as $version(x, p)$. This is the version that corresponds to the value of $top(stacks_x)$ when the renaming algorithm is at the program point p during its traversal of the CFG. Clearly, the following relations hold:

1. If the statement a_1 is followed by the statement a_2 in a block, then

$$version(x, after(a_1)) = version(x, before(a_2))$$

2. If a is the last statement in a block n, then

$$version(x, after(a)) = version(x, after(n))$$

LEMMA 6.6
Let x be a variable and $n \rightarrow m$ be an edge in the CFG such that m does not have a ϕ-instruction for x. Then

$$version(x, after(n)) = version(x, after(idom(m)))$$

PROOF If $n = idom(m)$, there is nothing to be proven. So assume that $n \neq idom(m)$. Since n dominates a predecessor of m (namely itself) and does not strictly dominate m, $m \in df(n)$. Further, from Lemma 6.4, since m does not have a ϕ-instruction for x, n does not have a definition for x.

Observe that $idom(m)$ strictly dominates n; otherwise there would be a path from *Start* to m through n which bypasses $idom(m)$. Consider the node o that is closest to m, strictly dominates m and defines x. Then

$$version(x, after(n)) = version(x, after(idom(m))) = version(x, after(o))$$

∎

Given a variable x and a control flow path ρ from *Start* to a program point p, let $val(x, \rho)$ denote the value of x at program point p when execution takes place along ρ.

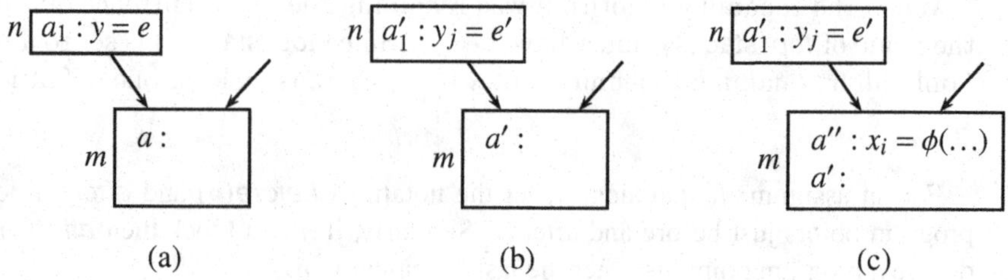

FIGURE 6.13
Figure illustrating Lemma 6.7. (a) represents the original program and (b) and (c) represent the transformed program.

LEMMA 6.7
Consider a path ρ in the original program from **Start** *to an assignment statement a. Let ρ' and a' be the corresponding path and statement in the SSA-transformed program. Then, for any variable x,*

$$\mathit{val}(x,\rho) = \mathit{val}(\mathit{version}(x, \mathit{before}(a')),\rho')$$

PROOF The proof is by induction on number of statements in the path ρ. In the proof, a will denote the last statement of ρ and a' and ρ' will denote the corresponding statement and path in the transformed program. Further $\rho - \{a\}$ will denote the path obtained by deleting the last statement a from ρ.

Basis: Consider the path ρ from *Start* to the first statement a of the successor node of *Start*. Clearly for any variable x,

$$\begin{aligned}\mathit{val}(x, \rho) &= \mathit{undef}\\ &= \mathit{val}(x_0, \rho')\\ &= \mathit{val}(\mathit{version}(x, \mathit{before}(a')), \rho')\end{aligned}$$

Inductive step: Now assume that the lemma holds for all paths of length $k-1$ or less. Consider a path ρ of length k. We consider the following cases.

1. *a is not the first statement of the containing block m.* Consider the statements before a and a' as shown below. e' has been obtained from e by renaming each variable y in e to $\mathit{version}(y, \mathit{before}(x_i = e'))$

$$\begin{array}{ll} x = e & x_i = e' \\ a: & a': \end{array}$$

By the induction hypothesis, for any variable y,

$$\mathit{val}(y, \rho - \{x = e\}) = \mathit{val}(\mathit{version}(y, \mathit{before}(x_i = e')), \rho' - \{x_i = e'\})$$

Thus from the induction hypothesis and the semantics of the assignment statement,

$$\mathit{val}(x, \rho) = \mathit{val}(\mathit{version}(x, \mathit{before}(a')), \rho')$$

Variables other than x remain unchanged and the statement of the lemma holds for them because of the induction hypothesis.

2. *a is the first statement of the containing block m.* Assume that the control flows along the edge $n \rightarrow m$. This situation is shown in Figure 6.13. The original program is shown in part (a) and the two cases of the transformed program are shown in parts (b) and (c). Let the paths to the end of node n be denoted as ρ_1 and ρ_1'. We first show that for any variable x, $\mathit{val}(x, \rho_1) = \mathit{val}(\mathit{version}(x, \mathit{after}(n)), \rho_1')$. Consider the last statement of n denoted as a_1 and the corresponding statement in the transformed program a_1'. Because of the induction hypothesis, we have for any variable y,

$$\mathit{val}(y, \rho_1 - \{a_1\}) = \mathit{val}(\mathit{version}(y, \mathit{before}(a_1')), \rho_1' - \{a_1'\})$$

Once again, using the induction hypothesis and the semantics of assignment, we have:

$$\mathit{val}(x, \rho_1) = \mathit{val}(\mathit{version}(x, \mathit{after}(a_1')), \rho_1')$$

and therefore

$$\mathit{val}(x, \rho_1) = \mathit{val}(\mathit{version}(x, \mathit{after}(n)), \rho_1')$$

We now have to show that the values of any variable x and its renamed version $\mathit{version}(x, \mathit{before}(a'))$ match. For this consider two subcases:

(a) m does not have a ϕ-instruction for x. Let the path to the immediate dominator of m be ρ_1''. Then:

$$\begin{aligned}\mathit{val}(x,\rho) &= \mathit{val}(x, \rho_1)\\ &= \mathit{val}(\mathit{version}(x, \mathit{after}(n)), \rho_1')\\ &= \mathit{val}(\mathit{version}(x, \mathit{after}(\mathit{idom}(m))), \rho_1'') && \text{(Lemma 6.6)}\\ &= \mathit{val}(\mathit{version}(x, \mathit{before}(a')), \rho')\end{aligned}$$

(Renaming algorithm, line 22)

(b) If m has a ϕ-instruction for x, then:

$$\begin{aligned}\mathit{val}(x, \rho) &= \mathit{val}(x, \rho_1)\\ &= \mathit{val}(\mathit{version}(x, \mathit{after}(n)), \rho_1')\\ &= \mathit{val}(\mathit{version}(x, \mathit{before}(a'')), \rho_1')\end{aligned}$$

(Renaming algorithm, lines 18-20)

$$\begin{aligned}&= \mathit{val}(x_i, \rho') && \text{(Semantics of } \phi\text{-instruction)}\\ &= \mathit{val}(\mathit{version}(x, \mathit{before}(a')), \rho')\end{aligned}$$

(Renaming algorithm, line 8-9)

∎

The following theorem ties the previous results into an statement of correctness of the entire algorithm.

THEOREM 6.1
The algorithms for ϕ-placement and renaming together constitute a valid SSA-transformation.

PROOF Follows from Lemmas 6.5 and 6.7. ∎

We finally prove a property about programs in SSA form that will be used in later sections. Let the program point associated with the definition of a variable x be represented as $\mathsf{def}(x)$. This is the point just before the statement that has a definition of x, where the defining statement may also be a ϕ-instruction. Program points associated with the uses of a variable x are denoted as $\mathsf{use}(x)$, and are defined as follows:

DEFINITION 6.6 *A program point p is in* $\mathsf{use}(x)$ *iff*

1. *The statement just after p is an ordinary assignment (not a ϕ-instruction) and x occurs on the right hand side of the assignment.*
2. *p is* $\mathsf{after}(n)$, *n is the ith predecessor of a block m and m contains a ϕ-function with x as the ith argument.*

We shall use the term $\mathsf{use}(x)$ to refer to any of the points denoted by it.

LEMMA 6.8
(SSA dominance property) *Consider the SSA transformation of a strict program. For any variable x in the transformed program,* $\mathsf{def}(x) \geq \mathsf{use}(x)$.

PROOF Because of the semantic invariance property of an SSA transformation, the SSA of a strict program is also strict. Now assume that there is a use of a variable that is not dominated by its definition. By Lemma 6.5, the variable has a single definition. If this definition does not dominate the use, then the SSA form program is not strict, a contradiction. ∎

The program in SSA form must be finally converted into executable code. However no real processor has instructions that can directly capture the semantics of ϕ-instructions. Therefore the ϕ-instructions have to be replaced by code fragments inserted at appropriate places. The elimination of ϕ-instructions from a program in SSA form is called *SSA destruction*. The intermediate form of the program that

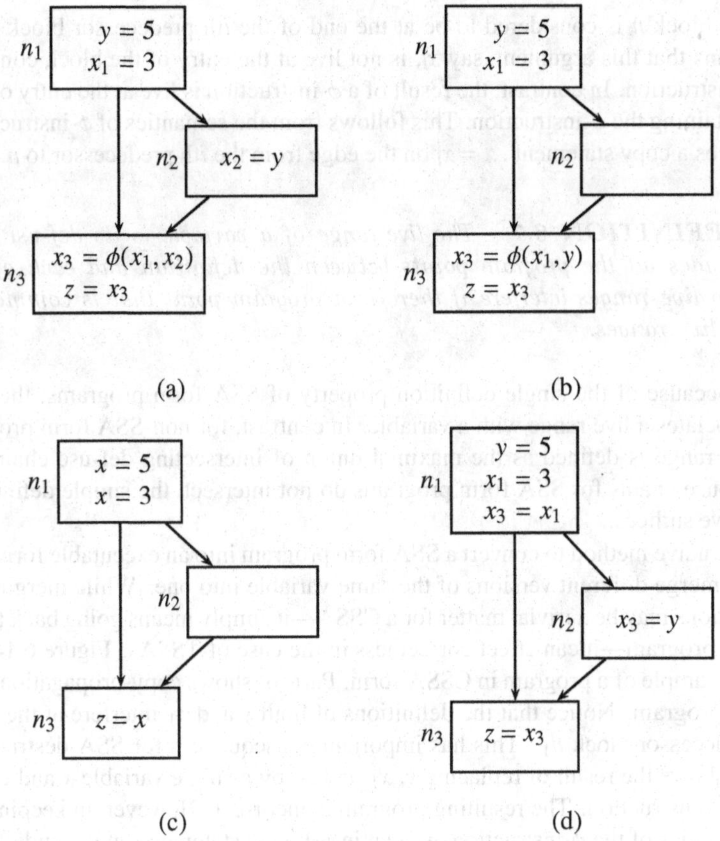

FIGURE 6.14
(a) A program in CSSA form. (b) The same program in TSSA form after copy propagation. (c) Eliminating ϕ assignments by merging variable versions results in an incorrect program. (d) A correct program obtained by inserting copy statements.

emerges as the result of applying the SSA construction algorithm discussed earlier is called *canonical SSA (CSSA)*. This is to distinguish it from the SSA form after optimizations called *transformed SSA (TSSA)*.

6.3 Destruction of SSA

Before embarking on the issues related to SSA destruction, we define live ranges for SSA form programs. Recall that the last use of the ith argument of a ϕ-function in a block n is considered to be at the end of the ith predecessor block of n. This means that this argument, say x_i, is not live at the entry of the block containing the ϕ-instruction. In contrast, the result of a ϕ-instruction is live at the entry of the block containing the ϕ-instruction. This follows from the semantics of ϕ-instruction which places a copy statement $\ldots = x_i$ on the edge from the ith predecessor to n.

DEFINITION 6.7 *The live range of a variable is its def-use chain. It includes all the program points between the definition and each of its uses. Two live ranges interfere if there is a program point that is common to both the live ranges.*

Because of the single definition property of SSA form programs, the definition associates a live range with a variable. In contrast, for non-SSA form programs, the live range is defined as the maximal union of intersecting def-use chains[‡]. Since def-use chains for SSA form programs do not intersect, the simple definition given above suffices.

A naive method to convert a SSA form program into an executable form may simply merge different versions of the same variable into one. While merging variable versions may be a trivial matter for a CSSA—it simply means going back to the original program—it can affect correctness in the case of TSSAs. Figure 6.14(a) shows an example of a program in CSSA form. Part (b) shows copy-propagation applied to the program. Notice that the definitions of both y and x_1 interfere at the end of the predecessor block n_1. This has important consequences for SSA destruction. Part (c) shows the result of replacing y, x_1 and x_3 by a single variable x and eliminating the ϕ-instruction. The resulting program is incorrect. However, in keeping with the semantics of the ϕ-instruction, we can insert copy statements at the end of blocks n_1 and n_2. This is shown in part (d). While this is correct for this example, we shall show later that removing ϕ-instructions by inserting copy statements may still result in incorrect programs. Besides, the copy at the end of n_1 is obviously redundant. The subtleties involved in SSA destruction through insertion of copy statements are illustrated through two well-known problems called the *lost-copy problem* and the *swap problem.*

The lost copy problem is illustrated in Figure 6.15 on the next page. The original program and its SSA form are shown in Figures 6.15, parts (a) and (b). The program after copy propagation and dead-code elimination is shown in part (c). Finally, part (d) shows the program after insertion of copy statements. The resulting program is incorrect because it prints the value of x in the last iteration instead of the penultimate iteration.

The reason for the incorrectness is a departure from the semantics of ϕ-instructions. This requires us to insert the copy $x_3 = x_2$ on the back edge from node n_2 to itself. This edge is a *critical edge.* An edge $n \to m$ is a critical edge if n has more than one successor and m has more than one predecessor. What we have done is to hoist the

[‡]Also called a web.

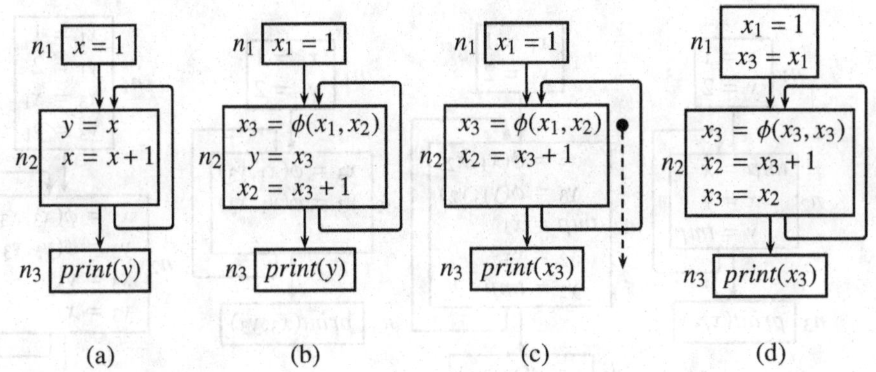

FIGURE 6.15
The lost copy problem.

copy statement across the critical edge. As a result this copy interferes with the live range of x_3 (shown using the dotted arrow).

The swap problem: The swap problem is illustrated in Figure 6.16 on the following page. In this case also the problem arises because the process of SSA destruction does not follow the semantics of ϕ-instructions. The program in Figure 6.16(c) is correct because of the implied translation of the ϕ-instruction to the simultaneous assignment $x_3 = y_3 \parallel y_3 = x_3$. The actual translation, however, replaces the simultaneous assignment by a sequence of assignments resulting in a dependence between them.

6.3.1 An Algorithm for SSA Destruction

Since the algorithm will require us to talk about variables which are related through ϕ-instructions, we introduce the following definitions.

DEFINITION 6.8 *A pair of variables are ϕ-related if they occur in the same ϕ-instruction.*

The idea of variables related through ϕ-instructions, which we have been informally calling variable versions, is captured through ϕ-*congruence*.

DEFINITION 6.9 *For a SSA variable x, ϕ-congruence(x) is the least set defined by the following two rules:*

1. *if y and x are ϕ-related, then y is in ϕ-congruence(x).*
2. *if y and z are ϕ-related and z is in ϕ-congruence(x) then y is in ϕ-congruence(x).*

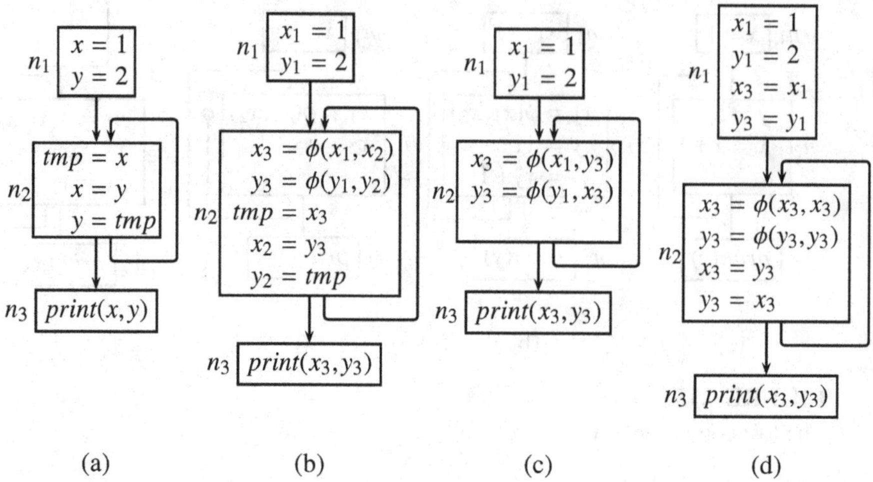

FIGURE 6.16
(a) The original program (b) After conversion to SSA form (c) After copy propagation (d) Destruction of the SSA form program through copying results in an incorrect program.

In other words, variables in ϕ-*congruence*(x) are directly or transitively connected to x through ϕ-instructions. Further, if y is in ϕ-*congruence*(x) then x is also in ϕ-*congruence*(y), and we say that x and y are in the same ϕ-*congruence* class. The notion of ϕ-*congruence* class is very similar to the notion of live range (or web) for programs which are not in SSA form.

For a program in CSSA form, all variables that are in the same ϕ-*congruence* class can be replaced by a common variable and the ϕ-instruction can be eliminated. Our objective now is to modify TSSA programs so that ϕ-instructions can be eliminated in the same way as CSSA programs, i.e., by renaming ϕ-*congruence* variables to the same name.

The reason why SSA-destruction through merging of ϕ-*congruent* variables poses problems in the case of TSSA programs can be better explained through live ranges. Observe in part (a) of Figure 6.17 on the next page that the ϕ-*congruent* variables x_1 and y interfere with each other and thus cannot be replaced by the same variable. Replacing both the variables by a single variable effectively kills the earlier definition. So a key idea might be to make the ϕ-*congruent* variables non-interfering by inserting copy statements. As shown in part (b) of the figure, this has been achieved for the example by inserting the copy statement $x'_1 = x_1$ in block n_1, $x'_2 = y$ in block n_2 and $x_3 = x'_3$ in n_3. Further, the ϕ-instruction has been rewritten to refer to the new variables x'_1, x'_2 and x'_3. Since the live ranges of these ϕ-variables are non-interfering, they can be renamed to a single variable x and the ϕ-instruction can be eliminated. The result is shown in Figure 6.17(c).

A further refinement of the idea is to minimize the number of copy instructions by

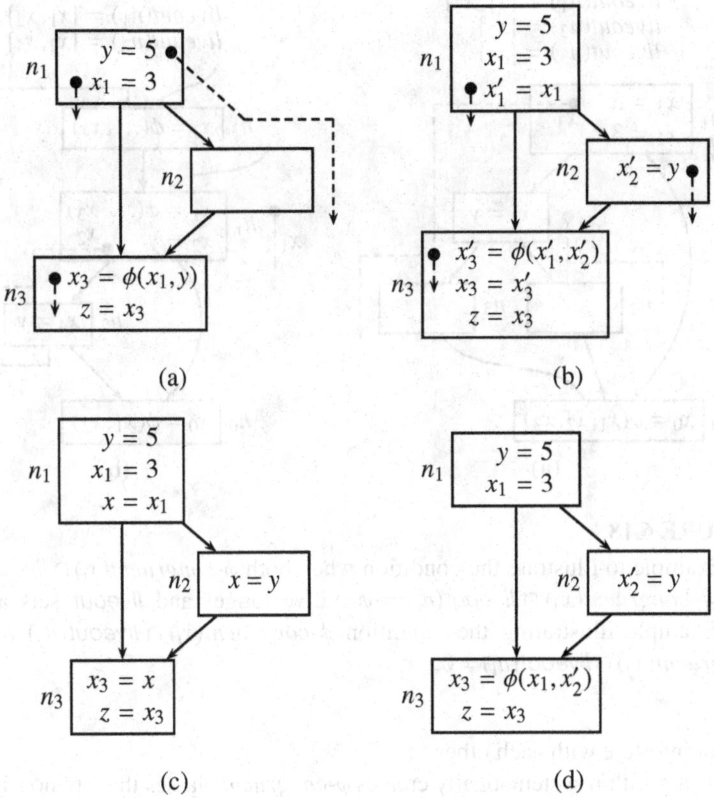

FIGURE 6.17
(a) Interference of Live ranges of the ϕ variables x_1 and y. The dashed lines represent live ranges of variables. (b) Breaking the interference through copy statements. The new ϕ variables x'_1 and x'_2 do not interfere. (c) Eliminating ϕ assignments now results in a correct program. (d) The copy statement for x_1 is redundant.

introducing the copy statement $x'_2 = y$ only. This also makes the live ranges of the ϕ-variables x_1, x'_2 and x_3 non-interfering. The result of this minimization is shown in Figure 6.17(d). Observe that inserting a copy statement $x'_1 = x_1$ at the end of block n_1 instead of $x'_2 = y$ does not break the interference between the live ranges of the variables x'_1 and y which are now *ϕ-congruent*.

The basis for the decision that the insertion of a single copy statement $x'_2 = y$ is enough is as follows. First notice that the only interference that has to be broken is between x_1 and y; x_3 does not interfere with these variables. Now y is live at the exit of n_1. Therefore insertion of a copy statement $x'_1 = x_1$ at the end of n_1 is useless since the new *ϕ-congruent* variables x'_1 and y will still continue to interfere. However insertion of the statement $x'_2 = y$ creates the *ϕ-congruent* variables x_1 and x'_2 which

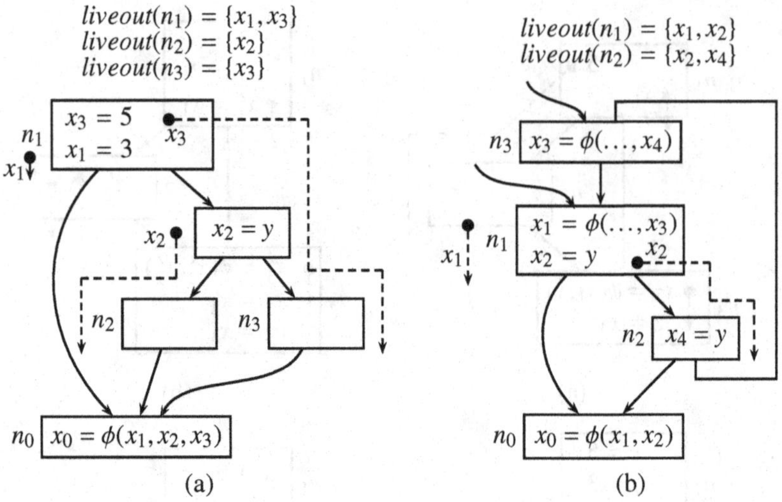

FIGURE 6.18
(a) Example to illustrate the condition when both ϕ-*congruent*$(x_i) \cap$ *liveout*$(n_j) = \phi$ and ϕ-*congruent*$(x_j) \cap$ *liveout*$(n_i) = \phi$. Live ranges and *liveout* sets are shown. (b) Example illustrating the condition ϕ-*congruent*$(x_i) \cap$ *liveout*$(n_j) \neq \emptyset$ and ϕ-*congruent*$(x_j) \cap$ *liveout*$(n_i) \neq \emptyset$.

do not interfere with each other.

The algorithm systematically creates ϕ-*congruent* classes that are non-interfering. Initially ϕ-*congruent*(x) is set to $\{x\}$ for every variable x. It considers in sequence all the ϕ-instructions. For each pair of operands x_i and x_j mentioned in a ϕ-instruction, it checks whether ϕ-*congruent*(x_i) interferes with ϕ-*congruent*(x_j). If it does not, ϕ-*congruent*(x_i) and ϕ-*congruent*(x_j) are merged into the same ϕ-*congruent* class. Otherwise copy statements are inserted to change the variables in the ϕ-instruction itself so that the ϕ-*congruence* classes of the new variables are non-interfering. The method for choosing the copy statement to be inserted is described below. In the description below, n is the block that contains the ϕ-instruction, n_i refers to the ith predecessor of n, and x_i and x_j are the interfering variables. We first consider the case when both x_i and x_j are arguments of the ϕ-instruction:

1. ϕ-*congruent*$(x_i) \cap$ *liveout*$(n_j) \neq \emptyset$ and ϕ-*congruent*$(x_j) \cap$ *liveout*$(n_i) = \emptyset$: This situation is similar to Figure 6.17 with y playing the role of x_i and x_1 playing the role of x_j. In this case, a copy statement $x_i' = x_i$ is needed at the end of n_i. x_i is marked to record this fact.

2. ϕ-*congruent*$(x_j) \cap$ *liveout*$(n_i) \neq \emptyset$ and ϕ-*congruent*$(x_i) \cap$ *liveout*$(n_j) = \emptyset$: This is similar to the previous situation and the variable x_j is marked.

3. ϕ-*congruent*$(x_i) \cap$ *liveout*$(n_j) = \emptyset$ and ϕ-*congruent*$(x_j) \cap$ *liveout*$(n_i) = \emptyset$: This situation is as shown in Figure 6.18(a), where x_2 and x_3 play the roles of x_i

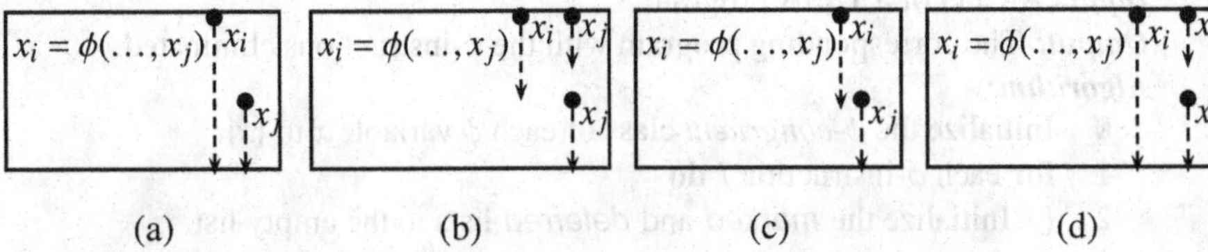

FIGURE 6.19
Interference between argument and result variables of a ϕ-instruction.

and x_j. In this case, either a copy statement $x'_2 = x_2$ at the end of n_2 or a copy statement $x'_3 = x'_3$ at the end of n_3 will break the interference. The better choice is to insert $x'_2 = x_2$ as it will also break the interference between x_3 and x_1. Since we cannot know this till we examine the pairs x_1 and x_2, we defer the insertion of the copy statement till we have examined all the pairs.

4. ϕ-*congruent*$(x_i) \cap$ *liveout*$(n_j) \neq \emptyset$ and ϕ-*congruent*$(x_j) \cap$ *liveout*$(n_i) \neq \emptyset$: This situation is represented by Figure 6.18(b) with x_1 and x_2 playing the roles of x_i and x_j. Note that x_4 is in ϕ-*congruence*(x_1). In this situation copy statements are needed for both x_i and x_j, so both the variables are marked.

When one of the interfering variables, say x_i, is the result and the other variable x_j is an argument of the ϕ-instruction, the situation is slightly more complex. The program point for inserting the copy statement involving the result variable is just after the ϕ-instruction. Consider the block which has the ϕ-instruction. As shown in Figure 6.19(a)–(d), there are four cases:

1. ϕ-*congruent*$(x_i) \cap$ *liveout*$(n) \neq \emptyset$ and ϕ-*congruent*$(x_j) \cap$ *livein*$(n) = \emptyset$: We have to insert the copy statement $x_i = x'_i$ just after the ϕ-instruction. The result variable of the ϕ-instruction is changed to x'_i.

2. ϕ-*congruent*$(x_i) \cap$ *liveout*$(n) = \emptyset$ and ϕ-*congruent*$(x_j) \cap$ *livein*$(n) \neq \emptyset$: As we shall see later when we re-examine the swap problem, this situation occurs when x_j is also the result of a subsequent ϕ-instruction. This requires the copy statement $x'_j = x_j$. The argument variable x_j is changed to x'_j.

3. ϕ-*congruent*$(x_i) \cap$ *liveout*$(n_j) = \emptyset$ and ϕ-*congruent*$(x_j) \cap$ *liveout*$(n_i) = \emptyset$: Here we can insert either a copy statement for x_i or for x_j. As explained earlier, the choice is deferred.

4. ϕ-*congruent*$(x_i) \cap$ *liveout*$(n_j) \neq \emptyset$ and ϕ-*congruent*$(x_j) \cap$ *liveout*$(n_i) \neq \emptyset$: In this situation copy statements are needed for both x_i and x_j.

The variables for which copy statements are to be inserted are added to a marked or deferred list as before. After all variables have been considered, we obtain two lists—a list of variables which have been marked and for which we need copy statements

Input: A CFG of a TSSA program.
Output: The corresponding program with the ϕ-instructions eliminated.
Algorithm:

Initialize the *ϕ-congruent* class of each ϕ variable x to $\{x\}$.
for each ϕ-instruction I **do**
{ Initialize the *marked* and *deferred* lists to the empty list.
  for each pair x_i and x_j of argument variables in I **do**
    if x_i and x_j interfere, **then** proceed according to the four cases described in Section 6.3.1.
  for the result variable x_i and each argument variable x_j **do**
    if x_i and x_j interfere, **then** proceed according to the four cases described in Section 6.3.1.
  if a variable x is in the *marked* list, **then** remove all pairs which have x as one of the components from the *deferred* list.
  while there are elements in the *deferred* list **do**
  { Select the variable x that appears maximum number of times in the *deferred* list.
    Insert x in the *marked* list.
    Remove all pairs which have x as one of the components from the *deferred* list
  }
  for each element x in the *marked* list **do**
  { Insert the copy statement $x' = x$ at the appropriate program point.
    Update I to contain x' instead of x.
    Modify the interference graph to reflect this change.
  }
  Put all the variables of I in the same congruence class.
}
Eliminate all ϕ-instructions.

FIGURE 6.20
An algorithm for SSA destruction.

and the other a list of pair of variables, the choice from which has been deferred. We now choose a variable which appears the largest number of times in the deferred list and enter it in the marked list. All pairs in which it appears are removed from the deferred list. This is repeated till the deferred list is empty.

The last step consists of taking each variable from the marked list, inserting a copy statement for the variable, updating the ϕ-instruction, and updating the live ranges of the old and the new variables. The ϕ-instructions which now contain variables in the same *ϕ-congruent* class are now eliminated. The algorithm for breaking interference through insertion of copy statements is shown in Figure 6.20.

We now explain how the algorithm works on the lost-copy problem and the swap

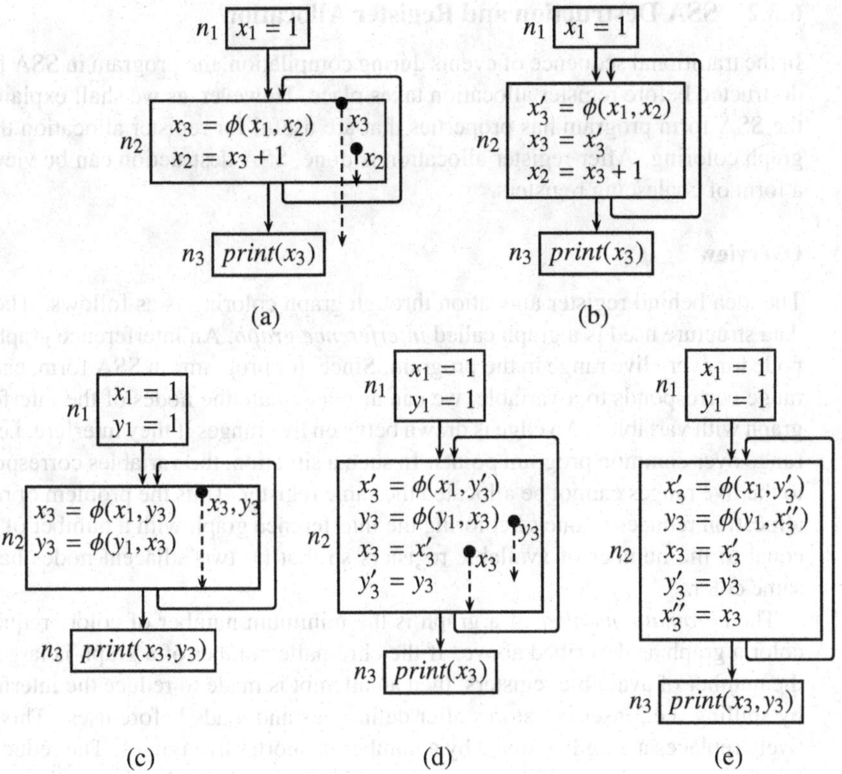

FIGURE 6.21
Illustrating the effect of the algorithm on the lost-copy (Figures (a) and (b)) and the swap problem (Figures (c), (d) and (e)).

problem. Consider the SSA corresponding to the lost-copy problem shown in part (a) of Figure 6.21. The live ranges of x_2 and x_3 interfere. While x_3 is in *liveout*(n_2), x_2 is not in *livein*(n_2). Therefore, as shown in Figure 6.21(b), a copy $x_3 = x'_3$ inserted after the ϕ-instruction breaks the interference.

The SSA form of the program illustrating the swap problem is shown in Figure 6.21(c). The live ranges of both x_3 and y_3 span the entire block n_2. Now consider the first assignment. Since x_3 is in *liveout*(n_2) a copy is needed for x_3. Similarly, since y_3 is in *livein*(n_2), a copy is needed for y_3. Now there is no interference between the variables of the first assignment. Considering the second assignment in Figure 6.21(d), we see that the live ranges of y_3 and x_3 interfere. However, neither y_3 is in *liveout*(n_2) nor x_3 is in *livein*(n_2). Therefore a copy statement for either x_3 or y_3 can be inserted. We choose x_3 and the result is shown in Figure 6.21(e).

6.3.2 SSA Destruction and Register Allocation

In the traditional sequence of events during compilation, the program in SSA form is destructed before register allocation takes place. However, as we shall explain later, the SSA form program has properties that are useful for register allocation through graph coloring. After register allocation is done, SSA destruction can be viewed as a form of coalescing registers.

Overview

The idea behind register allocation through graph coloring is as follows. The main data structure used is a graph called *interference graph*. An interference graph has a node for every live range in the program. Since, for programs in SSA form, each live range corresponds to a variable, we can also associate the nodes of the interference graph with variables. An edge is drawn between live ranges if they interfere, i.e., they range over common program points. In such a situation, the variables corresponding to the live ranges cannot be allocated the same register. Thus the problem of register allocation reduces to one of coloring the interference graph with a number of colors equal to the number of available registers so that no two adjacent nodes have the same color.

The *chromatic number* of a graph is the minimum number of colors required to color a graph as described above. If the chromatic number of a graph is larger than the number of available registers, then an attempt is made to reduce the interference by spilling, i.e., inserting stores after definitions and loads before uses. This effectively replaces a long live range by a number of shorter live ranges. The reduction in interference has the possible consequence of bringing down the chromatic number.

As shown in Figure 6.22, a typical register allocator that uses graph coloring repeats the following steps till the graph is colored.

1. Constructing or updating the interference graph.

2. Coalescing live ranges. If the live range of x ends with a copy statement to y, then the live ranges for x and y can be combined by replacing subsequent references to the uses of y in the live range by x and eliminating the copy. As this will change the interference graph, it has to be updated.

3. Attempt to color nodes. If this requires a node to be spilled, the interference graph has to be updated. So we go back to step 1.

There are two problems with this approach. While coalescing eliminates copy statements, it might also result in a graph with a larger chromatic number. Moreover, since every spill may not reduce the chromatic number of the graph, the interference graph may have to be constructed several times. This can be costly.

Now consider register allocation for a program in SSA form. We shall show that the interference graph of a SSA form program is a special kind of graph called chordal graph. The chromatic number of such a graph is the same as the size of the largest clique. Moreover, the largest clique in a SSA form program is equal to

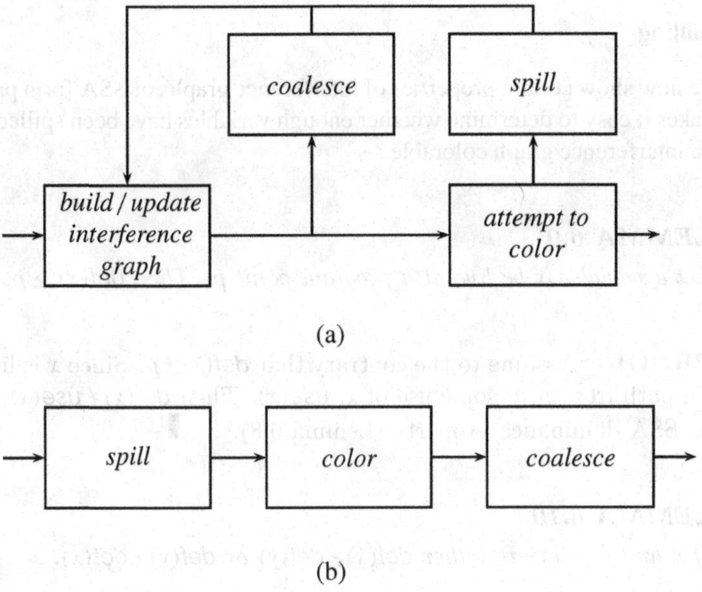

FIGURE 6.22
(a) Traditional register allocation. (b) Register allocation for SSA form programs.

the maximum number of variables live at a program point. So we can spill variables till the largest number of variables live at any program point equals the given number of registers. The interference graph of the resulting program is now guaranteed to be colorable with colors equal to the available number of registers. In fact, for the SSA form program, there is also an efficient algorithm to find the coloring.

While variables are replaced by registers after coloring, the ϕ-instructions are still present. As mentioned earlier, SSA destruction is a form of coalescing. For instance, assume that the ϕ-instructions in a basic block are:

$$R_1 = \phi(R_1, R_3)$$
$$R_2 = \phi(R_2, R_4)$$

For both the ϕ-instructions, the first operand is the same as the result and therefore no transfer of values need take place. An attempt is made to recolor R_3 to R_1 and R_4 to R_2. If this succeeds, then the ϕ-instructions can simply be eliminated. Otherwise copy instructions must be inserted.

The overall scheme for register allocation for SSA form programs is shown in Figure 6.22(b). Note that the process is not iterative. More importantly, all the above steps can be carried without constructing the interference graph.

Spilling

We now show certain properties of interference graphs of SSA form programs which makes it easy to determine whether enough variables have been spilled so as to make the interference graph colorable.

LEMMA 6.9

Let a variable x be live at a program point p. Then $\mathsf{def}(x) \geq p$.

PROOF Assume to the contrary that $\mathsf{def}(x) \not\geq p$. Since x is live at p, there is a path from p to some use of x, $\mathsf{use}(x)$. Then $\mathsf{def}(x) \not\geq \mathsf{use}(x)$ contradicting the SSA dominance property (Lemma 6.8). ∎

LEMMA 6.10

If x and y interfere either $\mathsf{def}(x) \geq \mathsf{def}(y)$ or $\mathsf{def}(y) \geq \mathsf{def}(x)$.

PROOF Since x and y interfere, there is a program point p where they are both live. From Lemma 6.9, both $\mathsf{def}(x)$ and $\mathsf{def}(y)$ dominate p. The result then follows from Observation 6.1. ∎

LEMMA 6.11

Assume $\mathsf{def}(x) \geq \mathsf{def}(y)$. Then x and y interfere if and only if then x is live at $\mathsf{def}(y)$.

PROOF The if part is obvious. For the only if part observe that under the condition $\mathsf{def}(x) \geq \mathsf{def}(y)$ if x is not live at $\mathsf{def}(y)$ then there is no point p such that x is live at p and there is a path from $\mathsf{def}(y)$ to p. It follows that x and y cannot interfere, leading to a contradiction. ∎

LEMMA 6.12

Let $x — y$ and $y — z$ be edges in the interference graph G of a SSA form program. Further, assume that $x — z$ is not an edge in G. If $\mathsf{def}(x) \geq \mathsf{def}(y)$, then $\mathsf{def}(y) \geq \mathsf{def}(z)$.

PROOF Since x and y interfere and $\mathsf{def}(x) \geq \mathsf{def}(y)$, x must be live at $\mathsf{def}(y)$. Further, since y and z interfere, either $\mathsf{def}(y) \geq \mathsf{def}(z)$ or $\mathsf{def}(z) \geq \mathsf{def}(y)$. If $\mathsf{def}(z) \geq \mathsf{def}(y)$, then z must also be live at $\mathsf{def}(y)$ and x and z interfere. This is a contradiction and we must have $\mathsf{def}(y) \geq \mathsf{def}(z)$. ∎

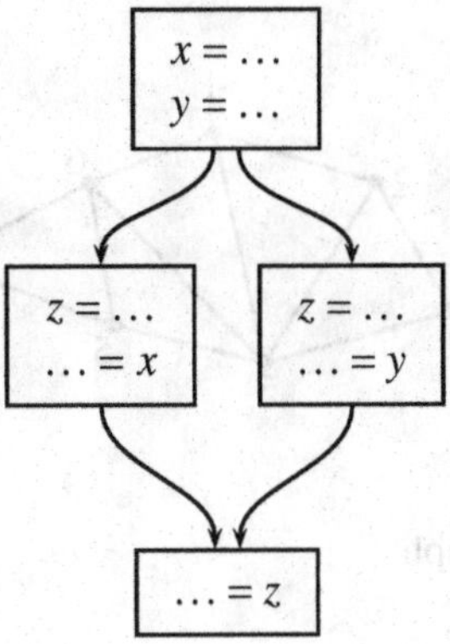

FIGURE 6.23
An example to show that Lemma 6.14 does not hold for programs not in SSA form.

LEMMA 6.13
Let G be the interference graph of a program in SSA form and let $C \subseteq G$ be a clique whose vertex set is $\{x_1, \dots, x_n\}$. Then there is a permutation π of $\{1, \dots, n\}$ such that $def(x_{\pi(1)}) \geq, \dots, \geq def(x_{\pi(n)})$.

PROOF For $i, j \in \{1, \dots n\}$, x_i and x_j interfere. Therefore from Lemma 6.10, either $def(x_i) \geq def(x_j)$ or $def(x_j) \geq def(x_i)$. π can be obtained by sorting $\{x_1, \dots, x_n\}$ on $\geq$. ∎

LEMMA 6.14
Let G be the interference graph of a program in SSA form and let $C \subseteq G$ be a induced subgraph with vertex set $\{x_1, \dots, x_n\}$. C is a clique if and only if there is a program point where $x_1, \dots, x_n$ are all live.

PROOF The if part is trivial. Let C be a clique. By Lemma 6.13, there is a permutation π of $\{1, \dots, n\}$ such that $def(x_{\pi(1)}) \geq \dots \geq def(x_{\pi(n)})$. Therefore, from Lemma 6.11, $x_1, \dots, x_n$ are all live just after $def(x_{\pi(n)})$. ∎

The above lemma does not hold for programs which are not in SSA form. Consider, for example, Figure 6.23. The live ranges of x, y and z form a clique in the interference graph. However, there is no program point where all three variables are live.

DEFINITION 6.10 A chordal graph *is a graph which does not have any induced cycle of length more than three.*

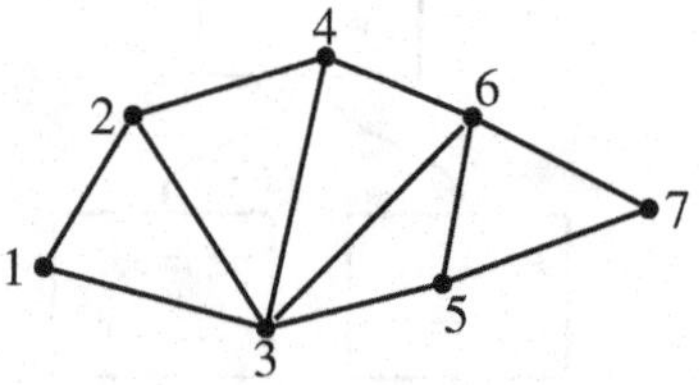

FIGURE 6.24
Example of a chordal graph.

Figure 6.24 gives an example of a chordal graph.

An interesting property of a chordal graph is its chromatic number is the same as the size of its largest clique. This can be seen in the example graph where the maximum clique size is three which is also the minimum number of colors required to color the graph. Therefore, if we can show that the interference graph of a program in SSA form is chordal, then, by Lemma 6.14, its chromatic number will be determined by the largest liveness set at any point in the program.

LEMMA 6.15

Let G be an interference graph of a program in SSA form. Then G is chordal.

PROOF Assume to the contrary that it is not. Then there will be at least one induced cycle $C = x_1, x_2, \ldots, x_n, x_1$ with $n \geq 4$. Now consider the sequence $x_1, x_2, \ldots, x_n$. Clearly, we do not have an edge $x_i — x_j$, such that $j > i+1$, or C would not be a cycle.

Since x_1 and x_2 interfere, either $\mathit{def}(x_1) \geq \mathit{def}(x_2)$ or $\mathit{def}(x_2) \geq \mathit{def}(x_1)$ by Lemma 6.10. Assume without loss of generality, $\mathit{def}(x_1) \geq \mathit{def}(x_2)$. Since $x_2 — x_3$ is an edge and $x_1 — x_3$ is not an edge, by Lemma 6.12, $\mathit{def}(x_2) \geq \mathit{def}(x_3)$. Using this idea, we can show by induction that there is a chain of dominance $\mathit{def}(x_1) \geq \mathit{def}(x_2) \geq \ldots \geq \mathit{def}(x_n)$.

Now since x_1 and x_n interfere, there is a program point p where both x_1 and x_n are live. Further, by Lemma 6.9, $\mathit{def}(x_n)$ dominates p. Because of the chain of dominances each $\mathit{def}(x_i)$ dominates p.

Consider a x_i, where i is not 1 or n. Since $\mathit{def}(x_i)$ dominates p and does not dominate $\mathit{def}(x_1)$, there is at least one path from $\mathit{def}(x_i)$ to p that does not have a definition of x_1. Thus x_1 is live at $\mathit{def}(x_i)$. This means there is an interference edge between 1 and i, leading to a contradiction. ∎

The Spilling Algorithm

The chromatic number of an SSA form program is the same as the maximum number of variables that are live at any point in the program. Hence we should ensure through spilling that the size of the set of live variables at any program point is no larger than the available number of registers. This is done without constructing the interference graph.

For every variable x we assume that there is a memory location x. These memory locations are not in contention for registers. A spill is an assignment $\mathsf{x} = x$. A reload of a variable is an assignment $x = \mathsf{x}$. For every basic block, the spilling algorithm decides:

1. The variables that get into registers at the entry of the basic block.
2. For every assignment statement, the variables that have to be spilled so that the operands on the right hand side of the assignment can be accommodated into registers, by reloading if necessary.

The spilling decision at a program point is based on the nearest distance at which a variable is subsequently used. We call this the next use of the variable and is captured through a function called *nextuse*. The next variable to be spilled at a program point is the one whose next use is the farthest. This is with the expectation that a free register can be found for the variable by the time the next use is reached.

For a basic block n and a variable x, the function *nextuse* is defined as follows:

$$\mathit{nextuse}(n,x) = \begin{cases} \infty & x \text{ is not live} \\ 0 & x \text{ is used in } n \\ 1 + \min\limits_{n' \in \mathit{succ}(n)} \mathit{nextuse}(n',x) & \end{cases}$$

Assume that the number of available registers is k. At the entry of each block, we consider only the variables that are live and select k variables with the lowest *nextuse*. These are the variables to be held in registers at the entry of the block.

Similarly, for an assignment $p: x = \mathit{op}(y_1, \ldots y_i)$, if any of the variables $y_1, \ldots, y_i$ have to be brought into a register, the variable z with the highest value of $\mathit{nextuse}(p,z)$ value is spilled. Since the assignment to x takes place after the computation of $\mathit{op}(y_1, \ldots y_i)$, to find a register for x, we spill the variable z with the highest value of $\min_{p' \in \mathit{succ}(p)} \mathit{nextuse}(p',z)$.

Let us assume that based on the above consideration, we have decided to assign registers to the set of variables I at the beginning of a basic block n. Consider any predecessor n' of n. If O is the set of variables that have been decided to be kept in registers at the exit of the predecessor, we have to reload the variables in $I - O$ at the edge connecting n' and n.

Reloads introduce definitions that were not present in the original program. As a result of reloads, the program may not be in SSA form. However, for the PEO based coloring that we discuss later to be applicable, the program must be brought back to SSA form. We explain with an example how this is done.

Assume that in Figure 6.25(a), the variable x_1 had to be reloaded in block n_3 so that the program is no longer in SSA form. We have to bring the program back to SSA form and rewrite the uses of x_1. We start by calculating the iterated dominance frontier of the node n_3 which contains the reload. Next, the variable x_1 in n_3 is

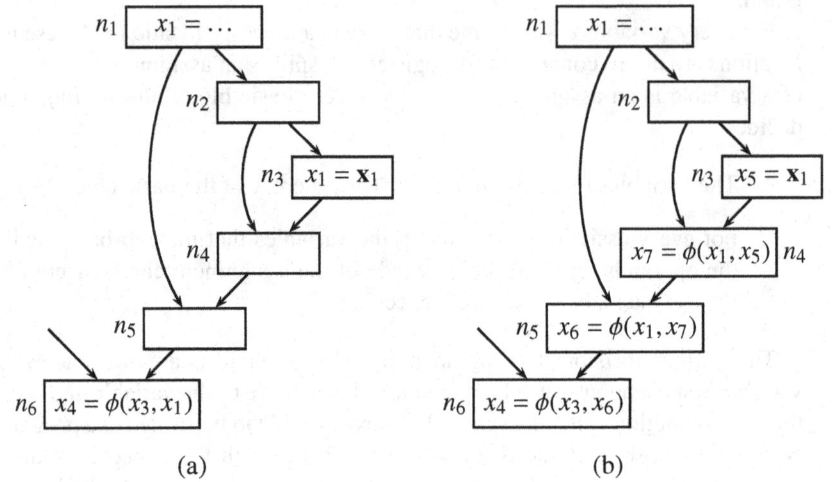

FIGURE 6.25
Example to illustrate SSA reconstruction.

renamed to a new variable x_5 to bring back the single definition property of SSA form. We now rewrite the use occurrence of each variable to the definition reaching it. In the process ϕ-instructions are inserted wherever necessary.

To start with, we have to decide how to rewrite the use of x_1 in n_6. We observe that the predecessor n_5 of n_6 is in the iterated dominance frontier of n_3. Since this does not have a ϕ-instruction for x_1, we have to insert one. The result of this ϕ-instruction, x_6, is the definition reaching x_1 and thus will replace x_1. Now we recursively try to find the definitions reaching the first and second argument of the inserted ϕ-instruction at n_5. The definition reaching the first argument comes from x_1 at n_1. The search for the definition reaching the second argument results in the insertion of another ϕ-instruction at n_4. The result of this ϕ instruction, x_7, reaches the second argument of the ϕ function at n_5. The arguments of the ϕ function at n_4 are similarly found to be x_1 and x_5.

Coloring

We now describe properties of a chordal graph due to which it can be colored efficiently.

DEFINITION 6.11 *A node in a graph G is called simplicial if its neighboring nodes induce a clique in G.*

DEFINITION 6.12 A perfect elimination order (*PEO*) *of a graph G is an order based on elimination of the nodes of G as follows: At each step eliminate a simplicial node in the remaining graph.*

It can be verified that 1,2,4,3,6,5,7 is a *PEO* for the graph in Figure 6.24.

Let the maximum size of a clique in a graph be k. Consider the following procedure to color the graph with k colors using a *PEO* ordering: Starting with the empty graph, at each step we color and add a node, say n, in reverse order of *PEO*. While adding n we are assured that its neighbors form a clique of size at most $k-1$. Thus a color can always be found for n.

A graph is chordal if and only if it admits of a *PEO* ordering. If a graph has a *PEO*, not only is its colorability equal to the maximum size over all cliques of the graph, there is a polynomial time algorithm to obtain the coloring.

In the context of programs in SSA form, the following result gives a *PEO* of interference graphs and thus forms the basis of the coloring algorithm.

LEMMA 6.16

Let G be the interference graph of a program in SSA form. Consider an ordering of the nodes of the graph in which a node v is included only if all the nodes whose definitions are dominated by the definition of v have been already added to the ordering. Then the ordering is a PEO.

PROOF We have to show that v is simplicial at the point when it is included in the ordering. Consider two nodes u and x both of which interfere with v. Then we have to show that u and x interfere with each other.

Since the nodes v and u interfere, following Lemma 6.10 we have either $def(v) \geq def(u)$ or $def(u) \geq def(v)$. Since all definitions that are dominated by u have already been added to the ordering and eliminated from the interference graph, it must be the case that $def(u) \geq def(v)$. Therefore u is live at $def(v)$. For similar reasons x is also live at $def(u)$. Thus u and x interfere. ∎

The function *colorNode* uses the dominator based *PEO* to color the interference graph and is shown in Figure 6.26. The function is initially called with *Start*. It processes a node in the dominator tree before processing its children, and within a node it processes the statements in sequence. This ensures that the corresponding interference graph is colored in reverse *PEO* order. Observe that this happens without actually constructing the interference graph.

Coalescing by Recoloring

At the end of the coloring phase, the residency of variables in registers is as follows:

1. Some variables which do not participate in any ϕ-instruction could be assigned registers. If such a variable is live across a join node, it is held in a register

Input: A node n of the CFG of the SSA form program, the dominator tree of the CFG and the set of live variables at the entry of n. The function *color* returns the color of a already colored node.
Output: A coloring of the variables in n.
Algorithm:

```
function colorNode(n)
{ allocated = ∅
  for each variable x in livein(n) do
  { allocated = allocated ∪ color(x)
    for each statement s in n in sequence do
        for each variable y used in s do
        { if the last use of y is in s then
                allocated = allocated − {color(y)}
            let x be the variable defined in s and c be an unallocated color
            in
            { color(x) = c
                allocated = allocated − {c}
            }
        }
  }
  for each child m of node n do colorNode(m)
}
```

FIGURE 6.26
Algorithm for coloring the interference graph.

along all paths reaching the join node. This situation is different for a ϕ variable which could be held in a register along one of the paths reaching the join point.

2. If the result of a ϕ-instruction is in a register, then it is ensured that the arguments of the ϕ-instruction are also in registers. Since the number of registers available for allocation to ϕ-variables is the same along all paths to a join node, the result of the coloring algorithm can always be altered to satisfy this condition. Similarly, if the result of a ϕ-instruction is a memory location, then the arguments of the ϕ-instruction are also made to reside memory locations.

The destruction of ϕ-instructions is viewed as a form of coalescing. Let *alloc* be an assignment of variables to registers and consider the ϕ-instruction

$$\mathit{alloc}(y) = \phi(\mathit{alloc}(x_1), \ldots, \mathit{alloc}(x_i), \ldots, \mathit{alloc}(x_n))$$

Destruction of this ϕ-instruction is the transfer of values from the registers $\mathit{alloc}(x_i)$ to $\mathit{alloc}(y)$ through register copies. If $\mathit{alloc}(y)$ is the same as $\mathit{alloc}(x_i)$, then no transfer of value needs take place. Otherwise, a copy statement has to be issued to transfer the value from $\mathit{alloc}(x_i)$ to $\mathit{alloc}(y)$. The problem is to color the interference graph of a program so as to minimize the transfer cost. This problem is called the *SSA-coalescing* problem. We shall now define it formally.

SSA coalescing

Call a pair of variables *ϕ-assigned*, if one of them is an argument and the other the result of a ϕ-instruction. Assume that we have a function c which associates a cost with every pair of edges that are *ϕ-assigned*. This cost takes into account (i) the cost of transferring a value x to y, assuming the variables are in separate registers, and (ii) the frequency of execution of the basic block which has the ϕ-instruction containing x and y. Given a coloring alloc, we define the cost of the coloring for the *ϕ-assigned* pair (x, y) as

$$\mathsf{cost}_{\mathsf{alloc}}(x,y) = \begin{cases} 0 & \mathsf{alloc}(x) = \mathsf{alloc}(y) \\ c(x,y) & \text{otherwise} \end{cases}$$

And the cost of the coloring for the entire program P as:

$$\mathsf{cost}_{\mathsf{alloc}}(P) = \sum_{(x,y)\in P,\ \phi\text{-}assigned(x,y)} \mathsf{cost}_{\mathsf{alloc}}(x,y)$$

DEFINITION 6.13 *Given a program in SSA form and its interference graph, the SSA-coalescing problem is to find a coloring* alloc *for which* $\mathsf{cost}_{\mathsf{alloc}}(P)$ *is minimum.*

Since this problem is NP-hard, we now present a heuristic for solving the problem. The idea is that we take the output of the coloring algorithm described before and modify the coloring so as to minimize the cost of transfer of values.

To start with, the algorithm forms groups of variables. Each group consists of maximal number of *ϕ-congruence* variables that are non-interfering. Interfering variables cannot be given the same color. Define the cost of each such group g as the cost of all the ϕ-related edges between variables in the group g, i.e.,

$$\mathsf{cost}_{group}(g) = \sum_{x,y\in g,\ \phi\text{-}assigned(x,y)} \mathsf{cost}_{\mathsf{alloc}}(x,y)$$

Clearly, a successful coloring of a costlier group will yield more benefits in transfer costs. Therefore, the groups are sorted by decreasing cost and entered into a priority queue for recoloring in this order.

Now the groups in the priority queue are attempted to be recolored. We take each color c in turn and attempt a recoloring with c. Not all nodes in the group G can be colored with c. As a result, the recoloring attempt results in several subgroups $g_1, g_2, \ldots, g_n$ such that:

1. Each variable in each subgroup can be recolored to c.
2. Each g_i forms a *ϕ-congruence* class.

The subgroup g_i with maximum value of $\mathsf{cost}_{group}(g_i)$ is the candidate subgroup sg_c for the color c. This is done for all colors and the final decision is to chose c' with the maximum $sg_{c'}$. The corresponding subgroup's color is fixed at c' and never changed thereafter. This ensures the termination of the algorithm. A new group $G - sg_{c'}$ is formed and entered in the priority queue at an appropriate place depending on its cost. This process is repeated till the priority queue is empty.

To recolor a node with the color c, the algorithm checks that none of its neighbors have the color c. If this is true then the recoloring attempt is successful. Otherwise the algorithm recursively attempts to recolor the offending neighbor with a color different from c. The recoloring attempt fails if the color of the node is already fixed to a color that is different from the color for which the recoloring attempt is being made, or the node cannot be colored because of a lack of color.

It might appear that the recoloring step requires construction of the interference graph to, for example, determine non-interfering *ϕ-congruence* groups. However, this is not the case. Assume that we want to decide whether x interferes with y. We first determine whether $\mathsf{def}(x)$ and $\mathsf{def}(y)$ are related by a dominance relationship. If they are not, then by Lemma 6.10 they do not interfere. On the other hand, if there is a dominance relationship and $\mathsf{def}(x) \geq \mathsf{def}(y)$, for example, then by Lemma 6.11, x and y interfere if x is live at $\mathsf{def}(y)$.

Register Copies

The last step in the method is to arrange for transfer of value for *ϕ-congruent* variables that could not be colored with the same color. To take into account that ϕ-instructions within the same basic block are to be simultaneously executed, we consider all the ϕ-instructions in the basic block together. As an example consider the ϕ-instructions

$$
\begin{aligned}
R_1 &= \phi(\ldots, R_2, \ldots)\\
R_2 &= \phi(\ldots, R_2, \ldots)\\
R_3 &= \phi(\ldots, R_5, \ldots)\\
R_4 &= \phi(\ldots, R_3, \ldots)\\
R_5 &= \phi(\ldots, R_4, \ldots)
\end{aligned}
$$

In the example, we limit ourselves to the registers at one of the argument positions. We can represent this transfer of value through a graph shown in Figure 6.27. While in the example, we have restricted ourselves to the registers at one of the argument positions, the graph has to be extended to other argument positions. The resulting graph is called the *register transfer graph*. Now we generate instructions to effect the value transfers suggested by the register transfer graph. Each step is repeated as many times as possible.

1. If there is a edge $R_i \rightarrow R_j$ in the graph such that R_j does not have any out edges, then a copy statement $R_j = R_i$ is issued. This is illustrated by the edge $R_2 \rightarrow R_1$ in the example, for which a copy statement $R_1 = R_2$ has to be issued.

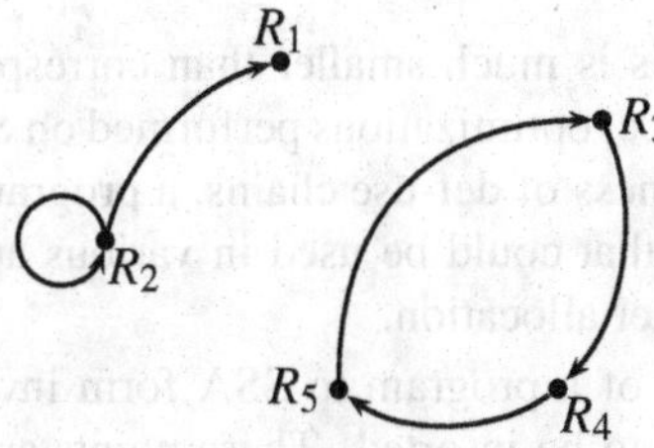

FIGURE 6.27
Graph indicating transfer of values between registers.

2. Now the register transfer graph will consist of one or more cycles. The cycles of length 1 like R_2 are eliminated.

3. The cyclic transfers values indicated by loops of length more than one like R_3, R_4, R_5 can be effected in more than one way:

   (a) Transfer using a free register as a temporary. For the example, assuming R_0 is a free register, the instructions generated are:

$$R_0 = R_3$$
$$R_3 = R_4$$
$$R_4 = R_5$$
$$R_5 = R_0$$

   (b) If there is no free register, then pairwise swap operations can be used. For the example, the transfer can be effected through the following swaps:

$$\textit{swap}\ R_3\ \ R_4$$
$$\textit{swap}\ R_4\ \ R_5$$
$$\textit{swap}\ R_5\ \ R_3$$

   If the underlying machine does not directly support a swap operation, it may be simulated through *xor* operations.

6.4 Summary and Concluding Remarks

In this chapter we described a useful intermediate representation of programs called the SSA form. In this representation every variable has exactly one definition, and this definition dominates each use of the variable. The number of def-use chains in SSA form programs is much smaller than corresponding programs not in SSA form. As a consequence, optimizations performed on SSA form programs are faster. Apart from the sparseness of def-use chains, a program in SSA form also has other interesting properties that could be used in various applications. An example that was presented is register allocation.

The transformation of a program to SSA form involves finding program points where ϕ-functions are to be inserted. These points are identified by iterated dominance frontiers. After ϕ-functions are inserted, variables are renamed to satisfy the single definition property. Both these steps can be done efficiently. The transformation of programs to their SSA form can be thought of as being the result of some form of data flow analysis. Destruction of SSA form programs is based on creating *ϕ-congruence* variables that are also non-interfering. This is through insertion of copy statements. The *ϕ-congruence* variables are then renamed to the same variable and the ϕ-instruction is removed.

We also presented register allocation as a way of destructing SSA form programs. Register allocation of SSA form programs through graph coloring is convenient because the interference graphs of such programs have properties that enable us to (a) determine how much spilling is required so that the interference graph becomes colorable, and (b) obtain a coloring. Removal of ϕ-instructions is through register coalescing. Interestingly, all these steps can be done without actually constructing the interference graph.

SSA-based optimizations are more difficult when the entity involved in the optimization is not a variable, as in the redundancy elimination optimizations. The problem is that the expressions representing redundant computations may not be lexically the same; they may have different versions of a variable. Detecting these occurrences and eliminating the redundant ones by exploiting the sparseness of def-use chains is not straightforward.

6.5 Bibliographic Notes

The earliest papers on SSA form are by Rosen, Wegman and Zadeck [85] and Alpern, Wegman and Zadeck [8]. The first comprehensive method for construction of SSA form programs is by Cytron, Ferrante, Rosen, Wegman, and Zadeck [28]. The method described in this chapter is based on this paper. A later paper by Sreedhar and Gao [95] gives a linear time algorithm for placing ϕ-instructions using a data structure called DJ-graphs. Both methods involve finding the dominator tree of a program. Lengauer and Tarjan [68] give a fast algorithm for finding dominators in a graph. The methods above construct minimal SSA. Choi, Cytron and Ferrante [22] present a method to create programs in pruned SSA form and Briggs, Cooper, Harvey, and Simpson [18] describe construction of semi-pruned SSA.

While Cytron, Ferrante, Rosen, Wegman, and Zadeck [28] discuss destruction of

SSA, the method that they suggest has shortcomings. The method discussed here is based on the work by Sreedhar, Dz-Ching Ju, Gillies and Santhanam [96]. Briggs, Cooper, Harvey, and Simpson [18] discuss SSA-destruction by placing copy statements along edges. The method for SSA destruction by register allocation is by Hack [41] and by Hack, Grund, and Goos [42].

Many applications of SSA form can be found in literature. Rosen, Wegman and Zadeck [85] describe a method to eliminate redundant computations among expressions that may not be lexically identical. Alpern, Wegman and Zadeck [8] describe how to conservatively detect equality of variables in a program. Kennedy, Chan, Liu, Lo, Tu, and Chow [58] use SSA for partial redundancy elimination and Wegman and Zadeck [103] for conditional constant propagation. As mentioned earlier, Hack, Grund, and Goos [42] perform register allocation over SSA form programs while Knobe and Sarkar [64] use a variation of SSA form for parallelization.

Appel [11] describes the similarity between SSA programs and functional programs written in continuation passing style and Dhamdhere, Rosen and Zadeck [31] point out the difficulties in using SSA form for partial redundancy elimination.

Part II

Interprocedural Data Flow Analysis

7

Introduction to Interprocedural Data Flow Analysis

The intraprocedural optimizations that we have discussed so far have ignored the effect of a call under the assumption that a safe approximation of the effect of a call can be incorporated without inspecting the called procedures. This was illustrated in Section 1.1.2. A possible improvement of using interprocedural data flow information by analyzing the called procedures was also demonstrated in the same section. In this chapter we evolve the basic concepts of the latter.

7.1 A Motivating Example

We use the program in Figure 7.1 as a running example in this chapter. We perform constant propagation and dead code elimination over this program and introduce common variants of interprocedural analyses. Figure 7.1(a) shows our program. From the viewpoint of interprocedural analysis, its simplifying features are that it is non-recursive and contains global variables only.

The optimized program after performing interprocedural constant propagation is shown in part (b). Modified statements are shown in gray background. Constant propagation replaces uses of variables by their known values and potentially creates dead code. The statements shown in gray background in part (c) are the assignments that become dead code and can be deleted. Observe that when procedure p is called from procedure q, the value of variable d is 14. However, p is also called from main and the value of d in that call is not known. Hence we cannot conclude that d is constant in procedure p. Also observe that when procedure p is called the second time, since the values of b and d are known to be 2 and 14 respectively, the condition on line 17 is true and the assignment on line 18 is executed. Since a is assigned 1 in procedure q, the value of c becomes 3 and remains 3 in expression $a+c$ on line 12. Our analysis does not perform conditional constant propagation and fails to discover that the value of c is 3. However, it discovers the value of a in expression $a+c$ on line 12 to be 2 due to the assignment in line 25.

0. int a,b,c,d;	0. int a,b,c,d;	0. int a,b,c,d;
1.	1.	1.
2. void main()	2. void main()	2. void main()
3. { a = 5;	3. { a = 5;	3. { a = 5;
4. b = 3;	4. b = 3;	4. b = 3;
5. c = 7;	5. c = 7;	5. c = 7;
6. read(d);	6. read(d);	6. read(d);
7. p();	7. p();	7. p();
8. a = a+2;	8. a = 7;	8. a = 7;
9. print(c+d);	9. print(7+d);	9. print(7+d);
10. d = a*b;	10. d = 14;	10. d = 14;
11. q();	11. q();	11. q();
12. print(a+c);	12. print(2+c);	12. print(2+c);
13. }	13. }	13. }
14.	14.	14.
15. void p()	15. void p()	15. void p()
16. { b = 2;	16. { b = 2;	16. { b = 2;
17. if (b<d)	17. if (2<d)	17. if (2<d)
18. c = a+b;	18. c = a+2;	18. c = a+2;
19. print(c+d);	19. print(c+d);	19. print(c+d);
20. }	20. }	20. }
21.	21.	21.
22. void q()	22. void q()	22. void q()
23. { a = 1;	23. { a = 1;	23. { a = 1;
24. p();	24. p();	24. p();
25. a = a*b;	25. a = 2;	25. a = 2;
26. }	26. }	26. }
(a) Original program	(b) Discovered constants	(c) Discovered dead code

FIGURE 7.1

An example program with interprocedural constant propagation and subsequent interprocedural dead code elimination. For simplicity, we assume built-in operations to read and print data.

7.2   Program Representations for Interprocedural Analysis

Figure 7.2 shows two intermediate representations of our example. A *call multigraph* is a directed graph which captures the caller-callee relationships in a program. Nodes in a call multigraph represent procedures whereas edges represent procedure calls and are labeled by the call sites. Since each call to a procedure is represented by a distinct edge, a call multigraph contains parallel edges when a procedure contains multiple calls to some procedure. Recursion in a program would cause cycles in the call multigraph. The call multigraph for our program does not contain parallel edges or cycles.

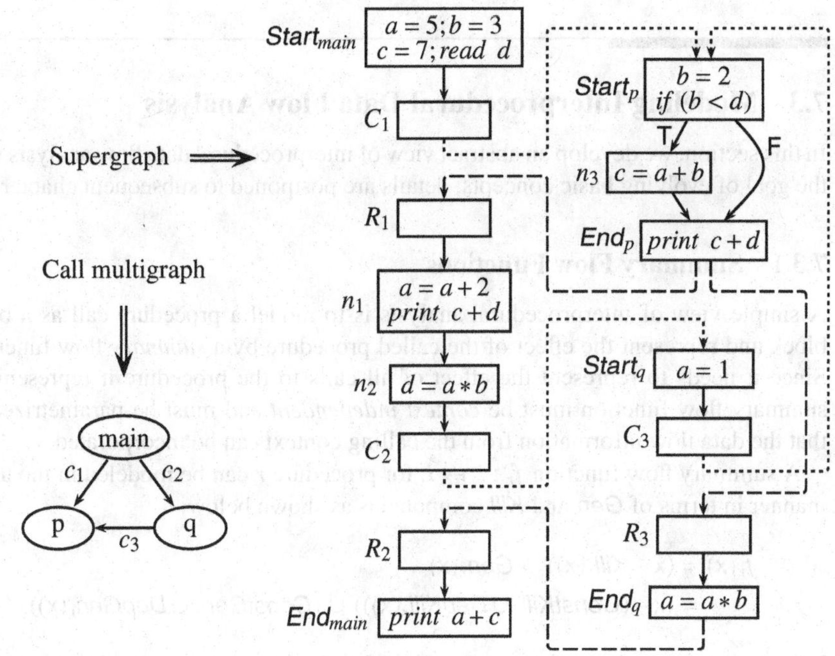

FIGURE 7.2
Common intermediate representations for interprocedural data flow analysis.

The second intermediate representation is also a directed graph called a *supergraph* which connects CFGs of callers and callees by edges indicating interprocedural control transfers. A simpler version of supergraph was introduced in Chapter 1. As illustrated in Figure 1.3 on page 5, it represented a call by a single basic block. Now we split a call site c_i into a *call node* C_i and the corresponding *return node* R_i. A call to procedure r at call site c_i is represented by an edge from C_i to $Start_r$. The corresponding return from procedure r is represented by an edge from End_r to R_i. These edges are interprocedural edges. The edges in the individual CFG are intraprocedural edges. The supergraph in Figure 7.2 shows the interprocedural edges by dashed lines and intraprocedural edges by solid lines. The program entry and exit is denoted by $Start_{main}$ and End_{main}.

A supergraph and the corresponding call multigraph are related to each other by a simple graph transformation. If every procedure in a supergraph of a program is represented by a single node by combining all blocks of a procedure and all return edges are removed, a supergraph reduces to the call multigraph of the program.

Observe that blocks $Start_{main}$, n_1, and $Start_p$ in our supergraph contain multiple statements in spite of the fact that for constant propagation a basic block consists of a single statement. However, it is possible to combine assignment statements into a single block when they do not have data dependence between them; we have done so for convenience.

7.3 Modeling Interprocedural Data Flow Analysis

In this section, we develop an abstract view of interprocedural data flow analysis with the goal of evolving basic concepts; details are postponed to subsequent chapters.

7.3.1 Summary Flow Functions

A simple view of interprocedural analysis is to model a procedure call as a basic block and represent the effect of the called procedure by a *summary* flow function. Since it needs to represent the effect of all calls to the procedure it represents, a summary flow function must be *context independent* and must be parametrized so that the data flow information from the calling context can be incorporated.

A summary flow function $f_r : L \mapsto L$ for procedure r can be modeled in the usual manner in terms of *Gen* and *Kill* components as shown below:

$$\begin{aligned} f_r(\mathsf{x}) &= (\mathsf{x} - \mathit{Kill}_r(\mathsf{x})) \cup \mathit{Gen}_r(\mathsf{x}) \\ &= (\mathsf{x} - (\mathit{ConstKill}_r \cup \mathit{DepKill}_r(\mathsf{x}))) \cup (\mathit{ConstGen}_r \cup \mathit{DepGen}_r(\mathsf{x})) \end{aligned}$$

Note that this merely models the function f_r; whether f_r is actually constructed by identifying *ConstKill*, *DepKill*, *ConstGen*, and *DepGen* is an independent matter and is discussed in Section 7.3.3. Chapter 8 discusses how it is constructed; we introduce some intuitions related to it in Section 7.6.

Although the notions of Gen_r and Kill_r for a procedure r are similar to the notions of Gen_i and Kill_i for a basic block i, there are some differences arising from the fact that the execution of a procedure may involve control transfers whereas a basic block involves a strictly sequential execution. Thus we need to distinguish between *may* and *must* properties. For example, when performing liveness analysis, Kill_r must ensure that a variable is modified along all paths in r. This is represented by $\mathit{MustKill}_r$ which is different from $\mathit{MayKill}_r$; the latter says that a variable is modified along some path but not necessarily all. For available expressions analysis, Kill_r should be $\mathit{MayKill}_r$ rather than $\mathit{MustKill}_r$.

We now describe the summary flow functions for constant propagation and liveness analysis of our example program. Consider the instance of constant propagation framework involving our example program. Let $\mathsf{x} \in L$ be the tuple $\langle \widehat{\mathsf{x}}_a, \widehat{\mathsf{x}}_b, \widehat{\mathsf{x}}_c, \widehat{\mathsf{x}}_d \rangle$ representing the constantness information of the four variables in our example program. Thus, $\widehat{\mathsf{x}}_a$, $\widehat{\mathsf{x}}_b$, $\widehat{\mathsf{x}}_c$, and $\widehat{\mathsf{x}}_d$ are values in the component lattice $\widehat{L}$ for constant propagation (Figure 4.5 on page 110).

From the supergraph in Figure 7.2, it is clear that the data flow values of a and d remain unaffected by procedure p since it does not modify them. Further, variable b is always 2 at the end of procedure p regardless of the flow of execution. The data flow value of variable c depends on result of the condition in block Start_p. If the execution follows edge $\mathit{Start}_p \rightarrow n_3$, the data flow value of c becomes $\widehat{\mathsf{x}}_a + 2$. The alternative execution path involving edge $\mathit{Start}_p \rightarrow \mathit{End}_p$ does not modify c. Static summarization of the two possibilities results in $\widehat{x}_c \sqcap (\widehat{x}_a + 2)$. Thus, the flow function that summarizes the effect of procedures p is:

$$f_p(\langle \widehat{x}_a, \widehat{x}_b, \widehat{x}_c, \widehat{x}_d \rangle) = \langle \widehat{x}_a, 2, \widehat{x}_c \sqcap (\widehat{x}_a + 2), \widehat{x}_d \rangle$$

To see the flow function in terms of *Gen* and *Kill*, observe that the data flow information $x = \langle \widehat{x}_a, \widehat{x}_b, \widehat{x}_c, \widehat{x}_d \rangle$ is merely a convenient notation for the set representation $x = \left\{ \langle a, \widehat{x}_a \rangle, \langle b, \widehat{x}_b \rangle, \langle c, \widehat{x}_c \rangle, \langle d, \widehat{x}_d \rangle \right\}$. Thus, the *Gen* and *Kill* components of f_p are:

$$\begin{aligned} ConstGen_p &= \{\langle b, 2 \rangle\} \\ ConstKill_p &= \emptyset \\ DepGen_p(x) &= \{\langle c, \widehat{x}_c \sqcap (\widehat{x}_a + 2) \rangle\} \\ DepKill_p(x) &= \{\langle b, \widehat{x}_b \rangle, \langle c, \widehat{x}_c \rangle\} \end{aligned}$$

Since procedure q calls procedure p, the definition of f_q depends on the definition of f_p. In particular, procedure q assigns 1 to a and then passes on the resulting data flow information $\langle 1, \widehat{x}_b, \widehat{x}_c, \widehat{x}_d \rangle$ to f_p. The resulting intermediate flow function defines the data flow at R_3 in terms of the assumed input value $x = \langle \widehat{x}_a, \widehat{x}_b, \widehat{x}_c, \widehat{x}_d \rangle$ available at $Start_q$. When the flow function of block End_q is composed with it, we get

$$f_q(\langle \widehat{x}_a, \widehat{x}_b, \widehat{x}_c, \widehat{x}_d \rangle) = \langle 2, 2, \widehat{x}_c \sqcap 3, \widehat{x}_d \rangle$$

For live variables analysis, $\mathbb{V}ar = \{a, b, c, d\}$ and L is $2^{\mathbb{V}ar}$. We leave it for the reader to verify that the flow functions for procedures p and q are:

$$\begin{aligned} f_p(x) &= (x - \{b\}) \cup \{a, c, d\} \\ f_q(x) &= (x - \{a, b\}) \cup \{c, d\} \end{aligned}$$

where $x \subseteq \{a, b, c, d\}$.

7.3.2 Inherited and Synthesized Data Flow Information

For a given call to procedure r in the body of procedure s, let x be the data flow information reaching the call point. Then, x represents the data flow information *inherited* by procedure r from the call site in s and $f_r(x)$ represents the data flow information *synthesized* by r at the call site in s. This is illustrated in Figure 7.3. The inherited data flow information is context sensitive. The synthesized data flow information has a context insensitive component represented by $ConstGen_p$ and a context sensitive component represented by $DepGen_p(x)$ and $x - \left(ConstKill_p \cup DepKill_p(x)\right)$. The final data flow information at a program point u in procedure r is influenced by

- interprocedural data flow information inherited by r from all calls to r,
- interprocedural data flow information synthesized by calls appearing on the paths from $Start_r$ to u for forward flows and from u to End_r for backward flows, and

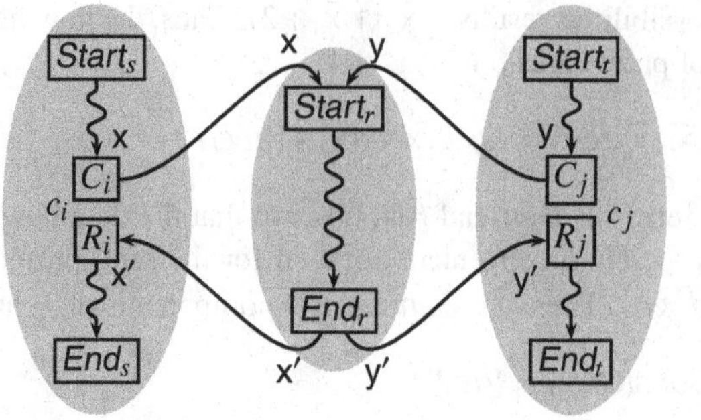

Data Flow Information	
x	Inherited by r from call site c_i in s
y	Inherited by r from call site c_j in t
x′	Synthesized by r in s at call site c_i
y′	Synthesized by r in t at call site c_j

FIGURE 7.3
Inherited and synthesized data flow information.

- intraprocedural data flow information along the paths from $Start_r$ to u for forward flows and from u to End_r for backward flows.

In Part I of the book, the interprocedural data flow information was approximated as follows: The inherited data flow information was approximated by a conservative value of *BI* and the synthesized data flow information was approximated by using fixed conservative values for *Gen*(x) and *Kill*(x). These approximations were independent of calls and were same for all calls to all procedures in the program. Interprocedural data flow analysis tries to replace the above approximations by more precise values.

For constant propagation in our example, procedure p has a call from *main* and a call from q. The context insensitive synthesized data flow information of p is $\{\langle b,2\rangle\}$. It inherits $\mathsf{x} = \langle 5,3,7,\bot\rangle$ from its call in *main*. Since we wish to separate the data flow information associated with different variables, we view x as $\{\langle a,5\rangle,\langle b,3\rangle,\langle c,7\rangle,\langle d,\bot\rangle\}$. The context sensitive synthesized data flow information for this call is $\{\langle a,5\rangle,\langle c,7\rangle,\langle d,\bot\rangle\}$. This is the data flow information associated with block R_1 in the caller procedure *main*. The data flow information inherited by p from its call in q is $\langle 1,2,7,14\rangle$. The corresponding context sensitive synthesized data flow information associated with block R_3 in the caller procedure q is $\{\langle a,1\rangle,\langle c,\bot\rangle,\langle d,14\rangle\}$.

7.3.3 Approaches to Interprocedural Data Flow Analysis

Various methods of interprocedural data flow analysis can be divided into two broad categories: *functional* approach or a *value-based* approach.

A functional approach to interprocedural analysis consists of two steps: In the first step, the summary flow functions that represent the effects of a call are computed. These functions are context independent and are parametrized. In the second step, inherited data flow information of a procedure is computed from its calling contexts. Then, the body of the procedure is analyzed and the summary flow functions corresponding to the callee are used to compute the synthesized data flow information.

Observe that using the summary functions does not require traversing the body of the caller procedures represented by the functions. In practice, computation of summary flow functions is possible only for a limited class of frameworks. In particular, it is easy for separable frameworks. In non-separable frameworks, it may not be possible to automatically construct summary flow functions unless the lattice is finite and flow functions are distributive. This is because constructing summary flow functions requires reducing expressions involving function compositions and intersections. Whether a systematic method of reductions can be devised or not depends on the nature of the flow functions and data flow values.

A *value-based* approach avoids computing summary flow functions. Instead, it directly computes data flow values by traversing a program during analysis. In particular, when it encounters a procedure call, the inherited data flow information is propagated to the callee and the method starts examining the callee's body. At the end of the analysis of the callee's body, synthesized data flow information is propagated back to the caller and the analysis of caller's body is resumed. This approach requires traversing a procedure repeatedly for different calling contexts. Conceptually, this approach is simpler than functional approach except that it may have to distinguish between a large number of contexts.

Both these approaches inherently handle recursion so long as the frameworks involve finite lattices. Although our example program in this chapter is non-recursive, subsequent chapters present these approaches for recursive programs.

7.4 Compromising Precision for Scalability

Recall that the scope of intraprocedural data flow analysis is restricted to individual procedures. By contrast, interprocedural data flow analysis needs to examine entire programs. Although this increases the precision of data flow information, practically interprocedural analysis could be very inefficient both in terms of space as well as time. Since real life applications often contain hundreds or thousands of procedures, a supergraph is many times larger than a single CFG. Hence efficiency and scalability issues assume much more significance in interprocedural data flow analysis than in intraprocedural data flow analysis. Most approaches that achieve efficiency and scalability, compromise on precision in one way or the other. Two common tradeoffs that enhance efficiency and scalability are:

- Not distinguishing between actual and spurious control flow paths.
  This manifests itself in the form of flow or context insensitivity.
- Restricting the influences between caller and callees.
  This results in side effects analysis instead of whole program analysis.

In this section we explore these tradeoffs and explain how they affect the precision of interprocedural data flow analysis. Empirical investigations have revealed that

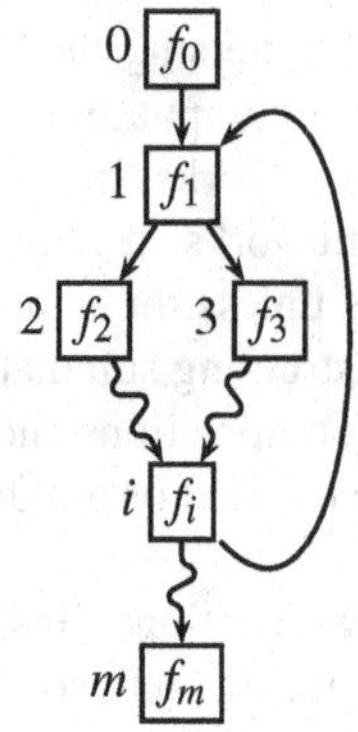

(a) CFG

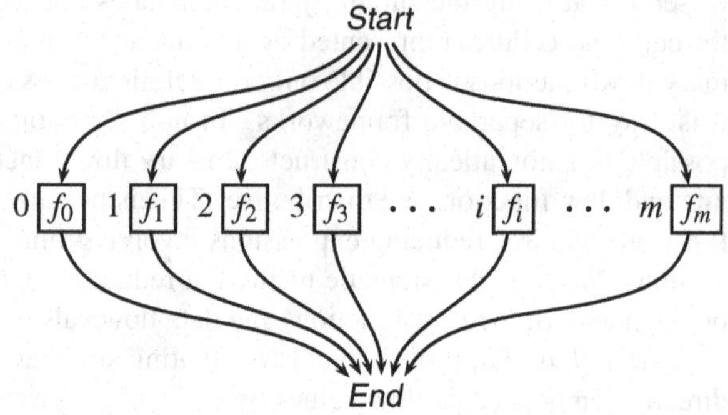

(b) Flow insensitive analysis

FIGURE 7.4
Modeling flow insensitive analysis.

these tradeoffs enhance the efficiency of analysis significantly. The resulting loss of precision has been found to be tolerable in many cases but not all.

7.4.1 Flow and Context Insensitivity

Recall that the *MOP* value associated with a program point u is the *glb* of data flow information computed along all paths reaching u (Definition 3.20). Let $P(u)$ denote the set of paths used for computing data flow information at u. If $P(u) \supseteq \mathit{paths}(u)$, then a data flow value computed along all paths in $P(u)$ is weaker than MOP_u and hence is safe. Precision of the data flow value computed by traversing paths in $P(u)$ depends on how close $P(u)$ is to $\mathit{paths}(u)$. The larger the number of spurious paths in $P(u)$, the more imprecise the computed data flow value is likely to be.

As observed in Section 3.4.3, computing the *MOP* assignment for arbitrary monotone frameworks is undecidable. Thus the algorithms that need to cover all potential paths can at best compute the *MFP* solution (Section 3.4.2). This involves merging data flow information at shared program points in $\mathit{paths}(u)$. If the flow functions are non-distributive, this has the effect of creating combinations of data flow values across paths (Example 4.6). This can be seen as traversing some paths that are not present in $\mathit{paths}(u)$. This source of imprecision shows the limit of static analysis and hence is accepted as inevitable.

We now describe two features called *flow* and *context insensitivity* that a method can employ as a matter of choice for achieving efficiency. They are orthogonal but are similar in the sense that both of them relate to spurious paths; they are different in the nature of paths they consider.

Flow insensitivity

As mentioned in Section 1.2, flow insensitive analysis disregards the flow of control by implicitly assuming that the block can be executed in all possible orders. This is achieved by accumulating the effect of each block in the same data flow value and the resulting value is a safe approximation of data flow information at each point.

For convenience, let the blocks in a procedure be numbered from 0 to m in any arbitrary order. Then, flow insensitive analysis computes $\mathsf{x} \in L$ as defined below:

$$\mathsf{x} = \prod_{i=0}^{m} f_i(\mathit{BI}) \tag{7.1}$$

where $\mathit{BI} \in L$ is the boundary information. This is illustrated in Figure 7.4.

Intuitively, the operation of function composition employed in the usual flow sensitive data flow analysis is replaced by the operation of function confluence; the latter is commutative while the former is not. Thus just a single visit to each block in any arbitrary order approximates all possible orders between blocks. Section 8.1.2 shows that the value x computed by Equation (7.1) is a safe approximation of the corresponding flow sensitive data flow information at each program point.

In the case of flow functions with dependent parts, the above model of flow insensitive computation needs to be modified slightly. This is because the dependent component of f_i could depend on a value computed by some f_j and since the statements are assumed to be executed in an arbitrary order, this dependence must be taken care of. For example, consider flow insensitive *may* points-to analysis for the pointer assignments in Figure 7.5(a). Block n_3 generates a points-to pair $b \rightarrow d$ and since we assume that n_2 could be potentially executed after n_1 or n_3, our analysis should discover the points-to pairs $a \rightarrow c$ and $a \rightarrow d$. Following the strategy of Figure 7.4(b) we would get the flow graph in Figure 7.5(b) and it will not compute the desired points-to pairs. A simple way of modeling flow insensitive analysis in such a situation is to extend the graph by adding edges from n_1 and n_3 to n_2 as shown in Figure 7.5(c). Observe that these are data flow dependences captured by the primitive entity functions and the composite entity functions described in Section 4.5. They are different from the dependences of values of variables at run time which may or may not create dependences of data flow values.

In practice, instead of creating such flow graphs, the required dependences are remembered in a global data structure. Points-to analysis constructs a graph that contains points-to edges as well as constraints that result in points-to edges. Thus, edge $b \rightarrow c$ is added while processing n_1. When n_2 is processed, edge $a \rightarrow *b$ is also remembered apart from adding the edge $a \rightarrow c$. Whenever new points-to information for b becomes available, an appropriate points-to edge is added to the graph.

We now introduce the issues that arise when we wish to construct a flow insensitive summary flow function instead of computing a flow insensitive data flow value. These issues are handled in details in Chapter 8. We consider the following two cases in constructing flow insensitive summary functions:

- *When the flow functions do not have dependent parts.*

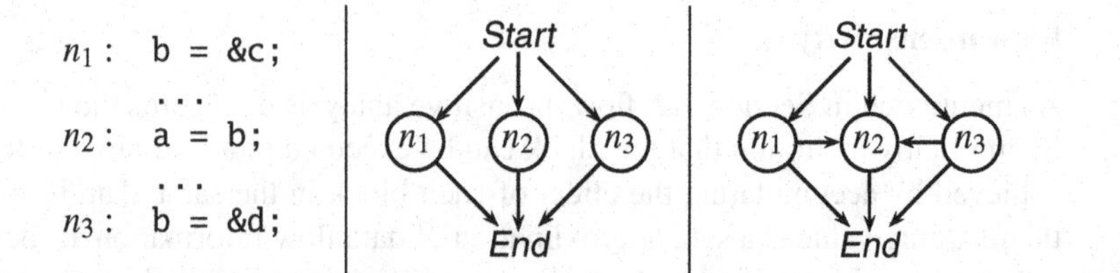

(a) Pointer assignment | (b) Default modeling | (c) Required modeling

FIGURE 7.5
Modeling flow insensitive analysis in presence of dependent parts in flow functions. Edges $n_1 \rightarrow n_2$ and $n_3 \rightarrow n_2$ represent the fact that $DepGen_{n_2}(x)$ depends on the data flow information computed at n_1 and n_3.

If flow functions have only constant parts (as in liveness analysis), then the summary flow function can be constructed by computing the values of the constant parts. In particular, for constructing side effect function of procedure r for liveness analysis, we need to compute only $ConstKill_r$ and $ConstGen_r$ sets.

The *ConstKill* set for live variables should include only those variables that are guaranteed to be modified within the called procedure regardless of the order of execution of basic blocks. This is represented by flow insensitive *MustKill* set which is computed using Equation (7.1) by intersecting the *Kill* sets of the individual basic blocks in the procedure. This should be contrasted with *ConstGen* computation which must record every variable that becomes live locally within the called procedure regardless of the control flow. This is represented by flow insensitive *MayUse* set which is computed using Equation (7.1) by taking a union of the *Gen* sets of individual basic blocks in the procedure. Then,

$$f_r(x) = (x - MustKill_r) \cup MayUse_r$$

where $x \in L$. Both these approaches are demonstrated for our example program in Section 7.6 although their detailed formal definitions are provided later in Chapter 8.

- *When the flow functions have dependent parts.*

  In this case, merely combining the *Gen* and *Kill* sets does not work. Instead, we will have to replace $BI \in L$ by a symbolic value that represents the data flow value in the calling context and parametrizes the summary flow function. For simplicity, we describe this for liveness analysis. A symbolic value for liveness analysis could be the following set:

$$BI = \left\{ \langle a, \widehat{x}_a \rangle \mid a \in \mathbb{G}\text{var} \right\}$$

where $\widehat{x}_a$ is a symbolic value that will be replaced by a concrete value *true* or *false* from the calling context. The flow function f_i to be used in Equation (7.1) will also have to be re-written as:

$$\begin{aligned} f_i(x) &= (x - Remove_i) \cup Add_i \\ Remove_i &= \{\langle a, \widehat{x}_a \rangle \mid a \in Kill_i, a \notin Gen_i\} \\ Add_i &= \{\langle a, true \rangle \mid a \in Gen_i\} \cup \\ &\quad\; \{\langle a, false \rangle \mid a \in Kill_i, a \notin Gen_i\} \end{aligned}$$

$\langle a, true \rangle \in x$ indicates that variable a is live and $\langle a, false \rangle \in x$ indicates that variable a is not live; exactly one of them is in x by construction. The confluence operation over the sets of pairs is defined as follows for liveness analysis:

$$x \cup y = \{\langle a, \widehat{x}_a + \widehat{y}_a \rangle \mid \langle a, \widehat{x}_a \rangle \in x, \langle a, \widehat{y}_a \rangle \in y\}$$

where + denote the boolean OR operation.

In the presence of dependent parts in flow functions, it may not always be possible to construct summary flow functions. In Chapter 8 we characterize the class of frameworks for which summary flow functions can be directly constructed. For others, either it is not possible to construct summary flow functions or some adhoc mechanism may have to be employed. For example, it is not possible to construct flow sensitive summary flow functions for points-to analysis. However, flow insensitive summary flow functions can be constructed by building a points-to graph which has been explained before. An application of such a summary flow function requires traversing the graph.

In our example program, assuming that it is known that the value of b is 2 after every call to procedure p, a flow insensitive analysis of procedure q would conclude that a could be both 1 and 2 and hence is not constant in q. This is a safe conclusion when only gross information instead of fine grained point-specific information about q is desired.

In general, flow insensitive analysis is not common at the intraprocedural level.

Context insensitivity

A calling context is represented by the snapshot of the control stack at run time. During program analysis, it is determined by the sequence of unfinished calls in a path in the supergraph.

As explained in Chapter 1, context insensitive analysis does not distinguish between different calling contexts. Instead, the inherited data flow information from all contexts is merged and the resulting synthesized data flow information is propagated to all calling contexts indiscriminately. This implies traversing interprocedurally invalid paths—paths in which calls and returns do not match. In essence, there is no distinction between the interprocedural and intraprocedural edges in a supergraph.

In our program, procedure p inherits $\langle 5,3,7,\bot \rangle$ from its call in the *main* and $\langle 1,2,7,14 \rangle$ from its call in procedure q. The merged value is $\langle \bot,\bot,7,\bot \rangle$ and the resulting synthesized value $\langle \bot, 2, 7, \bot \rangle$ is propagated back to both the callers of p. As a consequence, such an analysis fails to discover the fact that a is constant with value 5 at the entry of block n_1. Effectively, this is a consequence of propagating the value $a = 1$ from Start_q to n_1. Although there is a path from Start_q to n_1 in the supergraph, it does not represent matching calls and returns: Data flow information computed along the path from Start_q to End_p should be propagated to R_3 and not to R_1 because the last call in this path represents a call to p from q and not from *main*. Context sensitive analysis excludes such paths and restricts $P(u)$ to interprocedurally valid paths.

The issue of context sensitivity does not arise at the intraprocedural level.

7.4.2 Side Effects Analysis

Interprocedural analysis requires incorporating the mutual influence of callers and callees on each other. This requires computing both inherited and synthesized part of data flow information. We call such an analysis, a *whole program* analysis. This should be contrasted with the situation when only callee's influence on callers is computed. This is achieved by computing the synthesized part of interprocedural data flow information; the inherited part is approximated by a fixed value for each procedure. Traditionally, such analyses have been called *side effects* analyses.

A side effects analysis can also have some variations depending upon whether only the context insensitive side effects are computed or the context sensitive side effects are also computed. For a given procedure p, the context insensitive side effects are represented by $\mathsf{ConstGen}_p$ while the context sensitive side effects are represented by $\mathsf{DepGen}_p(\mathsf{x})$ and $\mathsf{x} - (\mathsf{ConstKill}_p \cup \mathsf{DepKill}_p(\mathsf{x}))$. The former is much simpler but less useful compared to the latter.

For a given procedure call, side effect analysis restricts the scope of optimization to the caller whereas whole program analysis facilitates optimization in both caller and callee. For example, if interprocedural live variables analysis is performed using side effects, it is possible to decide whether a value in a register should be preserved across a procedure call. The transformation resulting from this decision is restricted to a caller's body. However, if whole program analysis is performed, it may be possible to assign the same register to a variable both within a caller and its callee.

7.5 Language Features Influencing Interprocedural Analysis

Interprocedural data flow analysis is influenced by language features that support high level abstractions related to procedure calls.

In this chapter, we have deliberately used a non-recursive program to introduce interprocedural data flow analysis. In the presence of recursion, functional approaches require fixed point computation to construct summary flow functions. Convergence of this computation needs to be established by examining the flow functions and data flow values in the framework. Since the value-based approaches have to explicitly remember contexts, a mechanism of summarizing the contexts needs to be devised. For the frameworks with finite lattices, it is possible to bound the number of contexts by a finite number without compromising on precision. However, the number of contexts remains very large. Thus recursion affects both the feasibility and the efficiency of interprocedural data flow analysis significantly. Many practical value-based approaches perform context insensitive analysis in the recursive portions of programs. However, it is possible to perform context sensitive interprocedural analysis in the presence of recursions. We present such methods in Chapters 8 and 9.

The other simplifying feature of our program was that it did not involve parameters and local variables. In practice, parameterless procedures are rare and it is important to handle the parameter passing mechanism because computation of inherited data flow information requires transferring the data flow information of actual parameters to that of the corresponding formal parameters. For this purpose, the call by value parameter passing mechanism can be modeled by simple assignments whereas call by reference parameter passing mechanism should be modeled by pointer assignments. Further, distinction should be made between global variables and local variables for inherited and synthesized data flow information. Unless local variables are involved in the actual parameters of a procedure call, synthesized data flow information should not be computed for local entities nor should their data flow information be propagated as a part of the inherited data flow information of the callee. Recall that the motivating example of heap data analysis presented in Section 1.1 contains local pointer variables that are passed as actual parameters. Section 9.5 performs interprocedural liveness analysis for that example and describes how transfer of data flow information between actual and formal parameters can be modeled.

Further, in the presence of parameter passing by reference, depending upon the actual parameters a particular call may create aliasing between formal parameters or between formal parameters and global variables within the callee's body. This may affect the correctness or precision of the data flow information discovered. Section 8.2 shows how such aliasing can be discovered.

Some languages support local functions. This influences interprocedural analysis in the following ways: (a) The possible call structure in a program is governed by the scope rules of the language that restrict the visibility of local procedures. (b) The notion of global variables must now be replaced by the notion of non-local variables that depend on the scope of a procedure.

Function pointers and subtyping mechanism resulting in dynamic dispatch of function calls hide the identity of the called procedures at compile time making the static call structure imprecise. Exception handling mechanisms of a language have a similar effect. Interprocedural data flow analyses are restricted to single threads, similar to intraprocedural data flow analysis. Use of library functions imply that the entire source is not available to an interprocedural analyzer and a summary of their effects must be provided explicitly.

7.6 Common Variants of Interprocedural Data Flow Analysis

We introduce the following common variants using our running example.

- *Intraprocedural analysis with conservative approximation.* We use conservative approximation of inherited and synthesized data flow information for handling procedure calls.
- *Intraprocedural analysis with side effects.* We compute flow sensitive as well as flow insensitive side effects and represent them by context independent flow functions.
- *Whole program analysis.* We perform context sensitive as well as context insensitive analysis.

In each case, the data flow information in the caller procedures is computed in flow sensitive manner and the data flow value associated each program point is computed separately. In the case of flow insensitive side effects, only the effect of a call is flow insensitive—the data flow values computed in the caller's body are flow sensitive.

Although flow insensitive analysis of all procedures has also been used in practice, it computes a single summary data flow value per procedure which is usually very imprecise. For example, a flow insensitive constant propagation of our program computes the data flow value $\langle \widehat{\bot}, \widehat{\bot}, \widehat{\bot}, \widehat{\bot} \rangle$ for procedures *main* and *q* and, $\langle \widehat{\bot}, 2, \widehat{\bot}, \widehat{\bot} \rangle$ for procedure *p*. This value is same regardless of the variant. Flow sensitive version of these variants compute data flow values with varying degrees of precision.

7.6.1 Intraprocedural Analysis with Conservative Interprocedural Approximation

Intraprocedural analysis with conservative interprocedural approximation involves using safe values for inherited and synthesized data flow information. This approach was introduced in Section 1.1 analysis of heap data.

The inherited data flow information for constant propagation is represented by $BI_{main} = \langle 0, 0, 0, 0 \rangle$ and $BI_p = BI_q = \langle \widehat{\bot}, \widehat{\bot}, \widehat{\bot}, \widehat{\bot} \rangle$. This distinction arises from the fact that all our variables are global variables which are initialized to 0; however, their values cannot be assumed to be known when other procedures are invoked. For local variables, the value in BI is $\widehat{\top}$ but our program does not have local variables. For live variables analysis, $BI_{main} = \emptyset$ because no variable is live at the end of the program. However, all global variables should be conservatively assumed to be live at the end of other procedures, hence $BI_p = BI_q = \{a, b, c, d\}$.

The synthesized data flow information for constant propagation is conservatively represented by $\langle \widehat{\bot}, \widehat{\bot}, \widehat{\bot}, \widehat{\bot} \rangle$ under the assumption that a function call could modify all variables. For live variables analysis, the synthesized data flow information is $\{a, b, c, d\}$ because it is conservatively assumed that all global variables are live at the

Block and associated data flow value		Intraprocedural analysis with conservative interprocedural approximation	Side Effects Analysis: Flow sensitivity of synthesized information		Whole Program Analysis: Context sensitivity of inherited information	
			Insensitive	Sensitive	Insensitive	Sensitive
Start$_m$	*In*	$\langle 0,0,0,0\rangle$	$\langle 0,0,0,0\rangle$	$\langle 0,0,0,0\rangle$	$\langle 0,0,0,0\rangle$	$\langle 0,0,0,0\rangle$
	Out	$\langle 5,3,7,\widehat{\bot}\rangle$	$\langle 5,3,7,\widehat{\bot}\rangle$	$\langle 5,3,7,\widehat{\bot}\rangle$	$\langle 5,3,7,\widehat{\bot}\rangle$	$\langle 5,3,7,\widehat{\bot}\rangle$
C_1	*In, Out*	$\langle 5,3,7,\widehat{\bot}\rangle$	$\langle 5,3,7,\widehat{\bot}\rangle$	$\langle 5,3,7,\widehat{\bot}\rangle$	$\langle 5,3,7,\widehat{\bot}\rangle$	$\langle 5,3,7,\widehat{\bot}\rangle$
R_1	*In, Out*	$\langle \widehat{\bot},\widehat{\bot},\widehat{\bot},\widehat{\bot}\rangle$	$\langle 5,\widehat{\bot},\widehat{\bot},\widehat{\bot}\rangle$	$\langle 5,2,7,\widehat{\bot}\rangle$	$\langle \widehat{\bot},2,\widehat{\bot},\widehat{\bot}\rangle$	$\langle 5,2,7,\widehat{\bot}\rangle$
n_1	*In*	$\langle \widehat{\bot},\widehat{\bot},\widehat{\bot},\widehat{\bot}\rangle$	$\langle 5,\widehat{\bot},\widehat{\bot},\widehat{\bot}\rangle$	$\langle 5,2,7,\widehat{\bot}\rangle$	$\langle \widehat{\bot},2,\widehat{\bot},\widehat{\bot}\rangle$	$\langle 5,2,7,\widehat{\bot}\rangle$
	Out	$\langle \widehat{\bot},\widehat{\bot},\widehat{\bot},\widehat{\bot}\rangle$	$\langle 7,\widehat{\bot},\widehat{\bot},\widehat{\bot}\rangle$	$\langle 7,2,7,\widehat{\bot}\rangle$	$\langle \widehat{\bot},2,\widehat{\bot},\widehat{\bot}\rangle$	$\langle 7,2,7,\widehat{\bot}\rangle$
n_2	*In*	$\langle \widehat{\bot},\widehat{\bot},\widehat{\bot},\widehat{\bot}\rangle$	$\langle 7,\widehat{\bot},\widehat{\bot},\widehat{\bot}\rangle$	$\langle 7,2,7,\widehat{\bot}\rangle$	$\langle \widehat{\bot},2,\widehat{\bot},\widehat{\bot}\rangle$	$\langle 7,2,7,\widehat{\bot}\rangle$
	Out	$\langle \widehat{\bot},\widehat{\bot},\widehat{\bot},\widehat{\bot}\rangle$	$\langle 7,\widehat{\bot},\widehat{\bot},\widehat{\bot}\rangle$	$\langle 7,2,7,14\rangle$	$\langle \widehat{\bot},2,\widehat{\bot},\widehat{\bot}\rangle$	$\langle 7,2,7,14\rangle$
C_2	*In, Out*	$\langle \widehat{\bot},\widehat{\bot},\widehat{\bot},\widehat{\bot}\rangle$	$\langle 7,\widehat{\bot},\widehat{\bot},\widehat{\bot}\rangle$	$\langle 7,2,7,14\rangle$	$\langle \widehat{\bot},2,\widehat{\bot},\widehat{\bot}\rangle$	$\langle 7,2,7,14\rangle$
R_2	*In, Out*	$\langle \widehat{\bot},\widehat{\bot},\widehat{\bot},\widehat{\bot}\rangle$	$\langle \widehat{\bot},\widehat{\bot},\widehat{\bot},\widehat{\bot}\rangle$	$\langle 2,2,\widehat{\bot},14\rangle$	$\langle \widehat{\bot},2,\widehat{\bot},\widehat{\bot}\rangle$	$\langle 2,2,\widehat{\bot},14\rangle$
End$_m$	*In, Out*	$\langle \widehat{\bot},\widehat{\bot},\widehat{\bot},\widehat{\bot}\rangle$	$\langle \widehat{\bot},\widehat{\bot},\widehat{\bot},\widehat{\bot}\rangle$	$\langle 2,2,\widehat{\bot},14\rangle$	$\langle \widehat{\bot},2,\widehat{\bot},\widehat{\bot}\rangle$	$\langle 2,2,\widehat{\bot},14\rangle$
Start$_p$	*In*	$\langle \widehat{\bot},\widehat{\bot},\widehat{\bot},\widehat{\bot}\rangle$	$\langle \widehat{\bot},\widehat{\bot},\widehat{\bot},\widehat{\bot}\rangle$	$\langle \widehat{\bot},\widehat{\bot},\widehat{\bot},\widehat{\bot}\rangle$	$\langle \widehat{\bot},\widehat{\bot},\widehat{\bot},\widehat{\bot}\rangle$	$\langle \widehat{\bot},\widehat{\bot},7,\widehat{\bot}\rangle$
	Out	$\langle \widehat{\bot},2,\widehat{\bot},\widehat{\bot}\rangle$	$\langle \widehat{\bot},2,\widehat{\bot},\widehat{\bot}\rangle$	$\langle \widehat{\bot},2,\widehat{\bot},\widehat{\bot}\rangle$	$\langle \widehat{\bot},2,\widehat{\bot},\widehat{\bot}\rangle$	$\langle \widehat{\bot},2,7,\widehat{\bot}\rangle$
n_3	*In*	$\langle \widehat{\bot},2,\widehat{\bot},\widehat{\bot}\rangle$	$\langle \widehat{\bot},2,\widehat{\bot},\widehat{\bot}\rangle$	$\langle \widehat{\bot},2,\widehat{\bot},\widehat{\bot}\rangle$	$\langle \widehat{\bot},2,\widehat{\bot},\widehat{\bot}\rangle$	$\langle \widehat{\bot},2,7,\widehat{\bot}\rangle$
	Out	$\langle \widehat{\bot},2,\widehat{\bot},\widehat{\bot}\rangle$	$\langle \widehat{\bot},2,\widehat{\bot},\widehat{\bot}\rangle$	$\langle \widehat{\bot},2,\widehat{\bot},\widehat{\bot}\rangle$	$\langle \widehat{\bot},2,\widehat{\bot},\widehat{\bot}\rangle$	$\langle \widehat{\bot},2,\widehat{\bot},\widehat{\bot}\rangle$
End$_p$	*In, Out*	$\langle \widehat{\bot},2,\widehat{\bot},\widehat{\bot}\rangle$	$\langle \widehat{\bot},2,\widehat{\bot},\widehat{\bot}\rangle$	$\langle \widehat{\bot},2,\widehat{\bot},\widehat{\bot}\rangle$	$\langle \widehat{\bot},2,\widehat{\bot},\widehat{\bot}\rangle$	$\langle \widehat{\bot},2,\widehat{\bot},\widehat{\bot}\rangle$
Start$_q$	*In*	$\langle \widehat{\bot},\widehat{\bot},\widehat{\bot},\widehat{\bot}\rangle$	$\langle \widehat{\bot},\widehat{\bot},\widehat{\bot},\widehat{\bot}\rangle$	$\langle \widehat{\bot},\widehat{\bot},\widehat{\bot},\widehat{\bot}\rangle$	$\langle \widehat{\bot},2,\widehat{\bot},\widehat{\bot}\rangle$	$\langle 7,2,7,14\rangle$
	Out	$\langle 1,\widehat{\bot},\widehat{\bot},\widehat{\bot}\rangle$	$\langle 1,\widehat{\bot},\widehat{\bot},\widehat{\bot}\rangle$	$\langle 1,\widehat{\bot},\widehat{\bot},\widehat{\bot}\rangle$	$\langle 1,2,\widehat{\bot},\widehat{\bot}\rangle$	$\langle 1,2,7,14\rangle$
C_3	*In, Out*	$\langle 1,\widehat{\bot},\widehat{\bot},\widehat{\bot}\rangle$	$\langle 1,\widehat{\bot},\widehat{\bot},\widehat{\bot}\rangle$	$\langle 1,\widehat{\bot},\widehat{\bot},\widehat{\bot}\rangle$	$\langle 1,2,\widehat{\bot},\widehat{\bot}\rangle$	$\langle 1,2,7,14\rangle$
R_3	*In, Out*	$\langle \widehat{\bot},\widehat{\bot},\widehat{\bot},\widehat{\bot}\rangle$	$\langle 1,\widehat{\bot},\widehat{\bot},\widehat{\bot}\rangle$	$\langle 1,2,\widehat{\bot},\widehat{\bot}\rangle$	$\langle \widehat{\bot},2,\widehat{\bot},\widehat{\bot}\rangle$	$\langle 1,2,\widehat{\bot},14\rangle$
End$_q$	*In*	$\langle \widehat{\bot},\widehat{\bot},\widehat{\bot},\widehat{\bot}\rangle$	$\langle 1,\widehat{\bot},\widehat{\bot},\widehat{\bot}\rangle$	$\langle 1,2,\widehat{\bot},\widehat{\bot}\rangle$	$\langle \widehat{\bot},2,\widehat{\bot},\widehat{\bot}\rangle$	$\langle 1,2,\widehat{\bot},14\rangle$
	Out	$\langle \widehat{\bot},\widehat{\bot},\widehat{\bot},\widehat{\bot}\rangle$	$\langle \widehat{\bot},\widehat{\bot},\widehat{\bot},\widehat{\bot}\rangle$	$\langle 2,2,\widehat{\bot},\widehat{\bot}\rangle$	$\langle \widehat{\bot},2,\widehat{\bot},\widehat{\bot}\rangle$	$\langle 2,2,\widehat{\bot},14\rangle$

FIGURE 7.6

Constant propagation in our example program using flow sensitive version of common variants of interprocedural data flow analysis.

entry of p and q. This does not contradict the assumption made for constant propagation because although a global variable may be modified in the callee procedure, it cannot be guaranteed to be modified along all paths before being used. These assumptions are safe because they cannot enable incorrect optimizations.

From Figure 7.6, it is easy to see that intraprocedural analysis limits the scope of constant propagation to a single procedure and disables it across function calls. As illustrated in Figure 7.7 on the following page, only variable b in blocks *Start*$_p$ and n_3 is replaced by its value which happens to be 2. The result of performing liveness analysis on the program obtained after constant propagation is shown in Figure 7.7 on the next page. Our analysis concludes that all left hand side variables in the assignments are live after the assignments. Thus this variant of analysis fails to enable dead code elimination in our example program.

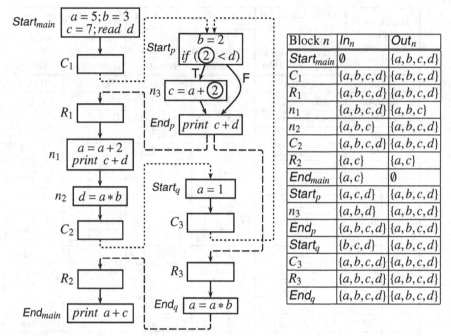

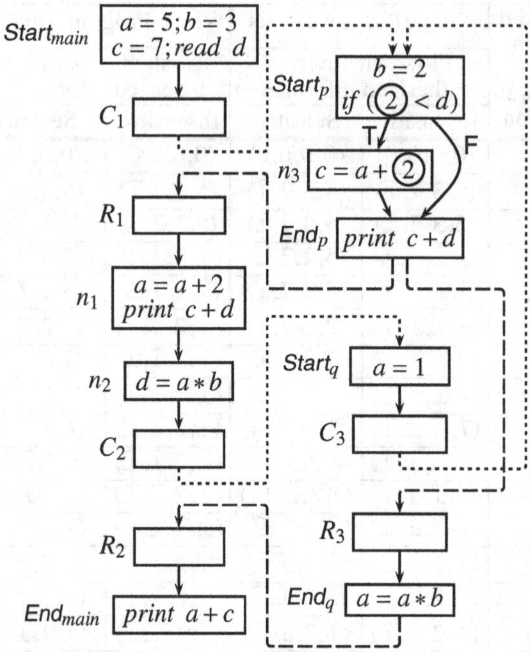

Block n	In_n	Out_n
$Start_{main}$	$\emptyset$	$\{a,b,c,d\}$
C_1	$\{a,b,c,d\}$	$\{a,b,c,d\}$
R_1	$\{a,b,c,d\}$	$\{a,b,c,d\}$
n_1	$\{a,b,c,d\}$	$\{a,b,c\}$
n_2	$\{a,b,c\}$	$\{a,b,c,d\}$
C_2	$\{a,b,c,d\}$	$\{a,b,c,d\}$
R_2	$\{a,c\}$	$\{a,c\}$
End_{main}	$\{a,c\}$	$\emptyset$
$Start_p$	$\{a,c,d\}$	$\{a,b,c,d\}$
n_3	$\{a,b,d\}$	$\{a,b,c,d\}$
End_p	$\{a,b,c,d\}$	$\{a,b,c,d\}$
$Start_q$	$\{b,c,d\}$	$\{a,b,c,d\}$
C_3	$\{a,b,c,d\}$	$\{a,b,c,d\}$
R_3	$\{a,b,c,d\}$	$\{a,b,c,d\}$
End_q	$\{a,b,c,d\}$	$\{a,b,c,d\}$

FIGURE 7.7
Intraprocedural liveness analysis after intraprocedural constant propagation. Propagated constants are shown in circles.

7.6.2 Intraprocedural Analysis with Side Effects Computation

Side effect analysis discovers which variables are actually modified in a procedure calls. Hence it can compute more precise synthesized data flow information. Side effect computation could be flow insensitive or flow sensitive. We compute the data flow information in the body of a caller in a flow sensitive manner. In either case, since no data flow information is inherited, the value of *BI* is same as in intraprocedural analysis.

After computing the side effects, function calls are treated as basic blocks and conventional intraprocedural analysis is performed.

Flow insensitive side effects

We present two methods of computing flow insensitive side effects. The first method uses symbolic values to parametrize the context. The other method works for frameworks in which the flow functions do not contain dependent parts. This method computes the values of *ConstGen* and *ConstKill* components of the summary side effect flow function of a procedure explicitly. We illustrate the former method for constant propagation and the latter for live variables analysis.

- *Flow insensitive side effects for constant propagation.*

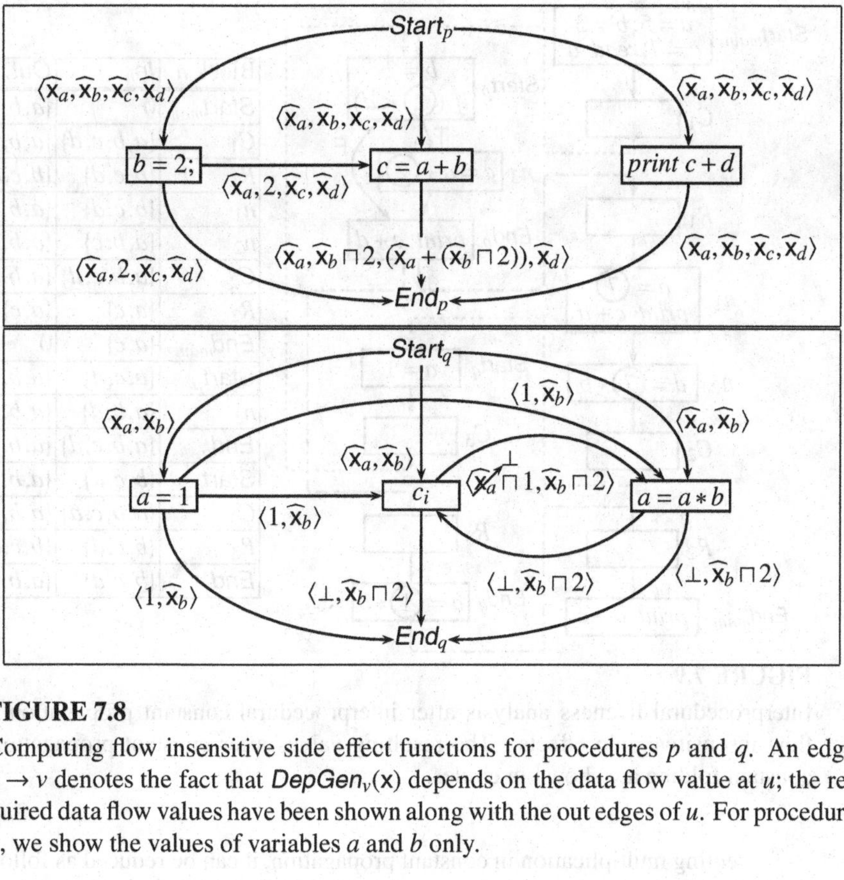

FIGURE 7.8
Computing flow insensitive side effect functions for procedures p and q. An edge $u \rightarrow v$ denotes the fact that $\mathit{DepGen}_v(\mathsf{x})$ depends on the data flow value at u; the required data flow values have been shown along with the out edges of u. For procedure q, we show the values of variables a and b only.

Recall that a systematic construction of summary flow functions is possible only for a limited set of data flow frameworks; in general, it is not possible for full constant propagation. Here we use Equation (7.1) intuitively to symbolically compute summary function for constant propagation and illustrate the difficulty in automatic construction of flow functions for constant propagation.

Computation of flow insensitive side effect summary flow functions for procedure p and q are illustrated in Figure 7.8. It is easy to see that:

$$f_p(\langle \widehat{x}_a, \widehat{x}_b, \widehat{x}_c, \widehat{x}_d \rangle) = \langle \widehat{x}_a, \widehat{x}_b \sqcap 2, \widehat{x}_c \sqcap (\widehat{x}_a + (\widehat{x}_b \sqcap 2)), \widehat{x}_d \rangle$$

For computing the summary side effect function for q, we need to incorporate the effect of procedure p too. For simplicity, only the computation for variables a and b for procedure p is illustrated in Figure 7.8. The expression that represents the data flow value of a after processing the assignment $a = a * b$ is $\left(\widehat{x}_a \sqcap 1 \sqcap \left((\widehat{x}_a \sqcap 1) * (\widehat{x}_b \sqcap 2)\right)\right)$. Using monotonicity of the flow function repre-

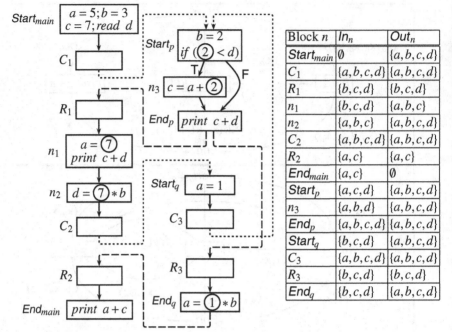

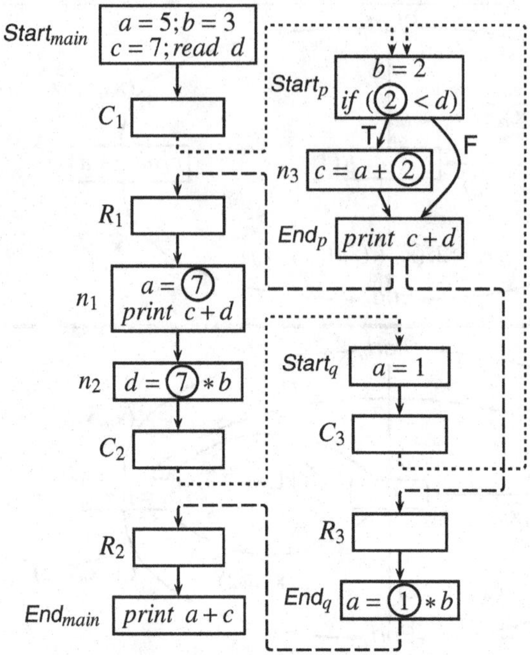

Block n	In_n	Out_n
$Start_{main}$	$\emptyset$	$\{a,b,c,d\}$
C_1	$\{a,b,c,d\}$	$\{a,b,c,d\}$
R_1	$\{b,c,d\}$	$\{b,c,d\}$
n_1	$\{b,c,d\}$	$\{a,b,c\}$
n_2	$\{a,b,c\}$	$\{a,b,c,d\}$
C_2	$\{a,b,c,d\}$	$\{a,b,c,d\}$
R_2	$\{a,c\}$	$\{a,c\}$
End_{main}	$\{a,c\}$	$\emptyset$
$Start_p$	$\{a,c,d\}$	$\{a,b,c,d\}$
n_3	$\{a,b,d\}$	$\{a,b,c,d\}$
End_p	$\{a,b,c,d\}$	$\{a,b,c,d\}$
$Start_q$	$\{b,c,d\}$	$\{a,b,c,d\}$
C_3	$\{a,b,c,d\}$	$\{a,b,c,d\}$
R_3	$\{b,c,d\}$	$\{b,c,d\}$
End_q	$\{b,c,d\}$	$\{a,b,c,d\}$

FIGURE 7.9
Interprocedural liveness analysis after interprocedural constant propagation using flow insensitive side effects. The resulting values after constant propagation and constant folding are shown in circles.

senting multiplication in constant propagation, it can be reduced as follows:

$$\begin{aligned}\widehat{\mathsf{x}}_a \sqcap 1 \sqcap \big((\widehat{\mathsf{x}}_a \sqcap 1) * (\widehat{\mathsf{x}}_b \sqcap 2)\big) &\sqsubseteq \widehat{\mathsf{x}}_a \sqcap 1 \sqcap \big((\widehat{\mathsf{x}}_a * \widehat{\mathsf{x}}_b) \sqcap (\widehat{\mathsf{x}}_a * 2) \sqcap (1 * 2) \sqcap (1 * \widehat{\mathsf{x}}_b)\big)\\ &\sqsubseteq \widehat{\mathsf{x}}_a \sqcap 1 \sqcap (\widehat{\mathsf{x}}_a * \widehat{\mathsf{x}}_b) \sqcap (\widehat{\mathsf{x}}_a * 2) \sqcap 2 \sqcap \widehat{\mathsf{x}}_b\\ &\sqsubseteq \widehat{\bot}\end{aligned}$$

Intuitively, a can be both 1 and 2, hence it must be $\widehat{\bot}$. Using this, the final summary side effect function is:

$$f_q(\langle \widehat{\mathsf{x}}_a, \widehat{\mathsf{x}}_b, \widehat{\mathsf{x}}_c, \widehat{\mathsf{x}}_d \rangle) = \langle \widehat{\bot}, \widehat{\mathsf{x}}_b \sqcap 2, \widehat{\bot}, \widehat{\mathsf{x}}_d \rangle$$

Observe that devising a systematic method that can perform the reductions such as above is not easy.

The details of constants discovered in each basic block are shown in Figure 7.6 on page 247. The resulting constant propagation is shown in Figure 7.9. Observe that the number 7 in blocks n_1 and n_2 is a result of constant folding. The use of flow insensitive side effects in intraprocedural analysis results in more precise data flow information compared to the data flow information computed using the conservative approximation of function calls.

- *Flow insensitive side effects for live variables analysis.*

  We need to compute *MustKill* and *MayUse* sets for procedures p and q. We compute them for the program in Figure 7.9 on the facing page.

$$
\begin{aligned}
\mathit{MustKill}_p &= \mathit{Kill}_{\mathit{Start}_p} \cap \mathit{Kill}_{n_3} \cap \mathit{Kill}_{\mathit{End}_p} &&= \emptyset \\
\mathit{MustKill}_q &= \mathit{Kill}_{\mathit{Start}_q} \cap \mathit{MustKill}_p \cap \mathit{Kill}_{\mathit{End}_q} &&= \emptyset \\
\mathit{MayUse}_p &= \mathit{Gen}_{\mathit{Start}_p} \cup \mathit{Gen}_{n_3} \cup \mathit{Gen}_{\mathit{End}_p} &&= \{a,c,d\} \\
\mathit{MayUse}_q &= \mathit{Gen}_{\mathit{Start}_q} \cup \mathit{MayUse}_p \cup \mathit{Gen}_{\mathit{End}_q} &&= \{a,b,c,d\} \\
f_p(\mathsf{x}) &= (\mathsf{x} - \mathit{MustKill}_p) \cup \mathit{MayUse}_p &&= \mathsf{x} \cup \{a,c,d\} \\
f_q(\mathsf{x}) &= (\mathsf{x} - \mathit{MustKill}_q) \cup \mathit{MayUse}_q &&= \mathsf{x} \cup \{a,b,c,d\}
\end{aligned}
$$

  Note that $f_p(\mathsf{x})$ is a little better than the conservative approximations used in Section 7.6.1 in that it does not contain b. However, due to flow insensitivity, it does not recognize that b is killed in procedure p. Hence, the use of b in block n_2 cause b to be considered live at the exit of Start_{main}. The resulting data flow information after performing constant propagation using flow insensitive side effects is shown in Figure 7.9 on the preceding page. Observe that no variable is dead immediately after its assignment hence dead code elimination is not possible using this variant also in spite of the fact that some more constant are discovered and liveness information has become more precise.

Flow sensitive side effects

As in the previous section, we compute *Kill* and *Gen* implicitly for constant propagation and explicitly for live variables analysis.

Flow sensitive side effects for constant propagation can be computed by performing data flow analysis over a called procedure with $\mathit{BI} = \langle \widehat{\mathsf{x}}_a, \widehat{\mathsf{x}}_b, \widehat{\mathsf{x}}_c, \widehat{\mathsf{x}}_d \rangle$. The resulting flow functions are represented by the symbolic data flow values at the exit of the function. It is easy to see that:

$$
\begin{aligned}
f_p(\langle \widehat{\mathsf{x}}_a, \widehat{\mathsf{x}}_b, \widehat{\mathsf{x}}_c, \widehat{\mathsf{x}}_d \rangle) &= \langle \widehat{\mathsf{x}}_a, 2, \widehat{\mathsf{x}}_c \sqcap (\widehat{\mathsf{x}}_a + 2), \widehat{\mathsf{x}}_d \rangle \\
f_q(\langle \widehat{\mathsf{x}}_a, \widehat{\mathsf{x}}_b, \widehat{\mathsf{x}}_c, \widehat{\mathsf{x}}_d \rangle) &= \langle 2, 2, \widehat{\mathsf{x}}_c \sqcap 3, \widehat{\mathsf{x}}_d \rangle
\end{aligned}
$$

It is clear from Figure 7.6 on page 247 that flow sensitive side effects enable detecting more constants than flow insensitive side effects. The resulting constant propagation and constant folding is shown in Figure 7.10 on the next page.

For liveness analysis, we compute flow sensitive *MustKill* and *MayUse* by traversing the CFG in post order. *MustKill* is computed by discovering the sets of variables that are modified in basic blocks such that these modifications are upwards exposed. If a variable is used in a basic block, it is removed from the set. By contrast, *MayUse*

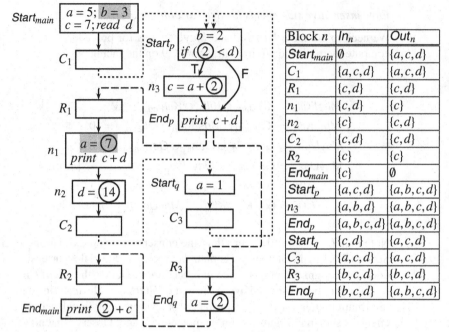

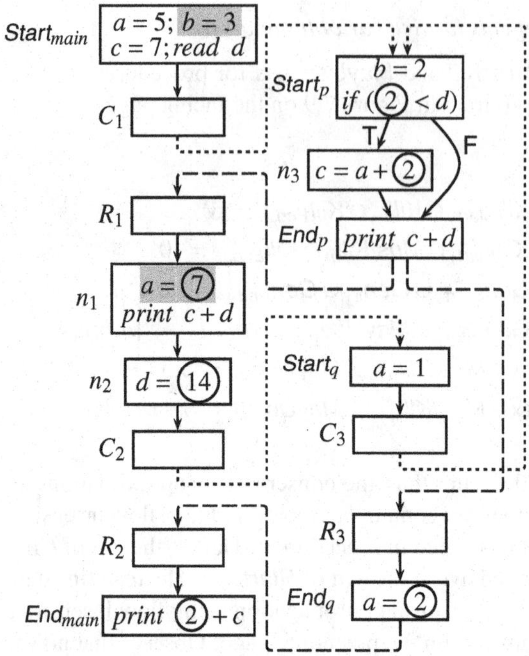

Block n	In_n	Out_n
$Start_{main}$	$\emptyset$	$\{a,c,d\}$
C_1	$\{a,c,d\}$	$\{a,c,d\}$
R_1	$\{c,d\}$	$\{c,d\}$
n_1	$\{c,d\}$	$\{c\}$
n_2	$\{c\}$	$\{c,d\}$
C_2	$\{c,d\}$	$\{c,d\}$
R_2	$\{c\}$	$\{c\}$
End_{main}	$\{c\}$	$\emptyset$
$Start_p$	$\{a,c,d\}$	$\{a,b,c,d\}$
n_3	$\{a,b,d\}$	$\{a,b,c,d\}$
End_p	$\{a,b,c,d\}$	$\{a,b,c,d\}$
$Start_q$	$\{c,d\}$	$\{a,c,d\}$
C_3	$\{a,c,d\}$	$\{a,c,d\}$
R_3	$\{b,c,d\}$	$\{b,c,d\}$
End_q	$\{b,c,d\}$	$\{a,b,c,d\}$

FIGURE 7.10
Interprocedural liveness analysis after interprocedural constant propagation using flow sensitive side effects. Highlighted statements are dead assignments and can be eliminated.

is computed using live variables analysis. *BI* is $\emptyset$ for both *MustKill* and *MayUse*. The resulting flow functions are:

$$
\begin{aligned}
MustKill_p &= \{b\} \\
MayUse_p &= \{a,c,d\} \\
f_p(\mathsf{X}) &= (\mathsf{X} - \{b\}) \cup \{a,c,d\} \\
MustKill_q &= \{a,b\} \\
MayUse_q &= \{c,d\} \\
f_q(\mathsf{X}) &= (\mathsf{X} - \{a,b\}) \cup \{c,d\}
\end{aligned}
$$

Figure 7.10 shows the liveness analysis on the program in which constant propagation has been performed. Both analyses use flow sensitive side effects to incorporate the effect of a procedure call. The results of both analyses are more precise compared to the results obtained by using flow insensitive side effects. Further, dead code elimination also becomes possible. Variable b is not live at the exit of $Start_{main}$ and $Start_p$. Hence the assignments to these variables in the respective blocks can

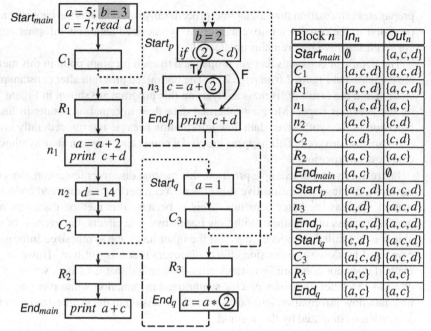

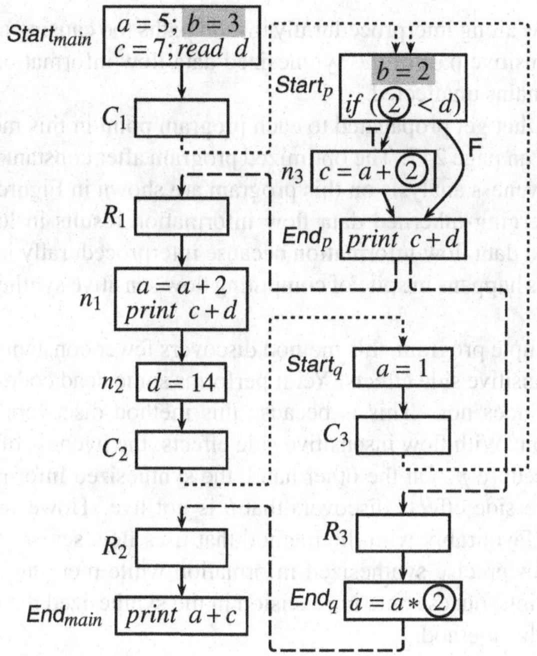

Block *n*	In_n	Out_n
$Start_{main}$	$\emptyset$	$\{a,c,d\}$
C_1	$\{a,c,d\}$	$\{a,c,d\}$
R_1	$\{a,c,d\}$	$\{a,c,d\}$
n_1	$\{a,c,d\}$	$\{a,c\}$
n_2	$\{a,c\}$	$\{c,d\}$
C_2	$\{c,d\}$	$\{c,d\}$
R_2	$\{a,c\}$	$\{a,c\}$
End_{main}	$\{a,c\}$	$\emptyset$
$Start_p$	$\{a,c,d\}$	$\{a,c,d\}$
n_3	$\{a,d\}$	$\{a,c,d\}$
End_p	$\{a,c,d\}$	$\{a,c,d\}$
$Start_q$	$\{c,d\}$	$\{a,c,d\}$
C_3	$\{a,c,d\}$	$\{a,c,d\}$
R_3	$\{a,c\}$	$\{a,c\}$
End_q	$\{a,c\}$	$\{a,c\}$

FIGURE 7.11
Interprocedural liveness analysis after interprocedural constant propagation using context insensitive whole program analysis.

be deleted. Observe that this still does not cover all dead assignments shown in Figure 7.1 on page 234.

7.6.3 Whole Program Analysis

We now present interprocedural analyses that compute both inherited and synthesized data flow information. As usual, the analyses are flow sensitive. Since inherited data flow information depends on the callers alone, we present two possible variants: (a) Context insensitive analysis, and (b) Context sensitive analysis.

Context insensitive whole program analysis

Conceptually, the simplest method of performing context insensitive whole program analysis is to treat a supergraph as single control flow graph and compute data flow properties with a block from all its neighbours without distinguishing between interprocedural and intraprocedural edges. Thus, the constants reaching $Start_p$ are a merge of the constants available at C_1 and C_3. This merged information is then used to compute the synthesized information which is then propagated to both R_1 and R_3. Thus the data flow information at C_3 influences the data flow information at R_1 in spite of the fact that there is no control flow from C_3 to R_1. Thus this method propagates information flow along interprocedurally invalid paths too causing an imprecision in the context sensitive part of the synthesized data flow information; the context insensitive part remains unaffected.

The details of constants that get propagated to each program point in this method are presented in Figure 7.6 on page 247. The optimized program after constant propagation and the result of liveness analysis on this program are shown in Figure 7.11 on the previous page. Merging inherited data flow information results in loss of precision in the synthesized data flow information because interprocedurally invalid paths are also covered. This happens in spite of computing flow sensitive synthesized data flow information.

Interestingly, in our example program, this method discovers fewer constants than the method using flow insensitive side effects. Yet it performs some dead code elimination whereas the latter does not. This is because this method discovers more precise liveness information: With flow insensitive side effects, the liveness of variable b is not killed in procedure p. On the other hand, the synthesized information computed by flow sensitive side effects discovers that b is not live. However, this method does not compare favourably with the method that uses flow sensitive side effects—the latter computes precise synthesized information while merging inherited data flow information introduces some imprecision in the synthesized data flow information computed by this method.

Context sensitive whole program analysis

Our final method of interprocedural data flow analysis does not merge inherited data flow information while computing the synthesized data flow information. Thus the context sensitive part of synthesized data flow information is more precise than in the context insensitive whole program analysis.

It uses the same flow functions as used by the flow sensitive side effects. The main difference is that in that method, the inherited data flow information was represented by a conservative approximation. This method computes the inherited information from calling contexts and propagates it within the callee's body.

The resulting optimization is shown in Figure 7.12 on the facing page. The dead code discovered by this method matches the dead code shown in Figure 7.1 on page 234.

Observe that this method fails to discover that the value of c is 3 in End_{main}. It can be discovered by context sensitive whole program conditional constant propagation.

7.7 An Aside on Interprocedural Optimizations

A lot of work that analyses programs at the interprocedural level is directed at interprocedural optimizations like procedure inlining and cloning. The analyses required for these optimizations are different from the analyses that are presented in

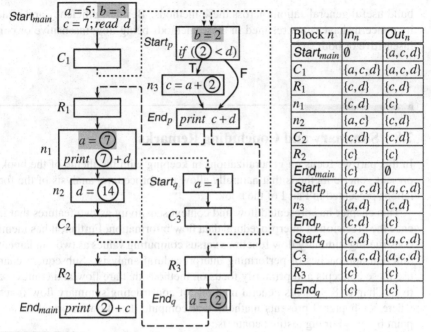

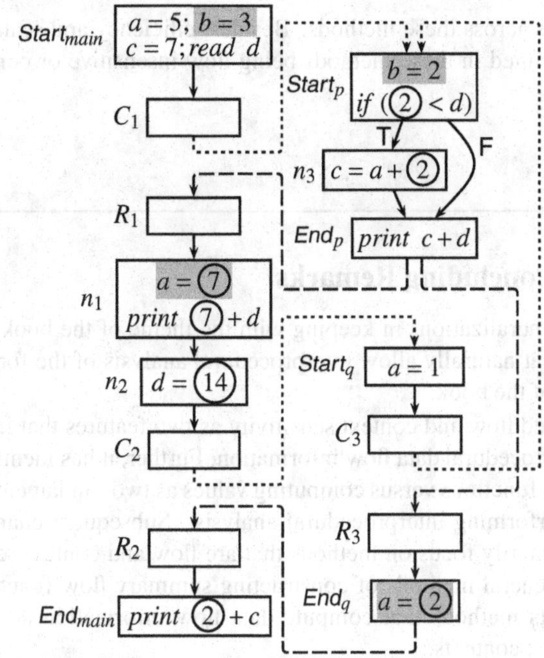

Block n	In_n	Out_n
$Start_{main}$	$\emptyset$	$\{a,c,d\}$
C_1	$\{a,c,d\}$	$\{a,c,d\}$
R_1	$\{c,d\}$	$\{c,d\}$
n_1	$\{c,d\}$	$\{c\}$
n_2	$\{a,c\}$	$\{c,d\}$
C_2	$\{c,d\}$	$\{c,d\}$
R_2	$\{c\}$	$\{c\}$
End_{main}	$\{c\}$	$\emptyset$
$Start_p$	$\{a,c,d\}$	$\{a,c,d\}$
n_3	$\{a,d\}$	$\{c,d\}$
End_p	$\{c,d\}$	$\{c\}$
$Start_q$	$\{c,d\}$	$\{a,c,d\}$
C_3	$\{a,c,d\}$	$\{a,c,d\}$
R_3	$\{c\}$	$\{c\}$
End_q	$\{c\}$	$\{c\}$

FIGURE 7.12
Interprocedural liveness analysis after interprocedural constant propagation using context sensitive whole program analysis.

this book. Often they involve a single traversal over program representation. For example, procedure inlining analyses parameters and checks that there is no recursive call. The final decision to inline is taken based on a collection of heuristics supported by empirical evidence. Then a transformation pass renames global variables and performs inlining by traversing the call graph bottom up. Procedure cloning is based on analyzing actual parameters from different call sites and their effects on the called procedures. Typically, the option of cloning is considered when constant values are passed as actual parameters. Again, the final decision depends on a collection of thumb rules. Most production compilers gainfully employ these optimizations. An additional advantage of these optimizations is that they enhance the possibility of intraprocedural optimizations.

The next set of interprocedural optimizations employed by production compilers are actually more aggressive intraprocedural optimizations using side effects of procedure calls. The common side effect that most compilers try to detect is potential modifications of global variables and reference parameters.

Finally, many interprocedural optimizations do involve systematic analyses. However, for reasons of efficiency and scalability, most of these analyses are rooted in specific optimizations e.g., constant propagation, side effect analysis, points-to analysis etc. There is a large body of work along these lines but it seems difficult to build useful generalizations across these methods. Besides, efficiency and scalability concerns have often resulted in these methods being flow insensitive or context insensitive or both.

7.8 Summary and Concluding Remarks

In this part we focus on generalizations in keeping with the theme of the book and present generic methods that naturally allow interprocedural analysis of the formulations presented in Part I of the book.

This chapter has presented flow and context sensitivity as two features that influence the precision of interprocedural data flow information. Further, it has identified constructing summary flow functions versus computing values as two fundamentally different approaches of performing interprocedural analysis. Subsequent chapters use these concepts and primarily focus on methods that are flow and context sensitive. Chapter 8 presents general methods of constructing summary flow functions whereas Chapter 9 presents methods that compute data flow information at each point by maintaining distinct contexts.

7.9 Bibliographic Notes

The earliest studies of interprocedural data flow analysis were motivated by the need of discovering side effects. The work by Spillman [94] was directed at finding out side effects in terms of values modified by the called procedure. This analysis was performed by traversing a call graph from callees to callers. Allen [6] addressed a slightly more general problem of additionally finding out values used by callees also. However, unlike Spillman's method, Allen's method was not suited for recursive programs. Barth [13, 14] introduced a much more general formulation based on computing transitive closures of relationships. This method allowed asking a wider range of questions such as whether variables shared storage or not, whether variables were modified or used etc. More importantly, he introduced the notions of *must* and *may* in the data flow information discovered. Banning [12] was the first to make a distinction between flow sensitive and flow insensitive side effect computation.

The concept of context sensitivity was introduced by Sharir and Pnueli [93] which can be easily called the most influential work on interprocedural data flow analysis. We present their concepts in greater details in the next two chapters.

Effectiveness of interprocedural data flow analysis was studied by Richardson and Ganapathi [83], Grove and Torczon [39], and Martin [72]. Lhoták and Hendren [69] have empirically observed that in the presence of recursive calls, context insensitivity leads to significant imprecision.

Duesterwald, Gupta and Soffa [32, 33] present an interesting alternative of computing interprocedural data flow information incrementally on demand.

An important issue in interprocedural data flow analysis is precise call graph construction. This becomes difficult in the presence of function pointers in a language like C and virtual functions and dynamic dispatch of methods in object oriented languages. Early works along these lines were done by Hall and Kennedy [43] and by Callahan, Carle, Hall and Kennedy. [20]. Grove and Chambers [38] present a more recent detailed treatment of call graph construction. We do not address this issue in this book.

8

Functional Approach to Interprocedural Data Flow Analysis

Functional approach to interprocedural data flow analysis constructs context independent summary flow functions which are then used in the calling contexts to compute the data flow information synthesized by called procedures in the body of the caller procedures. Data flow information inherited by a procedure is computed from the calling contexts of the procedure. The main advantage of constructing context independent summary flow functions is that a procedure needs to be analyzed only once regardless of the number of calls to it.

We begin by presenting the classical side effects analysis for bit vector frameworks as a special case of constructing summary flow functions. This is followed by context and flow sensitive whole program analysis. Finally we show how the explicit construction of summary flow functions can be avoided by enumerating the function in terms of pairs of input output values.

For simplicity, we focus on data flow analysis of global variables. We present orthogonal techniques of handling the effects of parameters. We restrict the analysis to languages that do not contain nested procedures.

8.1 Side Effects Analysis of Procedure Calls

Classical side effects analysis focuses on computing the effect of a callee procedure on the variables of the caller procedure in order to discover more optimization opportunities in the caller procedures. In particular, the following side effects are directly relevant: For a given variable v and a given callee s in a procedure r

- Is the execution of r guaranteed to modify the value of v?
- Can the execution of r modify the value of v?
- Is the execution of r guaranteed to use the value of v before modifying it?
- Can the execution of r use the value of v before modifying it?

The variables for which the above answers are in affirmative are contained in $\mathit{MustKill}_r$, $\mathit{MayKill}_r$, $\mathit{MustUse}_r$, and MayUse_r respectively. Clearly, the *must* properties are all paths properties whereas *may* properties are some path properties.

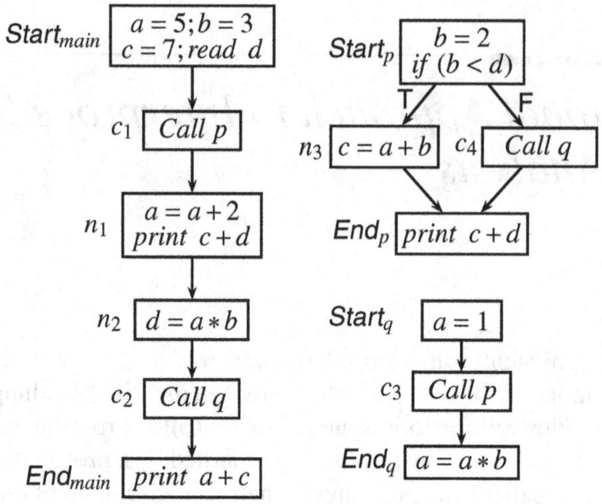

FIGURE 8.1
Modified version of the program in Figure 7.2.

These basic side effects of a procedure can be used to answer a variety of questions. For example, liveness analysis can handle call to procedure r by computing In_n of the call block as follows:

$$\mathit{In}_n = (\mathit{Out}_n - \mathit{MustKill}_r) \cup \mathit{MayUse}_r$$

Observe that liveness information of a variable is killed only when it is guaranteed to be modified in the callee along all execution paths. Available expression analysis, on the other hand, should use kill the availability of expressions whose operands are in $\mathit{MayKill}_r$. The variables that are guaranteed to preserve their values across a call to procedure r are contained in $\mathbb{G}\mathsf{var} - \mathit{MayKill}_r$ where $\mathbb{G}\mathsf{var}$ denotes the set of global variables. The variables that may preserve their values along some path through procedure r are contained in $\mathbb{G}\mathsf{var} - \mathit{MustKill}_r$.

The $\sqcap$, $\top$ and $\bot$ values for computing the above side effect properties are:

Property	$\sqcap$	$\top$	$\bot$	Explanation of $\bot$
$\mathit{MustKill}_r$	$\cap$	$\mathbb{G}\mathsf{var}$	$\emptyset$	No variable can be guaranteed to be necessarily killed by r
$\mathit{MustUse}_r$	$\cap$	$\mathbb{G}\mathsf{var}$	$\emptyset$	No variable can be guaranteed to be necessarily used in r before being modified
MayUse_r	$\cup$	$\emptyset$	$\mathbb{G}\mathsf{var}$	Any variable may be used in r along some path or the other
$\mathit{MayKill}_r$	$\cup$	$\emptyset$	$\mathbb{G}\mathsf{var}$	Any variable may be killed in r along some path or the other

We use the program in Figure 8.1 as a running example in this section. This program is same as the program in the previous chapter except that we have now included a call to procedure q in procedure p to make the program recursive.

8.1.1 Computing Flow Sensitive Side Effects

The side effect properties *MustKill*, *MayKill*, *MustUse*, *MayUse* are computed by assuming *BI* to be empty set.

For computing the *MustKill* and *MayKill*, a simple data flow analysis gathers the variables that are killed on the paths from $Start_r$ to End_r. The sets so computed do not include local variables of r because they are not visible in the caller procedures even if r is called recursively. The data flow value Out_r defines $MayKill_r$ or $MustKill_r$ as the case may be. The data flow equations for computing $MustKill_r$ are given below.

$$
\begin{aligned}
In_n &= \begin{cases} BI & n \text{ is } Start \text{ block} \\ \bigcap\limits_{p \in pred(n)} Out_p & \text{otherwise} \end{cases} \\
Out_n &= \begin{cases} In_n \cup MustKill_s & n \text{ is a call to } s \\ In_n \cup Gen_n & \text{otherwise} \end{cases} \qquad (8.1) \\
MustKill_r &= Out_{End_r}
\end{aligned}
$$

The initial values of In_n, Out_n, and $MustKill_s$ are $\top = \mathbb{G}var$.

For computing $MayKill_r$, $\sqcap$ is $\cup$, and the initial values of In_n, Out_n, and $MayKill_s$ are $\top = \emptyset$.

Example 8.1

The computation of *MustKill* and *MayKill* properties of procedures p and q of our program in Figure 8.1 are shown in Figure 8.2 on the following page. Since procedures p and q are mutually recursive, their data flow values are mutually dependent and require a fixed point computation with $\top$ as the initial value. When procedure p is being analyzed $MustKill_q$ is assumed to be $\{a,b,c,d\}$. This results in $MustKill_p = \{b,c\}$ which is then used in computing $MustKill_q$. The resulting value $MustKill_q = \{a,b,c\}$ is used in the second iteration over p. Although it causes a change in Out_{c_4}, Out_{End_p} does not change. Thus neither $MustKill_p$, not $MustKill_q$ changes. For computing *MayKill*, $\top$ is $\emptyset$. Thus the initial value of $MayKill_q$ is $\emptyset$ resulting in $MayKill_p = \{a,b,c\}$. When this is used to compute $MayKill_q$, the result is $\{a,b,c\}$. However, the new value of $MayKill_q$ does not result in a change in the value of $MayKill_p$.

Observe that c is contained in $MustKill_p$ in spite of the fact that it is computed conditionally. This is because every path from $Start_p$ to End_p must pass through n_3: Even if the execution were to follow edge $Start_p \rightarrow c_4$, the only way to unwind the recursive call to q is to execute the path involving n_3. Since there is only one path through procedure q (with varying depths of recursion), $MustKill_q = MayKill_q$. Also observe that a is contained in $MayKill_p$ but not in $MustKill_p$. □

Procedure	Node	*MustKill*				*MayKill*			
		Iteration #1		Changes in Iteration #2		Iteration #1		Changes in Iteration #2	
		In	*Out*	*In*	*Out*	*In*	*Out*	*In*	*Out*
p	$Start_p$	$\emptyset$	$\{b\}$			$\emptyset$	$\{b\}$		
	n_3	$\{b\}$	$\{b,c\}$			$\{b\}$	$\{b,c\}$		
	c_4	$\{b\}$	$\{a,b,c,d\}$		$\{a,b\}$	$\{b\}$	$\{b\}$		$\{a,b,c\}$
	End_p	$\{b,c\}$	$\{b,c\}$			$\{b,c\}$	$\{b,c\}$	$\{a,b,c\}$	$\{a,b,c\}$
		$MustKill_p = End_p = \{b,c\}$				$MayKill_p = End_p = \{a,b,c\}$			
q	$Start_q$	$\emptyset$	$\{a\}$			$\emptyset$	$\{a\}$		
	c_3	$\{a\}$	$\{a,b,c\}$			$\{a\}$	$\{a,b,c\}$		
	End_q	$\{a,b,c\}$	$\{a,b,c\}$			$\{a,b,c\}$	$\{a,b,c\}$		
		$MustKill_q = End_q = \{a,b,c\}$				$MayKill_q = End_q = \{a,b,c\}$			

FIGURE 8.2
Computing flow sensitive *MustKill* and *MayKill* for the program in Figure 8.1.

The data flow equations for computing *MayUse* have been provided below. Intuitively, $MayUse_r$ contains the variables that are live at the entry of r assuming that no variable is live at the exit of r. Thus except for a call statement, the data flow equations are identical to the data flow equations of liveness analysis. Gen_n contains the set of variables with upwards exposed uses in block n.

$$In_n = \begin{cases} (Out_n - MustKill_t) \cup MayUse_t & n \text{ is a call to } t \\ (Out_n - Kill_n) \cup Gen_n & \text{otherwise} \end{cases} \tag{8.2}$$

$$Out_n = \begin{cases} BI & n \text{ is } End \text{ block} \\ \bigcup_{s \in succ(n)} In_s & \text{otherwise} \end{cases}$$

$$MayUse_r = In_{Start_r}$$

For a call statement, the variables in *MustKill* set of the callee cease to be live whereas the variables in *MayUse* set of the callee become live. For *MustUse*, $\sqcap$ is $\cup$ and *Kill* for a call statement is *MayKill* instead of *MustKill*.

Example 8.2

The data flow analysis for computing *MayUse* and *MustUse* of our example program is provided in Figure 8.3 on the next page. Observe that for computing $MayUse_p$ we use $\top = \emptyset$ as the initial value of $MayUse_q$ whereas for computing $MustUse_p$ we use $\top = \{a,b,c,d\}$ as the initial value of $MustUse_q$. The data flow values for computing *MayUse* do not change in the second iteration whereas the data flow values for computing *MustUse* do. □

Procedure	Node	*MayUse*		*MustUse*			
		Iteration #1		Iteration #1		Changes in Iteration #2	
		Out	*In*	*Out*	*In*	*Out*	*In*
p	End_p	$\emptyset$	$\{c,d\}$	$\emptyset$	$\{c,d\}$		
	n_3	$\{c,d\}$	$\{a,b,d\}$	$\{c,d\}$	$\{a,b,d\}$		
	c_4	$\{c,d\}$	$\{d\}$	$\{c,d\}$	$\{a,b,c,d\}$		$\{d\}$
	$Start_p$	$\{a,b,d\}$	$\{a,d\}$	$\{a,b,d\}$	$\{a,d\}$	$\{d\}$	$\{d\}$
		$MayUse_p = End_p = \{a,d\}$		$MustUse_p = End_p = \{d\}$			
q	End_q	$\emptyset$	$\{a,b\}$	$\emptyset$	$\{a,b\}$		
	c_3	$\{a,b\}$	$\{a,d\}$	$\{a,b\}$	$\{a,d\}$		$\{d\}$
	$Start_q$	$\{a,d\}$	$\{d\}$	$\{a,d\}$	$\{d\}$	$\{d\}$	
		$MayUse_q = End_q = \{d\}$		$MustUse_q = End_q = \{d\}$			

FIGURE 8.3
Computing flow sensitive *MayUse* and *MustUse* for the program in Figure 8.1.

8.1.2 Computing Flow Insensitive Side Effects

Recall that flow insensitive computation accumulates the effect of each block using Equation (7.1). As explained in Figure 7.5 on page 242 and Figure 7.8 on page 249, dependence of data flow values on other data flow values has to be explicitly handled by adding dependence edges. In the general situation, a path in $paths(u)$ could consist of fragments where the dependent parts in the flow functions are $\emptyset$ as illustrated in Figure 8.4 on the following page.

The following lemma shows that if dependent parts are handled explicitly, flow insensitive analysis computes a safe approximation of the corresponding flow sensitive data flow information.

LEMMA 8.1
Consider a path fragment $\rho = (p_0, p_1, \ldots, p_k)$ along which the dependent parts of flow functions $f_{p_i \to p_{i+1}}$ are $\emptyset$. Then,

$$\forall x \in L : \bigsqcap_{i=0}^{k} f_i(x) \ \sqsubseteq \ f_\rho(x)$$

where $f_i = f_{p_i \to p_{i+1}}$ and $f_\rho = f_k \circ f_{k-1} \circ \ldots \circ f_1 \circ f_0$.

PROOF We prove this by induction on path length.

- *Basis:* Consider path of length of 1. We need to show that

$$\forall x \in L : \ f_1(x) \sqcap f_0(x) \ \sqsubseteq \ f_1(f_0(x))$$

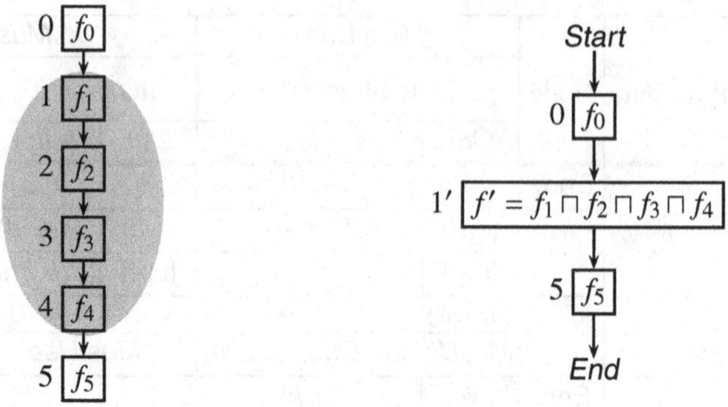

(a) A path for flow sensitive analysis. Dependent parts in f_1, f_2, f_3, f_4 are $\emptyset$.

(b) Modeling the path for flow insensitive analysis. $In_{5'} \sqsubseteq In_5$.

FIGURE 8.4
Safety of flow insensitive analysis with dependent parts.

Since there are no dependent parts in flow functions, the flow function is separable. Thus we can prove the lemma for independent entities. Further, absence of dependent parts imply that entity functions are constant functions or the identity function; a non-constant non-identity flow function requires dependent part. Thus the proof obligation reduces to

$$\forall \alpha \in \Sigma, \forall \widehat{x} \in \widehat{L} : \widehat{f_0}^{\alpha}(\widehat{x}) \mathbin{\widehat{\sqcap}} \widehat{f_1}^{\alpha}(\widehat{x}) \mathrel{\widehat{\sqsubseteq}} \widehat{f_0}^{\alpha}\left(\widehat{f_1}^{\alpha}(\widehat{x})\right)$$

We consider the following two cases.

- $\widehat{f_0}^{\alpha}$ is the identity function. Then the proof obligation reduces to

  $$\forall \widehat{x} \in \widehat{L} : \widehat{x} \mathbin{\widehat{\sqcap}} \widehat{f_1}^{\alpha}(\widehat{x}) \mathrel{\widehat{\sqsubseteq}} \widehat{f_1}^{\alpha}(\widehat{x})$$

  which trivially holds.

- $\widehat{f_0}^{\alpha}$ is some constant function resulting in a particular value $\widehat{y} \in \widehat{L}$. Then the proof obligation reduces to

  $$\forall \widehat{x} \in \widehat{L}_{\alpha} : \widehat{y} \mathbin{\widehat{\sqcap}} \widehat{f_1}^{\alpha}(\widehat{x}) \mathrel{\widehat{\sqsubseteq}} \widehat{y}$$

  which also trivially holds.

- *Inductive step:* Assume that the lemma holds for path of length i. Then, it follows that for $f_{\rho'} = f_i \circ f_{i-1} \circ \ldots \circ f_1 \circ f_0$,

  $$\forall x \in L : \prod_{i=0}^{i} f_i(x) \sqsubseteq f_{\rho'}(x)$$

Property	Defining expression	Result	
		Iteration #1	Changes in iteration #2
$MustKill_p$	$Kill_{Start_p} \cap Kill_{n_3} \cap MustKill_q \cap Kill_{End_p}$	$\emptyset$	
$MayKill_p$	$Kill_{Start_p} \cup Kill_{n_3} \cup MayKill_q \cup Kill_{End_p}$	$\{b,c\}$	$\{a,b,c\}$
$MustUse_p$	$Gen_{Start_p} \cap Gen_{n_3} \cap MustUse_q \cap Gen_{End_p}$	$\emptyset$	
$MayUse_p$	$Gen_{Start_p} \cup Gen_{n_3} \cup MayUse_q \cup Gen_{End_p}$	$\{a,b,c,d\}$	
$MustKill_q$	$Kill_{Start_q} \cap MustKill_p \cap Kill_{End_q}$	$\emptyset$	
$MayKill_q$	$Kill_{Start_q} \cup MayKill_p \cup Kill_{End_q}$	$\{a,b,c\}$	
$MustUse_q$	$Gen_{Start_q} \cap MustUse_p \cap Gen_{End_q}$	$\emptyset$	
$MayUse_q$	$Gen_{Start_q} \cup MayUse_p \cup Gen_{End_q}$	$\{a,b,c,d\}$	

FIGURE 8.5
Flow insensitive computation of side effects for the program in Figure 8.1.

We need to show that

$$f_{i+1}(\mathsf{x}) \sqcap \left(\prod_{i=0}^{i} f_i(\mathsf{x}) \right) \sqsubseteq f_{i+1}\left(f_{\rho'}(\widehat{\mathsf{x}})\right)$$

Since the flow functions are separable we can prove this independently for different entities by considering constant and identity entity functions $\widehat{f}_{i+1}^{\alpha}$ in a manner similar to that in the basis case.

∎

Recall that for flow insensitive analysis, we merge $f_i(BI)$ (Equation 7.1). Since BI is $\emptyset$ the flow functions defined in Equations (8.1) and (8.2) reduce to:

Property	Flow Function	Flow Function with $\mathsf{x} = BI = \emptyset$
$MustKill_r, MayKill_r$	$\mathsf{x} \cup Kill$	$Kill$
$MustUse_r, MayUse_r$	$(\mathsf{x} - Kill) \cup Gen$	Gen

Example 8.3
The flow insensitive computations of side effects for our example program of Figure 8.1 is shown in Figure 8.5. Observe the mutual dependence of the data flow values of procedures p and q due to mutual recursion. We first compute the values for procedure p by using $\top$ values for procedure q. The resulting values for procedure p are then used to compute the values of procedure q. The resulting values for procedure q are different from the initially assumed $\top$ values. However, they do not cause any change in the values of procedure p except for $MayKill_p$. When this changed value is used for recomputing $MayKill_q$, there is no change. □

```
int a,b;
main()
{  int c,d;
   read (a,b,c);
   q(a,b,c,d);          /* Call site c1 */
   p(c,c);              /* Call site c2 */
}
q(int w, int x, int y, int z)
{  int e;
   x = x + 1;
   if (x < y)
   {  q(x,y,z,e);  /* Call site c3 */
      p(w,x);      /* Call site c4 */
   }
}
p(int m, int n)
{ n=m; }
```

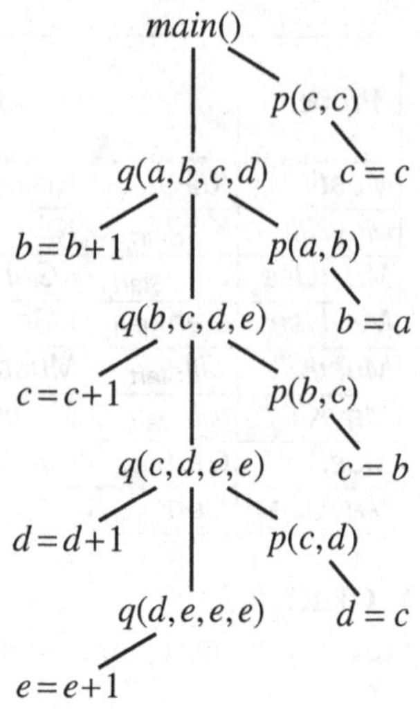
main()
p(c,c)
q(a,b,c,d)
c = c
b=b+1
p(a,b)
q(b,c,d,e)
b = a
c=c+1
p(b,c)
q(c,d,e,e)
c = b
d=d+1
p(c,d)
q(d,e,e,e)
d = c
e=e+1

FIGURE 8.6
A C program assuming parameter passing by reference. A possible activation tree shows how variables may be modified in the program.

8.2 Handling the Effects of Parameters

Recall that we have excluded the effects of parameters from our descriptions of analyses by restricting them to global variables only. If the parameter passing mechanism is by value, the basic techniques do not change much except that the data flow information of actual parameters must be propagated as the data flow information of formal parameters. Thus formal parameters can be considered similar to local variables except that *BI* for formal parameters is computed from the calling contexts. Section 9.5 shows a way of modeling the effect of parameters to capture the transfer of data flow information between actual and formal parameters.

In this section we look at aliasing between formal parameters in the presence of parameter passing by reference. In this case the actual parameter and the formal parameter share the same address and hence are aliased. The main difference between this aliasing and the aliasing created by pointer assignments (Section 4.3.2) is that in pointer assignments, both variables involved in an alias are simultaneously visible; in the case of parameters this need not hold always. Thus discovering such aliases requires a different technique.

8.2.1 Defining Aliasing of Parameters

We discover *may* aliases created by call statements only. Further, we restrict the aliases to scalar variables only. Hence, all other statements including the control flow statements are ignored and our analysis is flow insensitive. Observe that there is no way of killing such aliases; they just become invisible when the variables involved go out of scope.

Example 8.4

We consider the program in Figure 8.6 for performing side effects analysis of procedure q. If we assume parameter passing by reference, it is easy to see that q will modify variable b. However, it is clear from the activation tree of the program that q can also modify the local variables of *main* (c and d) and q (e). This happens because the recursive call to q at the call site c_3 passes its formal parameters as actuals in a different order. As a consequence, the formal parameter x gets aliased to y and z in nested recursive calls. Observe that it does not get aliased to w and the global variable a cannot be modified anywhere in the program. The first call to p modifies c whereas the second call to p modifies b, c, and d. ▯

Our primary goal is to find out aliasing of formal parameters of a procedure. Consider two formal parameters x and y of procedure r. They may be aliased to each other because of any of the following reasons:

- *Direct generation*. There are two ways in which direct aliases are generated:
  - The actual parameters of both x and y are same in some call. They may well be global variables, local variables of the caller, or formal parameters of the caller.
  - In some call, the actual parameter for x (alternatively, y) is a global variable v and the actual parameter of y (alternatively, x) is a formal parameter of the caller and is aliased to v. Observe that a formal parameter of a procedure can never be aliased to a local variable of the same procedure.
- *Indirect generation*. x may be passed as y (or vice-versa) in a call in r in a recursive call sequence.
- *Propagation*. The actual parameters of x and y may be aliased in a caller's body.

We restrict ourselves to languages that do not support nested procedures. In the case of nested procedures, the formal parameters of an outer procedure are visible within the nested procedures and must be treated as global variables within them rather than as formal parameter of the outer procedure.

8.2.2 Formulating Alias Analysis of Parameters

We solve the problem in two steps. In the first step we find out the variables that may be aliased to formal parameters of a procedure along some call chain leading to the procedure. These variables may be global variables and formal parameters of callers. In the second step, we augment this information with the aliasing between formal parameters of the same procedure.

Let the local variables and formal parameters of procedure r be contained in Local_r and Formal_r respectively; we assume that formal parameter names are distinct for each procedure. We define a function ψ to map a formal parameter to the corresponding actual parameter at a call site. Let a call site c_i in procedure s call procedure r. Given $x \in \mathit{Formal}_r$, $\psi(c_i, x) = y$ where $y \in \mathbb{G}\mathsf{var} \cup \mathit{Local}_s \cup \mathit{Formal}_s$.

Our lattice consists of data flow values denoted by $x \overset{c_i}{\mapsto} y$ where x is a formal parameter of a procedure being called at call site c_i and y is a variable which is represented by x in the called procedure; in the simplest case, y is the actual parameter corresponding to x. In order to compute data flow information inherited by the callee, the data flow information of y must be copied to the data flow information of x in BI of the callee. To compute the data flow information synthesized by the callee, the data flow information of x must be copied to the data flow information of y. In particular, if the callee modifies x, y should be considered to be modified in the caller's body. Similarly, if the callee uses x, y should be considered to be used in the caller's body. Thus the relation $x \overset{c_i}{\mapsto} y$ is not symmetric; the exact direction of dependence is governed by the intended use of the data flow information.

The relation $x \overset{c_i}{\mapsto} y$ between x and y becomes symmetric if both x and y are visible within the called procedure. This is possible only when y is a global variable or when y is a formal parameter that encloses the called procedures. In such a situation, a modification in y in the callee is should be considered a modification in x and vice-versa. This situation is more appropriately modeled by considering y as a global variable for the callee rather than as a formal parameter of the caller.

The flow function for a call site c_i in procedure s calling a procedure r is defined as follows:

$$
\begin{aligned}
f_{c_i}(\mathsf{X}) &= \mathsf{X} \cup \mathit{ConstGen}_{c_i} \cup \mathit{DepGen}_{c_i}(\mathsf{X}) \\
\mathit{ConstGen}_{c_i} &= \{x \overset{c_i}{\mapsto} y \mid x \in \mathit{Formal}_r,\ y = \psi(c_i, x),\ y \in \mathbb{G}\mathsf{var} \cup \mathit{Formal}_s\} \\
\mathit{DepGen}_{c_i}(\mathsf{X}) &= \{x \overset{c_i}{\mapsto} z \mid x \in \mathit{Formal}_r,\ y = \psi(c_i, x),\ y \in \mathit{Formal}_s,\ y \overset{c_i}{\mapsto} z \in \mathsf{X}\}
\end{aligned}
$$

Observe that $\mathit{ConstGen}_{c_i}$ excludes $y \in \mathit{Local}_r$ and z in DepGen_{c_i} could well be a formal parameter of a caller of s or some other ancestor of s along a call chain reaching c_i.

Let Calls denote all call sites in a program. In the first step, the aliasing information is computed as the MFP solution of the following equation with $\top = \emptyset$:

$$
\mathit{PVA} = \bigcup_{c_i \in \mathit{Calls}} f_{c_i}(\mathit{PVA}) \tag{8.3}
$$

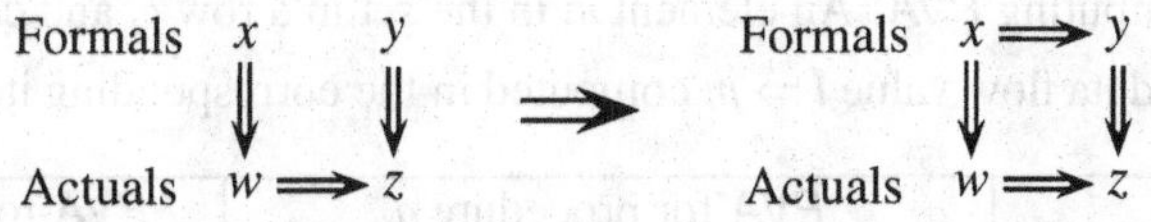

FIGURE 8.7
Aliasing relation between actual parameters should be propagated to the corresponding formal parameters.

where *PVA* is an abbreviation of "Parameters to Variables Aliasing". *PVA* contains the variables to which formal parameters of a function may be aliased. These variables could be global variables, formal parameters of caller procedures, or formal parameters of the same procedure in the case of recursion.

To see why *PVA* contains the indirectly generated aliases of formal parameters in the presence of recursion, consider $x, y \in \mathit{Formal}_r$ for procedure r that is part of a recursive call chain. There must be a sequence of corresponding formal parameters x', y', x'', y'', etc. of the procedures called in the call sequence. If one of these parameters (say y'') is passed as an actual parameter at a different position (say in the place of x''') in the subsequent call, it will result in a pair $x''' \overset{c_j}{\Mapsto} y''$ in *PVA*. Due to transitive propagation defined in $\mathit{DepGen}_{c_j}(\mathsf{x})$, we will also have the pair $x''' \overset{c_j}{\Mapsto} y$ in *PVA*. When this pair is propagated to r, we will get the pair $x \overset{c_k}{\Mapsto} y$ in *PVA*. The pairs x, y'', y, x'' in *PVA* are not meaningful by themselves because they represent formal parameters of different procedures; their use is mainly in detecting and propagating indirectly generated aliases.

The semantics captured by the pair $x \overset{c_k}{\Mapsto} y$ in *PVA* when both x and y are in Formal_r requires some explanation. Recall that this relation is not symmetric because it denotes the fact that y is represented by x in a nested call. Since both x and y are formal parameters of the same procedure, this is possible only when an incarnation of y in a call to r is represented by an incarnation of x in a nested recursive call to r. Thus, if we have $x \overset{c_k}{\Mapsto} y$ in *PVA* and x is modified in r, we can conclude that y is modified in r. However, if y is modified in r, then we cannot conclude that x is modified in r unless we have $y \overset{c_k}{\Mapsto} x$ in *PVA*. Observe that this is consistent with our semantics of $x \overset{c_k}{\Mapsto} y$ when x and y are formal parameters of different procedures.

Let $\mathit{VPA}_r(x)$ (abbreviation for "Variables to Parameters Aliasing") denote the set of formal parameters of r that are aliased to variable x. It is defined as:

$$\mathit{VPA}_r(x) = \begin{cases} \{y \mid x \overset{c_i}{\Mapsto} y \in \mathit{PVA},\ y \in \mathit{Visible}_r,\} & \text{if } x \in \mathit{Formal}_r \\ \{y \mid y \overset{c_i}{\Mapsto} x \in \mathit{PVA},\ y \in \mathit{Formal}_r,\} & \text{if } x \in \mathbb{G}\mathsf{var} \end{cases} \tag{8.4}$$

The meaning of $y \in \mathit{VPA}_r(x)$ is that whenever x is modified in r, y should also be considered to be modified in r; similarly, whenever x is used in r, y should be considered to be used in r. Clearly, $\mathit{VPA}_r(x)$ as defined by Equation (8.4) is not symmetric.

- Computing *PVA*. An element m in the set in a row c_i and column l represents the data flow value $l \overset{c_i}{\mapsto} m$ computed in the corresponding iteration.

Iteration	*PVA* for procedure q					*PVA* for procedure p		
	Call site	w	x	y	z	Call site	m	n
#1	c_1	$\{a\}$	$\{b\}$	$\emptyset$	$\emptyset$	c_2	$\emptyset$	$\emptyset$
	c_3	$\{x\}$	$\{y\}$	$\{z\}$	$\emptyset$	c_4	$\{w\}$	$\{x\}$
#2	c_1	$\{a\}$	$\{b\}$	$\emptyset$	$\emptyset$	c_2	$\emptyset$	$\emptyset$
	c_3	$\{b,x,y\}$	$\{y,z\}$	$\{z\}$	$\emptyset$	c_4	$\{a,w,x\}$	$\{b,x,y\}$
#3	c_1	$\{a\}$	$\{b\}$	$\emptyset$	$\emptyset$	c_2	$\emptyset$	$\emptyset$
	c_3	$\{b,x,y,z\}$	$\{y,z\}$	$\{z\}$	$\emptyset$	c_4	$\{a,b,w,x,y\}$	$\{b,x,y,z\}$

- Computing VPA_r for calls with different set of actual parameters at call site c_2.

Call at c_2	VPA_q						VPA_p			
	w	x	y	z	a	b	m	n	a	b
`p(c,c)`	$\{x,y,z\}$	$\{y,z\}$	$\{z\}$	$\emptyset$	$\{w\}$	$\{w,x\}$	$\{n\}$	$\{m\}$	$\{m\}$	$\{m,n\}$
`p(c,d)`	$\{x,y,z\}$	$\{y,z\}$	$\{z\}$	$\emptyset$	$\{w\}$	$\{w,x\}$	$\emptyset$	$\emptyset$	$\{m\}$	$\{m,n\}$

FIGURE 8.8
Computing aliasing resulting from reference parameters for our example program.

The aliases contained in $\mathit{VPA}_r(x)$ are not complete. What remains is to detect and propagate the directly generated aliases of formal parameters. When x is a formal parameter, we augment $\mathit{VPA}_r(x)$ as shown below:

$$\mathit{VPA}_r(x) = \mathit{VPA}_r(x) \cup \left(\bigcup_{c_i \in \mathit{CallsTo}_r} \mathit{propVPA}_r(c_i, x) \right)$$

$\mathit{propVPA}_r(c_i, x)$ denotes the set of aliases that are propagated to $c_i \in \mathit{CallsTo}_r$: When two aliased formal parameters of a caller of r are passed as actual parameters in a call to r, the corresponding formal parameters of r get aliased; this has been illustrated in Figure 8.7. The identification of directly generated aliases and their propagation is achieved by:

$$\begin{aligned} \mathit{propVPA}_r(c_i, x) = {} & \mathit{directVPA}_r(c_i, x) \;\cup \\ & \{y \mid x \overset{c_j}{\mapsto} w \in \mathit{PVA},\; y \overset{c_j}{\mapsto} z \in \mathit{PVA},\; z \in \mathit{VPA}_s(w), \\ & \quad c_j \in \mathit{CallsTo}_r,\; x \in \mathit{Formal}_r,\; y \in \mathit{Formal}_r\,\} \end{aligned}$$

where c_j is a call site in procedure s calling r, and

$$\begin{aligned}\mathit{directVPA}_r(c_i,x) = \; & \{y \mid \psi(c_i,x) = \psi(c_i,y),\ x \in \mathit{Formal}_r,\ y \in \mathit{Formal}_r\} \cup \\ & \{y \mid ((\psi(c_i,x) = v,\ y \overset{c_i}{\mapsto} v \in \mathit{PVA}) \text{ or } (\psi(c_i,y) = v,\ x \overset{c_i}{\mapsto} v \in \mathit{PVA})), \\ & \quad v \in \mathbb{G}\mathit{var},\ x \in \mathit{Formal}_r,\ y \in \mathit{Formal}_r\}\end{aligned}$$

Observe that the propagation of aliases to callees results in context insensitive aliases because the aliases from all callers are combined. This is similar to the context insensitivity observed in *PVA*.

Example 8.5

The computation of aliases resulting from reference parameters in the program of Figure 8.6 has been shown in Figure 8.8 on the facing page. Beginning with $\top = \emptyset$, we compute successive approximations of *PVA* using Equation (8.3). Observe that the indirect aliases for procedure q capture the fact that w represents x, y, and z in recursive calls and x represents y and z. However, w is not represented by any other variable. What this means is that the assignment to x in procedure q cannot modify w although it can modify y and z and their actual parameters.

We augment this information with aliasing between formal parameters of the same procedure, under two different situations:

- When the call at call site c_2 is `p(c,c)`, and
- when it is `p(c,d)`.

When the call is `p(c,c)`, the formal parameters m and n of procedure p get aliased. Since the data flow information is context insensitive, our analysis assumes that this aliasing holds for all calls to p. If we change the call to `p(c,d)`, m and n are not aliased anymore. □

8.2.3 Augmenting Data Flow Analyses Using Parameter Aliases

Now $\mathit{VPA}_r(x)$ can be used to augment the data flow information computed by other analyses. We illustrate it for computing $\mathit{MayKill}_r$.

We define $\mathit{MayKill}_r$ to consist of two components:

$$\mathit{MayKill}_r = \mathit{Kill}_r \cup \left(\bigcup_{c_j \in \mathit{CallsIn}_r} \mathit{MayKill}_t(c_j) \right) \cup \left\{ y \mid y \in \mathit{VPA}_r(x),\ x \in \mathit{MayKill}_r \right\} \tag{8.5}$$

where $\mathit{MayKill}_r$ represents all variables visible in r that are killed by execution of r. They include local and global variables as well as formal parameters of r. This information, augmented with the killing of actual parameters by a call to r at call

Procedure	*Kill*	When call at c_2 is p(c,c)			When call at c_2 is p(c,d)		
		MayKill	Call specific *MayKill*		*MayKill*	Call specific *MayKill*	
			Call site c_i	$MayKill(c_i)$		Call site c_i	$MayKill(c_i)$
p	$\{n\}$	$\{m,n\}$	c_2	$\{c,c\}$	$\{n\}$	c_2	$\{d\}$
			c_4	$\{w,x\}$		c_4	$\{x\}$
q	$\{x\}$	$\{w,x,y,z\}$	c_1	$\{a,b,c,d\}$	$\{y,z\}$	c_1	$\{b,c,d\}$
			c_3	$\{w,x,y,z\}$		c_3	$\{x,y,z\}$

FIGURE 8.9
Side effects for the example program of Figure 8.6.

site c_i is contained in $\mathit{MayKill}_r(c_i)$ which is defined below in Equation (8.6). Kill_r represents the variables that may be directly killed within r without incorporating the effect of calls made in r. The variables killed by a call to procedure s made at call site c_j in r are contained in $\mathit{MayKill}_s(c_j)$.

From the gross information $\mathit{MayKill}_r$, we extract $\mathit{MayKill}_r^G$ and $\mathit{MayKill}_r^F$ that denote the global variables and formal parameters of r killed by r. They are defined as shown below:

$$\mathit{MayKill}_r^F = \mathit{MayKill}_r \cap \mathit{Formal}_r$$
$$\mathit{MayKill}_r^G = \mathit{MayKill}_r \cap \mathbb{G}\mathit{var}$$

Now we need to find out the local variables of the caller that may be killed by r. This can happen only through the formal parameters of r. The complete side effect of a call to r made at call site c_i is represented by $\mathit{MayKill}_r(c_i)$ which is defined in terms of $\mathit{MayKill}_r^G$ and $\mathit{MayKill}_r^F$ as shown below:

$$\mathit{MayKill}_r(c_i) = \mathit{MayKill}_r^G \cup \left\{ y \mid \psi(c_i, x) = y,\ x \in \mathit{MayKill}_r^F \right\} \quad (8.6)$$

Observe that the definition of $\mathit{MayKill}_r$ (Equation 8.5) is flow insensitive. It can be made flow sensitive by computing In_i and Out_i along the control flow and using $\mathit{MayKill}_r(c_i)$ as the flow function for call site c_i. However, the aliases contained in $\mathit{VPA}_r(x)$ and PVA remain context and flow insensitive.

Example 8.6
The side effects computed for our example have been shown in Figure 8.9. When the call at c_2 is p(c,c), our analysis concludes that the call at c_4 kills both w and x. Hence it concludes that q can kill the global variable a which has been passed as an actual parameter of w at call site c_1. If we change the call at c_2 to p(c,d), m and n are not aliased. Hence our analysis concludes that the call at c_4 kills only x and not w. As a consequence, a is not contained in the side effect of call at c_1. □

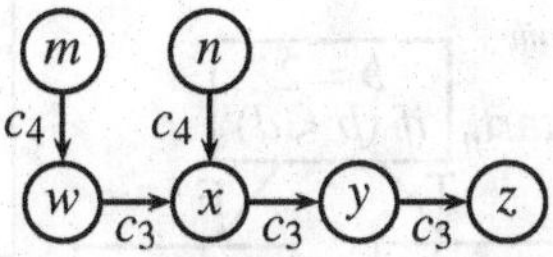

FIGURE 8.10
Parameter binding graph for the program in Figure 8.6.

8.2.4 Efficient Parameter Alias Analysis

The parameter analysis presented in Section 8.2.2 models the required computation instead of designing an efficient algorithm for performing the analysis. The resulting data flow analysis is non-separable and requires a lot of transitive computation that may be redundant. To see this, consider an alias $x \overset{c_i}{\Mapsto} y$ computed by Equation (8.3). If the analysis discovers $y \overset{c_j}{\Mapsto} z_1$ and $y \overset{c_k}{\Mapsto} z_2$, it implies adding the pairs $x \overset{c_i}{\Mapsto} z_1$ and $x \overset{c_i}{\Mapsto} z_2$. Now if $w \overset{c_l}{\Mapsto} x$ is discovered, the analysis computes $w \overset{c_l}{\Mapsto} y$, $w \overset{c_l}{\Mapsto} z_1$, and $w \overset{c_l}{\Mapsto} z_2$. Thus every possible transitive effect of parameters is detected. Observe that it is not necessary to store all these relations. The core relations that need to be stored are $w \overset{c_l}{\Mapsto} x$, $x \overset{c_i}{\Mapsto} y$, $y \overset{c_j}{\Mapsto} z_1$, and $y \overset{c_k}{\Mapsto} z_2$; other aliases can be discovered from these relations when required.

A simple way of speeding up the analysis is to identify the dependence of formal parameters on each other and store them in a graph called *parameter binding graph*. For our example program, it has been illustrated in Figure 8.10. An edge $x \rightarrow y$ represents the relation $x \overset{c_i}{\Mapsto} y$. This graph directly captures the dependence arising out of non-separability and hence avoid redundant traversals over a call graph. Constructing this graph is efficient because we only need to construct individual edges; computing *PVA* involves identifying all paths in the graph. After this graph is constructed, aliasing with global variables require only propagating them in the graph along the edges in the graph starting from the formal parameter for which the global variable is an actual parameter. Further, indirect aliases are represented by edges between the formal parameters of the same procedure. Thus *PVA* involves mapping formal variables to global variables. There is no need to record mapping between formal variables. This is particularly useful if there are very few recursive procedures; for non-recursive procedures, these mappings are irrelevant.

Observe that a use of parameter binding graph is similar to the use of points-to graph in that both these data structures capture the effect of the dependent part of flow functions and facilitate a flow insensitive computation in a single pass over the underlying control flow structure. The only difference between them is that for points-to analysis the control flow structure is either a CFG or a supergraph whereas for a parameter binding graph, it is a call graph.

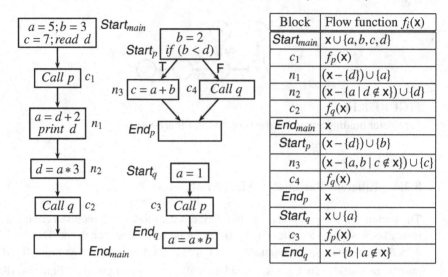

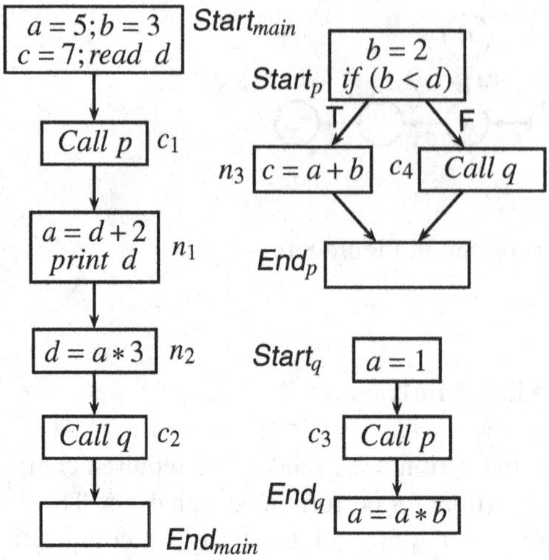

Block	Flow function $f_i(\mathsf{x})$
$Start_{main}$	$\mathsf{x} \cup \{a,b,c,d\}$
c_1	$f_p(\mathsf{x})$
n_1	$(\mathsf{x} - \{d\}) \cup \{a\}$
n_2	$(\mathsf{x} - \{a \mid d \notin \mathsf{x}\}) \cup \{d\}$
c_2	$f_q(\mathsf{x})$
End_{main}	x
$Start_p$	$(\mathsf{x} - \{d\}) \cup \{b\}$
n_3	$(\mathsf{x} - \{a,b \mid c \notin \mathsf{x}\}) \cup \{c\}$
c_4	$f_q(\mathsf{x})$
End_p	x
$Start_q$	$\mathsf{x} \cup \{a\}$
c_3	$f_p(\mathsf{x})$
End_q	$\mathsf{x} - \{b \mid a \notin \mathsf{x}\}$

FIGURE 8.11
Example program for interprocedural faint variables analysis. This is a modified version of the program in Figure 8.1.

8.3 Whole Program Analysis

In the previous section, we constructed summary flow functions for specific analyses. In this section we present the general method of constructing summary flow functions. We consider flow sensitive methods; the flow insensitive versions can be devised along the lines described earlier.

We use liveness analysis and faint variables analysis to explain the method. For liveness analysis, we use the program of Section 8.1. Since it does not have much scope for faint variables analysis, we use the program in Figure 8.11.

8.3.1 Lattice of Flow Functions

Defining a data flow analysis requires setting up a lattice of the values that are to be computed by the analysis. This greatly simplifies reasoning about the analysis. The same approach can be used to define analyses to construct summary flow functions. The main difference is that the data flow values computed by other analyses we have seen so far represent certain semantics of the entities appearing in the program. The data flow values for the analysis that constructs summary flow functions are flow functions that compute the data flow values desired in the end.

When we view the set of flow function F as a lattice, we define the partial order relation over flow functions in terms of the partial order relation between the values

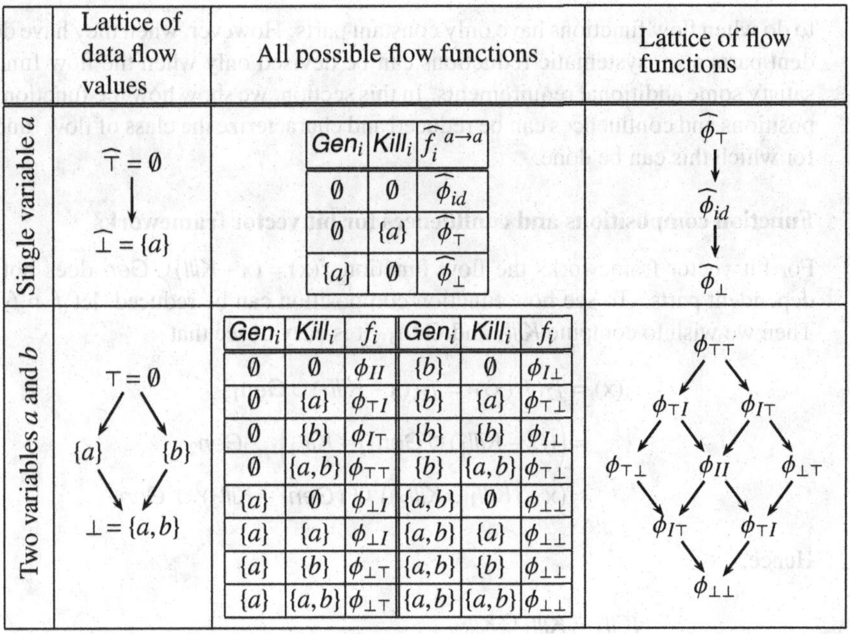

Lattice of data flow values
All possible flow functions
Lattice of flow functions
Single variable a
$\widehat{\top} = \emptyset$
$\widehat{\bot} = \{a\}$
$\widehat{\phi}_\top$
$\widehat{\phi}_{id}$
$\widehat{\phi}_\bot$
Two variables a and b
$\top = \emptyset$
$\{a\}$
$\{b\}$
$\bot = \{a,b\}$
$\phi_{\top\top}$
$\phi_{\top I}$
$\phi_{I\top}$
$\phi_{\top\bot}$
ϕ_{II}
$\phi_{\bot\top}$
$\phi_{I\top}$
$\phi_{\top I}$
$\phi_{\bot\bot}$

Gen_i	$Kill_i$	$\widehat{f_i}^{a\to a}$
$\emptyset$	$\emptyset$	$\widehat{\phi}_{id}$
$\emptyset$	$\{a\}$	$\widehat{\phi}_\top$
$\{a\}$	$\emptyset$	$\widehat{\phi}_\bot$

Gen_i	$Kill_i$	f_i	Gen_i	$Kill_i$	f_i
$\emptyset$	$\emptyset$	ϕ_{II}	$\{b\}$	$\emptyset$	$\phi_{I\bot}$
$\emptyset$	$\{a\}$	$\phi_{\top I}$	$\{b\}$	$\{a\}$	$\phi_{\top\bot}$
$\emptyset$	$\{b\}$	$\phi_{I\top}$	$\{b\}$	$\{b\}$	$\phi_{I\bot}$
$\emptyset$	$\{a,b\}$	$\phi_{\top\top}$	$\{b\}$	$\{a,b\}$	$\phi_{\top\bot}$
$\{a\}$	$\emptyset$	$\phi_{\bot I}$	$\{a,b\}$	$\emptyset$	$\phi_{\bot\bot}$
$\{a\}$	$\{a\}$	$\phi_{\bot I}$	$\{a,b\}$	$\{a\}$	$\phi_{\bot\bot}$
$\{a\}$	$\{b\}$	$\phi_{\bot\top}$	$\{a,b\}$	$\{b\}$	$\phi_{\bot\bot}$
$\{a\}$	$\{a,b\}$	$\phi_{\bot\top}$	$\{a,b\}$	$\{a,b\}$	$\phi_{\bot\bot}$

FIGURE 8.12
Example of lattices of functions for live variables analysis. ϕ_{xy} indicates that the component flow function for variable a is x and that for variable b is y. The possible values for x and y are: I for $\widehat{\phi}_{id}$, $\top$ for $\widehat{\phi}_\top$, and $\bot$ for $\widehat{\phi}_\bot$.

computed by the functions:

$$\forall f_i, f_j \in F:\ f_i \sqsubseteq_f f_j \ \Leftrightarrow\ \forall \mathsf{x} \in L:\ f_i(\mathsf{x}) \sqsubseteq f_j(\mathsf{x})$$

The function composition and confluence operations required for constructing flow functions are:

$$\begin{aligned}
\forall f_i, f_j, f_k \in F:&\ f_k = f_i \sqcap_f f_j \ \Leftrightarrow\ \forall \mathsf{x} \in L:\ f_k(\mathsf{x}) = f_i(\mathsf{x}) \sqcap f_j(\mathsf{x})\\
\forall f_i, f_j, f_k \in F:&\ f_k = f_i \circ f_j \ \Leftrightarrow\ \forall \mathsf{x} \in L:\ f_k(\mathsf{x}) = f_i(f_j(\mathsf{x}))\\
\forall f \in F:&\ f \sqcap_f \phi_\top = f\\
\forall f \in F:&\ f \sqcap_f \phi_\bot = \phi_\bot
\end{aligned}$$

Recall that $\phi_\top$ and $\phi_\bot$ are constant functions.

8.3.2 Reducing Function Compositions and Confluences

Constructing flow functions requires reducing expressions involving compositions and confluences of flow functions to a canonical form. This is different from function applications to actual data flow values. As observed in Section 7.6.2, this is easy to do when flow functions have only constant parts. However, when they have dependent parts also, systematic reductions can be devised only when the flow functions satisfy some additional requirements. In this section, we show how the function compositions and confluences can be reduced and characterize the class of flow functions for which this can be done.

Function compositions and confluences for bit vector frameworks

For bit vector frameworks the flow function $f(x) = (x - Kill) \cup Gen$ does not have dependent parts. To see how function composition can be reduced, let $f_2 \circ f_1 = f_3$. Then we wish to compute $Kill_3$ and Gen_3. It is easy to see that

$$\begin{aligned} f_3(x) = f_2(f_1(x)) &= f_2((x - Kill_1) \cup Gen_1) \\ &= \Big(((x - Kill_1) \cup Gen_1) - Kill_2\Big) \cup Gen_2 \\ &= (x - (Kill_1 \cup Kill_2)) \cup (Gen_1 - Kill_2) \cup Gen_2 \end{aligned}$$

Hence,

$$Kill_3 = Kill_1 \cup Kill_2 \tag{8.7}$$
$$Gen_3 = (Gen_1 - Kill_2) \cup Gen_2 \tag{8.8}$$

To see how function confluences can be reduced, let $f_2 \sqcap f_1 = f_3$. First we consider the case when $\sqcap$ is $\cup$.

$$\begin{aligned} f_3(x) = f_2(x) \cup f_1(x) &= ((x - Kill_2) \cup Gen_2) \cup ((x - Kill_1) \cup Gen_1) \\ &= (x - (Kill_1 \cap Kill_2)) \cup (Gen_1 \cup Gen_2) \end{aligned}$$

implying that

$$Kill_3 = Kill_1 \cap Kill_2 \tag{8.9}$$
$$Gen_3 = Gen_1 \cup Gen_2 \tag{8.10}$$

When $\sqcap$ is $\cap$,

$$\begin{aligned} f_3(x) = f_2(x) \cap f_1(x) &= ((x - Kill_2) \cup Gen_2) \cap ((x - Kill_1) \cup Gen_1) \\ &= (x - (Kill_1 \cup Kill_2)) \cup (Gen_1 \cap Gen_2) \end{aligned}$$

Kill and *Gen* are defined by

$$Kill_3 = Kill_1 \cup Kill_2 \tag{8.11}$$
$$Gen_3 = Gen_1 \cap Gen_2 \tag{8.12}$$

Thus the reduction of function composition and confluences for bit vector frameworks can be defined in terms of $\cup$ and $\cap$ alone.

Function compositions and confluences for general frameworks

When the flow functions have dependent parts also the dependence of data flow values must also be brought in. This dependence may be dependence of values of the same entity or across different entities. Using the notation from Definition 4.1,

$$f_i = \langle \widehat{f_i}^{\alpha}, \widehat{f_i}^{\beta}, \cdots, \widehat{f_i}^{\eta} \rangle$$

where $\widehat{f_i}^{\alpha} : L \mapsto \widehat{L}$ is a component function computing the data flow value of entity α. Given $f_2 \circ f_1 = f_3$, we need to construct $\widehat{f_3}^{\alpha}$ for all α. We know that:

$$\widehat{f_2}^{\alpha} = \bigsqcap_{\beta \in \Sigma} \left(\overline{f_2}^{\beta \to \alpha} \right)$$

where $\overline{f_2}^{\beta \to \alpha}$ is a primitive entity function computing the data flow value of α from β. In order to compute $\widehat{f_3}^{\alpha}$, we will need to compose $\overline{f_2}^{\beta \to \alpha}$ with every component function $\widehat{f_1}^{\beta}$ which is defined as:

$$\widehat{f_1}^{\beta} = \bigsqcap_{\gamma \in \Sigma} \left(\overline{f_1}^{\gamma \to \beta} \right)$$

In other words, we need to compose the *pef*s of various components function. This gives us the first restriction on the flow functions for systematic reduction of compositions: It is not possible to compose flow functions unless the component functions can be defined in terms of *pef*s. This rules out full constant propagation and points-to analysis.

For primary framework $\widehat{f_3}^{\alpha}$ can be constructed as follows:

$$\begin{aligned} \widehat{f_3}^{\alpha} &= \bigsqcap_{\beta \in \Sigma} \left(\overline{f_2}^{\beta \to \alpha} \circ \widehat{f_1}^{\beta} \right) \\ &= \bigsqcap_{\beta \in \Sigma} \left(\overline{f_2}^{\beta \to \alpha} \circ \left(\bigsqcap_{\gamma \in \Sigma} \overline{f_1}^{\gamma \to \beta} \right) \right) \end{aligned}$$

The need to reduce this suggests the second restriction: The *pef*s must be distributive. Although, it is not difficult to construct non-distributive *pef*s of the form $\widehat{L} \mapsto \widehat{L}$, most of the known such *pef*s in practical data flow frameworks are indeed distributive. Thus $\widehat{f_3}^{\alpha}$ reduces to

$$\widehat{f_3}^{\alpha} = \bigsqcap_{\beta, \gamma \in \Sigma} \left(\overline{f_2}^{\beta \to \alpha} \circ \overline{f_1}^{\gamma \to \beta} \right) \tag{8.13}$$

Function confluences are relatively easy to define. Given $f_3 = f_1 \sqcap f_2$,

$$\widehat{f_3}^{\alpha} = \widehat{f_1}^{\alpha} \sqcap \widehat{f_2}^{\alpha} \tag{8.14}$$

$$= \bigsqcap_{\beta \in \Sigma} \left(\overline{f_1}^{\beta \to \alpha} \sqcap \overline{f_2}^{\beta \to \alpha} \right) \tag{8.15}$$

due to distributivity.

When we restrict ourselves to primary frameworks, compositions can be reduced using the following identities. We use the superscript $\alpha \to \beta$ to show the dependency of entity β on the entity α only when required.

$$\forall \widehat{f}, \forall \widehat{\mathsf{z}} \in \widehat{L}: \quad \widehat{\phi}_{\mathsf{z}} \circ \widehat{f} = \widehat{\phi}_{\mathsf{z}}$$

$$\forall \alpha, \beta \in \Sigma: \widehat{\phi}_{id}^{\beta \to \gamma} \circ \widehat{\phi}_{id}^{\alpha \to \beta} = \widehat{\phi}_{id}^{\alpha \to \gamma}$$

$$\forall \alpha, \beta \in \Sigma: \quad \widehat{\phi}_{id}^{\beta \to \gamma} \circ \widehat{\phi}_{\mathsf{z}} = \widehat{\phi}_{\mathsf{z}}$$

$$\forall \alpha, \beta \in \Sigma, \forall a, b \in \mathbb{C}\mathsf{onst}: \widehat{\phi}_{id}^{\beta \to \gamma} \circ \widehat{\phi}_{ab}^{\alpha \to \beta} = \widehat{\phi}_{ab}^{\alpha \to \gamma}$$

$$\forall a, b \in \mathbb{C}\mathsf{onst}, \forall \widehat{\mathsf{z}} \in \widehat{L}: \quad \widehat{\phi}_{ab}^{\alpha \to \beta} \circ \widehat{\phi}_{\mathsf{z}} = \widehat{\phi}_{\mathsf{y}} \qquad \text{where } \widehat{\mathsf{y}} = a \times \widehat{\mathsf{z}} + b$$

$$\forall a, b, c, d \in \mathbb{C}\mathsf{onst}: \widehat{\phi}_{ab}^{\beta \to \gamma} \circ \widehat{\phi}_{cd}^{\alpha \to \beta} = \widehat{\phi}_{mn}^{\alpha \to \gamma} \qquad \text{where } m = a \times c,\ n = a \times d + b$$

Thus all compositions of *pef*s can be reduced to a single *pef*. In some cases, function confluences can also be reduced:

$$\forall \widehat{f}: \quad \widehat{f} \sqcap \widehat{\phi}_{\top} = \widehat{f}$$

$$\forall \widehat{f}: \quad \widehat{f} \sqcap \widehat{\phi}_{\bot} = \widehat{\phi}_{\bot}$$

$$\forall \widehat{\mathsf{x}}, \widehat{\mathsf{y}} \in \widehat{L}: \quad \widehat{\phi}_{\mathsf{x}} \sqcap \widehat{\phi}_{\mathsf{y}} = \widehat{\phi}_{\mathsf{z}} \quad \text{where } \widehat{\mathsf{z}} = \widehat{\mathsf{x}} \sqcap \widehat{\mathsf{y}}$$

$$\forall a, b, c, d \in \mathbb{C}\mathsf{onst}, a \neq c, b \neq d: \widehat{\phi}_{ab} \sqcap \widehat{\phi}_{cd} = \widehat{\phi}_{\bot}$$

$$\forall a, b \in \mathbb{C}\mathsf{onst}, \widehat{\mathsf{z}} \neq \widehat{\top}: \quad \widehat{\phi}_{ab} \sqcap \widehat{\phi}_{\mathsf{z}} = \widehat{\phi}_{\bot}$$

$$\forall a, b \in \mathbb{C}\mathsf{onst}, a \neq 1, b \neq 0: \widehat{\phi}_{ab} \sqcap \widehat{\phi}_{id} = \widehat{\phi}_{\bot}$$

Note that $\widehat{\phi}_{id}^{\alpha \to \beta} \sqcap \widehat{\phi}_{id}^{\beta \to \gamma}$ cannot be reduced any further.

Recall that in the case of bit vector frameworks,

$$\forall \alpha \neq \beta: \widehat{\phi}_{id}^{\alpha \to \beta} = \widehat{\phi}_{\top}$$

Hence every component function $\widehat{f}^{\alpha}$ in bit vector frameworks is guaranteed to be reduced to one of the following three functions: $\widehat{\phi}_{\top}$, $\widehat{\phi}_{\bot}$, and $\widehat{\phi}_{id}^{\alpha \to \alpha}$.

8.3.3 Constructing Summary Flow Functions

Having defined the reductions involving function compositions and confluences, it is now possible to construct summary flow functions by traversing the CFG. Let $\Phi_v^r : L \mapsto L$ denote the summary flow function associated with program point v in procedure r. It represents the effect of all paths from *Entry*(*Start*$_r$) to v and from v to *Exit*(*End*$_r$). If appropriate *BI* is computed for procedure r, applying Φ_v^r to it results in the desired data flow information associated with v.

Φ_v^r is computed from Φ_u^r of $u \in \mathsf{neighbours}(v)$ as defined below:

$$\Phi_v^r = \bigsqcap_{u \in \mathsf{neighbours}(v)} f_{u \to v} \circ \Phi_u^r$$

Block	Flow functions $f_i(x)$ in terms of *pefs*															
	pefs computing faintness of a from a, b, c, d				*pefs* computing faintness of b from a, b, c, d				*pefs* computing faintness of c from a, b, c, d				*pefs* computing faintness of d from a, b, c, d			
	a	b	c	d	a	b	c	d	a	b	c	d	a	b	c	d
$Start_m$	$\widehat{\phi}_\top$	$\widehat{\phi}_\top$	$\widehat{\phi}_\top$	$\widehat{\phi}_\top$	$\widehat{\phi}_\top$	$\widehat{\phi}_\top$	$\widehat{\phi}_\top$	$\widehat{\phi}_\top$	$\widehat{\phi}_\top$	$\widehat{\phi}_\top$	$\widehat{\phi}_\top$	$\widehat{\phi}_\top$	$\widehat{\phi}_\top$	$\widehat{\phi}_\top$	$\widehat{\phi}_\top$	$\widehat{\phi}_\top$
n_1	$\widehat{\phi}_{id}$	$\widehat{\phi}_\top$	$\widehat{\phi}_\top$	$\widehat{\phi}_\top$	$\widehat{\phi}_\top$	$\widehat{\phi}_{id}$	$\widehat{\phi}_\top$	$\widehat{\phi}_\top$	$\widehat{\phi}_\top$	$\widehat{\phi}_\top$	$\widehat{\phi}_{id}$	$\widehat{\phi}_\top$	$\widehat{\phi}_\bot$	$\widehat{\phi}_\bot$	$\widehat{\phi}_\bot$	$\widehat{\phi}_\bot$
n_2	$\widehat{\phi}_{id}$	$\widehat{\phi}_\top$	$\widehat{\phi}_\top$	$\widehat{\phi}_{id}$	$\widehat{\phi}_\top$	$\widehat{\phi}_{id}$	$\widehat{\phi}_\top$	$\widehat{\phi}_{id}$	$\widehat{\phi}_\top$	$\widehat{\phi}_\top$	$\widehat{\phi}_{id}$	$\widehat{\phi}_\top$	$\widehat{\phi}_\top$	$\widehat{\phi}_\top$	$\widehat{\phi}_\top$	$\widehat{\phi}_\top$
End_m	$\widehat{\phi}_{id}$	$\widehat{\phi}_\top$	$\widehat{\phi}_\top$	$\widehat{\phi}_\top$	$\widehat{\phi}_\top$	$\widehat{\phi}_{id}$	$\widehat{\phi}_\top$	$\widehat{\phi}_\top$	$\widehat{\phi}_\top$	$\widehat{\phi}_\top$	$\widehat{\phi}_{id}$	$\widehat{\phi}_\top$	$\widehat{\phi}_\top$	$\widehat{\phi}_\top$	$\widehat{\phi}_\top$	$\widehat{\phi}_{id}$
$Start_p$	$\widehat{\phi}_{id}$	$\widehat{\phi}_\top$	$\widehat{\phi}_\top$	$\widehat{\phi}_\top$	$\widehat{\phi}_\top$	$\widehat{\phi}_\top$	$\widehat{\phi}_\top$	$\widehat{\phi}_\top$	$\widehat{\phi}_\top$	$\widehat{\phi}_\top$	$\widehat{\phi}_{id}$	$\widehat{\phi}_\top$	$\widehat{\phi}_\bot$	$\widehat{\phi}_\bot$	$\widehat{\phi}_\bot$	$\widehat{\phi}_\bot$
n_3	$\widehat{\phi}_{id}$	$\widehat{\phi}_\top$	$\widehat{\phi}_{id}$	$\widehat{\phi}_\top$	$\widehat{\phi}_\top$	$\widehat{\phi}_{id}$	$\widehat{\phi}_{id}$	$\widehat{\phi}_\top$	$\widehat{\phi}_\top$	$\widehat{\phi}_\top$	$\widehat{\phi}_\top$	$\widehat{\phi}_\top$	$\widehat{\phi}_\top$	$\widehat{\phi}_\top$	$\widehat{\phi}_\top$	$\widehat{\phi}_{id}$
End_p	$\widehat{\phi}_{id}$	$\widehat{\phi}_\top$	$\widehat{\phi}_\top$	$\widehat{\phi}_\top$	$\widehat{\phi}_\top$	$\widehat{\phi}_{id}$	$\widehat{\phi}_\top$	$\widehat{\phi}_\top$	$\widehat{\phi}_\top$	$\widehat{\phi}_\top$	$\widehat{\phi}_{id}$	$\widehat{\phi}_\top$	$\widehat{\phi}_\top$	$\widehat{\phi}_\top$	$\widehat{\phi}_\top$	$\widehat{\phi}_{id}$
$Start_q$	$\widehat{\phi}_\top$	$\widehat{\phi}_\top$	$\widehat{\phi}_\top$	$\widehat{\phi}_\top$	$\widehat{\phi}_\top$	$\widehat{\phi}_{id}$	$\widehat{\phi}_\top$	$\widehat{\phi}_\top$	$\widehat{\phi}_\top$	$\widehat{\phi}_\top$	$\widehat{\phi}_{id}$	$\widehat{\phi}_\top$	$\widehat{\phi}_\top$	$\widehat{\phi}_\top$	$\widehat{\phi}_\top$	$\widehat{\phi}_{id}$
End_q	$\widehat{\phi}_{id}$	$\widehat{\phi}_\top$	$\widehat{\phi}_\top$	$\widehat{\phi}_\top$	$\widehat{\phi}_{id}$	$\widehat{\phi}_{id}$	$\widehat{\phi}_\top$	$\widehat{\phi}_\top$	$\widehat{\phi}_\top$	$\widehat{\phi}_\top$	$\widehat{\phi}_{id}$	$\widehat{\phi}_\top$	$\widehat{\phi}_\top$	$\widehat{\phi}_\top$	$\widehat{\phi}_\top$	$\widehat{\phi}_{id}$

FIGURE 8.13

Flow functions for faint variables analysis of the program in Figure 8.11 expressed in terms of *pefs*.

where the flow function at the entry point is ϕ_{id} and does not change any further. More specifically, $\Phi^r_w = \phi_{id}$ and $\forall u: f_{u \to w} = \phi_\top$; such that w is *Entry*(*Start*$_r$) for forward flows and *Exit*(*End*$_r$) for backward flows. Φ^r_v is iteratively computed by taking the initial value as $\phi_\top$.

If edge $u \to v$ represents a basic block calls procedure s, $f_{u \to v}$ is replaced by the summary flow function for procedure s. It is defined by Φ^s_w where w is chosen based on the following criterion:

- If $f_{u \to v}$ is a forward flow function mapping the data flow information before the call to the data flow information after the call, w is *Exit*(*End*$_s$).
- If $f_{u \to v}$ is a backward flow function mapping the data flow information after the call to the data flow information before the call, w is *Entry*(*Start*$_s$).

The termination of construction of summary flow functions depends on the nature of component flow functions and the structure of lattice of data flow values. Since we require the *pefs* to be distributive and closed under composition, each component flow function $\widehat{f}^{\,\alpha}$ constituting Φ^p_v can be reduced to the following canonical form

$$\widehat{f}^{\,\alpha} = \prod_{i \geq 0, j \geq 0} (\phi^0_i \circ \phi^1_i \circ \ldots \circ \phi^j_i) \tag{8.16}$$

where ϕ^j_i could be any *pef* in the framework.

Procedure	Flow Function	Defining Expression	Iteration #1		Changes in iteration #2	
			Gen	Kill	Gen	Kill
p	$\Phi^p_{End_p}$	f_{End_p}	$\{c,d\}$	$\emptyset$		
	$\Phi^p_{n_3}$	$f_{n_3} \circ \Phi^p_{End_p}$	$\{a,b,d\}$	$\{c\}$		
	$\Phi^p_{c_4}$	$f_q \circ \Phi^p_{End_p}$	$\emptyset$	$\{a,b,c,d\}$	$\{d\}$	$\{a,b,c\}$
	$\Phi^p_{Start_p}$	$f_{Start_p} \circ (\Phi^p_{n_3} \sqcap \Phi^p_{c_4})$	$\{a,d\}$	$\{b,c\}$		
	f_p	$\Phi^p_{Start_p}$	$\{a,d\}$	$\{b,c\}$		
q	$\Phi^q_{End_q}$	f_{End_q}	$\{a,b\}$	$\{a\}$		
	$\Phi^q_{c_3}$	$f_p \circ \Phi^q_{End_q}$	$\{a,d\}$	$\{a,b,c\}$		
	$\Phi^q_{Start_q}$	$f_{Start_p} \circ \Phi^q_{c_3}$	$\{d\}$	$\{a,b,c\}$		
	f_q	$\Phi^q_{Start_q}$	$\{d\}$	$\{a,b,c\}$		

FIGURE 8.14
Summary flow functions of procedures p and q required for interprocedural liveness analysis of the program in Figure 8.1 on page 260. The flow functions compute the value at the entry of the blocks.

In order to guarantee the termination of construction of $\widehat{f}^{\,\alpha}$, it should be possible to bound both the number of terms as well as the size of each term in any expression of the form in Equation (8.16). Bounding the size of each term requires that it should be possible to reduce every unbounded sequence of compositions by a bounded sequence. Bounding the number of terms requires that an infinite meet must be equivalent to the meet of a finite number of terms.

For the primary frameworks, the sequence of compositions always reduces to a single *pef*. Note that this does not bound the number possible *pef*s. For example, consider the *pef* $\widehat{\phi}_{11}$ in linear constant propagation. It increments the value of its argument by 1. If we compose k such *pef*s, the resulting *pef* is $\widehat{\phi}_{1k}$ and the length of the sequence of compositions is bounded by 1 for all k. However, there is an unbounded number of $\widehat{\phi}_{1k}$; in particular, one for each k. Thus bounding the size of each term does not automatically bound the number of terms in the canonical form.

Thus it becomes important to ensure that the confluence of the terms in an expression of the form in Equation (8.16) can be reduced to a canonical form. This is possible because of the following reason. In the worst case, each term in the canonical form could compute a distinct value in L. Although, the number of such values may not be finite, we restrict our analysis to those frameworks in which every descending chain in L is finite. Thus every descending chain ending on a distinct i in the canonical form can be represented by a finite chain. All that remains is to identify

Flow function	*pefs* computing faintness of a from a,b,c,d				*pefs* computing faintness of b from a,b,c,d				*pefs* computing faintness of c from a,b,c,d				*pefs* computing faintness of d from a,b,c,d			
	a	b	c	d	a	b	c	d	a	b	c	d	a	b	c	d
$\Phi^p_{End_p}$	$\widehat{\phi}_{id}$	$\widehat{\phi}_{\top}$	$\widehat{\phi}_{\top}$	$\widehat{\phi}_{\top}$	$\widehat{\phi}_{\top}$	$\widehat{\phi}_{id}$	$\widehat{\phi}_{\top}$	$\widehat{\phi}_{\top}$	$\widehat{\phi}_{\top}$	$\widehat{\phi}_{\top}$	$\widehat{\phi}_{id}$	$\widehat{\phi}_{\top}$	$\widehat{\phi}_{\top}$	$\widehat{\phi}_{\top}$	$\widehat{\phi}_{\top}$	$\widehat{\phi}_{id}$
$\Phi^p_{n_3}$	$\widehat{\phi}_{id}$	$\widehat{\phi}_{\top}$	$\widehat{\phi}_{id}$	$\widehat{\phi}_{\top}$	$\widehat{\phi}_{\top}$	$\widehat{\phi}_{id}$	$\widehat{\phi}_{id}$	$\widehat{\phi}_{\top}$	$\widehat{\phi}_{\top}$	$\widehat{\phi}_{\top}$	$\widehat{\phi}_{\top}$	$\widehat{\phi}_{\top}$	$\widehat{\phi}_{\top}$	$\widehat{\phi}_{\top}$	$\widehat{\phi}_{\top}$	$\widehat{\phi}_{id}$
$\Phi^p_{c_4}$	$\widehat{\phi}_{\top}$	$\widehat{\phi}_{\top}$	$\widehat{\phi}_{\top}$	$\widehat{\phi}_{\top}$	$\widehat{\phi}_{\top}$	$\widehat{\phi}_{\top}$	$\widehat{\phi}_{\top}$	$\widehat{\phi}_{\top}$	$\widehat{\phi}_{\top}$	$\widehat{\phi}_{\top}$	$\widehat{\phi}_{\top}$	$\widehat{\phi}_{\top}$	$\widehat{\phi}_{\top}$	$\widehat{\phi}_{\top}$	$\widehat{\phi}_{\top}$	$\widehat{\phi}_{\top}$
$\Phi^p_{Start_p}$	$\widehat{\phi}_{id}$	$\widehat{\phi}_{\top}$	$\widehat{\phi}_{id}$	$\widehat{\phi}_{\top}$	$\widehat{\phi}_{\top}$	$\widehat{\phi}_{\top}$	$\widehat{\phi}_{\top}$	$\widehat{\phi}_{\top}$	$\widehat{\phi}_{\top}$	$\widehat{\phi}_{\top}$	$\widehat{\phi}_{\top}$	$\widehat{\phi}_{\top}$	$\widehat{\phi}_{\bot}$	$\widehat{\phi}_{\bot}$	$\widehat{\phi}_{\bot}$	$\widehat{\phi}_{\bot}$
$\Phi^q_{End_q}$	$\widehat{\phi}_{id}$	$\widehat{\phi}_{\top}$	$\widehat{\phi}_{\top}$	$\widehat{\phi}_{\top}$	$\widehat{\phi}_{id}$	$\widehat{\phi}_{id}$	$\widehat{\phi}_{\top}$	$\widehat{\phi}_{\top}$	$\widehat{\phi}_{\top}$	$\widehat{\phi}_{\top}$	$\widehat{\phi}_{id}$	$\widehat{\phi}_{\top}$	$\widehat{\phi}_{\top}$	$\widehat{\phi}_{\top}$	$\widehat{\phi}_{\top}$	$\widehat{\phi}_{id}$
$\Phi^q_{c_3}$	$\widehat{\phi}_{id}$	$\widehat{\phi}_{\top}$	$\widehat{\phi}_{id}$	$\widehat{\phi}_{\top}$	$\widehat{\phi}_{\top}$	$\widehat{\phi}_{\top}$	$\widehat{\phi}_{\top}$	$\widehat{\phi}_{\top}$	$\widehat{\phi}_{\top}$	$\widehat{\phi}_{\top}$	$\widehat{\phi}_{\top}$	$\widehat{\phi}_{\top}$	$\widehat{\phi}_{\bot}$	$\widehat{\phi}_{\bot}$	$\widehat{\phi}_{\bot}$	$\widehat{\phi}_{\bot}$
$\Phi^q_{Start_q}$	$\widehat{\phi}_{\top}$	$\widehat{\phi}_{\top}$	$\widehat{\phi}_{\top}$	$\widehat{\phi}_{\top}$	$\widehat{\phi}_{\top}$	$\widehat{\phi}_{\top}$	$\widehat{\phi}_{\top}$	$\widehat{\phi}_{\top}$	$\widehat{\phi}_{\top}$	$\widehat{\phi}_{\top}$	$\widehat{\phi}_{\top}$	$\widehat{\phi}_{\top}$	$\widehat{\phi}_{\top}$	$\widehat{\phi}_{\top}$	$\widehat{\phi}_{\top}$	$\widehat{\phi}_{\bot}$

FIGURE 8.15
First iteration of constructing summary flow functions of procedure p and q for interprocedural faint variables analysis of the program in Figure 8.11 on page 274. The flow functions compute the value at the entry of the blocks. Highlighted entries show the *pefs* that differ from the corresponding *pefs* in the local flow function $f_i(\mathsf{x})$ provided in Figure 8.13 on page 279.

this when summary flow functions are being constructed.

If we examine the primary *pefs*, the only *pef* that may give rise an infinite number of terms in the canonical form is $\widehat{\phi}_{ab}$. Fortunately, its confluence with every flow function can be reduced due to the structure of $\widehat{L}$ in constant propagation. All other *pefs* are guaranteed to be finite in number. Hence the canonical form is always bounded and the construction of summary flow functions follows for primary frameworks.

Example 8.7

Figure 8.14 on the preceding page provides the summary flow functions for our example program. We first analyze procedure p. We compute summary flow functions associated with *Entry*(n) of each block n; the flow function associated with *Exit*(n) is left implicit. Each flow function is constructed by computing *Kill* and *Gen* sets for function composition using Equations (8.7) and (8.8). The confluence required in computing $\Phi^p_{Start_p}$ uses Equations (8.9) and (8.10) to compute *Kill* and *Gen* sets. The analysis initially uses $\phi_\top(\mathsf{x}) = (\mathsf{x} - \{a,b,c,d\})$ for f_q while computing $\Phi^p_{c_4}$. Hence the *Gen* and *Kill* sets of $\Phi^p_{c_4}$ are approximate in the first iteration. Using these sets, f_p is computed and is used in analyzing procedure q. The resulting f_q is different from $\phi_\top$. This causes change in $\Phi^p_{c_4}$ in the second iteration. However, this change does not affect Φ^p_{Start}, and hence

f_p remains same implying that f_q computed in the first iteration does not change.

It is not surprising that Kill_p and Kill_q computed above are identical to $\mathit{MustKill}_p$ and $\mathit{MustKill}_q$ computed in Figure 8.2 on page 262. Similarly, Gen_p and Gen_q computed here are identical to MayUse_p and MayUse_q computed in Figure 8.2 on page 262. □

Example 8.8

Figure 8.15 on the preceding page shows the first iteration in constructing summary flow functions for faint variables analysis. Since the description of the functions is very verbose, the relevant entries have been highlighted. While analyzing procedure p, the summary flow function for c_4 is assumed to be $\phi_\top$. When $\Phi^p_{\mathit{Start}_p}$ is computed, we discover that the faintness of a now depends on c also. This is a result of the composition $\overline{f}^{\,a\to a}_{\mathit{Start}_p} \circ \overline{f}^{\,c\to a}_{n_3}$. When this is merged with the earlier *pef* $\overline{f}^{\,c\to a}_{\mathit{Start}_p}$ which was $\widehat{\phi}_\top$, it becomes $\widehat{\phi}_{id}$. When procedure q is analyzed, the flow function for c_3 is f_p which is the same as $\Phi^p_{\mathit{Start}_p}$. The summary flow function as $\Phi^q_{\mathit{Start}_q}$ so computed represents the fact that b and c are faint at the entry of Start_q and d is not faint. Observe that this is due to the effect of the called procedure p. The resulting f_q is different from the earlier $\phi_\top$.

When the new value of f_q is used in the second iteration, it changes the *pef* $\overline{f}^{\,d\to d}_{c_3}$ from $\widehat{\phi}_\top$ to $\widehat{\phi}_\bot$ suggesting that d is not faint at the entry of c_4. However, this does not cause any change in $\Phi^p_{\mathit{Start}_p}$ and the process of constructing summary flow functions terminates. □

8.3.4 Computing Data Flow Information

Φ^r_u represents the effect of the paths from $\mathit{Entry}(\mathit{Start}_r)$ to u for forward problems and from u to $\mathit{Exit}(\mathit{End}_r)$ for backward problems. This effect includes the intraprocedural data flow information as well as synthesized data flow information resulting from the calls along these paths. Thus the data flow information associated with u can be computed by the function application $\Phi^r_u(\mathit{BI}_r)$ where BI represents the data flow information inherited by r from its callers.

Let $\mathit{CallsTo}_r$ denote the set of callers of r. These are simply the predecessors of r in the call graph. Let $\mathit{CallsTo}_r(s)$ denote the call sites calling r from procedure s. Given BI_{main}, the data flow information associated with program point u in procedure r, denoted x^r_u, is computed as follows:

$$\mathit{BI}_r = \prod_{\substack{s\in \mathit{CallsTo}_r \\ c_i\in \mathit{CallsTo}_r(s)}} \Phi^r_{c_i}(\mathit{BI}_s) \tag{8.17}$$

$$\mathsf{x}^r_u = \Phi^r_u(\mathit{BI}_r) \tag{8.18}$$

Procedure	BI	Data flow variable	Summary flow function		Data flow value
			Name	Definition	
main	$\emptyset$	In_{End_m}	$\Phi^m_{End_m}$	$BI_m \cup \{a,c\}$	$\{a,c\}$
		In_{c_2}	Φ^m_{c2}	$(BI_m - \{a,b,c\}) \cup \{d\}$	$\{d\}$
		In_{n_2}	Φ^m_{n2}	$(BI_m - \{a,b,c,d\}) \cup \{a,b\}$	$\{a,b\}$
		In_{n_1}	Φ^m_{n1}	$(BI_m - \{a,b,c,d\}) \cup \{a,b,c,d\}$	$\{a,b,c,d\}$
		In_{c_1}	Φ^m_{c1}	$(BI_m - \{a,b,c,d\}) \cup \{a,d\}$	$\{a,d\}$
		In_{Start_m}	$\Phi^m_{Start_m}$	$BI_m - \{a,b,c,d\}$	$\emptyset$
p	$\{a,b,c,d\}$	In_{End_p}	$\Phi^p_{End_p}$	$BI_p \cup \{c,d\}$	$\{a,b,c,d\}$
		In_{n_3}	Φ^p_{n3}	$(BI_p - \{c\}) \cup \{a,b,d\}$	$\{a,b,d\}$
		In_{c_4}	Φ^p_{c4}	$(BI_p - \{a,b,c\}) \cup \{d\}$	$\{d\}$
		In_{Start_p}	$\Phi^p_{Start_p}$	$(BI_p - \{b,c\}) \cup \{a,d\}$	$\{a,d\}$
q	$\{a,b,c,d\}$	In_{End_q}	$\Phi^q_{End_q}$	$(BI_q - \{a\}) \cup \{a,b\}$	$\{a,b,c,d\}$
		In_{c_3}	Φ^q_{c3}	$(BI_q - \{a,b,c\}) \cup \{a,d\}$	$\{a,d\}$
		In_{Start_q}	$\Phi^q_{Start_q}$	$(BI_q - \{a,b,c\}) \cup \{d\}$	$\{d\}$

FIGURE 8.16
Data flow information computed by interprocedural liveness analysis of the program in Figure 8.1 on page 260 using the summary flow functions defined in Figure 8.14 on page 280.

The initial value of BI_s is assumed to be $\top$; it is assumed that appropriate boundary point is chosen depending on the flows i.e., $Entry(Start_p)$ for forward flows and $Exit(End_p)$ for backward flows.

Example 8.9
Figure 8.16 shows the result of interprocedural liveness analysis of the program in Figure 8.1 on page 260 using the summary flow functions defined in Figure 8.14 on page 280. For simplicity, we show the information associated with block entries only. The liveness information of the *main* procedure (abbreviated by *m*) can be computed in a single iteration from $BI = \emptyset$. For live variables analysis

$$BI_p = In_{n_1} \cup In_{End_q} \quad = In_{n_1} \cup \Phi^q_{End_q}(BI_q)$$
$$BI_q = In_{End_m} \cup In_{End_p} = In_{End_m} \cup \Phi^p_{End_p}(BI_p)$$

Procedure	BI	Data flow variable	Summary flow function Name	Summary flow function Definition	Data flow value
main	$\{a,b,c,d\}$	In_{Start_m}	$\Phi^m_{Start_m}$	$BI_m \cup \{a,b,c,d\}$	$\{a,b,c,d\}$
		In_{c_1}	$\Phi^m_{c_1}$	$(BI_m - \{d\}) \cup \{b,c\}$	$\{a,b,c\}$
		In_{n_1}	$\Phi^m_{n_1}$	$(BI_m - \{d\}) \cup \{a,c\}$	$\{a,b,c\}$
		In_{n_2}	$\Phi^m_{n_2}$	$(BI_m - \{a\}) \cup \{c,d\}$	$\{b,c,d\}$
		In_{c_2}	$\Phi^m_{c_2}$	$(BI_m - \{d\}) \cup \{a,b,c\}$	$\{a,b,c\}$
		In_{End_m}	$\Phi^m_{End_m}$	BI_m	$\{a,b,c,d\}$
p	$\{a,b,c\}$	In_{Start_p}	$\Phi^p_{Start_p}$	$(BI_p - (\{d\} \cup \{a \mid c \notin BI_p\})) \cup \{b,c\}$	$\{a,b,c\}$
		In_{n_3}	$\Phi^p_{n_3}$	$(BI_p - \{a,b \mid c \notin BI_p\}) \cup \{c\}$	$\{a,b,c\}$
		In_{c_4}	$\Phi^p_{c_4}$	$(BI_p - \{d\}) \cup \{a,b,c\}$	$\{a,b,c\}$
		In_{End_p}	$\Phi^p_{End_p}$	BI_p	$\{a,b,c\}$
q	$\{a,b,c\}$	In_{Start_q}	$\Phi^q_{Start_q}$	$(BI_q - \{d\}) \cup \{a,b,c\}$	$\{a,b,c\}$
		In_{c_3}	$\Phi^q_{c_3}$	$(BI_q - (\{d\} \cup \{a \mid c \notin BI_q\})) \cup \{b,c\}$	$\{a,b,c\}$
		In_{End_q}	$\Phi^q_{End_q}$	$BI_q - \{b \mid a \notin BI_q\}$	$\{a,b,c\}$

FIGURE 8.17
Interprocedural faint variables analysis for the program in Figure 8.11 on page 274 using the summary flow functions constructed in Example 8.8.

Thus BI_p and BI_q are mutually dependent on each other. Since In_{n_1} is $\{a,b,c,d\}$ which is the $\perp$ element of the lattice, BI_p cannot change any further. From this, In_{End_p} is computed which turns out to be $\{a,b,c,d\}$. Thus BI_q is also $\{a,b,c,d\}$ and does not change any further.

Our analysis shows that Out_{Start_m} contains only a and d. Thus the assignments to b and c in $Start_m$ are redundant and can be eliminated. Observe that although c is used in End_p, it is found to be dead at the entry of c_4. This is because the recursion ending path must pass through block n_3 before the execution reaches End_p from c_4. Due to the assignment in n_3, c is not live at the entry of c_4. □

Example 8.10

Figure 8.17 shows the result of interprocedural faint variables analysis of the program in Figure 8.11 on page 274 using the summary flow functions computed in Example 8.8. In faint variables analysis, BI for *main* is $\{a,b,c,d\}$

because every variable is faint at the end of the program. The data flow information in *main* can be computed in a single iteration. BI for p and q is defined by:

$$\begin{aligned} \mathsf{BI}_p &= \mathsf{In}_{n_1} \cap \mathsf{In}_{\mathsf{End}_q} &&= \mathsf{In}_{n_1} \cap \Phi^q_{\mathsf{End}_q}(\mathsf{BI}_q) \\ \mathsf{BI}_q &= \mathsf{In}_{\mathsf{End}_m} \cap \mathsf{In}_{\mathsf{End}_p} &&= \mathsf{In}_{\mathsf{End}_m} \cap \Phi^p_{\mathsf{End}_p}(\mathsf{BI}_p) \end{aligned}$$

For computing BI_p, In_{n_1} is $\{a,b,c\}$ and $\Phi^q_{\mathsf{End}_q}(\mathsf{BI}_q)$ is assumed to be $\top$ which is $\{a,b,c,d\}$ for faint variables analysis. Thus $\mathsf{BI}_p = \{a,b,c\}$ and the data flow information for all blocks in p also turns out to be $\{a,b,c\}$. Thus BI_q is also $\{a,b,c\}$ and so is the data flow information for all blocks in q.

Thus we conclude that the only relevant assignment in procedures p and q is the assignment to b in Start_p for local use in the condition. Local constant propagation can make even this assignment redundant. To see why the assignment in End_q is redundant, consider the paths starting at End_q. If all recursive calls to q are not over, the execution can only reach End_p and from there End_q. When all recursive calls to q finish, the execution reaches End_{main} directly or n_1 through End_p. Thus there is no use of the value assigned to a in End_q other than in the same assignment. Hence this assignment is redundant. This makes both a and b faint making the assignment to c in n_3 redundant. Discovering this through live variable analysis would require repeatedly performing dead code elimination and live variables analysis. □

8.3.5 Enumerating Summary Flow Functions

The construction method explained in previous sections requires the component flow functions to consist of primitive flow functions only. If a component flow function requires composite entity functions, the method is not applicable to the framework. The main difficulty is in being able to compose entity functions and reduce the compositions. Function applications on the other hand do not require any reduction to be performed. This leads to an interesting possibility: Instead of constructing closed form summary flow functions, the flow functions can be enumerated in terms of input output pairs by identifying the data flow values that could appear in the program as inputs to a flow function. This is possible because every program has a well defined BI and starting from BI the relevant data flow values can be constructed.

We write the enumerated form of function Φ^r_u as follows:

$$\mathcal{E}[\![\Phi^r_u]\!] = \{\mathsf{x} \mapsto \mathsf{y} \mid \mathsf{x} \mapsto \mathsf{x} \in \Phi^r_w, \mathsf{y} = \Phi^r_u(\mathsf{x})\}$$

where w is the boundary point of r which is chosen depending upon the direction of flows. For backward flows w is $\mathsf{Exit}(\mathsf{End}_r)$ whereas for forward flows w is $\mathsf{Entry}(\mathsf{Start}_r)$.

Enumeration for the entire program begins at the boundary point w of the *main* procedure and is chosen to be the identity function restricted to BI.

$$\mathcal{E}\left[\!\left[\Phi^{main}_w\right]\!\right] = \{\mathsf{BI} \mapsto \mathsf{BI}\}$$

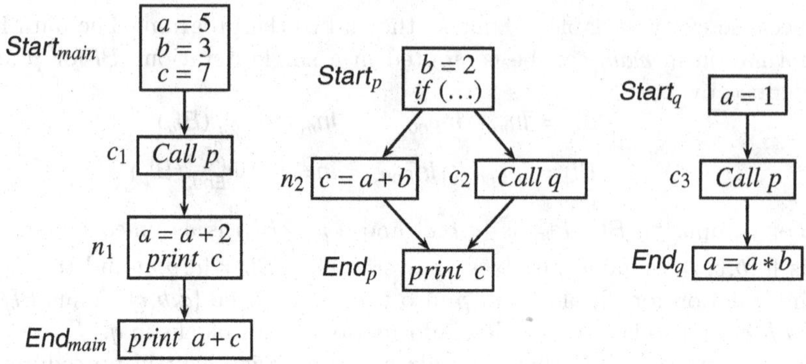

FIGURE 8.18
Program to illustrate enumeration of flow functions for full constant propagation.

Similarly, enumeration for a given procedure r also begins at its boundary point w; however, it gets defined by the enumerated summary flow functions corresponding to the call sites that call procedure r:

$$\mathcal{E}[\![\Phi^r_w]\!] = \left\{\mathsf{x} \mapsto \mathsf{x} \mid \mathsf{y} \mapsto \mathsf{x} \in \mathcal{E}[\![\Phi^s_{c_i}]\!],\ c_i \text{ is a call to } r \text{ in procedure } s\right\} \tag{8.19}$$

For other program points v in p:

$$\mathcal{E}[\![\Phi^r_v]\!] = \left\{\mathsf{x} \mapsto \mathsf{y} \mid \mathsf{y} = \bigsqcap_{u \in neighbours(v)} f_{u\to v}(\mathsf{z}),\ \mathsf{x} \mapsto \mathsf{z} \in \mathcal{E}[\![\Phi^r_u]\!]\right\} \tag{8.20}$$

If edge $u \to v$ represents a basic block calls procedure s, $f_{u\to v}$ is replaced by the summary flow function for procedure s. It is defined by $\mathcal{E}[\![\Phi^s_w]\!]$ where w is chosen based on the following criterion:

- If $f_{u\to v}$ is a forward flow function mapping the data flow information before the call to the data flow information after the call, w is *Exit*(*End$_s$*).
- If $f_{u\to v}$ is a backward flow function mapping the data flow information after the call to the data flow information before the call, w is *Entry*(*Start$_s$*).

Equations (8.19) and (8.20) are computed with $\emptyset$ as the initial value.

Once all summary flow functions are enumerated, the final data flow values are computed by simply merging the output of a summary flow function for each relevant input that has already been identified:

$$\mathsf{X}_u = \bigsqcap_{\mathsf{x} \mapsto \mathsf{y} \in \mathcal{E}[\![\Phi^r_u]\!]} \mathsf{y} \tag{8.21}$$

Observe that this is different from the method of using the closed form summary flow functions; Equations (8.17) and (8.18) require a fixed point computation whereas Equation (8.21) does not.

Procedure	Block	$\mathcal{E}[\![\Phi^r_u]\!]$		
		Iteration #1	Iteration #2	Iteration #3
	$Start_p$	$\langle 5,3,7\rangle \mapsto \langle 5,3,7\rangle$	$\langle 5,3,7\rangle \mapsto \langle 5,3,7\rangle$ $\langle 1,2,7\rangle \mapsto \langle 1,2,7\rangle$	$\langle 5,3,7\rangle \mapsto \langle 5,3,7\rangle$ $\langle 1,2,7\rangle \mapsto \langle 1,2,7\rangle$
	n_2	$\langle 5,3,7\rangle \mapsto \langle 5,2,7\rangle$	$\langle 5,3,7\rangle \mapsto \langle 5,2,7\rangle$ $\langle 1,2,7\rangle \mapsto \langle 1,2,7\rangle$	$\langle 5,3,7\rangle \mapsto \langle 5,2,7\rangle$ $\langle 1,2,7\rangle \mapsto \langle 1,2,7\rangle$
p	c_2	$\langle 5,3,7\rangle \mapsto \langle 5,2,7\rangle$	$\langle 5,3,7\rangle \mapsto \langle 5,2,7\rangle$ $\langle 1,2,7\rangle \mapsto \langle 1,2,7\rangle$	$\langle 5,3,7\rangle \mapsto \langle 5,2,7\rangle$ $\langle 1,2,7\rangle \mapsto \langle 1,2,7\rangle$
	End_p	$\langle 5,3,7\rangle \mapsto \langle 5,2,7\rangle$	$\langle 5,3,7\rangle \mapsto \langle 5,2,7\rangle$ $\langle 1,2,7\rangle \mapsto \langle 1,2,3\rangle$	$\langle 5,3,7\rangle \mapsto \langle 5\sqcap 2,2,7\sqcap 3\rangle$ $\langle 1,2,7\rangle \mapsto \langle 1\sqcap 2,2,3\rangle$
	f_p	$\langle 5,3,7\rangle \mapsto \langle 5,2,7\rangle$	$\langle 5,3,7\rangle \mapsto \langle 5,2,7\rangle$ $\langle 1,2,7\rangle \mapsto \langle 1,2,3\rangle$	$\langle 5,3,7\rangle \mapsto \langle \widehat{\bot},2,\widehat{\bot}\rangle$ $\langle 1,2,7\rangle \mapsto \langle \widehat{\bot},2,3\rangle$
	$Start_q$	$\langle 5,2,7\rangle \mapsto \langle 5,2,7\rangle$	$\langle 5,2,7\rangle \mapsto \langle 5,2,7\rangle$ $\langle 1,2,7\rangle \mapsto \langle 1,2,7\rangle$	$\langle 5,2,7\rangle \mapsto \langle 5,2,7\rangle$ $\langle 1,2,7\rangle \mapsto \langle 1,2,7\rangle$
	c_3	$\langle 5,2,7\rangle \mapsto \langle 1,2,7\rangle$	$\langle 5,2,7\rangle \mapsto \langle 1,2,7\rangle$ $\langle 1,2,7\rangle \mapsto \langle 1,2,7\rangle$	$\langle 5,2,7\rangle \mapsto \langle 1,2,7\rangle$ $\langle 1,2,7\rangle \mapsto \langle 1,2,7\rangle$
q	End_q	$\emptyset$	$\langle 5,2,7\rangle \mapsto \langle 1,2,3\rangle$ $\langle 1,2,7\rangle \mapsto \langle 1,2,3\rangle$	$\langle 5,2,7\rangle \mapsto \langle \widehat{\bot},2,3\rangle$ $\langle 1,2,7\rangle \mapsto \langle \widehat{\bot},2,3\rangle$
	f_q	$\emptyset$	$\langle 5,2,7\rangle \mapsto \langle 2,2,3\rangle$ $\langle 1,2,7\rangle \mapsto \langle 2,2,3\rangle$	$\langle 5,2,7\rangle \mapsto \langle \widehat{\bot},2,3\rangle$ $\langle 1,2,7\rangle \mapsto \langle \widehat{\bot},2,3\rangle$

FIGURE 8.19
Enumerated summary flow functions for constant propagation over procedure p and q of the program in Figure 8.18.

Example 8.11

Consider the program in Figure 8.18 on the preceding page for constant propagation analysis. When procedure p is called from *main*, the values of a, b, and c are 5, 3, and 7 respectively. If p does not call q at all, then the values of a, b, and c at End_p are 5, 2, and 7 respectively. However, if q is called, then the value of a is modified in $Start_q$ and End_q. When the recursion unwinds, the value of c gets modified. Variable b is assignment 2 in every call to p. Thus when p returns in *main*, the value of b is 2 whereas a and c are not constants.

Iterative computation of $\mathcal{E}[\![\Phi^r_u]\!]$ for procedures p and q is shown in Figure 8.19. In the first iteration, $\mathcal{E}\left[\!\left[\Phi^q_{End_q}\right]\!\right]$ remains $\emptyset$: mapping $\langle 5,2,7\rangle \mapsto \langle 1,2,7\rangle$ at c_3 indicates that the value $\langle 5,2,7\rangle$ reaching $Start_q$ is mapped to the value $\langle 1,2,7\rangle$ at c_3. However, the mapping for $\langle 1,2,7\rangle$ in procedure p has not been discovered so far; the only mapping for procedure p discovered in first iteration is $\langle 5,3,7\rangle \mapsto \langle 5,2,7\rangle$. Second iteration discovers $\langle 1,2,7\rangle \mapsto \langle 1,2,3\rangle$ for p. This leads to $\langle 5,2,7\rangle \mapsto \langle 2,2,3\rangle$ and $\langle 1,2,7\rangle \mapsto \langle 2,2,3\rangle$ for procedure q due the assignment $a = a * b$ in End_q. This influences c_2 and End_p where it is discovered that a can be mapped to 5 if no call to q is made, 1 when p is called from q, and 2 when q returns in p. Similarly, c can be 7 and 3 depending upon whether q is called or not. Thus f_p records $\langle 5,3,7\rangle \mapsto \langle \widehat{\bot},2,\widehat{\bot}\rangle$ and $\langle 1,2,7\rangle \mapsto \langle \widehat{\bot},2,\widehat{\bot}\rangle$ whereas f_q contains $\langle 5,2,7\rangle \mapsto \langle \widehat{\bot},2,3\rangle$ and $\langle 1,2,7\rangle \mapsto \langle \widehat{\bot},2,3\rangle$. □

Although we have presented the enumeration of summary flow function as a fixed point computation performed using a round-robin iterative method, in practice, this may not be efficient since a program may consist of hundreds of procedures. The data flow values discovered as inputs to summary flow functions may reach limited portions of the program. In such situation, it is preferable to use a work list method and propagate the values to the relevant portions of the program.

We outline a work list based method in the following. The work list contains pairs (u, x) that represents the fact that $\mathcal{E}[\![\Phi^r_u]\!]$ has been computed for input value x and its effect needs to be propagated further. The work list is initialized with the pair (w, BI) where w is the boundary of the *main* procedure. As is typical in a work list based method, an entry from work list is removed, its effect is propagated to its neighbours, and new entries whose effect needs to be propagated are added to the work list. This process is repeated until the work list becomes empty.

We use the following notation to describe propagation.

- The meaning of $\mathcal{E}[\![\Phi^r_u]\!](\mathsf{x}) = y$ is that the mapping $\mathsf{x} \mapsto \mathsf{y}$ is included in $\mathcal{E}[\![\Phi^r_u]\!]$. Initially, $\mathcal{E}[\![\Phi^r_u]\!]$ is assumed to be empty.

- When $\mathcal{E}[\![\Phi^r_u]\!](\mathsf{x})$ appears on the right hand side of an assignment, it denotes y such that $\mathsf{x} \mapsto \mathsf{y} \in \mathcal{E}[\![\Phi^r_u]\!]$. If there is no mapping for x in $\mathcal{E}[\![\Phi^r_u]\!]$, $\mathcal{E}[\![\Phi^r_u]\!](\mathsf{x})$ denotes $\top$.

The meaning of propagating the effect of a pair (u, x) to its neighbour v is that the summary flow function $\mathcal{E}[\![\Phi^r_v]\!]$ should be constructed. Observe that v need not be in the same procedure. It could be a program point in a caller procedure or a called procedure. More precisely, propagation of (u, x) for forward flows is defined as follows.

- When u is a call node c_i calling procedure s. Let the successor of u be node v in the same procedure. Then $\mathcal{E}[\![\Phi^r_v]\!]$ should be updated with the value of the result of applying f_s to the value reaching c_i.

$$\mathcal{E}[\![\Phi^r_v]\!](\mathsf{x}) = \mathcal{E}[\![\Phi^r_v]\!](\mathsf{x}) \sqcap \mathcal{E}[\![\Phi^s_w]\!]\left(\mathcal{E}[\![\Phi^r_{c_i}]\!](\mathsf{x})\right)$$

where w is $Exit(End_s)$. It is possible that the $\mathcal{E}[\![\Phi^s_w]\!]$ may not have been defined for x. Thus the effect should be propagated to $Start_s$ as follows:

$$\mathcal{E}[\![\Phi^s_{w'}]\!]\left(\mathcal{E}[\![\Phi^r_{c_i}]\!](\mathsf{x})\right) = \mathcal{E}[\![\Phi^r_{c_i}]\!](\mathsf{x})$$

where w' is $Entry(Start_s)$. If $\mathcal{E}[\![\Phi^r_v]\!]$ changes, add the pair (u, x) to the work list. If $\mathcal{E}[\![\Phi^r_{w'}]\!]$ changes, add the pair $\left(w', \mathcal{E}[\![\Phi^r_{c_i}]\!](\mathsf{x})\right)$ to the work list.

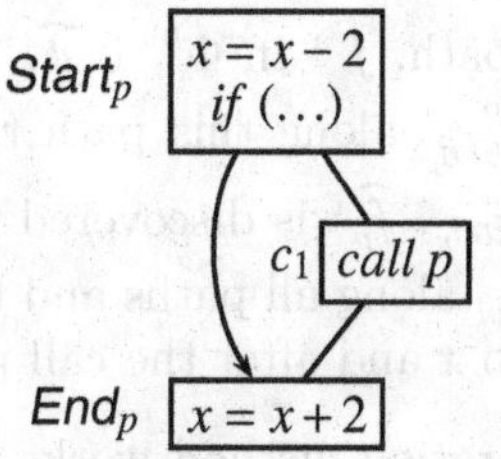

FIGURE 8.20
Example of linear constant propagation for which a closed form summary flow function can be created but summary flow functions cannot be enumerated.

- When u is *Exit*(*End*$_r$). In this case, the summary flow function of callers need to be updated. Find out all callers t of r such that $\mathcal{E}\left[\!\left[\Phi^t_{c_j}\right]\!\right](\mathsf{y}) = \mathsf{x}$. Let the successor of c_j in t be v. Then,

$$\mathcal{E}[\![\Phi^t_v]\!](\mathsf{y}) = \mathcal{E}[\![\Phi^t_v]\!](\mathsf{y}) \sqcap \mathcal{E}[\![\Phi^r_u]\!](\mathsf{x})$$

  If $\mathcal{E}[\![\Phi^t_v]\!]$ changes, add the pair (v, y) to the work list.

- When u is some other program point. Update the summary flow function of every neighbour v of u:

$$\mathcal{E}[\![\Phi^r_v]\!](\mathsf{x}) = \mathcal{E}[\![\Phi^r_v]\!](\mathsf{x}) \sqcap f_{u\to v}(\mathcal{E}[\![\Phi^r_u]\!](\mathsf{x}))$$

  If $\mathcal{E}[\![\Phi^r_v]\!]$ changes, add the pair (u, x) to the work list.

The main difference between the two methods of enumerating the summary flow function is the fundamental difference between a round-robin method and a work list method: In a round-robin method, the relevant computation for a given program point u is performed by incorporating the effect of all its neighbours. In a work list method, the influence of a program point u is propagated to all its neighbours v and the value at u is updated.

The main advantage of enumerating summary flow functions is that there is no need to reduce function compositions because the method relies on computing actual values. However, the main limitation of computing values is that it may not terminate for a lattice with infinite values. If flow functions can be reduced, the closed form summary flow functions can be used for lattices with infinite values also.

Example 8.12

Figure 8.20 shows an example of linear constant propagation. If we construct closed form summary flow functions, we discover that $\widehat{f}^{\,x}$ in the summary flow function at *Exit*(*End*$_p$) along the edge *Start*$_p$ → *End*$_p$ is a composition of $\widehat{\phi}_{1,-2}$ and $\widehat{\phi}_{1,2}$. Thus the flow function representing p along the call free path is $\widehat{\phi_{id}}$. Along the other path, $\widehat{f}^{\,x}$ in $\Phi^p_{c_1}$ is $\widehat{\phi_{1,-2}}$. This is composed with the $\widehat{f_p}^{\,x} = \widehat{\phi_{id}}$ to construct $\Phi^p_{End_p}$ along this path resulting in $\Phi^p_{End_p} = \widehat{\phi_{1,-2}}$ when this is composed with f_{End_p}, $\widehat{f_p}^{\,x}$ is discovered to be $\widehat{\phi_{id}}$ along this path also. Thus f_p is found to be $\widehat{\phi_{id}}$ along all paths and the method concludes that the value of x before a call to x and after the call remains same.

To see how the enumeration method works for this program, we will need to know the value of x when the outermost call to p is made. Assume that x is 10 when p is called from outside. Let w denote *Exit*(End_p). Then we have $\langle 10 \rangle \mapsto \langle 10 \rangle$ in $\mathcal{E}\left[\!\left[\Phi^p_{Start_p}\right]\!\right]$ and $\langle 10 \rangle \mapsto \langle 8 \rangle$ in $\mathcal{E}\left[\!\left[\Phi^p_{c_1}\right]\!\right]$. Along the other path, we get $\langle 10 \rangle \mapsto \langle 10 \rangle$ in $\mathcal{E}\left[\!\left[\Phi^p_w\right]\!\right]$. In order to propagate the effect of $\langle 10 \rangle \mapsto \langle 8 \rangle$ in $\mathcal{E}\left[\!\left[\Phi^p_{c_1}\right]\!\right]$, we find out if have $\langle 8 \rangle \mapsto \langle \ldots \rangle$ in $\mathcal{E}\left[\!\left[\Phi^p_w\right]\!\right]$. Since we don't have it, we have to propagate this effect to $Start_p$ thereby adding $\langle 8 \rangle \mapsto \langle 8 \rangle$ to both $\mathcal{E}\left[\!\left[\Phi^p_{Start_p}\right]\!\right]$ and $\mathcal{E}\left[\!\left[\Phi^p_w\right]\!\right]$. In the next iteration we check if have $\langle 6 \rangle \mapsto \langle \ldots \rangle$ in $\mathcal{E}\left[\!\left[\Phi^p_w\right]\!\right]$. The process does not terminate because the recursive calls generate an infinite number of values for x. □

8.4 Summary and Concluding Remarks

In this chapter we have presented methods that construct context independent summary flow functions. Side effects analysis constructs summary flow functions for a fixed set of side effects. The key idea of this approach is to reduce expressions of sets representing flow functions. These reductions compute the sets that represent the required summary flow functions.

A natural extension of this idea results in a whole program analysis method that computes context independent summary flow functions for a given data flow framework. This extension attempts to reduce expressions of functions instead of expressions of sets. The feasibility of reducing expressions consisting of function compositions and confluences can be established in terms of the *pef*s that make up flow functions of a given data flow framework. A related concern of this method is that the canonical form of reduced expressions may not be compact and may require a lot of space. Both these concerns are addressed by the method that enumerates functions in terms of observed input output behaviour. This method does not need to reduce expressions of functions. However, its main limitation is that it may not terminate if the lattice of data flow values is not finite.

An orthogonal issue presented in this chapter is to construct functions that represent mappings of formal parameters across call sequences.

8.5 Bibliographic Notes

The side effect analysis presented in this chapter is a generalization of the work by Barth [13, 14] and Banning [12]. Callahan [19] has tried to solve the same problem using a different representation called *program summary graph.* The alias analysis of parameters is based on the work by Cooper [25] and by Cooper and Kennedy [26]. The whole program analysis is based on the classical functional approach defined by Sharir and Pnueli [93]. However, unlike Sharir and Pnueli, we use primitive entity functions to describe reductions of flow functions. The alternative approach of enumerating summary flow functions is an abstract model of the tabulation method proposed by Sharir and Pnueli. The concept of *partial transfer functions* by Wilson and Lam [107] can be viewed as similar to the tabulation method. However, it is context insensitive in recursive calls.

Another interesting method of interprocedural data flow analysis that belongs to the category of functional approaches is the method based on *graph reachability* proposed by Reps, Horwitz and Sagiv [82, 87]. This approach handles exactly the same class of frameworks that are handled by the method presented in this chapter.

9

Value-Based Approach to Interprocedural Data Flow Analysis

In this chapter, we present the other paradigm of context and flow sensitive whole program analysis. This approach does not involve precomputation of summary flow functions. Instead, it directly computes the data flow information and propagates the inherited data flow information from callers to callees and the synthesized data flow information from callees to callers.

We first present the program model and some basic concepts underlying this approach. Then we present a method for precise flow and context sensitive interprocedural data flow analysis for bit vector frameworks. The subsequent section generalizes this method to general frameworks.

9.1 Program Model for Value-Based Approaches to Interprocedural Data Flow Analysis

A value-based approach of interprocedural data flow analysis views a program as a single large procedure with different kinds of paths rather than as a collection of independent procedures. With this view of programs, interprocedural data flow analysis reduces to identifying the origins of *ifp*s and traversing them; the only difference is that these *ifp*s are interprocedural rather than intraprocedural and hence must be sensitive to the calling contexts. This is required to distinguish between inherited data flow information propagated from different callers. This enables propagation of synthesized information to appropriate callers.

A value-based approach uses a supergraph which has been explained in Section 7.2. Let a given call site c_i in procedure r call procedure s. Then, logically the program points *Entry*(C_i) and *Exit*(R_i) belong to the caller procedure r in that the data flow information associated with these program points holds for procedure r. The program points *Exit*(C_i) and *Entry*(R_i) belong to the callee procedure s as the data flow information associated with these points holds for procedure s.

The roles of call and return nodes in a supergraph cannot be abstracted out into a single kind of node; they must be explicated for value-based interprocedural data flow analysis. Hence unlike intraprocedural data flow analysis, a general formulation that is uniformly applicable to both forward and backward data flow frameworks does not seem natural; the flow function of the proposed abstract node representing call and return nodes will have to be predicated on whether the formulation is being used for forward flows or backward flows. Hence we restrict our formulations to forward data flow problems for simplicity of exposition,

As observed in Chapter 7, traversing all paths in a supergraph results in context insensitive analysis. Context sensitivity requires that the propagation of data flow information must be restricted to interprocedurally valid paths.

DEFINITION 9.1 *A path from* Start_{main} *to a block* n *in a supergraph is an interprocedurally valid path if*

1. *for every edge* $\mathsf{End}_r \rightarrow R_i$ *in the path, there is a matching edge* $C_i \rightarrow \mathsf{Start}_r$ *in the path, and*
2. *if the subpath from* C_i *to* R_i *does not contain any other call or return node, then after replacing this subpath by a single (fictitious) edge, the reduced path is interprocedurally valid.*

At the base level, a path consisting of only intraprocedural edges is a valid interprocedural path. Similarly, a path in which there is no return edge is also a valid interprocedural path; the validity constraint arises only when a return edge is encountered. This is because a return edge that appears in a path must correspond to the last call edge in the path. This constraint facilitates ensuring that the data flow information from a callee procedure is propagated back to the correct caller procedure.

Let call site c_i call procedure r. In an interprocedurally valid path, this procedure call is represented by a path segment starting with the call edge $C_i \rightarrow \mathsf{Start}_r$ and ending in the corresponding return edge $\mathsf{End}_r \rightarrow R_i$. Every such call appearing in an interprocedurally valid path can be abstracted out by a basic block making the call; a path containing this basic block remains an interprocedurally valid path.

We view call and return nodes as being *significant* nodes because they define the structure of an interprocedural path. Often we will restrict a path to the significant nodes appearing in it. For interprocedural validity, the structure of a path in terms of significant nodes should be derivable from the following context free grammar with *IPVP* as its start symbol:

$$
\begin{aligned}
\mathit{IPVP} &\rightarrow \mathit{finishedCalls}\ \ \mathit{unFinishedCalls} \\
\mathit{finishedCalls} &\rightarrow C_i\ \ \mathit{finishedCalls}\ \ R_i \\
&\mid\ \mathit{finishedCalls}\ \ \mathit{finishedCalls} \\
&\mid\ \epsilon \\
\mathit{unFinishedCalls} &\rightarrow C_i\ \ \mathit{finishedCalls}\ \ \mathit{unFinishedCalls} \\
&\mid\ \epsilon
\end{aligned}
$$

where C_i and R_i are placeholders for terminal symbols representing corresponding call and return nodes in a supergraph.

DEFINITION 9.2 *An* ifp *ρ from a program point u to a program point v is a an interprocedurally valid* ifp *if it is a suffix of some interprocedurally valid path.*

An important requirement of traversing interprocedurally valid *ifp*s is discovering matching C_i for every R_i encountered in a path in the supergraph in order to establish interprocedural validity of the *ifp*. Value-based interprocedural analyses achieve this by embedding the information about contexts within the data flow values being computed. This information represents the call nodes C_i encountered in the paths traversed for computing the data flow value. In the presence of recursion, precise embedding of context information becomes an important issue in value-based interprocedural data flow analysis. The methods presented in this chapter handle recursive program without compromising on precision.

DEFINITION 9.3 *A calling context of procedure r is defined as a sequence of callers of r starting from the main procedure.*

A calling context σ is denoted by a string $c_1 \cdots c_k$ of call site names. This string represents a call sequence $r_1, \ldots, r_k$ starting from the main procedure, such that $c_i \in \mathsf{CallsIn}_{r_i}$ and $c_i \in \mathsf{CallsTo}_{r_{i+1}}$. Note that the call sites in a call string or the called procedures in a call chain need not be distinct.

Value-based interprocedural data flow analysis is defined in terms of data flow values that are pairs of the form $\langle \sigma, \mathsf{x} \rangle$ where σ represents the context and $\mathsf{x} \in L$ is the actual data flow value. We call a pair $\langle \sigma, \mathsf{x} \rangle$ a *qualified data flow value* and denote it by X to distinguish it from x. In some cases, X may be a set of pairs $\langle \sigma, \alpha \rangle$ where $\alpha \in \Sigma$ is an entity. Where the context of usage is sufficient to distinguish between the two, we drop the adjective "qualified" and refer to both X and x as data flow values.

DEFINITION 9.4 *A path ρ in a supergraph is:*

- *An intraprocedural segment if ρ contains intraprocedural nodes only.*
- *A call segment if ρ contains intraprocedural nodes and at least one call node but no return node.*
- *A return segment if ρ contains intraprocedural nodes and at least one return node but no call node.*
- *A symmetric segment if ρ is an interprocedurally valid path from a call node C_i in procedure r to a return node R_j also in procedure r.*

An intraprocedural segment does not alter the context in a qualified data flow value whereas call and return segments do. A symmetric segment represents a sequence of finished calls—it alters the context within the segment but restores it at the end of the segment.

Apart from handling context, an interprocedural analysis must also handle scope rules and parameter passing mechanisms. These issues are handled as explained in Section 8.2. For simplicity, we assume that our programs have only global variables.

9.2 Interprocedural Analysis Using Restricted Contexts

Bit vector frameworks have special properties that make it possible to perform interprocedural analysis by remembering a restricted amount of context. The two key insights that this algorithm uses are:

- For bit vector frameworks, the default value of an entity α at a program point u, denoted $\widehat{\mathsf{x}}_u^{\alpha}$, can be considered as $\widehat{\top}$. If it becomes $\widehat{\bot}$, then it is sufficient to make $\widehat{\mathsf{x}}_v^{\alpha} = \widehat{\bot}$ for all $v \in \mathsf{neighbours}(u)$ such that $\widehat{f_\alpha}^{u \to v}$ is $\widehat{\phi}_{id}$. This effect needs to be propagated transitively.
- This propagation can be done independently of any other *ifp*. Thus there is no need to consider any other *ifp* of α or any *ifp* of some other entity β.

This allows fully context sensitive analysis by restricting the length of calling context σ to 1 at each call point in a sequence of calls. Reconstructing the calling contexts transitively along a call chain does not introduce any imprecision—it is possible to propagate different synthesized data flow information from a procedure to different callers of the procedure.

Let the qualified data flow value X_u at a program point u in procedure r be a set of tuples $\langle \psi, \alpha \rangle$ where α is the entity whose data flow value at u is $\widehat{\bot}$ and ψ is the context information which is either a call site $c_i \in \mathit{CallsTo}_r$ or "$*$". When ψ is c_i, the data flow value $\widehat{\mathsf{x}}_u^{\alpha} = \widehat{\bot}$ is inherited by r from the call at c_i. When ψ is $*$, the data flow value $\widehat{\mathsf{x}}_u^{\alpha} = \widehat{\bot}$ is synthesized in r or in some procedure called from within r. The main difference between the two is that a data flow value qualified by c_i can only be propagated to the caller containing the call site c_i whereas the data flow value qualified by $*$ should be propagated to all callers of r.

The exact criteria of propagation of $\widehat{\bot}$ values in a supergraph for a forward data flow framework is as described below. For backward data flows, the roles of C_i and R_i should be interchanged.

- When a pair $\langle \psi, \alpha \rangle$ reaches an intraprocedural node n,
  - If $\widehat{f_n}^{\alpha} = \widehat{\phi}_{\top}$, $\langle \psi, \alpha \rangle$ should not be propagated any further.
  - If $\widehat{f_n}^{\alpha} = \widehat{\phi}_{\bot}$, it indicates generation of synthesized data flow information. Hence the pair $\langle \psi, \alpha \rangle$ must be replaced by the pair $\langle *, \alpha \rangle$.
  - If $\widehat{f_n}^{\alpha} = \widehat{\phi}_{id}$, the pair $\langle \psi, \alpha \rangle$ must be propagated further.

- When a pair $\langle\psi,\alpha\rangle$ reaches a call node C_i in procedure r, the $\widehat{\bot}$ value of α must be propagated to the called procedure with c_i as the calling context. Thus the pair $\langle c_i,\alpha\rangle$ must be propagated further.
- When a pair $\langle\psi,\alpha\rangle$ reaches R_i in procedure r,
  - If ψ is $*$, the pair $\langle *,\alpha\rangle$ must be propagated further in r.
  - If ψ is c_i, the value $\widehat{\bot}$ of α has been inherited by r through the call site C_i so the $\widehat{\bot}$ value of α must be propagated further in the rest of r. However, the context from where its $\widehat{\bot}$ value reached C_i must be recovered. This is easily done by examining the pairs reaching C_i—if a pair $\langle\psi',\alpha\rangle$ reached C_i, then the required context is ψ'. Observe that ψ' could be another call site or could be $*$.
  - If ψ is some c_j other than c_i, it indicates traversal of an interprocedurally invalid path and the data flow value must be discarded. This is because the context information c_j represents the fact that C_j was the last call node traversed in the path so this qualified data flow value cannot reach any other return node; it must reach R_j where the calling context will be reconstructed.

We use IN_n and OUT_n to compute the qualified data flow values X; the conventional variables In_n and Out_n continue to contain the underlying data flow values $\mathsf{x} \in L$. The data flow equations are:

$$\mathsf{IN}_n = \begin{cases} \{\langle *,\alpha\rangle \mid \alpha \text{ is } \widehat{\bot} \text{ in } \mathsf{BI}\} & n \text{ is } \mathsf{Start}_{main} \\ \bigcup\limits_{p \in pred(n)} \mathsf{OUT}_p & \text{otherwise} \end{cases} \tag{9.1}$$

$$\begin{aligned} \mathsf{OUT}_n = {} & \mathsf{ConstGEN}_n \cup \mathsf{DepGEN}_n(\mathsf{IN}_n) - \\ & (\mathsf{X} - (\mathsf{ConstKILL}_n - \mathsf{DepKILL}_n(\mathsf{IN}_n))) \end{aligned} \tag{9.2}$$

where the constant and dependent components are defined as follows:

$$\mathsf{ConstGEN}_n = \begin{cases} \emptyset & n \text{ is } C_i \text{ or } R_i \\ \{\langle *,\alpha\rangle \mid \widehat{f_n}^{\alpha} = \widehat{\phi}_{\bot}\} & \text{otherwise} \end{cases}$$

$$\mathsf{DepGEN}_n(\mathsf{X}) = \begin{cases} \{\langle c_i,\alpha\rangle \mid \langle\psi,\alpha\rangle \in \mathsf{X}\} & n \text{ is } C_i \\ \{\langle *,\alpha\rangle \mid \langle *,\alpha\rangle \in \mathsf{X}\} \cup \\ \{\langle\psi,\alpha\rangle \mid \langle c_i,\alpha\rangle \in \mathsf{X}, \langle\psi,\alpha\rangle \in \mathsf{IN}_{C_i}\} & n \text{ is } R_i \\ \emptyset & \text{otherwise} \end{cases}$$

$$\mathsf{ConstKILL}_n = \{\langle\psi,\alpha\rangle \mid \alpha \in \mathsf{Gen}_n \text{ or } \alpha \in \mathsf{Kill}_n\}$$

$$\mathsf{DepKILL}_n(\mathsf{X}) = \emptyset$$

Observe the use of the component function $\widehat{f_n}^{\alpha}$ for $\mathsf{ConstGEN}_n$. For data flow frameworks that use $\cup$ as $\sqcap$, $\widehat{f_n}^{\alpha}$ is $\widehat{\phi}_{\bot}$ if $\alpha \in \mathsf{Gen}_n$ whereas for data flow frameworks that

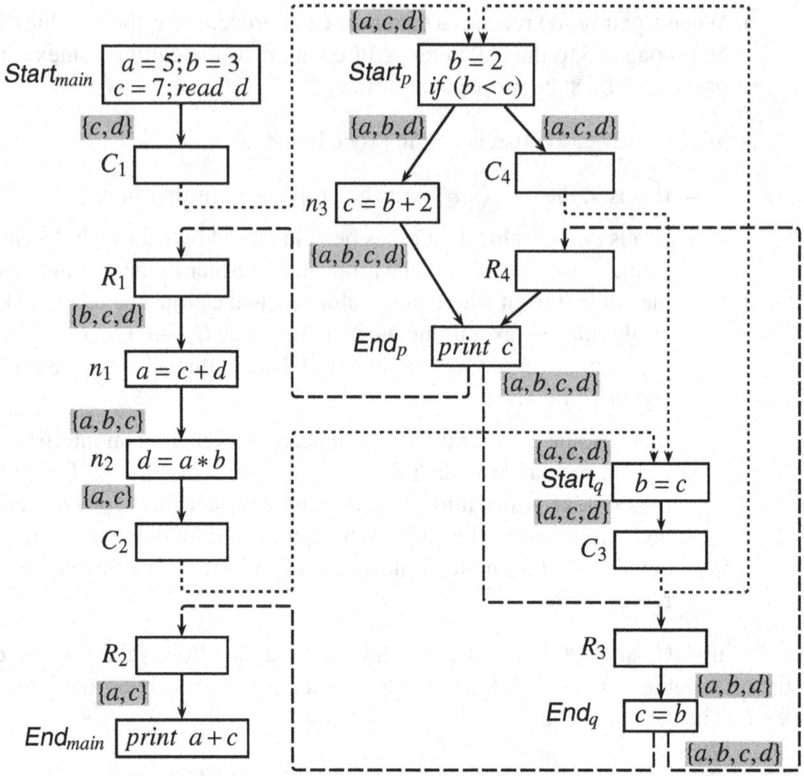

FIGURE 9.1
An example program for interprocedural live variables analysis.

use $\cap$ as $\sqcap$, it is $\widehat{\phi}_\perp$ if $\alpha \in Kill_n$ and $\alpha \notin Gen_n$. Also observe the use of IN_{C_i} in the definition of $DepGEN_n(X)$.

The final set of entities whose data flow values are $\widehat{\top}$ are extracted from

$$In_n = \left\{\alpha \mid \langle \psi, \alpha \rangle \in IN_n,\ \psi \in CallsTo_r \cup \{*\}\right\} \tag{9.3}$$

$$Out_n = \left\{\alpha \mid \langle \psi, \alpha \rangle \in OUT_n,\ \psi \in CallsTo_r \cup \{*\}\right\} \tag{9.4}$$

Example 9.1

Consider the program in Figure 9.1 for interprocedural liveness analysis. All variables are global variables. Variables that are live at a program point are shown in graph boxes. Observe that variable d is live in procedure q at $Start_q$ but not before its call in the *main* procedure. The use of d in block n_1 makes it live in procedure p. Since q is called from p and neither p nor q modify d,

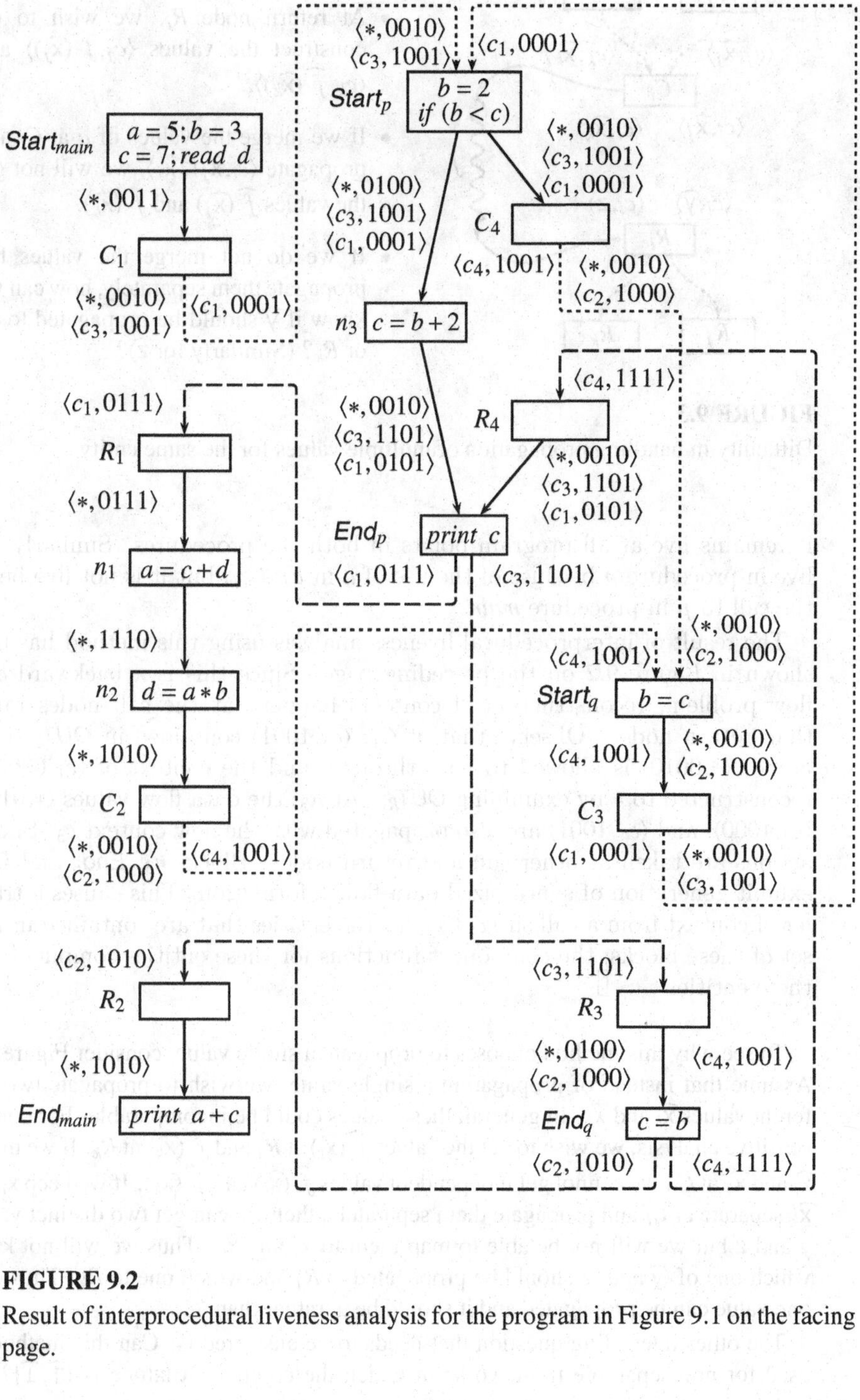

FIGURE 9.2

Result of interprocedural liveness analysis for the program in Figure 9.1 on the facing page.

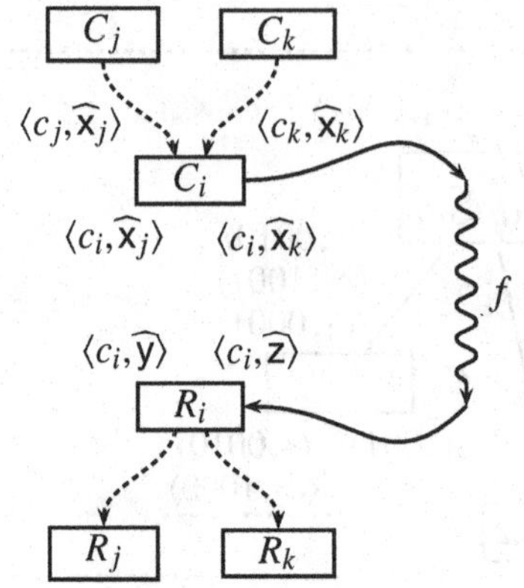

- At return node R_i, we wish to reconstruct the values $\langle c_j, \widehat{f}\,(\widehat{\mathsf{x}_j})\rangle$ and $\langle c_k, \widehat{f}\,(\widehat{\mathsf{x}_k})\rangle$.
- If we merge the values of a at C_i and propagate $\langle c_i, \widehat{\mathsf{x}_j} \sqcap \widehat{\mathsf{x}_k}\rangle$, we will not get the values $\widehat{f}\,(\widehat{\mathsf{x}_j})$ and $\widehat{f}\,(\widehat{\mathsf{x}_k})$.
- If we do not merge the values but propagate them separately, how can we know if $\widehat{\mathsf{y}}$ should be propagated to R_j or R_k? (Similarly for $\widehat{\mathsf{z}}$)?

FIGURE 9.3
Difficulty in handling propagation of multiple values for the same entity.

it remains live at all program points in both the procedures. Similarly, a is live in procedure p because of the use of a in $\textsf{End}_{main}$ but it is not live before the call to p in procedure *main*.

The result of interprocedural liveness analysis using this method has been shown in Figure 9.2 on the preceding page. Since this is a backward data flow problem, reconstruction of contexts happens at the call nodes rather than return nodes. Observe that at C_1, $\langle c_3, 1001\rangle$ contained in $\textsf{OUT}_{C_1}$ is ignored, $\langle *, 0010\rangle$ is allowed to pass through, and the context of $\langle c_1, 0001\rangle$ is reconstructed to $*$ by examining $\textsf{OUT}_{R_1}$. At R_3, the data flow values $\langle *, 0100\rangle$, $\langle c_2, 1000\rangle$, and $\langle c_4, 1001\rangle$ are also propagated with the new context c_3. Similar actions are taken at other call and return nodes. Blocks n_3, $\textsf{End}_p$ and $\textsf{End}_q$ exhibit generation of synthesized data flow information. This causes a transfer of context from a call site c_i to $*$ for the entities that are contained in $\textsf{Gen}$ set of these blocks; the component functions for these entities compute $\widehat{\bot}$ for these entities. □

To see why this method chooses to propagate a single value, consider Figure 9.3. Assume that instead of propagating a single value, we wish to propagate two different values $\widehat{\mathsf{x}_i}$ and $\widehat{\mathsf{x}_k}$. In general, these values could be incomparable. For context sensitive analysis, we wish to get the values $\widehat{f}\,(\widehat{\mathsf{x}_i})$ at R_j and $\widehat{f}\,(\widehat{\mathsf{x}_k})$ at R_k. If we merge $\widehat{\mathsf{x}_i}$ and $\widehat{\mathsf{x}_k}$ at C_i, we cannot get independent values $\widehat{f}\,(\widehat{\mathsf{x}_i})$ and $\widehat{f}\,(\widehat{\mathsf{x}_k})$. If we keep $\widehat{\mathsf{x}_i}$ and $\widehat{\mathsf{x}_k}$ separate at C_i and propagate them separately, then we can get two distinct values $\widehat{\mathsf{y}}$ and $\widehat{\mathsf{z}}$ but we will not be able to map them to $\widehat{\mathsf{x}_j}$ and $\widehat{\mathsf{x}_k}$. Thus we will not know which one of $\widehat{\mathsf{y}}$ and $\widehat{\mathsf{z}}$ should be propagated to R_j and which one to R_k. Thus only one value can be propagated and it should be $\widehat{\bot}$ rather than $\widehat{\top}$.

The other interesting question that needs to be answered is: Can this method be used for non-separable frameworks in which the component lattice is $\{\widehat{\top}, \widehat{\bot}\}$? To

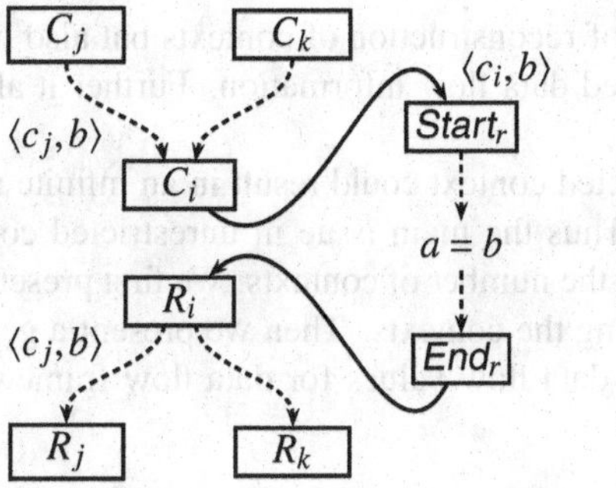

- From the calling context c_j, variable a is initialized but b is not.
- From the calling context c_k, both a and b are initialized.
- At R_i, data flow values of only the following forms are valid: $\langle *, \alpha \rangle$ and $\langle c_i, \alpha \rangle$.
- Our method can construct $\langle c_j, b \rangle$ at R_i but not $\langle c_j, a \rangle$.

FIGURE 9.4
Difficulty in reconstructing contexts for possibly uninitialized variables analysis.

see why propagating $\widehat{\bot}$ values using this method is not sufficient in the presence of non-separability, consider the problem of performing possibly uninitialized variables analysis as illustrated in Figure 9.4. A pair $\langle \psi, x \rangle$ indicates that variable x is possibly uninitialized and this fact has been discovered along the context ψ. The assignment $a = b$ dictates that a must be considered possibly uninitialized in all contexts in which b has been discovered to be possibly uninitialized. Even if we generate the pair $\langle c_i, a \rangle$ from the pair $\langle c_i, b \rangle$ after encountering the assignment statement $a = b$, there is no context information about a at C_i. Further, this method cannot handle general constraints that copy the context of b into the context of a whenever a context of b is reconstructed.

For the qualified data flow value X, the $\top$ is $\emptyset$. In order to establish that this method computes *MFP* assignment in terms of X, we only need to argue about the termination. It follows from the fact that at each call node, the incoming context information is overwritten by the call site. During analysis, the number of tuples representing the synthesized data flow information at any node in procedure r can at most be $|\mathbb{G}\mathsf{var}|$ and the number of tuples representing the inherited data flow information is bounded by $|\mathit{CallsTo}_r| \times |\mathbb{G}\mathsf{var}|$.

Since Equations (9.1) and (9.2) cover all paths, they cover all interprocedurally valid *ifp*s also. This ensures safety of data flow analysis. The precision follows from the fact that data flow analysis is restricted to interprocedurally valid paths only.

9.3 Interprocedural Analysis Using Unrestricted Contexts

The main limitation of interprocedural data flow analysis using a restricted context is that it requires reconstruction of context. This restricts the method to bit vector frameworks only. In this section we generalize the method to use unrestricted context. This not only eliminates the need of reconstruction of contexts but also of the special context $*$ to represent synthesized data flow information. Further it allows propagation of any data flow value.

In the presence of recursion, unrestricted context could result in an infinite number of unbounded length call strings. Thus the main issue in unrestricted context approach is how to bound the length and the number of contexts. We first present the method without any concern for bounding the contexts. Then we present a general method of bounding contexts based on data flow values for data flow frameworks with finite lattices.

9.3.1 Using Call Strings to Represent Unrestricted Contexts

The call strings method uses $X = \langle \sigma, \mathsf{x} \rangle$ as a qualified data flow value where σ is a call string representing a calling context. Special symbol λ denotes the empty call string. Concatenation $\lambda \cdot c_i$ results in the call string c_i.

The computation and propagation of qualified data flow value X is simpler in this method than in the previous method:

- If a pair $\langle \sigma, \mathsf{x} \rangle$ reaches C_i, the context σ is extended and the pair $\langle \sigma \cdot c_i, \mathsf{x} \rangle$ is propagated further.
- If a pair $\langle \sigma, \mathsf{x} \rangle$ reaches R_i, there are two possibilities:
  - If the last call site in σ is c_i, i.e. $\sigma = \sigma' \cdot c_i$, it indicates a matching C_i and R_i and thus represents an interprocedurally valid path. In such a situation, the pair $\langle \sigma', \mathsf{x} \rangle$ is propagated further. Note that σ' could be λ.
  - If the last call site in σ is not c_i, or σ is λ, it indicates an interprocedurally invalid path and the pair $\langle \sigma, \mathsf{x} \rangle$ should not be propagated further.
- If a pair $\langle \sigma, \mathsf{x} \rangle$ reaches an intraprocedural node n, the context does not change, only the data flow value changes. Let the flow function for block n be f_n. Then the pair $\langle \sigma, f_n(\mathsf{x}) \rangle$ should be propagated further.

There is no need of the special context $*$ because a call string remembers the call sites corresponding to all unfinished calls. This makes it possible to propagate synthesized data flow information to appropriate callers without the need of reconstructing contexts. Note that the above description does not guarantee termination of call strings in recursive programs; we address this issue independently.

Since this method propagates all values in L rather than only $\widehat{\top}$, multiple qualified data flow values reaching a node cannot be combined by plain set union. Instead, the data flow values associated with the same context must be merged. Thus the confluence of qualified data flow values is defined as follows:

$$
\begin{aligned}
X \uplus Y = \; & \{ \langle \sigma, \mathsf{x} \sqcap \mathsf{y} \rangle \mid \langle \sigma, \mathsf{x} \rangle \in X, \; \langle \sigma, \mathsf{y} \rangle \in Y \} \; \cup \\
& \{ \langle \sigma, \mathsf{x} \rangle \mid \langle \sigma, \mathsf{x} \rangle \in X, \; \forall \mathsf{z} \in L, \langle \sigma, \mathsf{z} \rangle \notin Y \} \; \cup \\
& \{ \langle \sigma, \mathsf{y} \rangle \mid \langle \sigma, \mathsf{y} \rangle \in Y, \; \forall \mathsf{z} \in L, \langle \sigma, \mathsf{z} \rangle \notin X \}
\end{aligned}
$$

The resulting data flow equations computing the qualified data flow values IN_n and OUT_n are as defined below:

$$IN_n = \begin{cases} \langle \lambda, BI \rangle & n \text{ is a } Start_{main} \\ \biguplus_{p \in pred(n)} OUT_p & \text{otherwise} \end{cases}$$

$$OUT_n = ConstGEN_n \cup DepGEN_n(IN_n) - (X - (ConstKILL_n - DepKILL_n(IN_n)))$$

where $ConstGEN_n = ConstKILL_n = DepKILL_n(X) = \emptyset$ and

$$DepGEN_n(X) = \begin{cases} \{\langle \sigma \cdot c_i, \mathsf{x} \rangle \mid \langle \sigma, \mathsf{x} \rangle \in X\} & n \text{ is } C_i \\ \{\langle \sigma, \mathsf{x} \rangle \mid \langle \sigma \cdot c_i, \mathsf{x} \rangle \in X\} & n \text{ is } R_i \\ \{\langle \sigma, f_n(\mathsf{x}) \rangle \mid \langle \sigma, \mathsf{x} \rangle \in X\} & \text{otherwise} \end{cases}$$

The above data flow equations should be taken as a specification of the computation to be performed. In practice, we use a work list based iterative algorithm for computed IN_n and OUT_n rather than a round-robin iterative algorithm. This is because the effect of a change does not affect the entire supergraph directly.

The final data flow values at a node n are:

$$In_n = \bigsqcap_{\langle \sigma, \mathsf{x} \rangle \in IN_n} \mathsf{x} \quad (9.5)$$

$$Out_n = \bigsqcap_{\langle \sigma, \mathsf{x} \rangle \in OUT_n} \mathsf{x} \quad (9.6)$$

Example 9.2

Consider the program in Figure 9.1 on page 298 for call strings based interprocedural liveness analysis. A partial result of this analysis is shown in Figure 9.5 on the next page. It is complete in the sense that it includes all live variables at all program points. However, it is partial in the sense that it does not enumerate all call strings. For example, $\langle c_2c_3c_4, 1010 \rangle$ and $\langle c_1c_4, 0011 \rangle$ contained in IN_{Start_q} could be propagated to OUT_{C_2}, only to be ignored at C_2 because these call strings do not end with c_2. However, some pairs that will not be ignored by the algorithm are $\langle c_2c_3c_4c_3, 1110 \rangle$ and $\langle c_1c_4c_3, 0111 \rangle$ that should be propagated from IN_{End_p} to OUT_{R_4} where new pairs $\langle c_2c_3c_4c_3c_4, 1110 \rangle$ and $\langle c_1c_4c_3c_4, 0111 \rangle$ would be created. This will further result in call strings $c_2c_3c_4c_3c_4c_3$ and $c_1c_4c_3c_4c_3$ and the construction of call strings will not terminate in spite of the fact that no new data flow information is generated.

Observe that in OUT_{Start_p}, the data flow information has been shown as $1100 + 1010$ and $0101 + 0011$ to highlight the fact that it is a merge of the data flow information propagated from the two successors of $Start_p$. □

Block	OUT_n	IN_n
End_m	$\langle\lambda, 0000\rangle$	$\langle\lambda, 1010\rangle$
R_2	$\langle\lambda, 1010\rangle$	$\langle c_2, 1010\rangle$
C_2	$\langle c_2, 1010\rangle$	$\langle\lambda, 1010\rangle$
n_2	$\langle\lambda, 1010\rangle$	$\langle\lambda, 1110\rangle$
n_1	$\langle\lambda, 1110\rangle$	$\langle\lambda, 0111\rangle$
R_1	$\langle\lambda, 0111\rangle$	$\langle c_1, 0111\rangle$
C_1	$\langle c_2c_3, 1010\rangle, \langle c_1, 0011\rangle$	$\langle\lambda, 0011\rangle$
$Start_m$	$\langle\lambda, 0011\rangle$	$\langle\lambda, 1111\rangle$
End_q	$\langle c_2, 1010\rangle, \langle c_2c_3c_4, 1110\rangle, \langle c_1c_4, 0111\rangle$	$\langle c_2, 1100\rangle, \langle c_2c_3c_4, 1100\rangle, \langle c_1c_4, 0101\rangle$
R_3	$\langle c_2, 1100\rangle, \langle c_2c_3c_4, 1100\rangle,$ $\langle c_1c_4, 0101\rangle$	$\langle c_2c_3, 1100\rangle, \langle c_2c_3c_4c_3, 1100\rangle,$ $\langle c_1c_4c_3, 0101\rangle$
C_3	$\langle c_2c_3, 1010\rangle, \langle c_1, 0011\rangle,$ $\langle c_2c_3c_4c_3, 1010\rangle, \langle c_1c_4c_3, 0011\rangle$	$\langle c_2, 1010\rangle,$ $\langle c_2c_3c_4, 1010\rangle, \langle c_1c_4, 0011\rangle$
$Start_q$	$\langle c_2, 1010\rangle, \langle c_2c_3c_4, 1010\rangle, \langle c_1c_4, 0011\rangle$	$\langle c_2, 1010\rangle, \langle c_2c_3c_4, 1010\rangle, \langle c_1c_4, 0011\rangle$
End_p	$\langle c_2c_3, 1100\rangle, \langle c_1, 0111\rangle,$ $\langle c_2c_3c_4c_3, 1100\rangle, \langle c_1c_4c_3, 0101\rangle$	$\langle c_2c_3, 1110\rangle, \langle c_1, 0111\rangle,$ $\langle c_2c_3c_4c_3, 1110\rangle, \langle c_1c_4c_3, 0111\rangle$
n_3	$\langle c_2c_3, 1110\rangle, \langle c_1, 0111\rangle,$ $\langle c_2c_3c_4c_3, 1110\rangle, \langle c_1c_4c_3, 0111\rangle$	$\langle c_2c_3, 1100\rangle, \langle c_1, 0101\rangle,$ $\langle c_2c_3c_4c_3, 1100\rangle, \langle c_1c_4c_3, 0101\rangle$
R_4	$\langle c_2c_3, 1110\rangle, \langle c_1, 0111\rangle$	$\langle c_2c_3c_4, 1110\rangle, \langle c_1c_4, 0111\rangle$
C_4	$\langle c_2, 1010\rangle, \langle c_2c_3c_4c_3, 1110\rangle,$ $\langle c_1c_4c_3, 0111\rangle, \langle c_2c_3c_4, 1010\rangle,$ $\langle c_1c_4, 0011\rangle$	$\langle c_2c_3, 1010\rangle, \langle c_1, 0011\rangle$
$Start_p$	$\langle c_2c_3, 1100 + 1010\rangle, \langle c_1, 0101 + 0011\rangle,$ $\langle c_2c_3c_4c_3, 1100\rangle, \langle c_1c_4c_3, 0101\rangle$	$\langle c_2c_3, 1010\rangle, \langle c_1, 0011\rangle,$ $\langle c_2c_3c_4c_3, 1010\rangle, \langle c_1c_4c_3, 0011\rangle$

FIGURE 9.5

Some call strings and associated values for interprocedural live variables analysis of our example program Figure 9.1 on page 298.

Example 9.3

Figure 9.6 on the facing page provides a recursive procedure *r* that reverses a linked list pointed to by the *head* pointer. Every call to *r* reverses the pointer of the *head* node by assigning the *previous* pointer and then moves the three pointers forward. As the recursion unwinds, the same operations are repeated nullifying the effect of the operations carried out before a recursive call was made. Thus, at the end of every call to *r*, regardless of the depth of recursion, the list is identical to what it was before the call.

Figure 9.7 on page 306 shows the points-to graphs for some contexts discovered by the call strings method. Call site c_1 represents a call from *main*, whereas c_2 represents the recursive call. The points-to graph associated with

```
0. void r()
1. {  /* Reverse the list */
2.    n = *h;
3.    *h = p;
4.    p = h;
5.    if (n != NULL)
6.    {  h = n;
7.       r();
8.    }
9.    else
10.   {  /* Reversed */
11.   {  p = NULL;
12.      n = NULL;
13.      /* Process it */
14.   }
15.      /* Reverse it again */
16.      n = *h;
17.      *h = p;
18.      p = h;
19.      h = n;
20. }
```


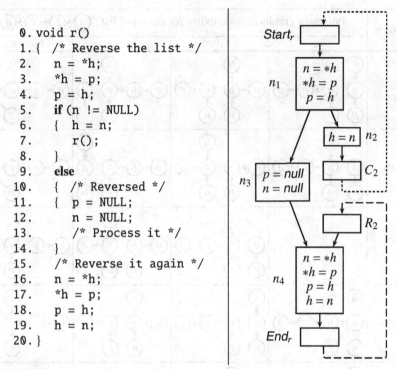

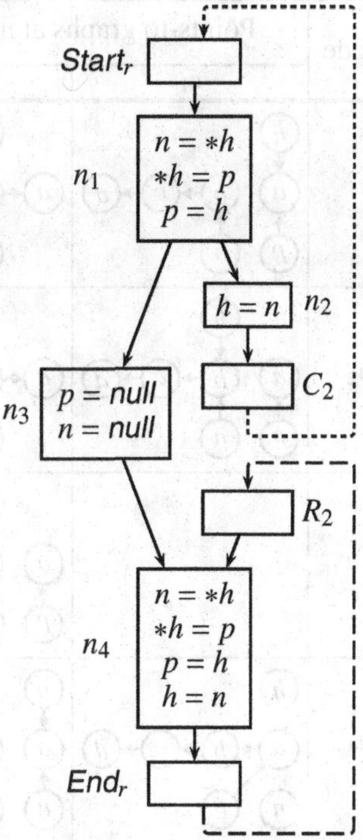

FIGURE 9.6

Example program for interprocedural points-to analysis. Pointer h is the *head* pointer, p is the *previous* pointer, and n is the *next* pointer.

End_r for the call string c_1 represents the data flow information returned to the *main* procedure confirming that two reversals of the list have restored the list to its original structure. This is possible because the call strings method remembers the history of calls. This ensures that the method traverses interprocedurally valid paths only: In every path reaching the *main* procedure, for every occurrence of $Start_r$ there is a matching End_r and vice-versa. Thus the number of times the flow function representing a single step of list reversal is applied remains equal for the control flow path entering the recursion and the control flow path leaving the recursion. ▯

9.3.2 Issues in Termination of Call String Construction

In non-recursive programs, only a finite number of call strings can be constructed and the termination of the method is governed solely by the convergence of data flow values associated with the call strings. In recursive programs, termination of call string construction needs to be ensured explicitly. Once the termination of call strings is ensured, the usual fixed point criterion of data flow values can be applied

Node	Points-to graphs at node exists for the input list $a \to b \to c \to d$			
	c_1	$c_1 c_2$	$c_1 c_2 c_2$	$c_1 c_2 c_2 c_2$
n_1				
n_2				
C_2				
n_4				
R_2				

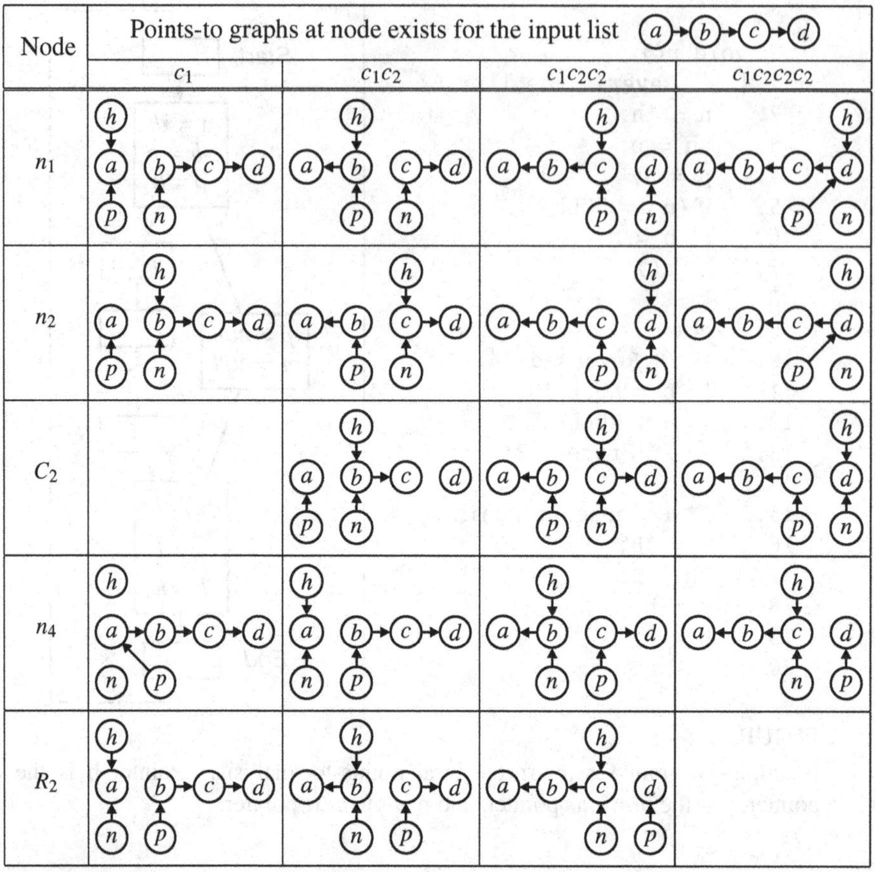

FIGURE 9.7

Points-to graphs in selected calling contexts. The *head* pointer points to variable a in the linked list.

to ensure the termination of analysis exactly as in iterative intraprocedural analysis.

A natural question that needs to be answered is whether call string construction can be terminated based on convergence of data flow values. In particular, we need to ascertain whether we need to continue constructing new call strings even when no new data flow information is generated for the new call strings. We have observed that in the case of intraprocedural analysis it is possible to compute the data flow values by a fixed point computation of the data flow variables associated with the nodes in a loop. The main difference between recursive contexts and loops is separation of data space. However, if we restrict ourselves to global variables only, is it possible to perform a fixed point computation of call strings? The next example shows that if call strings construction is stopped when data flow values reach a fixed point, it may result in an unsafe solution.

```
 0. int a,b,c;
 1.
 2. void main()
 3. { c = a*b;
 4.    p();
 5. }
 6.
 7. void p()
 8. { if (...)
 9.    { p();
10.       a = a*b;
11.    }
12. }
```


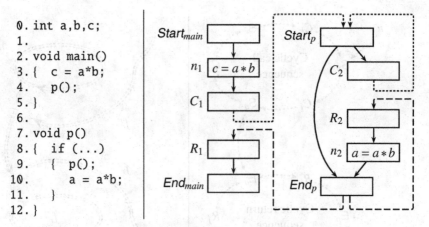

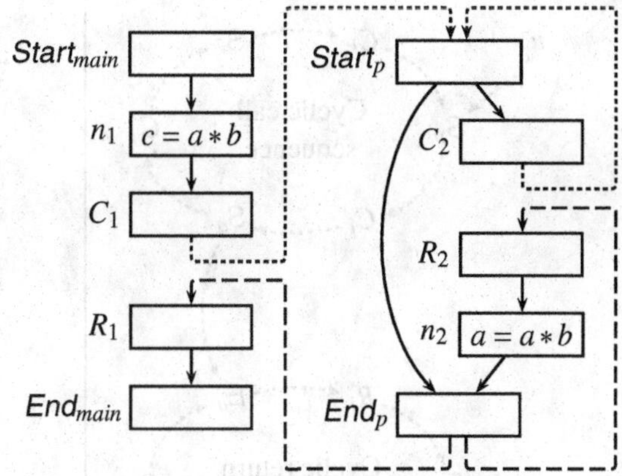

Constructed call strings	Block	Iteration #1		Iteration #2	
		IN_n	OUT_n	IN_n	OUT_n
$\langle c_1,1 \rangle$, $\langle c_1 c_2,1 \rangle$	R_2	$\langle c_1,1 \rangle$, $\langle c_1 c_2,1 \rangle$	$\langle c_1,1 \rangle$	$\langle c_1,0 \rangle$, $\langle c_1 c_2,1 \rangle$	$\langle c_1,1 \rangle$
	n_2	$\langle c_1,1 \rangle$	$\langle c_1,0 \rangle$	$\langle c_1,1 \rangle$	$\langle c_1,0 \rangle$
	End_p	$\langle c_1,0 \rangle$, $\langle c_1 c_2,1 \rangle$	$\langle c_1,0 \rangle$, $\langle c_1 c_2,1 \rangle$	$\langle c_1,0 \rangle$, $\langle c_1 c_2,1 \rangle$	$\langle c_1,0 \rangle$, $\langle c_1 c_2,0 \rangle$
$\langle c_1,1 \rangle$, $\langle c_1 c_2,1 \rangle$, $\langle c_1 c_2 c_2,1 \rangle$	R_2	$\langle c_1,1 \rangle$, $\langle c_1 c_2,1 \rangle$, $\langle c_1 c_2 c_2,1 \rangle$	$\langle c_1,1 \rangle$, $\langle c_1 c_2,1 \rangle$	$\langle c_1,0 \rangle$, $\langle c_1 c_2,0 \rangle$, $\langle c_1 c_2 c_2,1 \rangle$	$\langle c_1,0 \rangle$, $\langle c_1 c_2,1 \rangle$
	n_2	$\langle c_1,1 \rangle$, $\langle c_1 c_2,1 \rangle$	$\langle c_1,0 \rangle$, $\langle c_1 c_2,0 \rangle$	$\langle c_1,0 \rangle$, $\langle c_1 c_2,1 \rangle$	$\langle c_1,0 \rangle$, $\langle c_1 c_2,0 \rangle$
	End_p	$\langle c_1,0 \rangle$, $\langle c_1 c_2,0 \rangle$, $\langle c_1 c_2 c_2,1 \rangle$	$\langle c_1,0 \rangle$, $\langle c_1 c_2,0 \rangle$, $\langle c_1 c_2 c_2,1 \rangle$	$\langle c_1,0 \rangle$, $\langle c_1 c_2,0 \rangle$, $\langle c_1 c_2 c_2,1 \rangle$	$\langle c_1,0 \rangle$, $\langle c_1 c_2,0 \rangle$, $\langle c_1 c_2 c_2,1 \rangle$

FIGURE 9.8

Available expressions analysis using call strings approach. Unless call string $c_1 c_2 c_2$ is constructed, it is not possible to find out that $a * b$ is not available at $Entry(n_2)$.

Example 9.4

Consider the program in Figure 9.8. Since variable a is modified in n_2 and is a global variable, the expression $a * b$ is not available at the entry of n_2 in any call of procedure p except for the most deeply nested call from which the recursion starts unwinding. When the call strings based method constructs call string $c_1 c_2$, the expression is available. When the pair $\langle c_1 c_2,1 \rangle$ reaches R_2, call site c_2 is removed and the data flow value is passed on through the pair $\langle c_1,1 \rangle$. At the exit of n_2, the qualified data flow value becomes $\langle c_1,0 \rangle$ and is propagated to both R_1 and R_2. However since the last call site c_1 does not

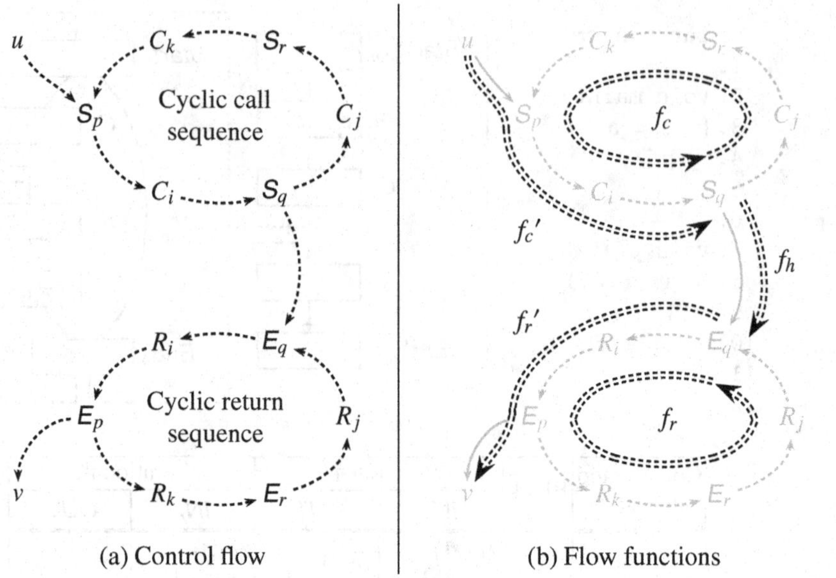

FIGURE 9.9
Modelling recursion. *Start*$_r$ and *End*$_r$ for procedure r are abbreviated by S_r and E_r.

correspond to R_2, this qualified value is ignored at R_2. Thus the only way we can get the data flow value 0 at *Entry*(n_2) is by ensuring that the cycle ($R_2, n_2, \mathit{End}_p, R_2$) is traversed at least once more. This is not possible unless call string $c_1c_2c_2$ is constructed in the cycle ($C_2, \mathit{Start}_p, C_2$).

In terms of information flow paths, our analysis must cover the following *ifp*: $O_{n_2} \rightarrow I_{End_p} \rightarrow O_{End_p} \rightarrow I_{R_2} \rightarrow O_{R_2} \rightarrow I_{n_2}$ where I_{n_i} and O_{n_i} denote *Entry*(n_i) and *Exit*(n_i) respectively. Observe that node n_2 can be reached only via R_2 and the two occurrence of R_2 require at least two occurrences of C_2. The shortest interprocedurally valid path that covers this *ifp* is:

$$(\mathit{Start}_m, n_1, C_1, \mathit{Start}_p, C_2, \mathit{Start}_p, C_2, \mathit{Start}_p, \mathit{End}_p, R_2, n_2, \mathit{End}_p, R_2, n_2)$$

The call string corresponding to this *ifp* is $c_1c_2c_2$. □

This situation arises because a recursive call sequence in a program consists of two loops rather than one as illustrated in Figure 9.9. The first loop represents the control flow entering the recursive call while the other loop represents the control flow leaving the recursive calls. We call them as *cyclic call sequence* and *cyclic return sequence* respectively. We denote the flow functions associated with them by f_c and f_r respectively. The dashed line from *Start*$_q$ to *End*$_q$ represents the recursion ending control flow path and the flow function associated with it is denoted by f_h. Since we do not require the call sites along a cyclic call sequence to be distinct, this figure models a general recursive path. In the most general case, there could be a path from the cyclic return sequence to the cyclic call sequence if there exists a recursive

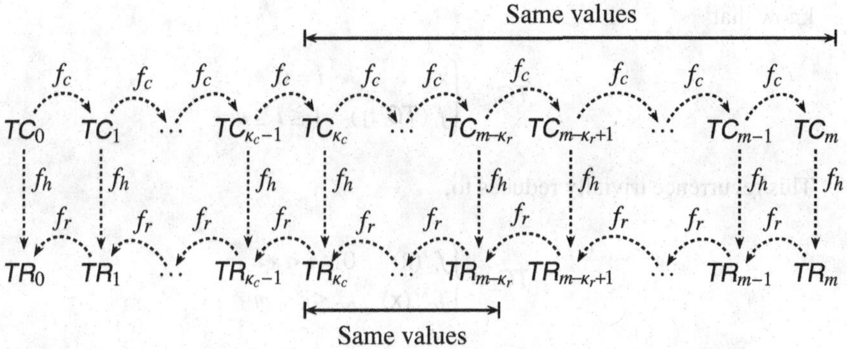

FIGURE 9.10
Computation of data flow values along recursive paths. Dashed arrows indicate function applications.

call within a loop. Since we do not require f_c, f_r, and f_h to be independent, this does not affect our Modelling.

In a valid interprocedural path from u to any program point in the recursive procedures, the cyclic call sequence must be traversed at least as many times as the cyclic return sequence. For a valid interprocedural path from u to v, the cyclic call sequence must be traversed exactly as least as many times as the cyclic return sequence.

For forward data flow problems, call strings are constructed when the cyclic call sequence is traversed. Let the sequence of call sites $(\ldots c_i \ldots c_j \ldots c_k \ldots)$ along the cyclic call sequence from $Start_q$ back to $Start_q$ be represented by σ_c. Each application of f_c suffixes σ_c to every call string reaching $Start_q$. These call strings are consumed when the corresponding cyclic return sequence is traversed. Each application of f_r requires traversing the cyclic return sequence once. In the process, the last occurrence of σ_c is removed from every call string. Thus, f_r can be applied only as many times as the maximum number of σ_c in any call string reaching the entry of End_p. Note that the application of f_c does not have such a requirement because the call strings are constructed rather than consumed while applying f_c.

In order to guarantee safety of interprocedural data flow analysis, the call strings should be long enough to allow computation of all possible data flow values in both cyclic call and return sequences. We quantify this length in terms of a *fixed point closure bound*. A fixed point closure bound of a function h is the smallest number $n > 0$ such that $\forall x, h^{n+1}(x) = h^n(x)$.

Let the fixed point closure bound of f_c be κ_c and that of f_r be κ_r. Let the number of occurrences of σ_c in the longest call string be $m > \kappa_c$. Let the qualified data flow value reaching $Start_q$ in Figure 9.9 on the facing page be $\langle \sigma, \mathsf{x} \rangle$. Let the sequence of the qualified data flow values computed at $Start_q$ be denoted by $\langle \sigma \cdot \sigma_c^i, TC_i \rangle$. We know that

$$TC_i = \begin{cases} \mathsf{x} & i = 0 \\ f_c(TC_{i-1}) & 1 \le i \le m \end{cases}$$

This recurrence trivially reduces to:

$$TC_i = \begin{cases} f_c{}^i(\mathsf{x}) & 0 \le i < \kappa_c \\ f_c{}^{\kappa_c}(\mathsf{x}) & \kappa_c \le i \le m \end{cases}$$

Let the sequence of the qualified data flow values computed at End_q be denoted by $\langle \sigma \cdot \sigma_c^i, TR_i \rangle$. Then,

$$TR_i = \begin{cases} f_h(TC_i) \sqcap f_r(TR_{i+1}) & 0 \le i < m \\ f_h(TC_i) & i = m \end{cases}$$

The first term of $\sqcap$ represents the data flow value along the path from $Start_q$ to End_q whereas the second term represents the data flow value computed along the cyclic return sequence. On substituting the values of TC_i, we get

$$TR_i = \begin{cases} TR_i \sqcap f_r(TR_{i+1}) & 0 \le i < \kappa_c \\ TR_m \sqcap f_r(TR_{i+1}) & \kappa_c \le i < m \\ f_h(f_c{}^{\kappa_c}(\mathsf{x})) & i = m \end{cases} \tag{9.7}$$

Since TR_i depends on TR_{i+1}, the final computation in cyclic return sequence starts from the last call string as illustrated in Figure 9.10 on the previous page. Clearly, m should be at least $\kappa_c + \kappa_r$. If $m < \kappa_c + \kappa_r$, then some data flow values corresponding to unbounded recursion may not be computed. However, the values of κ_c and κ_r are not known a priori, and there should be some way of terminating the construction of call strings.

Example 9.5

Consider the program of Figure 9.6 on page 305. Flow function f_c is the composition of the flow functions for n_1 and n_2, f_h is the composition of the flow functions for n_1, n_3, and n_4, whereas f_r is the flow function for block n_4. If we ignore the *head* pointer which is conditionally advanced in the cyclic call sequence, $f_r{}^i(f_h{}^i(\mathsf{x})) = \mathsf{x}$. Further, for the given input value x (consisting of a linked list of 4 elements), $\kappa_c = \kappa_r = 4$. Because of these reasons, it is sufficient to use $m = 4$ in this special case and stop call string construction when $c_1c_2c_2c_2c_2$ is created. This can be readily verified from Figure 9.7 on page 306. In the general case, m should be larger then $\kappa_c + \kappa_r$ for all values of κ_c and κ_r. □

9.4 Bounding Unrestricted Contexts Using Data Flow Values

A simple approach of allowing unrestricted call strings and yet bounding the overall set of call strings is to maintain in each procedure r, a single representative call string for each possible value in the lattice. This technique is deceptively simple and requires elaborate explanation. We outline the basis of this simple idea in terms of the following fundamental invariants of the call strings method:

- We observe that the same set of call strings reaches all program points in a procedure although they may have different values associated with them. As a consequence, if a mechanism is devised to ignore some call strings in a procedure (e.g., to represent them by other call strings), it would be possible to reconstruct them wherever they are required.

- If the call strings reaching a procedure are partitioned on the basis of data flow values, the equivalence classes remain unchanged in the procedure (the data flow value associated with an equivalence class may be different at different program point). More call strings may be included in an equivalence class across procedure calls because of construction of additional call strings.

- Finally, if there is a way of computing the correct value of $\sigma \cdot \sigma_c^{\kappa_c}$ at End_p, call strings $\sigma \cdot \sigma^i$, $\kappa_c < i \leq m$ need not be constructed. Further, there is not need to regenerate them explicitly; their implicit regeneration can be simulated by iterative computation of data flow values.

9.4.1 Call String Invariants

This section proves the call string invariants; the actual details of the method are presented in Section 9.4.2.

DEFINITION 9.5 *A context defining path from program point u to program point v is a valid interprocedural path from u to v that consists of only intraprocedural segments, call segments, or symmetric segments.*

If a context defining path contains return segments, they are suffixes of symmetric segments. For the purpose of our discussion, we restrict a context defining path to the significant nodes appearing in it. Thus each adjacent pair of nodes in a context defining path may correspond to many distinct intraprocedural segments.

DEFINITION 9.6 *A program point v is context dependent on program point u, denoted $v \in Cd(u)$, if there is a context defining path from u to v.*

Given procedure r, $\mathsf{Cd}(\mathsf{Start}_r)$ contains all program points within r and all program points within all callees in every call chain starting in r. For $v \in \mathsf{Cd}(u)$, we use $\mathsf{Cdp}(u,v)$ to denote the set of context defining paths from u to v and $\mathsf{Cs}(u,v)$ to denote the set of call strings corresponding to paths in $\mathsf{Cdp}(u,v)$.

Let $\mathsf{dfVal}(\sigma,u)$ denote the value associated with call string σ at program point u.

DEFINITION 9.7 *Call strings σ_1 and σ_2 are equivalent at program point u, denoted $\sigma_1 \stackrel{u}{=} \sigma_2$, if $\{\sigma_1,\sigma_2\} \subseteq \mathsf{Cs}(\mathsf{Start}_{main},u)$ and $\mathsf{dfVal}(\sigma_1,u) = \mathsf{dfVal}(\sigma_2,u)$.*

We assume that the work list based interprocedural analysis traverses interprocedural paths such that all intraprocedural segments are processed completely before propagating data flow information from a significant node to another significant node. This can be achieved by maintaining two separate work lists: One for intraprocedural nodes and the other for significant nodes. A significant node is selected for processing only after ensuring that the work list of intraprocedural nodes is empty. We call such an interprocedural analysis algorithm as being *intraprocedurally eager*.

LEMMA 9.1
The calling contexts of all intraprocedural program points in a procedure are identical.

PROOF Obvious. ▮

Calling contexts of a procedure depend on the callers so they cannot be different for different program points within the procedure. For a given call site $c_i \in \mathsf{CallsIn}_r$, $\mathsf{Exit}(C_i)$ and $\mathsf{Entry}(R_i)$ are assumed to logically belong to the callee procedure rather than r.

The following lemma shows that if σ_1 and σ_2 are transformed in the same manner by following the same set of paths, the values associated with them will also be transformed in the same manner and will continue to remain equal.

LEMMA 9.2
Consider a program point $v \in \mathsf{Cd}(u)$. Assume that the recursive paths in $\mathsf{Cdp}(u,v)$ are unbounded. When the work list of intraprocedural nodes is empty in an intraprocedurally eager call strings based method,

$$\sigma_1 \stackrel{u}{=} \sigma_2 \Rightarrow \forall \sigma \in \mathsf{Cs}(u,v),\ (\sigma_1 \cdot \sigma) \stackrel{v}{=} (\sigma_2 \cdot \sigma)$$

PROOF There are two cases to consider:

1. There is only one context defining path in $\mathsf{Cdp}(u,v)$ leading to a single sequence σ of call nodes that can be suffixed to both σ_1 and σ_2.

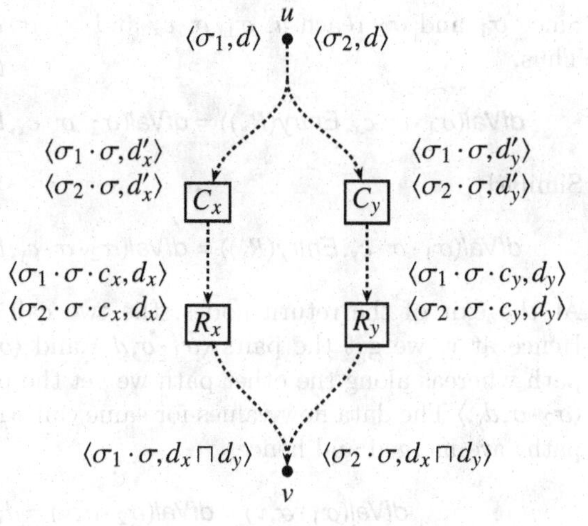

FIGURE 9.11
Case 2 for Lemma 9.2.

In this case, the eager interprocedural analysis algorithm traverses exactly the same set of paths from u to v for computing the data flow information associated with the call strings $\sigma_1 \cdot \sigma$ and $\sigma_2 \cdot \sigma$. Thus the data flow values along the call strings $\sigma_1 \cdot \sigma$ and $\sigma_2 \cdot \sigma$ undergo the same change. Clearly,

$$\mathit{dfVal}(\sigma_1, u) = \mathit{dfVal}(\sigma_2, u) \Rightarrow \mathit{dfVal}(\sigma_1 \cdot \sigma, v) = \mathit{dfVal}(\sigma_2 \cdot \sigma, v)$$

2. $\mathit{Cdp}(u, v)$ contains multiple context defining paths corresponding to σ.
   We prove this case by induction on the length of the maximal common suffix of all paths in $\mathit{Cdp}(u, v)$ which correspond to σ.

   - *Basis*. The basis is the case when there is no common suffix.
     For simplicity, assume that we have only two paths corresponding to σ as illustrated in Figure 9.11. Without any loss of generality, assume that R_x and R_y are the last nodes which are different.* Since both the paths from u to v correspond to a common call string σ, $\mathit{Cs}(u, \mathit{Entry}(R_x))$ contains a call string $\sigma \cdot c_x$ and $\mathit{Cs}(u, \mathit{Entry}(R_y))$ contains a call string $\sigma \cdot c_y$.
     Let $\mathit{dfVal}(\sigma_1, u) = \mathit{dfVal}(\sigma_2, u) = d$. Assume that the path segment from u to $\mathit{Entry}(R_x)$ changes this value to d_x and the path segment from u to $\mathit{Entry}(R_y)$ changes this value to d_y.

*If two context defining paths differ in call nodes which are not followed by matching return nodes, then the two paths would not correspond to the same call string.

Since σ_1 and σ_2 reach u, $\sigma_1 \cdot \sigma \cdot c_x$ and $\sigma_2 \cdot \sigma \cdot c_x$ reach $\mathit{Entry}(R_x)$. Thus,

$$\mathit{dfVal}(\sigma_1 \cdot \sigma \cdot c_x, \mathit{Entry}(R_x)) = \mathit{dfVal}(\sigma_2 \cdot \sigma \cdot c_x, \mathit{Entry}(R_x)) = d_x$$

Similarly,

$$\mathit{dfVal}(\sigma_1 \cdot \sigma \cdot c_y, \mathit{Entry}(R_y)) = \mathit{dfVal}(\sigma_2 \cdot \sigma \cdot c_y, \mathit{Entry}(R_y)) = d_y$$

At the exit of the return nodes, the two call sites are removed. Hence at v, we get the pairs $\langle \sigma_1 \cdot \sigma, d_x \rangle$ and $\langle \sigma_2 \cdot \sigma, d_x \rangle$ along one path whereas along the other path we get the pairs $\langle \sigma_1 \cdot \sigma, d_y \rangle$ and $\langle \sigma_2 \cdot \sigma, d_y . \rangle$ The data flow values for same call strings from different paths are merged and hence

$$\mathit{dfVal}(\sigma_1 \cdot \sigma, v) = \mathit{dfVal}(\sigma_2 \cdot \sigma, v) = d_x \sqcap d_y$$

This proves the basis case for two paths. Extending it to more than two paths is easy due to the finiteness of L. If there is a recursive call in a path from u to v, there will be infinitely many context defining paths corresponding to σ, each with a different number of matchings of some call and return nodes. However, since L is finite, these paths can be partitioned based on the data flow values corresponding to the call strings $\sigma_1 \cdot \sigma$ and $\sigma_2 \cdot \sigma$. Thus we will have a finite merge and inducting on the number of values (or number of partitions of paths from u to v) serves the purpose.

- *Inductive step.* Assume that all paths in $\mathit{Cdp}(u, v)$ which correspond to σ have a non-empty common suffix. Assume further that the lemma holds for a maximal common suffix consisting of k nodes. To show that it holds for a common suffix of $k+1$ nodes, observe that since all call strings traverse essentially the same path segment from node k to node $k+1$, the data flow values associated with the call string will be modified in the same way. Since the data flow values are equal after k nodes, they remain equal after $k+1$ nodes.

∎

Note that this lemma assumes unbounded recursion. If call string construction is terminated after some repetition of cyclic call sequence (say m), then as illustrated in Figure 9.10 on page 309, the values of TR_i for $(m - \kappa_r + 1) \leq i \leq m$ are likely to be different in spite of the fact that the values of TC_i for the same range of i are identical $(f_c^{\kappa_c}(\mathsf{x}))$. The lemma holds for the values of TR_i for $\kappa_c \leq i < (m - \kappa_r + 1)$. However, this exception arising due to bounded call strings does not matter because the associated values follow a strictly descending chain and converge on the least value. Hence the result of the merge of $\mathit{TR}_i, \kappa_c \leq i \leq m$ is the same as the values in those ranges of i for which the above lemma holds.

Intuitively, the values of TR_i for $(m - \kappa_r + 1) \le i \le m$ follow a strictly descending chain because they are repeatedly computed using the same function and are merged with the same value ($f_c^{\kappa_c}(\mathsf{x})$ in our case) at each step. We prove this in the following lemma.

LEMMA 9.3
Assume that the call strings method constructs call strings long enough so that all call strings $\sigma \cdot \sigma_c^i$, $0 \le i \le m$ are constructed where $m \ge \kappa_c + \kappa_r$ for all possible values of κ_c and κ_r. Then,

$$\forall \kappa_r, \quad TR_{m-\kappa_r} \sqsubseteq TR_i, \quad m - \kappa_r \le i \le m$$

PROOF We prove this by inducting on the distance of i from m by rewriting TR_i, $m - \kappa_r \le i \le m$ as $TR_{m-j}, 0 \le j \le \kappa_r$ and by showing that

$$TR_{m-(j+1)} \sqsubseteq TR_{m-j}, \; 0 \le j < \kappa_r$$

The basis of induction is $j = 0$. Since $TR_{m-1} = TR_m \sqcap f_r(TR_m)$ it trivially follows that $TR_{m-1} \sqsubseteq TR_m$. For the inductive hypothesis, assume that $TR_{m-(j+1)} \sqsubseteq TR_{m-j}$. We need to show that $TR_{m-(j+2)} \sqsubseteq TR_{m-(j+1)}$. From the definition of TR_i,

$$TR_{m-(j+2)} = TR_m \sqcap f_r(TR_{m-(j+1)}) \qquad 0 \le j \le \kappa_r,\; m > \kappa_c + \kappa_r \qquad (9.8)$$
$$TR_{m-(j+1)} = TR_m \sqcap f_r(TR_{m-j}) \qquad 0 \le j \le \kappa_r,\; m > \kappa_c + \kappa_r \qquad (9.9)$$

From the inductive hypothesis and monotonicity of flow functions,

$$TR_{m-(j+1)} \sqsubseteq TR_{m-j} \Rightarrow f_r(TR_{m-(j+1)}) \sqsubseteq f_r(TR_{m-j})$$

The inductive step follows by comparing the right hand sides of Equations (9.8) and (9.9). ∎

Observe the role of κ_c in the above proof. Since TR_{κ_c-1} does not have the first term as $f_h(f_c^{\kappa_c}(\mathsf{x}))$ unlike TR_{κ_c}, a partial order relation between TR_{κ_c-1} and TR_{κ_c} cannot be established and lemma may not hold.

We have defined TC_i and TR_i for $Start_q$ and End_q in Figure 9.9 on page 308. In particular, the term TR_i for End_q involves a merge of the data flow values along the recursion ending path and the cyclic return sequence. For some other pair of program points, say $Start_r$ and End_r, the term TR_i may not be a merge of data flow values along two paths. However, the data flow values at all program point in the cyclic return sequence must converge. When the computation of a data flow value converges at a program point in a cycle, it must converge at each program point in the cycle. Further, the direction of convergence must be same for each program point.

This convergence immediately suggests that the data flow values associated with call strings $\sigma \cdot \sigma_c^i$, $\kappa_c \le i \le m$ are not required for the final data flow value in cyclic return sequences. This happens because when the data flow values that are being

$$x = \{a{\rightarrow}\{b\}, b{\rightarrow}\{c\}, c{\rightarrow}\{b\}\}$$
$$f^1(x) = \{a{\rightarrow}\{c\}, b{\rightarrow}\{c\}, c{\rightarrow}\{b\}\}$$
$$f^2(x) = \{a{\rightarrow}\{b\}, b{\rightarrow}\{c\}, c{\rightarrow}\{b\}\}$$
$$f^3(x) = \{a{\rightarrow}\{c\}, b{\rightarrow}\{c\}, c{\rightarrow}\{b\}\}$$

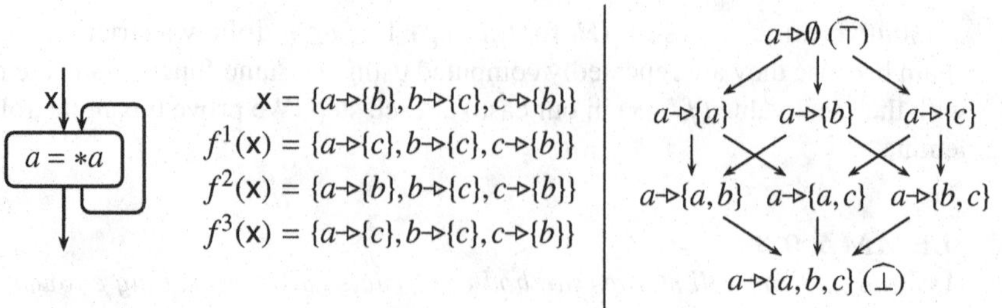

(a) x is a periodic point with a period 2 for the flow function for pointer assignment $a = *a$.

(b) Lattice of *may* points-to information for variable a

FIGURE 9.12

Flow functions in Points-to analysis. Data flow value $v{\rightarrow}S$ indicates that variable v may point to the variables contained in S.

merged follow a descending chain, only the last value in the chain matters in the overall merge and since our lattices are finite, all descending chains are finite and such a last value is guaranteed to exist.

THEOREM 9.1

Assume that the call strings method constructs call strings long enough so that all call strings $\sigma \cdot \sigma_c^i$, $0 \le i \le m$ constructed where $m \ge \kappa_c + \kappa_r$ for all possible values of κ_c and κ_r. Then for each program point v in a return sequence

$$\prod_{i=0}^{m} dfVal(\sigma \cdot \sigma_c^i, v) = \prod_{i=0}^{\max(\kappa_c)} dfVal(\sigma \cdot \sigma_c^i, v)$$

PROOF   The values $dfVal(\sigma \cdot \sigma_c^i, v)$, $0 \le i < \kappa_c$ may be different. However, due to the convergence of data flow values for subsequent call strings,

$$dfVal(\sigma \cdot \sigma_c^i, v) = dfVal(\sigma \cdot \sigma_c^{i+1}, v), \ \kappa_c \le i < m - \kappa_r$$

Thus $dfVal(\sigma \cdot \sigma_c^{\kappa_c}, v)$ is the least value for $\kappa_c \le i \le m$. Hence it is sufficient to merge the values of all call strings up to κ_c number of occurrence of σ_c.   ∎

An aside on flow function with periodic points

For a given function h and a value x, if $h^n(x) = x$ and $h^i(x) \ne x$, $0 < i < n$, then x is a *periodic point* of h with period n. A fixed point is a periodic point of period one. In general, flow functions can have periodic points of larger periods even if the functions are monotonic. This is possible only when functions compute incomparable values. Figure 9.12 shows an example of such a flow function from *may* Points-to analysis. x is the data flow information reaching statement n from outside of the loop. Observe that f_n computes incomparable values in all successive applications.

We have restricted the discussion in this chapter to flow functions with period one. Extending the arguments to functions of larger periods is easy. Consider a flow

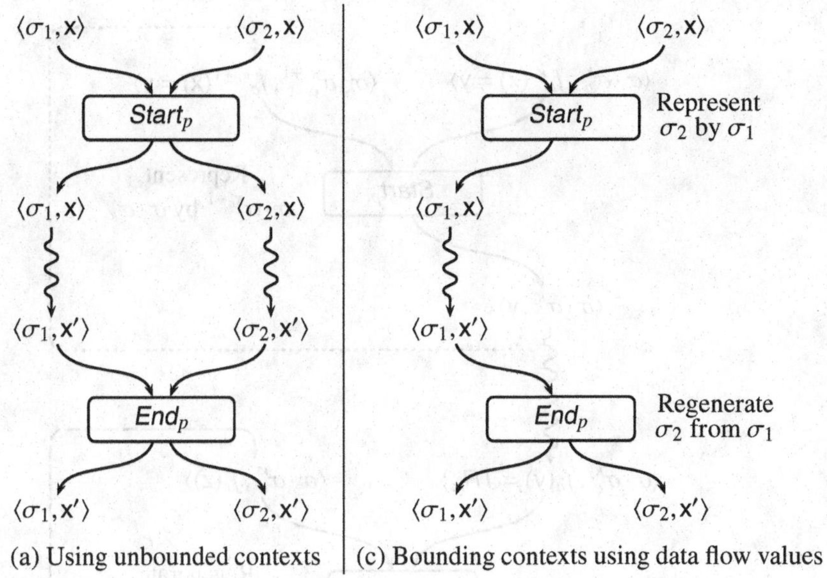

FIGURE 9.13
Representation and regeneration of equivalent call strings.

function which has period n for the incoming data flow value. Then, there are n periodic points instead of 1. In such a situation, instead of

$$\mathit{dfVal}(\sigma \cdot \sigma^{i+1}, \mathit{Start}_p) = \mathit{dfVal}(\sigma \cdot \sigma^{i}, \mathit{Start}_p), \ \ \kappa_c \le i \le m$$

we have

$$\mathit{dfVal}(\sigma \cdot \sigma^{i+n}, \mathit{Start}_p) = \mathit{dfVal}(\sigma \cdot \sigma^{i}, \mathit{Start}_p), \ \ \kappa_c \le i \le m-n$$

The convergence holds for call strings corresponding to each periodic point independently. For periodic point i, Lemma 9.3 can be proved by inducting on the distance of the call string from the call string $\sigma \cdot \sigma^{m-i}$.

9.4.2 Value-Based Termination of Call String Construction

Given a set of cyclic call strings, Theorem 9.1 allows us to distinguish between two types of call strings:

- The call strings whose data flow values are relevant for the final result of data flow analysis. These call strings involve up to κ occurrences of any cyclic call sequence where κ is the largest possible value of κ_c.
- The call strings which facilitate a sufficient number of traversal over return segment to allow convergence of data flow values. These are the call strings

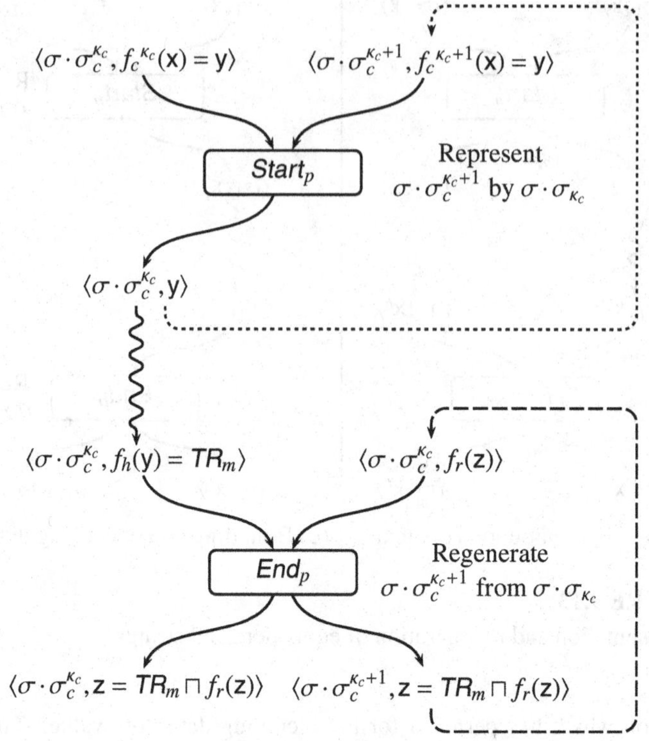

FIGURE 9.14
Representation and regeneration of cyclic call strings whose data flow values reach convergence in a cyclic call sequence. These call strings are used for convergence of data flow values in the corresponding cyclic return sequence.

> that contain κ' additional occurrences of cyclic return sequences where κ' is the largest possible value of κ_r.

If there is some way of allowing traversal of a cyclic return sequence as many times as may be required, we may be able to terminate construction of redundant call strings in the corresponding cyclic call sequence. This is achieved as follows:

> A single representative call string for an equivalence class within the scope of a maximal context dependent region is maintained and at the end of the region, all call strings belonging to each equivalence class are reconstructed. Some of them are constructed explicitly while some of them are constructed implicitly.

For procedure p, the decision of representation is taken at *Start$_p$*. This representation remains valid at all program points which are context dependent on *Start$_p$*.

End_p is the last such point and the call strings must be regenerated so that appropriate data flow values can be propagated to different callers of p. Similar to the scope of variables in a program, this representation may be "shadowed" by other context dependent regions created by procedure calls in the outer context dependent region.

Let $representative(x, Start_p)$ denote a uniquely selected call string which has value x at $Start_p$. The selection can be made based on some well defined criterion and the choice of this criterion is immaterial so long as it identifies a unique call string. One example of selecting a unique call string is to select the shortest call string from among the set of call strings that have the same data flow value. Another criterion could be to select the first call string that is listed in the associated data structure. The representation of call strings at $Start_p$ is defined as follows:

$$\forall \langle \sigma, x \rangle \in IN_{Start_p} : represent(\sigma, Start_p) = representative(x, Start_p)$$

The regeneration at End_p is performed as follows:

$$\begin{aligned} OUT_{Start_p} &= \{\langle represent(\sigma, Start_p), x\rangle \mid \langle \sigma, x\rangle \in IN_{Start_p}\} \\ regenerate(\sigma, End_p) &= \{\langle \sigma', y\rangle \mid represent(\sigma', Start_p) = \sigma, \langle \sigma, y\rangle \in IN_{End_p}\} \\ OUT_{End_p} &= \bigcup_{\langle \sigma, y\rangle \in IN_{End_p}} regenerate(\sigma, End_p) \end{aligned}$$

Regeneration copies the same data flow value to all call strings belonging to the same equivalence class. For general call strings this process has been illustrated in Figure 9.13 on page 317. For call strings in recursive programs, this process facilitates iterative computation of data flow values in cyclic return sequences without having to construct redundant call strings in the corresponding cyclic call sequence. This has been illustrated in Figure 9.14 on the preceding page.

The call string invariants presented in Section 9.4.1 are based on the following assumptions that should be honoured by work list based method used for call strings based interprocedural data flow analysis:

- The work list algorithm is assumed to be intraprocedurally eager. Hence data flow information should be propagated across procedure boundaries only when no further intraprocedural propagation is possible.

  This can be handled by maintaining separate work lists for intraprocedural nodes and significant nodes. A significant node should be selected by the method only when there is no pending intraprocedural node.

- It is assumed that the functions in cyclic return sequence are applied only after the data flow values in the corresponding cyclic call sequence have reached a convergence. This matters only in those cases when there is a path from a cyclic return sequence to a cyclic call sequence e.g., when a function call is contained in a loop.

  This can be handled by maintaining the following invariant in the work list of significant nodes: A call node always precedes any return node in the work list, regardless of when it is included in the work list.

Step No.	Selected Node	Qualified Data Flow Value IN_n	Qualified Data Flow Value OUT_n	Remaining Work List: Intraproc. Nodes	Remaining Work List: Significant Nodes
1	$Start_p$	$\langle c_1, 1\rangle$	$\langle c_1, 1\rangle$	End_p	C_2
2	End_p	$\langle c_1, 1\rangle$	$\langle c_1, 1\rangle$		C_2, R_2
3	C_2	$\langle c_1, 1\rangle$	$\langle c_1c_2, 1\rangle$	$Start_p$	R_2
4	$Start_p$	$\langle c_1, 1\rangle \langle c_1c_2, 1\rangle$	$\langle c_1, 1\rangle$	End_p	C_2, R_2
		(c_1c_2 is represented by c_1)			
5	End_p	$\langle c_1, 1\rangle$	$\langle c_1, 1\rangle\langle c_1c_2, 1\rangle$		C_2, R_2
		(c_1c_2 is regenerated from c_1)			
6	C_2	No change	No change		R_2
7	R_2	$\langle c_1, 1\rangle \langle c_1c_2, 1\rangle$	$\langle c_1, 1\rangle$	n_2	
8	n_2	$\langle c_1, 1\rangle$	$\langle c_1, 0\rangle$	End_p	
9	End_p	$\langle c_1, 0\rangle$	$\langle c_1, 0\rangle \langle c_1c_2, 0\rangle$		R_2
		(c_1c_2 is regenerated from c_1)			
10	R_2	$\langle c_1, 0\rangle \langle c_1c_2, 0\rangle$	$\langle c_1, 0\rangle$	n_2	
11	n_2	$\langle c_1, 0\rangle$	No change		

FIGURE 9.15
Interprocedural data flow analysis of example program in Figure 9.8 on page 307 using value-based termination of call string construction.

- When representation is performed, it is assumed that the corresponding regeneration is guaranteed to be performed.

  This can be ensured by adding End_r to the work list whenever representation is performed at $Start_r$; this includes the situation when an equivalence class remains same but the data flow value associated with the call strings in that equivalence class changes. It is possible that the data flow values do not change within procedure r after representation and hence End_r may never be added to the work list. In such a case, the new qualified data flow value may not be generated at End_p.

Example 9.6

Call strings based interprocedural data flow analysis using representation and regeneration of call strings for the example program in Figure 9.8 on page 307 has been illustrated in Figure 9.15. Observe that in step 2, R_2 is inserted in the work list after C_2 rather than before it. In step 4, $\langle c_1c_2, 1\rangle \in IN_{Start_p}$ is not propagated to OUT_{Start_p} as it is represented by $\langle c_1, 1\rangle$. At End_p $\langle c_1c_2, 1\rangle$ is regenerated. This reaches R_2 where c_2 is removed and the resulting qualified data flow value $\langle c_1, 1\rangle$ is propagated to n_2. Due to the assignment to a in n_2, this data flow value changes to $\langle c_1, 0\rangle$ and is propagated to End_p where it is merged with $\langle c_1, 1\rangle$ arriving from $Start_p$. This causes the value 0 to be propagated as $\langle c_1c_2,0\rangle$ and $\langle c_1,0\rangle$. A subsequent traversal over the return sequence ensures that the data flow value become 0 at $\mathit{Entry}(n_2)$ also. □

Representation and regeneration discards only those call strings which contain redundant values and performs the desired computation iteratively.

Recall that for the points-to analysis of program of Figure 9.6 on page 305, additional call strings are not required for convergence in cyclic return sequence. This does not influence our algorithm in any way; we leave it for the reader to verify that this method computes identical result as in Figure 9.7 on page 306.

THEOREM 9.2

The final data flow values computed by representing and regenerating call strings are identical to the values computed by a call strings method with an unbounded length call strings.

PROOF Regeneration explicitly constructs all acyclic call strings and all cyclic call strings containing κ_c+1 occurrences of σ_c. At End_p, $\sigma\cdot\sigma_c^{\kappa_c+1}$ is regenerated and the data flow value associated with $\sigma\cdot\sigma_c^{\kappa_c}$ is propagated to it. From Equation (9.7) and Figure 9.14 on page 318, this value is TR_m. This value is then propagated as $\langle\sigma\cdot\sigma_c^{\kappa_c+1}, \mathsf{z} = \mathit{TR}_m\rangle$ along the cyclic return sequence. This traversal removes the last occurrence of σ_c from $\sigma\cdot\sigma_c^{\kappa_c+1}$, computes $f_r(\mathsf{z})$, which is merged with the value of $\sigma\cdot\sigma_c^{\kappa_c}$ along the recursion ending path. Thus $\mathit{dfVal}(\sigma\cdot\sigma_c^{\kappa_c}, \mathit{End}_p) = \mathit{TR}_m \sqcap f_r(\mathit{TR}_m)$ after one traversal. This is same as the value associated with call string $\sigma\cdot\sigma_c^{m-1}$ where $m \geq \kappa_c+\kappa_r$. At End_p, this is again copied to the call string $\sigma\cdot\sigma_c^{\kappa_c+1}$ overwriting the previous value and the pair $\langle\sigma\cdot\sigma_c^{\kappa_c+1}, \mathsf{z} = \mathit{TR}_m \sqcap f_r(\mathit{TR}_m)\rangle$ is propagated along the cyclic return sequence. The process repeats as long as new values are computed for $\sigma\cdot\sigma_c^{\kappa_c}$; effectively, traversal i over the cyclic return sequence computes the value T_{m-i} for $\sigma\cdot\sigma_c^{\kappa_c}$. The process terminates after κ_r traversals. This computes the desired value for $\sigma\cdot\sigma_c^{\kappa_c}$. ∎

After the convergence of data flow values in a cyclic call sequence has been reached, this method replaces construction of the subsequent call strings by iteratively computing the data flow values in the corresponding cyclic return sequence using a pair of last two call strings.

Observe that representation is performed afresh every time any *Start* node is visited. On a subsequent visit to Start_p of procedure p, representation could change because of the following reasons:

- A new call string with the value of an existing call string reaches Start_p.
- A new call string with a new value reaches Start_p.
- A call string that had reached Start_p with a value x now reaches Start_p with a different value x'.

```
int a,b,c;

void main()
{  c = a*b;
   p();
}

void p()
{  while (...)
   {  p();
      a = a*b;
   }
}
```

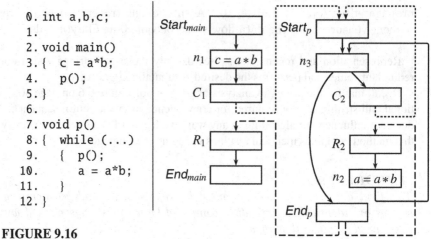

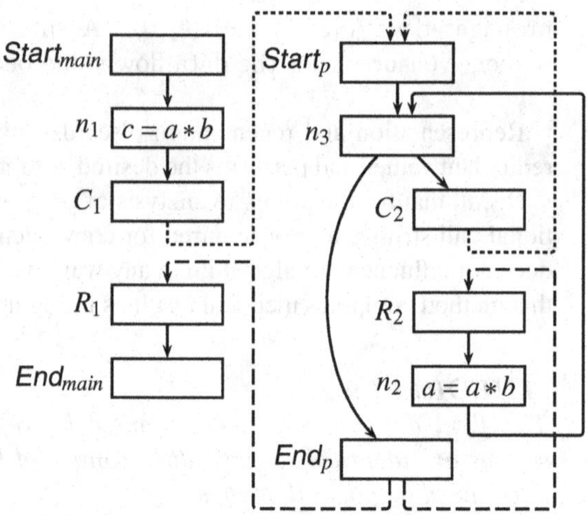

FIGURE 9.16

Modified program of Figure 9.8 on page 307. Expression $a * b$ is not available anywhere in procedure p.

In either case, End_p will be added to the work list. Thus all call strings will get regenerated with appropriate data flow values at End_p.

Example 9.7

Figure 9.16 contains a modified version of the program in Figure 9.8 on page 307. Since now the recursive call is in the loop, expression $a * b$ is unavailable in nodes Start_p and C_2 also. A trace of the call strings method using value-based termination has been provided below.

Step No.	Selected node	Qualified data flow value: IN_n	Qualified data flow value: OUT_n	Remaining work list: Intra. nodes	Remaining work list: Sig. nodes
1	Start_p	$\langle c_1, 1\rangle$	$\langle c_1, 1\rangle$	n_3	
2	n_3	$\langle c_1, 1\rangle$	$\langle c_1, 1\rangle$	End_p	C_2
3	End_p	$\langle c_1, 1\rangle$	$\langle c_1, 1\rangle$		C_2, R_2
4	C_2	$\langle c_1, 1\rangle$	$\langle c_1 c_2, 1\rangle$	Start_p	R_2
5	Start_p	$\langle c_1, 1\rangle \langle c_1 c_2, 1\rangle$	$\langle c_1, 1\rangle$	n_3, End_p	R_2
		($c_1 c_2$ is represented by c_1)			
6	n_3	$\langle c_1, 1\rangle$	$\langle c_1, 1\rangle$	End_p	C_2, R_2
7	End_p	$\langle c_1, 1\rangle$	$\langle c_1, 1\rangle \langle c_1 c_2, 1\rangle$		C_2, R_2
		($c_1 c_2$ is regenerated from c_1)			
8	C_2	No change	No change		R_2
9	R_2	$\langle c_1, 1\rangle \langle c_1 c_2, 1\rangle$	$\langle c_1, 1\rangle$	n_2	
10	n_2	$\langle c_1, 1\rangle$	$\langle c_1, 0\rangle$	n_3	

Step No.	Selected node	Qualified data flow value IN_n	Qualified data flow value OUT_n	Remaining work list: Intra. nodes	Remaining work list: Sig. nodes
11	n_3	$\langle c_1,0\rangle$	$\langle c_1,0\rangle$	End_p	C_2
12	End_p	$\langle c_1,0\rangle$	$\langle c_1,0\rangle$ $\langle c_1c_2,0\rangle$		C_2, R_2
		(c_1c_2 is regenerated from c_1)			
13	C_2	$\langle c_1,0\rangle$	$\langle c_1c_2,0\rangle$	$Start_p$	R_2
14	$Start_p$	$\langle c_1,1\rangle$ $\langle c_1c_2,0\rangle$	$\langle c_1,1\rangle$ $\langle c_1c_2,0\rangle$	n_3	R_2
		(Representation has changed)			
15	n_3	$\langle c_1,0\rangle$ $\langle c_1c_2,0\rangle$	$\langle c_1,0\rangle$ $\langle c_1c_2,0\rangle$	End_p	C_2, R_2
16	End_p	$\langle c_1,0\rangle$ $\langle c_1c_2,0\rangle$	No change		C_2, R_2
17	C_2	$\langle c_1,0\rangle$ $\langle c_1c_2,0\rangle$	$\langle c_1c_2,0\rangle$ $\langle c_1c_2c_2,0\rangle$	$Start_p$	R_2
18	$Start_p$	$\langle c_1,1\rangle$ $\langle c_1c_2,0\rangle$ $\langle c_1c_2c_2,0\rangle$	No change	End_p	R_2
		($c_1c_2c_2$ is represented by c_1c_2)			
19	End_p	No change	$\langle c_1,0\rangle$ $\langle c_1c_2,0\rangle$ $\langle c_1c_2c_2,0\rangle$		R_2
		($c_1c_2c_2$ is regenerated from c_1c_2)			
20	R_2	$\langle c_1,0\rangle$ $\langle c_1c_2,0\rangle$ $\langle c_1c_2c_2,0\rangle$	$\langle c_1,0\rangle$ $\langle c_1c_2,0\rangle$	n_2	
21	n_2	$\langle c_1,0\rangle$ $\langle c_1c_2,0\rangle$	$\langle c_1,0\rangle$ $\langle c_1c_2,0\rangle$	n_3	
22	n_3	No change	No change		

Observe that first the call string c_1c_2 is represented by c_1 but since the call is in a loop, after unwinding the recursion once, the data flow value 0 reaches C_2 along the call string c_1. This changes the representation at $Start_p$ and the call string c_1c_2 must be explicitly propagated further. Eventually, call string $c_1c_2c_2$ has the same value as c_1c_2. This results in a different representation and the data flow analysis terminates after a few steps. □

THEOREM 9.3

Using the value-based termination of call strings, the maximum number of call strings at any internal program point is $|L|$.

PROOF At $Exit(Start_p)$ for any procedure p, the call strings are partitioned by the data flow values associated with them and there can be at most $|L|$ distinct data flow values. ∎

THEOREM 9.4

Let the maximum number of call sites in any acyclic call chain be K. Then, using the value-based termination of call strings, the maximum length of any *call string is* $K \times (|L| + 1)$.

PROOF Consider a call string $\sigma = \ldots(C_i)^1 \ldots (C_i)^2 \ldots (C_i)^3 \ldots (C_i)^j \ldots$ where $(C_i)^j$ denotes j^{th} occurrence of C_i. Let $j \geq |L| + 1$ and let C_i call procedure p. The set of call strings reaching p is prefix closed in the following sense: All prefixes of σ ending in C_i must reach entry $Start_p$. Since only $|L|$ distinct values are possible, by the pigeon hole principle, at least two prefixes ending with C_i will carry the same data flow value to $Start_p$ and the longer prefix will get represented by the shorter prefix. Since one more C_i is suffixed to discover fixed point, $j \leq |L| + 1$. In the worst case, all call sites may occur in σ thus the worst case length of any call string is $K \times (|L| + 1)$. ∎

9.5 The Motivating Example Revisited

It is appropriate that our explanation of data flow analysis in this book should end with the example that it began with. This section presents context sensitive interprocedural liveness analysis of the program in Section 1.1.

The examples in this part have considered programs with global variables. However, our motivating example from Figure 1.1 on page 2 contains local pointer variables that are passed as actual parameters. As observed in Section 7.5, this requires data flow information to be propagated between the actual parameters and formal parameters. We model this using a couple of assignments and a special edge in the supergraph as illustrated in Figure 9.17 on the facing page.

For correct Modelling of local pointer variables as actual parameters, we need to assign them to formal variables in the call node (C_2 in our case) and restore them in the return node (R_2 in our case). The assignment in C_2 indicates that the heap memory reachable from `succ` is reachable from `n` in a recursive call. The assignment in R_2 indicates that the heap memory reachable from `n` in a recursive call is reachable from `succ` in an outer call. Besides, we need to bypass the call by an edge because the local variables are available in the program fragment beyond the call due to call by copy semantics. We have achieved this by adding edge $n_2 \rightarrow n_4$. In the absence of this edge, if formal parameter `n` is made *null* in procedure `dfTraverse` our assignment in R_2 will make `succ` *null* in node n_4. Since the pointer has been passed by copy, this is incorrect. The assignment is required because the heap cells reachable from `succ` could be influenced by `n` but the address contained in `succ` is not modified because `succ` is a local variable and is not passed by reference.

Liveness analysis is a backward analysis. Hence we interchange the roles of call nodes and return nodes. Now a call site is appended and call strings grow when a return node is visited. Call sites are removed at the call nodes. By the same token, representation is performed at End_r of procedure r and regeneration is performed

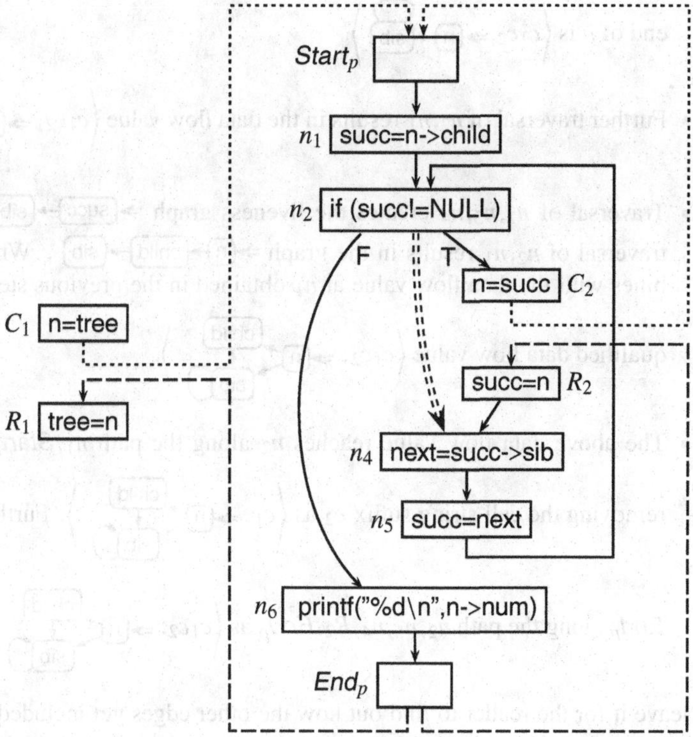

FIGURE 9.17
Supergraph for procedure `dfTraverse` from the program in Figure 1.1 on page 2. Observe the assignments in call and return nodes and the edge $n_3 \rightarrow n_4$ for handling parameters.

at *Start_r*. Besides, a return node always precedes the corresponding call node in the work list of significant nodes. Note that the recursive call in this example is contained in a loop and hence we can expect the representation made at *End_p* to change.

Our data flow values are access graphs as defined in Section 4.4.3. We use the data flow equations defined in Section 4.4.4 for computing the effect of intraprocedural nodes on access graphs representing explicit liveness. Since field name `sib` is dereferenced only in node n_4, summarization can be achieved without subscripting this field name with the node number. Similar remarks apply to the field name `child`. Hence, we drop the subscripts of field names.

The final data flow information is provided in Figure 9.18 on page 327. Below we list some path fragments to show the flow of information:

- $\rho = (End_p, n_6, n_2, n_5, n_4, n_2, n_5, n_4, R_2, n_6, n_2)$

  The data flow value at the start of ρ is $\langle c_1, \mathcal{E}_G \rangle$ and the data flow value at the end of ρ is $\left\langle c_1c_2, \right.$ 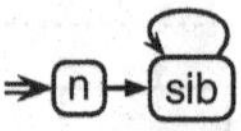 $\left.\right\rangle$.

- Further traversal of n_2, n_1 results in the data flow value $\left\langle c_1c_2, \right.$ 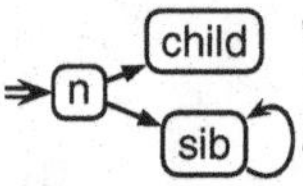 $\left.\right\rangle$.

- Traversal of n_2, n_5, n_4 creates the liveness graph 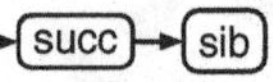. A further traversal of n_2, n_1 results in the graph . When this combines with the data flow value at n_1 obtained in the previous step, we get the qualified data flow value $\left\langle c_1c_2, \right.$ 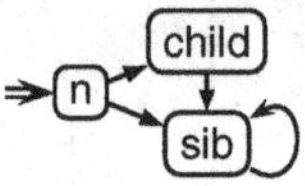 $\left.\right\rangle$.

- The above data flow value reaches n_2 along the path n_1, *Start*$_p$, C_2, n_1 after removing the call string suffix c_2 as $\left\langle c_1, \right.$ 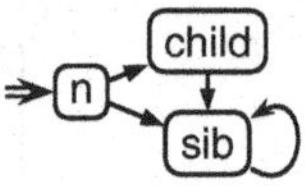 $\left.\right\rangle$. Further, it reaches *End*$_p$ along the path n_2, n_5, n_4, R_2, *End*$_p$ as $\left\langle c_1c_2, \right.$ 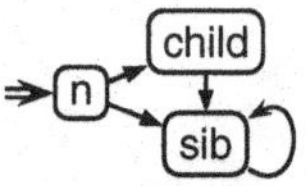 $\left.\right\rangle$.

We leave it for the reader to find out how the other edges get included in the above liveness graph and how the graphs are propagated to various nodes in the supergraph.

Observe that in the liveness graphs at the entry of n_4, there is no edge from `succ` to `child`. Further, there is no graph rooted at `succ` at the entry of n_5. This confirms our conclusion in Section 1.1 that the pointer `succ` can be freed between n_4 and n_5.

Also note that the access path *n→child* is not live in nodes n_2, n_4, n_5, and n_6 in the data flow information in Figure 9.18. However, it is live in the same nodes in the data flow information computed with conservative interprocedural summarization in Section 4.4.5. This is because *n→child* is not explicitly live; it is only implicitly live in that it is aliased to an access path that is explicitly live.

9.6 Summary and Concluding Remarks

This chapter has explored the approach of computing distinct values for distinct contexts instead of constructing context independent functions. Bit vector frameworks are amenable to such an analysis when the context is restricted to immediate caller. This method overwrites the context at every call and recovers it after the call is over.

A natural generalization of this method is to remember the entire call history in the form of a call string. This method is attractive because it is simple and general. Beside, it is context sensitive and hence computes precise data flow information. The

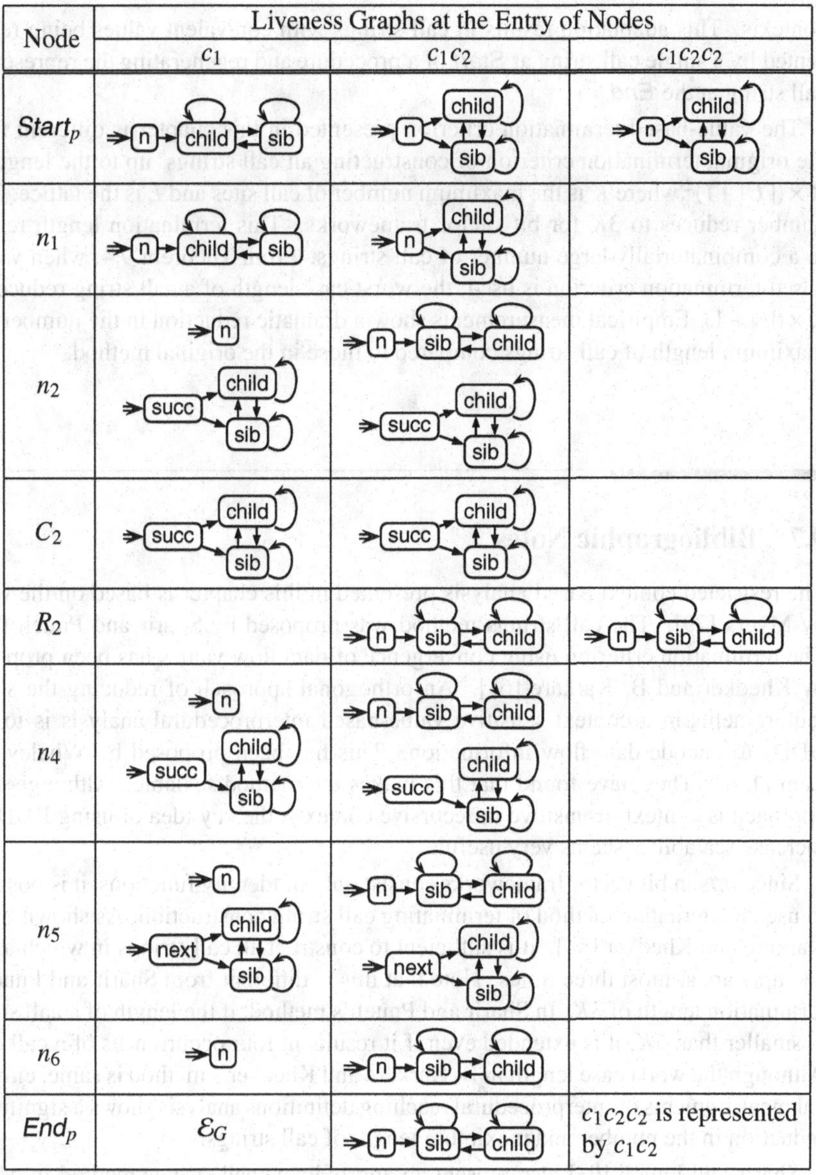

FIGURE 9.18
Interprocedural liveness analysis of heap data for the program in Figure 9.17.

main difficulty in this method is that the number and length of call strings could be exponentially large. Further, in the case of recursive programs, the termination of the construction of call strings must be explicitly ensured. This can be achieved by adapting the "overwrite-and-recover" technique from the method that uses restricted contexts. This adaptation results in call strings with equivalent values being represented by a single call string at *Start* of a procedure and regenerating the represented call string at the *End*.

The value-based termination criterion presented in this chapter is different from the original termination criterion of constructing all call strings up to the length of $K \times (|L|+1)^2$ where K is the maximum number of call sites and L is the lattice. This number reduces to $3K$ for bit vector frameworks. This termination length results in a combinatorially large number of call strings. From Theorem 9.4, when value-based termination criterion is used, the worst case length of a call string reduces to $K \times (|L|+1)$. Empirical measurements show a dramatic reduction in the number and maximum length of call strings compared to those in the original method.

9.7 Bibliographic Notes

The restricted context based analysis presented in this chapter is based on the work by Myers [79]. The call strings method was proposed by Sharir and Pnueli [93]. The termination criterion using convergence of data flow values has been proposed by Khedker and B. Karkare [61]. An orthogonal approach of reducing the space requirements in a context sensitive value-based interprocedural analysis is to use BDDs to encode data flow information. This has been proposed by Whaley and Lam [104]. They have found that this makes the method scalable. Although their approach is context insensitive in recursive contexts, the key idea of using BDDs to increase scalability seems very useful.

Since *ifp*s in bit vector frameworks consist only of identity functions, it is possible to use an alternative method of terminating call string construction. As shown by B. Karkare and Khedker [54], it is sufficient to construct all call strings in which a call site appears at most three times. Note that this is different from Sharir and Pnueli's termination length of $3K$. In Sharir and Pnueli's method, if the length of a call string is smaller than $3K$, it is extended even if it results in four occurrences of a call cite. Although the worst case length in B. Karkare and Khedker's method is same, empirical measurements of interprocedural reaching definitions analysis shows a significant reduction in the number and maximum length of call strings.

Sharir and Pnueli [93] also present an approximate call strings method in which call string suffix of a fixed length k is remembered. This retains context sensitivity for call depths of k but for the call sequences beyond this depth, the method essentially becomes context insensitive. Effectiveness of this method has been empirically measured by Martin [72] who concluded that a value of $k > 2$ did not increase the precision significantly for constant propagation. Khedker and B. Karkare [61] have also presented an approximate version where the imprecision can be adjusted on demand. The basic idea is to allow say k occurrences of a call site in a call string and use representation and regeneration for all such call strings. When the call string grows and the number of occurrences of a call site exceeds k, the data flow values are computed iteratively by retaining the same call string instead of extending it. Unlike Sharir and Pnueli's approximate method, this method is context sensitive until k unfoldings of recursive calls.

The interprocedural points-to analysis by Emami, Ghiya and Hendren [34] can be viewed as a value-based approach. It uses a variant of call graph called an *invocation graph* in which recursive invocations of procedures result in creating two nodes for a procedure: One node is recursive whereas the other node is approximate. Thus it is context sensitive in the first unfolding of recursion but context insensitive beyond that. We leave it for the reader to verify that the Emami's method computes imprecise points-to graphs for the program in Figure 9.6 on page 305 compared to the points-to graphs in Figure 9.7 on page 306 computed using call strings method.

Part III

Implementing Data Flow Analysis

10

Implementing Data Flow Analysis in GCC

This chapter presents a *g*eneric *d*ata *f*low *a*nalyzer for *p*er *f*unction (i.e., intraprocedural) *b*it *v*ector *d*ata *f*low *a*nalysis in GCC 4.3.0. We call this infrastructure *gdfa*. The analyzers implemented using *gdfa* are called *pfbvdfa*. *gdfa* has been used to implement several bit vector data flow analyses.

The design and implementation of *gdfa* is motivated by the following objectives:

- Demonstrating the practical significance of the following important generalization: Instead of implementing specific analyses directly, it is useful to implement a generic driver that is based on a carefully chosen set of abstractions. The task of implementing a particular analyzer then reduces to merely specifying the analysis by instantiating these abstractions to concrete values.

- Providing an easy to use and easy to extend data flow analysis infrastructure. The goal is to facilitate experimentation in terms of studying existing analyses, defining new analyses, and exploring different analysis algorithms.

Section 10.1 describes the specification mechanism of *gdfa* and shows how the resulting pass can be included in GCC 4.3.0. We illustrate it for the bit vector analyses implemented using *gdfa*. Section 10.2 demonstrates how *pfbvdfa* can be used. Section 10.3 describes the implementation of *gdfa*. This section also shows how local property computation can be driven by specifications. Finally Section 10.4 suggests some possible enhancements to *gdfa*.

The GCC related details in this chapter are interleaved with the description of *gdfa*. Appendix A provides a short introduction to GCC, its installation, and how to obtain its patch for *gdfa*.* The code presented in this chapter is a slightly edited version of the original code. This was required to fit a page size constraints.

10.1 Specifying a Data Flow Analysis

In this section we look at how we can use the generic data flow analysis driver to implement a data flow analysis pass in GCC. The implemented pass has to be registered

*We use GCC to denote the GNU compiler generation framework using which a compiler can be built for a given processor. The compiler so generated is denoted by `gcc`.

with the pass manager in GCC so that it can be executed by the compiler.

10.1.1 Registering a Pass With the Pass Manager in GCC

gdfa works on the gimple version of the intermediate representation used by GCC. We have included *pfbvdfa* passes such that they are invoked by default when gcc is used for compiling a program. When gcc is built, this causes *pfbvdfa* passes to run on the entire source of gcc which consists of over a million lines of C code. This helps in ensuring that these do not cause any exception in the compilation sequence.

After constructing the gimple representation, gcc views the rest of the compilation as sequential execution of various passes. This is carried out by traversing a linked list whose nodes contain pointers to the entry functions of these passes. A pass is registered with the pass manager through the following steps:

- Instantiating a variable as an instance of `struct tree_opt_pass` in some file.
- Declaring this variable as an `extern` variable in header file `tree-pass.h`.
- Inserting this variable in the linked list of passes using the macro `NEXT_PASS` in function `init_optimization_passes` in file `passes.c`.

Here is the declaration of `struct tree_opt_pass`. For convenience comments have been removed and are used in the explanation that follows.

```
 0 struct tree_opt_pass
 1 {
 2   const char *name;
 3   bool (*gate) (void);
 4   unsigned int (*execute) (void);
 5   struct tree_opt_pass *sub;
 6   struct tree_opt_pass *next;
 7   int static_pass_number;
 8   unsigned int tv_id;
 9   unsigned int properties_required;
10   unsigned int properties_provided;
11   unsigned int properties_destroyed;
12   unsigned int todo_flags_start;
13   unsigned int todo_flags_finish;
14   char letter;
15 };
```

The `name` of the pass (line 2) is used as a fragment of the dump file name. We have used the names like `gdfa_ave`. The `gate` function (line 3) is used to check whether this pass and all its sub-passes should be executed or not. They are executed only if this function returns `true`. If no such checking is required, this function pointer can be NULL. The execute function (line 4) is entry function of the pass. If this function pointer is NULL, there should be sub-passes otherwise this pass does nothing. The return value tells gcc what more needs to be done. The variable sub (line 5) is a list of sub-passes that should be executed depending upon the gate predicate. If there are sub-passes that must be executed unconditionally, then they are listed in next (line 6). The static pass number (line 7) is used as a fragment of the dump file name. If it is specified as 0, the pass manager computes its value depending on the position of the pass. It is this that generated numbers 15, 16, 17, 18, and 19 for our data flow analyses. Variable tv_id is the variable that can be used as a time variable. The rest of the variables are self-explanatory. The last variable letter is used to annotate RTL code that is emitted.

We have registered available expressions analysis by creating a structure variable called pass_gimple_pfbv_ave_dfa as shown below.

```
struct tree_opt_pass pass_gimple_pfbv_ave_dfa =
{
  "gdfa_ave",              /* name */
  NULL,                    /* gate */
  gimple_pfbv_ave_dfa,     /* execute */
  NULL,                    /* sub */
  NULL,                    /* next */
  0,                       /* static_pass_number */
  0,                       /*tv_id */
  0,                       /* properties_required */
  0,                       /* properties_provided */
  0,                       /* properties_destroyed */
  0,                       /* todo_flags_start */
  0,                       /* todo_flags_finish */
  0                        /* letter */
};
```

This variable is declared as follows in file tree-pass.h

```
extern struct tree_opt_pass pass_gimple_pfbv_ave_dfa;
```

The next step in registering this pass is to include it in the list of passes. We show below the relevant code fragment from function init_optimization_passes in file passes.c:

```
  NEXT_PASS (pass_build_cfg);
/* Intraprocedural dfa passes begin */
  NEXT_PASS (pass_init_gimple_pfbvdfa);
  NEXT_PASS (pass_gimple_pfbv_ave_dfa);
  NEXT_PASS (pass_gimple_pfbv_pav_dfa);
  NEXT_PASS (pass_gimple_pfbv_ant_dfa);
  NEXT_PASS (pass_gimple_pfbv_lv_dfa);
  NEXT_PASS (pass_gimple_pfbv_rd_dfa);
  NEXT_PASS (pass_gimple_pfbv_pre_dfa);
/* Intraprocedural dfa passes end */
```

Finally, we need to include the new file names in the GCC build system. This is done by listing the file names and their dependencies in `Makefile.in` in the `gcc-4.3.0/gcc` directory. Appendix A provides the steps for building `gcc`.

10.1.2 Specifying Available Expressions Analysis

The specification mechanism supported by *gdfa* is simple and succinct. It follows the GCC mechanism of specification by using a `struct` as a hook and by requiring the user to create a variable by instantiating the members of the `struct` defined for the purpose.

For available expressions analysis, we define a variable called `gdfa_ave` which is of the type `struct gimple_pfbv_dfa_spec gdfa_ave`.

```
struct gimple_pfbv_dfa_spec gdfa_ave =
{
      entity_expr,                      /* entity             */
      ONES,                             /* top_value          */
      ZEROS,                            /* entry_info         */
      ONES,                             /* exit_info          */
      FORWARD,                          /* traversal_order    */
      INTERSECTION,                     /* confluence         */
      entity_use,                       /* gen_effect         */
      down_exp,                         /* gen_exposition     */
      entity_mod,                       /* kill_effect        */
      any_where,                        /* kill_exposition    */
      global_only,                      /* preserved_dfi      */
      identity_forward_edge_flow,       /* forward_edge_flow  */
      stop_flow_along_edge,             /* backward_edge_flow */
      forward_gen_kill_node_flow,       /* forward_node_flow  */
      stop_flow_along_node              /* backward_node_flow */
};
```

Before we explain the above, we present the rest of the code required to complete the specification.

```
18 pfbv_dfi ** AV_pfbv_dfi = NULL;
19
20 static unsigned int
21 gimple_pfbv_ave_dfa(void)
22 {
23
24         AV_pfbv_dfi = gdfa_driver(gdfa_ave);
25
26         return 0;
27 }
```

Nothing more is required for specifying available expressions analysis apart from registering it with the pass manager with function `gimple_pfbv_ave_dfa` as its entry point as described in Section 10.1.1. This function calls the *gdfa* driver passing the specification variable `gdfa_ave` as actual parameter. The data flow information computed by the driver is stored in a pointer to an array called `AV_pfbv_dfi`; each element of this array represents the data flow information for a basic block and is an instance of the following type defined by *gdfa*.

```
typedef struct pfbv_dfi
{
        dfvalue gen;
        dfvalue kill;
        dfvalue in;
        dfvalue out;
} pfbv_dfi;
```

The semantics expressed by `struct gimple_pfbv_dfa_spec gdfa_ave` is as described below: Line 2 declares that the relevant entities for this analysis are expressions (`entity_expr`). Line 3 specifies that $\top$ is "all `ONES`" implying the universal set $\mathbb{E}\text{xpr}$. The specification "all `ZEROS`" on line 4 initializes the BI_{Start} to $\emptyset$ whereas `ONES` on line 5 renders BI_{End} irrelevant because it is same as $\top$. Line 6 declares the direction of traversal to be `FORWARD`. Note that this is independent of the direction of flow and only influences the number of iterations. If we choose the direction of traversal as `BACKWARD`, the resulting data flow information will remain same except that it may take a much larger number of iterations. Line 7 declares the $\sqcap$ to be $\cap$. Line 12 directs the driver to preserve only the global data flow information (*In* and *Out*); the driver can reclaim the space occupied by the local data flow information (*Gen* and *Kill*).

The most interesting elements of the specification are the specifications of local properties and flow functions:

- *Local property specification.*

  Lines 8 to 11 define the *Gen* and *Kill* kill sets for a block. Observe that this mechanism closely follows the description in Section 2.2.

  - Lines 8 and 9 say that when a downwards exposed (`down_exp`) use of an entity (`entity_use`) is found in a basic block, it is included in the *Gen* set of the block. From line 2 we know that the entity under consideration is an expression (`entity_expr`).
  - Lines 10 and 11 say that when a modification of an entity (`entity_mod`) is found in a basic block, it is included in the *Kill* set of the block. This modification need not be upwards exposed or downwards exposed, it can appear `any_where`.

  This is possible because the *gdfa* driver is aware of the fact that the use of an entity could be affected by its modification and hence the notion of exposition of an entity is explicated in the specification.

- *Flow function specification.*

  Lines 13 to 16 specify the flow functions for available expressions analysis as required by the generic data flow Equations (5.1) and (5.2). The forward edge flow function $\overrightarrow{f}_{n\to m}$ in available expressions analysis is ϕ_{id} (line 13) whereas the forward node flow function $\overrightarrow{f_n}$ is the conventional *Gen*-*Kill* function $f(X) = Gen \cup (In - Kill)$. Further, there is no backward flow i.e., $\overleftarrow{f_n}$ and $\overleftarrow{f}_{n\to m}$ are $\phi_\top$ (Section 5.1). This is specified by lines 14 and 16. All these functions are supported by *gdfa* and it is enough to associate the function pointers with appropriate functions.

  When the nature of data flow is different from the default flows, it is also possible to write custom functions—we show how it is done for partial redundancy elimination in Section 10.1.3.

10.1.3 Specifying Other Bit Vector Data Flow Analyses

Given the specification of available expressions analysis, it is easy to visualize specifications for other bit vector frameworks. We describe the required changes in the following:

- *Partially available expressions analysis.*

  Confluence should be `UNION`, $\top$ and BI_{End} should be `ZEROS`.

- *Reaching definitions analysis.*

  Entity should be `entity_defn`, confluence should be `UNION`, $\top$ and BI_{End} should be `ZEROS`.

- *Anticipable expressions analysis.*

  The data flow equations for anticipable expressions analysis are Equations (2.9) and (2.10). In this case it is desirable, though not necessary, to choose the direction of traversal as `BACKWARD`. The exposition for *Gen* should be changed to up_exp. BI_{Start} should be `ONES` and BI_{End} should be `ZEROS`. Flow functions would change as follows:

  - forward edge flow function $\overrightarrow{f_{n \to m}}$ should be `stop_flow_along_edge`,
  - forward node flow function $\overrightarrow{f_n}$ should be `stop_flow_along_node`, and
  - backward node flow function $\overleftarrow{f_n}$ should be the default *Gen-Kill* function `backward_gen_kill_node_flow`.

- *Live variables analysis.*

  This specification would be similar to that of anticipable expressions analysis except that the entity should be `entity_var`, confluence should be `UNION`, $\top$ and BI_{End} should be `ZEROS`.

- *Partial redundancy elimination.*
  Here it would useful to change the `gate` function to this pass to check that available expressions analysis and partially available expressions analysis has been performed.

  The specification of data flow analysis would be similar to that of anticipable expressions analysis except that the flow functions would change. The data flow equations for anticipable expressions analysis are Equations (2.9) and (2.10) whereas the data flow equations for partial redundancy elimination are Equations (2.11) and (2.15). Clearly, the change is only in the flow function in the equation for In_n. In particular, the forward edge flow function $\overrightarrow{f_{n \to m}}$ and the backward node flow function $\overleftarrow{f_n}$ cannot be chosen from the default functions supported by *gdfa*. We define the required functions as shown below.

```
dfvalue
forward_edge_flow_pre(basic_block src, basic_block dest)
{
        dfvalue temp;

        temp = union_dfvalues (OUT(AV_pfbv_dfi,src),
                                         CURRENT_OUT(src));

        return temp;
}
```

In this function, src and dest indicate the source and destination of an edge. Since this flow function is used in computing In_n, dest represents n and src represents the given predecessor node p. Under the assumption that the data flow information of available expressions analysis is stored in the variable AV_pfbv_dfi, the term OUT(AV_pfbv_dfi,src) represents $AvOut_p$ whereas the Out_p is represented by the term CURRENT_OUT(src). Thus this flow function computes $AvOut_p \cup Out_p$ for a given predecessor p.

The definition of backward node flow is similar to that of the default node flow except that we need to include the value of $PavIn_n$. This is easily achieved by the function defined below:

```
dfvalue
backward_node_flow_pre(basic_block bb)
{
        dfvalue temp1, temp2;

        temp1 = backward_gen_kill_node_flow(bb);

        temp2 = intersect_dfvalues (IN(PAV_pfbv_dfi,bb),
                                    temp1);

        if (temp1)
                free_dfvalue_space(temp1);

        return temp2;
}
```

Here bb is the current node n. The default backward node flow function is used to compute the data flow information in the variable temp1. Under the assumption that the data flow information of partially available expressions analysis is stored in the variable PAV_pfbv_dfi, the term IN(PAV_pfbv_dfi,bb) represents $PavIn_n$. All that further needs to be done is to intersect them.

This completes the specification of partial redundancy elimination.

10.2 An Example of Data Flow Analysis

We use the example program from Figure 2.1 on page 27 in Chapter 2 to demonstrate the use of analyzer implemented using *gdfa*. We show the result of live variables analysis and available expressions analysis. A C program that represents the CFG in Figure 2.1 is given below.

```
int x, y, z;

int exmp(void)
{   int a, b, c, d;

    b = 4;
    a = b + c;
    d = a * b;
    if (x < y)
        b = a -c;
    else
    {   do
        {   c = b + c;
            if (y > x)
            {   do
                {   d = a + b;
                    f(b + c);
                } while(y > x);
            }
            else
            {   c = a * b;
                f(a - b);
            }
            g (a + b);
        } while(z > x);
    }
    h(a-c);
    f(b+c);
}
```

Since the original example does not show conditions explicitly, we have used global variables in conditions; these variables are ignored by intraprocedural data flow analysis. Further, the functions f, g, and h are unspecified. Since C uses call by value mechanism, we have ignored the effects of function calls under the assumption that arrays and addresses of variables are not passed as parameters.

10.2.1 Executing the Data Flow Analyzer

Our example program is not a complete program hence we cannot compile it into an executable program. For such programs we must use the `-c` option that creates only an object file for the given input C file. Alternatively, we can use the `-S` option that stops the compilation after generating the corresponding assembly file. We use the following command to generate text files that provide the results of our passes.

```
$ gcc -S -fdump-tree-all -fgdfa exmp.c
```

The option `-fdump-tree-all` enables generation of the dump files for passes implemented on gimple representation. The option `-fgdfa` emits the results of our data flow analysis passes in respective dump files. The dump files that are of interest to us are:

Name	Description of the output
`exmp.c.013t.cfg`	CFG
`exmp.c.015t.gdfa_ave`	available expressions analysis
`exmp.c.016t.gdfa_pav`	partially available expression analysis
`exmp.c.017t.gdfa_ant`	anticipable expressions analysis
`exmp.c.018t.gdfa_lv`	live variables analysis
`exmp.c.018t.gdfa_rd`	reaching definitions analysis
`exmp.c.019t.gdfa_pre`	partial redundancy elimination

The numbers indicate the position of the pass in the sequence of passes. Pass number 014 processes the CFG to discover the entities of interest to us and performs depth first numbering of basic blocks so that post order or reverse post order traversal can be used by our data flow analysis passes. These numbers would change depending upon the exact sequence of passes in a given version of GCC.

10.2.2 Examining the Gimple Version of CFG

The gimple representation used by GCC consists of three address code statements. The CFG version of gimple representation identifies basic blocks and explicates control flow between basic blocks. It also shows the declarations of temporary variables. There are two categories of temporary variables in gimple:

- *Artificial variables.* These variables are created to store the values of global variables. Subsequently, these variables are used in expressions. Any assignment to a global variable uses the original global variable so that the latest value can be read into a new artificial variable for a subsequent use.

  Artificial variables are also created for those instances of local variables that are assigned a value returned by a function call. The value of these artificial variables is then assigned to the local variables.

- *Temporary variables.* These are the traditional temporary variables which hold the intermediate results of expression computations. The parameters passed to functions are also represented by temporary variables.

The declaration part of gimple CFG in `exmp.c.013t.cfg` is:

```
0
1 ;; Function exmp (exmp)
2
3 exmp ()
4 {
5     int d;
6     int c;
7     int b;
8     int a;
9     int D.1205;
10    int D.1204;
11    int x.7;
12    int z.6;
13    int D.1201;
14    int D.1200;
15    int x.5;
16    int y.4;
17    int D.1197;
18    int x.3;
19    int y.2;
20    int y.1;
21    int x.0;
```

The gimple representation of our program initially contains eight artificial variables: $x.7$, $z.6$, $x.5$, $y.4$, $x.3$, $y.2$, $y.1$, and $x.0$. Each use of a global variable causes a distinct number to be suffixed to the variable. The temporary variables are: $D.1205$, $D.1204$, $D.1201$, $D.1200$, and $D.1197$. They represent the parameters of the five calls made in our program. There are no temporary variables for holding intermediate results of computations because our expressions consist of a single operation—temporaries are created for expressions containing more than one operation.

The CFG contains a unique ENTRY block which does not contain any computation and does not have any predecessor block. Similarly, there is an EXIT block which does not contain any computation and does not have any successor. An unconditional control transfer from a block to another block is recorded as fallthru whereas a conditional transfer is labeled true or false. All auxiliary information about a block e.g., block number, list of successors and predecessors, nature of control flow etc. is shown with a # mark as the first symbol on a line.

ENTRY and EXIT blocks are not listed explicitly in the dump. Internally they are numbered block 0 and block 1 respectively. Hence the first block that appears in the CFG is block 2 as shown below. It corresponds to block n_1 in Figure 2.1 on page 27. Observe the use of artificial variables $x.0$ and $y.1$ in the block.

```
22   # BLOCK 2
23   # PRED: ENTRY (fallthru)
24   b = 4;
25   a = b + c;
26   d = a * b;
27   x.0 = x;
28   y.1 = y;
29   if (x.0 < y.1)
30      goto <bb 3>;
31   else
32      goto <bb 4>;
33   # SUCC: 3 (true) 4 (false)
```

This block has a conditional control transfer at the end of it. Its successor blocks are blocks 3 and 4 which correspond to blocks n_2 and n_3 respectively in the CFG in Figure 2.1. Note that the predecessors of a block are also labeled to indicate the nature of control transfer (i.e., fallthru, true, or false).

```
34   # BLOCK 3
35   # PRED: 2 (true)
36   b = a - c;
37   goto <bb 9>;
38   # SUCC: 9 (fallthru)
39
40   # BLOCK 4
41   # PRED: 2 (false) 8 (true)
42   c = b + c;
43   y.2 = y;
44   x.3 = x;
45   if (y.2 > x.3)
46      goto <bb 5>;
47   else
48      goto <bb 7>;
49   # SUCC: 5 (true) 7 (false)
```

The structure of the control flow between the remaining blocks is a little different from the CFG shown in Figure 2.1. Block 5 in the gcc generated CFG combines blocks n_5 and n_6 of Figure 2.1 because there is a strictly sequential control flow between them. Block 6 consists of a single goto that will be optimized away later. Figure 2.1 does not have this block. Block 7 corresponds to block n_4 and block 8 corresponds to block n_7 in Figure 2.1. The last block containing some program code is block 9 which corresponds to n_8 in Figure 2.1. Observe that it has EXIT as its successor. The details of these blocks are as follows:

```
  # BLOCK 5
  # PRED: 4 (true) 5 (true)
  d = a + b;
  D.1197 = b + c;
  f (D.1197);
  y.4 = y;
  x.5 = x;
  if (y.4 > x.5)
    goto <bb 5>;
  else
    goto <bb 6>;
  # SUCC: 5 (true) 6 (false)

  # BLOCK 6
  # PRED: 5 (false)
  goto <bb 8>;
  # SUCC: 8 (fallthru)

  # BLOCK 7
  # PRED: 4 (false)
  c = a * b;
  D.1200 = a - b;
  f (D.1200);
  # SUCC: 8 (fallthru)

  # BLOCK 8
  # PRED: 6 (fallthru) 7 (fallthru)
  D.1201 = a + b;
  g (D.1201);
  z.6 = z;
  x.7 = x;
  if (z.6 > x.7)
    goto <bb 4>;
  else
    goto <bb 9>;
  # SUCC: 4 (true) 9 (false)

  # BLOCK 9
  # PRED: 3 (fallthru) 8 (false)
  D.1204 = a - c;
  h (D.1204);
  D.1205 = b + c;
  f (D.1205);
  return;
  # SUCC: EXIT

}
```

In essence, the CFGs constructed by `gcc` are quite similar to the CFGs that we have seen in the earlier parts of the book.

10.2.3 Examining the Result of Data Flow Analysis

The results of an analysis are available in internal data structures in a ready to use form. Section 10.1.3 shows how they can be used when we describe the implementation of partial redundancy elimination which needs the result of available expressions analysis and partially available expressions analysis. Here we present the textual dump of the results produced by the options `-fdump-tree-all` and `-gdfa`.

File `exmp.c.018t.gdfa_lv` contains the result of liveness analysis. It indicates that for this example $\mathbb{V}\mathsf{ar} = \{\mathtt{a}, \mathtt{b}, \mathtt{c}, \mathtt{d}\}$ intraprocedural liveness analysis. It also indicates the bit position for each variable. Variable `d` is the first to be considered. This is because internally, the variables are added to the head of the list of variables rather than its tail. Observe that the other three category of variables (global, artificial, and local) have been eliminated from consideration.†

```
;; Function exmp (exmp)

Number of relevant entities: 4

 Bit position and entity mapping is   ********************
        0:(d),1:(c),2:(b),3:(a)

 Initial values ****************************************

Basic Block 2. Preds:  ENTRY. Succs:  3 4
        ----------------------------
        GEN Bit Vector:    0100
        GEN Entities:      (c)
        ------------------------------
        KILL Bit Vector:  1011
        KILL Entities:     (d),(b),(a)
        ------------------------------
        IN Bit Vector:     0000
        IN Entities:
        ------------------------------
        OUT Bit Vector:    0000
        OUT Entities:
        ------------------------------
```

The In_n and Out_n properties have been initialized to $\emptyset$ which is $\top$ for live variables analysis. In the following, we produce only the lines that enumerate the Gen_n and

†At the moment, our implementation does not consider formal parameters.

$Kill_n$ in terms of entity names rather than bit vectors.

```
Basic Block 2. Preds:  ENTRY. Succs:  3 4
         ------------------------------
         GEN Entities:      (c)
         KILL Entities:     (d),(b),(a)
         --------------------------------
Basic Block 3. Preds:  2. Succs:  9
         ------------------------------
         GEN Entities:      (c),(a)
         KILL Entities:     (b)
         --------------------------------
Basic Block 4. Preds:  2 8. Succs:  5 7
         ------------------------------
         GEN Entities:      (c),(b)
         KILL Entities:     (c)
         --------------------------------
Basic Block 5. Preds:  4 5. Succs:  5 6
         ------------------------------
         GEN Entities:      (c),(b),(a)
         KILL Entities:     (d)
         --------------------------------
Basic Block 6. Preds:  5. Succs:  8
         ------------------------------
         GEN Entities:
         KILL Entities:
         --------------------------------
Basic Block 7. Preds:  4. Succs:  8
         ------------------------------
         GEN Entities:      (b),(a)
         KILL Entities:     (c)
         --------------------------------
Basic Block 8. Preds:  6 7. Succs:  4 9
         ------------------------------
         GEN Entities:      (b),(a)
         KILL Entities:
         --------------------------------
Basic Block 9. Preds:  3 8. Succs:  EXIT
         ------------------------------
         GEN Entities:      (c),(b),(a)
         KILL Entities:
         --------------------------------
```

It can be readily verified from the table in Example 2.3 on page 27 that the local data flow values given below are identical to the values discovered earlier.

The final values are also generated in the same format. We show selected lines from the final result of liveness analysis of our example program:

```
Total Number of Iterations = 2 *********

Basic Block 2. Preds:  ENTRY. Succs:  3 4
        ----------------------------
        IN Entities:        (c)
        OUT Entities:       (c),(b),(a)
        ------------------------------
Basic Block 3. Preds:  2. Succs:  9
        ----------------------------
        IN Entities:        (c),(a)
        OUT Entities:       (c),(b),(a)
        ------------------------------
Basic Block 4. Preds:  2 8. Succs:  5 7
        ----------------------------
        IN Entities:        (c),(b),(a)
        OUT Entities:       (c),(b),(a)
        ------------------------------
Basic Block 5. Preds:  4 5. Succs:  5 6
        ----------------------------
        IN Entities:        (c),(b),(a)
        OUT Entities:       (c),(b),(a)
        ------------------------------
Basic Block 6. Preds:  5. Succs:  8
        ----------------------------
        IN Entities:        (c),(b),(a)
        OUT Entities:       (c),(b),(a)
        ------------------------------
Basic Block 7. Preds:  4. Succs:  8
        ----------------------------
        IN Entities:        (b),(a)
        OUT Entities:       (c),(b),(a)
        ------------------------------
Basic Block 8. Preds:  6 7. Succs:  4 9
        ----------------------------
        IN Entities:        (c),(b),(a)
        OUT Entities:       (c),(b),(a)
        ------------------------------
Basic Block 9. Preds:  3 8. Succs:  EXIT
        ----------------------------
        IN Entities:        (c),(b),(a)
        OUT Entities:
        ------------------------------
```

We leave it for the reader to verify that these values are identical to the values in the table in Example 2.3 on page 27.

If the option `-fgdfa` is replaced by `-fgdfa-details`, data flow values after each iteration are generated.

The result of data flow analyses involving expressions is produced much the same way. File `exmp.c.015t.gdfa_ave.` contains the details of available expressions analysis. The initial information in this file is:

```
;; Function exmp (exmp)

Number of relevant entities: 5

 Bit position and entity mapping is   ***********************
    0:(b + c),1:(a * b),2:(a - c),3:(a + b),4:(a - b)

 Initial values ****************************************

Basic Block 2. Preds:  ENTRY. Succs:  3 4
       ----------------------------
       GEN Bit Vector: 11000
       GEN Entities:    (b + c),(a * b)
       ----------------------------
       KILL Bit Vector:11111
       KILL Entities:   (b + c),(a * b),(a - c),(a + b),(a - b)
       ----------------------------
       IN Bit Vector:   11111
       IN Entities:     (b + c),(a * b),(a - c),(a + b),(a - b)
       ----------------------------
       OUT Bit Vector: 11111
       OUT Entities:    (b + c),(a * b),(a - c),(a + b),(a - b)
       ----------------------------
```

Unlike live variables analysis for which bit vectors of four bits are created, *gdfa* has created a bit vector of five bits for available expressions analysis of our example because our example has five expressions that qualify as local expressions. Observe that the expressions have been numbered in a different order compared to the order in Figure 2.1 on page 27. This is because *gdfa* forms the set $\mathbb{E}\text{xpr}$ by making a forward pass over the program.

The initialization for available expressions analysis uses the entire $\mathbb{E}\text{xpr}$ set which represents the $\top$ value. The value of *BI* is $\emptyset$. Although basic block 2 corresponds to block n_1 for which we had chosen *In* as *BI* for initialization, for the CFG constructed by `gcc`, *BI* is associated with the fictitious blocks `ENTRY` and `EXIT` as the case may be.

The local data flow properties for available expressions analysis of our example program for all blocks are:

```
Basic Block 2. Preds:  ENTRY. Succs:  3 4
    ----------------------------
    GEN Entities:   (b + c),(a * b)
    KILL Entities:  (b + c),(a * b),(a - c),(a + b),(a - b)
    ----------------------------
Basic Block 3. Preds:  2. Succs:  9
    ----------------------------
    GEN Entities:     (a - c)
    KILL Entities:    (b + c),(a * b),(a + b),(a - b)
    ------------------------------
Basic Block 4. Preds:  2 8. Succs:  5 7
    ----------------------------
    GEN Entities:
    KILL Entities:    (b + c),(a - c)
    ------------------------------
Basic Block 5. Preds:  4 5. Succs:  5 6
    ----------------------------
    GEN Entities:     (b + c),(a + b)
    KILL Entities:
    ------------------------------
Basic Block 6. Preds:  5. Succs:  8
    ----------------------------
    GEN Entities:
    KILL Entities:
    ------------------------------
Basic Block 7. Preds:  4. Succs:  8
    ----------------------------
    GEN Entities:     (a * b),(a - b)
    KILL Entities:    (b + c),(a - c)
    ------------------------------
Basic Block 8. Preds:  6 7. Succs:  4 9
    ----------------------------
    GEN Entities:     (a + b)
    KILL Entities:
    ------------------------------
Basic Block 9. Preds:  3 8. Succs:  EXIT
    ----------------------------
    GEN Entities:     (b + c),(a - c)
    KILL Entities:
    ------------------------------
```

Since block 6 consists of only an unconditional `goto` statement, $Gen_6 = Kill_6 = \emptyset$. For other block, the *Gen* and *Kill* values are same as in Example 2.9 on page 34. The final data flow values for available expressions analysis have been shown below.

```
Total Number of Iterations = 3 *********

Basic Block 2. Preds:  ENTRY. Succs:  3 4
   ---------------------------
    IN Entities:
    OUT Entities:     (b + c),(a * b)
    ---------------------------
Basic Block 3. Preds:  2. Succs:  9
    ---------------------------
    IN Entities:      (b + c),(a * b)
    OUT Entities:     (a - c)
    ---------------------------
Basic Block 4. Preds:  2 8. Succs: 5 7
    ---------------------------
    IN Entities:      (a * b)
    OUT Entities:     (a * b)
    ---------------------------
Basic Block 5. Preds:  4 5. Succs:  5 6
    ---------------------------
    IN Entities:      (a * b)
    OUT Entities:     (b + c),(a * b),(a + b)
    ---------------------------
Basic Block 6. Preds:  5. Succs:  8
    ---------------------------
    IN Entities:      (b + c),(a * b),(a + b)
    OUT Entities:     (b + c),(a * b),(a + b)
    ---------------------------
Basic Block 7. Preds:  4. Succs:  8
    ---------------------------
    IN Entities:      (a * b)
    OUT Entities:     (a * b),(a - b)
    ---------------------------
Basic Block 8. Preds:  6 7. Succs:  4 9
    ---------------------------
    IN Entities:      (a * b)
    OUT Entities:     (a * b),(a + b)
    ---------------------------
Basic Block 9. Preds:  3 8. Succs:  EXIT
    ---------------------------
    IN Entities:
    OUT Entities:     (b + c),(a - c)
    ---------------------------
```

We leave it for the reader to verify that these values are identical to the values obtained in Example 2.9 on page 34.

10.3 Implementing the Generic Data Flow Analyzer *gdfa*

We describe the implementation in terms of the specification primitives, interface with GCC, the generic functions for global property computation, and generic functions for local property computation.

10.3.1 Specification Primitives

The main data structure used for specification is:

```
0 struct gimple_pfbv_dfa_spec
1 {
2        entity_name                  entity;
3        initial_value                top_value_spec;
4        initial_value                entry_info;
5        initial_value                exit_info;
6        traversal_direction          traversal_order;
7        meet_operation               confluence;
8        entity_manipulation          gen_effect;
9        entity_occurrence            gen_exposition;
10       entity_manipulation          kill_effect;
11       entity_occurrence            kill_exposition;
12       dfi_to_be_preserved          preserved_dfi;
13
14       dfvalue (*forward_edge_flow)(basic_block src,
15                                       basic_block dest);
16       dfvalue (*backward_edge_flow)(basic_block src,
17                                        basic_block dest);
18       dfvalue (*forward_node_flow)(basic_block bb);
19       dfvalue (*backward_node_flow)(basic_block bb);
20
21 };
```

The types appearing on lines 2 to 12 are defined as enumerated types with the following possible values.

Enumerated Type	Possible Values
entity_name	entity_expr, entity_var, entity_defn
initial_value	ONES, ZEROS
traversal_direction	FORWARD, BACKWARD, BIDIRECTIONAL
meet_operation	UNION, INTERSECTION
entity_manipulation	entity_use, entity_mod
entity_occurrence	up_exp, down_exp, any_where
dfi_to_be_preserved	all, global_only, no_value

The type dfvalue is just another name for the type sbitmap supported by GCC. We have used a different name to allow for the possibility of extending *gdfa* to other kinds of data flow values.

The entry point of each data flow analysis invokes the driver with its specification. The driver creates space for current data flow values in current data flow analysis in a variable current_pfbv_dfi which is declared as shown below:

```
typedef struct pfbv_dfi
{
        dfvalue gen;
        dfvalue kill;
        dfvalue in;
        dfvalue out;
} pfbv_dfi;

pfbv_dfi ** current_pfbv_dfi ;
```

For a basic block bb, different members of the data flow information are accessed using the following macros:

Data flow variable	current_pfbv_dfi	Given dfi
Gen	CURRENT_GEN(bb)	GEN(dfi,bb)
Kill	CURRENT_KILL(bb)	KILL(dfi,bb)
In	CURRENT_IN(bb)	IN(dfi,bb)
Out	CURRENT_OUT(bb)	OUT(dfi,bb)

Now we can describe the default functions that can be assigned to the function pointers on lines 14 to 19 in struct gimple_pfbv_dfa_spec. Alternatively, the users can define their own functions which have the same interface. The default functions supported by *gdfa* are:

Function	Returned value
identity_forward_edge_flow(src, dest)	CURRENT_OUT(src)
identity_backward_edge_flow(src, dest)	CURRENT_IN(dest)
stop_flow_along_edge(src, dest)	top_value
identity_forward_node_flow(bb)	CURRENT_IN(bb)
identity_backward_node_flow(bb)	CURRENT_OUT(bb)
stop_flow_along_node(bb)	top_value
forward_gen_kill_node_flow(bb)	CURRENT_GEN(bb) ∪ (CURRENT_IN(bb) - CURRENT_KILL(bb))
backward_gen_kill_node_flow(bb)	CURRENT_GEN(bb) ∪ (CURRENT_OUT(bb) - CURRENT_KILL(bb))

where top_value is of the type initial_value and is constructed based on the value of top_value_spec (line 3 in struct gimple_pfbv_dfa_spec).

This completes the description of the specification primitives.

10.3.2 Interface with GCC

The top level interface of *gdfa* with GCC is through the pass manager as described in Section 10.1.1. At the lower level, *gdfa* uses the support provided by GCC for traversals over CFGs, basic blocks etc.; discovering relevant features of statements, expressions, variables etc.; constructing and manipulating data flow values; and printing entities appearing in statements.

Traversal Over CFG and Basic Blocks

In a round-robin iterative traversal, the basic blocks in a CFG are usually visited in the order of along control flow or against the order of control flow. In GCC, this is achieved as follows:

```
basic_block bb;

FOR_EACH_BB_FWD(ENTRY_BLOCK_PTR)
{      /* process bb */
}
FOR_EACH_BB_BKD(EXIT_BLOCK_PTR)
{      /* process bb */
}
```

In the above code, basic_block is a type supported by GCC. ENTRY_BLOCK_PTR and EXIT_BLOCK_PTR point to ENTRY and EXIT blocks of the current function being compiled. These macros have been defined by GCC. The two other macros used above are defined as follows:

```
#define FOR_EACH_BB_FWD(entry_bb)              \
    for(bb=entry_bb->next_bb;                  \
        bb->next_bb!=NULL;                     \
        bb=bb->next_bb)
#define FOR_EACH_BB_BKD(exit_bb)               \
    for(bb=exit_bb->prev_bb;                   \
        bb->prev_bb!=NULL;                     \
        bb=bb->prev_bb)
```

Given a basic block bb, its predecessor and successor blocks are traversed using an edge_iterator variable, an edge variable, and the macro FOR_EACH_EDGE as described below. All these are directly supported by GCC.

```
edge_iterator ei ;
edge e ;
basic_block succ_bb, pred_bb;

FOR_EACH_EDGE(e,ei,bb->preds)
{      pred_bb = e->src;
       /* process the predecessor pred_bb */
}
FOR_EACH_EDGE(e,ei,bb->succs)
{      succ_bb = e->dest;
       /* process successor succ_bb */
}
```

A statement is of the type `tree`. Further, all entities appearing in a statement are also of the type `tree`. All statements in a basic block can be traversed using a `block_statement_iterator` variable.

```
basic_block bb;
block_stmt_iterator bsi;
tree stmt;

FOR_EACH_STMT_FWD
{     stmt = bsi_stmt(bsi);
      /* process stmt */
}
FOR_EACH_STMT_BKD
{     stmt = bsi_stmt(bsi);
      /* process stmt */
}
```

The macros used in the above code are defined as follows:

```
#define FOR_EACH_STMT_FWD                    \
    for(bsi=bsi_start(bb);                   \
        !bsi_end_p(bsi);                     \
         bsi_next(&bsi))

#define FOR_EACH_STMT_BKD                    \
   for(bsi=bsi_last(bb);                     \
        bsi.tsi.ptr!=NULL;                   \
        bsi_prev(&bsi))
```

Discovering the Entities in a Statement

Statements can be of many types but only a few types are relevant to local data flow analysis. The lvalue and rvalue of a given statement `stmt` are of the type `tree` and are extracted as shown below:

```
tree expr=NULL, lval=NULL;

switch(TREE_CODE(stmt))
{  case COND_EXPR:
             expr = TREE_OPERAND(stmt,0);
             break;
   case MODIFY_EXPR:
             lval = TREE_OPERAND(stmt,0);
             expr = TREE_OPERAND(stmt,1);
   case GIMPLE_MODIFY_STMT:
             lval = GIMPLE_STMT_OPERAND(stmt,0);
             expr = GIMPLE_STMT_OPERAND(stmt,1);
             break;
   default:
             break;
}
```

The operands of relevant expressions are extracted as shown below:

```
tree op0=NULL, op1=NULL;

switch(TREE_CODE(expr))
{  case MULT_EXPR:
   case PLUS_EXPR:
   case MINUS_EXPR:
   case LT_EXPR:
   case LE_EXPR:
   case GT_EXPR:
   case GE_EXPR:
   case NE_EXPR:
   case EQ_EXPR:
          op1 = TREE_OPERAND(stmt,1);
          op0 = TREE_OPERAND(stmt,0);
          break;
   default:
           break;
}
```

Observe that this covers the set of expressions that is currently supported by *gdfa*.

Clearly, extending this set is easy.

Local variables are discovered by traversing `cfun->unexpanded_var_list` using `TREE_VALUE` and `TREE_CHAIN` macros supported by GCC. Here `cfun` represents the current function being compiled.

```
tree var,list;

list = cfun->unexpanded_var_list;
while (list)
{     var = TREE_VALUE (list);
        /* process variables *
        list = TREE_CHAIN(list);
}
```

Discovering definitions is easy: A statement with `TREE_CODE` as `MODIFY_EXR` or `GIMPLE_MODIFY_STMT` is detected as a definition.

Constructing and Manipulating Data Flow Values

We define the type `dfvalue` as follows:

```
typedef sbitmap dfvalue;
```

`sbitmap` is a type supported by GCC to represent sets. We use the following `sbitmap` functions to construct and manipulate bitmaps. Note that these functions are not directly used in *gdfa*. Instead, *gdfa* code calls `dfvalue` functions that are defined in terms of these functions.

Name of the Function	Action
`sbitmap_equal(v_a,v_b)`	is v_a equal to v_b?
`sbitmap_a_and_b(t, v_a, v_b)`	t = v_a ∩ v_b
`sbitmap_union_of_diff(t, v_a, v_b, v_c)`	t = v_a ∪ (v_b − v_c)
`sbitmap_a_or_b(t, v_a, v_b)`	t = v_a ∪ v_b
`sbitmap_ones(v)`	set every bit in v to 1
`sbitmap_zero(v)`	set every bit in v to 0
`sbitmap_alloc(n)`	allocate a bitmap of n bits
`sbitmap_free(v)`	free the space occupied by v

Facilities for Printing Entities

We use the function `dump_sbitmap` to print bitmaps. For printing a statement, the function `print_generic_stmt` is used whereas function `print_generic_expr` prints an expression `expr`.

10.3.3 The Preparatory Pass

Before the *gdfa* driver is invoked, some preparatory work has to be performed by an earlier pass. The top level function of this pass is:

```
static unsigned int
init_gimple_pfbvdfa_execute (void)
{
        local_var_count=0;
        local_expr_count=0;
        number_of_nodes = n_basic_blocks+2;

        assign_indices_to_var();
        assign_indices_to_exprs();
        assign_indices_to_defns();

        dfs_ordered_basic_blocks = NULL;
        dfs_numbering_of_bb();

        return 0;
}
```

Function `assign_indices_to_var` assigns a unique index to each local variable by traversing `cfun->unexpanded_var_list` as explained in Section 10.3.2. These indices represent the bit position of a local variable. This requires adding an `integer` field to the `tree` data structure. The variables which are not interesting are assigned index `-1`. Function `assign_indices_to_defns` assigns a unique index to each statement that is a definition.

Function `assign_indices_to_exprs` assigns a unique index to each expression whose operands are restricted to constants and variables that have been assigned a valid index. These indices represent the bit position of relevant expressions. Other expressions are assigned index `-1`. Unlike local variables, there is no ready list of expressions. Hence function `assign_indices_to_exprs` traverses the CFG visiting each statement and examining the expressions appearing in relevant statements. If the expression used in a statement qualifies as a local expression, it is first checked whether an index has already been assigned to it. This could happen because an expression could appear multiple times in a program.

Finally, function `dfs_numbering_of_bb` performs depth first numbering of the blocks in a CFG.

10.3.4 Local Data Flow Analysis

In production compilers, implementing global data flow analyzers is much easier compared to implementing local data flow analyzers. This is because local data flow analysis has to deal with the lower level intricate details of the intermediate representation and intermediate representation are the most complex data structures in practical compilers. Global data flow analyzers are insulated from these lower level details; they just need to know CFGs in terms of basic blocks. Thus most data flow analysis engines require the local property computation to be implemented by the user of the engine.

This situation can change considerably if we view local data flow analysis as a special case of global data flow analysis. The objective of local data flow analysis is to compute Gen_n and $Kill_n$ of a block n. This computation can be performed by traversing statements in block n in a manner similar to traversing blocks in a CFG. The only difference is that statements in a block cannot have multiple predecessors of successors.

The way In_{Start} (or Out_{End}) is computed by incorporating the effect of blocks in a CFG, Gen_n and $Kill_n$ can also be computed by incorporating the effects of individual statements in block n. The effect of statement s can be defined in terms of Gen_s and $Kill_s$. However, we need to overcome the following conceptual difficulty: When we compute Gen_n for block n, Gen_s of a statement s must be added to the cumulative effect of the statements processed so far. However, when we compute $Kill_n$, $Kill_s$ of statement s should be *added* to the cumulative effect instead of being removed. This deviates from the normal meaning of *Kill* which represents the entities to be removed.

We overcome this conceptual difficulty by renaming Gen_s and $Kill_s$ as Add_s and $Remove_s$ respectively. Now local data flow analysis does not depend on knowing whether the data flow property being computed is Gen_n or $Kill_n$. Given a local property specification such as below:

```
typedef struct lop_specs
                {
                        entity_name entity;
                        entity_manipulation stmt_effect;
                        entity_occurrence exposition;
                } lp_specs;
```

Local data flow analysis searches for the effect of a given statement specified through `stmt_effect` and stores it in `add_entities`. If the specified `stmt_effect` is `entity_use`, the entities that qualify for `entity_mod` are stored in the variable `remove_entities`. Depending upon the `exposition`, the final decision of removal is taken.

Thus computation of Gen_n and $Kill_n$ depends upon setting up a variable of the type `lp_specs` and the solving the following recurrence

$$\texttt{accumulated\_entities} = (\texttt{accumulated\_entities} - \texttt{remove\_entities}) \cup \texttt{add\_entities}$$

Function `effect_of_a_statement` performs the above computation for a given statement. It is called by the top level function local_dfa_of_bb. The relevant code fragment for downwards exposed entities is:

```
FOR_EACH_STMT_FWD
{   stmt = bsi_stmt(bsi);
    accumulated_entities = effect_of_a_statement(lps_given,
                                      stmt, accumulated_entities);
}
```

For upwards exposed entities, the accumulation is against the control flow and the above traversal is performed using the macro FOR_EACH_STMT_BKD.

The main limitation of this approach is that it requires independent traversal of a basic block for computing *Gen* and *Kill*. However, by using a slightly more complicated data structure that passes both *Gen* and *Kill* to function local_dfa_of_bb, will solve this problem. The other limitation is that due to the generality, there are many checks that are done in the underlying functions. There are two possible solutions to this problem of efficiency:

- This is used as a rapid prototyping tool for a given data flow analysis. Once the details are fixed, one could spend time writing a more efficient data flow analyzer.

- Instead of interpreting the specifications, a program can generate a customized C code that is compiled with GCC source.

10.3.5 Global Data Flow Analysis

As observed earlier, implementation of global data flow analyzer is much simpler once local data flow analysis and interface with the underlying compiler infrastructure is in place. The fact that *gdfa* use generic data flow Equations (5.1) and (5.2) makes it possible to execute a wide variety of specifications without having to know the name of a particular analysis being performed. In other words, *gdfa* driver is not a collection of data flow analysis implementations but is capable of executing any specification within the limits of the possible values of specification primitives.

At the top level, the *gdfa* driver needs to perform the following tasks:

- Create special values like $\top$, BI_{Start}, and BI_{End}.

- Create space for data flow values

- Perform local data flow analysis

- Select flow functions

- Perform global data flow analysis

Function gdfa_driver performs the above tasks:

```
0 pfbv_dfi **
1 gdfa_driver(struct gimple_pfbv_dfa_spec dfa_spec)
2 {
3     if (find_entity_size(dfa_spec) == 0)
4         return NULL;
5     initialize_special_values(dfa_spec);
6     create_dfi_space();
7     traversal_order = dfa_spec.traversal_order;
8     confluence = dfa_spec.confluence;
9
10    local_dfa(dfa_spec);
11
12    forward_edge_flow = dfa_spec.forward_edge_flow;
13    backward_edge_flow = dfa_spec.backward_edge_flow;
14    forward_node_flow = dfa_spec.forward_node_flow;
15    backward_node_flow = dfa_spec.backward_node_flow;
16
17    perform_pfbvdfa();
18
19    preserve_dfi(dfa_spec.preserved_dfi);
20    return current_pfbv_dfi;
21 }
```

Lines 12 to 15 select the flow functions from the specifications. Below we show the code fragment of function perform_pfbvdfa when the direction of traversal is FORWARD.

```
do
{   iteration_number++;
    change = false;
    FOR_EACH_BB_IN_SPECIFIED_TRAVERSAL_ORDER
    {   bb = VARRAY_BB(dfs_ordered_basic_blocks,visit_bb);
        if(bb)
        {   if (traversal_order == FORWARD)
            {   change_at_in = compute_in_info(bb);
                change_at_out = compute_out_info(bb);
                change = change||change_at_out||change_at_in;
            }
            else  /* compute in the opposite order */
        }
    }
} while(change);
```

The main code fragment of function compute_in_info is as shown below. It calls function backward_node_flow which is extracted from the specification.

```
if (!bb->preds)
    temp = combine(entry_info, backward_node_flow(bb));
else
    temp = combine(combined_forward_edge_flow(bb),
                            backward_node_flow(bb));
old = CURRENT_IN(bb);
change = is_new_info(temp,old);

if (change)
{
     CURRENT_IN(bb) = temp;
     if (old)
         free_dfvalue_space(old);
}
return change;
```

Function combined_forward_edge_flow computes the following term

$$\prod_{p \in pred(n)} \overrightarrow{f}_{p \to n}(Out_p)$$

Its main code fragment is shown below. It calls function forward_edge_flow which is extracted from the specification.

```
edge_vec = bb->preds;
temp = make_initialized_dfvalue(top_value_spec);

if (forward_edge_flow == &stop_flow_along_edge)
    return temp;

FOR_EACH_EDGE(e,ei,edge_vec)
{   pred_bb = e->src;
    new = combine(temp,forward_edge_flow(pred_bb,bb));
    if (temp)
        free_dfvalue_space(temp);
    temp = new;
}
return temp;
```

The code sequence corresponding to function compute_out_info is an exact dual of the above code sequence. This completes the description of generic global data flow analysis in *gdfa*.

10.4 Extending the Generic Data Flow Analyzer *gdfa*

Many extensions and enhancements of *gdfa* are possible. We suggest some of them by dividing them into the following categories.

- *Extensions that do not require changing the architecture of gdfa.*
  - Include space and time measurement of analyses.
  - Consider scalar formal parameters for analysis.
  - Support a work list based driver.
  - Extend *gdfa* to support other entities such as statements (e.g., for data flow analysis based program slicing), and basic blocks (e.g., for data flow analysis based dominator computation). Both these problems are bit vector problems.
  - Improve the implementation of *gdfa* to make it more space and time efficient. This may require compromising on the simplicity of the implementation but generality should not be compromised.
- *Extensions that may require minor changes to the architecture of gdfa.*
  - Implement incremental data flow analysis and measure its effectiveness by invoking in just before gimple is expanded into RTL.

    This would require a variant of a work list based driver.
  - Explore the possibility of extending *gdfa* to the data flow frameworks where data flow information can be represented using bit vectors but the frameworks are not bit vector frameworks because they are non-separable e.g., faint variables analysis, possibly undefined variables, analysis, strongly live variables analysis.

    This would require changing the local data flow analysis. One possible option is using matrix based local property computation [53]. The other option is to treat a statement as an independent basic block.
- *Extensions that may require major changes to the architecture of gdfa.*
  - Extend *gdfa* to non-separable frameworks in which data flow information cannot be represented by bit vectors e.g., constant propagation, signs analysis, points-to analysis, alias analysis, heap reference analysis etc. Although the main driver would remain same, this would require making fundamental changes to the architecture.
  - Extend *gdfa* to support some variant of context and flow sensitive interprocedural data flow analysis.

A

An Introduction to GCC

A.1 About GCC

GCC is an acronym for GNU Compiler Collection (`http://gcc.gnu.org`) which is the de-facto standard compiler generation framework for a number on GNU/Linux and many other variants of Unix/Linux on a wide variety of machines and is one of the most dominant softwares in the free software community.

GCC started as C compiler, and was the acronym for *GNU C Compiler* in the early days. Over the years, it has been continuously upgraded to support a number of back end machines. Similarly, on the front end side, it has grown to support a number of front end languages like C++, Objective C, Java, and FORTRAN to name a few. As a consequence, it has been renamed as *GNU Compiler Collection*.

As of 2008, GCC supports six front end languages, and 34 back end machines. This results in a quite huge code base, and GCC has earned a reputation of being one of the most complex and major free software/open source projects. A rough line count of all the C source files (including header files) of just the compiler code (i.e., only the `gcc` directory) with the major block comments removed is about 1440336 lines. This does not include the code that describes the supported back end machines, as well as code for other purposes like the build system, libraries etc.

GCC generates production quality optimizing compilers from descriptions of target platforms. It supports a wide variety of source languages and target machines (including operating system specific variants) in a ready-to-deploy form. Besides, new machines can be added by describing instruction set architectures and some other information e.g., calling conventions. This retargetability requirement implies that target information is incorporated into the compiler at build time rather than at design time. The GCC sources consist of

- Language dependent front end.
- Language and target independent modules.
- Target architecture specification.

A compiler for specific language-target pair is generated by selecting front end for desired language and generating back end for specified target.

A.2 Building GCC

There are four directories that are useful to describe the user level building of GCC. They are not required to be defined in practice.

- The directory where we have downloaded the compressed sources. We denote this by `$DOWNLOADDIR`
- The directory where we extract the downloaded sources. We denote this by `$GCCHOME`
- The directory where we build the compiler for the chosen source language and target machine. We denote this by `$BUILDDIR`
- The directory where the built compiler is installed for use. We denote this by `$INSTALLDIR`

The GCC build instructions in `$GCCHOME/INSTALL/index.html` recommend the use of a distinct build directory and discourages building GCC in `$GCCHOME`. Any directory with suitable permissions that is different from `$GCCHOME` may be used.

The binaries, libraries, headers and documentation that is built is installed as a directory tree under `$INSTALLDIR`. This is any convenient directory with suitable permissions, and usually distinct from the others. The default is a system wide installation directory e.g., `/usr/local`, but can be specified when GCC is configured for building.

There are four steps to building the compiler.

- change to the `$BUILDDIR`,
- configure the pristine GCC sources,
- build the compiler binaries, libraries etc., and
- install the compiler.

In the description below, unless otherwise stated, we assume a GNU/Linux system running on an i386 with the GNU Bourne Again SHell (`bash`) as the command shell. All commands are issued at the bash shell prompt, and shell commands or scripts are bash scripts.

Configuring GCC

The pristine GCC sources must be informed about some details like the system on which it will eventually run. A shell script called `configure` is used for this. Most pieces of required information have reasonable default values, and the usual way is to simply issue the `configure` command, which uses the defaults. However, specific non default values can be given to the `configure` command through command line switches. Being a retargetable compiler that supports a number of high level languages (HLLs), the sources need to be informed about the particular source language and the target hardware on which the built compiler is to be used. By default, GCC is configured to build a compiler for the target on which it is being compiled. If a compiler for a specific language is desired, then the switch `--enable-languages` can be used. The install directory defaults to `/usr/local`, but can also be specified using the `--prefix` switch. The configure `--help` command lists out various such options whose details are documented in `$GCCHOME/INSTALL/index.html`.

To build only a C compiler for a i386 for running on a GNU/Linux operating system and `/home/gcc/gcc-trial-install` as the installation directory, we configure as follows:

1. Change to the build directory

   ```
   cd $BUILDDIR
   ```

2. Specify that we need only the C compiler, to run on an i386 machine running GNU/Linux and `/home/gcc/gcc-trial-install` as the installation directory (each option is shown on a separate line for clarity, but is one single command line)

   ```
   $GCCHOME/configure
   --enable-languages=c
   --target=i386-linux-gnu
   --prefix=/home/gcc/gcc-trial-install
   ```

The `configure` program makes a number of checks for a successful build and generates a `Makefile` (as `$BUILDDIR/Makefile`) if all checks pass. It is useful to redirect the output of `configure` to some file for later study as follows:

```
$GCCHOME/configure > configure.log 2> configure.errors
```

Compiling GCC

Once the configuration successfully generates the `Makefile`, the GCC source is compiled by issuing the `make` command. The steps are:

1. `cd $BUILDDIR`
2. `make`

Compiling GCC involves building the compiler for each source language, the driver program `gcc`, the associated header files, support libraries, and the documentation. The driver program `gcc` so generated is the command that users use to compile their source programs. The driver takes the user's source file to be compiled and invokes a sequence of programs (the compiler, the assembler and the linker) that generate its binary.

It is useful to redirect the output of `make` to some file for later study as follows:

```
$BUILDDIR/make > make.log 2> make.errors
```

Installing GCC

Final installation installs various components of the compiler like the driver, the compiler, libraries, the documentation etc., in a well-defined directory structure in the `$INSTALLDIR` directory. The following structure is typically used:

- `$INSTALLDIR/bin`: Directory where the various executables are installed.
- `$INSTALLDIR/include`: Directory where the various headers are installed.
- `$INSTALLDIR/lib`: Directory where the various libraries are installed.
- `$INSTALLDIR/man`: Directory where the various online manual pages are installed.
- `$INSTALLDIR/info`: Directory where the various online info pages are installed.

To install the built sources, use the following command:

```
$BUILDDIR/make install
```

It is useful to redirect the output of install to some file for later study as follows:

```
$BUILDDIR/make install > install.log 2> install.errors
```

Downloading and Installing *gdfa*

A patch of GCC 4.3.0 for *gdfa* is available at the following URL. Patches for later versions will be made available on this page whenever possible.

`http://www.cse.iitb.ac.in/uday/dfaBook-web`

Following steps patch up GCC with *gdfa* code.

1. `cd $GCCHOME`
2. `patch -p0 < patch_file_with_path`

Now GCC can be configured, compiled, and installed.

A.3 Further Readings in GCC

Here we list further resources for learning about GCC.

- GCC Internals
  `http://gcc.gnu.org/onlinedocs/gccint.html`
  This is the official internals document which exhaustively describes most details and is a part of the documentation distributed with the compiler code.

- GCC Internals documents developed at IIT Bombay
  `http://www.cse.iitb.ac.in/grc/`
  This is the website of *GCC Resource Center* at IIT Bombay. It hosts the GCC documents developed at IIT Bombay.

- The GCC Wiki
  `http://gcc.gnu.org/wiki/`
  The official GCC Wiki pages where the various aspects of GCC, including some description of the internals, are being developed by the GCC developers and others.

- The GCC Internals workshop held at IIT Bombay
  `http://www.cse.iitb.ac.in/~uday/gcc-workshop/`
  This workshop that focused mainly on the machine descriptions was held at IIT Bombay in June 2007. The slides and some associated software is available on the `Downloads` page of the workshop.

- The GCC on Wikipedia
  `http://en.wikipedia.org/wiki/GNU_Compiler_Collection`

- The GCC Internals on Wikipedia
  `http://en.wikibooks.org/wiki/GNU_C_Compiler_Internals`

References

[1] O. Agesen, D. Detlefs, and J. E. Moss. Garbage collection and local variable type-precision and liveness in Java virtual machines. In *Proceedings of the ACM SIGPLAN Conference on Programming Language Design and Implementation*, pages 269–279. ACM, 1998.

[2] A. V. Aho, J. E. Hopcroft, and J. D. Ullman. *The Design and Analysis of Computer Algorithms*. Addison-Wesley, 1974.

[3] A. V. Aho, M. S. Lam, R. Sethi, and J. D. Ullman. *Compilers: Principles, Techniques, and Tools (2/e)*. Addison-Wesley Longman Publishing Co., Inc., 2006.

[4] F. E. Allen. Control flow analysis. *ACM SIGPLAN Notices*, 5(7):1–19, 1970.

[5] F. E. Allen. A basis for program optimization. In *IFIP Congress (1)*, pages 385–390. North Holland Publishing Company, 1971.

[6] F. E. Allen. Interprocedural data flow analysis. In *Proceedings of IFIP Congress 74*, pages 398–408. North Holland Publishing Company, 1974.

[7] F. E. Allen and J. Cocke. A program data flow analysis procedure. *Communications of the ACM*, 19(3):137–147, 1976.

[8] B. Alpern, M. N. Wegman, and F. K. Zadeck. Detecting equality of variables in programs. In *Proceedings of the ACM SIGPLAN-SIGACT Symposium on Principles of Programming Languages*, pages 1–11. ACM, 1988.

[9] L. O. Andersen. *Program Analysis and Specialization for the C Programming Language*. PhD thesis, DIKU, University of Copenhagen, 1994.

[10] A. W. Appel and M. Ginsburg. *Modern Compiler Implementation in C*. Cambridge University Press, 1998.

[11] Andrew W. Appel. SSA is functional programming. *ACM SIGPLAN Notices*, 33(4):17–20, 1998.

[12] J. Banning. An efficient way to find the side effects of procedure calls and aliases of variables. In *Proceedings of the ACM SIGPLAN-SIGACT Symposium on Principles of Programming Languages*, pages 29–41. ACM, 1979.

[13] J. M. Barth. An interprocedural data flow analysis algorithm. In *Proceedings of the ACM SIGPLAN-SIGACT Symposium on Principles of Programming Languages*, pages 119–131. ACM, 1977.

[14] Jeffrey M. Barth. A practical interprocedural data flow analysis algorithm. *Communications of the ACM*, 21(9):724–736, 1978.

[15] B. Blanchet. Escape analysis for object-oriented languages: application to Java. In *Proceedings of the ACM SIGPLAN Conference on Object-oriented Programming Systems, Languages, and Applications*, pages 20–34. ACM, 1999.

[16] B. Blanchet. Escape analysis for Java^{TM}: Theory and practice. *ACM Transactions on Programming Languages and Systems*, 25(6):713–775, 2003.

[17] R. Bodik, R. Gupta, and M. L. Soffa. Complete removal of redundant computations. In *Proceedings of the ACM SIGPLAN Conference on Programming Language Design and Implementation*, pages 1–14. ACM, 1998.

[18] P. Briggs, K. D. Cooper, T. J. Harvey, and L. T. Simpson. Practical improvements to the construction and destruction of static single assignment form. *Software—Practice and Experience*, 28(8):859–881, 1998.

[19] D. Callahan. The program summary graph and flow-sensitive interprocedural data flow analysis. In *Proceedings of the ACM SIGPLAN Conference on Programming Language Design and Implementation*, pages 47–56. ACM, 1988.

[20] D. Callahan, A. Carle, M. W. Hall, and K. Kennedy. Constructing the procedure call multigraph. *IEEE Transactions on Software Engineering*, 16(4):483–487, 1990.

[21] J. Choi, M. Burke, and P. Carini. Efficient flow-sensitive interprocedural computation of pointer-induced aliases and side effects. In *Proceedings of the ACM SIGPLAN-SIGACT Symposium on Principles of Programming Languages*, pages 232–245. ACM, 1993.

[22] J. Choi, R. Cytron, and J. Ferrante. Automatic construction of sparse data flow evaluation graphs. In *Proceedings of the ACM SIGPLAN-SIGACT Symposium on Principles of Programming Languages*, pages 55–66. ACM, 1991.

[23] J. Choi, M. Gupta, M. Serrano, V. C. Sreedhar, and S. Midkiff. Escape analysis for Java. In *Proceedings of the ACM SIGPLAN Conference on Object-oriented Programming Systems, Languages, and Applications*, pages 1–19. ACM, 1999.

[24] J. Cocke. Global common subexpression elimination. *ACM SIGPLAN Notices*, 5(7):20–24, 1970.

[25] K. Cooper. Analyzing aliases of reference formal parameters. In *Proceedings of the ACM SIGPLAN-SIGACT Symposium on Principles of Programming Languages*, pages 281–290. ACM, 1985.

[26] K. D. Cooper and K. Kennedy. Fast interprocedural alias analysis. In *Proceedings of the ACM SIGPLAN-SIGACT Symposium on Principles of Programming Languages*, pages 49–59. ACM, 1989.

[27] T. H. Cormen, C. E. Leiserson, R. L. Rivest, and C. Stein. *Introduction to Algorithms, (2/e)*. The MIT Press and McGraw-Hill Book Company, 2001.

[28] R. Cytron, J. Ferrante, B. K. Rosen, M. N. Wegman, and F. K. Zadeck. Efficiently computing static single assignment form and the control dependence graph. *ACM Transactions on Programming Languages and Systems*, 13(4):451–490, 1991.

[29] B. A. Davey and H. A. Priestley. *Introduction to Lattices and Order (2/e)*. Cambridge University Press, 2002.

[30] D. M. Dhamdhere and U. P. Khedker. Complexity of bidirectional data flow analysis. In *Proceedings of the ACM SIGPLAN-SIGACT Symposium on Principles of Programming Languages*, pages 397–408. ACM, 1993.

[31] D. M. Dhamdhere, B. K. Rosen, and F. K. Zadeck. How to analyze large programs efficiently and informatively. In *Proceedings of the ACM SIGPLAN Conference on Programming Language Design and Implementation*, pages 212–223. ACM, 1992.

[32] E. Duesterwald, R. Gupta, and M. L. Soffa. Demand-driven computation of interprocedural data flow. In *Proceedings of the ACM SIGPLAN-SIGACT Symposium on Principles of Programming Languages*, pages 37–48. ACM, 1995.

[33] E. Duesterwald, R. Gupta, and M. L. Soffa. A practical framework for demand-driven interprocedural data flow analysis. *ACM Transactions on Programming Languages and Systems*, 19(6):992–1030, 1997.

[34] M. Emami, R. Ghiya, and L. J. Hendren. Context-sensitive interprocedural points-to analysis in the presence of function pointers. In *Proceedings of the ACM SIGPLAN Conference on Programming Language Design and Implementation*, pages 242–256. ACM, 1994.

[35] M. Fähndrich, J. S. Foster, Z. Su, and A. Aiken. Partial online cycle elimination in inclusion constraint graphs. In *Proceedings of the ACM SIGPLAN Conference on Programming Language Design and Implementation*, pages 85–96. ACM, 1998.

[36] M. Fähndrich, J. Rehof, and M. Das. Scalable context-sensitive flow analysis using instantiation constraints. In *Proceedings of the ACM SIGPLAN Conference on Programming Language Design and Implementation*, pages 253–263. ACM, 2000.

[37] S. Graham and M. Wegman. A fast and usually linear algorithm for global data flow analysis. *Journal of ACM*, 23(1):172–202, 1976.

[38] D. Grove and C. Chambers. A framework for call graph construction algorithms. *ACM Transactions on Programming Languages and Systems*, 23(6):685–746, 2001.

[39] D. Grove and L. Torczon. Interprocedural constant propagation: a study of jump function implementation. In *Proceedings of the ACM SIGPLAN Conference on Programming Language Design and Implementations*, pages 90–99. ACM, 1993.

[40] D. Grune, H. E. Bal, C. J. H. Jacobs, and K. G. Langendoen. *Modern Compiler Design*. John Wiley & Sons, 2000.

[41] S. Hack. *Register Allocation for Programs in SSA Form*. PhD thesis, Universität Karlsruhe, 2007.

[42] S. Hack, D. Grund, and G. Goos. Register allocation for programs in SSA-form. In *Proceedings of the International Conference on Compiler Construction*, pages 247–262. Springer-Verlag, 2006.

[43] M. W. Hall and K. Kennedy. Efficient call graph analysis. *ACM Letters on Programming Languages and Systems*, 1(3):227–242, 1992.

[44] M. S. Hecht. *Flow Analysis of Computer Programs*. Elsevier North-Holland Inc., 1977.

[45] M. S. Hecht and J. D. Ullman. Flow graph reducibility. In *Proceedings of the ACM Symposium on Theory of Computing*, pages 238–250. ACM, 1972.

[46] M. S. Hecht and J. D. Ullman. Characterization of reducible flow graphs. *Journal of ACM*, 21(3):367–375, 1974.

[47] M. Hind. Pointer analysis: haven't we solved this problem yet? In *Proceedings of the ACM SIGPLAN-SIGSOFT Workshop on Program Analysis for Software Tools and Engineering*, pages 54–61. ACM, 2001.

[48] M. Hind, M. Burke, P. Carini, and J. Choi. Interprocedural pointer alias analysis. *ACM Transactions on Programming Languages and Systems*, 21(4):848–894, 1999.

[49] J. B. Kam and J. D. Ullman. Global data flow analysis and iterative algorithms. *Journal of ACM*, 23(1):158–171, 1976.

[50] J. B. Kam and J. D. Ullman. Monotone data flow analysis frameworks. *Acta Informatica*, 7(3):305–317, 1977.

[51] A. Kanade, U. P. Khedker, and A. Sanyal. Heterogeneous fixed points with application to points-to analysis. In *Proceedings of the Asian Symposium on Programming Languages and Systems*, pages 298–314. Springer-Verlag, 2005.

[52] A. Karkare, A. Sanyal, and U. P. Khedker. Effectiveness of garbage collection in MIT/GNU Scheme. *CoRR*, abs/cs/0611093, 2006.

[53] B. Karkare. *Complexity and Efficiency Issues in Data Flow Analysis*. PhD thesis, Indian Institute of Technology, Bombay, 2007.

[54] B. Karkare and U. P. Khedker. An improved bound for call-strings based interprocedural analysis of bit vector frameworks. *ACM Transactions on Programming Languages and Systems*, 29(6):38, 2007.

[55] K. Kennedy. A global flow analysis algorithm. *International Journal of Computer Mathematic*, 3(1):5–15, 1971.

[56] K. Kennedy. Node listings applied to data flow analysis. In *Proceedings of the ACM SIGPLAN-SIGACT Symposium on Principles of Programming Languages*, pages 10–21. ACM, 1975.

[57] K. Kennedy. A survey of data flow analysis techniques, 1981. In [77].

[58] R. Kennedy, S. Chan, S. Liu, R. Lo, P. Tu, and F. Chow. Partial redundancy elimination in SSA form. *ACM Transactions on Programming Languages and Systems*, 21(3):627–676, 1999.

[59] U. P. Khedker. Data flow analysis. In Y. N. Srikant and Priti Shankar, editors, *The Compiler Design Handbook: Optimizations & Machine Code Generation*. CRC Press, 2002.

[60] U. P. Khedker and D. M. Dhamdhere. A generalized theory of bit vector data flow analysis. *ACM Transactions on Programming Languages and Systems*, 16(5):1472–1511, 1994.

[61] U. P. Khedker and B. Karkare. Efficiency, precision, simplicity, and generality in interprocedural data flow analysis: Resurrecting the classical call strings method. In *Proceedings of the International Conference on Compiler Construction*, pages 213–228. Springer-Verlag, 2008.

[62] U. P. Khedker, A. Sanyal, and A. Karkare. Heap reference analysis using access graphs. *ACM Transactions on Programming Languages and Systems*, 30(1):1, 2007.

[63] G. Kildall. A unified approach to global program optimization. In *Proceedings of the ACM SIGPLAN-SIGACT Symposium on Principles of Programming Languages*, pages 194–206. ACM, 1973.

[64] K. Knobe and V. Sarkar. Array SSA form and its use in parallelization. In *Proceedings of the ACM SIGPLAN-SIGACT Symposium on Principles of Programming Languages*, pages 107–120. ACM, 1998.

[65] J. Knoop, O. Rüthing, and B. Steffen. Lazy code motion. In *Proceedings of the ACM SIGPLAN Conference on Programming Language Design and Implementation*, pages 224–234. ACM, 1992.

[66] W. Landi and B. G. Ryder. A safe approximate algorithm for interprocedural pointer aliasing. In *Proceedings of the ACM SIGPLAN Conference on Programming Language Design and Implementation*, pages 235–248. ACM, 1992.

[67] W. Landi, B. G. Ryder, and S. Zhang. Interprocedural side effect analysis with pointer aliasing. In *Proceedings of the ACM SIGPLAN Conference on Programming Language Design and Implementation*, pages 56–67. ACM, 1993.

[68] T. Lengauer and R. E. Tarjan. A fast algorithm for finding dominators in a flowgraph. *ACM Transactions on Programming Languages and Systems*, 1(1):121–141, 1979.

[69] O. Lhoták and L. Hendren. Context-sensitive points-to analysis: is it worth it? In *Proceedings of the International Conference on Compiler Construction*, pages 47–64. Springer-Verlag, 2006.

[70] E. S. Lowry and C. W. Medlock. Object code optimization. *Communications of the ACM*, 12(1):13–22, 1969.

[71] T. J. Marlowe and B. G. Ryder. Properties of data flow frameworks. *Acta Informatica*, 28(2):121–163, 1990.

[72] F. Martin. Experimental comparison of call string and functional approaches to interprocedural analysis. In *Proceedings of the International Conference on Compiler Construction*, pages 63–75. Springer-Verlag, 1999.

[73] C. E. McDowell. Reducing garbage in java. *ACM SIGPLAN Notices*, 33(9):84–86, 1998.

[74] E. Morel and C. Renvoise. Global optimization by suppression of partial redundancies. *Communications of the ACM*, 22(2):96–103, 1979.

[75] R. Morgan. *Building an Optimizing Compiler*. Digital Press, 1998.

[76] S. S. Muchnick. *Advanced Compiler Design and Implementation*. Morgan Kaufmann Publishing Co., 1997.

[77] S. S. Muchnick and N. D. Jones. *Program Flow Analysis : Theory and Applications*. Prentice-Hall Inc., 1981.

[78] M. Müller-Olm and O. Rüthing. On the complexity of constant propagation. In *Proceedings of the European Symposium on Programming Languages and Systems*, pages 190–205. Springer-Verlag, 2001.

[79] E. M. Myers. A precise inter-procedural data flow algorithm. In *Proceedings of the ACM SIGPLAN-SIGACT Symposium on Principles of Programming Languages*, pages 219–230. ACM, 1981.

[80] F. Nielson, H. R. Nielson, and C. Hankin. *Principles of Program Analysis*. Springer-Verlag, 1998.

[81] A. Reid, J. McCorquodale, J. Baker, W. Hsieh, and J. Zachary. The need for predictable garbage collection. In *Proceedings of the ACM SIGPLAN Workshop on Compiler Support for System Software*. ACM, 1999.

[82] T. W. Reps, S. Horwitz, and S. Sagiv. Precise interprocedural dataflow analysis via graph reachability. In *Proceedings of the ACM SIGPLAN-SIGACT*

Symposium on Principles of Programming Languages, pages 49–61. ACM, 1995.

[83] S. E. Richardson and M. Ganapathi. Interprocedural optimizations : Experimental results. *Software Practice and Experience*, 19(2):149–169, 1989.

[84] B. K. Rosen. Monoids for rapid data flow analysis. *SIAM Journal of Computing*, 9(1):159–196, 1980.

[85] B. K. Rosen, M. N. Wegman, and F. K. Zadeck. Global value numbers and redundant computations. In *Proceedings of the ACM SIGPLAN-SIGACT Symposium on Principles of Programming Languages*, pages 12–27. ACM, 1988.

[86] B. G. Ryder and M. C. Paull. Elimination algorithms for data flow analysis. *ACM Computing Surveys*, 18(3):277–316, 1986.

[87] M. Sagiv, T. Reps, and S. Horwitz. Precise interprocedural dataflow analysis with applications to constant propagation. *Theoretical Computer Science*, 167(1–2):131–170, 1996.

[88] S. Sagiv, T. W. Reps, and R. Wilhelm. Parametric shape analysis via 3-valued logic. *ACM Transactions on Programming Languages and Systems*, 24(3):217–298, 2002.

[89] R. Shaham, E. K. Kolodner, and M. Sagiv. On effectiveness of GC in Java. In *International Symposium on Memory Management*, pages 12–17. ACM, 2000.

[90] R. Shaham, E. K. Kolodner, and M. Sagiv. Heap profiling for space-efficient java. In *Proceedings of the ACM SIGPLAN Conference on Programming Language Design and Implementation*, pages 104–113. ACM, 2001.

[91] R. Shaham, E. K. Kolodner, and M. Sagiv. Estimating the impact of heap liveness information on space consumption in Java. In *Proceedings of the International Symposium on Memory Management*, pages 64–75. ACM, 2002.

[92] R. Shaham, E. Yahav, E. K. Kolodner, and S. Sagiv. Establishing local temporal heap safety properties with applications to compile-time memory management. In *Proceedings of the International Static Analysis Symposium*, pages 483–503. Springer-Verlag, 2003.

[93] M. Sharir and A. Pnueli. Two approaches to interprocedural data flow analysis. In S. S. Muchnick and N. D. Jones, editors, *Program Flow Analysis : Theory and Applications*. Prentice-Hall Inc., 1981.

[94] T. C. Spillman. Exposing side effects in a PL/I optimizing compiler. In *Proceedings of IFIP Congress 71*, pages 376–381. North Holland Publishing Company, 1971.

[95] V. C. Sreedhar and G. R. Gao. A linear time algorithm for placing ϕ-nodes. In *Proceedings of the ACM SIGPLAN-SIGACT Symposium on Principles of Programming Languages*, pages 62–73. ACM, 1995.

[96] V. C. Sreedhar, R. Dz-Ching Ju, D. M. Gillies, and V. Santhanam. Translating out of static single assignment form. In *Proceedings of the International Symposium on Static Analysis*, pages 194–210, 1999.

[97] B. Steensgaard. Points-to analysis in almost linear time. In *Proceedings of the ACM SIGPLAN-SIGACT Symposium on Principles of Programming Languages*, pages 32–41. ACM, 1996.

[98] R. E. Tarjan. Fast algorithms for solving path problems. *Journal of ACM*, 28(3):594–614, 1981.

[99] A. Tarski. A lattice-theoretical fixpoint theorem and its applications. *Pacific Journal of Mathematics*, 5(2):285–309, 1955.

[100] J. D. Ullman. Fast algorithms for the elimination of common subexpressions. *Acta Informatica*, 2(3):191–213, 1973.

[101] V. Vyssotsky and P. Wegner. A graph theoretical FORTRAN source language analyzer. AT & T Bell Laboratories, Murray Hill, N. J., 1963. (Manuscript).

[102] M. N. Wegman and F. K. Zadeck. Constant propagation with conditional branches. *ACM Transactions on Programming Languages and Systems*, 13(2):181–210, 1991.

[103] M. N. Wegman and F. K. Zadeck. Constant propagation with conditional branches. *ACM Transactions on Programming Languages and Systems*, 13(2):181–210, 1991.

[104] J. Whaley and M. S. Lam. Cloning-based context-sensitive pointer alias analysis using binary decision diagrams. In *Proceedings of the ACM SIGPLAN Conference on Programming Language Design and Implementation*. ACM, 2004.

[105] R. Wilhelm and D. Maurer. *Compiler Design*. Addison-Wesley, 1995.

[106] R. Wilhelm, T. W. Reps, and S. Sagiv. Shape analysis and applications. In Y. N. Srikant and Priti Shankar, editors, *The Compiler Design Handbook: Optimizations & Machine Code Generation*, pages 175–218. CRC Press, 2002.

[107] R. P. Wilson and M. S. Lam. Efficient context-sensitive pointer analysis for C programs. In *Proceedings of the ACM SIGPLAN Conference on Programming Language Design and Implementation*, pages 1–12. ACM, 1995.

Index